This book may be checked
out for a limited time.

D1195579

Spanish &
Mexican
Records
of the
American
Southwest

Spanish & Mexican Records of the American Southwest

A Bibliographical Guide to Archive and Manuscript Sources

Henry Putney Beers

Published by the
UNIVERSITY OF ARIZONA PRESS   Tucson, Arizona

In Collaboration With
THE TUCSON CORRAL OF THE WESTERNERS

About the Author...

Henry Putney Beers, as archivist, historian, and editor for the United States government for more than thirty years, was involved in the publication of several scholarly references including the *Territorial Papers of the United States*. He has also compiled a number of standard reference works on his own such as *Bibliographies in American History: Guide to Materials and Research* and *The French and British in the Old Northwest: A Bibliographical Guide to Archive and Manuscript Sources*. He received degrees in history from Lafayette College and the University of Pennsylvania.

THE UNIVERSITY OF ARIZONA PRESS

Copyright © 1979
The Arizona Board of Regents
All Rights Reserved
Manufactured in the U.S.A.

Library of Congress Cataloging in Publication Data

Beers, Henry Putney, 1907–
    Spanish & Mexican records of the American Southwest.

    Bibliography: p.
    Includes index.
    1. Southwest, New — History — To 1848 — Archival resources — United States. 2. Southwest, New — History — To 1848 — Sources. I. Title.
Z1251.S8B4   [F799]   979'.01   79-4313
ISBN 0-8165-0673-6
ISBN 0-8165-0532-2 pbk.

To the precious memory of
Alice Tharpe Beers
= 1909 – 1976 =

Contents

MAPS

Preface

THE CHALLENGE OF PRESENTATION in this book has arisen in bringing together a historical account of the acquisition, preservation, and publication, by American institutions and individuals, of the original records created by Spanish and Mexican officials in what became the American Southwest, from the beginning of settlement in the early 1600s to the mid-nineteenth century. The historical treatment primarily concerns public records that have been preserved in official custody. Provincial records were accumulated at Santa Fe, San Antonio, and Monterey, but there were departmental headquarters, military headquarters, and many municipalities, presidios, and missions throughout the Southwest where records also accumulated. Descriptive information regarding the records, derived from a wide variety of finding aids and other publications, is included, and records of the Franciscan and Jesuit missions are also described.

The records include administrative papers of governor-commandants, judicial records, notarial records, land records, legislative records, and mission registers and other ecclesiastical records. To facilitate a proper understanding of the records, the government of the region and the land-grant system are described, as well as the organization of the Catholic church and its missionary orders and their missions. Many papers of officials, military officers, missionaries, businessmen, and others, containing communications from government officials, that have found their way into nongovernmental repositories, are also described.

The American Southwest was part of New Spain until 1821, when it became part of Mexico. Consequently, accounts are included of the procurement of reproductions from the archives of Spain and other places in Europe, and from Mexico, by American institutions and scholars, and some descriptions of the reproductions are included. Each section of the book — on New Mexico, Texas, California, and Arizona — contains chapters on history and government, provincial records, legislative records, archival reproductions, documentary publications, manuscript collections, land records, records of local jurisdictions, and ecclesiastical records. Three appendixes listing the lost records of California and a classified bibliography follow.

This work is based primarily on finding aids published by archival and manuscript repositories in the Southwest, but finding aids and publications outside of that region have also been utilized. Much California material exists in the Bancroft Library of the University of California, and much can be gleaned from the bibliography and pioneer register in H. H. Bancroft's *History of California*. The manuscript collections in the University of Arizona Library are extensive and additional materials exist at other institutions in Arizona. Many repositories in that state have furnished information in letters and lists concerning their holdings, in response to my specific inquiries. These places are too numerous to mention, but, in most cases, acknowledgment of their assistance has been made in footnotes.

I am indebted to several persons for various kinds of assistance. George S. Ulibarri, of the National Archives, and Handy Bruce Fant, now retired from that institution, made helpful suggestions after reading parts of the manuscript. The maps are the product of the cooperative efforts of the author, who gathered the data, of Herman R. Friis, formerly head of the Cartographic Records Division and director of the Center for Polar Archives of the National Archives, who delineated some preliminary maps, and of the Press which prepared the final maps. Dorothy G. Beers and Beverly Anne Beers assisted in the work on the index. Thanks is also due the University of Arizona Press for bringing about publication, supported in part by the Tucson Corral of the Westerners.

Research for this work was started many years ago and has been completed since I retired from the United States National Archives in 1968. Familiarity with federal records, that I acquired while working in that institution on *The Territorial Papers of the United States* and the preparation of finding aids, has greatly facilitated my research on this work. Also, many individuals on the staff of the National Archives have assisted me through the years by helping me to locate pertinent records and supplying useful items of information.

H. P. B.

Abbreviations

AGO	Adjutant General's Office
AG	Attorney General
arch.	archives
Bd. Land Commrs.	Board of Land Commissioners
BLM	Bureau of Land Management
coll.	collection
ct.	court
DI	Department of the Interior
DJ	Department of Justice
DLR	Division of Lands and Railroads
DS	Department of State
fasc.	fascicle
GAO	General Accounting Office
GLO	General Land Office
H.	House of Representatives
LC	Library of Congress
lets. recd.	letters received
lets. sent	letters sent
NA	National Archives
NARS	National Archives and Records Service
NRRB	National Resources Records Branch
O.F.M.	Order of Friars Minor (Franciscans)

PLC	Private Land Claims
PM	Patents and Miscellaneous
S.	Senate
SD	State Department
SF	Senate Files
SG	Surveyor General
SI	Secretary of the Interior
S.J.	Society of Jesus
SMRC	Southwestern Missions Research Center
stat.	statute
surv.	surveyor
SW	Secretary of War
terr.	territory
U.S. Sup. Ct.	United States Supreme Court
WD	War Department

Part I
The
Records
of
New Mexico

1

History & Government

SOON AFTER THE CONQUEST of Mexico by Hernando Cortés in 1519–21, the Spanish, attracted by rich silver mines, began a gradual advance to the north. Spanish settlements had expanded by 1590 to a line drawn from the mouth of the Río Grande to the Gulf of California.

Knowledge of New Mexico's physical features, resources, and native peoples was acquired through a number of expeditions. Cabeza de Vaca and three other survivors of the Pánfilo de Narváez colonization attempt in Florida in 1528 (and subsequent shipwreck and Indian massacre on the coast of Texas) made their way westward through the wilderness and across the Río Grande into New Mexico, from whence, after a period of captivity among the Indians, they fled south in 1534 to New Spain. Their reports of large settlements of Indians and signs of precious metals caused the viceroy to send Fr. Marcos de Niza and a small military escort on an exploratory trip to New Mexico in 1539. But the most important expedition of the century was that led by Francisco Vásquez de Coronado in 1540, through southeastern Arizona and east through New Mexico to the Zuñi villages. Exploratory parties sent out from this expedition discovered the Grand Canyon of the Colorado and the Pueblo Indian villages at Acoma and on the upper Río Grande. After wintering at the latter place, Coronado went on into eastern Kansas, but, failing to find the rich city that had been reported to him, returned to New Mexico and, in 1542, traveled back to New Spain.[1]

The failure of the Coronado expedition to find precious metals cooled the interest of the Spanish in the region, and little attention was

---

[1] Warren A. Beck, *New Mexico: A History of Four Centuries* (Norman, Okla., 1962), pp. 41–49.

Embudo

Abiquiú †

San Ildefonso
Peña Blanca

† San Juan

† Nambé

Jémez †

Santa Fe

San Ysidro ●

San Felipe †

† San Cristóbal

● San José del Vado

Bernalillo †

San Miguel del Vado

Zuñi †

Sandia †

San Marcos

Galisteo

Encinal †

Santo Domingo

Ácoma †

Alameda

Laguna

Isleta

Albuquerque

Tomé ●

Sabinal

● Belén

† Gran Quivira
(Humanas, Tabira)

Pecos River

San Antonio ●

New
Mexico

Sacramento Mountains

Rio Grande

Guadalupe
Mountains

San Lorenzo ●

● Las Cruces

Mesilla ●

El Paso del Norte ●

Mexico

N

● Town or settlement

† Mission

Scale in Miles

0   20   40   60   80

paid to it for the remainder of the century. A small party of soldiers and Indians, led by Francisco de Chamuscado and Fr. Agustín Rodríguez, visited New Mexico during 1581–82. In 1582, Antonio de Espejo, a wealthy rancher, went north to rescue Father Rodríguez and another friar who had remained there, and he continued on, after hearing of the death of the friars, to the Pueblos on the upper Río Grande, when an exploratory trip was made into Arizona. Espejo prepared a glowing report in which he sought royal authorization to explore and christianize New Mexico, but this undertaking was assigned to another Spaniard. A settlement was established in 1590 by Gaspar Castaño de Sosa, the lieutenant governor of Nuevo León, near the present Santo Domingo, but was withdrawn because his colonizing expedition of that year was unauthorized.[2]

At the end of the sixteenth century, the first settlements were made in New Mexico among the Pueblo Indians of the upper Río Grande. In July, 1598, an expedition led by Juan de Oñate of Zacatecas established colonists at San Juan and San Gabriel. Pedro de Peralta, shortly after succeeding Oñate as governor, founded Santa Fe as the capital in 1610.[3] The Indians at the numerous pueblos were subdued, and missions were established at many of them. The colony became primarily a center of missionary activity and buffer for the protection of the frontier.

The revolt of the Pueblo Indians in 1680 forced the Spanish to retire from the upper Río Grande valley to the neighborhood of El Paso del Norte, the present Mexican town of Ciudad Juárez, where a mission had been founded in 1659. The influx of fugitives from the north, including a considerable number of friendly Pueblos, resulted in the establishment of new settlements in this area. The Indian pueblos of Ysleta and Socorro and the presidio of San Elizario were located in this area on the Texas side of the Río Grande; these were the earliest settlements in Texas.[4]

While planning the reconquest of New Mexico, the Spanish kept the refugees and their Indian allies together at settlements near El Paso del Norte. Successive governors located at San Lorenzo endeavored to keep the dwindling band of refugees together.[5] Gov. Antonio de Otermín, who had led the retreat from Santa Fe, conducted an unsuccessful

---

2 Beck, *New Mexico*, pp. 50–51.

3 Ibid., pp. 52–54; Ralph E. Twitchell, *The Leading Facts of New Mexican History*, 5 vols. (Cedar Rapids, Iowa, 1911–17), 1:304.

4 Anne E. Hughes, *The Beginnings of Spanish Settlement in the El Paso District* (Berkeley, 1914), pp. 388–89.

5 Charles L. Sonnichsen, *Pass of the North: Four Centuries of the Rio Grande* (El Paso, 1968), pp. 50, 56.

expedition north to retake that settlement in the fall of 1691. Diego de Vargas, a more vigorous governor, set out in the summer of 1692 with a force of Spaniards and Indians to recover control of the area on the upper Río Grande. His rapid movements enabled him to reoccupy Santa Fe before the Indians could unite against him, and, during the campaigns in the fall of that year, twenty-three pueblos were recovered. The arrival of a large colonizing party in 1693 firmly reestablished Spanish control of the upper Río Grande.

Under Spanish dominion, New Mexico formed part of the vice-royalty of New Spain, one of the two principal governmental divisions into which Spanish possessions in the New World were divided during the sixteenth century. The governors of New Mexico were subordinate to the viceroy of New Spain until 1776, but, to a large degree, they functioned independently because of the great distance between Mexico City and Santa Fe. The governor was the chief political officer, commander of the military force, superintendent of Indian affairs, legislator on provincial matters, and the principal judge.[6] He appointed or approved the appointment of officials, and made land grants. He was assisted by a secretary who acted as an adviser, notary and custodian of the provincial records. The governor, from his headquarters at Santa Fe, administered affairs in the upper part of the Río Grande valley, and a lieutenant governor, stationed at El Paso del Norte, was the administrative officer in the lower part of the valley.

The governor of New Mexico was not always subject to the direct authority of the viceroy of New Spain. In 1776, New Mexico, Coahuila, Texas, Sonora, Sinaloa, Nueva Vizcaya, and the Californias were set up as the Interior Provinces, under a commandant general at Chihuahua.[7] As this was an effort to improve the defense of the frontier, the commandant general was primarily concerned with military affairs but he was also charged with political, judicial, and financial concerns. In 1787, New Mexico became part of the Western Interior Provinces, which included the Californias, Sonora, and Nueva Vizcaya, under a commandant general who was subordinate, to some extent, to the viceroy. The Eastern Interior Provinces, also established at that time, and the Western Interior Provinces were reunited in 1792, under a commandant at Chihuahua. In 1813, the Western Interior Provinces, consisting of Sonora, Sinaloa, Nueva Vizcaya, and New Mexico, were placed under a commandant at Durango, where the headquarters continued until the end of the Spanish regime.

---

[6] France V. Scholes, "Civil Government and Society in New Mexico in the Seventeenth Century," *New Mexican Historical Review* 10 (Apr. 1935):75; Marc Simmons, *Spanish Government in New Mexico* (Albuquerque, 1968), p. 54.

[7] Simmons, *Spanish Govt. in N. Mex.*, p. 25; Twitchell, *N. Mex. Hist.*, 1:448.

The governor rendered decisions in minor judicial cases appealed from local courts and had exclusive jurisdiction in cases involving Indians.[8] In more important cases, appeals from the judgments of the governor could be made at first to the Audiencia of Mexico, and after 1728, to the Audiencia of Guadalajara, which had jurisdiction over northern New Spain. The Audiencia of Guadalajara retained its judicial authority after the establishment of the commandancy general in 1776. Privileged courts considered cases involving the army, the church, and the royal treasury.

Until 1680, military protection evolved from the *encomendero* system, under which citizen-soldiers, whose normal occupations were farming and cattle raising, guarded missions and settlements and escorted travelers.[9] The Spanish citizens of the various settlements formed militia units under their own officers. Pueblo Indians also served as militiamen, and they and other former nomadic Indians (*genízaros*), who had become residents of the province, were organized into auxiliary companies.[10]

After the Indian rebellion of 1680 and the reconquest of New Mexico, defense of the province came from regular presidios established at El Paso del Norte in 1683 and Santa Fe in 1693. Efforts in the 1770s to stabilize the northern frontier resulted in the transfer of the garrison from El Paso del Norte south to Carrizal in Nueva Vizcaya. Despite appeals for the establishment of other presidios for the defense of New Mexico, none were authorized during the remainder of the Spanish regime. The presidial soldiers and militia guarded the horse herd, took part in patrol and reconnaissance missions, manned temporary outposts during the summer, served as couriers, and escorted the trade caravans from Chihuahua. The governor was commander of the Santa Fe presidio and of military forces throughout the province.

The governor was also responsible for financial matters connected with civil, military, and ecclesiastical establishments. He had general supervision of the supplymaster for the military garrison, the administrator of the tobacco and other monopolies, and, for a time, the friars who collected tithes.[11] In the absence of a treasury official, the supplymaster of the presidio served as treasurer for civil and ecclesiastical officials. After 1766, the sale of imported tobacco became a government monopoly, and the revenue received by the local administrator from

---

[8] Simmons, *Spanish Govt. in N. Mex.*, p. 67.

[9] Ibid., p. 112; Ted J. Warner, "Frontie⸱ Defense," *N. Mex. Hist. Rev.* 41 (Jan. 1966):15.

[10] Simmons, *Spanish Govt. in N. Mex.*, p. 147; Warner, "Frontier Defense," pp. 9, 15–16.

[11] Ibid., p. 88 ff.

sales was taken to Chihuahua by the presidial supplymaster for deposit with the office of the monopoly (administrador de rentas). The local administrator of the tobacco monopoly also received funds from the sale of gunpowder, playing cards, and, after 1786, stamped paper that was used for legal documents. The tithe for the support of the church was collected at times by the governor, by friars, or by private contractors engaged by the diocese of Durango.

Until late in the eighteenth century, New Mexico was dependent for its mail on the caravan that came under escort from Mexico City at irregular intervals. Soon after the establishment of an east-west mail service in the Interior Provinces in 1770, mail service was extended northward to El Paso del Norte, but communication with Santa Fe remained unsatisfactory. In 1783, on instruction from the commandant general, the governor of New Mexico inaugurated a courier service with military escort from Santa Fe to El Paso del Norte.[12] The lieutenant governor supervised the branch post office at El Paso del Norte, and, by 1788, there was a postmaster at Santa Fe, who was appointed by the chief postmaster at Chihuahua on the recommendation of the governor of New Mexico. The service between El Paso del Norte and Santa Fe was operated on a fairly regular schedule, and there seems to have been some kind of mail service within the province itself. The mission supply caravans that were initiated in 1609 brought not only mission and church supplies but also new settlers, missionaries, and public servants, and were used to export hides and blankets (prepared by Indians), piñon nuts, and, later, sheep, that were sent to supply the missionaries of New Spain.

After Mexico became independent of Spain, in 1821, New Mexico continued as part of the Interior Provinces, for a time, under the commandancy at Chihuahua, and Spanish laws remained in force. On January 31, 1824, New Mexico, together with Chihuahua and Durango, became the Interior State of the North.[13] The Mexican constitution of October, 1824, established Durango and Chihuahua as separate states and New Mexico as a territory. The El Paso district was assigned to the state of Durango, but, on the north, New Mexico extended to the boundary established by the treaty of 1821 between the United States and Spain. The Territory of New Mexico was governed by a political chief appointed by and responsible to the head of the Mexican government in Mexico City. A new Mexican constitution of 1836 established a centralized system of government under which the territory of the nation was divided into departments, which were subdivided into pre-

---

[12] Ibid., p. 105.

[13] Hubert H. Bancroft, *History of Arizona and New Mexico, 1530–1888* (San Francisco, 1889), p. 311.

fectures.[14] During the Mexican period, New Mexico was represented in the Mexican Congress by a deputy, chosen by an electoral junta composed of electors from the *alcaldias*.[15]

In New Mexico, under Mexican administration, there were other officials whose activities added to the accumulation of records in Santa Fe. Under the restrictive commercial policy of Spain, trade had been permitted only with the provinces to the south, but a Mexican law of 1822, allowing the entry of foreigners into the territory, resulted in the development of considerable commerce with the United States over the Santa Fe trail. Within a short time, customs duties collected on goods imported from Missouri became the chief source for support for the New Mexico government.[16] The general treasurer at Santa Fe kept the funds of the various subdivisions of the territorial government and acted as collector of customs and internal revenues.[17] Many American traders and trappers entered New Mexico during the Mexican regime, and a record of passports presented by or issued to them was kept.[18] During the territorial period, the treasury official in New Mexico was responsible to treasury officials in Chihuahua, but after the institution of the departmental system of government in 1837, he was subordinate to the minister of finance in Mexico City.

During the Mexican period, the military commander continued to be subordinate to the commandant general at Chihuahua. The governor sometimes filled that post, and at other times an army officer held it. In 1836, there were presidial troops at Santa Fe, San Miguel del Vabo, and Taos,[19] and militia continued to afford protection at other settlements. In 1839, New Mexico was made a separate commandancy general, responsible directly to the minister of war and the navy in Mexico City. Frequent campaigns had to be waged against the Indians, whose depredations continued during the Mexican period.

The alcaldes and the governor continued to be involved in the administration of justice. Early in the Mexican period, appeals of the governor's judicial decisions could be made to the court at Durango.

---

[14] Ibid., p. 314; Lansing B. Bloom, "New Mexico Under Mexican Administration," *Old Santa Fe* 1–2 (July 1913–Apr. 1915), 2:9–10. A Mexican Law of March 20, 1837, providing for the government of the departments, prescribed the duties of the governor, the departmental legislature, the prefects, and local officials (text in Matthew G. Reynolds, *Spanish and Mexican Land Laws: New Spain and Mexico* [St. Louis, 1895], pp. 211–21).

[15] Bloom, "N. Mex. Under Mex. Admin.," 1:145, 364; 2:10, 158, 234, 354.

[16] Bloom, "N. Mex. Under Admin.," 2:17.

[17] Ibid., 1:252; 2:15, 223, 235, 243, 245.

[18] Robert G. Cleland, *This Reckless Breed of Men: The Trappers and Fur Traders of the Southwest* (New York, 1950), p. 209.

[19] Bloom, "N. Mex. Under Mex. Admin.," 2:7, 135 n. 484.

Then a Mexican decree of May 20, 1826, established a circuit court at
Parral, for the states of Durango, Chihuahua, and the Territory of New
Mexico. The same decree provided for a district judge at Santa Fe, but
none was appointed until sometime towards the middle of the next
decade. In 1831, Antonio Barreiro arrived in New Mexico to act as
legal adviser to the government, but, in the absence of other legal
officers, it was not possible for him to accomplish much towards promoting the administration of justice. In 1844, courts of first resort were
established at Santa Fe, Los Luceros, and Valencia, with the alcaldes
of those places serving as judges and exercising civil and criminal jurisdiction.[20]

A postal service was maintained between Santa Fe and Chihuahua, and among the settlements in New Mexico. Juan Bautista Vigil
was the postmaster at Santa Fe during most of the Mexican period.
The mail was distributed from the post offices there and at Tomé to
other settlements.[21]

---

[20] Ibid., 1:45, 155 n. 119, 259; 2:12, 227 n. 571.
[21] Ibid., 1:14–15; 2:141, 158 n. 128, 179.

2

Provincial
Records

THE AMERICAN OCCUPATION of New Mexico occurred early in the Mexican War. Gen. Stephen W. Kearny, commander of the "Army of the West," after an overland march from the Missouri River, entered Santa Fe on August 18, 1846.[1] Lt. Gov. Juan Bautista Vigil y Alarid received him at the Governor's Palace and informed him that Gov. Manuel Armijo had fled into Chihuahua. On August 19, Kearny appointed Vigil as acting secretary of state, and Nicolas Quintana, the first clerk in the governor's office, became acting secretary.[2] Shortly afterwards, Kearny replaced the Mexicans who had served as treasurer and collector of customs with new appointees, who were instructed to take charge of the public funds, books, and property of those offices.[3] On September 22, before continuing his march to California, Kearny set up a civil government, appointing Charles Bent as governor, Donaciano Vigil as secretary, and other officials.

The designation of Donaciano Vigil as secretary placed the Spanish archives in experienced hands, for he had previously been their custodian. After Governor Bent's assassination in the Pueblo revolt at Taos in January, 1847, Vigil became acting governor, but in October,

---

[1] The instructions issued to Kearny by Winfield Scott, the commanding general of the Army, May 31, 1846, and those issued to him by Secretary of War William L. Marcy, June 3, 1846, relative to the occupation of New Mexico and California, contain no directions regarding the archives of those places (*House Exec. Doc. 60*, 30 Cong., 1 sess., pp. 241–45).

[2] Charles Bent to James Buchanan, Oct. 8, 1846, General Records of the Department of State, Miscellaneous Letters (Record Group 59), National Archives (hereinafter cited as NA, DS, Misc. Lets.).

[3] "Occupation of Mexican Territory," Dec. 22, 1846, *House Exec. Doc. 19*, 29 Cong., 2 sess., p. 22.

1848, he was succeeded by Lt. Col. John M. Washington. As secretary, Vigil continued in charge of the archives, which were housed in the Governor's Palace, until the establishment of the territorial government. During 1849–50, Vigil prepared an "index" to the Spanish archives, which is really a chronological listing.[4]

The treaty of Guadalupe Hidalgo of February 2, 1848,[5] ceded to the United States the territory in the Southwest (New Mexico, Arizona, and California) that had been occupied by its military forces. The treaty contained no stipulation with regard to the Spanish and Mexican archives of New Mexico, nor did the act of September 9, 1850 establishing the Territory of New Mexico.[6] The latter act did provide, however, for a territorial secretary, among whose duties was that of preserving the territorial records.

After the inauguration of the territorial government of New Mexico at Santa Fe in 1851, some attention was given to the Spanish archives. They came under the care of the secretary, a position having numerous incumbents during the early years of the territory. The appointment of David V. Whiting as translator and interpreter, on March 8, 1851, was confirmed by an act of the legislature on June 19.[7] Samuel Ellison succeeded Whiting on September 21, 1852. In his first message to the legislature on June 2, 1851, Gov. James S. Calhoun recommended the repair of the Governor's Palace in order to provide a safer repository for the records, which he felt needed a night guard or other measures for their security.[8] The secretary's quarters in the Governor's Palace consisted of two rooms; the inner one served as his office, and the outer room was used as an anteroom and a storeroom. "The latter is divided by a cotton curtain hanging down from the beams above, into two compartments, one of which is stored with the old manuscript records of the Territory which have been accumulating for nearly three hundred years."[9] On the recommendation of Gov. David

---

[4] The list is entitled "Indice General de Todos los Documentos del Tiempo de los Goviernos de Espana y de Méjico hasta el año de mil ochosientos cuarenta y seis" and is among the land records of New Mexico at Santa Fe. The list is also available on the microfilm of those records that is cited below. The list is valuable in showing the composition of the Spanish archives before they were divided between the territorial secretary's office and the surveyor general's office.

[5] United States, *Statutes at Large*, 9:922.

[6] U.S., *Stats.*, 9:447.

[7] Journal of the Executive Proceedings, Territory of New Mexico, General Records of the Department of State, Territorial Papers of New Mexico, I, (Record Group 59) National Archives, pp. 5, 45, 73, (hereinafter cited as NA, DS, N. Mex. Terr. Papers); New Mexico (Terr.), *Laws*, 1851–52, p. 107.

[8] NA, DS, N. Mex. Terr. Papers, 1:42.

[9] W. W. H. Davis, *El Gringo: or, New Mexico and Her People* (New York, 1857), p. 169. Davis became United States attorney at Santa Fe in November, 1863. As

Merriwether, the legislative council of New Mexico memorialized Congress, on February 4, 1854, for an appropriation of $15,000, to provide for the safekeeping and translation of the Spanish archives.[10] This appeal was unsuccessful, but nonetheless extensive repairs and remodeling were done on the Governor's Palace during the years 1860–68.[11]

The Spanish archives of New Mexico were subjected to neglect and destruction for many years under the territorial government. Poorly housed and improperly safeguarded in the Governor's Palace, their fate was a matter of indifference to most of the governors and secretaries of the territory. Following an appeal by Gov. William F. M. Arny, the legislative assembly passed an act, on January 28, 1863, which designated the librarian as "Librarian and Custodian of Archives."[12] Thus, the librarian became the keeper of the Spanish archives, of which he was directed to prepare a register. A room in the Governor's Palace was to be assigned for his use, and a small sum was provided for equipment and registers.

The territorial library, which had been established in 1850,[13] continued, however, to have a checkered career and did not make significant gains under the act of 1863. In his annual message of December, 1866, Governor Arny recommended the abolition of the position of territorial librarian, the transfer of the library to the secretary of the territory, and the appropriation of $500 for the proper arrangement of the old Spanish archives.[14] The next year, Gov. Robert B. Mitchell removed the librarian, and the archives passed into the hands of H. H. Heath, the secretary. That official was unsuccessful in soliciting funds from the government in Washington for the arrangement and preservation[15] of the archives, but he did manage to employ a Spanish-American scholar named Mariano Sena, for five and a half days, to

---

secretary of the territory from 1854–57, he found time to gather material from the Spanish archives which he later used in his book, *The Spanish Conquest of New Mexico* (Doylestown, Pa., 1869).

[10] Memorial to Congress by the Council and House of Representatives of the Territory of New Mexico, Records of the United States House of Representatives, HR33A–F24 (Record Group 233), National Archives; printed in *House Misc. Doc.* 50, 33 Cong., 1 sess.; *House Journal*, 33 Cong., 2 sess., p. 245.

[11] Clinton P. Anderson, "The Adobe Palace," *N. Mex. Hist. Rev.* 19 (Apr. 1944): 102–11.

[12] New Mexico (Terr.), *Acts*, 1862–63, p. 46.

[13] Arie Poldervaart, "The New Mexico Law Library — A History," *N. Mex. Hist. Rev.* 21 (Jan. 1946):47–48.

[14] New Mexico (Terr.), Governor, *Annual Message*, 1866, p. 31.

[15] H. H. Heath to William H. Seward, Aug. 8, Sept. 21, 1867, NA, DS, N. Mex. Terr. Papers, III; Seward to Heath, Sept. 2, Oct. 18, 1867, General Records of the Department of State, Domestic Letters, Bk. 77 (Record Group 59), National Archives (hereinafter cited as NA, DS, Dom. Lets.).

arrange and pack up the Spanish manuscripts and place the printed books of the library on shelves.[16]

During the course of alteration and repairs of the Governor's Palace in 1867–68, the secretary was without suitable quarters, and the archives were placed in an unfinished room. A new governor, with a big broom, arrived in the territory in 1869. Deciding that he needed the uncompleted room occupied by the archives, Gov. William A. Pile ordered their removal to an outhouse. A portion of the records was given to some convicts, and, on the governor's orders, the newly appointed librarian, Ira M. Bond, threw others out the windows for use by citizens, and sold the rest to merchants for wrapping paper.[17] A wood hauler, Eleuterio Barela, saw a pile of papers in the street and, with the permission of the governor, conveyed a load in his *carreta* to his home at Cienegita. The governor had not reckoned, however, with the historical consciousness of the local newspaper or the residents of Santa Fe, who formed a committee, investigated the ravaging of the archives, and then waited on the governor to request that steps be taken for their recovery.[18] Mr. Bond was sent on a salvaging mission and returned with a cart-load of records, obtained from the persons to whom they had been sold. The papers hauled off by Barela were also recovered at this time (except for a small quantity which he did not return to the archives until 1886).[19] Another committee of citizens drew up a resolution censoring the governor for the outrage he had partially succeeded in committing and demanding his removal by the president. Whether or not all this had any effect on the length of the governor's term is uncertain, but in little more than a year (June, 1871), he left the territory.[20] In 1872, the territorial librarian acknowledged the return of another lot of Spanish archives.

---

[16] Miscellaneous Treasury Accounts, No. 165317, Records of the United States General Accounting Office, (Record Group 217) National Archives (hereinafter cited as NA, GAO, Misc. Treas. Accts.).

[17] "Destruction of Spanish and Mexican Archives in New Mexico by United States Officials," Extract from the *Santa Fe Weekly Post*, Apr. 30, 1870, and the Albuquerque *Republican Review, n.d.;* Poldervaart, "N. Mex. Law Lib.," pp. 50–51. Bond claimed that he had consulted two prominent Spanish-Americans as to the value of the archives and that he had disposed of nothing of value, but he nevertheless published a notice in the newspaper requesting the return of the records that had been carried away (William A. Keleher, *Violence in Lincoln County, 1869–1881* [Albuquerque, 1957], pp. 7–8).

[18] J. Manuel Espinosa, "Memoir of a Kentuckian in New Mexico 1848–1884. *N. Mex. Hist. Rev.*, 13 (Jan. 1937):10–11.

[19] *N. Mex. Hist. Rev.* 10 (Apr. 1935):171–72. An act of the territorial legislature of New Mexico, approved Feb. 23, 1893, appropriated $200 to reward Barela for saving the archives (New Mexico [Terr.], *Laws,* 1893, p. 92).

[20] He was appointed minister resident to Venezuela on May 23, 1871.

Upon his arrival in the territory in 1871, the new governor, Marsh Giddings, found various manuscripts scattered about the Governor's Palace and Square, some of them in a lumber room exposed to the weather and to encroachments by children who trampled them underfoot and threw them about in play.[21] Learning that the records had long been exposed to pilfering by public and private parties, and aware of their historical value, Governor Giddings took measures for their protection. With the help of James C. McKenzie, the new librarian, the papers were gathered together, and some "three to five cords" of them were piled in a confused mass in boxes in the library room. An appropriation of $500 was requested by the governor for equipping a room for the archives and for their "proper selecting, folding, filing and packing." No funds were forthcoming, however, and, two years later, the governor could only report that the records, which had been rescued from open sheds, were still nailed up in twelve dry goods boxes.[22]

A program for the restoration of the archives was finally begun while Lewis Wallace, a retired general and historical novelist, was serving as governor. He reported the neglected condition of the Spanish archives to the secretary of the interior and, upon the basis of an examination of them by Samuel Ellison, translator and interpreter for a number of early territorial governors and the legislature, requested an appropriation of $5,000 for their care and preservation, but was turned down.[23]

Upon receiving the appointment of territorial librarian in October, 1880, Ellison was given custody of the Spanish archives and the task of rescuing them from further deterioration. He found them in a confused state, tied up in bundles without order or arrangement, dusty, worm-eaten, and partially rotted from exposure. Pointing out the considerable work that would be involved to put them in condition for preservation, their great value for historical research and the determination of titles to real estate, and the loss of documents resulting from vandalism and despoliation, he recommended to the governor that the legislature be urged to provide for their preservation.[24]

---

[21] New Mexico (Terr.), Governor, *Annual Message*, Dec. 1871, pp. 44–45.

[22] "Governor's [Annual] Message," Dec. 1873, in New Mexico (Terr.), Legislative Council, *Journal*, 1873–74, p. 27.

[23] Lewis Wallace to Carl Schurz, Aug. 25, Sept. 15, 1879, Records of the Office of the Secretary of the Interior, Patents and Miscellaneous Division, Letters Received Relating to the Territory of New Mexico (Record Group 48), National Archives. See also the appropriation acts for June 19, 1878, June 21, 1879, and June 15, 1880 (U.S., *Stats.*, 20:194; vol. 21, sect. 27, pp. 225–26).

[24] New Mexico (Terr.), Librarian, *Biennial Report*, 1880–81, Microfilm Collection of Early State Records, New Mexico D 25, Library of Congress.

A disinterested report on the condition of the Spanish archives, not long after Ellison took charge of them, is available in a description by Lt. John G. Bourke who was introduced to Ellison by Governor Wallace on April 18, 1881. Bourke wrote as follows:

> Next, we went into the archives' room and saw bundles upon bundles of paper, piled high above each other, in an inextricable confusion. There is no shelving, no glass-casing — nothing to retard the destroying influences of time and weather. Dust lies thick upon the leaves; mildew and decay have obliterated much of the writing and worst of all it is said that a former Governor — a drunken, political dead-beat named Pyle used many of these valuable documents for kindling the fires in his Office and sold cart-loads of others for waste paper! Mr. Ellison is laboring occasionally to bring order out of Chaos, and as he is not only a patient student, but has a fluent knowledge of Spanish, I look for much good from his exertions.[25]

Ellison was enabled, through the passage of acts by the territorial legislature, to undertake the first real program for the preservation of the Spanish archives. Two acts of March 1, 1882 ensured more adequate attention to the archives. Under one of these, the librarian was designated as custodian of the archives, and his salary was increased to $600, double the amount provided by the act of 1863 and making the position sufficiently remunerative to retain persons in office.[26] The other act directed the librarian to arrange the archives in either chronological order or by subjects, to have them bound in suitable volumes for preservation, and appropriated $400 for expenses.[27] During the next two years, Ellison arranged the papers by subjects and filed them in 144 pasteboard boxes, the limited appropriation making binding impossible.[28] In a large room in the eastern end of the Governor's Palace, the congested condition of which Ellison reported to the secretary of the territory in April, 1884, the librarian continued his labors for several years longer.

During the 1880s, historian Hubert Howe Bancroft obtained material from the Santa Fe archives. In 1881, he tried to have the archives

---

[25] Lansing B. Bloom, ed., "Bourke on the Southwest, VII," *N. Mex. Hist. Rev.* 10 (Oct. 1935):317.

[26] New Mexico (Terr.) *Laws*, 1882, pp. 85–87.

[27] Ibid., pp. 88–89.

[28] New Mexico (Terr.), Librarian, "Report of Samuel Ellison, Librarian of the Territory of New Mexico for the Years 1882 and 1883," in New Mexico (Terr.), *Official Reports of the Territory of New Mexico, for the Years 1882 and 1883* (Santa Fe, 1884), pp. 31–57.

of New Mexico deposited for a time in his own library. Failing in this, he was obliged to go to Santa Fe to have extracted such material as he wanted. In the winter of 1884–85, he went to Santa Fe to obtain more extracts for his history, and Samuel Ellison, then territorial librarian, was employed by him to make copies and extracts. Ellison engaged in this task for some time but, finding it laborious, finally consented to send bundles of archives to San Francisco by express so that Bancroft could have the copying done in his own library.[29] The material thus obtained was used by Bancroft in his *History of Arizona and New Mexico.*

Another extensive user of the Spanish archives of New Mexico was Adolph F. A. Bandelier, pioneer student of the ethnology, archaeology, and history of Pueblo and other Indians. His field and documentary studies of these Indians were initiated in 1880 with the support of the Archaeological Institute of America. During 1880–84 he made field investigations and examined and made copies and excerpts from the Spanish archives at Santa Fe.[30] As historiographer of the Hemenway Southwestern Archaeological Expedition, he investigated, during the years 1886–89, the Spanish archives at Santa Fe, Mexico City and elsewhere, taking copies, excerpts, and notes relative to both the Pueblos and the colonization and mission development of the Southwest and northern Mexico.[31] Besides extensive publications embodying much of the documentary material which he collected,[32] Bandelier also prepared a manuscript containing a 1400-page history, maps, original sketches, and photographs[33] of the colonization and

---

[29] Hubert H. Bancroft, *Literary Industries, a Memoir* (New York, 1891), pp. 628, 763.

[30] Charles H. Lange and Carroll L. Riley, eds., *The Southwestern Journals of Adolph F. Bandelier, 1880–1882* (Albuquerque, 1966), pp. 26, 72, 143–45, 180, 242, 245, 246; Charles H. Lange and Carroll L. Riley eds., *The Southwestern Journals of Adolph Bandelier, 1883–1884* (Albuquerque, 1970), pp. 333, 334. The transcripts of documents are in the Laboratory of Anthropology at Santa Fe.

[31] Frederick W. Hodge, "Biographical Sketch and Bibliography of Adolphe Francis Alphonse Bandelier," *N. Mex. Hist. Rev.* 7 (Oct. 1932):358–59.

[32] Adolph F. A. Bandelier, *Final Report of Investigations among the Indians of the Southwestern United States Carried on Mainly in the Years from 1880 to 1885 (Papers of the Archaeological Institute of America, American Series,* No. 3, pt. 1, and No. 4, pt. 2) (Cambridge, 1890, 1892); Bandelier, "An Outline of the Documentary History of the Zuñi Tribe," *Journal of American Ethnology and Archaeology* 3 (1892):1–115.

[33] A detailed description is in Ernest J. Burrus, S.J., "The Bandelier Collection in the Vatican Library," *Manuscripta* 10 (July 1966):67–84; Ernest J. Burrus, S.J. *A History of the Southwest: A Study of the Civilization and Conversion of the Indians in Southwestern United States and Northwestern Mexico from the Earliest Times to 1700, Volume I; A Catalogue of the Bandelier Collection in the Vatican Library* (Rome, 1969).

Franciscan missions of New Mexico, Arizona, Sonora, and Chihuahua, which was presented by Archbishop John B. Salpointe of Tucson, Arizona, to Pope Leo XIII and deposited in the Vatican Library. Photo-reproductions of the manuscripts are in the Bancroft Library of the University of California, the St. Louis University Library, the University of Arizona Library in Tucson, Arizona, and the Library of the Amerind Foundation in Dragoon, Arizona. Bandelier's collection of documents was presented to the Peabody Museum of Harvard University by Mary Hemenway, and soon after, a catalog of the collection was published.[34]

The provincial records remained in the custody of the territorial librarian for another twenty years. Then in 1888, the records were removed from the Governor's Palace to a newly completed capitol. Originally started in 1853, construction of this building was suspended in 1860 for more than a quarter of a century, leaving a roofless story-and-a-half structure in the basement of which fireproof vaults had been built for safekeeping the public archives.[35] The old Spanish archives seem not to have been kept in the vault, however, for when a fire started in the capitol on May 12, 1892, Ralph E. Twitchell and others, who knew where the archives were kept, rescued them.[36] The archives went back to the Governor's Palace again, until their removal in 1900 to a vault in the capitol prepared for the records in the charge of the territorial secretary.[37]

A new effort to improve the condition of the Spanish archives was made during the administration of Gov. L. Bradford Prince. An act of the territorial legislature, approved on February 26, 1891, authorized the governor to employ a competent person to catalog, number, index, bind, and translate the old Spanish and Mexican archives.[38] Only documents of historical interest to New Mexico were to be translated and transcribed into clean copies, which eventually were to be published. Bandelier was employed to execute this program, but

---

[34] "The Bandelier Collection of Copies of Documents Relative to the History of New Mexico and Arizona," in *Report of the United States Commission to the Columbian Historical Exposition at Madrid, 1892–93* (House Exec. Doc. 100, 53 Cong., 3 sess., Washington, 1895), pp. 305–26. A description of the collection is also in Ernest J. Burrus, S.J., "Bandelier's Manuscript Sources for the Study of the American Southwest," in *Homenaje a Don José María de la Peña y Cámara* (Madrid, 1969), pp. 38–48.

[35] W. F. M. Arny to O. H. Browning, Secretary of the Interior, May 15, 1867, *House Exec. Doc.* 33, 40 Cong., 2 sess., p. 11.

[36] "Ralph Emerson Twitchell," *N. Mex. Hist. Rev.* 1 (Jan. 1926):81.

[37] John H. Vaughan, "A Preliminary Report on the Archives of New Mexico," Amer. Hist. Assoc., *Ann. Rep.* (1909), p. 471.

[38] New Mexico (Terr.), *Acts of the Legislative Assembly*, 1891, pp. 201–02. This act appropriated $1200; another appropriation made by the act approved February 23, 1893 (ibid., 1893, p. 92) amounted to $600.

all that he accomplished was the preparation of a chronological list of 1,074 archival files.[39] A copy of this list, that came into the possession of the Historical Society of New Mexico, was used by Twitchell in compiling his *Spanish Archives of New Mexico.*

An inspection of the Spanish archives by out-of-town visitors in the summer of 1899 was to have a surprising outcome. Elliott Coues, an editor of journals of exploration, who was then on an ethnological expedition in the Southwest with Frederick W. Hodge of the Smithsonian Institution, showed the old records at Santa Fe to Charles Seymour, a lawyer of Knoxville, Tennessee. In April, 1900, after returning to his home, Seymour wrote to George P. Wetmore[40] who, as chairman of the Senate committee on the Library of Congress, logically referred the letter to Herbert Putnam, the librarian of Congress.[41] Putnam communicated with Hodge, who was back at his post in the Bureau of American Ethnology, and then wrote to the secretary of the Territory of New Mexico inquiring about the possibility of transferring the old manuscripts at Santa Fe to the Library of Congress.[42] The secretary answered favorably, saying that the archives consisted of forty-eight cubic feet.[43]

In 1902, the Library of Congress began negotiating for the acquisition of the Spanish archives of New Mexico, as part of its program for concentrating, among its holdings, the archives of the territories acquired from Spain and Mexico. The librarian of Congress wrote to the secretary of the interior, stressing the great importance of the records for historical research and the desirability of preserving them in the national library where they would be secure and accessible to scholars.[44] He suggested that the secretary forward a recommendation to the territorial legislature for the passage of an act providing for

---

[39] Ralph E. Twitchell, *The Spanish Archives of New Mexico*, 2 vols. (Glendale, Calif., 1914, 1:xv-xvi.

[40] Seymour to Wetmore, Apr. 18, 1900, Records of the Library of Congress, Office of the Librarian of Congress, Correspondence File, Miscellaneous (New Mexico Archives), Library of Congress. (hereinafter cited as LC, Librarian of Cong., Corres. File).

[41] A. R. Spofford to Herbert Putnam, May 31, 1900, ibid., commenting on the letter referred by Wetmore, the neglect of the archives in New Mexico, and recommending that negotiations be made through the proper channels to obtain the documents.

[42] Putnam to George H. Wallace, May 31, 1900, Records of the Office of the Secretary of the Interior, Patents and Miscellaneous Division, Letters Received (Record Group 48), National Archives (hereinafter cited as NA, SI, PM, Lets. Recd.); printed in the "Report of the Territorial Secretary," in New Mexico (Terr.), Governor, *Message of Governor Miguel A. Otero . . .* Jan. 21, 1901 (Albuquerque, New Mex., 1901), pp. 119–20.

[43] Wallace to Putnam, June 9, 1900, NA, SI, PM, Lets. Recd.

[44] Putnam to Ethan Allen Hitchcock, Dec. 18, 1902, NA, SI, PM, Lets. Recd.

the transfer of records selected by the librarian. This letter was sent by the secretary of the interior to the governor of New Mexico,[45] who referred it to the legislature.[46] Herbert Putnam visited Santa Fe in February, 1903, discussed the matter with members of the legislature and territorial officials, and made arrangements with the territorial librarian for shipping the records.[47] After his departure, protests were started against their removal. The New Mexico Historical Society aroused public sentiment to such an extent that the legislature was persuaded to amend the bill for the transfer of the archives, requiring the return of those relating to land titles or local personal matters within one year, and the return of all of the documents within five years.[48]

However, the Spanish archives were transferred to the Library of Congress anyway — but under other arrangements. The act of the territorial legislature approved March 19, 1903,[49] based on the bill mentioned above, was unacceptable to the librarian, who maintained that the records were subject to the control of the federal government. Upon his application, the secretary of the interior ordered the governor of New Mexico, on April 29, 1903, to ship the records to the Department of the Interior at Washington.[50] Consequently, on May 14, 1903, four packing cases of records were turned over to the Library of Congress under the authorization of an act of Congress of February 25, 1903.[51] Inasmuch as the transfer was finally effected by a direct order of the department, it was unconditional, and the records remained in the Library of Congress for twenty years. The records were cleaned, flattened, arranged chronologically without regard to provenance or subject matter, and placed in 180 half-leather portfolios. A card calen-

---

[45] Ethan A. Hitchcock to Miguel A. Otero, Dec. 24, 1902, LC, Librarian of Cong., Corres. File (Interior Dept.).

[46] New Mexico (Terr.), Governor, *Annual Message . . . , of Miguel A. Otero* Jan. 19, 1903, p. 57. Exhibit M (pp. 8–9) in this document contains the biennial report of the secretary of the territory for January 1, 1903, in which he stated that the Spanish archives were in danger of destruction from repeated handling by searchers who had to go through the unindexed packages of loose sheets looking for what interested them.

[47] Putnam to Lafayette Emmett, Territorial Librarian, Feb. 28, 1903, NA, SI, PM, Lets. Recd.

[48] New Mexico Historical Society, *Biennial Report* (1904), pp. 6–7. Herbert Putnam to James R. Garfield, Secretary of the Interior, Oct. 2, 1903, LC, Librarian of Cong., Corres. File (Interior Dept., Sec.).

[49] New Mexico (Terr.) *Acts*, 1903, p. 179.

[50] Thomas Ryan, Acting Secretary of the Interior, to Herbert Putnam, May 1, 1903, NA, SI, PM, Lets. Recd.

[51] Putnam to the Secretary of the Interior, May 15, 1903, SI, PM, Lets. Recd.; *Report of the Librarian of Congress*, 1903, pp. 26–27; New Mexico (Terr.), Secretary's Office, *Report of the Secretary of the Territory, 1903–1904, and Legislative Manual, 1905* (Santa Fe, 1905).

dar in English of the collection was completed as far as the year 1823 by Miss Elizabeth H. West.

The foregoing calendar became the basis of the catalog published by Ralph E. Twitchell, New Mexico lawyer and historian, in his publication entitled the *Spanish Archives of New Mexico* (volume II) published in 1914. Designed to facilitate the use of the Spanish records in Washington, this project was given some financial support by the state of New Mexico. The catalog contains 3,097 entries and covers the years 1621 to 1821.

The file of records known as the Spanish archives of New Mexico, 1621–1821, consists of the administrative records accumulated by the governor, including communications and decrees received from the viceroy and the commandant general, copies of communications to those officials, reports from local officials and instructions sent to them; censuses;[52] and appointments, governors' edicts, minutes, and petitions of the *cabildo* of Santa Fe.[53] The decrees and royal orders issued by the Spanish government in Spain and New Spain were usually printed and, being of general applicability, are useful for understanding Spanish administration in the whole Southwest.[54] Military records include lists of troops, muster rolls, orders, journals of operations, reports of inspections, and service records. Papers of a judicial nature include litigation proceedings in civil and criminal cases, judgments of the governor and the captain general, and auxiliary documents such as affidavits, declarations, petitions, writs, testimonies, depositions, pleas, sentences, orders, and judgments. Probate records on the settlement of estates and the protection of widows and minors are included.[55]

---

[52] A translation of a census of the several settlements in the El Paso del Norte district prepared from a copy of the document in the Archivo General de Indias in Seville is in J. Manuel Espinosa, trans., "Population of the El Paso District in 1692," *Mid-America*, n.s. 12 (Jan. 1941):61–84.

[53] New Mexico, State Records Center, *Guide to the Microfilm of the Spanish Archives of New Mexico, 1621–1821*, ed. by Myra Ellen Jenkins (Santa Fe, 1967), pp. 6–8; John H. Vaughan, "Archives of New Mexico," p. 473; U.S., Library of Congress, *Handbook of Manuscripts in the Library of Congress* (Washington, 1918), pp. 286–87.

[54] Bibliographic information concerning Spanish colonial legislation is in John T. Vance, *The Background of Hispanic American Law; Legal Sources and Juridical Literature of Spain* (Washington, 1937), pp. 127–65. Titles of Mexican Government publications containing decrees and other materials are in Annita M. Ker, *Mexican Government Publications; A Guide to the More Important Publications of the National Governments of Mexico, 1821–1936* (Washington, 1940), pp. 1–11, and the Historical Records Survey, Illinois, *Check List of New Mexico Imprints and Publications, 1784–1876* (Lansing[?] 1942), pp. 4–13.

[55] Reports on the arrival and departure of foreigners and a record of trade permits issued, 1826–28, are printed in David J. Weber, trans. and ed., *The Extranjeros: Selected Documents from the Mexican Side of the Santa Fe Trail, 1825–1828* (Santa Fe, 1967). These documents are important for the many names of Americans they contain.

The Spanish archives are useful not only for the political and social history of New Mexico, but also for ecclesiastical history, personal and family history, and as a record of the activities of foreigners.[56]

An act of the New Mexico legislature of February 19, 1909, established the State Museum of New Mexico at Santa Fe.[57] Its creation was the result of an agreement between the state and the Archaeological Institute of America, which wanted to locate its School of American Archaeology in the Southwest, a rich archaeological field. In return for a home in the Governor's Palace at Santa Fe, the school was to maintain there a museum of archaeology, ethnology, and history, which was to be the State Museum of New Mexico.[58] It was to be the depository of collections obtained by the school. Both the museum and the school were to be under a director provided by the institute, without cost to the state.[59]

In 1923, the State Museum of New Mexico became the depository of the Spanish archives of New Mexico, which, for the previous twenty years, had been in the Division of Manuscripts in the Library of Congress. Following a conference between Dr. Edgar L. Hewett, director of the School of American Archaeology and the State Museum of New Mexico, and Dr. Herbert Putnam, librarian of Congress, the former submitted an official request for the transfer of the archives to the State Museum of New Mexico.[60] Assurance was given of their continued safe custody and wise provision for use. The librarian, realizing that under the custodianship of the new institution the records would be properly cared for, interposed no objection to the transfer. He suggested to Dr. Hewett, in reply, that the governor of New Mexico apply to the secretary of the interior (to whom the transaction had already been explained by the acting chief of the Division of Manuscripts of the Library of Congress) for the return of the papers to Santa Fe.[61] After Putnam received a letter from the secretary of the interior, with

---

[56] Twitchell, *Spanish Arch. N. Mex.*, II. An intensive investigator in these records and in other records of colonial New Mexico, Fr. Angélico Chávez considers Twitchell's transcriptions of words and proper names, and his comments, often misleading (Chávez, *Origins of New Mexico Families in the Spanish Colonial Period* [Santa Fe, 1954], p. 338).

[57] New Mexico (Terr.), *Statutes*, 1909, pp. 4–7.

[58] Museum of New Mexico, *Report*, 1926, p. 3; New Mexico, Governor, *Report*, 1910, pp. 37–38; Bertha P. Dutton "The Museum of New Mexico," *El Palacio* 56 (Jan. 1949):3.

[59] The Governor's Palace was occupied by territorial governors until 1907 when an executive mansion was built. In 1911–13 the palace was restored for the use of the Museum of New Mexico, the School of American Archaeology, and the Historical Society of New Mexico.

[60] Hewett to Putnam, Jan. 10, 1923, LC, Librarian of Cong., Corres. File.

[61] Putnam to Hewett, June 26, 1923, LC, Librarian of Cong., Corres. File. (Misc., New Mex. Arch.).

a copy of a letter to him from Gov. James F. Hinkle of August 17,[62] three boxes of Spanish records and the catalog cards were shipped to Santa Fe, where they were received on October 30.[63] They were placed in a concrete vault in the Governor's Palace.

A New Mexico statute of April 1, 1959 authorized the appointment of a public records commission and the establishment of a State Records Center.[64] In 1960, a records administrator and an archivist were appointed, and a warehouse was purchased and converted for use as a records center. When the State of New Mexico Records Center and Archives (State Records Center) was opened in Santa Fe in the fall of 1960, it began receiving records from state agencies that had previously served as record depositories. Among the records transferred by the Museum of New Mexico were the Spanish and Mexican archives.[65]

During 1938–41, the Historical Records Survey of New Mexico, with material and equipment supplied by the University of New Mexico Library, microfilmed the Spanish and Mexican archives of New Mexico, which were then in the State Museum of New Mexico. Enlarged prints prepared from the microfilm were bound and made available at the University of New Mexico Library for ordinary research.[66] The fragile originals were retired from use in order to prevent further deterioration. The entire photoprint collection of the Spanish and Mexican archives of New Mexico, of which a copy was supplied to the Bancroft Library of the University of California at Berkeley, consists of 238 volumes. Documents pertaining to New Mexico in the Spanish period, 1621–1821, comprise 84 volumes, and those on the Mexican period, 1821–46, comprise 154 volumes.[67] Eighty-four volumes of the first part and

---

[62] Frank Springer, for the Board of Regents of the Museum of New Mexico, to James F. Hinkle, Aug. 13, 1923, Records of the Office of the Secretary of the Interior, Territorial Files, Miscellaneous Matters (Record Group 48), National Archives; Hinkle to Hubert Work, Aug. 17, 1923, ibid.; Work to Putnam, Oct. 5, 1923, transmitting the request of the governor, LC, Librarian of Congress, Corres. File. (Misc., New Mex. Arch.).

[63] Paul A. F. Walter to Putnam, Oct. 30, 1923, ibid. Professor Bloom started a card catalog of the documents in the Mexican archives of New Mexico in continuation of the earlier work by Twitchell, but if it was completed, its present whereabouts is unknown.

[64] New Mexico, *Laws* (1959), pp. 695–98.

[65] New Mexico, Commission of Public Records, *First Annual Report, 1960–1961* (Santa Fe, 1961), p. 3.

[66] George P. Hammond, "The Use of Microphotography in Manuscript Work in New Mexico," American Library Association, *Archives and Libraries, 1939* (Chicago, 1939), pp. 101–02.

[67] Albert J. Diaz, *Manuscripts and Records in the University of New Mexico Library* (Albuquerque, 1957), item 73; Dale L. Morgan and George P. Hammond, eds., *A Guide to the Manuscript Collections of the Bancroft Library (Bancroft Library Publications, Bibliographical Series, Volume I, Pacific and Western Manuscripts, Except California)* (Berkeley and Los Angeles, 1963), p. 90.

four volumes of the second part are calendared in Twitchell's *Spanish Archives of New Mexico,* (volume II). After the transfer of the original Spanish and Mexican archives of New Mexico to the State Records Center, they were again microfilmed.

In 1966, with a grant of $15,509 from the National Historical Publications Commission, the Archives Division of the New Mexico State Records Center again microfilmed the Spanish archives of New Mexico.[68] Myra Ellen Jenkins, the deputy for archives, directed the project and was assisted by J. Richard Salazar, who identified and calendared the miscellaneous documents and did much of the proofreading. Since Twitchell's inventory was only roughly chronological and has some errors in dates, the collection was recalendared in briefer form. Marc Simmons, of the University of New Mexico History Department, was engaged to calendar the documents for the years 1770–1821. The documents were renumbered in chronological order, but the Twitchell numbers were collated in the published calendar. The calendar for each roll of microfilm is reproduced at the beginning of the roll. The microfilm of the Spanish archives of New Mexico, 1621–1821, was published in 1967. Rolls one through twenty of the microfilm consist of the documents that were returned to Santa Fe by the Library of Congress in 1923, and the subject matter of each roll is described briefly in a published guide.[69] Roll twenty-one consists of miscellaneous Spanish archives of New Mexico not calendared by Twitchell, and official documents in special collections of the Archives Division of the New Mexico State Records Center and the Zimmerman Library of the University of New Mexico. Each item on that roll is identified by the name of the special collection in those repositories. Roll twenty-two is made up of orders and decrees, mostly printed, emanating from the governments of Spain and New Spain (1656, 1716–1821), that had been segregated and bound into two volumes by the Library of Congress, as well as others that were found in both the Historical Society of New Mexico collections and in private collections. A published calendar gives a brief description of each document, its date, the frame number, and the Twitchell number.[70]

---

[68] Holmes, "Southwestern Archival Legacy," pp. 532–33. An act of Congress of July 28, 1964 (78 Stat. pp. 335–36), authorized appropriations of up to $500,000 a year for a five-year period for grants to state and local agencies and nonprofit organizations and institutions for publication and microfilm projects. During the first four years of the program $350,000 was appropriated each year.

[69] Myra Ellen Jenkins, ed., *Guide to the Microfilm of the Spanish Archives of New Mexico, 1621–1821* (Santa Fe, 1967). Positive copies of the microfilm can be purchased from the New Mexico State Records Center, 404 Montezuma Ave., Santa Fe, New Mexico, 87501.

[70] New Mexico State Records Center, *Calendar of the Microfilm Edition of the Spanish Archives of New Mexico, 1621–1821* (Santa Fe, 1968).

A second grant of $16,852, from the National Historical Publications Commission, enabled the Archives Division to arrange, calendar, and microfilm the Mexican archives of New Mexico, 1821–46. These archives have been grouped, within each year, according to governmental agency or function. The material in each group has been arranged by subject matter and chronologically thereunder. Documents that extend over several years, such as letter books and judicial cases, are microfilmed under the earliest date. Printed circulars, orders, decrees, and handwritten manuscripts have been intermingled, as all are official documents. Executive papers form the first record group and are divided into (1) the governors' papers, and (2) the military commanders' papers — when there were two officials. When the governor held both positions, the papers are filed together. The executive papers include incoming communications, organized according to agency of origin, and outgoing communications, listed under names of correspondents. The legislative papers include correspondence, reports, incomplete copies of some proceedings of legislative bodies, *ayuntamiento* records, and election returns. Judicial proceedings were reviewed by the governor and were originally maintained separately, and are in a separate record group. Military records include company records, company accounts, soldiers' accounts, receipts, and service records. The company records include monthly muster rolls, supply records, correspondence sent to company commanders, military instruction notebooks, indexes of records, and special reports. The treasury (hacienda) series contains records of the fiscal department, including correspondence, account books, and customs records. A miscellaneous group contains materials that do not fit into the foregoing record groups, such as census reports, and incomplete files of official newspapers.

Official documents in private collections in the Archives Division of the State Records Center and in the Zimmerman Library of the University of New Mexico were collated with the Mexican archives of New Mexico and microfilmed. The provenance of documents from these collections is indicated on the microfilm. The journals of the legislative bodies and the governors' letter books in the State Records Center are also included on the microfilm. Finding aids were prepared to facilitate use of the microfilm. The published guide to the microfilm gives brief descriptions of the materials on each of the forty-two rolls of microfilm; individual documents are not listed.[71] A published calendar shows the date, a brief description of the document, frame number, and Twitchell number (for 1821 only).[72]

---

[71] Myra Ellen Jenkins et al., eds., *Guide to the Microfilm Edition of the Mexican Archives of New Mexico, 1821–1846* (Santa Fe, 1969).

[72] Myra Ellen Jenkins, *Calendar of the Mexican Archives of New Mexico, 1821–*

The collection of Spanish archives in the New Mexico State Records Center is not complete. The records for 1598–1680 were destroyed by the Pueblo Indians in the revolt of 1680.[73] They looted the government building and the church at Santa Fe and made a bonfire of the records, in the plaza. Only three documents, dated 1621, 1636, and 1664, are listed by Twitchell for the years before 1680. The flight of the Spaniards and friendly Indians from the Upper Río Grande, in 1680, was arrested at El Paso del Norte (Juárez, Mexico), where the seat of government was maintained until the reconquest of New Mexico was undertaken in 1692. The records that accumulated at El Paso del Norte were carried to Santa Fe at the time of the reoccupation of New Mexico, and those which survive now form part of the collection in the Records Center. Lacunae also exist in the records for this period.

The incompleteness of the New Mexico provincial records before 1693 renders especially valuable two historical reviews, based upon documentary sources, that were prepared in the next century. Villagutierre y Sotomayor, a *relator* of the Council of the Indies in Seville, wrote, about 1704, a history of the conquest, loss, and recovery of New Mexico, from contemporary documents.[74] Photoreproductions of the history, from the Biblioteca Nacional in Madrid, are in the Library of Congress and library of the Historical Society of New Mexico. A second study of the records in New Mexico was executed in 1778 at Santa Fe by Fray Silvestre Vélez de Escalante, a Franciscan missionary, at the request of his superior. While engaged in the examination of the records, Father Escalante wrote a letter (April 2, 1778) to his superior, Juan Agustín Morfi, which embodies historical data for the period 1680–92. The letter and a continuation for 1692–1717 are in the Archivo General de la Nación, Mexico. Copies of both are in the Bancroft Library of the University of California, and both have been printed.[75] The first part of the continuation is missing, but a complete

---

1846) (Santa Fe, 1970). The microfilm edition of the Spanish and Mexican archives of New Mexico had been acquired by some fifty purchasers by 1972 and thus has become available in numerous repositories.

[73] Vaughan, "Arch. N. Mex.," p. 469; Twitchell, *Spanish Arch. N. Mex.*, 1:vii–viii. During his lengthy examination of the archives at Santa Fe in 1778, Father Escalante found no documents for the years before 1680 (ibid., 2:268).

[74] Myra Ellen Jenkins, "The Juan de Villagutierre y Sotomayor Manuscript," *El Palacio* 67 (June 1960):108. A table of contents of this two-volume work is in Otto Maas, *Misiones de Nuevo Méjico; Documentos del Archivo General de Indias (Sevilla) publicados por primera vez y anotados* (Madrid, 1929), pp. x–lvi.

[75] Charles F. Lummis, trans. and ed., "Letter of Father Fray Silvestre Vélez de Escalante, Written on the 2d of April, in the Year 1778," *Land of Sunshine* 12 (Mar.–Apr. 1900):247-50, 309–14; printed also in Twitchell, *Spanish Arch. N. Mex.*, 2:268–80. Both are printed in *Documentos para la Historia de México*, 20 vols. (Mexico, 1853–57), 3d ser. 4:113–208.

copy, found by France V. Scholes in the Biblioteca Nacional in Mexico City, is considered to be the work of Escalante also, and a photostatic copy is in the Library of Congress.[76] The previously unknown part of this manuscript contains a detailed survey of the period from 1680 to 1692, with extracts from the provincial archives accumulated at El Paso del Norte during the years 1680 to 1693, and a copy of the diary of the Mendoza-López expedition to the Humanos in 1683–84. The value of this compendium is enhanced by the fact that most of the original records upon which it was based have disappeared. A copy of the Escalante letter of 1778 is filed with the manuscript.

Some original papers relating to the Pueblo revolt of 1680 and attempts at reconquest by Governor Otermín in 1680–82 were found by Herbert E. Bolton in the Archivo General de la Nación in Mexico early in the 1900s.[77] In the same repository, there is another group of documents in which the administrative relationships of the provincial government at El Paso del Norte with Mexico City, during 1680–85, are recorded.[78]

Original documents that once formed part of the Spanish archives of New Mexico are now in the Bancroft Library of the University of California. During his travels in the west, Alphonse Pinart, a French scholar, acquired manuscripts relating to New Mexico by purchase, gift, and copying, some of which may have been disposed of by the New Mexico territorial governor.[79] These and other manuscripts relating to New Mexico in the Bancroft Library cover the years 1681–1841 and include ninety-nine items.[80] Known in that repository as the "New Mexico Originals," the collection includes autos, censuses, complaints, correspondence, instructions, investigations, journals, judicial proceed-

[76] J. Manuel Espinosa, "Vélez de Escalante's Authorship of the So-Called 'Anonymous' Manuscripts in A. G. N., Historia, Tomo 2," *Hisp. Amer. Hist. Rev.* 22 (May 1942):422–25.

[77] Herbert E. Bolton, *Guide to Materials for the History of the United States in the Principal Archives of Mexico* (Washington, 1913), pp. 92, 94; Twitchell, *Spanish Arch. N. Mex.*, 2:5. Texts of some of these documents are printed in English: ibid., pp. 13–68. Reproductions from the collection are published in Charles W. Hackett, ed., Charmion C. Shelby, trans., *Revolt of the Pueblo Indians of New Mexico and Otermín's Attempted Reconquest, 1680–1682*, 2 vols. (Albuquerque, 1942).

[78] Hughes, *Spanish Settlement in the El Paso District*, p. 301.

[79] Letter from William M. Roberts, Reference Librarian, Bancroft Library, June 6, 1972, with a description of the Pinart Collection. Pinart loaned the collection to Bancroft who used it in preparing his *History of Arizona and New Mexico* (Bancroft, *Ariz. & N. Mex.*, p. 20). Bancroft later acquired the collection. He also had a transcript of the Historia section, volume 25, entitled Documentos para la Historia de Nuevo México from the Archivo General de la Nación (ibid.; Bolton, *Guide to Arch. of Mex.*, pp. 27–28).

[80] Morgan and Hammond, *Guide to Ms. Colls. of the Bancroft Lib.*, pp. 91–92. See also Bancroft, *Hist. Ariz. and N. Mex.*, p. 20.

ings, orders, petitions, reports, and residencias.[81] An eighty-four page volume, 1730–1748, contains acts, commissions, payments, and other documents on the administration and affairs of New Mexico.

The Henry E. Huntington Library at San Marino, California, has also acquired New Mexico records. In 1928, it obtained from the estate of William G. Ritch, secretary of the New Mexico territory in the 1870s, a collection of a few original documents, some typewritten copies and translations of documents which are still in the Spanish archives of New Mexico.[82] The collection includes correspondence, conveyances, autos de guerra, certificates, inventories of missions, decrees, appointments, censuses, proclamations, a record of vaccinations, a part of De Vargas's journal, naturalization papers, customs declarations, and court proceedings. The original records include the record book of passports presented by foreigners arriving at Santa Fe during 1828–1836 and of passports issued there to traders and trappers during the same period.[83] Some of the other documents also relate to trade and fur trapping in the Southwest, and, on the same subjects, there are microfilm reproductions in this repository from the Spanish archives of New Mexico. The Huntington Library also has documents of Manuel Armijo and Donaciano Vigil for 1837 and 1846. The University of New Mexico Library has microfilm copies of these materials from the Bancroft and Huntington Libraries.

The Spanish land-grant records in the New Mexico State Records Center contain other documents which apparently should be among the provincial records. Besides correspondence and reports pertaining to the Governor's Palace, these documents include papers relating to military matters, commissions, proclamations, and royal orders; papers relating to citizenship and naturalization; reports relating to Indians; letters from Mexican officials; the census of 1808; memorandums by the governor; and a copybook of letters sent by Gov. Manuel Armijo to officials in New Mexico, August 25, 1840–January 12, 1842.[84] Besides the foregoing small number of documents, there are others in a box labeled "Old Spanish Papers," which are not calendared in Twitchell's work. They consist of the following: documents on the appointment and commissioning of Mogollon as governor and an

---

[81] Angélico Chávez, "Some Original New Mexico Documents in California Libraries," *N. Mex. Hist. Rev.* 25 (July 1950):248–52.

[82] Ibid., pp. 245–48, contains a list of the Spanish originals, 1681–1837.

[83] Cleland, *Reckless Breed of Men*, p. 209.

[84] Report of Recommendations on New Mexican Private Land Claim Records, by Oliver W. Holmes, May 13, 1957, Records of the National Archives and Records Service (Record Group 64), Natural Resources Branch, Correspondence File, National Archives.

investigation of his administration; an order to Mogollon concerning the proposed visit to the Moqui pueblos of the Jesuit, Augustín de Campos, 1714; documents concerning the pueblos of San Juan, a proposed visit by Bernardo de Castro to Cerro de Oro to the Comanche nation, a silver mine at San Antonio in the Comanche nation, and the establishment of an Episcopal diocese in Santa Fe, 1813; letters of Pedro de Nava and others to the governors of New Mexico, 1794–1825; an order of the Marquis de Valero to Captain Félix Martínez, 1716; and a royal decree of May 31, 1789. These records have been microfilmed by the University of New Mexico Library and have been calendared and microfilmed by the State Records Center.

3

Legislative Records

THE FIRST LEGISLATIVE BODY of New Mexico met in Santa Fe on April 14, 1822.[1] The seven deputies who composed this provincial deputation were elected by an electoral junta that met in Santa Fe on January 29, 1822. The election was held in accordance with the provisions of the Spanish constitution of March 18, 1812, which had been reestablished by a liberal revolution in 1820.[2] A law of the Mexican Congress of June 17, 1823 renewed the decree of the Spanish Cortes adopting the constitution of 1812, and its provisions regarding the provincial deputation remained in force until 1837. After New Mexico became a territory in 1824, the legislative body became known as the territorial deputation, and, when the new constitution of 1837 established a system of departments, it became the departmental junta.[3] Under the Mexican constitution of 1843, the departmental junta was displaced by a departmental assembly in January, 1844; its last session was held on August 10, 1846.

The provincial deputation's enactments had an important impact on affairs in New Mexico. The provincial deputation established town councils, apportioned taxes among the towns, supervised the expenditures of their funds, and approved their regulations. With the con-

---

[1] Bloom, "N. Mex. under Mex. Admin.," 1:146–147. Bloom gives a roster of the members of the provincial deputation and successive bodies, from 1822 to 1846, in scattered footnotes. A complete list, prepared from Bloom's data, is in Twitchell, *N. Mex. Hist.*, 2:10–12.

[2] The provisions of the constitution of 1812 are in Reynolds, *Spanish and Mex. Land Laws*, pp. 79–82.

[3] See ibid., pp. 216–21, for a Mexican Law of March 20, 1837 regarding the functions of the departmental junta.

sent of the governor, it could adopt measures for executing new public works or repairing old ones. It enacted measures affecting education, agriculture, commerce, and industry, and provided for taking censuses. It watched over the activities of benevolent institutions and the progress of church missions in converting the Indians. It reported upon and approved land grants made by territorial officials. It transmitted proposals to the New Mexican deputy in the Mexican Congress for action by that body. The governor presided over the sessions of the deputation whenever he attended; at other times the senior deputy presided. A secretary, who prepared the minutes of the legislative proceedings and preserved other records, held office regularly after 1822.

The journals of the legislative bodies of New Mexico, formerly in the United States Bureau of Land Management Office in Santa Fe, are now in the State Records Center. These include the journal of provincial and territorial deputations, April 22, 1822–February 15, 1837 (three volumes, 90, 189, and 96 folios), and the journal of the departmental assembly, January 1, 1845–August 10, 1846 (two volumes, 46 and 56 folios).[4] Microreproductions of the journals are in the Microfilm Collection of Early State Records in the Library of Congress. Legislative minutes, 1837–1839, 1843–1846, relating to three or four departmental juntas and the departmental assembly, are in the Mexican archives of New Mexico in the State Records Center.[5] Land records of New Mexico in the same repository include extracts of legislative minutes relating to land grants[6] and a variety of other documents reflecting the participation of the territorial deputation in the land-grant procedure, such as petitions, reports of committees, correspondence, and decrees.[7] Besides journals embodying the minutes of legislative proceedings, there was a separate group of legislative archives at the end of the Mexican regime in 1846.[8] These now form part of the consolidated, chronological file of New Mexican archives in the State Records Center. The journals and other legislative records referred to above have been microfilmed by the State Records Center.[9]

---

[4] U.S. Library of Congress, Photoduplication Service, "Journals, Minutes, and Proceedings" *A Guide to the Microfilm Collection of Early State Records,* comp. by William S. Jenkins, ed. by Lillian A. Hamrick (Washington, 1950), p. 153.

[5] Bloom, "N. Mex. under Mex. Admin.," 2:34 n. 396, 130–33, 140, 165 n. 554; Jenkins, *Calendar of the Mex. Arch. of N. Mex.,* pp. 74, 81, 87, 122, 131, 140. Bloom located these sheets while the Spanish archives of New Mexico were still in the Library of Congress.

[6] Twitchell, *Spanish Archives,* 1:51, 330, 348.

[7] Ibid., passim.

[8] An inventory of the legislative archives was completed by order of the departmental assembly on June 15, 1846 (Bloom, "N. Mex. under Mex. Admin.," 2:354).

[9] New Mexico State Records Center, *Guide to Mex. Arch. N. Mex.,* pp. 12, 26.

4

Archival
Reproductions

THE GOVERNMENTS OF NEW SPAIN and Mexico, as well as the Spanish
government, accumulated masses of archives, from which reproductions have been obtained by institutions in New Mexico and other
places in the United States that substantially supplement the collections of original Spanish and Mexican archives in Santa Fe.

The bulk of Mexican records relating to the provinces on the
northern frontier are in the Archivo General de la Nación in the Palacio
Nacional in Mexico City. The holdings in that repository have been
classified into sections, which were determined partly by the subject
matter of the records and partly by the designation of the agencies
that created the records. Within the books or bundles comprising the
sections, the arrangement is usually chronological. Correspondencia
de los Virreyes, 1755–1821 (342 volumes), consists of copies of viceroy
dispatches to Spain, with copies of communications from provincial
governors, military officers, local authorities, and missionaries. Historia, 1697–1821 (565 volumes), a miscellaneous collection assembled
by an archivist, is of the highest importance for historical purposes.
Historia — Operaciones de Guerra, 1810–21 (1,025 volumes), relates
to the Mexican War of Independence and includes reports and correspondence of military officers. Misiones, 1616–1835 (27 volumes),
consists chiefly of correspondence of mission authorities with viceroys.
Provincias Internas, 1777–1821 (265 volumes), relates primarily to
the commandancy general authorized in 1776, and consists of correspondence of the viceroy with commandants general, provincial governors, and other provincial officials, with much transmitted material
of local origin. Californias, 1767–1821 (80 volumes), comprises mostly
files of correspondence of the viceroy with local officials of the Californias. Marina contains documents on maritime matters including

trade, vessels, ports, dockyards, and lighthouses. Other sections have only a general bearing on the history of what eventually became United States territory.[1]

In 1821, the newly independent Mexican government set up several ministries for administrative purposes. These included secretariats of justice and ecclesiastical affairs; war and navy; encouragement, colonization and industry; exterior and interior affairs; and hacienda, public credit, and commerce.[2] The archivo Histórico de Hacienda, also in the Palacio Nacional, contains more than 2200 *legajos* (files) of documents created by the Real Hacienda of the Viceroyalty of New Spain and early Mexico's Ministry of Hacienda. Though the collection is incomplete, it is important for the economic history of New Spain and, to a lesser extent, for the early years of the Mexican Republic, as well as for colonial financial administration.[3]

---

[1] Descriptions of materials on the southwestern United States in the various volumes of these sections are in Herbert E. Bolton, *Guide to Materials for the History of the United States in the Principal Archives of Mexico* (Washington, 1913), pp. 12–184. When Bolton investigated the Mexican archives for the Carnegie Institution of Washington in 1907–08, some of the records were stored in such a way that they were inaccessible, and all that he could report about them was the section titles (John F. Bannon, "Herbert E. Bolton: His Guide in the Making," *Southw. Hist. Quar.* 73 [July 1969]:47). Since Bolton made his survey, some records have been moved and others have been rearranged or lost, so that his descriptions are no longer as useful as they once were. However, some of the important sections on the American Southwest are in the Archivo General de la Nación, and Bolton's descriptions are still pertinent for these. Differently arranged descriptions of more recent date are in Jorge Ignacio Rubio Mañe, *El Archivo General de la Nación, México, D.F.* (México, D.F., 1940), pp. 127–44; Roscoe R. Hill, *The National Archives of Latin America* (Cambridge, 1945), pp. 115–19; and Manuel Carrera Stampa, *Archivalia Mexicana* (México, D.F., 1952), pp. 36–46. The last-named book also contains brief descriptions of other archives in Mexico City and the state capitals. Helpful as an introduction to archives in Mexico City is Richard E. Greenleaf and Michael C. Meyer, *Research in Mexican History: Topics, Methodology, Sources, and a Practical Guide to Field Research* (Lincoln, Nebr., 1973). Additional bibliography regarding Mexican archives is in Agustín Millares Carlo, *Reportorio bibliográfico de los archivos mexicanos y de los europeos y norteamericanos de interés para la historia de México* (México, D.F., 1959), pp. 157–317. No general descriptive guide to the records of the colonial period has been published by the Mexican Archivo General de la Nación. Since 1930 it has, however, published, in its *Boletín del Archivo General de la Nación*, indexes of uneven content and usefulness to the sections on Bishops and Archbishops, Colleges, Criminal, Inquisition, Interior Provinces, Lands, Laws, Proclamations and Ordinances, Secular and Regular Clergy, and Royal Dispatches and Orders. Other finding aids in manuscript form are available in the Archivo General de la Nación.

[2] Descriptions of pertinent materials in the records of these ministries are in Bolton, *Guide*, pp. 172–80, 269–98, 349–63, 370, 372, and *passim*. A chronologically arranged guide to the materials in the Archivo Histórico Militar has been published: Mexico, Dirección de Archivo Militar, *Guía del Archivo Histórico Militar de México* (México, D.F., 1948).

[3] Some of the materials in these archives are described in Mexico, Ministerio de Hacienda y Credito Público, *Guía del Archivo Histórico de Hacienda, siglos XVI a XIX* (México, D.F., 1940–45).

Adolph F. A. Bandelier, whose earlier investigations in the archives at Santa Fe and Mexico City have already been mentioned in chapter two, continued his investigations of the documentary sources on New Mexico. Late in 1911, Bandelier was appointed research associate of the Carnegie Institution of Washington to continue his archival work.[4] He worked with Mrs. Bandelier in Mexico City during 1912–13, and, in the latter year, went to Seville to search in the Archivo General de Indias.[5] After Bandelier's death there in March, 1914, Mrs. Bandelier continued to transcribe documents until the end of 1915. The transcripts from both the Spanish and Mexican archives were deposited by Mrs. Bandelier in the office of the Carnegie Institution in 1916. The following year, the institution engaged Charles W. Hackett, then a resident fellow of the University of California and after 1918 a member of the history department of the University of Texas, to edit the Bandelier transcripts for publication.[6] Hackett also used the Bandelier collection in the Peabody Museum and other transcripts from the Edward E. Ayer Collection of the Newberry Library, the Bancroft Library, and the University of Texas Library. The publication that resulted is valuable because it fills, to a large degree, the gap in the Spanish archives of New Mexico caused by the destruction of records by the Pueblo Indians in 1680.[7] The Bandelier transcripts, 1532–1780 (2,000 pages), are in the University of Texas Library.[8]

The Coronado Library of the University of New Mexico and the New Mexico Historical Society have acquired large collections of archival reproductions. After doing missionary work in Mexico and New Mexico, Lansing B. Bloom became interested in southwestern history and archaeology, joined the staff of the School of American Research at Santa Fe, and, after 1929, was on the history faculty of the University of New Mexico. Under the sponsorship of the School of American Research, the Museum of New Mexico, and the New Mexico Historical Society, Bloom and his wife worked for fourteen months (1928–29) in the Archivo General de Indias in Seville, and other reposi-

---

[4] Hodge, "Bandelier," p. 360.

[5] Roscoe R. Hill, *American Missions in European Archives* (México, D.F., 1951), p. 62. Brief descriptions of materials useful for genealogical research are in the Genealogical Society of the Church of Jesus Christ of Latter-Day Saints, *Major Genealogical Record Sources in Mexico* (Salt Lake City, 1970).

[6] Carnegie Institution of Washington, *Report of the Department of Historical Research*, 1922, p. 161.

[7] Charles W. Hackett, ed., *Historical Documents Relating to New Mexico, Nueva Vizcaya, and Approaches Thereto, to 1773*, 3 vols. (Washington, 1923, 1926, 1937).

[8] Carlos E. Castañeda and Jack A. Dabbs, *Guide to the Latin American Manuscripts in the University of Texas Library* (Cambridge, Mass., 1939), p. 163.

tories in Madrid,[9] listing documents relating primarily to New Mexico in the seventeenth century.[10] The Library of Congress, which at that time was initiating a microfilming program in the Spanish archives, later supplied Bloom with photostats of some of the documents he had listed. During 1938–39, while on leave from the University of New Mexico, Bloom spent six months in Seville microfilming documents in the Archives of the Indies relating to Coronado and De Vargas.[11]

In the fall of 1930, the university, with financial support from the Museum of New Mexico and the New Mexico Historical Society, sent

---

[9] In Spain the principal repositories for documentary materials relating to the southwestern United States are the Archivo General de Indias at Seville, the Archivo General at Simancas, and the Archivo Histórico Nacional at Madrid. In the Archivo General de Indias, the sections containing documents for the United States include (I) Audiencias, (II) Indiferente General (General Miscellaneous), (III) Ministerio de Ultramar (Ministry of the Colonies), (IV) Papeles de Estado (State Papers), (V) Patronato Real (Royal Patronage), and (IX) La Contaduria (Office of the Controller). The Archivo General contains records of the departments of the Spanish government, including the secretariat of state (custodian of the records of the crown), and the secretariats of war, marine, and finance. In the Archivo Histórico Nacional, the pertinent documents are the Papeles de Estado (state papers). Other repositories in Madrid having Hispanic American materials include the Biblioteca Nacional, Real Academia de la Historia, Biblioteca de Palacio, Museo Naval, Archivos Militares, Biblioteca Central Militar, Archivo General de Ministerio de Hacienda, Museo de Ciencias Naturales, and the Ministerio de Asuntos Exteriores. Descriptions of the archival materials are in William R. Shepherd, *Guide to the Materials for the History of the United States in Spanish Archives (Simancas, the Archivo Histórico Nacional, and Seville)* (Washington, 1907). Shepherd a member of the Columbia University faculty, made the investigation for the Carnegie Institution of Washington. A chronological catalog of materials in the Estado and Audiencia papers in the Archivo General de Indias is available in Charles E. Chapman, *Catalogue of Materials in the Archivo General de Indias for the History of the Pacific Coast and the American Southwest* (Glendale, Calif., 1919). Later searchers in this archive have found materials not listed by Chapman. Brief descriptions of the materials in Spanish repositories with citations to published and manuscript catalogs, guides, inventories, and indexes are in Ernest J. Burrus, S.J., "An Introduction to Bibliographical Tools in Spanish Archives and Manuscript Collections Relating to Hispanic America," *Hisp. Amer. Hist. Rev.* 35 (Nov. 1955):443-83. During the past twenty years, the Spanish Dirección General de Archivos y Bibliotecas has published a series of descriptions and inventories that include guides to the archives and libraries of Madrid, the Archivo General de Simancas, and the Archivo Histórico Nacional.

For information regarding the Spanish governmental agencies that created records containing material on Hispanic America, see Clarence H. Haring, *The Spanish Empire in America* (New York, 1947); Roger B. Merriman, *The Rise of the Spanish Empire in the Old World and in the New*, 4 vols. (New York, 1918–34), 3:618–69; and, Hubert H. Bancroft, *History of Mexico*, 6 vols. (San Francisco, 1883–88).

[10] France V. Scholes, "Research Activities of Lansing B. Bloom in Foreign Archives," *N. Mex. Hist. Rev.* 21 (Apr. 1946):100; Lansing B. Bloom, "A Student's Day in Seville," *El Palacio* 24 (June 9, 1928):446–49.

[11] Scholes, "Bloom," p. 102; [Letters of Lansing B. Bloom, Nov. 26, 1938, Apr. 1939], *N. Mex. Hist. Rev.* 14 (Jan., Apr. 1939):115–20, 200–03.

Bloom to Mexico, where he microfilmed documents on New Mexico and the Southwest in the Archivo General de la Nación and in the Biblioteca Nacional.[12] To the 17,000 exposures he obtained at that time, Bloom added 12,000 more during the summers of 1934 and 1935, with the further assistance of Mrs. Bloom. France V. Scholes, a colleague of Bloom's at the University of New Mexico and a historian of seventeenth century New Mexico also obtained transcripts on that period from Mexican archives and from the Spanish royal treasury records in the Archivo General de Indias in Seville, which Bloom had also searched.[13]

The collections of the Coronado Library of the University of New Mexico were further augmented by George P. Hammond, who was chairman of the university's history department from 1935 to 1946. At the suggestion of Herbert E. Bolton, he had chosen the founding of New Mexico as a subject for a doctoral dissertation at the University of California and had searched for pertinent documents in the archives in Seville in 1922–23.[14] While on sabbatical leave from the University of Southern California during the years 1933–34, Hammond microfilmed documents in the Archivo General de la Nación in Mexico City relating to the administration of Diego de Vargas, as well as other southwestern materials.[15] He subsequently made other visits to Mexico City to obtain microfilm for the University of New Mexico.

After Hammond joined the University of New Mexico faculty, a survey was made of the microfilms of foreign archives in the university's library, and plans were adopted for their preservation. To make the microfilms more readily available for use and prevent further damage to them, it was decided to have photographic enlargements made on paper. Workers of the Historical Records Survey made the enlargements on eleven-and-a-half-inch-wide Eastman haloid record paper.[16] The enlargements were bound and placed in the library for general use. Photoprints from the Archivo General de Indias in Seville are in 200 volumes; those from the Archivo General de la Nación in Mexico City are in 205 volumes; and those from the Biblioteca Nacional and the Museo Nacional in Mexico City are in 40 volumes.[17]

Reproductions from Spanish and Mexican archives relating to

---

[12] Scholes, "Bloom," pp. 102–08.

[13] France V. Scholes, "Royal Treasury Records Relating to the Province of New Mexico, 1596–1683," *N. Mex. Hist. Rev.* 50 (Jan. 1975):7, 22 n. 7.

[14] Friends of the Bancroft Library, *GPH: An Informal Record of George P. Hammond and His Era in the Bancroft Library* (Berkeley, 1965), p. 4.

[15] Ibid., p. 5.

[16] Hammond, "Microphotography in Ms. Work," pp. 99–101.

[17] Scholes, "Bloom," pp. 104–05.

New Mexico are also in the libraries of the Universities of Texas and California, and in the Library of Congress.[18] The materials in the Library of Congress include transcripts obtained during the years 1895–1903 by Woodbury Lowery, a retired Washington lawyer and historian of the Spanish settlements within the United States, from archives in Madrid, Seville, Paris, and London. The collection includes documents on New Mexico, 1538–1800 (5 volumes), and smaller quantities of documents on California, 1588–1800, and Texas, 1673–1803.[19]

Some repositories in New Mexico have collections of maps that include reproductions from Spanish and Mexican archives. A small collection in the School of American Research Library at Santa Fe includes maps dating from the sixteenth century. The Museum of New Mexico and the State Records Center also have reproductions of maps from the Spanish and Mexican periods.

Archival collections in the Mexican state of Chihuahua contain documents relating to New Mexico and Texas. Part of the state archives of Chihuahua were destroyed by fire in 1941, but many of the archives of the executive branch, the supreme tribunal of justice, and the tax administration, which had jurisdiction over New Mexico, were saved.[20] The University of Texas at El Paso has been microfilming the state archives of Chihuahua. The municipal archives of Chihuahua, dating from the eighteenth century, contain materials on New Mexico. In 1962, Charles L. Sonnichsen, of the University of Texas at El Paso, microfilmed the municipal archives of Ciudad Juárez. The Juárez archives, 1726–1904, consist of more than 100,000 items in 365 volumes on 91 rolls of microfilm.[21] Twelve of these rolls cover the years 1690 to 1821, and thirty-one are for the years 1821–46. A positive print is available for loan, and a classified index is being prepared.

---

[18] See the descriptions in chapter 13 in the section on Texas and chapter 22 in the section on California.

[19] Hill, *American Missions in European Archives*, p. 69.

[20] Carrera Stampa, *Archivalia mexicana*, p. 129–30. Description of the materials that existed earlier is in Bolton, *Guide to Archs. Mex.*, pp. 452–60.

[21] Holmes, "Southwestern Archival Legacy," p. 537.

5

Documentary Publications

GEORGE P. HAMMOND, before his transfer from California to New Mexico, became the editor-in-chief of a documentary publication series on the Spanish Southwest. In 1929, Hammond, Frederick W. Hodge, and Henry R. Wagner organized the Quivira Society, for the purpose of publishing documents, and obtained as its sponsors a number of well-known historians interested in the history of that region.[1] Between 1929 and 1958, thirteen volumes of Quivira Society Publications were issued. Contributions to the series, in English translation, by Hammond and his coworker, Agapito Rey of the University of Indiana, included the journal of Diego Pérez de Luxán of the Antonio de Espejo expedition of 1582–83, and Juan de Montoya's account of the discovery of New Mexico in 1602. Other volumes included De Villagrá's history of New Mexico, by Frederick W. Hodge and Gilberto Espinosa; three previously published chronicles of New Mexico by Pedro Bautista Pino (deputy of New Mexico in the Spanish Cortes in 1812) and Antonio Barreiro (a lawyer in New Mexico), with additions by José Agustín de Escudero (a Mexican lawyer), H. Bailey Carroll, and J. Villasana Haggard; Bernardo de Gálvez's instructions of 1786 for governing the Interior Provinces of New Spain, by Donald E. Worcester; and Nicolás de Lafora's account of the Margués de Rubí's tour of inspection of the northern frontier of New Spain during the years, 1766–68, by Lawrence Kinnaird.

The observance in 1940 of the 400th anniversary of the expedition

---

[1] Friends of the Bancroft Library, *Hammond*, p. 6. On pp. 95–97 of this work is a list of the Quivira Society Publications. Concerning Hammond, see also the news note in the *N. Mex. Hist. Rev.* 4 (Oct. 1929):411.

of Francisco Vásquez de Coronado provided an opportunity for inaugurating another documentary publication series.[2] George P. Hammond was designated editor-in-chief of the Coronado Cuarto Centennial Publications, which are comprised mainly of English translations of documents from the archives of Spain, Mexico, and New Mexico.[3] In collaboration with Agapito Rey, Hammond prepared compilations on the Coronado expedition, the founding of New Mexico, and the rediscovery of New Mexico, 1580–94, some of which were improved translations of previously publiṣhed documents. Charles W. Hackett, of the University of Texas, and Charmion Shelby, of the Library of Congress, prepared a two-volume compilation on the revolt of the Pueblo Indians. Alfred B. Thomas, of the University of Alabama, edited a volume on contacts with the Plains Indians.[4] Documents on De Vargas's expedition into New Mexico to initiate its reconquest were compiled by J. Manuel Espinosa, then of Loyola University, Chicago, Illinois. And Frederick W. Hodge, along with Hammond and Rey, issued Fray Alonso de Benavides's revised memorial of 1634, with supplementary documents.

Together, the Quivira and Coronado publication series provide extensive documentation, in English, on the Spanish period of New Mexico. All volumes didn't consist of documents, however, and some were related to other parts of the Southwest. Both series were inadequately financed; the editors received no compensation and largely contributed compilations on what they were intersted in, that often related to secondary works they had written. Use was made of longer documents, such as journals, reports, and narratives, but more routine correspondence from political and ecclesiastical archives was neglected. A systematic, chronological series, such as those published by some of the eastern and midwestern states on their colonial periods, would have been more satisfactory.[5]

Translations of censuses of New Mexico of 1790, 1823, and 1845 have been published from microfilm in the State Records Center.[6] These censuses provide important information regarding early white families in New Mexico, including their places of residence, the names

---

[2] James F. Zimmerman, "The Coronado Cuarto Centennial," *Hisp. Am. Hist. Rev.* 20 (Feb. 1940):158–62.

[3] The titles of the volumes published between 1940 and 1965 are in Friends of the Bancroft Library, *Hammond,* pp. 98–99, and in the bibliography of this book.

[4] Thomas compiled other documentary volumes on New Spain and New Mexico, that are listed in the bibliography.

[5] Jack P. Greene, "The Publication of the Official Records of the Southern Colonies," *William and Mary Quarterly,* 3d ser. 14 (Apr. 1957):268–80.

[6] Virginia L. Olmsted, trans. and ed., *New Mexico Spanish and Mexican Colonial Censuses, 1790, 1823, 1845* (Albuquerque, 1975).

of the heads of families, their marital status, wives' names and age; the places of birth, age, and sex of children; and the names of relatives and servants in the households.

Other documents in print are too numerous to be described here. The titles of contemporaneously published documents, and those in compilations by scholars, are in bibliographies.[7] Scholars continue to produce annotated translations of documents. A journal of an early expedition into New Mexico by Gaspar Castaño de Sosa, the lieutenant governor of Nuevo León, has been published.[8] English translations of documents relating to the travels of Pedro Vial from Santa Fe, during the years 1786–1808, that resulted in the opening of roads from that place to San Antonio, Natchitoches, and St. Louis, have been published.[9] These documents are by Vial and others who participated in his expeditions and were found during searches conducted by Abraham P. Nasatir, of San Diego State College, in the archives of Mexico, Spain, and other repositories.

---

[7] See the bibliographies by Haynes, the Historical Records Survey, Mecham, Steck, Wagner, and Winsor in the bibliography of this book. Particularly significant for the exploration of New Mexico is *Documentos para la Historia de México*, 20 vols. (Mexico, 1853–57), which consists largely of documents drawn from the Archivo General de la Nación, Mexico. A list of the individual volumes in this compilation is in Rubio Mañe, *El Archivo General de la Nación*, pp. 147–51; Joaquín García Icazbalceta, ed., *Colección de documentos para la Historia de México*, 2 vols. (Mexico, 1858–66); and Joaquín de Pacheco and Francisco de Cárdenas, eds., *Colección de documentos inéditos relativos al descubrimiento, conquista y colonización de la posessiones españolas en América y Oceania*, 42 vols. (Madrid, 1864–84), which was based chiefly on the Archivo General de Indias, Seville. Ernst Schafer, *Indice de la colección de documentos inéditos de Indias editada por Pacheco, Cárdenas, Torres de Mendoza, y otros (1 serie, tomos 1–42) y la Real Academia de la Historia (2 serie, tomos 1–25)*, 2 vols. (Madrid, 1946–47), contains an alphabetical index of persons and a chronological index of documents.

[8] Albert H. Schroeder, ed., and Dan S. Matson, trans., *A Colony on the Move: Gaspar Castaño de Sosa's Journal, 1590–1591* (Santa Fe, 1965). This is a different translation of the journal that is in George P. Hammond, ed. and Agapito Rey, trans., *The Rediscovery of New Mexico, 1580–1594: The Explorations of Chamuscado, Espejo, Costaño de Sosa, Morleto and Leyva de Bonilla and Humaña* (Albuquerque, 1966). Schroeder, an archaeologist, provides extensive notes that are interspersed with the text of the journal.

[9] Noel M. Loomis, ed., and Abraham P. Nasatir, trans., *Pedro Vial and the Roads to Santa Fe* (Norman, Okla., 1967).

6

Manuscript Collections

THE HISTORICAL SOCIETY of New Mexico, originally organized in 1859, was discontinued in 1863 and reestablished in 1880. Among its objectives was the collection and preservation of manuscripts, documents, records, and memoirs relating to the territory. In 1885, the secretary of the interior authorized the society to make its headquarters in two rooms in the east end of the Governor's Palace.[1] Beginning about 1884, the legislature of the New Mexico territory made small appropriations to the society to further its objectives. An act of the state legislature of March 14, 1927 made the society the official custodian of noncurrent public records that might be turned over to it by state or local officials.[2] No funds were provided to effectuate the act, and most of the records remained in the state capitol. By the 1920s, the Museum of New Mexico, which also had space in the Governor's Palace, was taking care of the society's collections and library. After the establishment of the *New Mexico Historical Review,* in 1926, more attention was paid to history, and the University of New Mexico (founded in 1882) became interested enough in the state's history to take over the editorship of the periodical in 1929.

The Historical Society of New Mexico has acquired, through gifts and purchases, manuscripts of an official nature from both the Spanish and Mexican periods. One group relates to the administration of Juan Ignacio Flores Mogollón, governor of New Mexico from 1712 to 1715.[3]

---

[1] Anderson, "Adobe Palace," p. 116.
[2] New Mexico, *Laws,* 1927. pp. 346–47.
[3] Vaughan, "Arch. N. Mex.," p. 474.

Benjamin M. Read, lawyer and historian of New Mexico, collected orders, decrees, letters, and other manuscripts on New Mexico, 1634–1821, that were bought by the society in 1936.[4] Microfilm of the Read collection is in the Bancroft Library of the University of California (3,143 exposures), and documents from the collection are printed in Read's *Illustrated History of New Mexico* (Santa Fe, 1912), in which there is a facsimile of the Santa Fe census of 1820.

In 1909, the society bought the papers of Manuel Alvarez, a man who had immigrated from St. Louis, Missouri, in 1825, to become a trader at Santa Fe and serve as American consul there from 1839 to 1846. The Alvarez papers, 1830–54 (6 volumes and 600 items), include correspondence, official reports, and business records (microfilm in the Bancroft Library and the University of New Mexico Library).[5] A ledger in the Alvarez papers contains both invoices of goods purchased by him in New York and Philadelphia in 1838–39, and in New York, Philadelphia, St. Louis, Independence, and Pittsburgh in 1841–42 and 1843–44, and an inventory of caravans at Independence.[6] A second ledger contains accounts of customers at Santa Fe, 1834–44[?]. And both books contain copies of letters that were sent. Charles Bent, a Virginian by birth but later a resident of St. Louis and Bent's Fort on the Arkansas River, established a store at Santa Fe in 1832 and settled at Taos, following his marriage there in 1835. Letters written by Bent to Manuel Alvarez, December 10, 1837–June 11, 1846, relating mostly to business affairs but also containing references to governmental matters in New Mexico, have been published.[7] Microfilm of the Bent papers is in the University of New Mexico Library.

Papers of Donaciano Vigil, military leader, member of the territorial deputation, and military secretary, contain military records, accounts, correspondence, and other documents, 1802–48 (140 items).[8] A collection assembled by Ralph E. Twitchell relates mainly to land grants in the Spanish and Mexican periods and includes other documents of more general interest, 1512, 1680–1870 (299 folders).[9] The Blackmore collection consists of translations of documents relating to

---

[4] Philip M. Hamer, ed., *A Guide to Archives and Manuscripts in the United States* (New Haven, 1961), p. 371.

[5] Ibid., p. 371.

[6] Lansing B. Bloom, ed., "Ledgers of a Santa Fe Trader," *N. Mex. Hist. Rev.* 21 (Apr. 1946):135–39.

[7] Frank D. Reeve, ed., "The Charles Bent Papers," *N. Mex. Hist. Rev.* 29–31 (1954–56).

[8] Hamer, *Guide to Arch. and Mss.*, p. 371.

[9] Ibid., p. 371; George P. Hammond, "Manuscript Collections in the Spanish Archives in New Mexico," *Archives and Libraries: Papers Presented at the 1939 Conference of the American Library Association* (Chicago, 1939), p. 87.

early land titles in northern New Mexico and southern Colorado. The Historical Society of New Mexico has also accumulated an extensive collection of miscellaneous documents, 1587, 1656–1894 (252 folders). In February, 1961, the society transferred manuscript collections that had been bought with territorial or state funds to the State Records Center.[10] These included the Vigil, Alvarez, Twitchell, Read, Martin Gardesky, Mrs. James Seligman, Maria G. Duran, Lewis Wallace, and the Historical Society Miscellaneous collections. Documents from these collections and other official documents from the Zimmerman Library of the University of New Mexico, including the L. Bradford Prince papers, the D'Armand papers, and the University of New Mexico Miscellaneous Collection, have been microfilmed on roll twenty-one of the microfilm of the Spanish archives of New Mexico.[11] Official documents from these collections have also been collated with the official records for the Mexican Period and microfilmed by the State Records Center. Other collections in the center that it has also microfilmed include the L. Bradford Prince papers, the Larkin G. Read papers, the Tyler Dingee Collection (Delgado family papers), Ortiz family papers, the Ina Sizer Cassidy Collection, the Ted Otero Collection, and the Valencia County records. The Ortiz family papers include a record book, January 1–November 19, 1830, of José Ignacio Ortiz, first alcalde of Santa Fe.

The University of New Mexico Library at Albuquerque also has collections of manuscripts and reproductions. Photoprints of documents relating to the Albuquerque family, 1462–1731 (16 items), were obtained from a member of that family.[12] The Louis d'Armand collection includes 1792 censuses of Santa Fe, Albuquerque, El Paso, Laguna, and other areas; a Taos census of April 17, 1796; a Santa Fe census of May 12, 1807; a roll of men able to bear arms in New Mexico, May 12, 1807; a muster roll of the permanent company of Santa Fe, December 31, 1837; and other documents.[13] The José Martínez collection consists of a few papers relating to civil suits, 1769–1845. Other Spanish language documents, 1826–87, relate to land grants. A memorandum book of Manuel Alvarez, ca. 1834–44, is available in photoprint. The L. Bradford Prince papers, the D'Armand papers, the Miguel Antonio Lovato papers, and the Julius Seligman papers were collated

---

[10] New Mexico, Commission of Public Records, *First Annual Report, 1960–61* (Santa Fe, 1961), pp. 4–5.

[11] New Mexico State Records Center, *Calendar of the Spanish Arch. of N. Mex.*, pp. 163–69.

[12] Albert J. Díaz, "University of New Mexico Special Collections," *N. Mex. Hist. Rev.* 33 (July 1958):235.

[13] Ibid., p. 242.

with the official records in the State Records Center and microfilmed for inclusion in the microfilm of the Spanish and Mexican archives of New Mexico.

Manuscripts relating to New Mexico are in repositories outside of New Mexico. In addition to the "New Mexico originals," described in chapter two of this section, the Bancroft Library of the University of California has some copies of royal orders relating to New Mexico and the northern provinces, 1609–1765 (716 pages); Lt. Col. Antonio Bonilla's "Apuntes sobre el Nuevo Mexico, September 3, 1776," with a 1642 census of the missions; extracts and notes of manuscript and printed matter on Chihuahua, 1786–1823 (2 volumes in 1), made by Pinart; documents and correspondence addressed to governors of Chihuahua, 1811–44 (134 pages) relating to civil and military administration; and a collection of historical documents relating to the ecclesiastical and civil history of Durango and other parts of the Interior Provinces, 1560–1847 (626 pages), assembled by José Fernando Ramírez.[14] The Henry E. Huntington Library in San Marino, California, has documents relating to Indians on the northern frontier of New Spain; speeches made by Donaciano Vigil to the departmental assembly, May 16 and June 22, 1846; and a letter from Gov. Manuel Armijo to Gen. Stephen W. Kearny, written at Apache Canyon on August 16, 1846.[15] The original dispatches written by Manuel Alvarez to the secretary of state, September 20, 1830–September 4, 1846 (1 volume), with copies of his correspondence with Mexican officials at Santa Fe, are in the records of the Department of State (Record Group 59) in the National Archives.[16] These documents contain considerable information regarding affairs in New Mexico. The volume is available on microfilm (microcopy number 199). In 1940, the Newberry Library of Chicago acquired by gift from William Greenlee some 600 pages of manuscripts relating to the Abiquiú area. In that same year, the Newberry Library also bought the Espinosa-Quintana collection, and in 1941, the Pablo Gonzales papers, and in 1942, the Joseph Chávez papers — all relating to land grants, Indians, and the church in the

---

[14] George P. Hammond, ed. *A Guide to the Manuscript Collections of the Bancroft Library. Volume II* (Berkeley and Los Angeles, 1972); pp. 21, 39–40, 173, 189, 229–30. Bonilla's work is an outline of the provincial annals during 1600–1776.

[15] Paul Horgan, *The Centuries of Santa Fe* (New York, 1956), pp. 343, 349. Mexican documents relating to the American conquest of New Mexico, including a letter from Armijo to the Minister of Foreign Relations, Sept. 8, 1846, and a report from Santa Fe, Sept. 26, 1846, signed by 105 citizens of New Mexico, have been published (Max. L. Moorhead, "Notes and Documents," *N. Mex. Hist. Rev.* 26 [Jan. 1951]: 68–82).

[16] Selections from this correspondence are in Harold H. Dunham, ed., "Sidelights on Santa Fe Traders, 1839–1846," *Westerners Brand Book Denver Annual* 6 (1950: 263–82).

Abiquiú area.[17] A few Manuel Armijo papers, 1837–45, in the State Historical Society of Wisconsin collection, consist of appointments of military and civil officers, a letter of commendation on his achievements, and a summary of his military record.

Mexican records in other repositories in the United States are of wider purport. Records of the Mexican state of Zacatecas, ca. 1561–1870 (43 feet or 300,000 pages) were purchased in 1952 by the William L. Clements Library of the University of Michigan.[18] Official letters of Viceroy Antonio María Bucareli y Ursua, 1771–78 (2 feet), in the same repository concern the administration of New Spain, expeditions against Apache Indians, and the development and fortification of the frontier provinces. Documents relating to the inspection tour by Brig. Gen. Pedro de Rivera y Villalón of the northern provinces of New Spain, 1724–28, are in the John Carter Brown Library, Providence, Rhode Island.[19] This was one of the most important inspections in the history of New Mexico, Texas, and Sonora, and resulted in two important contemporary publications.[20] Papers relating to military and civil affairs in Carrizal, Chihuahua, 1750s–1920s, are in the University of Texas at El Paso Archives.

---

[17] Newberry Library, *Report of the Trustees,* 1940, 1941 (Chicago, 1941–42), 1940, p. 16; 1941, p. 17; U.S. Library of Congress, *The National Union Catalog of Manuscript Collections, 1959–1961* (Ann Arbor, Mich., 1962), 1961, entries, 1016, 1017.

[18] William S. Ewing, *Guide to the Manuscript Collections in the William L. Clements Library* (Ann Arbor, Mich., 1953), p. 316.

[19] Damian Van den Eynde, O.F.M., "Calendar of Spanish Manuscripts in John Carter Brown Library," *Hisp. Am. Hist. Rev.* 16 (Nov. 1936):575.

[20] Mexico, Viceroyalty, Laws, Statutes, etc., *Reglamento para todos los presidios de las Provincias Internas de esta gobernación, hecho por el Excmo Señor de Casa-Fuerte* (Mexico, 1729); Pedro de Rivera y Villalón, *Diario y derrotero de lo caminado, visto y observado en el discurso de la visita general de presidios, situados en las Provincias Internas de Nueva España* (Guatemala, 1736; reprinted in Mexico City in 1946 under the editorship of Vito Alessio Robles). This reprint also contains the regulation for the presidios. See also Lawrence C. Wroth, "The Frontier Presidios of New Spain: Books, Maps, and a Selection of Manuscripts Relating to the Rivera Expedition, 1724–1727," Bibliographical Society of America, *Papers* 45 (3d Quar. 1951):191–218.

7

Land
Records

BOTH THE SPANISH AND MEXICAN governments adopted a liberal land-grant policy in order to promote settlement on the frontier. During the Spanish period, the viceroy of New Spain and governors of New Mexico granted land in New Mexico for settlement, agriculture, and mining.[1] A hundred grants were made to civilians, soldiers, towns, and Indian pueblos before 1822, three-fifths of them to individuals.

The Mexican colonization law of August 18, 1824 empowered the states to enact legislation governing land grants to individuals and communities. A large number of grants were made to individuals, towns, and ranchers during the Mexican period, so that by its end, all of the best lands along the Río Grande and its tributaries, having irrigation possibilities, had been granted. Many citizens of New Mexico held small strips of irrigated land fronting on rivers and streams by rights of possession, that were recognized by the United States. Pasture and woodlands back of the farming areas were held in common ownership.

The procedure for obtaining a grant of land in New Mexico was much the same under both the Spanish and Mexican regimes.[2] A petition of application for a grant addressed to an alcalde was forwarded by him to the governor, who directed the alcalde to make an investigation. After the alcalde had submitted a report and a sketch map to the governor, he ordered the alcalde to place the grantee in possession. On the land to be granted, the alcalde executed an act of possession before witnesses, whose presence was intended to prevent conflicts over

---

[1] Bloom, "N. Mex. under Mex. Admin.," 1:22.

[2] Simmons, *Spanish Govt. in N. Mex.*, pp. 179–80; William W. Morrow, *Spanish and Mexican Private Land Grants* (San Francisco, 1923), pp. 16–17.

boundaries. The original title paper was given to the grantee, and a copy, together with other documents, was filed in an *expediente* in the secretary's office at Santa Fe.[3] Final title papers were not issued until the alcalde certified to the governor that the land had been occupied for four years. The limits of the grants were natural boundaries and were so vague, overlapping, and confusing that much controversy did result. Surveys generally were not made and title papers not completed, so the *expedientes* remained incomplete. Transfers, exchanges, donations, and partitions of land were made before the governor or alcalde and recorded in the archives. Disputes over titles to lands, boundaries, and water rights were heard by the same officials.

The Mexican state of Chihuahua had jurisdiction over the southern part of New Mexico as far north as the Jornada del Muerte, near the present town of Las Cruces.[4] After the Mexican War and the transfer of New Mexico to United States jurisdiction, some New Mexicans, who preferred to remain Mexican citizens, moved to the Mesilla valley in Chihuahua. The United States then acquired this area in the Gadsden Purchase of 1853, and it was added to Doña Ana County, the Territory of New Mexico. The deed records of that county, in the county clerk's office in Las Cruces, contain data relating to Mexican land grants.[5]

The organic law for the government of the Territory of New Mexico, issued by General Kearny in 1846, created the office of register of lands. The secretary of the territory was to fill this office, which was "to record all papers and documents of and concerning lands and tenements situated in this Territory, which were issued by the Spanish or Mexican government, remaining in the archives of the secretary of the Territory, or which were in any office of the department of New Mexico under the Mexican Government."[6] Persons having documents relating to land claims could have them recorded upon payment of a fee, and those without written evidence of claims were required to have statements of them recorded within five years. The register of lands was authorized to furnish certified copies of documents and directed to safeguard the records in his possession.

Several registers of land titles were created as a result of the

---

[3] Samples in English translation of the documents in expedientes are printed in Twitchell, *Spanish Arch. N. Mex.*, 1:16–17, 36–39, 62–65, 71–73; Florence H. Ellis, "Tomé and Father J. B. R.," *N. Mex. Hist. Rev.* 30 (Apr. 1955):91–92; José León Padilla, *History of the Las Vegas Grant: Containing a Correct Literal Translation of the Original Spanish Papers* . . . (East Las Vegas, 1890); also in many Congressional documents listed in Bancroft, *Hist. Ariz. and N. Mex.*, 1:757 n. 3.

[4] J. J. Bowden, *Spanish and Mexican Land Grants in the Chihuahua Acquisition* (El Paso, 1971), pp. 1–2.

[5] Ibid., p. 217. Bowden presents histories of individual land grants.

[6] "Organic Law of the Territory of New Mexico," *House Exec. Doc.* 60, 30 Cong., 1 sess., pp. 220–21.

foregoing authorization, Donaciano Vigil initiating the work in 1847. Two registers, formerly in the custody of the surveyor general and the Bureau of Land Management Office at Santa Fe and now in the State Records Center there, include Book A, January 27, 1847–January 22, 1849, and Book C, January 1–July 25, 1849. Book D, December 18, 1851–July 26, 1853, is also in the State Records Center. Book B was lost. Reproductions of these registers are in the Microfilm Collection of Early State Records in the Library of Congress,[7] and microfilm of Books A and C are in the University of New Mexico Library.

The United States acquired sovereignty over New Mexico as a result of the Mexican War. The Treaty of Guadalupe Hidalgo, February 2, 1848, bound the United States to respect property of every kind that had belonged to Mexicans in the ceded territory.[8] So, the adjudication of land grants that had been made by the Spanish and Mexican governments and their survey became the responsibility of the United States. It was not until July 22, 1854, however, that Congress provided for the appointment of a surveyor general.[9] The appointment went to William Pelham who was instructed, on August 21, 1854, to apply to the governor of the territory for the archives relating to land grants made by former authorities of the country.[10] These were to be kept in a safe place, arranged, classified, bound, and used only under the supervision of a government employee. Pelham opened his office at Santa Fe about January 1, 1855.

In providing for the settlement of private land claims in the Territory of New Mexico and other territories formed in the Southwest, Congress abandoned the method, employed in older territories, of using land commissioners to investigate the archival evidence and documents filed by claimants and report upon the validity of the claims. Instead, the surveyor general of New Mexico, under the act of July 22, 1854, was to investigate the claims and report thereon to the secretary of the interior, who was to report to Congress. Many claimants, including the Pueblo Indians, were afraid to part with their documents, and

---

[7] William S. Jenkins, comp., and Lillian A. Hamrick, ed., *A Guide to the Microfilm Collection of Early State Records* (Washington, 1950), p. 67.

[8] U.S., *Stats.*, 9:929.

[9] U.S., *Stats.*, 10:308–310; Victor Westphall, *Public Domain in New Mexico, 1854–1891* (Albuquerque, 1965), p. 1.

[10] John Wilson to William Pelham Aug. 21, 1854, Records of the Bureau of Land Management, Letters Sent Relating to Private Land Claims, Bk. 20 (Record Group 49), National Archives (hereinafter cited as NA, BLM, Lets. Sent PLC). Wilson's letter is printed also in U.S. Dept. of the Interior, *Annual Report*, 1954, pp. 87–94; and in Thomas Donaldson, *The Public Domain: Its History* . . . (Washington, 1884), pp. 394–95.

hindered the examination by the surveyor general.[11] Thus, under this system very slow progress was made in confirming land grants,[12] and repeated recommendations were made by the surveyor general for the establishment of a commission.

The surveyor general quickly initiated work on the land records. When he called on Gov. David Merriwether to ask for the archives relating to private land claims, he was shown a mass of papers, put up in bundles as large as goods boxes, without any labels.[13] Asserting that it would be an enormous task to pick out the papers relating to land grants, the governor refused to order it done, but he did allow Pelham to take the entire collection, amounting to two wagon loads, to his own office, so that the selection could be made there. Two clerks familiar with Spanish immediately began picking out the land papers which were to be retained by the surveyor general, a task which lasted until the end of July, 1855.[14] From 168 packages containing 168,000 papers, 1,715 grants, conveyances of land, and other documents referring to grants of land were selected for retention. The arrangement and classification of the land papers was then undertaken. Altogether 1,014 land grants were found, of which 197 were private grants.

The surveyor general undertook other measures for the care of the records. David V. Whiting was engaged as translator and chief clerk and served until his resignation in 1860.[15] His successor in those positions, David J. Miller, continued until 1884. Arguing that the transportation of suitable safes from the east, across the plains to New

---

[11] William Pelham to Thomas A. Hendricks, May 27, 1856, Records of the Bureau of Land Management, Letters Received from Surveyors General (Record Group 49), National Archives (hereinafter cited as NA, BLM, Lets. Recd. SG); Twitchell, *Spanish Archives of New Mexico*, l:xii; Herbert O. Brayer, *William Blackmore: The Spanish-Mexican Land Grants of New Mexico and Colorado, 1863–1878*, 2 vols. (Denver, 1949), 1:17.

[12] Tables of private land claims are in Twitchell, *Spanish Arch. N. Mex.*, 1:484–502; in Bancroft, *Hist. Ariz. and N. Mex.*, pp. 758–63; and in Donaldson, *Public Domain*, pp. 405–06, 1153–54. See ibid., pp. 401–04 for translations of the documents relating to the grant for the town of Tomé. Much documentary evidence used in connection with the confirmation of land claims was published in Congressional documents; for lists of these see Twitchell, *N. Mex. Hist.*, 2:461–62 n. 383, and Bancroft, *Hist. Ariz. and N. Mex.*, pp. 649, 757.

[13] Pelham to Wilson, May 31, 1855, NA, BLM, Lets. Recd. SG.

[14] "Report of the Surveyor General of New Mexico," Sept. 30, 1855, in U.S. Dept. of the Interior, *Annual Report*, 1855, pp. 165–166; Twitchell, *Spanish Arch. N. Mex.*, 1:xi; Twitchell, *N. Mex. Hist.*, 2:459.

[15] *House Exec. Doc.* 14, 36 Cong., 1 sess., p. 16. It appears that Whiting carried off some documents which he later presented to the Historical Society of New Mexico (Lansing B. Bloom, ed., "Historical Society Minutes, 1859–1863," *N. Mex. Hist. Rev.* 18 [Oct. 1943]:398.

Mexico, would cost $10,000, Pelham sought funds, in 1856 and 1857 for the construction of a stone vault or other safe depository for the land records.[16] To assure their protection when he wasn't given the funds, he was obliged to sleep in one room of the adobe building which he had rented for his office, to require his porter to sleep in the room containing the records, and to keep a large watchdog in the backyard.[17] The walls of the office were lined with canvas to protect the documents, and the dirt floors were carpeted.

Fulfilling the original instructions from the commissioner of the General Land Office, the surveyor general had prepared a "Schedule of documents relating to grants of land by the Spanish and Mexican governments, forming the archives of the Surveyor General of New Mexico"[18] and an "Abstract of the grants of lands selected from the public records of the Territory, found in the archives of Santa Fe, New Mexico."[19] The earliest date in this chronological schedule is 1682 and in the abstract 1685, while the latest date in both is 1846. Somewhat later, a list of Spanish and Mexican governors of New Mexico was compiled,[20] which was revised at a much later date.[21] In 1885, another list of documents relating to grants of land, arranged alphabetically by name of grantee and containing 1,275 entries, was published.[22] A list of private land claims in New Mexico is in the same publication. Briefer lists of private land claims, compiled by David J. Miller, were also published.[23]

In 1862, upon the approach of Confederate forces up the Río Grande from Texas under Gen. Henry H. Sibley, an evacuation of Santa Fe occurred. Part of the records of the surveyor general's office, including original field notes, maps, copies of field notes, and other records, were packed into three boxes and conveyed in a train of wagons, under the charge of John M. Clark, a draftsman, 117 miles northeast to Fort Union.[24] Upon their arrival early in March, they were

16 Pelham to Thomas A. Hendricks, May 30, 1856, Sept. 30, 1856, NA, BLM, Lets. Recd. SG; "Report of the Surveyor General of New Mexico," Sept. 30, 1857, in U.S. Dept. of the Interior, *Annual Report*, 1857, pp. 182–183.

17 Pelham to Hendricks, Nov. 3, 1857, NA, BLM, Lets. Recd. SG.

18 "Report of the Surveyor General of New Mexico," Sept. 30, 1856, in U.S. Dept. of the Interior, *Annual Report*, 1856, pp. 227–46.

19 Ibid., pp. 247–53.

20 Ibid., Aug. 29, 1861, pp. 127–28.

21 Ibid., July 22, 1885, pp. 552–53.

22 Ibid., pp. 535–52.

23 David J. Miller, "Private Land Claims [Adjudicated]; Private Land Claims Not Yet Adjudicated," in New Mexico (Terr.), Secretary's Office, *The Legislative Blue-Book of the Territory of New Mexico* (Santa Fe, 1882), pp. 129–134.

24 John A. Clark to John M. Edmunds, Apr. 1, 1862, NA, BLM, Lets. Recd. SG;

placed in a storeroom in a secure portion of the fort, under the charge of its quartermaster. Before departing for Washington on March 3, as an emissary of the territorial government, John A. Clark, the surveyor general, placed the records left in his office at Santa Fe, which included the ancient archives relating to land grants, in charge of David J. Miller.[25] The Confederates entered Santa Fe on March 10, and, the following day, an officer occupied the surveyor general's office. Two days later, the office was usurped for quarters for additional Texans, as were all other public buildings in the town.[26] The invaders did not molest the records in the office; they did not even ask Miller for the keys to the desks containing the records so that they could examine them.

The northward advance of the Texans was checked by the arrival of Union reinforcements from the territory of Colorado, and, on April 8, Santa Fe was evacuated. After Clark's office was occupied for a time by paroled prisoners, it was returned to its original use and was cleaned up by Miller and John M. Clark, who had returned after serving with the Union forces. The records which had been sent to Fort Union were brought back to Santa Fe on May 20, none being damaged or missing.

Spanish and Mexican land-grant records that came into the custody of the surveyor general have remained in the possession of the federal government. On July 1, 1925, pursuant to the act of Congress of March 3 of that year,[27] the office of the surveyor general was abolished, and its duties and records were transferred to the district cadastral engineer in charge of the Public Survey Office at Santa Fe.[28] During the years 1934–35, the Civil Works Administration prepared a transcription and translation of the Spanish land-grant records.[29] These were in constant use thereafter by the land office and, for most purposes, served as adequate substitutes for the originals. Copies of

---

John M. Clark to John A. Clark, Aug. 7, 1862, NA, BLM, Lets. Recd. SG; George H. Well, "Saving the Archives, the Dash to Fort Union," *Our Public Lands* 3 (April 1953):4, 14.

[25] John A. Clark to John M. Edmunds, Aug. 7, 1862, enclosure John A. Clark to John M. Edmunds, Aug. 7, 1862, NA, BLM, Lets. Recd. SG.

[26] David J. Miller to John A. Clark, Aug. 7, 1862, enclosure John A. Clark to John M. Edmunds, Aug. 7, 1862, NA, BLM, Lets. Recd. SG.

[27] U.S., *Stats.*, sect. 1, 43:1144.

[28] As a result of the consolidation of the General Land Office and the Grazing Service of the Department of the Interior to form the Bureau of Land Management in 1946, the Public Survey Office at Santa Fe became known as the District Land Office. It has since become designated as the Bureau of Land Management, State Office.

[29] José D. Sena, "Archives in the Office of the Cadastral Engineer at Santa Fe," *El Palacio* 36 (Apr. 11–18, 1934):113; U.S. Dept. of the Interior, *Annual Report* 1935, p. 95.

the translation were supplied to the Historical Society of New Mexico and the Laboratory of Anthropology at Santa Fe. When the Spanish archives in the land office at Santa Fe were inventoried by the Survey of Federal Archives in the late 1930s, they filled forty-three document boxes.[30]

In October, 1955, in accordance with an agreement between the Bureau of Land Management and the University of New Mexico Library, as set forth in a letter of understanding, the Spanish and Mexican land-grant records of New Mexico were taken to Albuquerque for microfilming. They were conveyed by Eastburn R. Smith, state supervisor of the bureau at Santa Fe, in two station wagons, under state police escort. Mr. Smith had been making approaches to professors at the university since 1949, with this objective in view. In return for permission to add the land records to its collections of microfilmed source materials on the history of New Mexico, the university was to furnish the land office at Santa Fe with a positive copy of the microfilm. At the university, the records were arranged and prepared for filming by Dr. Davidson B. McKibbin, then special collections librarian, under the direction of David O. Kelley, the university librarian. The microfilming was done by the library's regular camera operator as an overtime job and consequently was not completed until September, 1957. At that time, the original records were transported back to Santa Fe by Mr. Smith and the state police, and were deposited in the old Federal Building in a vault adjoining Smith's office. Outside the office a "No Smoking" sign was posted.[31]

The microfilm produced by the university was considered technically superior by representatives of the Bureau of Land Management and the National Archives and Records Service who inspected it in May 1957, and is also regarded as usable by the bureau for official purposes. The sixty-six reels of microfilm contain not only the Spanish land-grant records which were taken over by the surveyor general in 1855, but also Pueblo land grants which include Spanish documents; the Vigil list of Spanish archives received by the Americans;[32] the register of land titles kept by Vigil from 1847–53; the case files of private land claims adjudicated by the surveyor general, 1855–90, and

---

[30] No inventory of the records was published by the Survey of Federal Archives, but the work sheets embodying the results of the survey are in the records of the national headquarters of the survey in the National Archives and in the New Mexico State Museum.

[31] Letter from Eastburn R. Smith, Dec. 23, 1957.

[32] E. R. Smith to Director, Bureau of Land Management, Sept. 17, 1957, Records of the National Archives and Records Service, Natural Resources Records Branch, Correspondence Files, National Archives (hereinafter cited as NARS, NRRB, Corres. Files, NA).

related dockets; a transcription in books of the documents filed with the surveyor general; the case files and other records of the Court of Private Land Claims; correspondence of the surveyor general; and the muniments of title of the claim of the Baron of Arizona.[33] (Further description of these records is in the following pages.) After acquiring the microfilm, the Bureau of Land Management Land Office at Santa Fe retired the original land-grant records from active use, thus preserving them from further damage. Copies of the microfilm are also in the Bancroft Library of the University of California at Berkeley, the Huntington Library at San Marino, California, the New York Public Library, and the National Archives, Washington, D.C.

In April, 1971, the regional director of the National Archives and Records Service proposed to the state director of the Bureau of Land Management at Santa Fe that the New Mexico land-grant records be transferred to the Federal Records Center at Denver, for preservation.[34] This proposal brought protests from the records administrator of the State of New Mexico, who argued that the records were important to local scholars who were studying land-tenure problems,[35] and from the chairman of the New Mexico Commission of Public Records, who asserted that the proposal was not in the best interest of the people of the state.[36] The state historian wrote the archivist of the United States that the transfer would fragment the historical records of New Mexico and impose great inconvenience on researchers, especially historians, graduate students, lawyers, and representatives from state agencies.[37] She pointed out that when the records had been microfilmed by the University of New Mexico in the 1950s, the documents in the case files had not been put into order before the microfilming, that, as a result, many documents had not been microfilmed in the correct case files, and that documents presented to the surveyor general had been confused with those that came before the Court of Private Land Claims. A memorandum of agreement, signed on April 10, 1972 by the state records administrator and a representative of the National Archives, provided for the deposit of the New Mexico land-grant records in the State Records Center. The records transferred to that repository were

---

[33] Albert J. Díaz, *A Guide to the Microfilm of Papers Relating to New Mexico Land Grants* (Albuquerque, 1960), p. 4.

[34] Harold Mundell to W. J. Anderson, Apr. 23, 1971, NARS, NRRB, Corres. Files, NA.

[35] Joseph F. Halpin to James B. Rhoads, Archivist of the United States, June 30, 1971, NARS, NRRB, Corres. Files, NA.

[36] Ward Alan Minge to J. B. Rhoads, July 1, 1971, NARS, NRRB, Corres. File, NA.

[37] Myra Ellen Jenkins to J. B. Rhoads, July 2, 1971, NARS, NRRB, Corres. File, NA.

those microfilmed by the University of New Mexico Library (listed in Díaz's *Guide*) and described below.

The Spanish land-grant records (calendared in Twitchell's *Spanish Archives of New Mexico*, volume I) consist of 1,384 numbered files, dated from 1685 to 1846 (section 2, microfilm rolls 1–6). These are folded papers (9,600 pages) enclosed in protective wrappers and placed in well-labeled, slip-cased boxes. It is presumed that these preservative measures were taken by Twitchell when he arranged and indexed the files, early in the present century. The Spanish land-grant records contain a variety of documents, including acts of possession, boundary proceedings, circular letters, correspondence, claims for lands, compromises, controversies over lands, confirmations of grants, conveyances, copartnerships, decrees, decisions and reports of the departmental assembly, deeds, distributions of estates, donations of lands, dowers, exchanges, gifts, grants, grants of lead mines, inventories and partitions of estates, lawsuits, laws and regulations relating to lands (mostly in print), letters, mining regulations, mining suits, mortgages, orders for possession, orders for the resettlement of towns, partitions of land, petitions for land, petitions for permission to remove, powers of attorney, proceedings for locations, proceedings regarding contested wills, proceedings regarding the establishment of towns, proceedings regarding the settlement of estates, protests against the sale of land, registrations of mines, reports, revocations of grants, titles, trespasses, and wills.[38] These documents provide data concerning local history, genealogy, biography, social and economic conditions, legal institutions, and governmental procedures.

Kept separately, but actually a part of the same series, are the miscellaneous archives consisting of 2,098 pages of flattened *expedientes* bound into twenty-seven canvas-covered volumes and bearing Twitchell "archive" numbers (section 5, rolls 8–9). The archives index volume is an alphabetic listing of documents in Twitchell's *Spanish Archives of New Mexico*, volume I (sect. 1, roll 1).[39]

Records of the surveyor general of New Mexico now in the State Records Center at Santa Fe are those accumulated or prepared while adjudicating land claims. The records (case files) of private land claims adjudicated by the surveyor general, 1855–90 (series 11, microfilm rolls 12–31), are the most extensive series and are filed in numerical order by report number. These separately jacketed files contain a variety of documents including petitions of claimants, sketch maps, original

---

[38] Twitchell, *Spanish Arch. N. Mex., I*, passim.

[39] This series and those that follow are described in Díaz, *Guide to Land Grants*. He refers to them as "sections," but the term more commonly used by archivists is series.

Spanish documents on the grants, translations, testimonies of witnesses, affidavits, survey documents, copies of decrees of the Court of Private Land Claims, copies of patents, correspondence, and memoranda. Indexes by case names, report numbers, and file numbers are in Díaz's *Guide*. A docket of private land claims (series 10, 1 volume, roll 11) lists the cases in the aforementioned file, and records documents submitted during the proceedings. This docket is indexed by report number and, alphabetically, by names of grantees. Land-claims records (series 12, 8 volumes, rolls 31 A–C, 32) contain copies of many of the documents recorded in the docket described above. An old grant docket (series 8, 1 volume, roll 11) contains 93 entries for claims adjudicated by the surveyor general, showing the dates of filing, boundaries of claims, and the action taken. A record of private land claims (series 9, 1 volume, roll 11) supplies extensive information on reports 1–139 of the total of 162 recorded in the docket.

Papers relating to grants made to Pueblo Indians (series 3, 1 volume, roll 7) contain Spanish documents relating to the Pueblo grants described in Twitchell's *Spanish Archives of New Mexico*, volume I, (pp. 451–83), and documents relating to the Acoma Pueblo survey investigation of 1884. A record of Pueblo grants (series 4, 1 volume, roll 7), contains copies of papers relating to Pueblo grants, followed by English translations. Some of these documents are described in Twitchell, and many of the original documents are in section three. Microfilm of the New Mexico surveyor general's letters sent, August 9, 1854–April 19, 1897 (series 18, 11 volumes, rolls 56–60), and his letters received, August 5, 1854–March 8, 1876 (series 19, 1 volume, roll 60), are included in the microfilm of the land records of New Mexico made by the University of New Mexico Library.

Records of the surveyor general of New Mexico in the Federal Records Center in Denver include letters sent to the registers and receivers at La Mesilla and Las Cruces, December 29, 1875–June 29, 1891 (microfilm in the University of New Mexico Library); letters sent relating to land grants, 1893–96 (2 volumes), concerning surveys, plats, conflicts in claims, and the status of cases before the Court of Private Land Claims; a volume showing the cost of grant surveys under confirmation by the Court of Private Land Claims; letters sent press copybooks, July 30, 1884–March 31, 1910 (117 volumes), containing letters to the General Land Office, private individuals, and surveyors; and for the land office at Las Cruces, letters received from the General Land Office, June 7, 1875–June 29, 1891 (3 volumes). Three volumes of the surveyor general's letters sent, October 31, 1887–April 19, 1897, part of the series referred to in the preceding paragraph, were later deposited in the Federal Records Center in Denver. In supervising land surveys, the surveyors general of New Mexico, Arizona, and Colorado accumulated other records that are in the Bureau of Land Management Land Offices at Santa Fe, Phoenix, and Denver. These records include field notes of surveys, survey plats, maps, contracts with deputy surveyors, accounts, annual reports, records of private surveys, and correspondence.[40]

The adjudication, survey, and patenting of private land claims based upon Spanish and Mexican land grants in New Mexico, Arizona, and Colorado, resulted in the accumulation of consolidated files relating to those claims in the Bureau of Land Management of the Department of the Interior in Washington, D.C. The surveyors' field notes form part of a large series in bound volumes arranged by state, and provide identifying information on private land claims and other areas of the public domain.[41] The survey plats prepared from the field notes contain general descriptions of the physical characteristics of the land and are filed by state, township, and range, in looseleaf form.[42] Tract books contain a record of the manner of disposal of every tract of land and serve as an index to the patents and case files of public land transactions.[43] Record copies of patents or title documents to land issued by the bureau are maintained in a huge series of volumes (about 7,000,000 patents in more than 12,000 volumes). The bureau has an index to private land claims. The tract books for the western states (except California) were transferred to the Washington National Records Center in 1970, and the record copies of patents, in 1971.

Other records relating to private land grants in New Mexico, Arizona, and Colorado are in the records of the Bureau of Land Management (Record Group 49) in the National Archives. Among the land-entry papers, which document separate actions relating to the public land, is the file of private land-claim papers. Grouped alphabetically by state, in heavy jackets bearing identification data, these case files include notices and evidence of claims, survey plats, field notes of surveys, patent certificates, affidavits, deeds, abstracts of title, testimony, copies of federal court decisions, appeals, correspondence, and related papers.[44] New Mexico and Colorado cases are

[40] U.S. Survey of Federal Archives, Arizona, *Inventory of Federal Archives in the States, Series VIII, the Department of the Interior, No. 3, Arizona* (Tucson, 1939). No inventories were published for New Mexico and Colorado. Some of the records of the Santa Fe office are listed in Westphall, *Public Domain in N. Mex.*, pp. 181–83.

[41] Clark M. Gumm, "The Foundation of Land Records," *Our Public Lands* 7 (Oct. 1957):4–5; William D. Pattison, "Use of the U.S. Public Land Survey Plats and Notes as Descriptive Sources," *Professional Geographer*, n.s. 8 (Jan. 1956):10–11.

[42] Robert W. Harrison, "Public Land Records of the Federal Government," *Miss. Valley Hist. Rev.* 41 (Sept. 1954): 279.

[43] Ibid., pp. 280–81.

[44] Harrison, "Public Land Records," p. 284; U.S. National Archives, *Preliminary*

in a single subseries of 215 cases in thirty-eight boxes. Arizona cases numbering 3–19 are in seven boxes. An index to field notes of New Mexico surveys gives the name or description of the grant, the private land-claim number, the plat volume number and the field-note volume. A set of tract books for New Mexico is incomplete. A docket of private land claims in New Mexico, 1861–90 (1 volume), gives the number of the survey, the designation in the act of confirmation, name of claimant or pueblo, location, and remarks. An old index to private land claims in New Mexico, Arizona, and Colorado, 1858–1905 (1 volume), gives the number of the claim, name of claimant, name of claim, locality, and remarks as to confirmation, rejection, or approval. "Private land claims and pueblos, New Mexico," 1823–90 (2 volumes), contains Spanish documents with English translations that were filed with the surveyor general. A file of miscellaneous records relating to private land claims in New Mexico, 1863–1918 (7 indexes), contains correspondence and other materials. There is a list of confirmed private land claims surveyed in Colorado, California, and New Mexico (1 volume). Extensive files of letters to and from surveyors general, relating to private land claims, further document the history of Spanish and Mexican titles.

Records relating to land surveys are also among the records of the Bureau of Land Management (Record Group 49) in the National Archives. Surveying contracts, bonds, and related papers, 1851–1913, include contracts with deputy surveyors, their bonds and oaths, and special instructions addressed to them. Arranged alphabetically by state or territory, this file includes materials for New Mexico, 1855–1913 (13 boxes), Arizona, 1871–1910 (9 boxes), and Colorado, 1861–1911 (10 boxes). These files include contracts for the survey of private land grants, and boundary lines of pueblos and town sites. Field notes of survey, ca. 1883–1918, include separately filed sections for New Mexico, Arizona, and Colorado.

Other records, of a cartographic nature, are in the records of the Bureau of Land Management in the Cartographic Records Branch in the National Archives. Plat books of private land grants, 1853–1915, contain manuscript, annotated, and lithographed plats of private land claims and other forms of land concessions from foreign governments, in areas taken over by the United States.[45] These plats were prepared in surveyor general offices from field notes made by deputy surveyors. For New Mexico, there are eight volumes, and for Arizona and Colo-

---

Inventory [No. 22] of the Land-Entry Papers of the General Land Office, comp. by Harry P. Yoshpe and Philip P. Brower (Washington, 1949), p. 12.

[45] U.S. National Archives, Preliminary Inventory of the Cartographic Records of the Bureau of Land Management (Record Group 49), comp. by Laura E. Kelsay (Washington, 1965).

rado, there is one volume each. The plats show the name of the grantee; the boundaries of the grant; its relationship to public land surveys; courses for the survey; topographic features; name of the deputy surveyor; date and number of the surveying contract; certificates from the surveyor general and Court of Private Land Claims approving the survey; date and record of patent; houses, ranches, or ruins of the same, and other structures; cultivated lands; and information as to lot, township, range, and number of acres. The Cartographic Records Branch has a photostat of a list of New Mexico private land claims made from a list in the Bureau of Land Management. This list is arranged alphabetically by name of claimant, Indian Pueblo, or town.

The old map files, 1790–1946, of the Division of Surveys (Division E) of the General Land Office, contain a variety of annotated, manuscript, and photoprocessed maps, relating to the disposal of public lands in the states and territories. Prepared mostly by deputy surveyors, these maps include some private land claims. Maps of states and smaller areas are arranged alphabetically by name of state, and thereunder, by map number.[46] The numerical order is a chronological one showing the development of surveying and mapping. A file of field notes related to maps in the old map files includes maps for private land claims. A record set of published maps of the United States, individual states, and territories, 1829–1944, contains maps showing public land surveys, private land claims and grants, publicly owned lands, and other lands.

During the 1950s, the Bureau of Land Management initiated a record improvement program designed to replace the worn-out records, based on a system dating back to the early years of the nineteenth century, with new records that could be more easily used to manage public lands and provide information and copies of documents. During 1950–52, the patents were microfilmed, and during 1952–53, the survey plats were microfilmed.[47] After a careful study, a plan was devised for preserving and modernizing the land records of the western states. As preparation for the inauguration of this program, additional records were microfilmed during 1955–56. Positive copies of individual documents on the microfilm, including patents, plats, and other control documents, were then made on 35 mm. microfilm and mounted in windows on tabulating cards.[48] Nearly 4,000,000 cards were key

[46] Lists of the maps for Arizona, Colorado, and New Mexico are in U.S. National Archives, *List of Cartographic Records of the General Land Office (Record Group 49)*, comp. by Laura E. Kelsay (Washington, 1964), pp. 12–17, 29–32, 60–66.

[47] U.S. Department of the Interior, *Annual Report*, 1950, p. 235; 1951, p. 268; 1952, p. 296; 1953, p. 78; 1954, p. 263.

[48] Ibid., 1956 p. 264; U.S. Bureau of Land Management, *The Public Land Records: Footnotes to American History* ([Washington], 1959).

punched and arranged by land descriptions. These cards for the western states were shipped to local land offices, which used them to construct all-inclusive new master title plats, accompanying use plats, and historical indexes for each township. Beginning in 1957, the work of conversion was done on a state-by-state basis. The New Mexico records were converted during 1957–59 at a cost of $695,595, and those for Arizona, during 1958–60 at a cost of $484,490.[49]

Deed books containing copies of deeds and other documents relating to conveyances of land in the Spanish and Mexican periods are in the custody of county clerks of New Mexico.[50] When new counties were created in the territory of New Mexico, it was the practice to provide them with copies of deeds from the records of counties from which they had been separated.[51] Deed books of some New Mexico counties, formerly in the University of New Mexico Library,[52] are now in the State Records Center.

Pueblo Indian land-suit papers, 1758–1905 (2 boxes), containing letters, court records, petitions, and other documents, are in the University of New Mexico Library.

COURT OF PRIVATE LAND CLAIMS

The experience of several decades showed that the approval of land grants by legislative enactment was an unsatisfactory procedure. Consequently, an act of Congress of March 3, 1891 provided for a Court of Private Land Claims to adjudicate titles to land in the regions acquired from Mexico by the Treaty of Guadalupe Hidalgo and the Gadsden Purchase Treaty of 1853.[53] This act required the commissioner of the General Land Office and the surveyors general of states and territories to supply papers presented to them, relative to land claims, to the court. The court consisted of a chief justice and four associate justices appointed by the president, and it also had an attorney, a clerk, and an interpreter and translator. The court was organized at Denver on July 1, 1891, but soon moved to Santa Fe because of the availability there of the records of the surveyor general of New Mexico.

---

[49] U.S. Department of the Interior, *Annual Report*, 1957, pp. 306–07; 1959, p. 318; 1960, 273.

[50] Inventories of county archives published by the Historical Records Survey are available for the counties of Colfax, Doña Ana, Mora, Sandoval, and Valencia; see the titles in the bibliography. Private land grants are also recorded in the deed books of Bernalillo, Grant, and Santa Fe Counties.

[51] See the acts approved January 8, 1874 and March 16, 1899 in New Mexico (Terr.), *Laws*, 1873–74, pp. 58–59; 1899, p. 145.

[52] *Natl. Union Catalog of Ms. Colls.*, 1966, entry 1762.

[53] U.S., *Stats.*, 26:854; Twitchell, *Hist. N. Mex.*, 2:465–66.

Sessions of the court were held in those places and in Tucson. The court found it necessary to employ agents to investigate and evaluate archival evidence regarding claims.[54] Of the 301 claims for more than 36,000,000 acres that were presented to the court, it confirmed 88, comprising a little over 2,000,000 acres.[55] Upon the conclusion of the court's sittings in 1904, its records were deposited with the surveyor general of New Mexico.

Records of the Court of Private Land Claims are in the State of New Mexico Records Center and Archives in Santa Fe. Records (case files) of private land claims adjudicated by the court (series 14, rolls 33–54) contain original grants or copies of grants, sketch maps, applications for survey, testimony of witnesses as to boundaries, reports of the surveyor general on surveys, notices of surveys, and decrees and opinions of the court.[56] An appearance docket or register of actions (series 13, roll 33) shows case numbers, title, nature, name of attorney, a memorandum of papers filed, and proceedings on the case. The docket includes an index by name of grant. The court's journal, December 1, 1899–June 15, 1904 (series 15, 4 volumes, roll 55), records the proceedings of the court by term and by days. The vacation minute book, 1893–1904 (series 16, 1 volume, roll 55), records proceedings during vacation periods, and the court's amended rules. The roll of attorneys (series 17, 1 volume, roll 55) contains the names of attorneys in alphabetical order. Muniments of title of the Baron of Arizona (series 22, rolls 62–63) contain documents relating to the spurious claims of James Addison Reavis, which are really a part of the claims papers in series 14 described above but were microfilmed separately.

---

[54] A comprehensive account of the formation and work of the court is in Richard W. Bradfute, *The Court of Private Land Claims: The Adjudication of Spanish and Mexican Land Grant Titles, 1891–1904* (Albuquerque, 1975).

[55] Lists of cases decided by the court are in U.S. Department of Justice, *Report of the Attorney General*, 1904, pp. 100–06, with lists of New Mexico and Arizona cases appealed to the Supreme Court, pp. 108, 109 (reprinted in Bradfute, *Court of Private Land Claims*, pp. 245–54). Other lists are in Anderson, *Hist. N. Mex.*, 1:204–08, and in Coan, *Hist. N. Mex.*, 1:477–79. Reports on cases decided by the Supreme Court are in the *United States Supreme Court Reports*. Many suits regarding land grants were considered by the territorial courts between 1891–1910 (Keleher, "Law of the N. Mex. Land Grant," p. 359). The records of these courts were transferred to the U.S. District Court at Santa Fe in 1912. Histories of land claims tried by the Court of Private Land Claims and lists of the cases referred to above, together with descriptions of the records of the court and the surveyor general of New Mexico, are in J. J. Bowden, *Private Land Claims in the Southwest*, 6 vols. (Houston, Tex., 1969).

[56] An alphabetical index to the cases, which include those for Arizona and Colorado as well as New Mexico, is in Díaz, *Guide*, pp. 17–57, and a list of case numbers is in ibid, pp. 59–65. A list of the cases is also in Twitchell, *Spanish Arch. N. Mex.*, 1:492–502. The series and roll numbers are for the microfilm of the court's records made by the University of New Mexico Library; see the description of the surveyor general's records in this chapter.

COLORADO

After the Texas revolution of 1836, the Mexican government made seven large land grants in northeastern New Mexico, as far as the international boundary along the Arkansas River in what is now southern Colorado. The grants were given to Mexican citizens, who were to colonize the area in an attempt to strengthen it against encroachment by the United States and Texas.[57]

The investigation of private land claims in Colorado, and the reporting thereon to Congress, was begun by the surveyor general of New Mexico and continued by the surveyor general of Colorado. Several grants reported on by the surveyor general of New Mexico were confirmed by an act of Congress of June 21, 1860.[58] An act of Congress of February 28, 1861 created the Territory of Colorado from that part of the Territory of New Mexico north of the thirty-seventh degree latitude and set it up as a separate surveying district.[59] That act authorized the president to appoint a surveyor general for the Territory of Colorado, with the same duties concerning the confirmation of private land claims as those given to the surveyor general of New Mexico by the act of July 22, 1854. The latter official was instructed, on April 22, 1861, to transmit all survey records and other official documents relating to public lands, private claims, or pueblos in the new territory to the newly appointed surveyor general of Colorado.[60] In January, 1862, all official documents (of which copies were retained) relating to the private land grants of Charles Beaubien, Ceran St. Vrain and Cornelio Vigil, and Gervacio Nolan and Pablo Montoya, which were believed to be in the Territory of Colorado, though possibly partly within the Territory of New Mexico, were sent to Denver.[61]

While investigating the private land claims in southern Colorado and preparing reports thereon for Congress, the surveyor general of Colorado accumulated a file of private land-claim records. The records received from Santa Fe probably constituted the beginning of this file, to which other documents were added by the surveyor general. The private land-grant records, 1820–1901, include petitions, grants, con-

---

[57] Ralph Carr, "Private Land Claims in Colorado," *The Colo. Mag.* 25 (Jan. 1948): 10–30; Harold H. Dunham, "New Mexican Land Grants with Special Reference to the Title Papers of the Maxwell Grant," *N. Mex. Hist. Rev.* 30 (Jan. 1955): 2. Carr gives histories of individual grants.

[58] Le Roy R. Hafen, "Mexican Land Grants in Colorado," *Colo. Mag.* 4 (May 1927):83–89; Joseph O. Van Hook, "Mexican Land Grants in the Arkansas Valley," *Southw. Hist. Quar.* 40 (July 1936):63–64.

[59] U.S., *Stats.*, 12:176–77.

[60] J. M. Edmunds to A. P. Wilbar, Apr. 22, 1861, Records of the Bureau of Land Management, Letters Sent to Surveyors General, Bk. 19 (Record Group 49), National Archives (hereinafter cited as NA, BLM, Lets. Sent to SG).

[61] John A. Clark to J. M. Edmunds, Sept. 13, 1862, NA, BLM, Lets. Recd., SG.

veyances, survey notes and reports, maps, lawsuit papers, affidavits, certificates of possession, copies of testimony presented before the surveyor general, estate records, and correspondence.[62] In 1969, this small collection of records was in the custody of the Colorado Land Office of the Bureau of Land Management, but the Court of Private Land Claim records in Santa Fe contain more complete files relating to land grants in Colorado.

Other records of the surveyor general of Colorado, now in the records of the Bureau of Land Management in the Federal Records Center in Denver, include materials containing references to private land grants. These records include letters sent to the commissioner of the General Land Office, 1861–68 (1 volume); miscellaneous letters sent, 1861–68 (1 volume); letters received by the Pueblo land office concerning claims to the Las Animas grant, 1871–90 (2 inches); letters received from the General Land Office, 1861–1934 (115 volumes); letters received from settlers claiming land within the Las Animas grant; and maps of land grants.

The Colorado Land Office of the Bureau of Land Management at Denver also has some records relating to private land grants in Colorado. Some miscellaneous papers and correspondence relate to the Baca, Nolan, Vigil-St. Vrain, Sangre de Cristo, Tierra Amarilla, Medano, and Zapato land grants. Other records include field notes of surveys and tract books. The records improvement program of the Bureau of Land Management, described above in the section on New Mexico, has also been applied to Colorado. Consequently, the Colorado Land Office has microfilm of the survey plats mounted in aperture cards, and the tract books have been replaced by new land-status plats.

The clerks and, later, the recorders of deeds in the counties that the Colorado legislature began setting up in 1861 also became the custodians of records relating to Mexican land grants.[63] Besides deed books, the county recorders have record books containing copies of United States patents.[64]

In the collections of the State Historical Society of Colorado, there are three volumes of materials on land grants in New Mexico and Colorado, gathered by collectors.

---

[62] Report on serials of the Survey of Federal Archives, No. 535, Apr. 23, 1936, for the supervisor of surveys of the General Land Office, Denver, Records of the Work Projects Administration (Record Group 69), National Archives.

[63] The clerks were required by a law of November 6, 1861 (Colorado [Terr.], Laws, 1861, pp. 92–94) to keep records of deeds and other instruments.

[64] Inventories by the Historical Records Survey of the records of Conejos, Costilla, and Alamosa Counties are listed in the bibliography.

8

Records of Local Jurisdictions

THE SYSTEM OF LOCAL GOVERNMENT in New Mexico during the Spanish period consisted of six to eight districts or jurisdictions. These were headed by *alcaldes mayores* appointed by the governor, generally for life. The districts were divided into *partidos* under *teniente alcaldes* who were also selected by the governor. The *alcalde mayor* resided in the principal town of his jurisdiction, and the *teniente alcalde* was located in the chief village of the *partido*. The *partidos* did not have definite boundaries, and the *tenientes* sometimes headed more than one partido. The people addressed themselves to the nearest official. In his judicial capacity, the *alcalde mayor* determined minor civil and criminal cases and, in more important ones, initiated the proceedings by collecting the depositions and testimonies of witnesses and forwarding them to the governor, whose sentences were executed by the *alcalde mayor*. The *alcaldes mayores* maintained law and order among Spanish citizens and Pueblo Indians, regulated travel within the province, proclaimed edicts and royal decrees, compiled census reports, accepted gifts for the king, collected levies from citizens to pacify nomadic Indians, and maintained a register of cattle brands. They notarized official documents and wills, maintained a depository for local archives, and handled applications for land grants. As the war captain, the *alcalde mayor* led expeditions against the Indians and made collections for the support of the military establishment. In temporal matters, the authority of the *alcalde mayor* extended over Indian pueblos where missionaries were stationed. The duties of the *teniente alcaldes* were similar to those of the *alcaldes mayores*.[1]

---

[1] Simmons, *Spanish Govt. in N. Mex.*, p. 170 ff.; France V. Scholes, "Civil Government and Society in New Mexico in the Seventeenth Century," *N. Mex. Hist. Rev.* 10 (Apr. 1935):91–92.

About 1718, the *alcaldías* consisted of the following settlements or groups of settlements: Santa Cruz de la Cañada; Albuquerque, Bernalillo, Santa Ana, Zía, and Jémez; Ysleta; Laguna, Acoma, Halona, and Zuñi; Pecos and Galisteo; and Taos. Later in the Spanish period, there was also an *alcalde mayor* at Alameda.

Ayuntamientos, or town councils, were also created in some settlements during the Spanish period. Santa Fe was governed by a council (referred to as the *cabildo* in early years) practically from the time of its establishment. The *ayuntamiento* consisted of four *regidores* (councilmen) who were elected by the citizens. They selected two *alcaldes ordinarios* (municipal magistrates), an *alguacil* (bailiff), a notary, an attorney, and a major-domo.[2] The presiding officer or his lieutenant was the governor, and in their absence, the *alcalde*. The *ayuntamiento* adopted ordinances for governing the villa of Santa Fe that had to be approved by the governor, delineated wards, and assigned town lots and lands in the vicinity to citizens for cultivation and grazing. In their judicial capacity, *alcaldes ordinarios* exercised civil and criminal jurisdiction over cases arising within the villa and its neighboring jurisdiction. Appeals could be taken from their courts to the *ayuntamiento* in minor matters, and to the governor and the Audiencia of Guadalajara in more serious cases. The governor was to request the advice of the council on all important matters. The *ayuntamiento* was inactive during much of the eighteenth century, and an *alcalde mayor* functioned in its place.

Toward the end of the Spanish regime in New Mexico, other *ayuntamientos* were established.[3] Decrees adopted by the Spanish Cortes in 1812, to effectuate the provisions of the Spanish constitution of 1812, were sent to the governor of New Mexico and put into effect there. These laws provided for *ayuntamientos* composed of constitutional *alcaldes*, *regidores*, an attorney and a secretary. Electors chosen by the citizens selected the municipal magistrates, councilors, and other officials. By 1814, *ayuntamientos* had been established at Albuquerque, Belén, Bernalillo, El Paso del Norte, Santa Cruz de la Cañada, and Santa Fe. Most of the councils had secretaries who kept the town records. Villages unable to maintain governments of their own were attached to the nearest *ayuntamiento*. In 1814, after regaining his throne, Ferdinand VII dissolved the Cortes, revoked the constitution and the decrees of 1812, and, on July 30, 1814, ordered the dissolution of the *ayuntamientos* and the restoration of the old officials. In 1815,

---

[2] Simmons, *Spanish Govt. in N. Mex.*, pp. 159–160; Scholes, "Civil Govt.," pp. 94–95; Lansing B. Bloom, "Beginnings of Representative Government in New Mexico," *N. Mex. Hist. Rev.* 21 (Apr. 1946):129–30.

[3] Simmons, *Spanish Govt. in N. Mex.*, pp. 205–12.

the town councils in New Mexico were dissolved, and local government was again in the hands of *alcaldes mayores* and their *tenientes*. In 1820, the king was forced by a liberal revolution to restore the constitution of 1812 and recall the Cortes, which reestablished the laws of the first Cortes. So, by 1820–21, most New Mexican towns and Indian pueblos had their own *ayuntamientos*.

Several rearrangements of the system of local government occurred during the Mexican period. In 1823, the provincial deputation divided the province into *partidos* headed by Santa Fe, Albuquerque, Santa Cruz de la Cañada, and El Paso del Norte.[4] Each *partido* comprised a number of pueblos designated as *ayuntamientos*, although few were really such. A decree of 1837 divided the department into districts, with capitals at Santa Fe and Albuquerque.[5] The districts were headed by prefects nominated by the governor; the prefects served, practically, as lieutenant governors. The settlements in each district were assigned to *partidos*, which were supervised by subprefects appointed by the governor. A decree of June 17, 1844, of the departmental assembly divided the department into the central district, comprising the *partidos* of Santa Fe, Santa Ana, and San Miguel del Vado, with the *cabecera* (headquarters) at Santa Fe; the northern district, comprising the partidos of Río Arriba and Taos, with the *cabecera* at Los Luceros; and the southeastern district, comprising Valencia and Bernalillo, with the *cabecera* at Valencia.[6] The governor was authorized to designate prefects for the three districts, but the subprefects were discontinued.

Most of the records of local jurisdictions for the period prior to American occupation have disappeared. The *partidos* and prefects established by the Mexicans in 1844 were continued under the Kearny code of 1846, which also provided for the continuation of prefects, alcaldes, and clerks. Their duties and such records as they possessed were transferred to officials of the counties that were created by an act of the first territorial legislature of New Mexico.[7] Neither the organic act of the congress for the government of the Territory of New Mexico, approved September 9, 1850, nor the acts of the territorial legislature, establishing local governments, contained specific provisions for the care of the Spanish and Mexican records.

A consequence of maintaining the colonial capital at Santa Fe

---

[4] Bloom, "N. Mex. under Mex. Admin.," 1:157–158.

[5] Ibid., 2:11–13.

[6] Ibid., pp. 226–27. The decree is printed in Twitchell, *N. Mex. Hist.*, 2:15–16, and shows the settlements in each district.

[7] The counties created by the act approved Jan. 9, 1852 were as follows: Bernalillo, Doña Ana, Río Arriba, San Miguel, Santa Ana, Santa Fe, Socorro, Taos, and Valencia (New Mexico [Terr.], *Laws*, 1851–52, p. 291).

and the close connection of the governor with the local government there is the preservation, in the Spanish archives of New Mexico, of documentation relating to the *cabildo* at Santa Fe, including fragments of its proceedings.[8] There is much material in these archives for the history of other *ayuntamientos*, but it is more voluminous for that of Santa Fe.[9]

There appears to have been some destruction of records during the Mexican War and the years following. While occupying El Paso del Norte during the winter of 1846–47, Missouri volunteers, under the command of Col. Alexander W. Doniphan, were quartered in public buildings and used records deposited in them for lighting candles and fires.[10] Some records from that settlement were saved by Mexican officials. Evidence that records were destroyed at Mora and Taos during the uprising of 1846–47 also exists.[11] Other losses were suffered as a result of the frequent removals of county seats, the indifference of local officials during both the colonial and American periods, and the failure of Mexican officials to turn records over to their successors. The few records of the colonial period that did survive are bound with other records, making them difficult to find.[12] Some records of the colonial period may have been destroyed in the wholesale burning of county records during the territorial period.[13]

Portions of the journal of proceedings of the *ayuntamiento* of Santa Fe, 1829–36, are in the Zimmerman Library of the University of New Mexico.[14] A typed translation of this journal is in the Bancroft Library of the University of California. This journal has been collated with other portions of the Santa Fe *ayuntamiento* proceedings in the New Mexico State Records Center and microfilmed.[15] Documents relat-

[8] Twitchell, *Spanish Arch., N. Mex.*, 2:passim. An inventory of cabildo archives relating to land grants is in ibid., 1:330–38, and Jenkins, *Calendar of the Mex. Arch. of N. Mex.*, passim. When the Santa Fe cabildo became inactive in the eighteenth century, its records were transferred to the governor's office.

[9] Coan, "Bernalillo County Documents in 'Santa Fe Archives,'" in his *Hist. N. Mex.*, 1:285–300. Prepared from Twitchell's *Spanish Arch. N. Mex.*, this list includes land papers, criminal proceedings and suits, inventories of property, muster rolls of militia, returns of arms and equipment, reports of war contributions, circulars, letters, and censuses.

[10] "To Confirm Certain Land Claims in the Territory of New Mexico, April 2, 1860," *House Rep.*, 321, 36 Cong., 1 Sess. (Washington, 1860), pp. 45, 72.

[11] "New Mexico Private Land Claims," Feb. 10, 1860, *House Exec. Doc.* 14, 36 Cong., 1 sess., p. 188; Vaughan, "Arch. N. Mex.," pp. 483–84.

[12] Vaughan, "Arch. N. Mex." p. 481.

[13] Hammond, "Ms. Coll. in N. Mex.," p. 83.

[14] Albert J. Díaz, *Manuscripts and Records in the University of New Mexico Library* (Albuquerque, 1957), entry 96.

[15] New Mexico State Records Center, *Guide to Mex. Arch. N. Mex.*, pp. 13, 17, 23.

ing to Santa Fe, in the Spanish archives of New Mexico in that repository, include land conveyances, petitions and other communications to the governor, and election returns for local officials.[16]

A fragmentary collection of the papers of Juan Gerónimo Torres, a militia lieutenant, farmer and deputy alcalde at Sabinal from 1819–27, a settlement 100 miles south of Santa Fe in the jurisdiction of Belén, has been preserved by the family. Photocopies of these papers were presented in 1950 to New Mexico Highlands University. In a series of articles, Lynn I. Perrigo, a history professor of that institution, has published translations of a number of documents from the collection, of a legal, economic, and personal nature, as well as information derived from other pieces.[17]

A few Río Arriba County documents, 1811–67, including bills of sale and records of court proceedings, are in the University of New Mexico Library. Some Valencia County records are in the State Records Center.

In 1909, the New Mexico Historical Society bought, with funds raised by public subscription and an appropriation by the territorial legislature, some records of Santa Cruz de la Cañada and the northern jurisdiction of New Mexico.[18] The records were placed in the Museum of New Mexico and were listed in its holdings in 1915, but, by 1926, they had disappeared. In 1960, Kenneth D. Sender, of the Smoky Hills Booksellers, Inc., Kansas City, Missouri, offered some 500 official records of the Spanish and Mexican governments of New Mexico to the Museum of New Mexico, for $50,000.[19] Sender had obtained the records for $3,400 from William Prince, the son of L. Bradford Prince, who, as president of the New Mexico Historical Society, had purchased the Santa Cruz records for the society in 1909. On February 22, 1961, the sheriff of Santa Fe County and the assistant attorney general of New Mexico, acting on a writ of replevin signed by the state records administrator, seized the records from Sender. The senior archivist of the State of New Mexico identified the documents as official correspondence, legislative proceedings, and other legal papers dealing largely with the area attached to Santa Cruz. Some 350 documents that were determined to be official were placed in the State Records Center, and the remainder was returned to Sender.

---

[16] Twitchell, *Spanish Arch. N. Mex.*, 2:passim. See the inventory of documents of 1750–51, ibid., pp. 320–21, and an index of documents on file, 1818–19, ibid., p. 603.

[17] The varying titles of these five compilations are in the bibliography.

[18] New Mexico Historical Society, *Biennial Report*, 1906–08, pp. 9–10; 1909–12, p. 8; Vaughan, "Arch. N. Mex.," p. 474.

[19] See the news note in the *American Archivist* 24 (July 1961):380.

The State of New Mexico based its claim to the Santa Cruz documents on grounds that it was the successor to previous custodial agencies of the State and Territory of New Mexico and the governments of Spain and Mexico. After the state lost jurisdiction in the case because of its failure to prosecute it within the prescribed two-year period, it obtained the assistance of the federal government in 1964. The Department of Justice and the National Archives collaborated on the preparation of the case, which was heard before the United States District Court for the Eastern District of Missouri. The jury verdict was in favor of Sender, and, after the United States government decided not to appeal the case, the records were returned to him early in 1969.[20]

---

[20] Paul V. Lutz, "Government Loses Suit for Documents," *Manuscripts* 19 (Fall 1967):9–11; *American Archivist* 31 (July 1968):337.

9

Ecclesiastical Records

THE SPANISH COLONIZING EXPEDITION under Juan de Oñate, that initiated the settlement of New Mexico in 1598, was accompanied by ten Franciscan missionaries. The Indians in New Mexico were living, for defensive purposes, in large, communal, stone or adobe structures containing many apartments, and, because of this manner of town dwelling, the Spaniards called them Pueblos, a term by which they have continued to be known. During the early years of Spanish colonization, the Franciscans established missions at a number of the Indian pueblos and supervised the construction of churches, conventos, and schools, where the Indians were taught the Catholic religion, the Spanish language, and useful occupations. During the first quarter century of Spanish occupation, missions or appendages known as *visitas* were founded at the pueblos of Abó, Acoma, Chililí, Cochití, Cuarac, Galisteo, Hawaikuh, Isleta, Jémez, Pecos, Picurís, Pojoaque, San Cristóbal, San Felipe, San Ildefonso, San Juan, San Lázaro, San Marcos, Sandía, Santa Ana, Santo Domingo, Taos, Tesuque, and Zía. Before the Pueblo revolt, other missions were established at the pueblos of Alameda, Halona, Humanos, Paako, Santa Clara, Senecú, Socorro, Tabira (Gran Quivira), Tajique, and Zuñi. The missions extended from El Paso del Norte (Ciudad Juárez), on the south, to Taos, on the north, and from points east of the Río Grande basin to as far west as the Hopi pueblos, in what is now northeastern Arizona.[1] During the Pueblo revolt against

---

[1] France V. Scholes and Lansing B. Bloom, "Friar Personnel and Mission Chronology, 1598–1629," *N. Mex. Hist. Rev.* 19 (Oct. 1944):319–36; Ibid. 20 (Jan. 1945): 58–82; Henry W. Kelly, *Franciscan Missions of New Mexico, 1740–1760* (Albuquerque, 1941); Edgar L. Hewett and Wayne L. Manuzy, *Landmarks of New Mexico* (Albuquerque, 1953). No complete history of the missions of New Mexico has been

the Spaniards in 1680, the Indians killed the majority of the Franciscans and destroyed the missions, including furnishings and records. The surviving missionaries and colonists fled to El Paso del Norte. After the reconquest of New Mexico by De Vargas in 1692–94, missions were reestablished at many pueblos. A new pueblo was built in 1697, west of Albuquerque at Laguna, where a mission was located. The ecclesiastical establishment in New Mexico in 1730 included Acoma, Albuquerque, Cochití, Galisteo, Isleta, Jémez, Laguna, Nambé, Pecos, Picurís, San Felipe, San Juan, San Ildefonso, Santa Ana, Santa Clara, Santa Fe, Santa Cruz, Santo Domingo, Taos, Zía, and Zuñi.[2] About 1747, Abiquiú, a settlement of genízaros (or Indian captives and fugitives) and a mission, was founded on the Chama River, northwest of Santa Fe. In 1760, when the bishop of Durango visited New Mexico, there were missions at the aforementioned pueblos as well as at Pojoaque, Sandía, San Lorenzo, Senecú, Socorro, and Tesuque.[3] The Indians subsisted by cultivating fields around the pueblos, that were irrigated to increase the output. Fruit and cotton were also produced where possible, and herds of sheep, cattle and hogs were raised. In 1749, missions were established at Cebolleta, north of Laguna, and at Encinal, north of Acoma, for the Navahos and Apaches, but lack of government support and the resistance of the Indians resulted in their evacuation. Efforts to persuade the nomadic Comanches to locate in permanent settlements were also unsuccessful.

When towns were founded in New Mexico, one of the earliest undertakings was the construction of a church. In the 1620s, a church was built on the plaza at Santa Fe,[4] and, later, San Miguel chapel was erected for the use of Indians who served Spanish officials at the

published. Descriptions of the locations of the pueblos and the tribal affiliations of the Indians are in Frederick W. Hodge, ed., *Handbook of American Indians North of Mexico*, 2 vols. (New York, 1959); and in John R. Swanton, *The Indian Tribes of North America* (Washington, 1952). Maps showing the locations of the missions are in Cleve Hallenbeck, *Spanish Missions of the Old Southwest* (Garden City, N. Y., 1926), p. 23; and Angelico Chávez, O.F.M., *Archives of the Archdiocese of Santa Fe 1678–1900* (Washington, 1957), which also show the names of the patron saints. The meager documentary records of the missions have been supplemented in recent years by archaeological investigations. The Franciscan Order (Order of Friars Minor) was established by Francis of Assisi in the thirteenth century and was the chief missionary order that the Spanish crown used to assist in the occupation of the Southwest.

[2] Frank D. Reeve, ed., "Documents Concerning Bishop Crespo's Visitation, 1730," *N. Mex. Hist. Rev.* 28 (July 1953):226–27.

[3] Eleanor Adams, ed. and trans., *Bishop Tamarón's Visitation of New Mexico, 1760* (Albuquerque, 1954), passim.

[4] Angelico Chávez, O.F.M., "Santa Fe Church and Convent Sites in the Seventeenth and Eighteenth Centuries," *N. Mex. Hist. Rev.* 24 (Apr. 1949):89.

capital.[5] Both edifices were destroyed by the Indians in 1680. St. Francis Church was built in 1714–17, and San Miguel was rebuilt in 1710. The Chapel of Our Lady of Light, also known as the Military Chapel or the Castrense, was built in 1760 on a site selected by the governor on the south side of the plaza.[6] Churches were also built at Albuquerque in 1706 and Santa Cruz de la Cañada in 1733, and later at Bernalillo and Socorro. Genízaro settlements where churches were built included Tomé, south of Santa Fe, nearby Belén, and Abiquiú, San Miguel del Vado, and San José del Vado, on the Pecos River southeast of Santa Fe. Spanish settlements north of Santa Fe with churches or chapels included Taos, Trampas, Truchas, Ojo Caliente, Embudo, Esquipulas, La Joya, Soledad, and Villita. Those south of Santa Fe were Alameda, Peña Blanca, Sabinal, San Andrés, San Clemente, San José, and San Ysidro. Franciscans officiated at these churches until they were replaced by secular clergy during the long period of secularization. Religious establishments in the El Paso area are treated in chapter eighteen, in the section on Texas.

After the arrival of another group of Franciscans in New Mexico in 1616 or early 1617, the missions of that new territory were constituted as the Custody of St. Paul of New Mexico.[7] It was subordinate to the Province of the Holy Gospel of Mexico which elected the custodian (custos) of St. Paul.[8] As chief prelate of New Mexico, the custodian represented the Catholic church in contacts with the provincial government.[9] He sometimes served as the agent of the Inquisition and investigated the conduct of governors.[10] He supervised the missionaries, issued instructions to them, corresponded with them, and received reports from them. He submitted reports on visitations to the missions and other matters to the Holy Gospel Province in Mexico. A friar served the custodian as secretary, and, when he was absent from his seat, a vice-custodian took his place. Another official of the custody was concerned with the procurement of supplies, which were brought overland from Mexico in caravans.

---

[5] George Kubler, *The Rebuilding of San Miguel at Santa Fe in 1710* (Colorado Springs, 1939):5–6.

[6] Eleanor B. Adams, "The Chapel and Cofradia of Our Lady of Light in Santa Fe," *N. Mex. Hist. Rev.* 22 (Oct. 1947):327–29.

[7] France V. Scholes, "Problems in the Early Ecclesiastical History of New Mexico," *N. Mex. Hist. Rev.* 7 (Jan. 1932):59, 61.

[8] Chávez, *Arch. Archdiocese of Santa Fe*, pp. 55, 157, 164, 165, 168, 169.

[9] Ibid., passim, contains many references to the names of custodians; no list has been found.

[10] Scholes, "Ecclesiastical Hist. N. Mex.," p. 43.

The missions of New Mexico declined in the second half of the eighteenth century, and, thereafter, the role of the Franciscans also declined in significance. In the report on his visitation to New Mexico in 1760, the bishop of Durango recommended that parishes be established at El Paso del Norte, Santa Fe, Albuquerque, and Santa Cruz de la Cañada, settlements that were in charge of secular clergy.[11] It was not until near the close of the century, however, that the bishop was able to send clergy to replace the missionaries at the villas.[12] In 1823, there were twenty-three Franciscans in New Mexico and still only four secular priests.[13] The missions at Abiquiú, Belén, San Juan, San Miguel del Vado, and Taos were secularized in 1826 when parish priests were appointed at those places.[14] A vicar forane at Santa Fe served as the channel of communication between the bishop and the parish priests, reported on visitations to the bishop, issued permits to build chapels, administered confirmations, and served as ecclesiastical judge.[15] Cura Juan Rafael Rascón was designated as vicar general and visitor to New Mexico in 1828, and reached Santa Fe in March, 1829.[16] Little financial support was given to the church, and it was reported in 1832 that most curacies and missions in the territory were vacant.[17]

Only part of the ecclesiastical records of the Spanish and Mexican periods of New Mexico have survived. Those antedating 1680 were presumably destroyed in the Pueblo revolt of that year.[18] Some seem to have survived, however, and were preserved in the archives at Santo Domingo mission, which served as a depository for the records of a number of the missions.[19] Records at that place may have been destroyed when the Río Grande washed away the mission and convent in 1886. Records of the Custody of St. Paul were preserved for many years in the mission at Santa Clara.[20] For over a hundred years after the secularization of the missions, their records were neglected and

[11] Adams, *Bishop Tamarón's Visitation*, p. 81.

[12] Chávez, *Arch. Archdiocese of Santa Fe*, pp. 55, 167.

[13] Ibid., p. 190.

[14] Ibid., pp. 191–92; Twitchell, *Hist. N. Mex.*, 2:185.

[15] Chávez, *Arch. Archdiocese of Santa Fe*, pp. 98, 179; Twitchell, *Hist. N. Mex.*, 2:185.

[16] Chávez, *Arch. Archdiocese of Santa Fe*, pp. 98, 179.

[17] Lansing B. Bloom, trans. and ed., *Antonio Barreiro's Ojeada sobre Nuevo-México* (Santa Fe, 1928).

[18] Bandelier, *Final Report*, 2:163, 273 n. 5.

[19] Eleanor B. Adams and Angelico Chávez, O.F.M., trans. and eds., *The Missions of New Mexico, 1776: A Description by Fray Francisco Atanasio Domínguez* (Albuquerque, 1956), pp. 234–37, 259–64, passim. Father Domínguez inspected the records of other missions and gives some information about them.

[20] Writers' Program, New Mexico, *New Mexico: A Guide to the Colorful State*, ed. by Henry G. Alsberg (New York, 1962), p. 352.

subjected to losses of various kinds. Finally, in 1934, Archbishop Rudolph A. Gerken had the extant records of the missions, the Custody of St. Paul, the vicar of New Mexico, and the parishes, up to the middle of the nineteenth century, assembled in the Archives of the Archdiocese of Santa Fe.[21]

The task of arranging and cataloguing the records was eventually undertaken by Fr. Angelico Chávez. He divided the loose documents into three chronological classifications: first, diligencias matrimoniales (1678–1869), or prenuptial investigations, which are bulkier than all the other materials; secondly, general, loose, mission documents and fragments (1680–1850); and thirdly, diocesan papers from 1850 to the present, but classified only to 1900.

The prenuptial investigations were designed to insure the validity of marriages by questioning the parties and witnesses under oath. The file contains two items for 1678; several items for 1680–93 (the years of exile at Guadalupe del Paso), 1694–1730, 1731; and the main body, covering the years 1760–1869. The documents supply much genealogical information and often supplant missing marriage registers. The genealogical and historical data in the prenuptial investigations has been incorporated into a published work.[22]

Chávez's calendar also presents information derived from the records of ecclesiastical establishments and the activities and assignments of friars.[23] The general, loose documents are varied in content. There is correspondence of missionaries, custodians, the vicar ecclesiastic and judge (Santiago Roybal), bishop of Durango, provincial fathers of the Province of the Holy Gospel at Mexico City, the commandant general of the Interior Provinces at Chihuahua, and civil authorities of New Mexico. Other materials include fragments of registers of missions and churches, and copybooks of official letters (*patentes*); inventories of mission property, libraries, archives, and lands; issuances of the bishop of Durango, the pope, the king, and the commandant general; accounts; censuses; circular letters to missionaries; acts of possession of church establishments; journals; proceedings of cases before the ecclesiastical courts or the governor; petitions of soldiers to marry; and treaties with the Indians.[24]

The copybooks of official communications, received from superior

---

[21] Chávez, *Arch. Archdiocese of Santa Fe*, p. 3.

[22] Chávez, *Origins of N. Mex. Families.* Further work by Chávez in cataloguing the archives resulted in his "Addenda to New Mexico Families," *El Palacio* 62–64 (1955–57); and "New Names in New Mexico, 1820–1850," *El Palacio* 64 (Sept.–Oct., Nov.–Dec. 1957):291–318, 367–80. The second addition contains not only New Mexican names but some French-Canadian, American, and North European names.

[23] Chávez, *Arch. Archdiocese of Santa Fe*, pp. 7–14.

[24] Ibid., pp. 15–113, contains a chronological calendar of the documents.

ecclesiastical and civil authorities, contain copies which the friars at missions entered in their books of *patentes* or which secular clergy entered in their books of edicts and circulars. These official communications included official letters from the father provincial of the Province of the Holy Gospel at Mexico City, the commissary general of the Indies at Mexico City, and the custodian or vice-custodian of New Mexico; edicts, pastorals, and other directives (circulars) received from the bishop of Durango; royal decrees (*cédulas, ordenes, decretos*) usually transmitted by an edict or order of the viceroy of New Spain; and orders from the governor of New Mexico and the commandant general of the Interior Provinces at Chihuahua.[25] The extant originals or duplicates (*cordilleras*), which were circulated among the missions and churches, are filed among the general, loose, mission documents described above.[26] The friars and secular clergy did not always copy the official communications in their copybooks, so the extant books and fragments were examined by Chávez and correlated with the originals in the general, loose, mission documents, and a chronological list containing cross references to the sources was prepared.[27] The books of *patentes* of the missions also contain other documents such as inventories of church property, censuses, transfers of missionaries, and licenses to build churches.

The mission and church records include registers of baptisms, marriages, and burials; books of official communications; inventory books; account books; books and lists of confirmation; and censuses. These registers constitute the only central body of information on births, marriages, and deaths, for, as in Texas and California during the Spanish and Mexican periods, no other vital statistics records were kept. The baptismal, marriage, and burial registers of the missions contain entries not only about Indians, but also about Spaniards living at nearby towns and ranches. The recordings in the baptismal records concerning Spaniards show the progress of settlement in the neighborhood of the missions. Burial registers show the effects of disease, epidemics, and Indian warfare. The registers contain notations regarding the deaths and successions of missionaries, and visitations by the custodian, the bishop of Durango, and the vicar forane. Many of the registers are still in bindings of leather, bisonhide, buckskin, or sheepskin, and all are boxed and labeled.

Confirmations were not administered locally, except by visiting bishops, until well into the Mexican period. In 1709, the custodian was

---

[25] Ibid., p. 149. The books of *patentes* for the individual missions are described on pp. 149–57.

[26] See the calendar in ibid., pp. 15–113.

[27] Ibid., pp. 157–86.

reminded by the provincial of the Holy Gospel Province that he was not authorized to administer confirmation.[28] Bishops on their visitations to New Mexico in 1730, 1737, 1760, 1833, and 1845 did administer confirmation. Fragments of books or lists of confirmations for Acoma (1737 and 1760); Alameda, Sandía, San Felipe, Nambé, Pojoaque, and Santa Cruz (1833); and Nambé, Truchas, Santo Domingo, and Cochití (1845); are in the Archives of the Archdiocese of Santa Fe.[29] In 1829, the Cathedral Chapter at Durango transmitted faculties for administering confirmation to Vicar Rascón, who did so at a number of places.[30]

Inventories were frequently made of church property, vestments, valuables, the sacristy, documents, and land, but for the most part, only fragments of inventory books have survived, and these are listed among the general, loose, mission documents in Chávez's calendar. Some inventories are entered in other record books, and notations regarding them are in the calendar. Inventories were sometimes recorded in the same books with accounts that were kept on the fabric (construction and maintenance of the church building), the sacristy, and the majordomos who received burial fees and made expenditures on behalf of the church. Other account books of church societies contain records of membership dues received and expenditures made.

Censuses are not numerous and are filed mostly as separate documents among the general, loose, mission documents.

In arranging the mission and church records in the Archives of the Archdiocese of Santa Fe, Chávez disregarded the fact that the records had originated at different establishments, and he arranged them by types of documents in the classifications described above. The present author has attempted to restore the original order (provenance) of the records by mission and church, insofar as is practicable, from the information supplied in Chávez's calendar. All types of records for individual church establishments have been brought together, including both book records and larger fragments from the general, loose, mission documents. Smaller fragments, scraps, and copies are not included, so Chávez's calendar must be consulted for a complete picture of the materials available on a particular mission. The calendar contains summaries of the loose documents and descriptions of the book records.

The collection of mission and church records in the Archives of the Archdiocese of Santa Fe is valuable not only for the ecclesiastical

---

[28] Ibid., p. 23.

[29] Ibid., pp. 104, 106, 111, 214, 220.

[30] Ibid., pp. 99, 100, 101, 102, 179–80, 214.

history of New Mexico but for the civil and military history of the province, including Indian affairs, local history, social and economic conditions, and genealogy. Following is a list of available records, arranged according to mission and church.

Abiquiú: Register of baptisms, May 7, 1754–Feb. 2, 1756; Feb. 20, 1756–May 2, 1761; May 28, 1761–Nov. 13, 1763; Aug. 3, 1762–Jan. 22, 1763; Sept. 13, 1765–Sept. 27, 1770; Feb. 23, 1772; May 29, 1772–Jan. 3, 1775; Jan. 22–Apr. 30, 1775; Mar. 14, 1775–Jan. 23, 1777; Feb. 5–12, 1777 (fragments); 1777–1811; Dec. 29, 1821–June 6, 1824; June 30, 1832–Mar. 23, 1833; Apr. 13, 1836–Aug. 26, 1842; June 29, 1845–Jan. 27, 1850 (fragments of books 10, 1a). Register of marriages, May 11, 1756–Feb. 4, 1770; Feb. 26–Apr. 20, 1772; Nov. 29, 1772–Oct. 16, 1774; Feb. 20–Mar. 27, 1775; July 27, 1775–Dec. 29, 1776 (fragments); 1777–1826 (bk. M–1). Book of official letters, 1822–41 (bk. LXXVI). Inventory book, 1777–1813 (bk. XLV).

Acoma: Register of baptisms, 1725–77 (bk. B–1). Register of marriages, 1726–70 (bk. M–2). Register of burials, 1726–77 (bk. Bur–1); Mar.–July 1810 (fragments). Register of confirmations, Sept. 26, 1737; June 30, 1760 (in register of marriages, 1726–70).

Albuquerque: Register of baptisms, 1706–36; 1743–1802; 1822–50 (bks. B–2–10); Apr.–July 26, 1736 (fragment). Register of marriages, 1726–1841; 1845–66 (bks. M–3, 4, 5, 6). Register of burials, 1726–1823; 1838–53 (bks. Bur–2, 3, 4, 6). Book of official letters, 1745–1810; 1818–51 (bks. V, XI). Account book of church fabric and majordomos and inventories, 1818–61 (bk. XXII). Accounts of church and majordomos, 1816–18 (fragment).

Belén: Register of baptisms, 1810–34; 1843–81 (bks. B–8, 10, 11, 12). Register of marriages, 1826–56 (bk. M–7). Index to register of baptisms and marriages; baptisms, 1793–1850; marriages, 1826–84. Register of burials, 1838–85 (bk. Bur–7). Register of baptisms, marriages, and burials, 1793–1826 (bk. B–54 with entries for Tomé). Book of official letters, 1819–51 (bk. XII).

Bernalillo: Register of baptisms, marriages, and burials, 1700–12 (bk. B–13).

Cochití: Register of baptisms, 1736–1829 (bks. 14, 15); Dec. 30, 1819–Jan. 1, 1820; Jan. 15, 1820–June 17, 1822; Feb. 20–Apr. 3, 1831 (fragments). Register of marriages, 1776–1827; 1846–73 (bks. M–8, 9). Register of burials, 1711 (fragment); 1776–1873 (bks. Bur–8, 8a, 9). Book of official letters, 1775–1817 (bk. LIX). Index to Spanish and Indian baptisms, 1845–73. Inventory book, 1753–1829 (bk. LXI).

Galisteo: Register of burials, 1711–29 (bk. B–11); July 18, Nov. 5, 1772 (fragment). Register of marriages, May 6, July 20, 1725; Feb. 12, Feb. 25, Oct. 14, 1726 (fragment); 1776–1828 (bk. M–10); May 6, July 20, 1725; Feb. 25, Oct. 14, 1726 (fragment); Feb. 12, 1727. Register of marriages and burials, 1727–74 (unbound). Register of burials, 1778–1829 (bk. Bur–9). Book of official letters, 1783–1815 (bound with register of burials, 1778–1829). Inventories, 1712; 1730; 1732 (fragment).

Isleta: Register of baptisms, 1720–76; 1829–42 (bks. B–57, 58). Register of marriages, 1726–1846 (bks. M–11, 49). Register of burials, 1726–76 (bk. Bur–10). Book of official letters, 1746–1818 (bk. IX); 1789-1823 (bk. LXXIX).

Jémez: Register of baptisms, 1701–1829 (bks. B–16, 17); Jan.–Dec. 1778; Jan. 1779; Apr. 15–May 18, 1821; Sept. 19–28, 1821 (fragment). Register of marriages, 1720–76 (bk. M–12). Register of burials, Jan. 17–Nov. 10, 1769 (fragment). Register of baptisms, marriages, and burials, 1701–26 (bk. B–16).

Laguna: Register of baptisms, 1720–76 (bk. 17a). Register of marriages, 1700–77 (bk. M–12). Register of burials, Jan. 15, 1715–Feb. 4, 1718; Feb. 23–Oct. 4, 1718; Dec. 28, 1718–Mar. 9, 1719 (fragments); 1726–76 (bk. Bur–13). Inventory book, 1736–77 (bk. LXXXIV).

Mansos: Register of marriages, Apr. 22–Oct. 16, 1691 (fragment).

Nambé: Register of baptisms, 1707–27; 1771–1837 (bk. B–18a, 21, includes some entries for Pojoaque and Tesuque; other Nambé entries, Apr. 27, 1784–Apr. 1789 are in Pojoaque register). Register of marriages, 1707–28; 1772–1862 (bks. M–16, 17). Register of burials, 1707–1869 (bks. Bur–15, 16, 17).

Pecos: Register of baptisms, 1726–63; 1776–1829 (bks. B–19, 20). Register of marriages, 1699–1765 (bks. M–18, 19, 20). Register of burials, 1726–72 (bk. Bur–18). Book of official letters, 1716–49 (bk. II).

Picurís: Register of baptisms, 1750–71; 1776–1830; 1835–52 (bks. B–21, 22, 50, 51; entries for Feb. 26, 1787–July 31, 1788 in San Juan register; 1750–71 (bk. B–21, mostly baptisms for nearby settlements of Embudo, Santa Barbara, and Trampas); Dec. 15–21, 1779 (fragment). Register of marriages, 1726–1837 (bks. M–21, 26). Register of burials, Mar. 10, 1712–Apr. 8, 1715; Apr. 16, Aug. 25, 1716; July 26, 1717–Jan. 29, 1718; Aug. 11, 1717; May 26, 1719; Mar. 5–Oct. 18, 1720; Apr. 20, 1721; July 20, 1721–Feb. 3, 1722; May 16, 1722; Mar., Apr., Dec. 19, 1843–Jan. 20, 1844 (fragments); 1727–1858 (bks. Bur–19, 20, 21). Inventory book, 1743–67 (fragment).

Pojoaque: Register of baptisms, 1779–1839 (bk. B–23). Register of marriages, 1744–1853 (bk. M–22). Register of burials, 1779–1852 (bk. Bur–22). Earlier marriages and burials are in Nambé registers.

Sandía: Register of baptisms, 1771–1846 (bks. B–60, 61). Register of marriages, 1722–1864 (bk. M–47, 48). Register of burials, 1771–1858 (bks. Bur–46, 47).

San Felipe: Register of baptisms, 1769–1829 (bk. B–22a, mostly Spanish entries from Bernalillo, Corrales, and nearby ranches, and, after 1804, also from Las Huertas and Angostura); May–Sept. 1782;

Aug. 1798–Jan. 1799 (fragment). Register of marriages, 1726–1814 (bk. M–23). Register of burials, Nov. 20, 1696–Feb. 2, 1697; Mar. 24, 1699; Jan. 21, 1700–July 20, 1703; Dec. 7, 1703–Feb. 27, 1704; Mar. 20, 1705; Sept. 26, 1707–Mar. 25, 1708 (fragments); 1726–32; July 15(?)–Oct. 8, 1796; 1841–70 (bks. Bur–25, 26). Book of official letters, Jan. 15, 1746–Sept. 23, 1747 (fragment); 1755–1823 (bk. VI). Inventory book, 1712–46; 1753; 1854 (fragments).

San Ildefonso: Register of baptisms, 1725–1834 (bks. B–24, 25). Register of marriages, 1700–1853 (bks. M–24, 25). Register of burials, 1840–55 (bk. Bur–24). Book of official letters, Apr. 30, 1824–Oct. 17, 1852 (fragment); 1817–34 (bk. LXXII).

San Juan: Register of baptisms, 1726–1837 (bks. B–27, 28, 29, 30, 42). Register of marriages, 1726–76; 1830–55 (bks. M–27, 28, 29). Register of burials, 1726–1826; 1836–57 (bks. Bur–27, 28, 36). Book of official letters, Aug. 1, 1779–Dec. 31, 1816; 1817–34 (fragments). Inventory of books and papers, 1818–46 (bk. XXXI), includes an inventory of church and sacristy, 1818.

San Miguel del Vado: Register of baptisms, 1829–47 (bks. B–1, 2, 3, 3a). Register of marriages, 1829–46 (bk. M–1). Register of burials, 1829–47 (bk. Bur–1). Account book, 1842–55 (bk. XXIX). Prenuptial investigations, 1829–34 (1 vol.). Inventory, Feb. 28, 1828 (fragment).

Santa Ana: Register of baptisms, 1771–1844 (bk. B–26). Register of marriages, 1694–1711, 1722–1828 (bks. M–28a, 35). Register of burials, 1739–52; 1765–71 (bks. Bur–27, 29a). Book of official letters, 1746–60 (bk. LX). Inventory book, 1712–53 (bk. LXXVIII).

Santa Clara: Register of baptisms, 1728–1805; 1841–45 (bks. B–31, 32); Feb. 5, 1845–June 1, 1845 (fragment). Register of marriages, 1726–1830 (bk. M–33); Feb.–Oct. 28, 1844; Mar. 6–Apr. 25, 1846 (fragment). Register of burials, July 24, 1712–Oct. 26, 1713; Sept. 20, 1714–July 3, 1719; Feb. 8, 1723; Feb. 14–Apr. 8, 1724; Jan. 31, 1800–Mar. 18, 1801; May 15–Nov. 18, 1801 (fragments); 1726–1843 (bk. Bur.–30). Book of official letters, 1815–32 (bk. LXXV). Inventory book, 1712–42 (fragment). Census book, 1818 (bk. XXXIII).

Santa Cruz de la Cañada: Register of baptisms, 1710–21 (fragment); 1731–67; 1769–1850 (bks. B–34, 35, 36, 37, 38, 39, 40); Aug. 5, 1758–Nov. 19, 1759; Mar., 1764; Mar. 23–May 30, 1764; Sept. 22, 1767–Jan. 30, 1768; Oct. 2, 1780–Jan. 21, 1781; Jan. 28–Feb. 19, 1844 (fragments). Register of marriages, 1726–1869 (bks. M–29, 30, 31, 32, 33a); Jan. 15, 1763; Feb. 14–Oct. 10, 1777 (fragment). Register of burials, 1726–89; 1795–1859 (bks. Bur–32, 33, 34, 35); Jan. 20–Feb. 26, 1794 (fragment). Book of official letters, 1721–95; 1803–33; 1834–53 (bks. III, XIX, LXXIII). Inventory of church, sacristy, and Carmel chapel, 1782–95 (bk. XLVI). Account book of fabric and majordomos, 1768; 1831 (bk. XXV), also contains burial entries Mar. 22, 1802–July 3, 1803; 1808–11). Account and inventory book of Carmel Confraternity, 1760–1860; 1761–1818 (bks. XXIV, XXIX). Account book and minutes of Sacrament Confraternity, 1803–60 (bk. XL). Fifteen baptismal entries, 1827; 1829; 1830, are in the Pojoaque burial register (bk. Bur–21).

Santa Fe: Register of baptisms, 1747–91; 1796–1848; 1848–51 (bks. B–62, 63, 64, 65, 67, 68, 69, 69a, 70, 71, 72). Register of marriages, 1728–1843; 1846–57 (bks. M–50, 52–55). Register of burials, 1726–1834; 1845–52 (bks. Bur–48, 49, 50, 52, 53). Book of official letters, 1697–1725 (bk. I); Nov. 8, 1769–Apr. 13, 1807 (1 bk.); 1816–33 (bk. LXIX). Parish account book, 1716–28 (1 bk.). Account book of the church fabric, 1813–50 (bk. LXXXI). Accounts of the Confraternity of La Conquistadora, 1716; 1720–23, 1727–28 (fragments); 1782–1852 (bk. LXXX). Account book of the Blessed Sacrament Confraternity, 1782–1852 (bk. LXXIX). Inventory books, 1730; 1734; 1735 (fragments). Books of the Confraternity of La Conquistadora, Feb. 1685–1718 (fragment).

Santa Fe Castrense: Register of baptisms, 1798–1833 (bk. B–66). Register of marriages of soldiers, 1779–1833 (bk. M–51). Register of burials, 1779–1833 (Bur–51).

Santo Domingo: Register of baptisms, 1771–73; 1829–46 (bks. B–44, 43c, 43a). Register of marriages, 1771–77; 1846–62 (bks. M–34a, 36); 1778–1845, marriages in Santa Ana register of marriages (bk. M–35). Register of burials, 1771–1846 (bk. Bur–37). Baptisms for 1777–1827 in Santa Ana register of marriages (bk. M–35). Register of baptisms, 1829–46, includes some confirmations and prenuptial investigations.

Socorro: Register of baptisms, 1821–50 (bks. B–74, 75, 76). Register of marriages, 1821–53 (bks. M–57, 58). Register of burials, 1821–63 (bks. Bur–55, 56). Book of official letters, 1831–50 (bk. XXVII).

Taos: Register of baptisms, 1701–27; 1777–1847 (bks. B–38, 45, 46, 47, 48, 48a, 49, 50, 52). Register of marriages, 1777–1822; 1827–56 (bks. M–37, 39, 40, 41); June 13–July 27, 1826; Aug. 27–Dec. 28, 1826 (fragment). Register of burials, 1827–50 (bks. Bur–39, 40, 41). Book of official letters, 1826–50 (bk. XV). Book of circulars, 1833–72 (bk. XXVIII). Account book of fabric, 1840–54 (bk. XX). Book of confirmations, 1830–50 (bk. XLI).

Tesuque: Register of baptisms, 1694–1724 (bk. B–53), includes some marriages and burials, Nov. 1694.

Tomé: Register of baptisms, 1793–1826; 1809–47 (bks. B–54, 71, 72; bk. 54 a mixed register of baptisms, marriages and burials, 1793–1826, of Belén and Tomé). Register of marriages, 1776–1846 (bk. M–56). Register of burials, 1809–55 (bk. M–54). Book of circulars, 1821–51 (bk. XCII).

Truchas: List of confirmations, July 20, 1845 (fragment).

Zía: Register of baptisms, 1694–1772 (bk. B–55). Register of burials, Mar. 9–May 2, 1709 (fragment); 1727–72 (bk. Bur–44). Register of marriages, 1697–1717 (bk. M–44).

Zuñi: Register of baptisms, Oct. 22, 1699–Apr. 2, 1700 (fragment); 1725–74 (bk. B–56). Register of marriages, 1705–76 (bk. M–45). Register of burials, 1706–19 (bk. Bur–45).

Other significant records relating to the activities of the vicars of New Mexico, the secular clergy, and missions are in the Archives of the Archdiocese of Santa Fe. A record of a visitation to New Mexico by Vicar Juan Bautista Guevara for the bishop of Durango, 1817–18 (book IX), includes reports and letters of the vicar to the bishop on his journey, visitation, and the condition of ecclesiastical establishments; letters to the governor of New Mexico and the commandant general; letters, orders and instructions to the clergy; and a list of matrimonial dispensations. A record of acts of the Guevara visitation to New Mexico, 1817–20 (book LXII), contains writs and circulars on the visitation; inventories of the churches and chapels at Santa Fe; a report on the parochial archives there; reports on visitations to Santa Cruz, San Juan, Picurís, Taos, Abiquiú, Santa Clara, San Ildefonso, and Tesuque; and Guevara's report to the bishop on the condition of New Mexico. A brief log of official acts of Juan Rafael Rascón, 1817–18 (book 74), contains official letters of appointment, faculties granted to clergy, and licenses for extra masses and the building and transfer of oratories. A record of the official acts of Vicar Augustín Fernández San Vicente's visitation to New Mexico, made for the bishop of Durango in 1826 (books LXIV, LXV, LXXIV, LXXVIII), contains announcements and circulars on the visitation; reports on visitations to Santa Cruz, San Juan, Picurís, Taos, Abiquiú, Santa Clara, San Ildefonso, and Santa Fe; and inventories of the churches, sacristies, fabrics, chapels, archives, and confraternities. A record of the official acts of the Fernández San Vicente visitation, 1826 ("Book for Cataloguing the Official Acts of Ecclesiastic Governor of New Mexico," book LXVI), contains a record of actions taken regarding various missions, parishes, chapels, faculties granted to clergymen, licenses for chapels, secularization of missions, matrimonial investigations, and other matters concerning lay congregations. Another record book of the Fernández San Vicente visitation, April–September 1826 ("Libro de oficios," book LXVII), contains a record of changes in pastorships, secularizations, marriage investigations, a general epidemic in July, and a controversy between the vicar and the governor about the legality of holding meetings of the clergy.

The first book of administration of Fernández San Vicente, May 1826 (book LXIII), contains copies of clergy faculties, licenses for building chapels, and renewals of chapel licenses. A record of the official acts of Vicar Juan Rafael Rascón, 1829–33 ("First Book of Government," book LXX), contains notifications of his appointment, circulars on the visitation, correspondence with pastors, faculties granted to pastors, licenses for building chapels and cemeteries, and copies of the bishop's edicts. A record of the official acts of the Rascón visitation of New Mexico, 1829–33 (book LXVIII), contains reports on visitations to Santa Fe and other missions, churches, and chapels. A record of the official acts of Vicar Juan Felipe Ortiz, 1832–46, 1837–45 (books LXXVI, LXXIII), contains information regarding resignations of pastors, appointments of pastors to succeed missionaries, difficulties between parishioners and parish priests, and marriage dispensations. Other record books include one containing bishop and vicar forane circulars, 1834–51 (book LXXI), and records of the official acts of the vicar of Santa Fe, 1832–51 (books LXXIII, LXXVI, C–1), with data relative to pastors, churches, graveyards, matrimonial investigations and dispensations, and other matters.[31]

The Archdiocese of Santa Fe can permit only limited use by accredited scholars of the mission records in its custody. To facilitate wider use, the State Records Center was allowed to microfilm the mission records, and copies are in the Henry E. Huntington Library in San Marino, California, the Genealogical Society of the Church of Jesus Christ of Latter-Day Saints in Salt Lake City, and the Archdiocesan Archives. Chávez's calendar serves as a guide to the microfilm.

Initially, the Franciscans in New Spain were supervised by a superior referred to as the *custos* (guardian), but in 1523, the Province of the Holy Gospel was established under a father provincial who directed the expanding missionary activities of the order.[32] The headquarters of the father provincial was in the monastery and church of San Francisco el Grande in Mexico City. The further expansion of Franciscan activities resulted later in the designation of a Commissary General of the order in Mexico City.

Mexican reform laws of 1856–61 and later years resulted in the confiscation of the property of religious orders and the dispersion of their records.[33] Monastic archives of monasteries and colleges, known as the Fondo Franciscano, that were obtained by the government, are in the library of the Museo Nacional and include documents relating to the Province of the Holy Gospel and the Franciscan Commissary General.[34] In 1919, the Biblioteca Nacional in Mexico City purchased the records of the Province of the Holy Gospel, which had been housed

---

[31] Ibid., pp. 150–51, 152, 153, 156, 157, 190–96.

[32] Marion A. Habig, O.F.M., "The Franciscan Provinces of Spanish North America," *The Americas* 1 (Oct. 1944):217.

[33] Carrera Stampa, *Archivalia mexicana*, p. 28.

[34] Ibid., p. 51; Bolton, *Guide Arch. Mex.*, pp. 205–09.

originally in the convent of San Francisco el Grande in Mexico City, from a private collector.[35] Now known as the Archivo Franciscano, this collection contains extensive materials on Franciscan missions on the northern frontier of Mexico, including the Interior Provinces, 1689–1804; Coahuila, 1673–1784; Texas, 1722–79; Nueva Vizcaya, 1564–1834; and New Mexico, 1527–1829.[36] Forty-one of the 159 boxes in the Franciscan Archives relate to the Interior Provinces.[37]

In the winter of 1927–28 France V. Scholes, of the University of New Mexico, examined the principal collection (Archivo Franciscano) of records of the Holy Gospel Province in the Biblicoteca Nacional in Mexico City, sorted out the items relating to New Mexico, arranged them in chronological order (1605–1818), and prepared a catalog which he published.[38] The 100 bundles in the collection included letters, reports, diaries, memorials, petitions, and relations of the missionaries; instructions of the custodian of New Mexico; governmental issuances, inventories, and decisions of the royal audiencia; letters of the governor; appointments; certifications; documents relating to the finance and supply service of the missions; investigations; a general muster of the citizens of New Mexico (1705); a census of New Mexico missions (1750); and census rolls of New Mexico (1779). Photoreproductions of the documents are in the Library of Congress, the University of New Mexico Library, and the Bancroft Library of the University of California. The same archives have been drawn on by Carlos E. Castañeda, whose collection of reproductions in the University of Texas Archives includes materials on New Mexico.

Records containing biographical information on postulants who entered the novitiate house of La Puebla de los Angeles, one of three such houses in the Province of the Holy Gospel, are in the John Carter Brown Library, Providence, Rhode Island. These records ("Informaciones noviciorum"), 1594–1829 (14 volumes), are important for the history of the church in Mexico and for the missions of New Mexico. The records were acquired in 1896 by John N. Brown, donor of the library to Brown University, from Dr. Nicolás León of Guadalupe Hidalgo, Mexico.[39]

---

35 Lino Gómez Canedo, O.F.M., "Some Franciscan Sources in the Archives and Libraries of America," The Americas 13 (Oct. 1956) :144.

36 Carrera Stampa, Archivalia mexicana, pp. 110–11. Ignacio del Río, a doctoral candidate at the Universidad Nacional de México, has published the first of three volumes of a comprehensive catalog of the Archivo Franciscano: Guía del Archivo Franciscano de la Biblioteca Nacional de México. Vol. 1, Guías, no. 3 (Mexico, 1975).

37 Greenleaf and Meyer, Research in Mexican History, p. 88.

38 France V. Scholes, "Manuscripts for the History of New Mexico in the National Library in Mexico City," N. Mex. Hist. Rev. 3 (July 1928) :301–23.

39 Damian Van den Eynde, O.F.M., "The Franciscan Manuscripts in the John

Some Querétaran missionaries went to New Mexico in 1693 to assist in restoring the missions there. The records of the College of Santa Cruz of Querétaro, from which these missionaries were dispatched, are described in chapter eighteen, in the section on Texas.

At first, New Mexico was part of the Diocese of Guadalajara, but when that diocese was divided in 1620, it became, along with Nueva Vizcaya (modern Durango, Chihuahua, Sinaloa, Sonora, and part of Coahuila), the Diocese of Durango.[40] The bishop of Durango claimed jurisdiction over New Mexico and made a number of visitations there, but his authority was disputed by the Franciscan Custody of St. Paul.[41] In 1730, the bishop appointed Santiago Roybal, a secular priest, as vicar ecclesiastic and judge at Santa Fe, but Roybal had no parish and exercised limited functions, as the Franciscans long remained the dominant religious force in the province.[42] Many directives and communications passed between Durango and New Mexico, which continued under the bishop of Durango until the arrival of a bishop responsible to the American hierarchy in 1851. In the archives of the Archdiocese of Durango, in the cathedral at Durango, there is an extensive collection of records that is important for the administration of church revenues.[43]

Important materials relating to the history of the Franciscan missions of New Mexico are in the Archivo General de la Nación in Mexico City. The Historia section (volumes 25–26) contains correspondence and reports of missionaries, diaries of expeditions by friars, reports from the provincial of the Province of the Holy Gospel to the viceroy, memorials to the viceroy, and other documents from the seventeenth and much of the eighteenth century.[44] Other documents of the missionaries, the provincial, and the custodian of New Mexico are in the sections on Misiones (27 volumes)[45] and in various volumes of the Provincias Internas[46] and Inquisición.[47] The records of the Inquisition,

---

Carter Brown Library, Providence, R. I., U.S.A.," *Archivum Franciscan Historicum*, annus 31 (fasc. I–II, Jan.–Apr. 1928):220–21.

[40] Bolton, *Guide to Arch. Mex.*, p. 406; *New Catholic Encyclopedia*, prep. by the editorial staff of the Catholic University, 15 vols. (New York, 1967), 4:1116–17.

[41] Kelly, *Franciscan Missions*, p. 69; Bancroft, *Hist. Ariz. & N. Mex.*, p. 240.

[42] Angelico Chávez, O.F.M., "El Vicario Don Santiago Roybal," *El Palacio* 55 (Aug. 1948):241–43.

[43] Bolton, *Guide to Arch. Mex.*, pp. 408–09.

[44] Ibid., pp. 27–28.

[45] Ibid., pp. 67–75.

[46] Ibid., p. 93 ff.

[47] France V. Scholes, "The First Decade of the Inquisition in New Mexico," *N. Hist. Rev.* 10 (July 1935):196, 197, 215, 217.

reflecting the investigation of officials and other persons in New Mexico, constitute the largest group of records relating to the history of New Mexico between 1610 and 1680, and, with other materials in the Mexican archives, help to fill the gap caused by the loss of records of New Mexico in the Pueblo revolt of 1680.[48] The records of the secretariat of the Hacienda contain accounts relating to New Mexico missions.[49] In 1927–28, France V. Scholes investigated the materials in the Mexican archives and obtained reproductions that are now in the Library of Congress, the Ayer Collection of the Newberry Library in Chicago, and the University of New Mexico Library.

Other repositories have documents relating to New Mexico missions. In the papers from monastic archives (Fondo Franciscano) in the Library of the Museo Nacional in Mexico City, there are letters from the Franciscan commissary general to the custodian of New Mexico; letters from the friars in New Mexico to the Province of the Holy Gospel; and correspondence and other documents relating to the missionaries.[50] Documents of scattered dates in the Santa Barbara Mission Archives include a report on Mission San Antonio de Senecú, 1779–80; a census of Mission Laguna, June 12, 1801; the custodian's circular letter of June 22, 1803; a general report on the missions of New Mexico, 1811; various other documents; and transcripts and translations.[51] In the Thomas Gilcrease Institute in Tulsa, Oklahoma, there are a letter of Domingo de Mendoza y Aguado to the father commissary, 1743, and three reports and letters of Ysidro Murillo, 1775–76, regarding the mission to the Moqui.[52] Frank H. Cushing, an ethnologist from the Bureau of American Ethnology, lived among the Zuñi Indians for five years and wrote books about them. At that time he apparently acquired the records of the mission which the Franciscans had conducted at the Zuñi pueblo. These books passed into the possession of his wife. Frederick W. Hodge, director of the Bureau of American Ethnology, obtained the books from Mrs. Cushing in November, 1902, and sent them to the Library of Congress, which apparently paid $250 for them.[53] The collection includes three registers of baptisms, marriages, and deaths, 1776–ca. 1850. At the end of the

---

[48] Bolton, *Guide to Arch. Mex.*, pp. 370–71.

[49] France V. Scholes, *Troublous Times in New Mexico, 1659–1670* (Albuquerque, 1942), pp. 1–2, 165–68.

[50] Bolton, *Guide to Arch. Mex.*, pp. 205–07, 209.

[51] Maynard J. Geiger, O.F.M., *Calendar of Documents in the Santa Barbara Mission Archives* (Washington, 1947), p. 262.

[52] Clevy L. Strout, *A Catalog of Hispanic Documents in the Thomas Gilcrease Institute* (Tulsa, 1962), pp. 33, 99.

[53] F. W. Hodge to W. C. Ford, Nov. 6, 15, 1902, Library of Congress, Manuscript Division, Correspondence File; W. C. Ford to the Order Division, Jan. 7, 1903, Lib. Cong., Ms. Div., Letters Sent Book, No. 3, p. 253.

first volume, there are copies of circular letters received from ecclesiastical superiors.

Other materials relating to the Franciscans in the Southwest were accumulated in the headquarters of the Roman Catholic church in Rome. The department of the Roman Catholic curia concerned with missions was the Congregation for the Propagation of the Faith (Propaganda Fide), established in 1622 to administer missionary activities of the Church throughout the world.[54] The missionary colleges founded by the Franciscans in Mexico had constitutions written by the Propaganda Fide and apostolic faculties derived from it, and these colleges eventually controlled the missionary activities in Texas, New Mexico, and California. The Archives of the Propaganda Fide, in the Palace of the Propaganda Fide on the Piazza di Spagna in Rome, contain reports and letters from missionaries, copies of decrees and instructions issued by the Propaganda Fide, and other Latin American materials that are very extensive.[55] Carl R. Fish, professor of American history at the University of Wisconsin, investigated these archives in 1908–09 and later published a guide in the Carnegie Institution of Washington series.[56]

Reproductions of documents in the Propaganda Fide archives are in a number of repositories in the United States. After the appearance of Fish's guide, Peter Guilday, of the Catholic University of America, obtained photostats of Benavides's revised memorial of 1634 and copies of related documents, and after the publication of these documents by F. W. Hodge, Guilday gave the copies to the Manuscript Division of the Library of Congress.[57] In 1938, Lansing B. Bloom microfilmed materials in the Propaganda Fide Archives in Rome.[58] The University of New Mexico Library and the State Records Center have photoprints (4 volumes) of selected documents from the Propaganda Fide Archives.[59] Extensive collections of microreproductions from these archives are in the St. Louis University Library[60] and the University

---

[54] *New Catholic Encyclopedia*, 11:840–42; Francis J. Weber, "Roman Archives of Propaganda Fide," Am. Cath. Hist. Soc., *Records* 76 (Dec. 1965):247–48.

[55] Ernest J. Burrus, S.J., "Research Opportunities in Italian Archives and Manuscript Collections for Students of Hispanic American History," *Hisp. Am. Hist. Rev.* 39 (Aug. 1959):436.

[56] Carl L. Fish, *Guide to the Materials for American History in Roman and Other Italian Archives* (Washington, 1911), pp. 119–95. See also Finbar Kenneally, O.F.M., *United States Documents in the Propaganda Fide Archives: A Calendar* (Washington, 1966).

[57] *Lib. Cong. Quar. Jour.* 3 (May 1946):46.

[58] [Letter of Lansing B. Bloom], *N. Mex. Hist. Rev.* 13 (July 1938):334–36.

[59] Díaz, *Mss. and Records in the Univ. of N. Mex. Lib.*, item 73.

[60] Lowrie J. Daly, "Microfilmed Materials from the Archives of the Sacred Congregation 'De Propaganda Fide'," *Manuscripta* 10 (Nov. 1966):139.

of Notre Dame Archives,[61] which also has reproductions of the documents listed in Kenneally's calendar.

Other materials relating to Franciscan missions in New Mexico are in other repositories in Europe. Documents in the Central Archives of the Franciscans in Rome include Gerónimo de Zárate Salmerón's relation on the years 1538–1626; Silvestre Vélez de Escalante's letter to Juan A. de Morfi, April 2, 1798; documents on the recovery of New Mexico by Diego de Vargas; and a 1686 opinion of Father Posada.[62] Other documents are in government repositories in Madrid,[63] and in the Archivo de Indias at Seville.[64]

The central archives of the Franciscans are housed in the headquarters of the general of the order in Rome (Via di S. Maria Mediatrice, 25). When the Tibertine Republic was set up in Rome by Napoleon in 1798, French soldiers occupied the Franciscan convent, and destroyed most of the records.[65] Documents relating to Texas and other parts of the American Southwest are in the central archives (Archivum Generale, O.F.M.) in Rome.[66] An important official for the management of Franciscan establishments in New Spain was the Franciscan commissary general of the Indies, who was stationed in Seville. Some of this official's records have also been lost; a description is available of surviving records.[67]

The Spanish crown controlled the Catholic church in America, except for the doctrine and discipline of clergymen serving there. A papal bull of 1501 gave the crown control of ecclesiastical tithes, and the crown assumed responsibility for introducing and maintaining the church, and instructing and converting the Indians. The exclusive right of patronage bestowed on the crown by a papal bull of 1508 gave it control over the founding and construction of ecclesiastical establishments and the nominating of ecclesiastical officials. The body of rights and privileges that evolved from these concessions by the pope became known as the Patronato Real and made the church a branch of the

---

[61] Natl. Union Catalog Ms. Colls., 1967, entry 889.

[62] Pedro Borges, O.F.M., "Documentación americana en el Archivo General O.F.M. de Rome," Archivo ibero-americano 19 (enero–junio 1959):17–18.

[63] Fidel de Lejarza, "Los Archivos españoles y la misionología," Missionalia Hispanica, año 4, num. 12 (1947):540, 555, 556, 565, 566.

[64] Chapman, Catalogue of Materials in the Archivo General de Indias, passim.

[65] Basile Pañdzic, "Les Archives Générales de l'Ordre des Frères Mineurs," Archivum 4 (1954):163; Ernest J. Burrus, S.J., "Research Opportunities in Italian Archives and Manuscript Collections for Students of Hispanic American History," Hisp. Amer. Hist. Rev. 39 (Aug. 1959):442.

[66] Borges, "Documentación americana," pp. 34, 40, 92, 105–06.

[67] Pedro Borges, O.F.M., "Notas sobre el desaparecido archivo matritense de la Comisaria General de Indias," Archivo ibero-americano 26 (Abr.–Sept. 1966): 113–64.

royal government. Thus, besides being proselytizing institutions, the missions were governmental agencies used to open and expand the northern frontier of New Spain for further colonization.[68] The exercise of the Patronato Real resulted in the accumulation, in archives in Spain, of important materials relating to Spanish missions in the Southwest. These documents are in the Archivo de Simancas, the Biblioteca Nacional, the Archivo Histórico Nacional, the Museo Naval, the Real Academia de la História, the Biblioteca de Palacio, the Archivo General de Indias, and other repositories.[69]

The Academy of American Franciscan History has transcripts of documents on the Franciscans (6 volumes) selected from various record groups in the Archivo General de Indias by Fr. Lázaro Lamadrid in 1955–56, and four volumes of other reproductions from the same repository.

Missionaries who served in New Mexico wrote extensively on mission activities in that province. They were the authors of letters, reports, journals and narratives of travels, relations, petitions, and memorials, that are in the archives of Spain and Mexico, and other repositories. Some of these documents, like the memorial of Alonso de Benavides and the narrative of Esteván de Perea, early superiors of the custody of New Mexico, were published contemporaneously in Madrid and Mexico; others are available only in manuscript.[70] Some Franciscan writings were published in the *Documentos para la Historia de México*, and have since been largely translated into English. Otto Maas, O.F.M., a professor at a German institution, collected eighteenth century travel writings of Franciscans from the Archivo General de Indias in Seville and edited them for publication.[71] Most of the materials in this volume had been printed before or were available in manuscript form in repositories in the United States. Maas later assembled other Franciscan documents from the same repository, on New Mexico missions in the seventeenth century, and published them, but omitted part of the texts of many documents.[72]

Other Franciscan writings, published in the United States, have

---

[68] Haring, *Spanish Empire in America*, pp. 180–82, 185, 292; Herbert E. Bolton, "The Mission as a Frontier Institution in the Spanish American Colonies," *Amer. Hist. Rev.* 23 (Oct. 1917):50; Simmons, *Spanish Govt. in N. Mex.*, pp. 20–21, 68–71.

[69] Fidel de Lejarza, "Los Archivos españoles y la misionología," *Misionalia hispanica*, año 4, num. 12 (1947):pp. 525–85.

[70] John M. Lenhart, "Franciscan Historians of North America," in *Franciscan History of North America (The Franciscan Educational Conference, Report of the Eighteenth Annual Meeting, August 2–4, 1936)* (Washington, 1937), pp. 8–14.

[71] Otto Maas, O.F.M., ed., *Viajes de misioneros franciscanos a la conquista del Nuevo México: Documentos del Archivo General de Indias (Sevilla)* (Sevilla, 1915).

[72] Otto Maas, O.F.M., ed. *Misiones de Nuevo México: Documentos del Archivo General de Indias (Sevilla)* (Madrid, 1929).

made significant contributions to the history of New Mexico. An account of Gerónimo de Zárate Salmerón, missionary at Jémez from 1621 to 1626, covers the years 1538–1626, but is most important for the years of his service in New Mexico, as it is the chief source of information.[73] This was the first printing in English in book form, but it had been translated and published earlier by Charles F. Lummis in the *Land of Sunshine* in 1899–1900. Zárate Salmerón obtained data from others who had served in New Mexico and from documents that were subsequently lost. Alonso de Benavides, custodian of New Mexico from 1626 to 1629, on his return to Spain in 1630, addressed a memorial to Philip IV, in which he reported on the development of missions in New Mexico.[74] It describes conditions in early seventeenth century New Mexico and Arizona and, like Zárate Salmerón's report, is valuable for the history of the Indians as well as that of the missions. A new translation from the Library of Congress copy of Benavides's memorial of 1630, designed to be more readable and to provide a version that would be more readily available in libraries, has been published.[75] A revised memorial of 1634 by Benavides, incorporating new information received from missionaries in New Mexico, was submitted to the pope and was also published, from the copy obtained by Peter Guilday, with other related documents obtained by him from the Propaganda Fide archives and the Archivo General de Indias in Seville, and the Archivo General de la Nación and the Biblioteca Nacional in Mexico.[76] Another contribution from the same period is the account of Esteván de Perea, which was written about 1629 after his many years of service at Sandía.[77]

Accounts of travels by Franciscans and reports of visitations by churchmen to New Mexico have attracted other translators and editors. Fr. Francisco de Escobar's account of Gov. Juan de Oñate's expedition

---

[73] Alicia R. Milich, trans., *Relaciones: An Account of Things Seen and Learned by Father Géronimo de Zarate Salmerón from the Year 1538 to the Year 1626* (Albuquerque, 1966). Copies of the relations are in the Bancroft Library of the University of California (Hammond, *Guide to Ms. Colls.*, pp. 127, 262).

[74] Frederick W. Hodge and Charles F. Lummis, eds., and Mrs. Edward E. Ayer, trans., *The Memorial of Fray Alonso de Benavides* (Chicago, 1916). Reprinted, Albuquerque, 1965.

[75] Peter P. Forrestal, trans., and Cyprian J. Lynch, ed., *Benavides' Memorial of 1630* (Washington, 1954).

[76] Frederick W. Hodge, George P. Hammond, and Agapito Rey, eds. and trans., *Fray Alonso de Benavides's Revised Memorial of 1634, with Numerous Supplementary Documents Elaborately Annotated* (Albuquerque, 1945). Remarks comparing the two Benavides memorials are in John F. O'Hara, C.S.C., "The Benavides Memorial," *Cath. Hist. Rev.* 3 (Apr. 1917):76–78.

[77] Lansing B. Bloom, ed. and trans., "Fray Estevan de Perea's Relación," *N. Mex. Hist. Rev.* 8 (July 1933):211–35. This is a revision of the version published by C. F. Lummis in the *Land of Sunshine* 15 (1901) from a facsimile reproduction of the original edition loaned by F. W. Hodge.

from the Río Grande to the Gulf of California, 1604–05, published from a copy of the original in the Archivo General de Indias, provides a primary source on that journey.[78] Fr. Alonso de Posada, who had served as a missionary in New Spain from 1650 to 1665, prepared a report on the country beyond New Mexico, where Sieur de La Salle had been active on the part of the French, in 1686–87, at the request of the crown.[79] In letters of September 8 and 25, 1730, to the viceroy, Bishop Benito Crespo described his activities on his visitation to New Mexico, during which he got as far as Taos.[80] More extensive is the report on Bishop Pedro Tamarón's visitation to New Mexico in 1760, containing considerable information on the condition of the church there, which has been translated from his larger account, published in Mexico in 1937 by Vito Alessio Robles from the manuscript in the Biblioteca Nacional.[81] An even lengthier report on the New Mexico missions, 1776, by Fr. Francisco A. Domínguez, father visitor of the Custody of St. Paul of New Mexico, found by France V. Scholes in the same repository, contains much detailed information on the missions and is accompanied by letters and other papers of Domínguez, 1775–95, and Silvestre Vélez de Escalante, 1775–76.[82] Fr. Juan Agustín Morfi, whose diary and history are mentioned in chapter fourteen, in the section on Texas, also prepared a geographical description of New Mexico that has been published from the manuscript in the Archivo General de la Nación, Mexico City.[83] Benavides's memorial of 1630, Zárate Salmerón's report on the years 1538–1626, Escalante's letter of April 2, 1778, and other documents, are in a volume of the Colleción Chimalistac.[84]

Vélez de Escalante was assigned to the pueblo of Zuñi in 1774

---

[78] Herbert E. Bolton, ed. and trans., "Father Escobar's Relation of the Oñate Expedition to California, 1605," *Cath. Hist. Rev.* 5 (Apr. 1919):19–41.

[79] H. Darrel Taylor, ed., and S. Lyman Tyler, trans., "The Report of Fray Alonso de Posada in Relation to Quivira and Teguayo," *N. Mex. Hist. Rev.* 33 (Oct. 1958): 285–314.

[80] Frank D. Reeve, ed. and trans., "Documents Concerning Bishop Crespo's Visitation, 1730," *N. Mex. Hist. Rev.* 28 (July 1953):222–33. Translated from the manuscript in the Archivo General de la Nación, Mexico City.

[81] Eleanor B. Adams, ed. and trans., *Bishop Tamarón's Visitation of New Mexico, 1760* (Albuquerque, 1954); Vito Alessio Robles, ed., *Demonstración del vastísimo Obispado de la Nueva Vizcaya–1765: Durango, Sinaloa, Sonora, Arizona, Nuevo México, Chihuahua y porciones de Texas, Coahuila y Zacatecas* (Mexico, 1937). A Spanish edition edited by Mario Hernández y Sánchez-Barba was published in Madrid in 1958.

[82] Eleanor B. Adams and Angelico Chávez, eds. and trans., *The Missions of New Mexico, 1776: A Description of Fray Francisco Atanasio Domínguez* (Albuquerque, 1956).

[83] Juan A. Morfi, *Descripción geográfica del Nuevo México* (Mexico, 1947).

[84] José Porrúa Turanzas, *Documentos para servir a la historia del Nuevo México, 1538–1778* (Madrid, 1962).

and, during his six years in New Mexico, did considerable traveling. In 1775, he journeyed westward to the Hopi pueblos and prepared a diary, that has been published from the manuscript in the Biblioteca Nacional.[85] The following year, he set out from Santa Fe with Francisco A. Domínguez and a small party of Spaniards and Indians to find a route from that place to Monterey. The expedition never reached California, but, in one of the most extensive explorations ever made in the Southwest, it traversed the interior basin, gathering new information about the geography and native life of New Mexico, Colorado, Utah, and Arizona. Escalante's journal, July 29, 1776–January 2, 1777, has been translated and published from the Spanish text in *Documentos para la Historia de México*, which was compared with the manuscript copy in the Edward E. Ayer Collection in the Newberry Library in Chicago.[86] Accompanying the journal is a report by Bernardo de Miera y Pacheco, a retired militia officer who traveled with Domínguez and Escalante and prepared a map of the exploration, that has been published from a photocopy in the Library of Congress.[87]

Auerbach's translation of Escalante's journal was soon out of print and its publisher, the Utah Historical Society, arranged with Herbert E. Bolton for another translation. Bolton prepared a new translation from reproductions of the manuscript journal in the Archivo General de la Nación in Mexico City and the Archivo General de Indias.[88] In preparation for that task, he personally retraced the course of the expedition and, in his annotations, identified the itinerary in terms of modern geography, preparing his own map of the route. The translated journal is preceded by a long introduction that places the journey in its historical setting. It also includes a larger, clearer reproduction, in color, of Miera's map.

Auerbach's and Bolton's translations of the account of the Domínguez-Escalante expedition are considered unsatisfactory, because they are based primarily on the Spanish text published in Mexico in 1854.[89]

---

85 Eleanor B. Adams, trans., "Fray Silvestre Vélez de Escalante to Provincial Fray Isidro Murillo, Zuñi, April 30, 1776, with a Literal Copy of the Diary He Kept during His Journey to the Hopi Pueblos in 1775," *N. Mex. Hist. Rev.* 38 (Apr. 1963):118–38.

86 Herbert S. Auerbach, ed. and trans., "Father Escalante's Journal with Related Documents and Maps," *Utah Hist. Quar.* 11 (Jan.–Oct. 1943):1–142.

87 J. Cecil Alter, "Father Escalante's Map," *Utah Hist. Quar.* 9 (Jan., Apr., 1941):64–72.

88 Herbert E. Bolton, *Pageant in the Wilderness: The Story of the Escalante Expedition to the Interior Basin, 1776, Including the Diary and Itinerary of Father Escalante Translated and Annotated* (Salt Lake City, 1950).

89 Angelico Chávez, trans., and Ted J. Warner, ed., *The Domínguez-Escalante Journal: Their Expedition through Colorado, Utah, Arizona and New Mexico in 1776* (Provo, Utah, 1976), p. xiii.

These authors also overplayed the part of Escalante in the leadership of the expedition and the authorship of the journal concerning it. Domínguez is now regarded as the actual leader of the expedition, as well as the joint author of the journal that had been credited solely to Escalante.[90] The original journal of the expedition has been lost, but a copy made by Domínguez's secretary is in the Newberry Library in Chicago, and a new translation based on it has been published.[91]

The Franciscans have not yet initiated a documentary publication series on the history of the order's missions in New Mexico, but the examples set for California and Texas may yet be followed.

---

[90] Ibid., pp. xiii–xiv; Eleanor B. Adams, "Fray Francisco Atanasio Domínguez and Fray Silvestre Vélez de Escalante," *Utah Hist. Quar.* 44 (Winter 1976):53.

[91] Chávez and Warner, *Domínguez-Escalante Journal*, pp. xiv, 201. The translation is on pp. 3–118, and the Spanish text on pp. 135–96.

Part II
The Records of Texas

10

History & Government

THE SPANISH ACQUIRED KNOWLEDGE of Texas long before it was permanently occupied. In 1519, Alonso Alvárez de Piñeda explored the coast of Texas, spending some time at the mouth of the Río Grande. Cabeza de Vaca and other survivors of the Pánfilo de Nárvaez expedition to Florida traveled through Texas in 1534 to the Río Grande. Coronado, the explorer of New Mexico, crossed the northern plains of Texas in 1541 on his way to Kansas. In the next year, Luis de Moscosco de Alvarado, a lieutenant of Hernando de Soto (who had died while exploring the region north of the Gulf of Mexico), marched through east Texas, returned to the Mississippi River, and then sailed along the coast of Texas to Mexico. In 1675, a small party led by Lt. Fernando del Bosque took possession of the east bank of the Río Grande for the Spanish crown and marched some distance into Texas. In 1683–84, Spaniards from El Paso del Norte established missions and pueblos at the junction of the Río Grande and the Río Conchos.[1]

Having learned from French pirates of the Sieur de La Salle's post on the coast of Texas, Gov. Alonso de León marched into Texas in 1689 and located a fort at Matagorda Bay. In 1691, Gov. Domingo Terán de los Ríos established other missions in Texas, among the Tejos Indians, but they and other missions in east Texas had to be abandoned in 1693 because of lack of protection.[2] Missions established in east Texas in 1716, by Franciscans who accompanied an expedition led by Capt. Domingo Ramón, had to be evacuated in 1719 during a war between Spain and France.

---

[1] Rupert N. Richardson, Ernest Wallace, and Adrian N. Anderson, *Texas, the Lone Star State* (Englewood Cliffs, N.J., 1970), pp. 13–15.

[2] Ibid., p. 18.

[93]

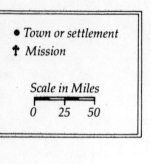

Texas

Colorado City

Colo

Santa Cruz de Sa

Corpus Christi de la Isleta

San Antonio de Senecú

NS de la Purísima Concepción del Socorro

El Paso del Norte
(Ciudad Juárez)

San Elizario

Menar

San S

NS de la Candelaria del Cañ

Rio

NS de Loreto • Presidio

Conchos

La Junta de los Ríos

Rio

Grande

Rio

CHIHUAHUA

San Juan Bautista

COAHUILA

Mexico

NUEV

LEÓ

DURANGO

Monter

Parras

Permanent occupation of Texas had to be undertaken in order to counter the French threat in Louisiana. Martín de Alarcón, the governor of Coahuila and Texas, conducted a party of soldiers, settlers, and Franciscans into Texas in 1718 and established a permanent settlement in the San Antonio area. The Mission San Antonio de Valero, the Presidio of San Antonio de Béxar, and the Villa de Béxar formed a combination settlement that developed into San Antonio.[3] By 1721, Spanish forces were back in east Texas under another governor, the Marqués de San Miguel de Aguayo. He reestablished the missions and founded a presidio, near present Robeline, Louisiana, to block French intrusion into Texas. A detachment from Aguayo's forces, under Capt. Domingo Ramón, also founded Nuestra Señora de Loreto Presidio at Matagorda Bay. Another post, on the Angelina River, that was occupied in 1722, was evacuated in 1727. Pedro Rivera's inspection tour, resulting in the reduction of garrisons in Texas, was followed by the withdrawal of missions in east Texas to San Antonio in 1731.

In the middle of the eighteenth century, Spain colonized the Río Grande valley and established other presidios and missions in Texas. The province of Nuevo Santander was created on the coast of the Gulf of Mexico, and in 1749 its governor, José de Escandón, led 3,000 colonists to occupy it.[4] In that same year, Camargo and Reynoso were founded south of the Río Grande, as was Revilla (Guerrero) in 1750, and Mier in 1753. North of the Río Grande, Dolores was settled in 1750, and, in 1755, Laredo was founded on the road from San Antonio to Monterrey and Mexico City.[5] The Presidio Nuestra Señora de Loreto and the mission it protected were moved, in 1749, to the San Antonio River, where they became the Presidio La Bahía and the La Bahía Mission, which developed into Goliad.[6] The San Francisco Xavier Mission and Presidio, that were established on the San Gabriel River in 1748, were moved to the San Marcos River in 1755, and the presidio was merged with the one at San Sabá in 1757. Col. Diego Ortiz Parrilla erected the Presidio San Luís de las Amarillas in 1757 in Apache country, near present Menard, where a mission and settlement were also located.[7] Indian hostility in 1768 forced the withdrawal of the garrison to the Nueces River, and later it was moved south of the Río Grande. To discourage French traders on the Texas coast, the Presidio

[3] Ibid., p. 20.

[4] Florence J. Scott, *Historical Heritage of the Lower Río Grande* (San Antonio, 1937), p. 5.

[5] Ibid., pp. 27–32, 40.

[6] Richardson, Wallace, and Anderson, *Texas*, p. 24.

[7] Ibid., p. 25.

of San Agustín de Ahumada and a mission were located near the mouth of the Trinity River in 1756.[8] Known also as El Orcoquisac, this garrison was abandoned in 1771. In 1759, the Presidio del Norte was constructed, of adobe, by Capt. Alonso Rubin de Celís at the junction of the Río Grande and the Río Conchos, three miles downstream from the present city of Presidio, Texas.[9] Abandoned in 1767, this presidio was rebuilt about 1773 on its original site and was occupied for about forty years.

A reexamination of the northern frontier of New Spain occurred after Spain acquired that part of Louisiana west of the Mississippi River and the River Iberville from France, under the terms of the Treaty of Paris of 1763 that concluded the Seven Years' War. Adopting the recommendations of the Marqués de Rubí, who inspected the presidios and settlements on the northern frontier in 1766–68, the Spanish crown issued new regulations on September 10, 1772 which provided for a realignment of the presidios. Accordingly, the missions in east Texas were abandoned in 1773, and the evacuees established a new settlement on the Trinity River.[10] Thenceforth, the easternmost presidios in the cordon extending from the Gulf of California were at San Antonio and La Bahía. In the same year, the presidio at El Paso del Norte was moved to San Elizario, on the Texas side of the Río Grande.

Like other provinces of New Spain, Texas was ruled by a governor appointed by the crown. He was a military officer and had charge of the soldiers, the militia, Indian relations, and Indian trade. The presidio officers, whom he appointed, managed the affairs of the settlements that grew up around the presidios and missions, until they developed into municipalities. The governor made land grants, issued licenses, considered appeals from alcalde courts, supervised fiscal matters, and administered laws and decrees.[11] He occupied a building on the military plaza in San Antonio that served as his residence, office, and judicial headquarters.

Under Spanish sovereignty, Texas formed part of the viceroyalty of New Spain. In 1689–90, the governor of Coahuila extended his authority over Texas, but after the withdrawal of the Spanish missions from east Texas in 1692, it was not until 1716 that the authority

---

[8] Ibid., pp. 22, 26, 30.

[9] Walter P. Webb, H. Bailey Carroll, and others, eds. *The Handbook of Texas*, 2 vols. (Austin, 1952), 2:409.

[10] Ibid., p. 30; Carlos E. Castañeda, *Our Catholic Heritage in Texas, 1519–1936*, 6 vols. (Austin, 1936–50), 4:288–9.

[11] Richardson, Wallace, and Anderson, *Texas*, p. 43.

of Coahuila was reestablished over Texas.[12] In 1726, Texas became a separate province. Its capital was at Los Adaes (now Robeline) until 1773, when it was moved to San Antonio.

In 1776, Texas and six other provinces on the northern frontier of New Spain were organized, for improved administration of military and civil affairs, into the Interior Provinces, under a commandant general who was responsible directly to the king rather than to the viceroy.[13] The capital of the commandancy general was initially at Arizpe, Sonora, but, after 1788, it was at Chihuahua, where there was a corps of administrative officials. In 1785, the authority of the viceroy over the northern provinces was partially restored and was continued to a limited extent under a rearrangement of 1787 which placed Texas, Coahuila, Nuevo León, and Nuevo Santander in the Eastern Interior Provinces. A royal order of November 22, 1792 created a new commandancy general, consisting of Nueva Vizcaya, Texas, Coahuila, New Mexico, Sonora, and Sinaloa.[14] This grouping was known also as the Interior Provinces, and the headquarters was at Chihuahua. A reorganization that occurred in 1813 set up Texas, Coahuila, Nuevo León, and Nuevo Santander as the Eastern Interior Provinces, under a commandant general at Monterrey, an office that was retained until the end of the Spanish regime.

Improvements in administration occurred after the establishment of the commandancy general. In 1779, an east-west mail service was established from La Bahía, on the Texas coast, through San Antonio, Monclova, and Parras, to Arizpe.[15] A few years later, a fortnightly mail service was established between Texas and Coahuila. Beginning in 1780, the government collected a head tax on unbranded cattle (mesteños) found on the king's domain.[16]

After the adoption of the Spanish constitution of 1812, a deputation was established in Texas and met for awhile, but was suspended.[17] Though Texas was eligible to send a deputy to the Spanish Cortes (congress), it failed to do so, but Miguel Ramos de Arizpe, the representative from Coahuila, spoke for all the Eastern Interior Prov-

---

[12] Dudley G. Wooten, ed., *A Comprehensive History of Texas 1685 to 1797*, 5 vols. (Dallas, 1898), 1:789; Webb, *Handbook of Texas*, 1:365.

[13] Hubert H. Bancroft, *History of the North Mexican States and Texas*, 2 vols. (San Francisco, 1884, 1889), 1:636–38; Herbert I. Priestley, *The Mexican Nation: A History* (New York, 1925), p. 178.

[14] Bancroft, *North Mexican States and Texas*, 1:641.

[15] Simmons, *Spanish Govt. in N. Mex.* p. 101; Chester V. Kielman, *Guide to the Microfilm Edition of the Béxar Archives, 1717–1803* (Austin, 1967), p. 18 ff.

[16] Castañeda, *Our Catholic Heritage in Texas*, 5:27.

[17] Chester V. Kielman, *Guide to the Microfilm Edition of the Béxar Archives, 1804–1821* (Austin, 1969), pp. 32, 33.

inces.[18] In 1820, after the restoration of the Spanish constitution of 1812, electors from Texas and the other Interior Provinces met in Monterrey to select representatives for the deputation that was to be set up in that place.[19] Ambrosio María de Aldasoro was selected to represent Texas, and two representatives were chosen for each of the other provinces. The deputation had authority to levy taxes, supervise municipalities, draft and equip militia, approve land grants, and select deputies for the national congress.

The presidios of Texas were never very numerous nor strongly manned. During the Spanish period, garrisons were maintained at San Antonio, Los Adaes until 1773, and Matagorda Bay, the last being relocated in 1749 to Goliad.[20] The San Francisco Xavier presidio, founded in 1747 on the San Gabriel River, was incorporated in 1757 into the newly founded San Sabá presidio, on the San Sabá River near present Menard.[21] The mission near the latter place was destroyed by the Comanches, and they continued their attacks on the presidio, forcing its removal in 1768 to El Cañon on the Nueces River, whence it was transferred in 1772 to Coahuila.[22] Presidio del Norte, an adobe fort, was built in 1759–60 near the junction of the Río Grande and the Río Conchos, three miles below present Presidio, Texas.[23] As a result of the king's regulation of 1772, providing for a realignment of presidios from Texas to Sonora, Presidio del Norte was moved to La Junta de Los Ríos, and the presidio at El Paso del Norte was moved to San Elizario on the Texas side of the Río Grande.[24] Small military detachments were continued at San Antonio and Goliad by the Mexican government, and it was obliged, after the Fredonian rebellion threatened control of the area, to establish a garrison at Nacogdoches in 1827.[25] An attempt by Mexico to control emigration from the United States led to the establishment of several more military posts at points along the coast of Texas, in 1830–31, but opposition from the Texans forced their abandonment in 1832.[26]

---

[18] Nettie L. Benson, "Texas Failure to Send a Deputy to the Spanish Cortes, 1810–1812," *Southw. Hist. Quar.* 64 (July 1960) :14, 28.

[19] Castañeda, *Our Catholic Heritage in Texas*, 6:221.

[20] Webb, *Handbook of Texas*, 1:699.

[21] Ibid., 2:552.

[22] Ibid., pp. 561–62.

[23] Ibid., p. 409.

[24] Ibid., p. 550.

[25] Eugene C. Barker, *The Life of Stephen F. Austin, Founder of Texas, 1793–1836: A Chapter in the Westward Movement of the Anglo-American People* (Nashville, 1925), pp. 326–27.

[26] Ibid., pp. 296, 304, 326, 327, 388, 400–01.

Both the Spanish and the Mexican governments followed a restrictive commercial system, under which the importation of certain goods was prohibited but others were admitted upon the payment of duties.[27] The only port of entry under the Spanish regime was located at San Bernard Bay and was too far west to benefit those colonies that were founded farther east in Texas during the 1820s. It was not until 1830 that a collector of customs was appointed at Galveston. Late in the next year, the collector, George Fisher, whose functions at Galveston had been suspended, was directed to open a branch at Anahuac. But armed opposition from the Texans forced the abandonment, in 1832, of attempts to collect customs duties.

In an effort to promote efficiency, a change in the governmental system of New Spain was decreed by the crown in 1786 and resulted in the replacement of gubernatorial districts with intendancies. Twelve intendancies were established under governor intendants who possessed civil, military, judicial, and financial authority under the viceroy, commandant general, or audiencia.[28] Subdelegates, who replaced the *alcaldes mayores* and *corregidores*, exercised similar jurisdiction in the district and county capitals. The extreme northern frontier of New Spain was comprised of several intendancies, which, like the others, were named after their seats of government. The intendancy of San Luís Potosí included Nuevo León, Nuevo Santander, and Coahuila and Texas.[29] The intendancy of Durango corresponded to Nueva Vizcaya (modern Durango and Chihuahua). The intendancy of Arizpe included the old provinces of Sonora and Sinaloa. The intendancies functioned throughout the remainder of the Spanish regime, and bodies of records which reflected their activities accumulated at the capitals.

Mexican rule succeeded Spanish rule in Texas, following the winning of Mexican independence in 1821. Gov. Antonio Marío Martínez, the last Spanish governor, turned over authority in Texas to Félix Trespalacios on August 24, 1822. Texas, like the other provinces of the Eastern Interior Provinces, became a separate political entity on August 18, 1823, and was authorized to have a provincial deputation and send a representative to the national congress.[30] The provincial deputation selected Erasmo Seguín as its representative to the Mexican Congress. A decree adopted by that body on May 7, 1824 united Coahuila and Texas as one state, allowing Texas one deputy in the assembly that

27 Ibid., p. 204.

28 Bancroft, *Hist. of Mexico*, 3:452–55; Bancroft, *Hist. of North. Mex. States and Texas*, 1:642–43.

29 Bancroft, *Hist. North Mexican States and Texas*, 1:605.

30 Charles A. Bacarisse, "The Union of Coahuila and Texas," *Southw. Hist. Quar.* 61 (Jan. 1958):342.

was to meet at Saltillo.[31] A state decree of August 28, 1824 abolished the provincial deputation and political chief of Texas and directed that their archives be transferred to corresponding officials of the state.[32] Although the deputation and political chief ceased to function, the archives apparently remained in Texas.[33] The Baron de Bastrop, who had been commissioner of colonization in Austin's colony, was admitted as the deputy of Texas in the state legislature in October, 1824, and served until his death in February, 1827.

Texas was set up as a department in December, 1824, under a "chief of the department of Texas" who was subordinate to the governor of Coahuila and Texas.[34] The chief of the department resided at San Antonio and had extensive powers. Besides being charged with the direction of political affairs in the province, he was chief of police, commander of the militia, guardian of the coast, presiding officer of the junta and the *ayuntamiento* at San Antonio, channel of communication between the *ayuntamientos* and the government, and overseer of the *ayuntamientos* and the administration of justice.[35]

The judicial system that had been in operation in Texas was continued by decree number 1 of the first constituent congress of Coahuila and Texas, adopted in August, 1824.[36] A superior court of three alcaldes was set up in Austin's colony in 1826 to handle the increased judicial business that had developed from the growth of the colony.[37] The permanent constitution, adopted in March, 1827, provided for a system of courts composed of inferior tribunals, hitherto existing (alcalde courts), and a supreme court, to be established at the capital (Saltillo).[38] Since appeals in civil and criminal cases had to be taken to Saltillo, 700 miles away from the Texas settlements, the administration of justice was inadequate.[39] Arbitration was to precede litigation, and petty offenses were dealt with summarily without formal trial or the right of appeal. According to decree number 277 of April 17, 1834,

---

[31] Bancroft, *Hist. North Mexican States and Texas,* 2:70.

[32] Hans P. N. Gammel, comp. and ed., *The Laws of Texas, 1822–1897,* 10 vols. (Austin, 1898), 1:118.

[33] Bacarisse,"Coahuila and Texas," pp. 347–49.

[34] Webb, *Handbook of Texas,* 1:365.

[35] Decree No. 13, Feb. 1, 1825, Gammel, *Laws of Texas,* 1:121–23.

[36] Gammel, *Laws of Texas,* 1:146–61; Barker, *Stephen F. Austin,* pp. 129–31, 137, 213; Bancroft, *Hist. North Mexican States and Texas,* 2:85.

[37] Barker *Stephen F. Austin,* p. 126.

[38] John C. Townes, "Sketch of the Development of the Judicial System of Texas," *Southw. Hist. Quar.* 2 (July 1898) :33–34.

[39] Charles S. Potts, "Early Criminal Law in Texas: From Civil Law to Common Law, to Code," *Texas Law Review* 21 (Apr. 1936) :396–97.

for the better regulation of the administration of justice, there was to be a supreme court for the state at Saltillo, a superior court for Texas, courts in each of the three districts of Béxar, Brazos, and Nacogdoches, courts presided over by primary judges in the municipalities, and inferior courts in smaller political subdivisions.[40] Thomas J. Chambers was appointed judge of the superior court, but because of disturbances resulting from the removal of the capital from Saltillo to Monclova, the court was never organized.[41] In the Brazos district, of which David C. Burnet was appointed judge, a court was organized and held several sessions at San Felipe.[42] Primary courts set up in the capitals of the municipalities functioned until the establishment of the provisional government of Texas in October, 1835.

A movement for Texas independence in the 1830s resulted in the establishment, late in 1835, of a provisional state government that was to be independent of Coahuila. At the same time, the Texans refused to recognize the Mexican government headed by Antonio López de Santa Anna. He led an army into Texas in 1836 but, after some initial successes, was defeated on April 21 at San Jacinto, by the Texas army commanded by Sam Houston. For the next few years, after its proposition for annexation to the United States was rebuffed by President Andrew Jackson, Texas governed itself. Later, political conditions in the United States became more favorable, and, on March 1, 1845, a joint resolution of Congress authorized the admission of Texas as a state.[43] Texas was to retain all vacant and unappropriated lands within its limits, as a means of paying its debts and other liabilities, and the lands remaining were to be disposed of under its own auspices. Late in the year, a Texas convention accepted the proposal, and an act of Congress of December 29, 1845 declared Texas to be an American State.[44]

[40] Townes, "Judicial System," pp. 35–36.

[41] Webb, *Handbook of Texas*, 1:326.

[42] Dorothy L. Fields, "David Gouverneur Burnet," *Southw. Hist. Quar.* 49 (Oct. 1945):221.

[43] U.S., *Stats.*, 5:797.

[44] U.S., *Stats.*, 9:108.

11

Provincial Records

THE BÉXAR ARCHIVES, provincial, departmental, and local, passed into the custody of the county of Béxar.[1] In 1841, certain papers from these archives were sent to the secretary of state at Austin where they became mixed with the Nacogdoches Archives.[2] Pursuant to acts of the legislature of 1853 and 1856, translations were made of Spanish documents in the Béxar Archives relating to early settlements in Texas and transferred, with the originals, to the secretary of state.[3] Both translations and originals were lost years later, but, about 1909, the translations were discovered by the state librarian among the Spanish Archives in the General Land Office and turned over to the state library, and the originals were found, largely in the Nacogdoches Archives, in the state library. The mass of Béxar Archives remained at the courthouse at San Antonio for many years and were neglected by state and local governments alike.

Not until after the establishment of the University of Texas at Austin in 1883 did an interest develop in the Béxar Archives. Members of the history faculty of that institution became interested in the archives as a source for the history of Texas. A young instructor, Lester G. Bugbee, acquired a firsthand knowledge of the great value of the Béxar Archives by working in them during the summer of 1898.

---

[1] Lester G. Bugbee, and Eugene C. Barker, "Report on the Béxar Archives," American Historical Association, *Annual Report*, 1902, 1 :359.

[2] Carlos E. Castañeda, *A Report on the Spanish Archives in San Antonio, Texas* (San Antonio, 1937), p. 15.

[3] Ernest W. Winkler, "Some Historical Activities of the Texas Library and Historical Commission," *Southw. Hist. Quar.* 14 (Apr. 1911) :303; acts approved Feb. 7, 1853 and Aug. 25, 1856 (Gammel, *Laws of Texas*, 3 :1322; 4 :468–69).

With the aid of the head of the history department, Prof. George P. Garrison, he sought the transfer of the archives from San Antonio to the university. A fireproof vault for their preservation was built in the library building, and, with the aid of friends of Bugbee in official positions at San Antonio, the commissioners of Béxar County were persuaded, on September 30, 1899, to approve the transfer of the archives.[4] The university obligated itself to house the records in a fireproof vault and to calendar and translate them within a reasonable time.

The provincial records of Texas (Béxar Archives), 1717–1836 (81 feet; 80,795 items), consist of more than 250,000 pages of manuscripts and more than 4,000 pages of printed material.[5] The collection includes correspondence of the chief of the Department of Texas, the governor of Coahuila-Texas, Mexican officials, the commandant general at Chihuahua, presidio commanders, other army officers, local officials, clergymen, enlisted men, and citizens. Other documents include reports, proceedings of the provincial deputation, election returns, diaries, petitions, cashbooks, inventories, lists of Indian presents and military supplies, passports, invoices, questionnaires, and cattle-branding licenses. Government ordinances of general applicability, such as royal orders, proclamations, laws, and regulations, are printed, and are also available in other archival collections and in libraries.[6] Censuses of Texas settlements, which usually show the names of heads of families; numbers of men, women, children, and slaves; and occupations; are interfiled among other documents. Judicial proceedings concern the trials of smugglers, highwaymen, traitors, murderers, foreigners, deserters, and others who violated Spanish and Mexican laws. These records reflect the administration of military and Indian affairs,

---

[4] Bugbee and Barker, "Béxar Archives," p. 357; Eugene C. Barker, "To Whom Credit Is Due," *Southw. Hist. Quar.* 54 (July 1950):6.

[5] Bugbee and Barker, "Béxar Archives," p. 363; Webb, *Handbook of Texas*, 1:154.

[6] Thomas W. Streeter, *Bibliography of Texas, 1795–1845*, 5 vols. (Cambridge, Mass., 1955–60), vols. 1–3; Annita M. Ker, *Mexican Government Publications: A Guide to the More Important Publications of the National Government of Mexico, 1821–1936* (Washington, 1940); John T. Vance, *The Background of Hispanic American Law: Legal Sources and Juridical Literature of Spain* (Washington 1937). These printed issuances were also published in newspapers: See Historical Records Survey, Texas, *Texas Newspapers 1813–1939: A Union List of Newspaper Files Available in Offices of Publishers, Libraries, and a Number of Private Collections* (Houston, 1941). Microfilm of Mexican and Texas broadsides, 1822–1836, is in the Library of Congress (U.S. Library of Congress, *A Guide to the Microfilm Collection of Early State Records, Supplement*, comp. and ed. by William S. Jenkins, [Washington, 1951], p. 101). The University of Texas Library has the following compilation: Grace A. Edman, trans., "A Compilation of Royal Decrees in the Archivo General de la Nación Relating to Texas and Other Northern Provinces of New Spain," 1719–1799 (University of Texas, Master's Thesis, 1930).

civil affairs, ecclesiastical matters, explorations, local history, immigration, colonization, agriculture, ranching, industry, commerce, postal service, activities of revolutionists and filibusters, American activities on the border, hospitals and health administration, education, genealogy, and the collection of the tax on unbranded cattle found in the king's domain.

The Béxar Archives were placed in the Old Main Building of the University of Texas, which was equipped with a vault. In the summer of 1900, Ernest W. Winkler, a fellow in history at the university, started arranging the documents.[7] In June, 1902, the university's board of regents authorized the employment of Mattie A. Hatcher, another fellow in history, to classify the records. It was decided to arrange the documents in several subgroups, each of which was to be in chronological order without regard to provenance:

1. Coahuila and Texas Official Publications, 1826–35.
2. General Governmental Publications, 1730–1836.
3. Nongovernmental Publications, 1778, 1811–36.
4. Undated and Undated Fragments.
5. General Manuscript Series, 1717–1836.

After the documents had been arranged in chronological order, the preparation of calendar cards for individual documents was begun; these were completed in 1932, with a total of 81,000 cards being amassed. The cards show the date, the number of pages, the writer's name, the place of writing, the addressee's name, a summary of the contents in English, and the type of document in symbols. An index is also available. A separate calendar of the printed laws and decrees of Coahuila and Texas, 1821–35, was also prepared. Translating was begun, but only a few hundred pages had been completed by 1933 when a full-time translator was appointed.[8] He was assisted in later years by students supplied by the Civil Works Administration and the National Youth Administration. By 1970, typed translations had been completed for the documents of 1717–79 and 1804–08, bound into indexed volumes, and deposited in the Béxar County Courthouse, the University of Texas Archives, and the Stephen F. Austin State College Archive Collection.

In January, 1966, the University of Texas Archives, with the aid

---

[7] Llerena Friend, "E. W. Winkler and the Texas State Library," *Texas Libraries* 24 (May–June 1962):90.

[8] Juan V. Haggard and Malcom D. McLean, *Handbook for Translators of Spanish Historical Documents* (Austin, 1941), p. x; Malcolm D. McLean, "The Béxar Archives," *Southw. Hist. Quar.* 50 (April 1947):494.

of grants from the National Historical Publications Commission, initiated a project to microfilm the Béxar Archives. Chester V. Kielman, the university archivist, directed the project, and Carmel Leal, formerly the translator, supervised the work. The arrangement that had been previously adopted for the Béxar Archives was retained.[9] The first segment, published in microfilm form in 1967, includes the four printed series (rolls 1–7) and the general manuscripts series, 1717–1803 (rolls 8–31).[10] The second segment includes the general manuscripts series, 1804–21 (rolls 32–69),[11] and the third segment includes the general manuscripts series, 1822–36 (rolls 70–172).[12] Guides accompanying each segment of the microfilm publication contain general descriptions of the material on each roll, with the names of places, Indian tribes, and officials and other persons. Calendar entries that introduce the rolls of microfilm enable researchers to locate documents related to their special fields of interest. The proceedings of the provincial deputation are included in the general manuscript series rolls 75–77.

In 1850, the Texas legislature authorized the secretary of state to order the clerk of Nacogdoches County to transfer the Spanish documents that were said to have been found in the office of the former political chief of the Department of Nacogdoches and the alcalde of the municipality of Nacogdoches.[13] The Nacogdoches Archives were transferred accordingly to the Texas State Library, which had been part of the Department of State since 1839. An act of August 21, 1876, established the Department of Insurance, Statistics, and History, made it the official archives repository of the state, and transferred the state library to it from the Department of State.[14] The Nacogdoches Archives were stored in a vault in the state library, where they survived a fire

---

[9] Chester V. Kielman, "The Béxar Archives Microfilm Project in the University of Texas Archives," *Texas Library Journal* 44 (Spring 1968):17–18; Oliver W. Holmes, "Managing Our Spanish and Mexican Southwestern Archival Legacy," *Southw. Hist. Quar.* 71 (April 1968):520–25.

[10] Chester V. Kielman, *Guide to the Microfilm Edition of the Béxar Archives, 1717–1803* (Austin, 1967).

[11] Chester V. Kielman, *Guide to the Microfilm Edition of the Béxar Archives, 1804–1821* (Austin, 1969). Positive copies of the microfilm can be purchased from the University of Texas Archives, The Library, Austin, Texas, 78712.

[12] Chester V. Kielman, *Guide to the Microfilm Edition of the Béxar Archives, 1822–1836* (Austin, 1971). Copies of the microfilm are in the county clerk's office of Bexar County at San Antonio, the University of Texas Archives at El Paso, and other places.

[13] Texas, Department of Agriculture, Insurance, Statistics, and History, *Twenty-Ninth Annual Report . . . 1903* (Austin, 1904), p. xiii; act of Jan. 24, 1850, Texas, Laws, 1850, pp. 71–72.

[14] Texas, Dept. of Agriculture, etc., *Twenty-Ninth Annual Report*, p. xiv; Texas, *General Laws*, 1876, pp. 219–26.

that burned the capitol in 1881. For many years, state librarians were more interested in published books in their charge than in the archives, and nothing was done to make the archives more usable.

After Ernest W. Winkler was appointed classifier and translator of manuscripts, on September 1, 1903, attention was at last given to the Nacogdoches Archives and other records in the custody of the state library.[15] It is believed that the archives at San Antonio were divided when the Department of Nacogdoches was created, and that some Béxar archives were improperly transferred to Nacogdoches.[16] So, the collection known as the Nacogdoches Archives contains records of the Department of Nacogdoches, the Department of Béxar, the Province of Texas, and the municipality of Nacogdoches.

The classification scheme that was adopted in 1903 for the Nacogdoches Archives was based on the administrative organization of the Mexican government from 1824 to 1836. According to that classification, the Nacogdoches Archives were divided into seven subgroups, which were further divided into series or files.[17] Subgroup (1), designated "Mexico," consisted of series (a) Spanish and Mexican decrees, 1812–35 (125 items); and (b) miscellaneous materials, 1756–1835 (140 items), consisting of communications from superior authorities in Mexico to the governors of Texas and Coahuila and Texas, and to the commandant general. Subgroup (2), designated "Chihuahua: Monterrey," consisted of communications from the commandant general of the Interior Provinces at Chihuahua or Monterrey to the governor of Texas or the governor of Coahuila and Texas, 1791–1835 (115 items). Subgroup (3), designated "San Antonio de Béxar: Saltillo (Leona Vicario): Monclova," consisted of series (a) *residencias* of Gov. Manuel de Sandoval, 1736 (125 folios), Gov. Francisco García Larios, 1748 (50 folios), and Gov. Pedro del Barrio Junco y Espriella, 1751 (83 folios); series (b) correspondence from the governors of Texas and Coahuila and Texas, 1749–1835 (435 items); series (c) decrees of Coahuila and Texas, 1834–35 (85 items); and series (d) miscellaneous material 1823–35, including monthly reports of the state treasury, communications from the clerk of the state supreme court to the alcalde (later to the primary judge) of Nacogdoches, and addresses and notices (160 items). Subgroup (4), designated "Béxar," consisted of series (a) correspondence of the political chief at Béxar, October 1823–

---

[15] Llerena Friend, "E. W. Winkler," p. 93.

[16] Seymour V. Connor, *A Preliminary Guide to the Archives of Texas* (Austin, 1956), p. 61.

[17] The classification scheme is published in Texas, Dept. of Agriculture, etc., *Twenty-Ninth Annual Report*, pp. xx–xxiii. Subgroup (6) is described under San Felipe.

October 1835 (1,065 items); series (b) miscellaneous material relating to the municipality of Béxar, 1825–35 (250 items), containing communications from the alcalde and *ayuntamiento* of Béxar to the alcalde and *ayuntamiento* of Nacogdoches, and letters to and from the Baron de Bastrop; and series (c) correspondence of the principal commandant, 1825–35 (30 items). Subgroup (5), designated "Nacogdoches," consisted of records of the municipality of Nacogdoches, that are described in chapter seventeen in this section. Subgroup (7), designated "General: Coahuila and Texas," consisted of series (a) census reports for various missions and towns, December 31, 1783–June 30, 1835 (210 items);[18] series (b) civil elections, September 1, 1824–December 16, 1835 (170 items), including tally sheets, returns of elections, minutes of electoral assemblies, and lists of officers elected, mostly for Nacogdoches but also for other places; series (c) reports of military companies stationed at Béxar, La Bahía, Bavia, Aguaverde, Río Grande, Monclova, Lampazos, and Trinity, 1773–1813, and the company at Monclova, 1835 (95 items); and series (d) miscellaneous material, September 1785–July 1835 (150 items). The Nacogdoches Archives totaled 6,728 items, and nine-tenths of them were loose papers. In 1905, 200 additional items were recovered from the vaults of the Department of Agriculture, Insurance, Statistics, and History, or transferred from the State Department.[19]

The state library undertook the job of putting the Nacogdoches Archives in better condition for use. It arranged them according to the classification scheme described above. Work on a card calendar of individual documents, giving summary information in English, was done by Elizabeth H. West and Katherine Elliott, but it was never completed. An inventory was prepared but lost its usefulness as a reference tool after the archives were rearranged chronologically. Translation of the documents was undertaken, those relating to censuses

---

[18] Microfilm of censuses, 1828–36, of Nacogdoches, Tenehaw and Sabine, Bevil's Settlement (Jasper), Williams' Settlement, and San Augustine, and other materials in the Nacogdoches Archives are in the Library of Congress (Jenkins, *Guide to the Microfilm Collection of Early State Records, Supplement*, pp. 5–6, 101).

[19] Disturbances in the Nacogdoches region, which was adjacent to the United States boundary, resulted in the depletion of the archives. A band of revolutionists, led by José Bernardo Guitiérrez de Lara and Augustus W. Magee, occupied Nacogdoches on Aug. 11, 1812, forcing the Spanish garrison to retreat. According to testimony presented years later by Gutiérrez, the public archives were carried off at that time by the Spanish and were not returned when they reoccupied Nacogdoches. Samuel Davenport, a resident of Nacogdoches at the time, testified to the same effect, as did José M. Mora and John Cortes ("Land Claims — Between the Rio Hondo and the Sabine," *House Exec. Doc.* 49, 24 Cong., 1 sess., p. 44). However, this testimony appears to have been exaggerated. Davenport was a member of the chief trading firm in east Texas, and Spanish Indian agent in Nacogdoches (J. Villasana Haggard, "The House of Barr and Davenport," *Southw. Hist. Quar.* 49 (July 1945):66–88).

being the first to be put into English. The documents were repaired with chiffon linings.

The Nacogdoches Archives were subsequently rearranged by the Archives Division of the Texas State Library and put in chronological order. Other Spanish documents and translations from the Béxar Archives were interfiled with them, and the new chronological file contains about 4,000 items.[20] To save the original Nacogdoches Archives from unnecessary handling and consequent wear, the Archives Division began typing transcriptions of them in the late 1920s. These transcriptions, 1731–1836, are in eighty-nine volumes, containing about 15,000 pages.[21] Sets of the transcriptions are in the University of Texas Archives, the Stephen F. Austin State College Library in Nacogdoches, the North Texas State College Library in Denton, and the Newberry Library in Chicago. A card index to the transcriptions, prepared by the Historical Records Survey of the Works Progress Administration, is in the University of Texas Archives.

Transcriptions of other Nacogdoches records, in the custody of the county clerk of Nacogdoches County, were made by Robert B. Blake, who once served as county clerk. The set of these transcriptions in the Texas State Archives makes up twenty volumes, containing about 4,000 pages.[22] Other sets of the transcriptions are in the University of Texas Archives, the Stephen F. Austin State College Library, the North Texas State College Library, and the Newberry Library.

Robert Blake made a lifetime hobby of transcribing archives and manuscripts relating to Spanish and Mexican Texas for a documentary history. After many years of calendaring, indexing, transcribing, and translating the records held by the county clerk at Nacogdoches, he became a court reporter at Austin in 1942 and worked thenceforth on the Nacogdoches Archives and other materials in the Texas State Archives, the General Land Office records, and the University of Texas Archives. After Blake's death in 1955, sets of his transcripts and translations were acquired by the Texas State Archives, the University of Texas Archives, the Stephen F. Austin State College Library, and the Houston Public Library. The Blake Collection in the Houston Public Library was bound into seventy-five volumes covering the years 1744 to 1837.[23] The collection includes correspondence, diaries, election

---

[20] Seymour V. Connor, *A Preliminary Guide to the Archives of Texas* ([Austin], 1956), p. 61.

[21] Ibid., p. 62.

[22] Ibid., p. 62.

[23] *Natl. Union Catalog of Ms. Colls.*, 1961, entry 1157. The set in the University of Texas Archives comprises 14 ft., including 93 vols. (Kielman, *Univ. of Texas Arch.*, p. 33).

returns, bills of sale, a record of foreigners who settled at Nacogdoches, 1827–34, lists of foreigners residing in Nacogdoches, judicial proceedings, marriage contracts, accounting and financial papers, orders, commissions, and other documents. Censuses for Nacogdoches and surrounding settlements, 1792–1835, show the name of the head of family, race, marital status, birthplace, age, occupation, name of wife, her race, birthplace, and age, and the number of children and their ages. Some censuses give information regarding servants, and others supply data on real estate.[24] Less numerous are returns of population giving the numbers of inhabitants at various settlements and missions. A calendar of the Blake collection is in the University of Texas Archives.

No extensive publication series based on the Béxar and Nacogdoches archives has been prepared, but documents from those archives have been included in a number of publications. Documents of 1801–22 from the Béxar Archives, relating to the struggle of the royalists to hold Texas against Americans and other foreign interlopers, have been translated and edited by Mattie A. Hatcher.[25] In 1811, Capt. Juan Bautista de las Casas led a faction at San Antonio, in support of the Hidalgo revolution. A counterrevolution, launched by Juan Manuel Sambrano in support of the legitimate government, resulted in the capture, trial, and execution of Casas. Documents from the Béxar, Nacogdoches, and Mexican archives relating to those revolutions have been published.[26] Translations of letters written by Gov. Antonio Martínez to Joaquín de Arredondo, the commandant general of the Eastern Provinces, have been published from the original manuscripts in the Nacogdoches Archives.[27] This publication actually contains only letters dated from May 28, 1817, to July 23, 1820, as the last two years of Martínez's correspondence are missing. Letters from him to the viceroy of New Spain, May 31, 1817, to January 20, 1821, were to be included in a later publication which has not yet appeared.[28]

---

[24] What appear to be consolidated lists of names from these censuses are in Marion D. Mullins, *The First Census of Texas, 1829–1836, to Which Are Added Texas Citizenship Lists, 1821–1835 and Other Early Records of the Republic of Texas* (Washington, 1959). An 1826 census of Austin's colony is in ibid., pp. 41–52.

[25] M. A. Hatcher, *The Opening of Texas to Foreign Settlement, 1801–1821* (Austin, 1927), pp. 295–358.

[26] Frederick C. Chabot, ed., *Texas in 1811: The Las Casas and Sambrano Revolutions* (San Antonio, 1941).

[27] Virginia H. Taylor and Juanita Hammons, trans. and eds., *The Letters of Antonio Martínez, Last Spanish Governor of Texas, 1817–1822* (Austin, 1957).

[28] A calendar covering letters to both the viceroy and *arredondo* has been published: Virginia H. Taylor, "Calendar of the Letters of Antonio Martínez, Last Spanish Governor of Texas, 1817–1822," *Southw. Hist. Quar.* 59–61 (Jan. 1956–Oct. 1957).

12

Departmental Records

THE EXPANSION OF SETTLEMENT in Texas during the 1820s resulted in changes in the governmental structure. The Department of Texas was divided by a legislative decree of January 31, 1831 into the districts of Béxar and Nacogdoches, whose mutual boundary was a line running northwesterly from Galveston Bay.[1] Another decree, of March 18, 1834, divided Texas into the Departments of Béxar, Brazos, and Nacogdoches, retaining for the last named department the boundary prescribed in 1831.[2] Despite the legislative provision of 1831, the political chief of Béxar governed all subdivisions until the summer of 1834, when political chiefs were provided for all departments. Juan N. Seguín then became head of the Department of Béxar at San Antonio. Henry Smith, who was appointed political chief of the Department of Brazos on July 24, 1834, resided at San Felipe de Austin, where he was succeeded in 1835 by James B. Miller. Henry Rueg took up his duties as head of the Department of Nacogdoches in October, 1834, and continued in office until January, 1836. A contemporary report lists the municipalities and towns assigned to each department as follows: Department of Béxar: Béxar, Goliad, Victoria, and San Patricio; Department of Brazos: San Felipe de Austin, Brazoria, Colombia, Matagorda, Gonzales, Harrisburg, Mina, Bolivar, and Velasco; and the Department of Nacogdoches: Nachogdoches, Liberty, San Augustine, Bevil, Terán, Tenehaw, Jonesboro, and Anáhuac.[3]

The organic law adopted by the Consultation of Representatives

---

[1] Gammel, *Laws of Texas*, 1:281.

[2] Ibid., p. 355.

[3] Carlos E. Castañeda, trans., "Statistical Report on Texas by Juan N. Almonte," *Southw. Hist. Quar.* 28 (Jan. 1925):186, 198, 206.

of Texas Settlements on November 13, 1835, for the organization of
the provisional government of Texas, abolished the political chiefs of
the Departments of Béxar, Brazos, and Nacogdoches and directed the
transfer of their archives to the governor and council.[4] Inasmuch as
Mexican military forces were in control in San Antonio, nothing could
be done immediately in regard to the records there. The Texans
neglected an opportunity to remove the records, during their occupation of San Antonio from December, 1835, to February, 1836, and,
after its recovery in 1836, took no steps to preserve these important
documents, which therefore remained part of the Spanish records at
San Antonio. Papers of Juan N. Seguín, political chief of the Department of Béxar after the reorganization of 1834, are in the Texas State
Library. Commissioners were appointed to take over the records of
the political chief at Nacogdoches, but the only one who reached that
place apparently failed to accomplish this mission, owing to the opposition of the people to the removal of the records from the locality.[5] The
political chief, Henry Rueg, transferred his records in January, 1836
to the alcalde of Nacogdoches.[6] Rueg's correspondence, August 12,
1834–March 5, 1836 (175 items), is in the Archives Division of the
Texas State Library.[7] Other correspondence of the Department of
Nacogdoches, in the Texas General Land Office, includes correspondence between Rueg and the secretary of state of Coahuila and Texas,
August 12, 1834–August 21, 1835 (75 pages); correspondence of Henry
Rueg, September 18, 1834–October 12, 1835 (39 pages); and correspondence of Vital Flores, August 12, 1834–November 28, 1835 (53
pages).[8] Flores served as political chief during the absence of Rueg.
Microfilm of the correspondence described above is in the Library of
Congress. For the short-lived Department of Brazos, headed by Henry
Smith, some records are available in print.[9] Other documents relating
to the departments are in the provincial records (Béxar Archives) and
in the records of municipalities.

---

[4] Gammel, Laws of Texas, 1:913; Seymour V. Connor, "The Evolution of County
Government in the Republic of Texas," Southw. Hist. Guar. 55 (Oct. 1951):163–66.

[5] William C. Binkley, ed., Official Correspondence of the Texas Revolution,
1835–1836, 2 vols. (New York, 1936), 1:131–40.

[6] Webb, Handbook of Texas, 2:513.

[7] "Report of the Classifier and Translator of Manuscripts in the Texas State
Library," in Texas, Dept. of Agriculture, etc., Twenty-Ninth Annual Report, 1903,
p. xxi.

[8] Jenkins and Hamrick, eds., "Administrative Records," in Guide to the Microfilm Collection of Early State Records, p. 89.

[9] Some documents from Smith's papers are in John H. Brown, Life and Times of
Henry Smith, the First American Governor of Texas (Dallas, 1887), and others are
in Charles A. Gulick et al. eds., The Papers of Mirabeau Bonaparte Lamar, from
the Original Papers in the Texas State Library, 6 vols. (Austin, 1921–28), 1:passim.

13

Archival Reproductions

Since Texas was governed by the viceroyalty of New Spain and, after 1821, by the republic of Mexico, the archives of both Spain and Mexico contain great quantities of pertinent documents. Various branches of the Spanish and Mexican governments were concerned with the administration of Texas, New Mexico, and California, and the records of both countries have long been in archival repositories. Their holdings have been investigated by American historians who have published guides describing the materials relating to the United States.[1]

The principal repository in Texas of reproductions from Mexican archives relating to Texas and the Southwest is the University of Texas Archives. George P. Garrison, of the university's history department, and Lilia M. Casís, who later became head of its Spanish department, initiated the copying of significant documents in the Archivo General de la Nación in Mexico City in 1897.[2] Systematic copying began in that depository in the following year.[3] Herbert E. Bolton, another member of the university's history department, investigated the Mexican archives during 1902–08 and obtained transcripts, of which copies went to the Universities of Texas, New Mexico, and California, and the Library of Congress.[4] In 1913, as a result of the efforts of Eugene

---

[1] For brief descriptions of materials in the Mexican and Spanish archives, and titles of guides to those archives and histories of Spanish and Mexican governmental administration, see chapter 4, in the section on New Mexico.

[2] Lota M. Spell, *Research Materials for the Study of Latin America at the University of Texas* (Austin, 1954), p. 2.

[3] Carlos E. Castañeda and Jack A. Dabbs, *Guide to the Latin American Manuscripts in the University of Texas Library* (Cambridge, Mass., 1939), p. vii.

[4] Vernon D. Tate, "Microphotography in Mexico," Interamerican Bibliographical and Library Association, *Proceedings*, 1940, pp. 355–56.

C. Barker, head of the history department of the University of Texas, a cooperative arrangement for obtaining transcripts from Mexican archives was entered into by the Universities of Texas and California, and the Library of Congress.[5] William E. Dunn, an instructor in Latin American history at the University of Texas, supervised the copying. Political disturbances in Mexico prevented continuous work in the Mexican archives during the next few years, but Dunn obtained transcripts from the Archivo General de la Nación relating to the northern provinces of New Spain.[6] When Dunn resigned from his position at the University of Texas in 1920, Charles W. Hackett took over the courses in Latin American history and the supervision of transcribing from the Mexican archives. He obtained additional transcripts relating to the Interior Provinces, and other documents,[7] and continued to supply the Library of Congress with copies. Transcripts obtained by Eugene C. Barker from the Archivo General de la Nación on the Anglo-American period of Texas history are also held by the University of Texas Archives.[8] Other holdings of that repository include typed transcripts from the "Marina" section of the Archivo General de la Nación, obtained by Charles H. Cunningham,[9] and photostatic copies of documents on the early history of Texas and Coahuila, selected by Carlos E. Castañeda from archives in Mexico City and Guadalajara.[10]

The extensive transcripts from the Archivo General de la Nación in the University of Texas Archives include the following classifications: Audiencia de Guadalajara, 1582–1821 (54 volumes); California, 1682–1807, 1823 (1 volume); Correspondencia de Virreyes, 1755–93 (1 volume); Fomento, Colonización, 1821–36 (17 volumes); Guerra, 1706–1831 (6 volumes); Guerra y Marina, 1827–45 (15 volumes); Historia, 1538–1820 (89 volumes); Inquisición, 1560–1662 (9 volumes); Marina, 1756–1814 (89 volumes); Misiones, 1623–1810 (2 volumes); Misiones de California, 1617–1821 (1 volume); Provincias Internas, 1617–1821 (88 volumes); Reales Cédulas, 1691–1792 (20 volumes); and Tierras, 1660–1719 (12 volumes).[11] Photocopies of these transcripts are in the University of Notre Dame Archives.

---

[5] Grace G. Griffin, "Foreign American History Ms. Copies in the Library of Congress," *Journal of Documentary Reproduction* 3 (March 1940):3.

[6] Castañeda and Dabbs, *Guide to the Latin American Mss.*, pp. 78, 117, 154; Kielman, *Univ. of Texas Archives*, p. 10.

[7] Castañeda and Dabbs, *Guide to the Latin American Mss.*, pp. 78, 118, 164.

[8] Ibid., p. 181.

[9] Ibid., p. 154.

[10] Ibid., p. 178.

[11] Kielman, *Univ. of Texas Arch.*, pp. 10–11.

Under the Texas Consortium, mentioned below, further micro-filming will be done in Mexico City by the University of Texas at Austin.

Other repositories in Texas also have reproductions from archives in Mexico City. Transcripts from the Secretariat of Fomento on the colonization of Texas, 1820–36, and from the Interior Provinces and Historia sections in the Archivo General de la Nación are in the Texas State Archives.[12] The University of Texas at El Paso and the El Paso Centennial Museum have microfilm from the Interior Provinces section.

The archives of the state of Tamaulipas in Ciudad Victoria have largely been destroyed,[13] but reproductions of other archives in that state have been obtained. In 1928, Carlos E. Castañeda, with the approval of federal and state authorities of Mexico, selected and had photostated a large collection of materials relating to Texas and New Mexico from the archives of Matamoros, a seaport near the mouth of the Río Grande.[14] The Matamoros *Ayuntamiento* Archives, 1720–1880 (67 volumes, 12,781 pages), include correspondence with various authorities, land records, notary records, royal decrees, communications and proclamations of the provincial governor and the comman-dant general, censuses, and lists of taxpayers, electors, etc.[15] Four sets of these reproductions were bound and placed in the University of Texas Archives, the Catholic Archives of Texas in the chancery office in Austin, the Bancroft Library of the University of California in Berkeley, and the Newberry Library in Chicago. A calendar of the collection was prepared by Castañeda, and a microfilm of the calendar is in the Manuscript Division of the Library of Congress. Photostats of vital statistics records from the archives of Camargo, Reynosa, and Mier, towns in Tamaulipas, on the Río Grande, are in the San Jacinto Museum Collections.

Since Texas was associated with Coahuila as a province during the eighteenth century and as a state after 1824, the archives of

---

[12] Texas, Library and Historical Commission, *Biennial Report*, 1911–12, pp. 15, 46–52 (list of transcripts from the Secretariat of Fomento); 1918–20, p. 32; 1920–22, p. 32; Connor, *Preliminary Guide*, p. 78. Some typescripts of documents in the Secretaría de Fomento relating to the colonization of Texas are also in the Bancroft Library of the University of California. (Hammond, *Guide to Ms. Colls. of the Bancroft Lib.*, p. 239).

[13] Carrera Stampa, *Archivalia mexicana*, pp. 182–83.

[14] Tate, "Microphotography in Mexico," p. 356.

[15] Castañeda and Dabbs, *Guide to the Latin American Mss.*, p. 180; Sister Claude Lane, *Catholic Archives of Texas: History and Preliminary Inventory* (Houston, 1961), p. 88.

Coahuila are important for the history of Texas.[16] In 1930–31 C. E. Castañeda selected and had photostated, in the archives of the government secretary in Saltillo, documents relating to colonization and missions in Coahuila and Texas.[17] The Saltillo Archives reproductions, 1689–1834 (50 volumes, 12,500 pages), in the University of Texas Archives are especially useful for the period of Anglo-American colonization of Texas.[18] These archives include commissions, autos, proclamations, inventories, lists of families, royal decrees, and Texas land grants and title transfers of American, Irish, German, and other colonies in Texas. Other sets of the Saltillo Archives photostats are in the Catholic Archives of Texas in Austin and the Bancroft Library of the University of California. Transcripts of Coahuila Archives, 1699–1824, in the Texas State Archives, were obtained by William E. Dunn.[19] Other copies from the Saltillo Archives, 1739–1876, are in the Archives of the Lady of the Lake College in San Antonio. Photocopies from the same archives are held by Trinity University, San Antonio, Texas.

An index and a calendar of the Coahuila photocopies have been prepared. The calendar was prepared in 1946, at the request of the Texas General Land Office, and contains volume and page numbers of the photostats as well as the *legajo* and *expediente* numbers of the originals. The University of Texas Archives also has proceedings of the Coahuila Congress, August, 1824–May, 1835 (1 foot, 2,026 pages).[20] This transcript of the congressional proceedings was obtained by Eugene C. Barker in 1922.[21] Microfilm of the congressional proceedings transcript is in the Library of Congress, where there is also a microfilm of the decrees of the congress, 1824–29, made from the photostat in the University of Texas Archives.[22]

Since 1962, the Instituto Tecnológico y de Estudios Superiores de Monterrey has been microfilming archives of municipalities in Nuevo León, Tamaulipas, and Coahuila. This program has been comprehensive, covering all civil and parish records in each municipality, and is being continued in cooperation with Trinity University of San

---

[16] Descriptions of archives in Saltillo containing materials relating to Texas are in Ethel Z. Rather, "Texas History Materials in Saltillo," *Southw. Hist. Quar.* 7 (Jan. 1904):244–45; Bolton, *Guide to Archives of Mexico*, pp. 422–40; Carrera Stampa, *Archivalia Mexicana*, p. 127.

[17] Castañeda, *Our Catholic Heritage in Texas*, 2:351–52; 5:442–71.

[18] Castañeda and Dabbs, *Guide to the Latin American Mss.*, p. 182.

[19] A list of the transcripts can be found in Texas, Library and Historical Commission, *Biennial Report*, 1911–12, pp. 57–63.

[20] Kielman, *Univ. of Texas Arch.*, p. 75.

[21] News note in *Southw. Hist. Quar.* 27 (April 1924):334.

[22] Jenkins and Hamrick, "Codes and Compilations," in *Guide to the Microfilm Collection of Early State Records*, p. 26. The decrees are printed in the compilations of Texas laws by H. P. N. Gammel and John and Henry Sayles.

Antonio.[23] Indexes relating to the municipal archives of Monterrey have been published, and indexes to the archives of other towns are in preparation.[24] An extension of the program into the neighboring states of Coahuila and Tamaulipas is planned. The archives of the commandancy general of the Interior Provinces have largely disappeared.[25] Early in the 1900s, there were a few documents of the commandancy general at Chihuahua, relating chiefly to the period when the headquarters was at Arizpe.[26] In the archives of the state of Nuevo León, at Monterrey, there are records of the commandancy general of the Interior Provinces and the Eastern Interior Provinces for the years since 1800.[27] Original letters and other documents relating to the administration of the Interior Provinces under Commandant General Teodoro de Croix, 1778–84 (9 folders, 257 pages), are in the Bancroft Library of the University of California, which also has a typescript of the correspondence of Commandant Teodoro de Croix, 1777–83 (5 volumes), obtained by Alfred B. Thomas from the Archivo General de Indias, Seville.[28]

Other more extensive microfilming programs in Mexican archives have since been planned and initiated. Since the early 1950s the Documentation Center of the Mexican National Institute of Anthropology and History has been microfilming selected materials from state and municipal archives.[29] The "Mexico on Microfilm" project was inaugurated in October, 1967 by a conference of forty-seven representatives from thirty institutions across the United States, held at Oyster Bay under the sponsorship of the State University System of New York. Its plan was to microfilm the extensive archives of the Real Audiencia of Guadalajara, the judicial archives of Jalisco, and other archives.[30] By 1970, the requisite number of institutions had been enlisted, and

[23] Jorge A. Manrique, "Una Colección importante para la historiografia del noroeste," *Historia mexicana* 16 (abril–junio 1967):636–43; Holmes, "Southwestern Archival Legacy," pp. 537–38.

[24] Eugenio del Hoyo, *Indice del Ramo de Causas Criminales del Archivo Municipal de Monterrey* (Monterrey, 1963); Israel Cavazos Garza, *Catálogo y síntesis de los protocolos del Archivo Municipal de Monterrey, 1599–1700* (Monterrey, 1966).

[25] Bolton, *Guide to Arch. of Mexico*, p. 460; Francisco R. Almada, "El Archivo de la Comandancia General de las Provincias Internas," *Boletín de la Sociedad Chihuahuense de Estudios Históricos* 1 (julio 1938):71–73; Carrera Stampa, *Archivalia Mexicana*, p. 129.

[26] Bolton, *Guide*, p. 452.

[27] Ibid., p. 413.

[28] Hammond, *Guide to Ms. Colls.*, pp. 49–50.

[29] Nettie L. Benson, "Microfilming Projects in Mexico," *News from the Center* [for the Coordination of Foreign Manuscript Copying, Library of Congress], No. 7, (Spring 1970), pp. 11–12.

[30] Ibid., p. 12.

the legal arrangements had been completed for this project, which is to be carried on with the assistance of the Mexican Academy of Genealogy and Heraldry. Texas Technological University became a full member of the consortium and will be the repository in Texas for the microfilm from Guadalajara.

The Texas representatives at the Oyster Bay meeting felt that it would be better for other Texas institutions to form their own consortium and arrange for microfilming in other areas of Mexico. After correspondence and meetings, the "Texas Consortium for Microfilming Mexican Archival Resources," composed of the Texas State Library and fifteen Texas academic institutions, was formed on March 6, 1969.[31] The members, or sometimes two or more in conjunction, agreed to microfilm within specific areas in Mexico. The University of Texas at Austin and the University of Houston are responsible for microfilming in Mexico State and México D.F. Trinity University at San Antonio has contracted with the Instituto Tecnológico y de Estudios Superiores de Monterrey for microfilming in the state of Nuevo León, including both the state archives and the municipal, judicial, and ecclesiastical records of Monterrey and three other municipalities. The Texas State Library is a partner in this arrangement. Pan American College, Texas A. & I., Abilene Christian College, and Southwestern Texas State University joined together in arranging a contract with Microfilmaciones Martineau S. A. to microfilm archives in the state of Tamaulipas. Other Texas institutions are to make arrangements for San Luís Potosí and Michoacán. The University of Texas at El Paso is to continue microfilming in Chihuahua and make arrangements for Durango. The object of this vast program is to microfilm all of Mexico's national, state, municipal, and ecclesiastical records. Even if only partly successful, it will add greatly to the microfilm holdings of Texas institutions.[32]

In 1914, a cooperative program for obtaining transcripts from Spanish archives was launched by the Universities of Texas and California, the Texas State Library, and the Library of Congress.[33] William E. Dunn directed the copying program in the Archivo General de Indias in Seville, from which materials relating to the American Southwest and

[31] Ibid., p. 13; Robert A. Houze, "The Texas Consortium for Microfilming the Mexican Archives," *Texas Library Journal* 45 (Fall 1969):120–22, 185–96.

[32] John M. Kinney. "The Texas Consortium to Microfilm Mexican Archival Resources," *College and Research Libraries* 32 (Sept. 1971):376–80.

[33] Griffin, "Foreign American History," p. 4; Lewis Hanke, "Mexican Microfilm Developments," *Library of Congress Quarterly Journal* 6 (Aug. 1949):11; U.S. Library of Congress, *Report of the Librarian of Congress*, 1915, p. 63; 1928, p. 230; Texas, Library and Historical Commission, *Report*, 1914–16, pp. 10, 45; 1918–20, p. 32.

the northern provinces of New Spain were obtained.[34] Charles H. Cunningham, a University of California fellow who worked in the Archivo General de las Indias during the years 1915–17, arranged for typewritten copies of documents, which he supplied to the Library of Congress, the Newberry Library, the University of Texas Library, and the Bancroft Library of the University of California.[35] Cunningham later directed copying in Spain for the Library of Congress.[36] The typewritten transcripts from the Archivo General de Indias, 1511–1850, in the University of Texas Archives amount to thirteen and one half feet.[37] A card index for the transcripts is available.

In 1927, as a result of a gift of $450,000 from John D. Rockefeller, Jr., the Library of Congress was able to inaugurate an extensive copying program in foreign archives.[38] Samuel F. Bemis, professor of history at George Washington University, was the general director of activities in Europe. In 1928, the initial agent of the Library in Spain was Lansing B. Bloom, of the University of New Mexico, with Roscoe R. Hill carrying on the work from October, 1928 to August, 1930. He was succeeded at Seville by Elizabeth H. West, and at Madrid by Charles C. Griffin. Using other funds, the library employed Irene A. Wright to continue the work in Spain until 1937, when the outbreak of civil war in that country forced her to leave. The Library of Congress Manuscript Division has selections on microfilm (some enlarged into photoprints for easier use) from the Archivo Histórico Nacional, Biblioteca Nacional, Biblioteca de Palacio, Archivo General de Indias, Biblioteca Colombina, Archivo General de Simancas, and the Biblioteca Pública de Toledo. Those from the Archivo General de Indias are on thirty-four reels and are from the following sections: Audiencias (Mexico), Contaduría, Contratación, Escribanía de Cámara, Justicia, Ministerio de Ultramar, and Papeles de Estado and Patronato Real.[39] The much smaller

---

[34] Castañeda and Dabbs, *Guide to Latin American Mss.*, p. 117; Lists of the Spanish transcripts appear in the *Report of the Librarian of Congress*, beginning in 1914. See also U.S. Library of Congress, *Handbook of Manuscripts in the Library of Congress*, (Washington, 1918), p. 458.

[35] Roscoe R. Hill, *American Missions in European Archives* (Mexico, 1951), p. 89; Castañeda and Dabbs, *Guide*, p. 117. The Cunningham transcripts have to be used with care, as the typists made many errors.

[36] U.S. Library of Congress, *Report of the Librarian of Congress*, 1923, p. 53; 1924, p. 65.

[37] Kielman, *Univ. of Texas Arch.*, p. 10.

[38] Hill, *American Missions*, pp. 71–73; U.S. Library of Congress, *Report of the Librarian of Congress*, 1928, pp. 236–37.

[39] Reproductions from the Archivo General de Indias relating to northern Mexico during the years 1600 to 1829 (103 reels) are in the State University of New York at Stony Brook.

selections from the Archivo General de Simancas are from the sections on Estado, Guerra Moderna, and Marina.

In the 1960s, the Library of Congress had an agent in Spain searching the archives for materials on the history of the Americas.[40] Additional microfilm selections obtained from the Archivo General de Indias came from the Audiencias (Guadalajara and Mexico), Indiferente General, and Patronato sections.[41]

The Rockefeller grant of 1927 also enabled the Library of Congress to send agents to Mexico. Beginning in 1929, France V. Scholes and, later, Robert S. Chamberlain and Vernon D. Tate, selected documents in the archives in Mexico City for photostating.[42] More than 50,000 pages of material were obtained from the Archivo General de la Nación, relating to the history of the American Southwest.[43] These were taken from the sections on the Californias, Civil, Guerra, Historia, Historia (Operaciones de Guerra), Inquisición, Marina, Provincias Internas, Reales Cédulas y Ordenes, Tierras, and Vinculos. The Library of Congress also has a large collection of photostats from the holdings of the Biblioteca Nacional.

The Library of Congress later obtained microfilm from Mexican archives. From 1948–51, a branch of the library's photoduplication section at the Benjamin Franklin Library in Mexico City microfilmed the official gazettes of the Mexican states.[44] In 1949, the Library of Congress itself microfilmed card catalogs in the Archivo General le la Nación for the following sections: Indios, Infidencia, Inquisición, Mercedes, Reales Cédulas (duplicadas), and Reales Cédulas (originales), and the Indice del Archivo de Cartas de Bienes Nacionales prepared by Jorge I. Rubio Mañé. In 1951, the Library of Congress made an agreement with the Instituto Nacional de Antropológia e Historia of Mexico City to microfilm in Mexico on a cooperative basis. From that arrangement, the library began receiving microfilm of Mexican state archives. Extensive microfilm in the Microfilm Reading Room of the Library of Congress from the archives at Guadalajara, Jalisco include Asuntos Eclesiasticos, 1575–1838 (21 reels); Civil, Sixteenth to early Nineteenth century (19 reels); Criminal, 1800, 1811, 1813, 1818 (2 reels); Libros

---

[40] U.S. Library of Congress, Report, 1963, p. 48.

[41] A Center for the Coordination of Foreign Manuscript Copying was operated in the Library of Congress from 1965 to 1970, to coordinate photocopying projects conducted in foreign libraries and archives by American scholars and institutions, and issued a news bulletin containing bibliographical titles on work that had been done in foreign archives.

[42] Hanke, "Mexican Microfilm Developments," p. 11.

[43] Hilton, Handbook of Hispanic Source Materials, p. 89; Hale, Guide to Photocopied Historical Materials, p. 210.

[44] U.S. Library of Congress, Report, 1951, p. 64; 1953, p. 21.

de Gobierno, 1676–1752 (29 reels); Reales Cédulas sobre diversos Asuntos, 1584–1695 (1 reel); Tierras y Aguas, 1584–1695 (3 reels); and a Catálogo del Archivo Civil y Administrativo. Some microfilm from the Archivo General de la Nación, Civil and Tierras ramos (5 reels), was received in 1967.

A union catalog of reproductions in American repositories from Mexican, and Spanish and other European archival and manuscript collections, would be of great assistance to American investigators.

Reproductions of maps relating to Texas in Mexican and Spanish archives are also held by American repositories. Several collections in the University of Texas Archives contain photographic copies of maps, as well as manuscript and printed maps.[45] The James Perry Bryan Map Collection in the University of Texas Archives consists of 122 maps, of which more than 30 are hand drawn copies of originals in the Archivo General de Indias in Seville.[46] Other maps are in the Latin American Collection in the University of Texas Library. An extensive collection of maps in the Texas State Archives includes photofilms of maps in the Archivo General de la Nación in Mexico, and photostats of maps in the S. F. Austin papers and other collections in the University of Texas Archives and the Texas Technological University Library.[47] The latter institution and the Stephen F. Austin College in Nacogdoches have copies of maps that are in the Texas State Archives. Copies of early maps of Texas are also in the Catholic Archives of Texas in Austin. Woodbury Lowery, historian of Spanish settlements in the United States, on trips to Europe between 1895 and 1903, obtained photographic copies of maps in archives in Madrid, Seville, London, and Paris, which passed into the possession of the Library of Congress.[48] Louis C. Karpinski, a professor of mathematics at the University of Michigan and interested in the history of American cartography, after working in the French archives, went to Spain and Portugal in 1927 and obtained photographic reproductions of maps relating to

---

[45] A description of early maps of Texas and a "List of Manuscript Maps of Texas 1822–1835" (pp. 44–55) are in Carlos E. Castañeda and Early Martin, Jr., *Three Manuscript Maps of Texas by Stephen Austin* (Austin, 1930).

[46] Ford Dixon, "Texas History in Maps: An Archival and Historical Examination of the James Perry Bryan Map Collection," *Texana* 5 (Summer, Fall, 1967):99–116, 238–67, presents historical data on Texas maps dated from 1813 to 1887, and a descriptive list of the maps in the Bryan collection.

[47] James M. Day, and others, *Maps of Texas, 1527–1900: The Map Collection of the Texas State Archives* (Austin, 1964), presents a chronological description.

[48] Henry P. Beers, *The French in North America: A Bibliographical Guide to French Archives, Reproductions, and Research Missions* (Baton Rouge, 1957), pp. 127–28; Woodbury Lowery, *The Lowery Collection: a Descriptive List of Maps of the Spanish within the Present Limits of the United States, 1502–1820*, ed. by Philip Lee Phillips (Washington, 1912).

America.[49] Sets of the photographs obtained by Karpinski are in the William L. Clements Library of the University of Michigan, the Map Division of the Library of Congress, the Henry E. Huntington Library, the Edward E. Ayer Collection of the Newberry Library, and the New York Public Library. This collection includes 200 photographs from repositories in Madrid and from the Archivo General de Indias in Seville.[50] The Map Division of the Library of Congress has photostats of other maps in Spanish repositories, including the Royal School of Navigation, relating to former Spanish possessions in the United States. James C. Massey is in charge, at the University of Pennsylvania, of the preparation of a guide to charts, maps, and plans of America in European archives, under the sponsorship of the Ford Foundation.

---

[49] Beers, *French in North America*, pp. 121–22.

[50] Louis C. Karpinski, "Manuscript Maps Relating to American History in French, Spanish and Portuguese Archives," *Mississippi Valley Hist. Rev.* 14 (Dec. 1927):438.

14

Documentary Publications

No SYSTEMATIC DOCUMENTARY SERIES on early Texas has been published, but there are extensive documentary materials in print.[1] A bibliography of travel accounts is available.[2] A treatise written between 1808–12, and related documents, collected by Frs. José Antonio Pichardo and Melchor de Talamantes under the direction of the king, to refute the contention of the United States that it acquired Texas with the Louisiana Purchase, are in print.[3] This compilation contains documents on the Spanish exploration and/or missionary settlement of Texas, New Mexico, Arizona, Oklahoma, and Kansas. Bolton's compilation on Athanase de Mézières contains documents on Spanish dominion in the Red River valley.[4] Many diaries, reports, and other documents from Mexican and Spanish archives and other repositories are in the *Southwestern Historical Quarterly*, for which cumulative indexes are

---

[1] The titles of these materials are in bibliographies by Mecham, Millares Carlo, Raines, Steck, Streeter, Wagner, and Winsor, listed in the bibliography. See also the bibliographies in the historical works by H. H. Bancroft. While at the University of Texas, Herbert E. Bolton corresponded with J. F. Jameson, director of the Carnegie Institution of Washington, and James A. Robertson, compiler of a guide for that institution, regarding a proposed documentary series on the Southwest composed of materials from the Mexican archives, but the series never materialized.

[2] Marilyn M. Sibley, *Travelers, in Texas, 1761–1860* (Austin, 1967), pp. 201–23.

[3] Charles W. Hackett, ed., *Pichardo's Treatise on the Limits of Louisiana and Texas*, 4 vols. (Austin, 1931–46).

[4] Herbert E. Bolton, trans. and ed., *Athanase de Mézières and the Louisiana-Texas Frontier, 1768–1780: Documents Published for the First Time, from the Original Spanish and French Manuscripts, Chiefly in the Archives of Mexico and Spain*, 2 vols. (Cleveland, Ohio, 1914).

available.[5] A chronological collection of letters and diaries by military officers and ecclesiastics, edited by Lino Gómez Canedo, on expeditions into Texas from Coahuila and Nuevo León in the late seventeenth century, includes some new materials from archives in Spain, Mexico, and Texas.[6] The Colección Chimalistac, edited by José Porrúa Turanzas, includes a volume relating in part to Texas.[7] A collection of selected illustrative documents from previously published compilations and Mexican and Spanish archives is also available.[8] Valuable for the history of northeastern Mexico and Texas is the report of Ramos de Arizpe, the deputy of Coahuila in the Spanish Cortes.[9]

Reconnoitering, planning for, and executing a realignment of the presidios on the northern frontier resulted in the preparation of a number of important documents that have been published. During 1766–68, on the instruction of Charles III of Spain, the Marqués de Rubí inspected the presidios on the northern frontier, from the Gulf of California to Louisiana, in order to recommend measures for improving the presidio system.[10] He was accompanied by Nicolás de Lafora, a captain of the Royal Engineers, who prepared a map and report of the tour that provides much information on the Indians and conditions along the frontier.[11] In 1772, the king issued a regulation based on the recommendations of the Marqués de Rubí, prescribing the manner of conducting relations with the Indians, the duties of the comman-

---

[5] The writers of these documents include Juan N. Almonte, Joaquín de Arredondo, Tienda de Cuervo, Juan B. Elguézabal, Pedro J. de la Fuente, Tadeo Ortiz de Ayala, Pierre M. F. de Pagès, and Manuel M. de Salcedo.

[6] Lino Gómez Canedo, ed., *Primeras exploraciones y poblamiento de Texas, 1686–1694* (Monterrey, 1968).

[7] José Porrúa Turanzas, ed., *Documentos para la historia eclesiastica y civil de la provincia de Texas, o Nuevas Philipinas, 1720–1779* (Madrid, 1962).

[8] Ernest Wallace and David M. Vigness, eds., *Documents of Texas History, Volume I (1528–1846)* (Lubbock, Texas, 1960).

[9] Nettie L. Benson, trans. and ed., *Report That Dr. Miguel Ramos de Arizpe, Priest of Bourbon and Deputy in the Present General and Special Cortes of Spain for the Province of Coahuila, One of the Four Eastern Interior Provinces of the Kingdom of Mexico, Presents to the August Congress on the Natural, Political and Civil Condition* . . . (Austin, 1950). Edition in Spanish: Vito Alessio Robles, ed., *Memoria [de Miguel Ramos de Arizpe] sobre el estado de las Provincias Internas de Oriente presentada a las Cortes de Cádiz* (México, 1932).

[10] David M. Vigness, "Don Hugo O'Conor and New Spain's Northeastern Frontier," *Journal of the West* 6 (Jan. 1967):30.

[11] Vito Alessio Robles, ed. *Relación del viaje que hizo a los presidios internos situados en la frontiera de la América septentrional* (Mexico, 1939); Lawrence Kinnaird, trans. and ed., *The Frontiers of New Spain: Nicolás de Lafora's Description, 1766–1768* (Berkeley, 1958). Lafora's map is reproduced in both of these publications. A large manuscript copy of the map (4½ ft. by 10½ ft.) is in the records of the Office of the Chief of Engineers (Record Group 77) in the National Archives, Washington, D.C.

dant inspector and other military personnel, and providing for a cordon of fifteen presidios, at intervals of about forty leagues, from Sonora to Texas.[12] The object was to prevent Apache raids from the north into settled areas and to bring the Indians under military control. In 1772, Hugo O'Conor was designated commandant inspector of the presidios in order to effectuate their rearrangement, a task that occupied him for several years and necessitated extensive traveling on the frontier. A report by O'Conor, submitted on the completion of the assignment in 1776, has been published.[13]

---

[12] "Rules and Regulations for the Presidios to be Established on the Frontier Line of New Spain, Ordered by Our Lord the King in a Decree of September 10, 1772," in John Galvin, ed., and Adelaide Smithers, trans., *The Coming of Justice to California: Three Documents* (San Francisco, 1963), pp. 3–45. This is a translation of the Mexican edition of 1773. A reprint of the Mexican edition of 1834, with English translation on opposite pages, is in Sidney B. Brinckerhoff and Odie B. Faulk, *Lancers for the King: A Study of the Frontier Military System of New Spain, with a Translation of the Royal Regulations of 1772* (Phoenix, 1965), pp. 11–67.

[13] Enrique González Flores and Francisco Almada, eds., *Informe sobre el estado de las Provincias Internas del Norte, 1771–1776* (Mexico, 1952). A manuscript copy of O'Conor's report is in the De Golyer Foundation Library, Southern Methodist University, Dallas, Texas.

15

Manuscript Collections

THE OFFICIAL RECORDS of colonial Texas can be supplemented by important collections of manuscripts in repositories in Texas and elsewhere. Many of these collections are papers of officials and contain official documents. The manuscripts of individuals often contain official documents or papers containing information about official matters.

Small collections of papers in the University of Texas Archives supply information about government affairs and other matters during the Spanish and Mexican periods.[1] The Canary Islanders' records, 1730–31 (8 inches), relate to the settlement of fifty-six persons from those islands at San Antonio. Legal papers of Manuel de la Fuente, 1770 (1 volume), relate to a suit between him and Manuel Delgado over a ranch at San Antonio. The Vicente Alvarez Travieso papers, 1771–83 (1 volume, English translation), contain protests against land claims made by San Antonio missions. A compendium by Lt. Antonio Bonilla on events in Texas from 1685 to 1772 was prepared, at the request of the viceroy, from archival sources in Mexico City.[2] Reports of Juan Bautista de Elguezábal, 1799–1805 (1½ inches), concern his activities as a Spanish colonial administrator and governor of Texas (1800–05). Correspondence of Philip Nolan, 1800–03 (copies from the collections of Frost Woodhull), relate to his activities in Texas and Louisiana. The Louis Aury papers, 1803–21 (1 inch), concern in part

---

[1] These collections sometimes consist of original manuscripts, photocopies, and typescript, and sometimes of only photocopies or typescript. Descriptions of the papers are in Kielman, *Univ. of Texas Arch.*

[2] Elizabeth H. West, trans. and ed., "Bonilla's Brief Compendium of the History of Texas, 1772," *Southw. Hist. Quar.* 8 (July 1904):3–78.

his activities as a privateersman under the Mexican Republic and as governor of Texas at Galveston. Gov. Manuel María de Salcedo's report, 1809, supplies information on conditions in Texas.[3] José Bernardo Gutiérrez de Lara, governor of Tamaulipas, commandant general of the Interior Provinces, and, later, a leader in the Mexican independence movement, is represented by papers, 1813–79 (30 items). Gov. Antonio María Martínez's letters, 1817–19 (2 volumes, typescript), relate to his official activities as the last Spanish governor of Texas.[4] Juan Antonio Padilla's report on the Indians of Texas, 1819, has been published.[5] Papers of Peter Ellis Bean, 1826–56 (10 items), pertain to his marriages and his estate. (After participating in the Mexican revolution, he settled near Nacogdoches in 1823 and was appointed Mexican Indian agent for east Texas in 1825.) The papers of José Juan Sánchez-Navarro, 1831–39 (3½ inches), are connected with the Office of Adjutant Inspector of Nuevo León and Tamaulipas and relate to military operations in Texas. Letters of Erasmo Seguín, 1823–24 (1 inch), are typed. (Seguín, a resident of San Antonio and first alcalde there in 1820, became a representative of Texas in the Mexican Congress in 1823, and participated in the framing of the Mexican Constitution in 1824.) Copies of diaries include the Marqués de Aguayo's diary of his expedition into Texas in 1720–22; Gov. Pedro del Barrio Junco y Espriella's inspection of La Bahía del Espíritu Santo in 1749; Juan Fernando de Palacio's diary of a visit by him and José de Ossorio y Llamas to San Agustín de Laredo in 1767; and Pedro Vial's diary, 1786–93, covering exploratory trips between San Antonio and Santa Fe.[6]

The Austin papers were scattered and partially destroyed during the Mexican invasion of Texas in 1836. After the death of Stephen F. Austin, near the end of that year, the papers became the property of his sister, Emily Austin Perry, who passed them on to her son, Guy M. Bryan. Bryan kept them in his home at Quintana and drew upon them for historical purposes. The papers were examined there by Lester G. Bugbee in 1896–97. Friendships which developed between Bryan, Bugbee, and Prof. G. P. Garrison resulted in Bryan's four children giving some of the papers to the University of Texas in 1902.[7]

---

[3] Nettie L. Benson, trans. and ed., "A Governor's Report on Texas in 1809," *Southw. Hist. Quar.* 71 (April 1968):603–15.

[4] Concerning Martínez, see material on the Nacogdoches archives in chapter 17.

[5] Mattie A. Hatcher, trans., "Texas in 1820: Report on the Barbarous Indians of the Province of Texas by Juan Antonio Padilla," *Southw. Hist. Quar.* 23 (July 1919):47–60.

[6] Concerning Pedro Vial, see Chapter 5, in the section on New Mexico.

[7] Barker, "To Whom Credit Is Due," p. 7.

At that time, a considerable part of the Austin papers was retained by Bryan's daughter, Mrs. Hally Bryan Perry; from this residue, which is largely of a personal nature, the university obtained transcripts of the more pertinent documents.

The Stephen F. Austin papers, 1793–1836 (7,600 items; 15,000 pages; manuscripts, typescripts, photocopies), consist of correspondence with Mexican authorities and others, personal correspondence, petitions and memorials addressed to the state and national governments of Mexico, political addresses, decrees, proclamations, legal documents, military papers, physiographical observations, accounts, receipts, licenses, lists of immigrants, business memoranda, censuses, and copies of state and federal laws.[8] Maps include not only maps of Texas prepared by Austin, but others collected by him.[9] Other records relating to land in Austin's colonies include field notes, surveys, grants, and deeds. Censuses that were submitted to Austin by the alcaldes of the settlements were sometimes merely statistical in content, but others supply the names of heads of families, data as to occupations, and the number of children and servants. Varied in subject matter, the Austin papers provide important information on the administration of Austin's and other Texas colonies, Austin's relations with the Mexican government and the government of Coahuila and Texas, military and Indian affairs, internal improvements, education, judicial administration, customs administration, commerce, slavery, and the Texas insurrection.

After years of preparation, during which the Austin papers were arranged and indexed, and reproductions of Austin materials were obtained from many other repositories, the publication of the Austin papers began in 1924, under the editorship of Eugene C. Barker of the University of Texas.[10] Containing the papers of both Stephen F. Austin and his father, Moses Austin, the *Austin Papers* are the most valuable source in print for the history of the Anglo-American colonization of Texas. The published documents cover numerous subjects and are significant not only for Austin's colonies, but for other colo-

---

[8] Kielman, *Univ. of Texas Arch.*, pp. 12–14, lists the names of persons and places associated with the papers.

[9] Jay W. Sharp, "The Maps of the Stephen F. Austin Collection," *Southw. Hist. Quar.* 64 (January 1961):388–97, contains an alphabetically arranged list of the maps; see also Castañeda and Martin, *Three Manuscript Maps of Texas by Stephen Austin.*

[10] Eugene C. Barker, ed., *The Austin Papers* (American Historical Association, *Annual Report*, 1919, vol. 2, pts. 1 and 2; 1922, vol. 2, [Washington, 1924 ,1928]); Eugene C. Barker, ed., *The Austin Papers, October 1834–January, 1837* (Austin, 1926). Other Austin manuscripts published by Barker include "Journal of Stephen F. Austin on His First Trip to Texas, 1821," *Southw. Hist. Quar.* 7 (Apr. 1904):286–

nies also, and for the operations of various *ayuntamientos*. Copies of Stephen F. Austin's outgoing letters are generally not available in his papers, but some obtained from other collections have been published. Limitations of space prevented the publication of all the papers; those not printed are briefed in a calendar in the printed volumes, and they have since been placed in a separate chronological file for easier reference.

Other manuscript collections in the University of Texas Archives also contain considerable Austin material. The papers of Moses Austin Bryan, a nephew of S. F. Austin, concern in part his activities as secretary to Austin after 1831. James Franklin Perry, Austin's brother-in-law, served as his agent during his absence in Mexico in 1833–35, and as the administrator of his estate. The J. F. Perry papers, 1825–74, include correspondence, legal papers, account books, surveys, maps, drawings, and other papers relating to land transactions, lawsuits over land in Austin's colony, early colonization and immigration in Texas, and politics of the Mexican period. The papers of Robert Peebles, 1832–87, relate in part to his activities as land commissioner for Austin's colony and include land surveys, and other land transactions. Other papers useful for land transactions in Austin's colony include those of Henry Austin, 1806–51; the account book of J. B. Austin, 1825–37; and the papers (1830–1908) of Gail Borden, Jr., who did surveying for S. F. Austin. The papers of Guy M. Bryan also contain material relating to Austin.

Papers in the University of Texas Archives of other Americans who immigrated to Texas during the Mexican period are useful for colonization and settlement, land transactions, business operations, governmental affairs, the movement for Texas independence, and the Texas revolution.[11] A photocopy of the grant made to Martín de León, and a related deposition, 1833, concern his colony at Victoria on the Guadalupe River. A collection of papers relating to James W. Fannin (1820–36, 310 leaves), a Georgian who settled at Velasco in 1834 and joined the Texas army in the war against Mexico, was assembled by Samuel Asbury. A few papers of George Fisher (1830–

307; "General Austin's Order Book for the Campaign of 1835," ibid. 11 (July 1907):1–55; "Descriptions of Texas by Stephen F. Austin," ibid. 28 (Oct. 1924):98–121; "The Prison Journal of Stephen F. Austin," ibid. 2 (1898–99):183–210. A hitherto undiscovered letter written by Austin from Mexico on March 31, 1835 is in Henry P. Beers, ed., "Stephen F. Austin and Anthony Butler, Documents," ibid. 62 (Oct. 1958):233–40.

[11] Biographical sketches of the persons mentioned here are in Webb, *Handbook of Texas*; Texas, Legislature, House of Representatives, *Biographical Directory of the Texas Conventions and Congresses, 1832–1845* (Austin, 1941); and in Louis W. Kemp, *The Signers of the Texas Declaration of Independence* (Salada, Tex., 1959).

48), customs officer at Galveston, are copies. The Sam Houston papers, 1814–61 (6 feet, 3 inches), are largely photocopies obtained from many repositories for use in preparing a published edition of his writings.[12] Though he had visited Nacogdoches before, Houston did not settle there until 1835, so his papers are useful for the movement for Texas independence, the war between Texas and Mexico, and his later career in Texas politics. Ira Ingram, an original settler of Austin's colony in 1824, was a merchant at San Felipe, a politician, and a landowner, whose letters, 1830–35 (10 items), concern political activities at Matagorda and Goliad that led up to the Texas revolution. Dr. Anson Jones arrived in Texas late in 1833, built up a medical practice in Brazoria, and embarked on a political career. The Anson Jones papers, 1809–1910 (3 feet), contain a variety of materials useful for his personal affairs, land transactions, business affairs, and political events of 1835 and later years. Collin McKinney settled on the Red River in 1831, farmed, and represented the area in the Texas Convention of 1836. McKinney's papers, 1809–54 (manuscripts and copies), relate to his farming, land, and political activities. Henry Raguet opened a mercantile firm, in partnership with William G. Logan, at Nacogdoches in 1833 and soon became active in politics there. The Raguet family papers, 1786–1924, contain materials relating to Henry Raguet's activities as a merchant, land speculator, and chairman of the committee of vigilance and safety at Nacogdoches. Thomas J. Rusk arrived in Nacogdoches in 1832 and became an attorney, soldier, and politician. The T. J. Rusk papers, 1824–59, are important for military and political events that terminated the allegiance of Texas to Mexico. Henry Smith settled in Brazoria in 1827, farmed, surveyed land, and was elected alcalde of Brazoria in 1833. Henry Smith's papers, 1834–79, relate largely to his land activities. In 1832, William B. Travis opened a law office in San Felipe de Austin, became secretary of the *ayuntamiento* there in 1834, and was killed at the Alamo in 1836. The Travis papers, 1831–1924 (1 foot, 7 inches), include some concerning his activities as a lawyer and soldier.[13] Correspondence and legal documents of Samuel May Williams, 1832–91 (1 inch), relate to his business activities.[14]

---

[12] Amelia W. William and Eugene C. Barker, eds., *The Writings of Sam Houston, 1813–1863*, 8 vols. (Austin, 1938–43). Documents relating to Texas affairs of 1835–36 are in vols. 1–4.

[13] A diary from the Travis papers has been published: Robert E. Davis, ed., and Thomas W. Walker, trans., *The Diary of William Barret Travis, August 30, 1833–June 26, 1834* (Waco, Tex., 1966).

[14] Selections from the manuscripts described above have been published in facsimile in Ernest W. Winkler, ed., *Manuscript Letters and Documents of Early Texians, 1821–1835* (Austin, 1937).

Several groups of miscellaneous manuscripts, assembled by collectors and acquired by the University of Texas Archives, provide further documentation on Texas history. The Alexander Dienst Collection, 1765–1927 (mainly 1826–1900; 4 feet; 3 inches), consists of correspondence, diaries, legal documents, and other materials on the personal and business affairs of numerous persons active in the Mexican period, and on education, politics, military affairs, and social matters. The Earl Vandale Collection, ca. 1819–ca. 1947 (23 feet), contains a wide variety of documents relating in part to the Mexican government of Texas, colonization, the consultation at San Felipe de Austin, the declaration of 1835, the convention of 1836, the war between Texas and Mexico, and the public career of Sam Houston.

After the death of Sterling C. Robertson in 1842, his papers passed into the hands of his son and remained in the possession of the family for many years. Some of the papers were carried off from the family homes at Salada and Temple by other relatives. Papers that were taken by Mrs. Cone Johnson were used for a publication that contains the texts of some documents.[15] In 1935, a granddaughter presented a small collection of Robertson papers, 1824–65 (17 items), including items relating to his colony, to the University of Texas Archives.[16] The principal collection of Robertson papers was presented to Texas Christian University in October, 1968, by a great granddaughter. These Robertson papers include plans for his colony, correspondence with officials in Mexico City and Saltillo, letters from prospective colonists, and lists of settlers.[17] Malcolm D. McLean, a great grandson of Robertson and professor of Spanish at Texas Christian University, Fort Worth, has custody of other papers, and has collected transcripts of papers relating to Robertson and his colony from family and other private collections, and archives and libraries in Texas, Kentucky, Washington, D.C. and Mexico, for more than thirty years, and prepared them for publication.[18]

---

[15] William C. Harllee, "Sterling Clack Robertson," in *A Genealogical and Biographical Record* . . . (New Orleans, 1937), 3:2813–65.

[16] Kielman, *Univ. of Texas Arch.*, pp. 302–03.

[17] News note in *Southw. Hist. Quar.* 72 (Jan. 1969):397.

[18] Malcolm D. McLean, "Report on the Compilation of the Sterling C. Robertson Papers," *Southw. Hist. Quar.* 47 (Apr. 1944):411–12; 48 (Apr. 1945):556–58; letter from Malcolm D. McLean, Apr. 7, 1954. A few documents relative to Robertson's efforts to recover his grant from Austin, derived apparently from the archives at Saltillo, are printed in Brown's *Hist. of Texas*. Malcolm D. McLean, ed., *Papers Concerning Robertson's Colony in Texas* (Fort Worth, 1974–75), vol. 1, 1788–1822, contains a variety of documents in chronological order with English translations of Spanish language documents. Volume 2, 1823–28, contains documents relating to Robert Leftwich's grant in central Texas, which became known as the Robertson colony.

Concerning the Galveston Bay and Texas Land Company, which took over the empresario contracts of Burnet, Vehlein, and Zavala, there are manuscripts in a number of collections. The company itself, in an effort to induce settlement, published documents relative to the grants and the organization of the company.[19] A photocopy of an 1834 circular describing the company's grant is in the University of Texas Archives. The original empresarios continued as trustees of the company, and two of them, David G. Burnet and Lorenzo de Zavala, became prominent in the affairs of Texas. Papers of David G. Burnet, 1798–1899 (1 foot, 2 inches), in the University of Texas Archives include correspondence, financial papers, legal documents, memorandum books, and other materials relating in part to the colonization of Texas and land claims. Other Burnet papers are in the Rosenberg Library in Galveston and the Texas State Archives. Papers of Lorenzo de Zavala in the University of Texas Archives include material on his activities as an empresario.[20] Letters of John Thomson Mason, agent of the company in Mexico during 1831–34, were used for a biographical article.[21] A lengthy search by E. C. Barker to locate Mason's papers ended in 1922 when Barker learned that they had been burned not long before.[22] A considerable collection of papers of George W. Smyth (1819–92), surveyor and then land commissioner for the company, was presented about 1932 to the University of Texas.[23] Anthony Butler, the United States chargé in Mexico City, 1829–35, was a large scrip holder in the company, and hence his papers, 1810–46, also in the University of Texas Archives, are of interest for its affairs.[24]

The management of the colony established by James Power and James Hewetson in Refugio County was left in the hands of Power. Hewetson continued to reside in Mexico in order to look after the large estates owned by his wife. In the course of research on the history of this colony, Father Oberste located several collections of papers of James Power that were in the hands of his grandchildren and were

[19] Galveston Bay and Texas Land Company, *Address to the Reader of the Documents Relating to the Galveston Bay & Texas Land Company, Which Are Contained in the Appendix* (New York, 1931).

[20] H. Bailey Carroll, "Texas Collection," *Southw. Hist. Quar.* 55 (Jan. 1952):405–06, contains a description of the De Zavala papers.

[21] Kate M. Rowland, "General John Thomson Mason," *Southw. Hist. Quar.* 11 (Jan. 1908):163–98.

[22] Barker, *Stephen F. Austin*, p. 324 n. 57. Two letters of Mason, April 18, 1831 and February 14, 1835, are in the Andrew Jackson Papers, Library of Congress. Correspondence of Thomson with his son and daughters, in the Detroit Public Library, relates partly to his business activities in Texas and Mexico. (*Natl. Union Catalog Ms. Colls.*, 1970, entry 1179).

[23] Kielman, *Univ. of Texas Arch.*, p. 340.

[24] Eugene C. Barker, "Private Papers of Anthony Butler," *The Nation* 92 (June 15, 1911):600–01; Kielman, *Univ. of Texas Arch.*, p. 58.

highly important for an adequate treatment of the subject. [25] A visit to Ireland, from whence colonists were brought to Texas, produced very little information, and no documents were found in public archives. Papers of James Hewetson that were found in Thomastown, County Kilkenny, Ireland, were later donated by the owner to the Most Rev. Lawrence J. FitzSimon, bishop of Amarillo, Texas, for his collection of Texana.[26] The Oberste collection, 1793–1830 (3 feet), in the Catholic Archives of Texas in the chancery office in Austin consists mainly of photocopies, transcripts, translations, and notes relating to the history of Refugio.[27] Father Oberste was unsuccessful in his attempts to locate papers of McMullen and McGloin, the colonizers of San Patricio County.

Documents also exist concerning the unsuccessful efforts of empresarios to establish colonies. For the colony of Beales and Grant at Dolores, there is documentation in both manuscript and printed form. A collection of documents relative to the estate of Dr. James Grant is in the records of the municipality of Brazoria at Angleton, Texas.[28] The John C. Beales papers, 1832–55 (1½ inches), in the University of Texas Archives, include material relative to his Río Grande colony and his efforts to secure the restoration of his Mexican land grants.[29] Papers pertaining to the colony of Beales and Grant are in the Lorenzo de Zavala papers in the University of Texas Archives, and photocopies of a few Beales papers are in the same repository. A journal by Beales for December, 1833, to March, 1834, the period of the establishment of the colony, soon found its way into print.[30] Additional documents relative to its founding, and other legal papers, have also been printed.[31] Papers relating to the varied career of Benjamin R. Milam, including some concerning his colonizing activities

---

[25] William H. Oberste, *Texas Irish Empresarios and Their Colonies, Power & Hewetson, McMullen & McGloin; Refugio — San Patricio* (Austin, 1953), pp. ix, 24 n. 11.

[26] Ibid., pp. x, 25 n. 13.

[27] Lane, *Catholic Arch. of Texas*, p. 83.

[28] Historical Records Survey, Texas, *Inventory of the Colonial Archives of Texas, 1821–1837, No. 3, Municipality of Brazoria, 1832–1837 (Brazoria County Courthouse, Angleton, Texas)* (San Antonio, 1937), p. 33.

[29] Kielman, *Univ. of Texas Arch.*, p. 24.

[30] William Kennedy, *Texas: The Rise, Progress, and Prospects of the Republic of Texas*, 2 vols. (London, 1841), pp. 30–56.

[31] *Documents Relating to a Grant of Land made to John Charles Beales and José Manuel Royuela in Texas* (New York, 1833); *An Abstract of the Constitution, Laws, and Other Documents Having Reference to, and Including the Impresario Grants and Contracts Made by the State of Coahuila and Texas to and with John Charles Beales; Also, Deeds of the Same from Him to John Woodward; to Which Is Appended an Argument Sustaining the Rights and Titles of John Woodward* (New York, 1842); John D. Freeman, *Memorial of Doctor John Charles Beales et al., vs.*

on the Red River, were preserved by several descendants.[32] Transcripts from one of these collections, and other Milam papers, 1819–35, including land papers, are in the University of Texas Archives.[33] A few of these documents have been published.[34] About 400 pages of typescript of Milam's letters and a genealogy are in the Texas State Archives.[35] Concerning the Arthur G. Wavell colony, there is a copy of the colonization contract and a register of settlers in the University of Texas Archives.[36] The A. G. Wavell papers in the Texas State Archives number about 250 items.[37] A prospectus issued by Wavell and Milam, in an effort to promote settlement in the Wavell grant, has been published.[38] Some notes and papers on the Wavell colony collected by the editor of that reprint are in the Texas State Archives. Not long before the original appearance of the prospectus in pamphlet form, Wavell contributed a description of Texas to an early English work on Mexico.[39]

Other manuscripts purchased by the University of Texas Library and now in its Latin American Collection contain documents relating to Texas and the Southwest. The Genaro García library comprises 350,000 pages of manuscripts for the years 1325–1921, including the papers of Vicente Guerrero, president of Mexico, April–December, 1829; Valentín Gómez Farías, acting president of Mexico, 1833–34; Antonio López de Santa Anna, commander of the Mexican army that invaded Texas in 1836; and many broadsides, pamphlets, and other publications.[40] The Juan E. Hernández y Dávalos (a historian) collection, 1700–1840 (5,000 items), comprises many documents supplementary to his published compilation on the war of independence.[41]

The United States, Narrating the Establishment of a Mexican Colony on the Rio Grande . . . (Washington[?], 1870). A history of the colony is in Carl C. Rister, Comanche Bondage: Dr. Charles Beales' Settlement of La Villa de Dolores on Las Moras Creek in Southern Texas . . . (Glendale, Calif., 1955), pp. 21–93.

[32] Lois Garver, "Benjamin Rush Milam," Southw. Hist. Quar. 38 (Oct. 1934, Jan. 1935):104 n. 31, 176 n. 117, 188 n. 8, 200.

[33] Kielman, Univ. of Texas, Arch., p. 248.

[34] Frederick C. Chabot, ed., Texas Letters (San Antonio, 1940), pp. 55–60.

[35] Connor, Guide to Arch. of Texas, p. 59.

[36] Kielman, Univ. of Texas Arch., p. 384.

[37] Connor, Guide to Arch. of Texas, p. 84. These materials include a list of family papers obtained from a grandson, Gen. Archibald Wavell.

[38] Robert Amsler, ed., "A Prospectus for the Wavell Colony in Texas," Southw. Hist. Quar. 56 (Apr. 1953):543–51.

[39] Arthur G. Wavell, "Account of the Province of Texas," in Henry George Ward, Mexico in 1827, 2 vols. (London, 1828), app. B, 1:547–59.

[40] Castañeda and Dabbs, Guide to Latin American Mss., p. vii; Carlos E. Castañeda, "A Great Literary Collection," Mexican Life 16 (Sept. 1940):30.

[41] News note in Univ. Texas Lib. Chron. 1 (Summer 1944):31. These documents were acquired by Hernández y Dávalos after the publication of his Colección de

The collection assembled by oil man William B. Stephens contains 20,000 pages relating to the Spanish Southwest, 1488–1860.[42] The Alejandro Prieto collection, 1823–80 (3,000 items), also concerns the Southwest but relates mainly to Tamaulipas.[43] The Sánchez-Navarro papers, 1658–1895 (4,000 items), concern the affairs of a family that once owned a large part of the state of Coahuila.[44] Original records of Janos, Chihuahua, 1706–1858 (8 feet), include presidial and parish records. Numerous maps are also in the Latin American Collection.

The Archives Division of the Texas State Library has records of the Republic of Texas that include manuscripts on the Mexican period. The State Department's domestic correspondence contains both official and personal manuscripts dating from 1822.[45] Less extensive is a file of papers of the Bureau of Indian Affairs and other departments on Indian affairs, 1825–45.[46] Another group is designated colonization papers, 1824–45. The beginnings of Texas administration are documented in the records of the provisional government of Texas, 1835–36.[47] Laws and decrees of the state of Coahuila and Texas, 1827–35, are also among the division's holdings.[48]

The Archives Division of the Texas State Library is also the repository of papers of men who were active in various official capacities.[49] The papers of George Fisher, 1829–56 (50 items), contain correspondence relating to the collection of customs at Galveston. Correspondence and other papers of José Bernardo Gutiérrez de Lara, 1811–42,

---

documentos para la historia de la Guerra de Independencia de México de 1808 a 1821, 6 vols. (Mexico, 1877–82), and have not been published. See Carlos E. Castañeda and Jack A. Dabbs, *Independent Mexico in Documents: Independence, Empire and Republic: A Calendar of the Juan B. Hernández y Dávalos Manuscript Collection* (Mexico, 1954).

[42] Spell, *Research Materials for the Study of Latin America,* p. 5.

[43] Philip M. Hamer, ed., *A Guide to Archives and Manuscripts in the United States* (New Haven, 1961), p. 585.

[44] News note in *Univ. Texas Lib. Chron.* 1 (Summer 1944):31–32; Spell, *Research Materials,* pp. 5, 7.

[45] Connor, *Guide to Arch. of Texas,* p. 72.

[46] These papers became so worn from use that they have been printed: Dorman H. Winfrey, and others, eds., *Texas Indian Papers, 1825–1843* (Austin, 1959).

[47] Described and published in William C. Binkley, ed., *Official Correspondence of the Texas Revolution, 1835–36,* 2 vols. (New York, 1936). See also Rupert N. Richardson, "Framing the Constitution of the Republic of Texas," *Southw. Hist. Quar.* 31 (Jan. 1928):191–221.

[48] Microfilm of the laws and decrees is in the Library of Congress (Jenkins and Hamrick, "Session Laws" *Guide to the Microfilm Collection of Early State Records,* p. 184. They are printed in Sayles, *Early Laws of Texas,* vol. 1, and Gammel, *Laws of Texas,* vol. 1.

[49] Brief entries regarding these papers are in Connor, *Guide to Arch. of Texas,* passim. Some of the papers are described in more detail in the *Natl. Union Catalog of Ms. Colls.*

concern his activities in 1811–12 in the movement for Mexican independence.[50] James R. Kerr, a physician and surveyor of DeWitt's and Milam's colonies, and a member of the Texas Convention of 1832, is represented by a small group of papers for 1813–66. Mirabeau Buonaparte Lamar, who arrived in Texas in 1836 and became an official of the Republic of Texas, preserved not only his own papers but collected other manuscripts relating to the earlier history of Texas and Mexico.[51] A 1795 account of expenses incurred by Gov. Manuel Muñoz relates to the maintenance of various Indian tribes. Letters received by Sam Houston from Andrew Jackson, 1825–44, are reproductions of privately held papers. A recent acquisition of Sam Houston papers, 1812–75 (4,800 items), that had been preserved by his son, Andrew Jackson Houston, and granddaughters, includes over 200 documents dated up to 1836 — some that have never been published. Correspondence of Eleazer L. R. Wheelock (1823–1911), who settled in Texas in 1833, surveyed land, and joined the Texas army, includes letters from S. F. Austin, Sam Houston, and other Texas leaders. Thomas J. Chambers was an official of Coahuila and Texas, a Texas land owner, a participant in the movement for Texas independence, an attorney, and a Texas army officer. The T. J. Chambers papers, 1833–92 (800 items), consist partly of photocopies and typed transcripts, and relate mainly to his land activities.

Other repositories in Texas have collections of papers containing official materials. The papers of Elisha M. Pease, secretary of the committee of safety at Mina and later of the General Council, are in the Austin Public Library. Correspondence and other papers of Charles S. Taylor, 1828–62 (2,000 items), are in the Catholic Archives of Texas in the Catholic chancery office in Austin.[52] In the 1830s, Taylor was successively a member of the *ayuntamiento of* Nacogdoches, alcalde of San Augustine, land commissioner of the municipality of San Augustine, and a member of the conventions of 1832 and 1836. The William E. Howard Collection of printed materials and 2,500 documents and letters, in the Dallas Historical Society, contains source

---

[50] A diary from these papers concerning a mission that Gutiérrez de Lara made to Washington to obtain aid from the U.S. government has been published: Elizabeth H. West, ed., "Diary of José Bernardo Gutiérrez de Lara, 1811–1812," *Am. Hist. Rev.* 34 (Oct. 1938, Jan. 1929):55–77, 281–94. A product of the Gutiérrez-Magee expedition into Texas in 1812–13 was the first constitution of Texas, which has been published from a manuscript copy in the records of the U.S. Department of State in Kathryn Garrett, ed., "The First Constitution of Texas, Apr. 17, 1813," *Southw. Hist. Quar.* 40 (Apr. 1937):305–08.

[51] Some of these earlier documents, including an account by Gutiérrez de Lara of August 1, 1815 of the progress of the revolution, are in Gulick, and others, *Papers of M. B. Lamar*, vol. 1.

[52] Lane, *Catholic Arch. of Texas*, p. 95.

material on Texas and Mexican history. The papers of Gail Borden, Jr., 1832–82 (2 volumes and 290 items), are in the Rosenberg Library in Galveston. Borden was a surveyor for S. F. Austin, collector of customs at Galveston, and a member of the convention of 1833 at San Felipe de Austin. The Samuel May Williams papers, 1819–84 (4,000 items) were presented to the Rosenberg Library by his daughter and grandson in 1922. Williams was secretary and recorder of Austin's colony from 1824 to 1834, postmaster at San Felipe after 1826, and agent there for the administrator of taxes at San Antonio. The Williams papers contain many letters from S. F. Austin and Mexican officials for the years before the Texas Revolution, account books for 1824–34, and various documents relating to the administration of the postal system. The collection was arranged chronologically, calendared, and indexed during 1945–55.[53] Other materials in the Rosenberg Library include correspondence between Mexican and Texas officials, and many printed orders and decrees issued by Mexican authorities.[54] The constitution of Gonzales, 1831, and Green DeWitt's empresario contract are in the Gonzales Memorial Museum.[55] An extensive East Texas Collection, dating from 1699, containing original manuscripts, photostats, typescripts, and microreproductions, is in the Stephen F. Austin College Library in Nacogdoches.[56] Some parts of this collection, such as the Béxar Archives and the Nacogdoches Archives, are described in earlier chapters in this section. The collection in that repository also includes papers of the Kuykendall family, 1822–97 (4 volumes), and letters and papers of Charles S. Taylor, 1810–93 (500 items). Another William E. Howard Collection, presented to the Alamo Museum in San Antonio in 1943, includes Spanish and Mexican documents.[57] The San Jacinto Museum has 500,000 pages of manuscript decrees; reports of missionaries; records of ranches, pueblos, convents, presidios, and colleges; grants and conveyances of land; reports of explorers; taxation schedules; manifestoes of political juntas; and personal, family, and business documents.[58] These holdings include materials relating

---

[53] A brief biography and calendar of the Williams papers are in Ruth G. Nichols and S. W. Lifflander, *Samuel May Williams, 1795–1858* (Galveston, 1956). A transcription of the Williams papers was completed by the Historical Records Survey of the Work Projects Administration in 1942.

[54] News note in *Miss. Valley Hist. Rev.* 10 (Dec. 1923):340–41.

[55] James M. Day and Donna Yarbrough, *Handbook of Texas Archival and Manuscript Depositories* (Austin, 1966), p. 46.

[56] Ibid., p. 56.

[57] Daughters of the Republic of Texas, Library, *Chronological List of Framed Documents from Dr. Wm. E. Howard Collection* (San Antonio, 1950).

[58] Ronald Hilton, ed., *Handbook of Hispanic Source Materials and Research Organizations in the United States* (Stanford, 1956), p. 375.

to Stephen F. Austin and Samuel Houston. Fifty Sam Houston items are in the Baylor University Library in Waco.

Repositories in places outside of Texas have important materials relating to Texas. Manuscripts in the Bancroft Library of the University of California include documents relating to the settlement of Canary Islanders in the San Antonio area, 1729–30 (210 pages); documents and letters relating to the Marqués de Rubí's inspection of the northern frontier, 1765–66 (76 pages); diaries by Hugo O'Conor, commandant inspector of presidios, of an expedition to locate presidio sites and check Indian hostilities, 1772–73 (10 pages), and diaries by O'Conor of expeditions against hostile Indians, 1774–75, 1776 (38, 51 pages); copies of documents submitted by Juan de Ugalde, former governor of Coahuila to Viceroy Bernardo de Gálvez, 1777–ca. 1788 (2 volumes), recommending reforms in the administration and military defense of the Interior Provinces; documents and letters of Mexican president Antonio López de Santa Anna, 1822–66 (15 pages);[59] and papers relating to Texas border activities, 1797–1806, involving American intruders, Indian hostilities, and Mexican reprisals.[60]

The new Henry R. Wagner Collection, purchased by the Yale University Library in 1919, contains several groups of manuscripts relating to Texas and the Southwest.[61] Letters of Spanish governors, 1784–1804 (40 items), relate to trade with Indians and Americans, and describe natural conditions and settlements. Another group of manuscripts (140 items), concerning Philip Nolan's expedition of Americans and Spaniards into Texas in 1801, consists of materials on the trial of the American survivors, and the diary of the leader of the Spanish force that captured them. Documents of 1805–16 (15 items) concern James Wilkinson's dealings with Spanish officials of Texas. Disturbances connected with the War of 1812 are the subject of eighteen other documents. Correspondence between Gov. Antonio María Martínez and Gaspar López, the military commander in east Texas, January–September, 1822 (300 items), is mainly concerned with American settlements in Texas. Other documents, 1825–40 (250 items), include letters to Stephen F. Austin and correspondence and other manuscripts of Mexican officials and American leaders regarding the movement for Texan independence.

---

[59] Hammond, *Guide to Ms. Colls.*, pp. 154, 202, 209, 238–39, 243.

[60] Friends of the Bancroft Library, *Hammond*, p. 50.

[61] This collection is described in Mary C. Withington, comp., *A Catalogue of Manuscripts in the Collection of Western Americana Founded by William Robertson Coe, Yale University Library* (New Haven, 1952), p. vi. Microfilm or photocopies of the Wagner Collection are in the University of Texas Archives. Information on Wagner's acquisition of the manuscripts is in his *Sixty Years of Book Collecting* (Los Angeles, 1952), pp. 13, 18–19.

The remainder of the Wagner Collection in the Yale University Library is composed of manuscripts of Jean Luis Berlandier, Swiss astronomer and naturalist who was attached to the Mexican commission that was appointed, in 1827, to investigate conditions in Texas and survey the boundary with the United States. The Berlandier manuscripts include papers of his own and others connected with the Mexican commission, and maps, plans of presidios, field sketches, and panoramic views by Berlandier, José M. Sánchez y Tapia, and Lino Sánchez y Tapia. Included also is a diary by Gen. Manuel de Mier y Terán, head of the commission, of a trip he made in east Texas during October and November, 1828, and his journey through Texas in 1829 to Matamoros.[62]

Berlandier manuscripts are also in other repositories. Berlandier manuscripts in the Manuscript Division of the Library of Congress (all in French) include his journal of travels in Mexico, 1826–34 (7 volumes, Phillips Collection number 15470); astronomical observations at places in Texas and Mexico, 1827–31 (1 volume, Phillips Collection number 15466); and papers, 1823–46 (2 volumes), including letters and geographical notes.[63] Other Berlandier manuscripts, in the Gray Herbarium of Harvard University, Cambridge, Massachusetts, are primarily botanical in content and include watercolor paintings of plants he collected in Texas and Mexico. Two journals of Berlandier containing notes on astronomical observations made by him at Goliad, Texas, December, 1832–May, 1834; Béxar, Texas, May–June, 1834; and Matamoros, Texas, August, 1834–November, 1835, are in the William L. Clements Library of the University of Michigan at Ann Arbor.[64] In the same repository, there is a journal containing notes on meteorological observations made at Goliad, December, 1832–December, 1833, by Rafael Chovell, mineralogist attached to the Mexican frontier commission. Berlandier's journals of the northeastern Mexican boundary survey, 1827–30 (4 volumes), and watercolor paintings of Indians and other inhabitants of Texas by Lino Sánchez y Tapia are in the Thomas Gilcrease Institute of American History Library in Tulsa, Oklahoma.[65] Berlandier's geographical and geological notes, and notes

---

[62] Another journal of General Mier y Terán, May 26–July 3, 1828, is in the Barker transcripts from the Mexican archives in the University of Texas Archives.

[63] Vicente Cortes Alonso, comp., and Mathias C. Kiemen, O.F.M., trans., "Manuscripts Concerning Mexico and Central America in the Library of Congress, Washington, D.C.," *Americas* 18 (Jan. 1962):266–67. The Library of Congress also has a collection of manuscript and printed edicts, proclamations, and other regulations of the viceroyalty of New Spain, 1720–72 (3 vols.).

[64] Howard H. Peckham, *Guide to the Manuscript Collections in the William L. Clements Library* (Ann Arbor, 1942), p. 23.

[65] *Natl. Union Catalog Ms. Colls.*, 1967, entry 120; Berlandier's 1830 journal and reproductions of the watercolors are in John C. Ewers, ed., and Patricia R. Leclercq,

of travels, ca. 1831, are in McGill University Library, Montreal, Canada.[66]

A few other manuscripts are in other repositories. An account of expenses incurred by Gov. Manuel Muñoz of Texas for gifts to Indian tribes in 1799 (12 pages) is in the Beinecke Collection of Western Americana in the Yale University Library.[67] Documents of the years 1630–1812, which are mostly copies assembled by Frs. Melchor de Talamantes and José Antonio Pichardo, in the Manuscript Division of the Library of Congress, relate to the boundaries of Louisiana and Texas. A collection of copies of documents for the ecclesiastical and civil history of Texas, 1689–1779 (2 volumes), made by Fr. Francisco García Figueroa for the Spanish government in 1790–92, was acquired by the same repository in 1892.[68] A census of Atascosita, July 31, 1826, is in the same repository. It is an unofficial census of a settlement of Americans on the lower Trinity River, in east Texas, that was renamed Liberty in 1831. Prepared for the purpose of accompanying a petition to the Mexican government asking for inclusion of the settlement in Austin's colony, the census lists the names of 331 people, and gives their sex, age, marital status, number of slaves, state of birth, state emigrated from, occupation or trade, and remarks as to the relationships of persons listed.[69] A report concerning the records of wine merchants and farmers of El Paso, 1762–68 (1 volume), kept by Pedro Varrios for the viceroy of New Spain, is in the New York Historical Society Collections.[70] A diary of a journey by Gov. Alonso de León into Texas, in 1690, is in the Thomas Gilcrease Institute of American History and Art in Tulsa, Oklahoma.

---

trans., *The Indians of Texas in 1830 by Jean Louis Berlandier* (Washington, 1969), which also has a bibliography containing titles of other documentary publications relating to the Mexican boundary commission. José María Sánchez y Tapia kept a journal that has been published in English: see Carlos E. Castañeda, trans. and ed., "A Trip to Texas in 1828," *Southw. Hist. Quar.* 29 (Apr. 1926):249–88.

[66] A catalog of the Berlandier manuscripts that was prepared while they were on deposit in the Smithsonian Institution has been published: Smithsonian Institution, *Catalogue of the Berlandier Manuscripts Deposited in the Smithsonian Institution, Washington, D.C.* (New York, 1853). The history of the manuscripts is traced in Jerry E. Patterson, "Spanish and Spanish American Manuscripts in the Yale University Library," *Yale Univ. Lib. Gazette* 31 (Jan. 1957):130–33.

[67] Jeanne E. Goddard and Charles A. Kritzler, comps., and Archibald Hanna, ed., *A Catalogue of the Frederick W. & Carrie S. Beinecke Collection of Western Americana, Volume I, Manuscripts* (New Haven, 1965), p. 72.

[68] For an account and description of the García Figueroa collection, see Bolton, *Guide to Arch. Mex.*, pp. 20–21, 28–31.

[69] The census is published in Mary M. Osborn, ed., "The Atascosita Census of 1826," *Texana* 1 (Fall 1963):299–321.

[70] New York Historical Society, *Survey of the Manuscript Collections in the New-York Historical Society* (New York, 1941), p. 83.

16

Land Records

A LIBERAL POLICY with respect to land grants was followed by the Spanish government, in order to promote settlement. Large grants were made to towns and missions, to distinguished soldiers, civilians, and public officials as rewards for service to the government, and to individual settlers for agricultural and grazing purposes.[1] The grants to the missions were not absolute and, for the most part, reverted to the government upon the secularization of the missions. The earliest grants, dating from 1731, were made in the San Antonio and Goliad region.[2] The towns established on the lower Río Grande (Mier, Reynosa, Revilla [later Guerrero], Camargo, and Laredo) held lands in common until the arrival of a royal commission, in 1767, which distributed some 400 allotments, or *porciones*, consisting of narrow strips of land extending back from the river.[3] By the close of the Spanish period, most of the desirable land between the Nueces and the Río Grande had been granted, either as *porciones* or as larger grants for grazing purposes.[4] Farther west, on the American side of the Río Grande near El Paso del Norte, grants were made by Spain, in 1751,

---

[1] Wooten, *Hist. Texas*, 2:786.

[2] Virginia H. Taylor, *The Spanish Archives of the General Land Office of Texas* (Austin, 1955), p. 21.

[3] Scott, *Lower Río Grande*, pp. 67–68; Taylor, *Spanish Arch.*, p. 82.

[4] Scott, *Lower Río Grande*, pp. 100, 130; Leroy P. Graf, "Colonizing Projects in Texas South of the Nueces, 1820–1845," *Southw. Hist. Quar.* 50 (Apr. 1947):431, 447. In Scott's work, there is a list of the original grantees of the Laredo *porciones* (pp. 74–76). A list of grantees on the delta of the Río Grande is in Foscue, "Lower Rio Grande," pp. 130–31.

to the towns of Socorro and Ysleta, and to the presidio of San Elizario.[5] The Spanish also made grants in east Texas, particularly in the neighborhood of Nacogdoches, whose commandant was authorized in 1792 to make grants.

The procedure for obtaining a land grant was the same in Texas as in Nuevo Santander, which had jurisdiction over the region south of the Nueces. An application was made to the governor, who then sent an order of approval to the local officer to make an examination, survey, and appraisal of the tract, and place the applicant in possession.[6] A record of the receipt of the order was made by the notary, who, together with the commissioned officer and the petitioner, signed a certification of the act. A visual inspection, survey, and demarcation of the tract was then made by a party composed of the local officer, the applicant, appraisers, witnesses, and adjacent land owners.[7] A written report of the proceedings, during which the applicant was put into possession, was prepared. All of the above documents made up the owner's title, which had to be approved by the viceroy of New Spain at Mexico City, and, after 1786, by the intendant. The files of *expedientes*, or land records, were archived in San Antonio, Nacogdoches, Laredo, and the other towns on the Río Grande, and the grants were registered in the provincial capital, the seat of the intendancy (San Luis Potosí) after 1786, and Mexico City.[8] During Spanish times, local officials permitted settlers to occupy land long before the legal requirements as to documentation were fulfilled, but eventually the documents were filed in the appropriate town archives.

Surveys of land grants were made in some areas, but in others they were long delayed. In July, 1731, Capt. Juan A. Pérez de Almazán, commandant of the presidio, surveyed San Fernando de Béxar, laying off streets, blocks for settlers' homes, the plaza, and lots for the church, the priest's house, and public and other buildings. He also surveyed neighboring fields, pastures, and farmlands, and, on completing his task, deposited the record of survey and the distribution of lands in the *cabildo* archives. In later years, other grants, transfers, and surveys of town lots were deposited in the municipal archives. After the distribution of *porciones* on the lower Río Grande in 1767, the farms and town sites in that area were surveyed. But little surveying was done

---

[5] Taylor, *Spanish Arch.*, p. 92; Robert G. West, "Validity of Certain Spanish Land Grants in Texas," *Texas Law Review* 2 (June 1924):435.

[6] Taylor, *Spanish Arch.*, pp. 17–19, 84.

[7] Thomas L. Miller, "A Note on the Spanish and Mexican Ceremony Conveying Possession of Land," *Agricultural History* 28 (Oct. 1954):168–70.

[8] Taylor, *Spanish Arch.*, pp. 83–84.

in east Texas before the arrival of Gov. Manuel Salcedo in 1810, when he gave old and new settlers possession of their lands by issuing title to plots, farms, and large ranches.[9]

Mexico also sought to stimulate the settlement of Texas by means of land grants. A national colonization law of August 18, 1824, turned the administration of public land, with certain restrictions, over to the states.[10] A law of the state of Coahuila and Texas of March 24, 1825, invited the settlement of foreigners and established the conditions under which colonies were to be founded.[11] Files relating to land grants in Texas are in the archives at Saltillo. Similar laws were adopted by the other border states of Tamaulipas (successor state to Nuevo Santander in 1824) and Chihuahua. The state of Tamaulipas continued to make grants north of the Río Grande until 1836, but attempts to establish colonies in that region were unsuccessful.[12] In Tamaulipas, the title papers were protocoled at Victoria, the capital, where record was made of the approval of the governor and payment to the treasurer, and copies were retained in the archives of the alcaldes of Reynosa, Matamoros, Laredo, Guerrero, Mier, Camargo, and Ciudad Victoria.[13] Town grants were made by Chihuahua to Ysleta, Socorro, and San Elizario, on the American side of the Río Grande near El Paso del Norte, and the *ayuntamiento* of that place made two grants to individuals for ranching, on the site of what became El Paso, Texas.[14]

Under the Coahuila-Texas law of 1825, numerous large grants were made in succeeding years to contractors or empresarios, who, as compensation for introducing settlers, were to receive premium lands from the government, which they could sell to settlers. The

---

[9] Houston, "Surveying in Texas," pp. 205–07. See also Lota M. Spell, trans. and ed., "The Grant and First Survey of the City of San Antonio," *Southw. Hist. Quar.* 66 (July 1962):73–89.

[10] Mary V. Henderson, "Minor Empresario Contracts for the Colonization of Texas, 1825–1834," *Southw. Hist. Quar.* 31 (Apr. 1928):206, 316; text printed in Joseph M. White, ed. *A New Collection of Laws, Charters, and Local Ordinances of the Governments of Great Britain, France and Spain, Relating to the Concessions of Land In Their Respective Colonies, Together with the Laws of Mexico and Texas on the Same Subject. . . .* 2 vols. (Philadelphia, 1839), 1:97–106, and in Gammel, *Laws of Texas,* 1:97–106.

[11] Henderson, "Minor Empresario Contracts," pp. 297–298; text in White, ed., *New Coll. Laws,* 1:433–440, 603–610.

[12] Taylor, *Spanish Arch.,* p. 89; Scott, *Lower Río Grande,* p. 153; Graf, "Colonizing Projects in Texas," p. 447; Paul S. Taylor, *An American-Mexican Frontier, Nueces County, Texas* (Chapel Hill, 1934), pp. 9–11, 179–180 (p. 180 contains a table of Spanish and Mexican land grants wholly or partly within Nueces County).

[13] Taylor, *Spanish Arch.,* p. 90.

[14] West, "Validity of Certain Spanish Land Grants in Texas," p. 435.

empresario contracts were issued in stereotyped form, differing only in the descriptions of the boundaries of the grants.[15] Chronological lists of the contracts have been published in various places;[16] for reference in the present study an alphabetical list is given here:

Arispe, Manuel R.	Nov. 12, 1828
Austin, Moses	1821
Austin, Stephen Fuller	Apr. 27, 1825
Austin, Stephen Fuller	Nov. 20, 1827
Austin, Stephen Fuller	Jul. 9, 1828
Austin, Stephen Fuller and Williams, Samuel	Feb. 1831
Beales, John Charles, and Royuela, José Manuel	Mar. 14, 1832
Beales, John Charles, and Mexicans	Apr. 13, 1832
Beales, John Charles, and Mexicans	Oct. 11, 1832
Beales, John Charles, and Grant, James	Oct. 9, 1832
Beales, John Charles. See Mexican Company.	
Burnet, David Gouverneur	Dec. 22, 1826
Cameron, John	May 21, 1827
Cameron, John	Aug. 18, 1828
Chambers, Thomas J. See Padilla, Juan A.	
Cherokee Indians	Sep. 1, 1831
De León, Martín	Oct. 6, 1825
De León, Martín	Apr. 30, 1829
DeWitt, Green	Apr. 15, 1825
Domínguez, Juan	Feb. 6, 1829
Domínguez, Marciano. See Mexican Company.	
Edwards, Haden	Apr. 15, 1825
Exeter, Richard, and Wilson, Stephen J.	Feb. 23, 1828
Filisola, Vicente	Oct. 15, 1831
Galveston Bay and Texas Land Co.	Oct. 16, 1830
Grant, James. See Beales, John C.	
Hewetson, James, and Power, James	Jun. 11, 1828
Johnson, Frank W. See Williams, Samuel	
Leftwich, Robert	Apr. 15, 1825
Lovell, Benjamin D. See Purnell, John G.	
McMullen, John, and McGloin, James	Aug. 17, 1828
Mason, John Thompson	Jun. 19, 1834
Mexican Company (Marciano Domínguez, Fortunato Soto, Juan Ramón Mila de la Rosa, John Charles Beales)	May 1, 1830
Milam, Benjamin R.	Jan. 12, 1826

---

[15] Austin's contract of Apr. 27, 1825 is printed in White, *New Coll. Laws*, 1:610–12; and his contract of July 9, 1828 is in ibid., pp. 616–18. Haden Edwards' contract of Apr. 15, 1825 is printed in Henderson Yoakum, *History of Texas from Its First Settlement in 1685 to Its Annexation to the United States in 1846*, 2 vols. (New York, 1855), 1:462–64.

[16] Henderson, "Minor Empresario Contracts", pp. 299–300; Curtis K. Bishop and Bascom Giles, *Lots of Land* (Austin, 1949), p. 41 n. 8.

Milan de la Rosa, Juan Ramón.	
See Mexican Company.	
Padilla, Juan Antonio, and Chambers,	
Thomas Jefferson	Feb. 12, 1830
Peebles, Robert. See Williams, Samuel.	
Power, James	Jun. 11, 1825
Power, James. See Hewetson, James.	
Purnell, John G., and Lovell, Benjamin D.	Oct. 22, 1825
Robertson, Sterling C.	May 22, 1834
Shawnee Indians	Apr. 16, 1825
Soto, Fortunato. See Mexican Company.	
Soto, Fortunato, and Henry Egerton	Jan. 1, 1834
Thorn, Frost	Apr. 15, 1825
Vehlein, Joseph. See Woodbury, John L.	
Vehlein, Joseph & Co.	Dec. 21, 1826
Vehlein, Joseph & Co.	Nov. 17, 1828
Wavell, Arthur Goodall	Mar. 9, 1826
Williams, Samuel. See Austin, Stephen F.	
Williams, Samuel; Peebles, Robert; and Johnson,	
Frank W.	May 11, 1835
Wilson, Stephen J. See Exeter, Richard.	
Wilson, Stephen J.	May 27, 1826
Woodbury, John L., and Joseph Vehlein & Co.	Nov. 14, 1826
Zavala, Lorenzo de	Mar. 12, 1829

The empresarios attained varying degrees of success. Only two — Austin and De León — settled the full number of families called for in their contracts, but others issued titles, had surveys made, and, consequently, accumulated land records. Nearly one-third of the empresarios failed to issue any titles at all, and, therefore, no mention will be made concerning land records for these colonies.[17] In the cases of some of these contractors, however, there is documentation relative to their efforts to make settlements, as will be noted.

The Coahuila-Texas law of 1825 also provided for direct grants of land to individuals, not exceeding eleven square leagues, in vacant lands, unrestricted areas, or within the empresarios' colonies with their consent. Applicants under this provision received their titles from special commissioners, alcaldes, or colony commissioners. After 1828, persons who had settled in border or coast reserves were also given concessions. And citizens of San Antonio and Goliad were given, under a law of April 28, 1832,[18] free grants of land as a reward for services rendered to the government.

---

[17] Information regarding the titles issued by the various empresarios can be found in Bishop and Giles, *Lots of Land, passim;* and Taylor, *Spanish Arch., passim.*

[18] Taylor, *Spanish Arch.*, p. 61.

The administration of the land system in the various colonies involved much labor, not only on the part of the empresarios, but by commissioners, surveyors, secretaries, and sometimes agents. Under the terms of the state colonization law and the empresarios' contracts, commissioners were appointed by the political chief of Texas. It was their function to supervise the admission of colonists, appoint surveyors to run off the land, issue land titles, lay off and establish new towns, and establish ferries.[19] The commissioners were to keep a record of titles issued in a book, which was to form part of the archives of the new colony, and an abstract prepared from it was to be transmitted to the government. In another book, they were to keep a record of town lots, and from it, attested copies were to be issued as title papers. Such a bound volume for land titles had previously been authorized on May 31, 1827, for use by Stephen F. Austin, who had recommended its adoption to prevent the loss of land records.[20] The empresarios became the custodians of the surveyors' papers — their field notes and plats, instructions and correspondence.

The procedure for obtaining titles was simplified by the state colonization law, and the *expediente* became standardized. The usual parts of the file were the petition by the applicant, decree of the governor or commissioner, report of the empresario, order of survey, field notes, and decree of possession.[21] Many surveyors were employed to prepare the field notes, and, since most of the notes were in English, they had to be translated into Spanish for submission to the government offices.[22] But the original English field notes are important for the examination of titles.

The grant made by the state of Coahuila and Texas to Stephen J. Wilson on May 27, 1826, included land in Oklahoma (present Cimarron County and the western part of Texas County) and large parts of Texas, New Mexico, and Colorado.[23] Wilson sold a half interest to Richard Exeter, a British merchant of Mexico City, and employed

---

[19] See the instructions of September 4, 1827, printed in White, *New Coll. Laws*, 1:487–91 and in Gammel, *Laws of Texas*, 1:180–83; see also Barker, *Stephen F. Austin*, pp. 157–58, and Ethel Z. Rather, "DeWitt's Colony," *Southw. Hist. Quar.* 8 (Oct. 1904):115, 119–20.

[20] Barker, *Stephen F. Austin*, p. 158 and n. 53; Texas, (Republic) Laws, Statutes, etc., *Translation of the Laws, Orders and Contracts, on Colonization, from Jan. 1821, up to 1829* (Columbia, Tex., 1837), pp. 22, 54–56.

[21] Taylor, *Spanish Arch.*, pp. 64–65.

[22] A list of the names of 103 surveyors who were employed in the colonies and districts in Coahuila and Texas is in Houston, "Surveying in Texas," pp. 215–16.

[23] Raymond Estep, "The First Panhandle Land Grant," *Chronicles of Oklahoma* 36 (Winter 1958):358.

Alexander Le Grand to survey the grant.[24] In 1830, after Exeter's death, his widow married Dr. John Charles Beales, a young English physician then residing in Mexico City. Beales obtained authority to act for his wife and, in 1831, transferred her interest in the grant to the Arkansas and Texas Land Company, which was formed in New York to develop the grant. But the company failed to obtain the colonists that were necessary to keep the grant in effect, and, in 1832, Beales and Josè Manuel Royuela obtained a concession to the same tract of land that Wilson had received in 1826. Wilson's application, his empresario contract, his agreement with Exeter, and documents relating to the transfer of power to Beales and others concerned with the formation of the Arkansas and Texas Land Company, are in print.[25] Efforts made by Beales to obtain confirmation of those parts of the grant outside of Texas resulted in another pamphlet, that also included the documents connected with the grant to Wilson, together with Le Grand's field notes and journal of survey, June 27–October 30, 1827, and documents relating to the grant to Beales and Royuela of March 14, 1832.[26]

Measures taken by the government of the Republic of Texas for the preservation of land records were only partially effectuated, and were tardily followed up. A resolution of October 27, 1835, by the permanent council, and article XIV of the organic act passed by the consultation on November 13,[27] ordered the suspension of all activities relating to lands and the closing of land offices, until conditions were more settled and arrangements could be made by the government for administering the lands. This legislation suspended the empresario contracts still in effect. Commissioners were designated for each of the departments, to see to the closing of the land offices and the suspension of the functions of the chiefs of department. Prompt obedience to the order was given by the land office in Austin's colonies at San Felipe de Austin, the commissioners reporting their success

---

[24] Raymond Estep, "The Le Grand Survey of the High Plains — Fact or Fancy," *New Mexico Historical Review* 29 (Apr. 1954):81–96, 141–53. Estep presents arguments indicating that Le Grand's survey notes and journal (printed on pp. 141–53, apparently from a copy found in the Archivo General de Relaciones Exteriores, Mexico) are fraudulent.

[25] *Documents Relating to Grants of Lands Made to Don Estevan Willson and Don Richard Exeter, in Texas* (New York, 1831).

[26] *Petition to Congress Made by the Heirs of Dr. John Charles Beales and the Howard University of Washington for the Confirmation of the Title to a Grant of Land in New Mexico Known as the Arkansas Grant* (New York, 1880). A copy of this pamphlet is in the Records of the United States House of Representatives (Record Group 233), National Archives.

[27] *Gammel, Laws of Texas*, 1:913.

on November 14.[28] William H. Steele, the land commissioner for the Robertson colony at Viesca, refused to comply.[29] In east Texas, where four land offices were in operation, George W. Smyth, land commissioner for the Galveston Bay and Texas Land Company, suspended his operations on December 19, 1835.[30] George A. Nixon closed his office and left the country. Radford Berry, the acting alcalde of Nacogdoches, and Charles S. Taylor, land commissioner for the municipality of San Augustine, refused to comply with the order of suspension.[31] In south Texas, which soon became the scene of active military operations, there was nothing to do but close the land offices.

Most of the records were allowed to remain for the time being in the hands of the commissioners for the various colonies. Those in Nixon's possession were insecurely housed, in February, 1836, in a box in the garret of an old wooden building at Nacogdoches.[32] It soon became necessary to remove the records from the path of the invading Mexicans. Those at San Felipe were packed up by Gail Borden and conveyed by Robert Peebles, one of the commissioners appointed by the permanent council, in April, 1836, to Fort Jesup, Louisiana, for safety.[33] After the fall of the Alamo, Robertson packed up the land records from his colony and sent them to a place of safety outside Texas, in the custody of his son.[34]

Under the laws of the Republic of Texas, which, in its constitution, recognized valid Spanish and Mexican land grants, the General Land Office was given the responsibility of collecting the records pertaining to those grants. The act of December 22, 1836, creating the land office, stipulated in section five that the commissioner of that office was to have custody and take charge of all records, books, and papers relating to the lands then in the hands of empresarios, polit-

---

[28] William C. Binkley, ed. *Official Correspondence of the Texas Revolution, 1835–36*, 2 vols. (New York, 1936), 1:71; see also Gammel, *Laws of Texas*, 1:621–22.

[29] Binkley, *Corres. Texas Revolution*, 1:149–50, 151 n. 6; Gammel, *Laws of Texas*, 1:614, 677, 947.

[30] Binkley, *Corres. Texas Revolution*, 1:221; George W. Smyth, "The Autobiography of George W. Smyth," *Southw. Hist. Quar.* 36 (Jan. 1933):212.

[31] Binkley, ed., *Corres. Texas Revolution*, 1:221, 513–14; Louis W. Kemp, *The Signers of the Texas Declaration of Independence* (Houston, 1944), pp. 342–43.

[32] William F. Gray, *From Virginia to Texas, 1835: Diary of Col. Wm. F. Gray....* (Houston, 1909), pp. 94–95.

[33] Robert Peebles to Thomas Barnett, Nov. 21, 1839, Robert Peebles Papers, University of Texas Library; Ibid., p. 119; Webb, *Handbook of Texas*, 2:356; Barker, *Austin Papers*, 3:370, 431, 437.

[34] Webb, *Handbook of Texas*, 2:488.

ical chiefs, alcaldes, commissioners, and others.[35] A more potent enactment of June 8, 1837, made it the duty of all empresarios, etc., to deliver
to the commissioner of the General Land Office all titles, surveys,
books, papers, and documents belonging to the republic, and imposed
a heavy penalty for failure to do so.[36] Agents were sent out by John
P. Borden, the newly appointed commissioner, in the summer of 1837,
to collect the land records.[37] He reported early in November, 1837,
that records had been received for the colonies of Austin, DeWitt,
Power and Hewetson, and Bevil's settlement, as well as a register from
Wavell's colony on the Red River.[38] Not all records for DeWitt's
colony were received, apparently, for the historian of that colony found
a record of town lots in Gonzales, in the office of Harwood and Walsh,
a law firm of that town, many years later.[39] The commissioner was
unable to find the land records for the colony of Martín de León in
1837, but he reported in 1840 that copies of titles issued during 1833–35
for fifty-one leagues in the colony, then Victoria County, had been
received.[40] (Subsequently, in 1850, the records of the colony were
obtained.) Having on hand at least some of the records necessary for
the transaction of business, the General Land Office opened its doors
on February 1, 1838.

The collection in that office was soon augmented with the original
records from the other colonies and sections of Texas. It acquired the

---

[35] Gammel, *Laws of Texas*, 1:1276–77.

[36] Ibid., p. 1324; see also sections 1 and 2 of the law of December 14, 1837, Ibid.,
p. 1386–87.

[37] John P. Borden to Asa Brigham, July 26, 1837, Virginia H. Taylor and Bertha
Brandt, eds., *Texas Treasury Papers; Letters Received in the Treasury Department
of the Republic of Texas 1836–1846*, 4 vols. (Austin, 1955–1956), 4:27.

[38] Bishop and Giles, *Lots of Land*, pp. 116–118; Taylor, *Spanish Arch.*, pp. 98–
105. The records of the General Land Office relating to Austin's colony have been
used as the basis of lists of settlers therein (Lester G. Bugbee, "The Old Three
Hundred, A List of Settlers in Austin's First Colony," *Southw. Hist. Quar.* 1 (Oct.
1897):108–17; reprinted in Wortham, *Texas*, 1:412–26; and in Ernest Wallace and
David M. Vigness, eds., *Documents of Texas History, Volume I (1528–1846)* (Lubbock, Tex., 1960), pp. 108–17. The records for the Power and Hewetson colony
were forwarded by James Power to the General Land Office (Oberste, *Irish Empresarios*, p. 257).

[39] Rather, "DeWitt's Colony," p. 168 n. 1. Lists of original settlers in this colony
and of grantees in the town of Gonzales, compiled from the original records, are
presented in Rather's study on pp. 163–172, and a documentary appendix includes
the petition by DeWitt for a grant, a title issued by him, and one issued directly by
the government. DeWitt's colonization contract is in the Gonzales Memorial
Museum.

[40] Texas (Republic), Congress, Joint Committee on Public Lands, *Evidence in
Relation to Land Titles Taken Before Joint Committee on Public Lands* (Austin,
1840), p. 33.

records of Milam's colony; those from the several land offices in east Texas conducted by George W. Smyth, Charles S. Taylor, George A. Nixon, and the alcalde of Nacogdoches; the Robertson colony;[41] the Austin and Williams colony; and the lands sold under the Williams, Johnson, and Peebles contracts, and the Durst and Williams contracts.[42] The General Land Office was thus able to publish, in 1838, an abstract containing lists of titles issued by the foregoing colonies and commissioners, as well as by the colonies of DeWitt, and Power and Hewetson.[43] The title records for the McMullen and McGloin colony were recovered in 1847 at Matamoros, where they had been carried at the time of the invasion of Texas in 1836, and deposited in the General Land Office.[44] That office also acquired records concerning the Beales and Grant colony, the Wavell colony, the unsuccessful colonies of Haden Edwards and John Cameron, settlements by Indians from the United States, and missions. From San Antonio, ten volumes of Spanish documents, consisting of laws, decrees, and orders of the governments of Spain, Mexico, and Coahuila and Texas, relating to land grants, colonization, and missions, were obtained about 1846–47 through the Texas secretary of state.

For certain areas of Texas, the General Land Office has only incomplete files of land-grant records, or no original records at all. The records for San Antonio and Goliad are few and fragmentary.[45] Papers for grants made at San Antonio from 1736–1836 were archived at that place, and land records are preserved in the county clerk's office there,[46] although these records were damaged to some extent during the revolutionary activities of 1813 and subsequent years. Original land records have also been retained at Nacogdoches. Since land grants made between the Nueces and the Río Grande were protocoled in Victoria, the capital of Tamaulipas, and copies were archived in Mexi-

---

[41] A brief description of the records of this colony in the General Land Office appears in William C. Harllee, *Kinfolks: A Genealogical and Biographical Record* (New Orleans, 1937), 3:2842.

[42] Taylor, *Spanish Arch.*, p. 105.

[43] Texas (Republic), General Land Office, *An Abstract of the Original Titles of Records in the General Land Office* (Houston, 1838). This publication was the first of a series of such abstracts, published in 1852, 1860, 1871, 1941–1942. The latest edition is the most correct. A few documents relative to the grant to Power and Hewetson are published in Oberste, *Irish Empresarios,* pp. 11–13, 16–20, 42–44.

[44] Oberste, *Irish Empresarios,* pp. 139 n. 18, 132; Taylor, *Spanish Arch.*, pp. 100, 121. Matamoros had been occupied by American soldiers under General Zachary Taylor in May, 1846.

[45] Taylor, *Spanish Arch.*, pp. 21–22.

[46] Ibid., pp. 23–24; Castañeda, *Spanish Arch. in San Antonio*, pp. 26–77.

can towns south of the Río Grande,[47] the General Land Office had to be satisfied with copies, which were eventually obtained.

The land records acquired by the General Land Office have been classified, indexed, and bound. The title papers of the various colonies are bound into separate volumes. Translations of empresario contracts and other materials, which were prepared by Thomas G. Western during 1838–40, fill twelve volumes. In all, there are about 175 volumes containing documents dated from 1720 to 1836 (mostly from 1800 to 1836).[48] The collection contains laws, decrees, resolutions, regulations, and treaties; empresario contracts and correspondence; census reports; lists of colonists; petitions and remonstrances; land grants, titles, surveys and field notes; messages of the governors of Coahuila and Texas; appointments of officers; reports of municipal officers; records relating to mission lands and property; registers of families; and oaths of allegiance. Some of these records are on microfilm in the Library of Congress and are available for borrowing.[49] These records constitute the most valuable collection of original documents for the history of the settlement of Texas during the period 1821–35, and one of the largest collections for the history of Texas.[50]

By the 1950s, the land records had become so damaged by constant use that it became necessary to undertake measures for their preservation. Microfilm copies were made; one copy has been made available for daily use by searchers, and another copy has been placed in security storage.[51] The Spanish titles are on forty-two rolls of microfilm, and the field notes of survey are on twelve rolls.[52] In 1958, the General Land Office began laminating the original Spanish archives with acetate film. This program disclosed 28,786 pages in the sixty-nine volumes of Spanish and Mexican titles, and 4,549 pages in the other twenty-three volumes. The data on the land records has been indexed on IBM cards, thus permitting easier access and less handling of the records and microfilm.

---

[47] Taylor, *Spanish Arch.*, p. 90.

[48] A description of the records in the General Land Office is in Eugene C. Barker, "Report on the Public Archives of Texas," *Amer. Hist. Assoc. Ann. Rep.*, 1901, 2:355–56; and in Taylor, *Spanish Arch.*, p. 68. No inventory of these records has been published.

[49] Jenkins and Hamrick, "Administrative Records," in *Guide to the Microfilm Collection of Early State Records*, pp. 87–89.

[50] Another list of Spanish and Mexican grants, arranged in alphabetical order and giving the date of the title, amount of land, name of the colony or commissioner, and present location, is in Taylor, *Spanish Arch.*, pp. 151–258.

[51] Texas, General Land Office, *Report*, 1954–56, pp. 11–14.

[52] Ibid., 1958–60, p. 63.

The land records in the General Land Office have been arranged and classified into a number of series. The title papers for the various colonies and municipalities have been bound into volumes as follows:[53]

Series	No. of Titles	Vol. nos.	Index vols.
Austin's first colony	301	1–2	A
Austin's second colony	483	3–6	A
Austin's third colony	185	7–8	A
Austin's fourth colony	76	9	A
Austin & Williams' colony	170	10–11	A
DeWitt's colony[54]	180	12–13	A
Robertson's colony		14–15	A–B
Milam's colony	54	16	A
Power & Hewetson's colony	220	17	A–B
Burnet's colony		18–19	A–B
Vehlein's colony		20–21	A–B
Zavala's colony		22–23	A–B
Frontier of Nacogdoches, George W. Smyth, commissioner		24–25	A–B
Frontier of Nacogdoches, Charles S. Taylor, commissioner		26–27	A–B
DeWitt, special grants	18	28	A–B
Austin & Williams, special grants	24	29	A–B
Large grants by various commissioners	24	30	B
Béxar authorities	25	31	A
Nacogdoches alcaldes and commissioners	25	32–33	A–B
Grants to volunteers under contracts with S. M. Williams, F. W. Johnson, Robert Peebles	41	34	B
224 leagues sold by the state	25	35	B
Concessions, titled, not titled	13	36	A
Titles issued by Spanish and Mexican authorities, 1791–1835		37–40	A–B
Titles deposited by individuals	172	41–43	B
Titles to Liberty town lots	35	44	
Titles to Refugio town lots	169	45	
Copies of titles not delivered and fragments	65	46	

---

[53] The data in the table was prepared from information supplied in a letter from Virginia H. Taylor, Spanish translator, Texas General Land Office, December 2, 1963, and an accompanying photostatic copy of a "Key to the Spanish Archives of the General Land Office of Texas." Regarding the blank spaces in the lists, all types of information are not always available.

[54] A list of the original settlers in DeWitt's colony prepared from this volume is in Rather, "DeWitt's Colony," pp. 163–67.

Series	No. of Titles	Vol. nos.	Index vols.
Frontier of Nacogdoches, George W. Smyth, commissioner		47–48	
Miscellaneous: petitions for lands upon which no final action was taken; land grants for which no titles were issued; titles for town lots at San Marcos de Neve and Santísima Trinidad de Salcedo		49	
Missions in Texas: establishment and distribution of lands of missions near San Antonio, Goliad, and Nacogdoches		50	
Appointments of officers, June 16, 1823–May 6, 1835, including state officers, department officers, land commissioners and instructions, and judicial officers		51	
Original and other documents in Spanish		52	
Appendix, empresario contracts, no. 1: general provisions relative to colonization in Texas under the Spanish and Mexican governments (I) measures relative to armed emigrants, (II) frontier and coast border leagues, (III) forfeited contracts and land sales annulled, (IV) La Vaca, Tenoxtitlán, and Galveston, (V) miscellaneous — laws and resolutions of the government of the state of Coahuila and Texas, etc.		53	
Appendix, empresario contracts, no. 2: general provisions relative to Austin's, DeWitt's, and Robertson's colonies		54	
Appendix, empresario contracts, no. 3: Milam's colony, Wavell's colony; Vehlein, Burnet, and Zavala's colonies; Cameron's colony; Haden Edwards' colony; McMullen and McGloin's colony; Grant and Beales' colony; extracts of sundry empresario contracts; Indian tribes (Shawnee, Coshatee, Alibamo, Choctaw, Cherokee)		55	
Appendix to empresario contracts, no. 4: documents relative to Power and Hewetson's colony and De León's colony		56	
Miscellaneous: (I) organization of the Mexican government, (II) treaty between U.S. and Mexico, (III) message of the governor of the State of Coahuila and Texas, (IV) Spanish marriage law, (V) slavery in the Spanish dominions and Mexico, (VI) copies of titles not delivered		57	
Titles deposited by individuals		58	
Titles in McMullen and McGloin's colony		59–60	
Unfinished titles in Milam's colony		61	
Unfinished business in Burnet's and Vehlein's colonies		62	
Unfinished business in Zavala's colony		63	
Unfinished business of Juan Antonio Padilla at San Felipe de Austin		64	
Unfinished business of Juan Antonio Padilla in 1829 and 1830, and of José Francisco Madero in 1831		65	

Series	No. of Titles	Vol. nos.	Index vols.
Titles in De León's colony		66–67	
Miscellaneous: (I) grants with possession but no title, (II) grants annulled, (III) transfers by donation, (IV) copies of titles, (V) original field notes, (VI) unfinished business, (VII) fragments and blanks, (VIII) itineraries in Texas, New Mexico, and Louisiana (Fragosa's diary)		68	
Titles between the Nueces and the Río Grande.		69	

The General Land Office also has other records in unnumbered volumes. These include a register of grants in Austin's colony, July 11, 1825–December 2, 1831 (1 volume); a register of grants in Wavell's colony, 1830–31 (1 volume); a register of grants in Milam's colony, 1830–31 (1 volume); a register of grants in Robertson's colony, 1835–36 (1 volume); a list of Charles S. Taylor's orders of survey, 1835–36 (1 volume); copies and translations of an examination as a result of which tracts of land were granted in Mier, Camargo, Reynosa, Guerrero, and Laredo in 1767; a file of character certificates of individual colonists, and records of San Felipe de Austin and Nacogdoches that are described with the other records of these municipalities.

A record of original titles in Austin's first tract, 1821–27 (1 volume), contains copies of decrees, dispatches, and laws relating to Austin's first tract and grants to settlers. A plat of the town is included in the book. An index to Spanish archives, 1823–37 (1 volume), is an alphabetical index by name of grantee to all land records.

Land records are also held by Texas counties. An act of the Texas Congress, passed December 20, 1836, required persons owning land to have their documents recorded by the clerks of the county courts, who were designated as recorders for their respective counties.[55] Accordingly, the documents held by individual land owners were recorded, and the collections thus developed have been used for research by many local historians. Some counties have obtained transcripts of records that are in the General Land Office.[56] Pursuant to an act of the state legislature of December 24, 1851,[57] volume forty-five of the Spanish archives of the General Land Office, containing

---

[55] Gammel, *Laws of Texas*, 1:1215.

[56] Descriptions of these transcripts are in the Historical Records Survey, Texas, *Inventory of the County Archives of Texas, No. 28, Caldwell County (Lockhart)* (Lockhart, Tex., 1941), p. 84; Historical Records Survey, Texas, *Inventory of the County Archives of Texas, No. 75, Fayette County (La Grange)* (La Grange, Tex., 1940), p. 132.

[57] Gammel, *Laws of Texas*, 3:900.

169 titles to town lots in Refugio, was deposited in the county clerk's office at that place. An act of the Texas legislature of May 11, 1893 authorized county commissioners to contract with clerks of county courts to prepare English translations of records in their offices relating to land titles, and to copy them into bound books.[58] The case files of county courts also contain papers relating to land grants about which litigation occurred.

The treaty of Guadalupe Hidalgo of February, 1848, established the Río Grande as the boundary between Mexico and the American state of Texas, and recognized authentic titles to land in the area between the Nueces River and the Río Grande.[59] Having retained her public lands under the terms of the annexation treaty of 1845 with the United States, the task of investigating land titles became the responsibility of Texas. Under acts of the Texas legislature, commissions were appointed to determine the validity of Spanish and Mexican grants and, on the basis of evidence collected, to report titles for confirmation.[60] The evidence had to be collected principally from the claimants themselves, since, due to the rancorous state of relations between Texas and Mexico, application could not be made to neighboring Mexican states. On the basis of a report made by the commissioners, the state legislature, under an act approved February 10, 1852, confirmed 192 grants in Kinney, Webb, Starr, Nueces, and Cameron counties.[61] The commissioners' report and the accompanying abstracts of titles, petitions, and testimony are in the Texas General Land Office, but the files collected as evidence have disappeared.[62] Under subsequent acts of the legislature providing for judicial determination of claims, some fifty additional Spanish and Mexican titles were confirmed.

The adjudication of titles to land between the Nueces River and Río Grande could have been promoted by the procurement of records relating to grants in that area, but very few copies or original land titles were presented to the General Land Office. Consequently, in April, 1871, the Texas legislature authorized the procurement of transcriptions of records useful in the settlement of land titles from the Mexican towns of Mier, Reynosa, Camargo, Laredo and Guerrero.[63] J. L. Haynes made copies of acts, charters, and grants, from the archives

[58] Texas, *General Laws*, 1893, p. 168.

[59] Scott, *Lower Río Grande*, p. 139.

[60] Wooten, *Hist. Texas*, p. 805 ff.; Scott, *Lower Río Grande*, pp. 146–153.

[61] Scott, *Lower Río Grande*, p. 152; Taylor, *Spanish Arch.* p. 132.

[62] Taylor, *Spanish Arch.*, pp. 132–33.

[63] Ibid., p. 83 n. 3.

of those towns, and translations by him were deposited within a year in the General Land Office.

Farther north, the United States supported the claim of Texas to the Río Grande as the western boundary against Mexico, but did not admit the Texas claim to the territory extending to that river, as it would have given Texas half of New Mexico. Since the matter became involved in the slavery controversy between the North and the South, it was not until the adoption by Congress of the Texas-New Mexico act of September 9, 1850 (the compromise act of 1850) that it was settled.[64] Texas received $10,000,000 for relinquishing its claim but retained 13,445,000 acres of land that had originally belonged to Chihuahua. Texas recognized Mexican land grants amounting to 66,519 acres, and the rest became part of the public lands of Texas.[65]

---

[64] Webb, *Handbook of Texas*, 1:388.

[65] Treatments of individual claims, with many citations to sources, are in J. J. Bowden, *Spanish and Mexican Land Grants in the Chihuahua Acquisition* (El Paso, 1970).

17

Records of Local Jurisdictions

THE EARLY SETTLEMENTS in Texas were missions, presidios, and pueblos. The missions were supervised by Franciscan friars assigned by superiors of that order in Mexico. At first, all phases of administration at the presidios were handled by military commanders. Later, civil settlements (pueblos) developed at many of the missions and presidios, and they eventually were accorded a large measure of self-government.[1]

The local governments included one or more towns and the surrounding territory, and were governed according to the system prescribed for all Spanish America by the *Recopilación de Leyes*.[2] Under instructions from the viceroy of New Spain, a *cabildo* (*ayuntamiento* or municipal council) was organized at San Antonio in 1731.[3] Composed of *regidores*, or councilmen, it was presided over by an alcalde who was also first *regidor*, with functions like those of the mayor of an American city and chief of police.[4] The *cabildo* elected two *alcaldes ordinarios*, or municipal judges, from whose decisions appeals could be taken to the *cabildo*, the governor, and to the Audiencia of Mexico

---

[1] Garrison, *Texas*, pp. 54–62.

[2] O. Garfield Jones, "Local Government in the Spanish Colonies as Provided by the Recopilación de Leyes de los Reynos de las Indias," *Southw. Hist. Quar.* 19 (July 1915):65.

[3] Mattie A. Hatcher, "The Municipal Government of San Fernando de Béxar, 1730–1800," *Southw. Hist. Quar.* 8 (Apr. 1905):297–98; Castañeda, *Our Catholic Heritage in Texas*, 2:309.

[4] A document from the Béxar archives relating to the election of the alcalde at San Fernando de Béxar is in Helen M. Hunnicutt, trans. and ed., "Election of Alcaldes in San Fernando, 1750," *Southw. Hist. Quar.* 54 (Jan. 1951):333–36.

(after 1779, to the Audiencia of Guadalajara). Other officials of the municipality included the *alguacil mayor* (sheriff) and the *mayordomo de propios* (administrator of public lands), who also functioned as the *procurador* (attorney). Less organized municipalities developed at other places during the Spanish regime. After 1768, Laredo was governed by an alcalde and two *regidores*.[5] Other local jurisdictions, in existence in 1810, included Nacogdoches, La Bahía (Goliad), Salcedo, San Marcos, and Bayou Pierre.[6] *Escribanos* kept the *cabildo* minutes and served as notaries, prepared legal documents, took depositions, and maintained the local archives. Subdivisions of municipalities, known as districts or precincts, were under *comisarios,* or subalcaldes, and *síndicos.* Under the tutelage of missionaries, the Indian pueblos also developed local governments fashioned after the Spanish pattern.

The system of local government established during the Spanish regime was continued, with modifications, by the Mexican government. Alcaldes presided over *ayuntamientos,* served as primary judges, and communicated with departmental and state authorities. The *ayuntamiento* was composed of the alcalde, two *regidores* (councilmen), the *procurador* (attorney), and a secretary or clerk. The *ayuntamiento* had wide responsibilities, including the supervision of finances and the police, collection of taxes, supervision of hospitals and public health, maintenance of roads and public buildings, regulation of weights and measures, organization of the militia, the holding of special elections, and the promotion of agriculture and industry.[7] The *ayuntamientos* were required by a decree of September 5, 1827, to submit annual reports to the chief of the department, but were lax in doing so.[8] Another law of the same year required the preparation of lists of slaves and the registration of births and deaths, but difficulty was encountered in getting the people to cooperate.[9] Secretaries served as interpreters and translators, notarized documents,[10] and kept local records, including the proceedings of the *ayuntamientos.*

---

[5] Sebron S. Wilcox, "The Spanish Archives of Laredo," *Southw. Hist. Quar.* 49 (Jan. 1946):346.

[6] Castañeda, *Our Catholic Heritage in Texas,* 5:400.

[7] Barker, *Stephen F. Austin,* pp. 210–11; Rather, "DeWitt's Colony," pp. 124–25; Castañeda, *Our Catholic Heritage in Texas,* 6:223.

[8] Gammel, *Laws of Texas,* 1:184; Rather, "DeWitt's Colony," p. 129.

[9] Decree no. 18, Sept. 15, 1827, Gammel, *Laws of Texas,* 1:188–89; Barker, *Stephen F. Austin,* pp. 273–74.

[10] The practice of notarizing documents was introduced in the Spanish colonies from Spain and was continued under the Mexican government. The notaries kept registers (*protocolos*), in which a variety of documents relating to legal and business transactions were recorded, that served as evidence in case of disputes or lawsuits. The diverse and numerous acts included bills of sales, exchanges, donations, and cessions; debts and receipts; wills and codicils; dowries; powers of

The establishment of new settlements by empresarios from the United States and other countries resulted in the founding of new municipalities. The state colonization act of March 24, 1825, provided for the election of *ayuntamientos* in the new colonies under certain conditions such as population and distance from other *ayuntamientos,* and under the supervision of the commissioners.[11] In east Texas, where the grants to Burnet, Vehlein, Zavala, Milam, Wavell, and Filisola were made, a repopulation of the country occurred in the 1820s, following the cessation of revolutionary disturbances. At the revived town of Nacogdoches, an alcalde was appointed in 1821, and an *ayuntamiento* was established in 1825.[12] Initially, its jurisdiction covered much of the neighboring country between the Sabine and Neches rivers, but with the growth of other settlements, these areas were elevated into municipalities. The Ayish Bayou district, lying to the east of Nacogdoches, increased sufficiently in population by 1834 to be organized into the municipality of San Augustine.[13] Bevil, established at the junction of the Neches and Angelina rivers in 1824, was also organized into a municipality in 1834, its name being changed the following year to Jasper. A somewhat older settlement at Anáhuac, on Galveston Bay, qualified for an *ayuntamiento* in 1831.[14] That year also marked the beginning of the municipality of Liberty, which had been settled some years before by squatters on the Trinity River.[15] Other settlements in east Texas that were established later as municipalities were Pecan Point, Jonesboro, and Tenehaw. All these places came under the Department of Nacogdoches.

Stephen F. Austin was given authority in 1823 to govern the settlement that he had located in 1821 between the Colorado and Brazos rivers, south of the San Antonio road.[16] Alcaldes and military commanders were elected in 1823 for the districts comprising the

---

attorney; contracts of service, obligations, compromises, agreements, guarantees, quitrents and mortgages; freights; and ratifications and confirmations. These instruments are valuable for economic history, social relations, cultural matters, and statistical, demographic, biographical, genealogical, and legal investigations (Aurelio Z. Tanodi, "Institución notarial hispanoamericana," *Archivum* 12 (1962): 31–34.

[11] Gammel, *Laws of Texas,* 1:131.

[12] Barker, *Stephen F. Austin,* pp. 170, 179–80; George L. Crockett, *Two Centuries in East Texas: A History of San Augustine County and Surrounding Territory from 1685 to the Present Time* (Dallas, 1932), p. 81.

[13] Crockett, *East Texas,* pp. 90–91; Webb, *Handbook of Texas,* 2:547; decree no. 265, March 6, 1834, in Gammel, *Laws of Texas,* 1:352.

[14] Barker, *Stephen F. Austin,* p. 380.

[15] Webb, *Handbook of Texas,* 2:54.

[16] Barker, *Stephen F. Austin,* p. 99 ff.; Garrison, *Texas,* p. 149; Eugene C. Barker, "The Government of Austin's Colony, 1821–1831," *Southw. Hist. Quar.* 21 (Jan. 1918):226.

colony, and instructions for alcaldes, which had been prepared by Austin and approved by the political chief in 1824, regulated the administration of justice in the districts and prescribed the forms of records to be used.[17] During the early years, Austin also conducted Indian relations, commanded the militia,[18] and superintended immigration. Late in the same year, the district of San Felipe was set up, and, in 1824, the districts of San Jacinto[19] and Mina were organized, and Victoria was formed out of part of San Felipe. San Felipe de Austin, founded on the Brazos River in 1824, became the headquarters of Austin's colony. Upon the formation of the *ayuntamiento* of San Felipe in February, 1828, the government of the colony passed into its hands. The southern portion of the municipality of San Felipe, near the mouth of the Brazos River, was organized by a state decree of April, 1832 as the municipality of Brazoria. It did not come into operation until early in 1833, however, when an alcalde, *regidores,* and a *sindico procurador* were elected.[20] The name Brazoria was changed to Columbia by a decree of April 25, 1834,[21] and changed back to Brazoria by a resolution of the consultation of November 14, 1835.[22]

Other settlements in Austin's colonies also developed into municipalities. After Austin obtained permission to locate a town at the mouth of the Colorado River, settlers were brought in from New York and New England in the late 1820s and established Matagorda. When it became a municipality in 1834, some of the territory of the municipality of Brazoria was given to it.[23] Far to the north, at the Colorado crossing of the San Antonio road in what was known as Austin's "Little Colony," a settlement named Mina opened about 1829. Established as a municipality with the same name in 1834,[24]

---

[17] Barker, *Stephen F. Austin,* p. 124. The regulations are printed in Louis J. Wortham, *A History of Texas: From Wilderness to Commonwealth,* 5 vols. (Fort Worth, 1924), 1:388–411; and in Wooten, *Hist. Texas,* 1:481–92.

[18] Barker, *Stephen F. Austin,* pp. 104–08; Henry W. Barton, "The Anglo-American Colonists under Mexican Militia Laws," *Southw. Hist. Quar.* 65 (July 1961):67.

[19] In August 1824, Humphrey Jackson, an emigrant from Louisiana who had received a land grant from the Baron de Bastrop, was elected alcalde of the San Jacinto district (Andrew F. Muir, "Humphrey Jackson, Alcalde of San Jacinto," *Southw. Hist. Quar.* 88 (Jan. 1965):361–62.

[20] Historical Records Survey, Texas, *Inventory of the Colonial Archives of Texas, 1821–1837; No. 3, Municipality of Brazoria 1832–1837* (San Antonio, 1937), p. 4.

[21] Ibid., p. 6; Gammel, *Laws of Texas,* 1:385.

[22] Historical Records Survey, Texas, *Inventory Col. Arch., No. 3: Municipality of Brazoria,* p. 8; Gammel, *Laws of Texas,* 1:535.

[23] Webb, *Handbook of Texas,* 1:208; 2:157; decree no. 265, March 6, 1834, Gammel, *Laws of Texas,* 1:352.

[24] Webb, *Handbook of Texas,* 1:121; decree no. 283, [1834], Gammel, *Laws of Texas,* 1:384.

it was changed by an act of the Texas Congress of December 18, 1837 to Bastrop.[25] A ferry service started in 1822 on the Brazos River, in the northern part of Austin's colony, took the name of Washington in 1834, and, in July, 1835, municipal officials were elected.[26] Velasco, at the mouth of the Brazos River, became the port of entry for Austin's colony. Most of the settlement of Harrisburg, on the right bank of Buffalo Bayou, was in Austin's colony, but the eastern part was in Vehlein's colony.[27] A decree of the Texas general council of December 30, 1835[28] established Harrisburg as a municipality, comprising what is now Harris County and parts of other counties. In the area granted to Robert Leftwich (Nashville Company) in 1825 and regranted in 1831 to Stephen F. Austin and Samuel Williams, no settlements were made before 1834, when the region was turned over to Sterling C. Robertson. He established Sarahville de Viesca, at the falls of the Brazos River, as the seat of his colony in 1834.[29] A resolution of the general council of December 27, 1935, changed the name of Viesca to Milam.[30] In 1835, Robertson founded Nashville, on the Brazos River below the mouth of the Little River.

DeWitt's colony, inaugurated in 1825 at Gonzales, west of San Felipe de Austin, was subject, at first, to authorities at San Antonio. That place was too distant, however, and in October, 1828, upon the petition of the colonists themselves, it was attached to the *ayuntamiento* of San Felipe de Austin, which appointed commissaries and *síndico procuradores* for the government of the neighboring colony.[31] By November, 1832, the settlement at Gonzales had progressed to the point of the commissioner's being able to hold an election for an *ayuntamiento*.

In south Texas, between the coast and San Antonio, there were several successful colonies. The earliest colonizer in this region, Martín de León, founded Victoria on the lower Guadalupe River in 1824, and it developed into a municipality.[32] Irish immigrants who were introduced by McMullen and McGloin founded the town of San Patricio

---

[25] Webb, *Handbook of Texas*, 1:121.

[26] Ernest W. Winkler, ed., "Documents Relating to the Organization of the Municipality of Washington, Texas," *Southw. Hist. Quar.* 10 (July 1906):96–100; Charles F. Schmidt, *History of Washington County* (San Antonio, 1949), p. 7.

[27] Andrew F. Muir, "The Municipality of Harrisburg, 1835–36," *Southw. Hist. Quar.* 56 (July 1952):39.

[28] Gammel, *Laws of Texas*, 1:1022.

[29] Barker, *Life of Stephen A. Austin*, p. 362; Webb, *Handbook of Texas*, 2:842.

[30] Gammel, *Laws of Texas*, 1:702.

[31] Rather, "DeWitt's Colony," pp. 102, 123–124, 126.

[32] Webb, *Handbook of Texas*, 2:839.

on the Nueces River in 1830, and it was made a municipality in 1834.[33] In the Power and Hewetson colony on the coast, the abandoned site of Refugio mission was chosen as the location of a settlement in 1834. A municipality began functioning there in July, 1834, while the town was still being surveyed.[34] A group of English and other colonists opened the Beales and Grant colony, which lay between the Nueces River and Río Grande above the San Antonio-Laredo road, with a settlement at Dolores on Los Moras Creek in March, 1834.[35] The founding also marked the inauguration of the municipality, of which Beales himself was elected the alcalde.

The town of El Paso, in west Texas, did not come into existence until after the Mexican War. Its site was occupied previously by ranches which had been granted by the alcalde of El Paso del Norte, acting for the Mexican state of Chihuahua.[36] Pueblos and missions had been established nearby, on the eastern side of the Río Grande, by Indians who had fled from the Pueblo revolt of 1680 in New Mexico. The pueblos included Socorro and Ysleta, south of El Paso, which are still in existence.[37] The Republic of Texas claimed the entire area north and east of the Río Grande but did not occupy it. American forces under Col. Alexander W. Doniphan did occupy El Paso del Norte in December, 1846.[38] Although the treaty of Guadalupe Hidalgo of February 22, 1848, between the United States and Mexico, established the Río Grande as the boundary between the two countries, it was not until 1850 that the dispute between Texas and New Mexico over their boundary was concluded, by an act of Congress which established it at 103° longitude and 32° latitude.[39]

At the consultation which met at San Felipe in November, 1835, to organize a provisional government for the Republic of Texas, the following municipalities were represented: (the Department of Brazos) — San Felipe, Brazoria, Gonzales, Harrisburg, Matagorda, Mina, Viesca,

---

[33] Gammel, *Laws of Texas*, 1:384.

[34] Hobart Huson, *Refugio County, Basic Titles: Refugio County General, Colonial Grants, Four League Grant to Town of Refugio* (Refugio, 1951), pt. 2, p. 6; pt. 3, pp. 3, 15.

[35] Joseph C. McConnell, *The West Texas Frontier: or, a Descriptive History of Early Times in West Texas. . . .* (Jacksboro, Tex., 1933), p. 32; Webb, ed., *Handbook of Texas*, 2:128.

[36] Webb, *Handbook of Texas*, 1:561–62; West, "Spanish Land Grants," p. 437.

[37] Anne E. Hughes, *The Beginnings of Spanish Settlement in the El Paso District* (Berkeley, 1914), p. 388; Charles S. Sonnichsen, *Pass of the North: Four Centuries on the Rio Grande* (El Paso, 1968), p. 107; Webb, *Handbook of Texas*, 2:415, 633, 949.

[38] Bancroft, *Hist. North Mexican States and Texas*, 2:607.

[39] Ibid., pp. 398–400.

Washington; (the Department of Nacogdoches) — Bevil, Liberty, Nacogdoches, San Augustine; and (the Department of Béxar) — Goliad, Refugio, San Patricio, and Victoria.[40] In the Department of Béxar, the elections for delegates were delayed by the presence of Mexican troops, but all the municipalities were admitted into the council (successor to the consultation) by December 1.[41] In addition, the following new municipalities were created during the period from November 11, 1835, to January 11, 1836: Red River, Tenehaw (Shelby), Jefferson, Jackson, Sabine, and Colorado.[42] However, since these municipalities were created by Texas rather than Mexico, they are of little concern in the present study.

The organic law of November, 1835, directed the transfer of the records held by the judges, alcaldes, and other municipal officials of the various jurisdictions to their successors in office.[43] Acts of the first congress of the Republic of Texas transformed the Mexican municipalities into counties patterned on the Anglo-American model familiar to American immigrants in Texas, and municipal officials were supplanted by their American counterparts.[44] The old *escribanos* were displaced by county clerks, who became the custodians of the records transferred from the *ayuntamientos* to the counties. The former seats of the Mexican municipalities were incorporated as towns and, in most cases, became the seats of the successor counties.

One of the largest collections of local records is at San Antonio. When Carlos E. Castañeda examined these records in 1923, he found part of them arranged in alphabetical order and others in disorder.[45] Two classifications, viz., land grants, deeds of sale, transfers, etc.,

---

[40] Binkley, *Corres. Texas Revolution*, 1:39–40. See also the lists in Gammel, *Laws of Texas*, 1:508–09, 551; Z. T. Fulmore, *History of the Geography of Texas* (n.p., 1897); Seymour V. Connor, "The Evolution of County Government in the Republic of Texas," *Southw. Hist. Quar.* 55 (Oct. 1951):176. There is doubt as to the status (at the end of the Mexican regime) of Harrisburg, Jasper, Liberty, Milam, Refugio, Shelby, Victoria, and Washington; some may have been only *comisario* districts (Eric L. Blair, *Early History of Grimes County*, Austin, 1930, p. 13 n. 13). That this aspect of the history of municipalities will be difficult to clarify is shown by Andrew F. Muir's article on "The Municipality of Harrisburg, 1835–36," *Southw. Hist. Quar.* 56 (July 1952):36–50.

[41] Binkley, *Corres. Texas Revolution*, 1:41; Connor, "Evolution of County Govt.," p. 177.

[42] Connor, "Evolution of County Govt.," pp. 177–79; Binkley, *Corres. Texas Revolution*, passim. The decrees are in Gammel, *Laws of Texas*, 1:614, 949–50, 1025–26, 1034–45.

[43] Gammel, *Laws of Texas*, 1:641.

[44] Connor, "Evolution of County Govt.," pp. 169–81; Binkley, *Corres. Texas Revolution*, 2:883.

[45] Carlos E. Castañeda, *A Report on the Spanish Archives in San Antonio, Texas* (San Antonio, 1937), pp. 16–17.

1736–1836, were arranged roughly in alphabetical order in twenty tin boxes, and wills and estate papers, 1742–1836, were arranged the same way in four tin boxes. In another tin box were papers concerning grants of land made outside Béxar County, 1778–1835, including some made in Nacogdoches, La Bahía, San Patricio, and other places, and many for locations outside the boundaries of Texas. These were arranged by Castañeda by names of places and dates. A box of protocols, 1782–1835, consisting of copies of deeds of sale, grants, judicial cases, and wills, was calendared on cards, which were arranged in chronological order.

In addition to the foregoing legal documents, there was a large group of disordered miscellaneous records in the Béxar County records, which was arranged in chronological order and listed. Varied in types of documents and subject matter, the miscellaneous records, 1760–1835, consisted of accounts, announcements, appointments, *bandos*, militia by-laws, circulars, correspondence, copies of instructions, decisions, deeds of sales, decrees of the Cortes, decrees of the Mexican Congress, decrees of Coahuila and Texas, index to laws and decrees, minutes of the *ayuntamiento*, notifications, orders, pardons, ordinances, petitions, proclamations, promulgations, receipts, recommendations, reports, reports and inventories of property, resolutions, royal *cédulas*, royal orders, royal dispatches, rules, speeches, transfers of property, and wills and testaments.[46] In his inventory of the collection, Castañeda followed the classification of the records described above. There was also a section on missions that will be mentioned later. The Béxar Archives in the University of Texas Archives contain proceedings of the *ayuntamiento* of San Antonio and other materials relating to that place.[47]

The Béxar County records concern not only the local municipality but also the civil and military administration of the province. Many documents in the miscellaneous records, particularly issuances of the king, viceroy, and Mexican Congress, are in printed form and were of general applicability in New Spain or Mexico. These records supplement, and in many cases duplicate, materials in the provincial records (Béxar Archives) of Texas in the custody of the University of Texas Archives.

The Béxar County Archives were partially transcribed by the Works Progress Administration Historical Records Survey of Texas. A copy of the typed transcript, 1716–1937 (9 volumes), is in the University of Texas Archives, where there are also original manuscripts,

---

[46] Ibid., pp. 108–56.

[47] Kielman, *Guide to the Béxar Archives, 1717–1803*, passim; Kielman, *Guide to the Béxar Archives, 1804–1821*, passim.

photocopies, and printed materials relating to San Antonio, dating from 1685.[48] A translation of the minutes of the *ayuntamiento* of San Antonio, 1815–35, also prepared by the WPA, is in the University of Texas Archives. Copies of the transcription and translation of the *ayuntamiento* minutes are in the Manuscript Division of the Library of Congress. The minutes concern the conduct of local affairs, the election and appointment of local officials, reports by officials, the transfer of public property, action on instructions received from the governor of the state, the administration of oaths to immigrants, and decisions of the *ayuntamiento*.

An archivist appointed by the county clerk of Béxar County in 1963 undertook a survey to determine the means of caring for the Spanish-Mexican archives of the county. Upon completing his examination, the archivist recommended that individual documents in the archives be placed in cotton covers in manila folders and kept in locked, fireproof cabinets; that the entire collection be reindexed to facilitate its use; that the size and content of the bulky and unmanageable "Miscellaneous" section be reduced; that the collection be microfilmed and enlargements made; and that the unfinished transcripts and translations begun by the WPA in the 1930s be completed, with copies being made available for public use. When the preparation of the materials was completed, the microfilming was started in September, 1965, on a Recordak camera under the supervision of an employee of the clerk's office, and was finished in January, 1966.[49]

The classification of works given in the archivist's report serves as a key to the microfilm and is as follows:[50]

A. Land Grants and Sales (*Tierras*), 1736–1836 (734 items) — papers relating to lands, arranged alphabetically by surnames of grantees and chronologically thereunder.

B. Mission Records (*Misiones franciscanos*), (93 items) — inventories of the San Antonio missions (San Antonio de Valero, San Juan de Capistrano, Purísima Concepción de Acuña, San Francisco de la Espada, and San José y San Miguel de Aguayo), 1793–94, and Mission Nuestra Señora

---

[48] Kielman, *Guide to the Univ. of Texas Arch.*, pp. 30, 314.

[49] Richard G. Santos, *A Preliminary Report on the Archival Project in the Office of the County Clerk of Bexar County* (San Antonio, [1966]).

[50] The Spanish titles and some of the dates for the different series are from Richard G. Santos, "Documentos para la historia de México en los Archivos de San Antonio, Texas," *Revista de Historia de América* 63–64 (jan.-dic. 1967):143–49. The classification "O" (*Colecciones especiales*) in this publication is described as special collections, consisting of various documents referring to persons important in the history of Texas, including José Antonio Navarro, Francisco Ruiz, James Bowie, David Crockett, Erastus "Deaf" Smith, etc.

del Refugio; and papers on the sale of the San Antonio mission lands by the provincial deputation 1823–30, arranged chronologically by mission.

C. Lands Outside Béxar County (*Concesiones fuera del municipio de Béxar*), 1778–1835 (124 items) — petitions and grants concerning land transactions in Victoria, 1800; junction of the Guadalupe and San Marcos rivers, 1809; Palo Alto Creek, 1817; La Bahía del Espíritu Santo (Goliad), 1778–1833; Villa de Nacogdoches, 1825–36; Villa de San Patricio, 1825–35.

D. Wills and Estates (*Homologaciones*), 1742–1836 (124 files) — papers regarding 124 estates, arranged alphabetically by name of estate and chronologically thereunder.

E. Rebel Property (*Tierras de los insurgentes*), 1813–19 (10 items) — inventories, directives, and public auctions of property confiscated from the insurgents by Brig. Gen. Joaquín de Arredondo, arranged chronologically.

F. Powers of Attorney (*Procuraciones*), 1770–1836 (84 items) — arranged alphabetically by surname of grantee and chronologically thereunder.

G. Contracts, Agreements, and Receipts (*Contratos y recibos*), (20 items) — instruments of a varied nature including adoptions, business partnerships, and marriage dowries, arranged chronologically.

H. Protocols (*Protocolos*), (dates not supplied; 59 folders) — various legal papers including land grants, wills, military discharges, and municipal accounts, arranged chronologically.

I. Litigations (*Litigios*), 1757–1830 (37 cases) — lawsuits, arranged chronologically.

J. Decrees, Edicts, Laws and Proclamations (*Edictos, decretos y proclamas*), 1761–1835 (619 items) — documents (largely printed) issued by the Spanish, Mexican, and Coahuila and Texas governments, arranged by government and chronologically thereunder.

K. Military Reports (*Partes militares*), 1781–1832 (15 folders) — papers concerning the activities of Spanish and Mexican military forces in Texas, arranged chronologically.

L. Postal Administration (*Administracion de correos*), 1816–35 (12 folders) — documents concerning postal administration, arranged chronologically.

M. Customhouse Reports (*Guías de la Aduana*), 1824–34 (16 folders) — arranged chronologically.

N. Oficios, 1770–1833 (153 items) — communications between the governor at Béxar and alcaldes and military officers, arranged chronologically.

O. Fragments. A few fragments of unidentified manuscripts.

P. & Q. consist of post–1836 records.

R. Broadsides (*Impresos*), 1761–1822 (74 items) —
large, odd-size issuances of the Spanish and Mexican governments, arranged chronologically.

The Republic of Texas claimed the Río Grande as its western boundary, following the treaty of Velasco of 1836 with General Santa Anna, under which he agreed to remove all Mexican troops south of that river.[51] Texas, however, failed to effectuate its claim, and the region south of the Nueces River, which had been established as the boundary between Texas and Nuevo Santander (Tamaulipas) in 1805, was not occupied. Traversed by military forces and raided by Indians, the region between the two rivers was evacuated by rancheros and became a no-man's-land. Abortive efforts were made by the Texans to occupy Laredo, but that place remained in Mexican hands until after the occupation of Texas by United States military forces and the outbreak of the Mexican War in 1846. The prolongation of Mexican rule at Laredo resulted in the further accumulation of Mexican records there.

The Spanish and Mexican archives of Laredo passed into the custody of the county clerk, after the American occupation, and were undisturbed for many years. The interest of Sebron S. Wilcox in the local history of Laredo, instigated by his work as a court reporter, caused him to undertake a search for the Spanish records in 1934.[52] A remodeling of the county clerk's office that year resulted in collections of old records being brought out from storage places, and Wilcox found a bundle of Spanish records containing documents signed by Tomás Sánchez, the founder of Laredo. In January, 1936, when the janitor was clearing old records out of the basement, he found, after being alerted by Wilcox, additional Spanish records.

The Laredo records were damaged and dirty, and Wilcox, in his spare time and aided by Father Florencio Andrés of the San Augustín church of Laredo, set about putting them in order.[53] The records were cleaned, placed in chronological arrangement in folders, and stored in steel boxes. The collection consists of some 8,000 documents for the years 1749 (mainly from 1768) to 1868. The importance of these records is indicated by the variety of documents (administrative, notarial, and judicial) disclosed by the examination, including correspondence between the officials of Laredo and civil and military officers of north-

---

[51] Scott, *Lower Río Grande*, pp. 132–33.

[52] Sebron S. Wilcox, "The Spanish Archives of Laredo," *Southw. Hist. Quar.* 44 (Jan. 1946):343.

[53] Ibid., p. 343; Letter of Sebron B. Wilcox to Walter P. Webb, Jan. 25, 1941, in Walter P. Webb, "The Texas Collection," *Southw. Hist. Quar.* 44 (Apr. 1941):499.

ern Mexico, decrees of the Spanish and Mexican governments, local decrees, laws, ordinances, trade statistics, census reports, vital statistics, Indian raids, allotments of land, boundary surveys, tax renditions, wills, settlements of estates, establishment of post offices and appointment of postmasters, civil and criminal litigation, and cattle brands.[54]

The Spanish Archives of Laredo were unearthed at an opportune time for work to be done on them. The transcription of these archives was started in 1936 as a Works Progress Administration project, under the direction of Ricardo de la Garza, a descendant of Tomás Sánchez, and the technical supervision of Wilcox. Taken over by the Historical Records Survey in 1940, the transcription was completed and collated with the originals in 1941. A set of the 15,000 pages of transcripts was bound by Wilcox for his personal use. At his suggestion, Witt B. Harwell, Texas state librarian, and an assistant drove to Laredo in August, 1958, and carried copies of the transcription back to Austin for the use of the Texas State Archives.[55] This set consists of about half of the total transcription, covering only 1755 to 1830 and with many gaps for those years. In January, 1960, the Texas State Library shipped another incomplete set of the transcripts to the National Archives, Washington, D.C. Another set is in St. Mary's University Library in San Antonio, and transcripts and photocopies are in the University of Texas Archives. At a later date, Mr. Wilcox obtained possession of the original records and used them for historical research.

Not long before his death in 1959, Wilcox permitted David M. Vigness to microfilm the Laredo Archives for the Southwest Collection of Texas Technological University, Lubbock, Texas. The twelve rolls of microfilm cover the Laredo Archives through 1847. A positive copy of this microfilm is in the Colorado State Archives.

In 1960, in accordance with her late husband's wishes, Mrs. Wilcox placed the Wilcox Collections and the Laredo Archives in St. Mary's University Library, San Antonio, to which Wilcox had already presented some materials. That repository has arranged the Laredo Archives in chronological order in acid-free folders, and placed them in a fireproof vault specially constructed for their preservation. The collection has been microfilmed on sixteen rolls (1749–1872; 13,347 pages). When the microfilm and the transcripts are not satisfactory, the University gives special permission to use the original manuscripts.

---

[54] Wilcox, "Spanish Arch. of Laredo," p. 345; Kielman, *Univ. Texas Arch.*, p. 216.

[55] Jaime S. Platon, "The Spanish Archives of Laredo," *Texas Libraries* 22 (Jan.-Feb. 1960):12–13.

Neither an index nor a calendar of the documents is available.[56] Copies of the microfilm have been purchased by the Texas State Archives and Laredo Junior College. A copy is also in the Béxar County Archives. In 1970, officials of St. Mary's University learned that the Wilcox family was attempting to withdraw the Wilcox Collections in its custody on grounds that they had been placed with the university as a loan rather than as a gift. A lawsuit over the ownership of the collections was heard by the District Court of Travis County in 1972, and, in 1973, the Court of Appeals of Texas at Austin upheld the trial court's judgment that the university had acquired and still held title to and ownership of the Wilcox Collections.[57] The judgment did not pass on the claims of the City of Laredo and State of Texas to the ownership of the Laredo Archives, and an appeal was made by the Wilcoxes to the Supreme Court of Texas, which decided that it was not an appealable judgment. Saint Mary's University has retained possession of the Laredo Archives and the other Wilcox materials.

Another town on the east side of the Río Grande, in Webb County, was Palafox, founded in 1810 by Capt. Juan J. Díaz and some families from Coahuila.[58] The town was abandoned because of Indian depredations during the years 1818–26, and was finally destroyed by Indians in 1829. Original records of the villa of San José de Palafox, 1810–27, are in the St. Mary's University Library, San Antonio, Texas. The records have been published in facsimile with translations.[59] This small collection includes instructions from Gov. Antonio Cordero of Coahuila to Captain Díaz, communications between the governor and the local official (referred to as the *justicia* and later as the *alcalde*), several lists of persons living in the town, and censuses of 1815 and 1816 showing the names of heads of families, and the numbers of children, men and women, mulattoes, mixed breeds, and Indians.

Many of the original records of the municipality of Nacogdoches were transferred in 1850 to the office of the secretary of state, from whence they eventually passed, as a result of administrative reorgani-

---

[56] Richard G. Santos, "An Annotated Survey of the Spanish Archives of Laredo at Saint Mary's University of Texas," *Texana*, (Spring 1966), fig. 4, p. 42. Besides a general description of the Laredo archives, this article contains a key to the microfilm rolls.

[57] *Mrs. Sebron S. Wilcox et al., Appellants,* v. *St. Mary's University of San Antonio, Inc., Appellee,* No. 12046, Court of Civil Appeals of Texas, 497 *Southwestern Reporter,* 2d series, p. 782.

[58] Webb, *Handbook of Texas,* 2:325.

[59] Carmen Perry, trans. and ed., *The Impossible Dream by the Rio Grande: A Documented Chronicle of the Establishment and Annihilation of San José de Palafox* (San Antonio, 1971).

zation, into the custody of the Archives Division of the Texas State Library. In 1903, these records were classified as subgroup (5), designated as "Nacogdoches" of the Nacogdoches Archives.[60] The several series that made up the subgroup were as follows: (a) alcalde's correspondence, October 1823–December 1836 (1,670 items); (b) primary judge's correspondence, June 1834–September 1835 (125 items); (c) political chief's correspondence, August 12, 1834–March 5, 1836 (175 items); (d) proceedings of the *ayuntamiento* of Nacogdoches, May 1826–March 1836 (315 entries);[61] (e) lawsuits, October 1824–December 1835 (4 volumes); (f) citizenship papers, November 1826–September 1836 (3 volumes); (g) miscellaneous material, 1758–1837 (1,175 items); (h) commandant of the frontier's correspondence, May 4, 1827–October 5, 1835 (150 items); and (i) places subordinate to Nacogdoches: Attoyac, Ayish Bayou, San Augustine, June 1824–October 1835 (160 items); Liberty, February 1831–July 8, 1835 (19 items); Neches, June 1824–August 1835 (18 items); Sabine, May 1824–July 1835 (27 items); and Anáhuac, 1832–35 (4 items).

Nacogdoches records are also in other repositories. Records of the county and district court, 1834–62 (500 items), and a daybook of Alcalde Vital Flores, 1834, are in the Stephen F. Austin State College Archives Collection.[62] Copies of the court proceedings are in the University of Texas Archives. Nacogdoches records, 1770–ca. 1900 (mostly from 1830; 2 feet), in the Texas History Collection of Baylor University include correspondence, orders, laws, land papers, and legal and tax records.[63] Nacogdoches records in the University of Texas Archives include a variety of manuscript, transcribed, and printed materials, some of which relate to the years before 1836.[64] These materials include a register of cattle brands, ca. 1806 (photostat), containing the names of stockmen and drawings of their marks and brands.

Records of other places in east Texas are also available. Records of San Augustine are in the custody of the local government.[65] Correspondence and legal documents of that municipality are in the Texas Technological College Library in Lubbock.[66] Copies of papers of the

---

[60] Texas, Dept. of Agriculture, Insurance, Statistics, and History, *Twenty-Ninth Annual Report*, 1903, pp. xxi–xxii.

[61] Microfilm of the proceedings is in the Library of Congress (Jenkins, *Guide to Early State Records, Supplement*, p. 5), and a translation is in the Archives Division of the Texas State Library.

[62] Day and Yarbrough, *Handbook*, p. 56.

[63] Letter from Guy B. Harrison, Baylor University, Nov. 20, 1963.

[64] Kielman, *Univ. of Texas Arch.*, p. 257.

[65] Crocket, *Two Centuries in East Texas*, pp. 95, 98.

[66] D. C. Arthur, "The San Augustine Collection in the Library of Texas Tech-

alcalde of San Augustine, 1833–37, are in the University of Texas Archives.[67] Papers of John A. Williams, president of the *ayuntamiento* at Liberty, concerning revolutionary activities in 1835, are in the Pinart Collection of the Bancroft Library of the University of California at Berkeley.[68] Copies of papers of the alcalde of Liberty, 1833–37, are in the University of Texas Archives.[69]

Records of the municipality of San Felipe de Austin are in the county clerk's office in Belleville. After Austin County was organized in 1837, San Felipe was the county seat, until Belleville became the county seat in 1848. Colonial archives, 1824–37 (7 boxes), contain 1,200 instruments and certified copies filed for record at San Felipe, including deeds, grants, powers of attorney, title bonds, acts of partition, agreements, mortgages, and bills of sale, arranged alphabetically by the first letter of the surname and numerically by file number thereunder. Colonial papers, 1810–37 (250 items in 2 envelopes), contain original instruments and certified copies, including powers of attorney, wills, articles of agreement, official letters and decrees, public and private accounts, mortgages, official bonds, affidavits, and promissory notes, arranged chronologically. A Spanish record of deeds, conveyances, mortgages, liens, etc., 1824–35 (1 volume), contains copies recorded after the establishment of the county government. Marriage bonds and contracts, 1824–36 (95 items), are documents that were executed by the participants before the judge and witnesses, to ensure religious marriage ceremonies by the priest when he arrived in the colony. Ferry bonds, 1830, 1832, 1836 (3 items), are instruments executed by purchasers of the right to operate ferries. A book of brands and marks, 1824–37 (1 volume), shows the names of persons recording brands, drawings of the brands, and the dates of recording. Many of the names for the 670 brands recorded are signatures.[70]

The judicial records of San Felipe, in Belleville, include those of the superior and alcalde courts. The docket of the alcalde court, Sep-

---

nological College" (Texas Technological College, Master's Thesis, 1931). Materials for 1834–36 are described in this manuscript, in which a few of the documents are reproduced.

[67] Kielman, *Univ. of Texas Arch.*, p. 6.

[68] C. Allen True, "John A. Williams, Champion of Mexico in the Early Days of the Texas Revolution," *Southw. Hist. Quar.* 47 (Oct. 1943), pp. 107–19.

[69] Kielman, *Univ. of Texas Arch.*, pp. 6–7.

[70] Final Inventory of State Historical Records Survey Files, May 4, 1942, file 651.3118 (Texas), entry 1200, pp. 49–50; Records of the Work Projects Administration (Record Group 69), National Archives; Historical Records Survey, Texas, Inventory of the Colonial Archives of Texas, 1821–1837; Municipality of San Felipe de Austin (Austin County Courthouse, Belleville, Texas) (San Antonio, Tex., 1938). The author has a xerox copy of the latter inventory from the University of Texas Archives.

tember 22, 1829–May 24, 1833 (3 volumes, books A–B, C, D) is a record of cases showing the names of plaintiff and defendant, kind of case, date, and amount of judgment; notations as to processes issued, stays, transfers, and appeals; amounts of fees due witnesses, arbitrators, alcalde, umpire, and sheriff; and signatures of the alcalde and arbitrators. The entries are arranged chronologically by date of filing. Dockets E to H, referred to in the case papers, have apparently been lost. The docket of the superior court, 1827–28 (pages 1–46 of docket A–B of the alcalde's court), contains a record of cases appealed from the alcalde's court, and minutes of proceedings of three sessions of the superior court held at San Felipe. Civil case papers ("Old Republic Papers"), 1834–37 (4 boxes), consist of original papers filed in civil actions in the alcalde's court, including plaintiffs' petitions, defendants' answers, orders for process, summonses, citations, executions, officers' returns, commissions for depositions, depositions, fee bills, inventories of property, returns of appraisers, arbitrators' awards, notes, title bonds, and a few judgments. The case jackets are arranged alphabetically by name of plaintiff. Probate case papers, 1824–37 (22 boxes), consist of original papers filed in the settlement of estates, including petitions, wills, bonds, notices in probate, citations, offers of sale, reports of sale, accounts of administration, awards, orders of partition, plats of survey, inventories, appraisements, fee bills, accounts and vouchers, and personal papers. The papers are arranged alphabetically by the name of the deceased.

Other records of the municipality of San Felipe are in other repositories. The proceedings of the *ayuntamiento* of San Felipe, February 12, 1828–January 3, 1832 (3 volumes), are in the Texas General Land Office. These proceedings were transferred by the county clerk to the district court clerk in 1849, and by the latter, pursuant to an act of the state legislature in 1852, to the General Land Office. Microfilm of the proceedings of 1828–32 is in the Library of Congress,[71] and the proceedings have been published.[72] The proceedings for 1832–35 are missing. Correspondence of the *ayuntamiento* is in the papers of individuals, including those of Austin and Lamar, described above. A volume of miscellaneous documents of San Felipe, October 20, 1823–October 17, 1835 (175 items), is among the Nacogdoches Archives in the Archives Division of the Texas State Library.[73] An 1826 census of San Felipe is in the Patrick I. Nixon papers in the University of Texas

---

[71] Jenkins and Hamrick, "Administrative Records," *Guide to Microfilm Collection of Early State Records*, p. 87.

[72] Eugene C. Barker, trans. and ed., "Minutes of the Ayuntamiento of San Felipe de Austin, 1828–1832," *Southw. Hist. Quar.* 21–24 (Jan. 1918–Oct. 1920).

[73] Texas, Dept. of Agriculture, etc., *29th Annual Report*, 1903, p. xxii.

Archives. In the same repository and in the Rosenberg Library in Galveston, there are papers of David G. Burnet, who became a judge of the municipality of San Felipe in 1834.

Records of the municipality of Brazoria were taken over by the clerk of Brazoria County upon its organization on February 20, 1837. The surviving records are in the county courthouse at Angleton, where the county seat was moved (from Brazoria) in 1897. Alcalde court papers, December 28, 1831–November 12, 1836 (148 items), consist of documents filed in civil, criminal, and probate cases.[74] The documents include contracts, affidavits, transfers of property, mortgages for slaves and real property, powers of attorney, promissory notes, inventories of property, subpoenas, accounts, petitions, injunctions, appraisements of land, apprentice indentures, bills of goods purchased, receipts for costs, and notices, authorizations, subpoenas, executions, orders, and judgments issued by the alcaldes. A final record of proceedings in the district court for the second judicial district, 1828–38 (1 volume), 457 pages, concerns cases originating in the alcalde, or primary, courts, or based on causes arising before February 20, 1837.[75] The proceedings include copies of instruments introduced as exhibits, copies of proceedings in which judgment was rendered by the alcalde court, copies of judgments rendered by the district court, and transcripts of decisions from the commissioner of civil appeals and the Texas Supreme Court. The entries are by case number, and there is an alphabetical index of the names of plaintiffs to case numbers. A file of civil cases, 1835 (921 cases), consists of papers of civil cases arising in the alcalde courts prior to 1837 and continuing in the district court of Brazoria County.[76] A docket of court cases for the precinct of Victoria, municipality of San Felipe, February 1, 1832–January 1, 1833 (1 volume, 101 pages), concerns cases tried before Asa Brigham, *comisario* of the precinct.[77] This record shows the names of plaintiffs and defendants, case numbers, recapitulations of fees assessed, a brief of the proceedings, orders of the court, and the dates of orders. A file docket of cases filed in the jurisdiction of Brazoria, 1834–35 (1 volume; 40 pages), contains entries regarding cases without numbers or dates, with the notation by cases of the amounts of fees for docketing.[78] A docket of the alcalde court of the jurisdiction of Brazoria, 1834–35 (1 volume, 200 pages), concerns

---

[74] Historical Records Survey, Texas, *Inventory of the Colonial Archives of Brazoria*, p. 86. Indexes of this file and/or lists of calendars of the files described below are in this inventory.

[75] Ibid., p. 102.

[76] Ibid., p. 108.

[77] Ibid., p. 34.

[78] Ibid., p. 39.

cases brought by or before alcalde Edwin Waller.[79] This docket shows the names of plaintiffs, defendants, and witnesses, a recapitulation of fees, a brief of proceedings, date of execution or execution returnable, and other notations. A general docket of all cases instituted in the primary court of the jurisdiction of Columbia, 1835 (1 volume, 268 pages), shows the names of the parties, number of cases, date of entries, recapitulation of fees, and, in some cases, notation of final settlement.[80] Another item is a docket of cases filed in the primary court of the jurisdiction of Columbia, 1835 (1 volume, last 53 pages of the execution docket, book B, of the district court, 1837–41).[81] Probate cases, 1787–1869, consist of original instruments, notices, and probate letters resulting from the administration of estates.[82] These cases include letters, receipts, orders of exchange, land grants and deeds, inventories, letters testamentary, notices of probate, appraisals, wills, notes, and accounts. Cases opening in the courts before the Texas Revolution were continued in Texas courts, pursuant to an act of the Texas Congress of December 29, 1837.[83] As it was the custom of early courts to take charge of the property of deceased persons who died intestate without heirs, private letters were filed with the case papers. Among the files for these cases are letters of Stephen F. Austin, 1823–51 (215 items); James W. Fannin, Jr., 1826–43 (115 items); and Dr. James Grant, 1833–36 (87 items).

Other records of the municipality of Brazoria are also in the courthouse at Angleton. A record of Spanish deeds, 1823–36 (1 volume, 500 pages), contains copies of land grants, deeds granted by Mexico to colonists, and transfers among the colonists for land within Brazoria County.[84] These chronologically entered instruments show the names of the grantor and grantee, date, quantity of land, location and description of the property, date of transfer, date of recording, and signature of the county clerk. Transcribed Spanish records, 1823–36 (1 volume), contain English translations of the land grants and deeds recorded in the volume described above. Marriage records, 1829–36 (29 items), consist of original marriage bonds and contracts executed under Mexican laws, permitting civil agreements until legal ceremonies could be held.[85] These records show the names of the parties, conditions of the

[79] Ibid., p. 39.

[80] Ibid., p. 63.

[81] Ibid., p. 77.

[82] Ibid., p. 27.

[83] Gammel, Law of Texas, 1:1462.

[84] Historical Records Survey, Texas, Inventory of the Colonial Archives of Brazoria, p. 19.

[85] Ibid., p. 23.

contract, amount of the agreement, and signature of the principals and witnesses.

Papers of the alcalde of the municipality of Brazoria, 1833–37 (typescript), in the University of Texas Archives, include reports on political, economic, and social matters.[86] Records of Gonzales, in DeWitt's colony, have been published by a historian of that colony. Minutes of the *ayuntamiento* from January 25, 1833, to sometime in 1834 were published from an incomplete record which was then in the law office of Harwood and Walsh in Gonzales.[87] A list of lots in Gonzales deeded by alcaldes from December 28, 1833, to September 16, 1835, was published from a volume entitled "Records of the Corporation of the Town of Gonzales," in the same office.[88] A list of inhabitants of Gonzales, 1828, obtained from the Nacogdoches Archives, is also in print.[89] Correspondence of the *ayuntamiento* with the governor, 1835, was also in the custody of Harwood and Walsh, and other correspondence was in a scrapbook in the University of Texas Library. Maps of the town of Gonzales, compiled in part from field notes of survey, are published in the study by Rather. The constitution of Gonzales, January 1, 1831, DeWitt's empresario contract, land sales and deeds, land surveys, and bills of sale of slaves, are in the Gonzales Memorial Museum.[90] Petitions for and deeds to lots in Gonzales, and a list of town lot purchasers, September–December, 1834 (31 pages, photocopies), are in the Texas State Archives.

The records of other municipalities in the Department of Brazos are more fragmentary. Minutes of the meetings of the proprietors of Matagorda, August 1, 1830–April 2, 1838, are in the custody of Matagorda County at Bay City, and a transcript (49 pages) is in the University of Texas Archives.[91] These minutes concern the election of officials, the distribution of lots in the town, instructions to surveyors, instructions for the sale of lots, the declaration of dividends on shares, statements of lots donated to individuals and the public, and a list of blocks selected by the proprietors as their own individual or private property. A copy of the constitution of the proprietors of Matagorda, July 8,

---

[86] Kielman, *Univ. Texas Arch.*, p. 6. Some printed broadsides were issued by the *ayuntamiento* of Brazoria during 1833–34, and others were issued by meetings of citizens of Columbia during June–September, 1833 (Streeter, *Bibliography of Texas*, pt. 1, 1:43, 47–49, 59–67).

[87] Rather, "DeWitt's Colony," pp. 181–88. A reprint of this study is available from the Gonzales Public Library for $2.25.

[88] Ibid., pp. 168–72.

[89] Ibid., pp. 189–91.

[90] Day and Harbrough, *Handbook of Texas Arch. and Ms. Depositories*, p. 46.

[91] William R. Hogan, *The Texas Republic: A Social and Economic History* (Norman, 1946), p. 304; Kielman, *Univ. Texas Arch.*, p. 121.

1830, is also in the University of Texas Archives. Minutes of the *ayuntamiento* of Mina (Bastrop), August 18–19, September 16–17, 1834 (photocopy), are in the same repository.[92] An 1875 hurricane is reported to have destroyed the records of the old town of Velasco.[93]

The Mexican forces under Gen. José Urrea, that invaded south Texas in 1836, destroyed the records in that area and carried off others. The minutes of the *ayuntamiento* of Goliad (La Bahía), 1821–35 (1 volume, 454 pages), are in the Archivo General de la Nación in Mexico City,[94] and a transcript is in the University of Texas Archives. The early records of San Patricio have been largely destroyed by fire.[95] The *síndico* of Refugio attempted to carry some of the records to safety in 1836, but was captured by Mexicans, who destroyed the records.[96] Most of the records that remained were thrown away by Mexican raiders in 1841. A few papers that escaped destruction are in the custody of the clerk of the district court at Refugio,[97] and others that fell into private hands are in the Dawgood Library at Refugio.[98] An account book of Martín de León, the founder of Victoria, is in the Victoria County archives.[99]

A transcription and translation of a segment of the records of the pueblo of Ysleta, in west Texas near El Paso, has been prepared.[100]

Microfilm publications should be prepared from the local records described above. Making these records more widely available for research would promote the writing of the history of Texas and the Southwest, and security copies of these valuable records would be assured.

---

92 Kielman, *Univ. Texas Arch.*, p. 22.

93 Webb, *Handbook of Texas*, 2:835.

94 Oberste, *Texas Irish Empresarios*, p. 31 n. 1.

95 Ibid., p. 256 n. 12.

96 Ibid., p. 216 n. 21; Huson, *Refugio County*, 1:3.

97 Oberste, *Texas Irish Empresarios*, p. 117 n. 6, p. 120 n. 12.

98 Huson, *Refugio County*, 1:3. Huson did not find any records dated before 1847.

99 Webb, *Handbook of Texas*, 1:484.

100 Elsie Campbell, "Spanish Records of the Civil Government of Ysleta, 1835" (Texas Western College, Master of Arts Thesis, 1950).

18

Ecclesiastical Records

MISSIONS ESTABLISHED by religious orders of the Catholic church were utilized throughout Spanish America to christianize the Indians and promote settlement. Franciscan friars accompanied the early Spanish conquerors of New Spain and were members of overland expeditions that were sent northward to explore and colonize. During 1683–84, Franciscan missionaries who accompanied Capt. Juan Domínguez de Mendoza to the junction of the Río Grande and the Río Conchos (La Junta de los Ríos) established six missions among the Humano Indians in that area, four of them on the Texas side of the Río Grande, near present Presidio.[1] These missions were not regularly occupied, and others that were established in 1715 were also irregularly tenanted.[2]

Several Franciscan missions were established among the Indians in the El Paso district. In 1659, the Mission Nuestra Señora de Guadalupe del Paso was founded among the Manso Indians at El Paso del Norte (Ciudad Juárez, Mexico).[3] Piro and Tompiro Indians who had fled from the Pueblo revolt in New Mexico settled in 1682 at the pueblo

---

[1] Castañeda, *Our Catholic Heritage in Texas*, 1:268–75; George B. Eckhart, "Missions in Texas Along the Río Grande and in Adjacent Areas," *Southw. Hist. Quar.* 63 (Jan. 1960):606. Castañeda presents the most detailed factual account of the establishment of the missions in Texas, incorporating much new information from manuscript sources. He includes several maps showing the locations of missions and presidios, and the routes of expeditions. H. E. Bolton's *Texas in the Middle Eighteenth Century* (Berkeley, 1915) contains a map of eighteenth century missions, presidios, towns, Indian villages, and roads.

[2] J. Charles Kelley, "The Historic Indian Pueblos of La Junta de los Ríos," *N. Mex. Hist. Rev.* 27 (Oct. 1952):268–70.

[3] Castañeda, *Our Catholic Heritage in Texas*, 1:248–49.

and mission of San Antonio de Senecú, below Guadalupe del Paso on the Texas side of the Río Grande. Tigua refugees from New Mexico settled at Corpus Christi de la Isleta, east of Senecú.[4] The Mission of Nuestra Señora de la Concepción del Socorro was also established in 1682 by Piro, Thano, and Jémez Indians from New Mexico. Missions were also located at this time at San Lorenzo and San Elizario, in what became El Paso County. Senecú and San Lorenzo have disappeared; the other pueblos still exist, the name of Isleta having been changed to Ysleta.[5]

Missionaries from the College of Santa Cruz of Querétaro established missions in various parts of Texas. In 1690, Fr. Damian Massanet and other missionaries founded San Francisco de los Tejas among the Tejas Indians in east Texas, near present-day Crockett.[6] In the fall of 1691, Santísimo Nombre de María was founded farther east on the bank of the Neches River. Within two years, Indian hostility forced the abandonment of both missions. San Francisco was reestablished in 1716, east of the Neches River, and, in the same year, San José de los Nazones and Nuestra Señora de la Purísima Concepción were established near Nacogdoches. When San Francisco de los Tejas was relocated in 1721, it was renamed San Francisco de los Neches.

The development of an intermediate cluster of missions began in 1718 with the removal of San Francisco Solano from the Río Grande to the San Antonio River, where it was refounded as San Antonio de Valero. A subordinate establishment known as San Francisco Xavier de Naxera was located nearby in 1722, but was closed in 1726. In 1731, the missions that had been established in east Texas were moved to the San Antonio area. Purísima Concepción became Purísima Concepción de Acuña, San José became San Juan Capistrano, and San Francisco de los Neches became San Francisco de la Espada. In 1773, the Querétarans transferred their missions at San Antonio to the Zacatecans.

In the mid-eighteenth century, the Querétaran missions were expanded into other areas of Texas. In 1748, San Francisco Xavier de Horcasitas was established on the San Gabriel River above its junction with Brushy Creek, near present-day Thorndale, and in 1749, San Ildefonso and Nuestra Señora de la Candelaria were established on the same river.[7] These missions, located northeast of Austin, endured only

---

[4] Ibid., p. 263.

[5] Webb, *Handbook of Texas*, 2:949.

[6] Castañeda, *Our Catholic Heritage in Texas*, 1:353.

[7] Herbert E. Bolton, "The Founding of Missions on the San Gabriel River, 1748–1749," *Southw. Hist. Quar.* 17 (Apr. 1914):340–41, 373, 375.

a few years before they were withdrawn, along with the presidio, because of unfavorable conditions. The properties belonging to the missions passed to Santa Cruz de San Sabá, which was established, with the assistance of missionaries from the College of San Fernando, with another presidio in 1757 in Apache country on the San Sabá River, near present Menard.[8] Comanche and other Indians attacked the mission in 1758, murdered most of the inhabitants, and burned the buildings. Another attempt, in 1762, to settle among the Apaches, by founding Nuestra Señora de la Candelaria del Cañon and San Lorenzo de Santa Cruz on the upper Nueces River, also resulted in failure in a few years.

Soon after the College of Guadalupe of Zacatecas was founded in 1707, its missionaries entered Texas and other parts of northern Mexico. In 1716, Fr. Antonio Margil de Jesús and other friars accompanied the expedition of Capt. Domingo Ramón that was sent to reoccupy Texas. Nuestra Señora de Guadalupe de Nacogdoches was established at the village of the Nacogdoches Indians, Nuestra Señora de los Dolores de los Ais was established halfway between Nacogdoches and Los Adaes,[9] and San Miguel was established at Los Adaes (Louisiana). These missions were maintained until the abandonment of east Texas in 1773. In 1720, San José y San Miguel de Aguayo was established at San Antonio, a short distance below San Antonio de Valero.[10] Abandoned in 1719 during the war with the French and reestablished in 1721, the east Texas missions were later moved to the San Antonio area. La Bahía del Espíritu Santo de Zuñiga, established among the Karankawa Indians on Matagorda Bay in 1722, was moved inland in 1726 to the Guadalupe River, and moved again in 1749 to the site of modern Goliad.[11] Nuestra Señora del Rosario was founded near Matagorda Bay in 1754 for work among the coast Indians.[12] About 1756, Nuestra Señora de la Purísima Concepción was established on the lower Trinity River, below present-day Liberty, near the presidio of San Agustín de Ahumada. About the same time, Nuestra Señora de la Luz was founded on the lower Trinity River. A site at

---

[8] Castañeda, *Our Catholic Heritage in Texas*, 3:397.

[9] Thomas P. O'Rourke, *The Franciscan Missions in Texas (1690–1793)* (Washington, 1927), pp. 22, 44; Robert B. Blake, "Locations of the Early Spanish Missions and Presidios in Nacogdoches County," *Southw. Hist. Quar.* 41 (Jan. 1938):213, and map.

[10] Marion A. Habig, O.F.M., "Mission San José y San Miguel de Aguayo," *Southw. Hist. Quar.* 71 (Apr. 1968):496.

[11] Castañeda, *Our Catholic Heritage in Texas*, 2:147.

[12] George B. Eckhart, "Spanish Missions of Texas, 1680–1800: An Outline of Spanish Mission History in Texas from 1680 to 1800," *The Kiva* 32 (Feb. 1967):89. Includes maps showing the locations of the missions.

the junction of the San Antonio and Guadalupe rivers, occupied by the Karankawa Indians, was selected for Nuestra Señora del Refugio in 1793.[13] Because of the unhealthfulness of the original site, this mission was moved in 1796 to the vicinity of present Refugio.

By the end of the eighteenth century, the missions were no longer needed to promote settlement on the frontier, and attempts were made to effect their secularization. This process involved the distribution of land, animals, and implements, the election of their own officials by the Indians, and the replacement of missionaries by regular clergymen, subordinate to the diocese.[14] On the instruction of Gov. Manuel Muñoz of Texas, San Antonio de Valero was secularized in 1793, and later, after its buildings were occupied as a military barracks, became known as the Alamo.[15] Missionaries continued to function at San José and the other missions in the San Antonio area, but the number of persons residing at them declined, and, in 1824, pursuant to a decree of the Mexican government, the mission churches and their properties were turned over to the military chaplain at the Alamo, who was also the substitute pastor of the San Fernando parish.[16] In 1831, the governor of Texas directed the alcalde of San Antonio to dispose of all remaining lands and buildings of the San Antonio missions except the chapels, which were to be used as churches.[17] The last missions to be secularized were those near Goliad (La Bahía), including Espíritu Santo del Zuñiga, N. S. del Refugio, and N. S. del Rosario, whose lands and property were distributed by 1830.[18]

The decree of 1793, directing the secularization of the San Antonio missions, resulted in the transfer of their records and appurtenances to the parish church of San Fernando.[19] The records that have survived are still in the custody of San Fernando Cathedral, the seat of the Archdiocese of San Antonio. The register of burials of San Antonio de Valero, 1703–82 (1 volume, 234 pages), includes a record of burials for San Francisco Solano, 1703–13, San Xavier de Naxera, 1722, and San Antonio de Valero, 1718–82.[20] The register of marriages and bap-

[13] Castañeda, *Our Catholic Heritage in Texas*, 5:80.

[14] Ibid., 5:46, 47, 115; 6:350–51.

[15] Ibid., 5:35.

[16] Marion A. Habig, O.F.M., *The Alamo Chain of Missions: A History of San Antonio's Five Old Missions* (Chicago, 1968), pp. 108–09.

[17] Castañeda, *Our Catholic Heritage in Texas*, 6:349.

[18] Paul H. Walters, "Secularization of the La Bahía Missions," *Southw. Hist. Quar.* 54 (Jan. 1951):287–300.

[19] Richard Santos, "A Preliminary Survey of the San Fernando Archives," *Texas Libraries* 28 (Winter 1966–67):153.

[20] Ibid., p. 154; Herbert E. Bolton, "Spanish Mission Records at San Antonio," *Southw. Hist. Quar.* 10 (Apr. 1907):303.

tisms of San Antonio de Valero, 1703–83 (1 volume, 351 pages), includes baptismal records of San Francisco Solano, October 6, 1703–June 17, 1708; and a register of baptisms of San Xavier de Naxera, March 12, 1721–July 20, 1726, includes baptisms of Hyerbipiamo Indians who were settled at the mission in 1722.[21] The register of marriages and marriage applications of San Antonio de Valero, 1709–1825 (1 volume, 400 pages), includes marriages recorded at San Francisco Solano, 1709–16.[22] The chaplain of the troops stationed at the Alamo after 1798 continued to use this book for recording marriages and marriage applications of troops. A register of baptisms, marriages, and burials of San Francisco Solano, 1703–08, is in the archives of the College of Santa Cruz of Querétaro.[23]

Records of other missions in the custody of San Fernando Cathedral, bound into one volume (490 pages), include a register of marriages of Purísima Concepción de Acuña, 1733–90 (72 pages); a register of baptisms of San José y San Miguel de Acuña, 1777–1823; a register of marriages of San José y San Miguel de Acuña, 1778–1822; and a register of burials, 1781–1824, and scattered entries, 1818–24, for San Juan Capistrano and San Francisco de la Espada.[24] Attached to the back of this volume is a report of a general visitation to the Villa San Fernando de Béxar and Texas, 1825–26. The baptismal and burial registers of Purísima Concepción de Acuña, and most of the records of San Francisco de la Espada, are missing. Fragments of registers of San Antonio de Valero, in the Bancroft Library of the University of California, include a baptismal and burial register, 1720–21 (2 pages), a marriage register, 1748 [?]–1754 (4 pages), and a burial register, 1757 (2 pages). In 1931, the Historical Commission of the Texas State Council of the Knights of Columbus had photostats made of the mission records in the San Fernando Cathedral. Sets of these photostats are in the San Fernando Archives, where they are used for research in place of the fragile originals, and another set is in the Catholic Archives of Texas in the Chancery Archives in Austin.[25] Microfilm of the mission registers is in the Genealogical Society of the Church of Jesus Christ of Latter-Day Saints in Salt Lake City. The mission records are useful

---

[21] Bolton, "Spanish Mission Records," pp. 298–300; Santos, "San Fernando Archives," p. 154.

[22] Bolton, "Spanish Mission Records," p. 302; Santos, "San Fernando Archives," p. 154.

[23] Bolton, *Guide Arch Mex.*, p. 392; Lino Gómez Canedo, "Some Franciscan Sources in the Archives and Libraries of America," *Americas* 13 (Oct. 1956):147.

[24] Bolton, "Spanish Mission Records," pp. 304–05; Santos, "San Fernando Archives," p. 154.

[25] Lane, *Catholic Archives of Texas*, pp. 89, 91. The chancery office is at 1600 Congress Ave., Austin, Tex. 78767.

not only for the history of the missions, the friars who served at them, and the many different Indian tribes connected with them, but also for data regarding the military and civilian populations.

Records of the parish church of San Fernando, which dates from the founding of the Villa San Fernando de Béxar in 1721, are also among the archives of the Archdiocese of San Antonio in the San Fernando Cathedral. These records include a register of baptisms, 1731–1858 (part of volume 1, volumes 2, 3, 8, 9); register of marriages, 1731–1856 (part of volume 1, volume 4); register of burials, 1731–1860 (part of volume 1, volume 5–7); register of confirmations, 1731–60 (part of volume 1).[26] The books of public administration (*libros de gobierno*), 1759–1826 (2 volumes), contain documents emanating from higher ecclesiastical and civil authorities, including proclamations, decrees, papal bulls, pastoral letters, directives and communications issued by the pope, the patriarch of the Indies, the dioceses of Guadalajara and Nuevo León, the king of Spain, the viceroy of New Spain, the commandant general of the Interior Provinces, the intendant of San Luís Potosí, and the Holy Inquisition of Mexico.[27] Miscellaneous unbound records include marriage records, 1775–78; marriage applications of citizens and soldiers of Texas, dating from 1763; and a lawsuit heard by an ecclesiastical tribunal at the San Fernando church, 1794–95.

Other records in the San Fernando Archives are those of a cavalry company, the Flying Company of San Carlos de Parras del Alamo, which was stationed at the secularized mission San Antonio de Valero in 1798. Its records were delivered by the chaplain to the parish church of San Fernando in 1812 and include a register of baptisms, 1798–1823 (1 volume, 180 pages), and unbound marriage applications, dating from 1798 (900 pages).[28]

Records of Nuestra Señora del Refugio, which was established in Refugio County in 1793, are in the parish church at Matamoros, Tamaulipas. These include a register of baptisms, April 21, 1807–February 21, 1827, and a register of burials, May 16, 1807–November 18, 1825.[29] Registers for the early years of the mission are missing. Photostats of the registers described above were obtained by the Texas Knights of Columbus in 1930 and are now in the Catholic Archives of Texas in the chancery office in Austin. Copies of the registers are also in the Church of Our Lady of Refuge at Refugio. The Catholic Archives of Texas also has a collection of reproductions and transla-

---

[26] Santos, "San Fernando Archives," p. 154.

[27] Ibid., pp. 154, 172 n. 3.

[28] Ibid., p. 155.

[29] Bolton, *Guide to Arch. Mex.*, p. 447; H. E. Bolton, "Records of the Mission of Nuestra Señora del Refugio," *Southw. Hist. Quar.* 14 (Oct. 1910):164–66.

tions of documents on the history of Refugio Mission assembled by Msgr. William H. Oberste,[30] who has also published data compiled from the mission registers, including lists of names of children baptized and the names of their Spanish parents, a statistical summary of baptisms, an index to burials, and a list of Spanish families residing in Refugio.[31]

Photostats of the records of St. Augustin Church of Laredo, obtained by the Texas Knights of Columbus in 1930, are in the Catholic Archives of Texas in the chancery office in Austin. These include registers of baptisms, 1788–1860 (4 volumes); registers of marriages, 1790–1881 (2 volumes); a register of burials, 1836–48 (volume II; volume I, 1789–1833 was missing in January, 1872); a book of confirmations, 1834–54 (1 volume); a book of public administration, 1789–1854 (1 volume); a book of orders and official correspondence, 1805–37 (1 volume); and a translation of a report on a general visitation of 1767.[32]

Records of missions and churches on the Mexican side of the Río Grande are useful for the history of Texas. The mission records supply information on the Indians of the Río Grande valley, and the parish records throw light on social conditions, racial intermixture (including mulattoes and mestizoes), and migration; both contain information on the ancestors of Mexican Americans, resident in Texas.

The records of the parish church of Nuestra Señora del Refugio de los Esteros, which was established at Matamoros in 1800, were found by Bolton in the curate's house. These records included complete books of baptisms, burials, marriages, confirmations, and government.[33] In the custody of that church there was also a book of episcopal and royal regulations, 1780–1804, that had originally belonged to the church at Camargo. This book contains episcopal and royal regulations issued principally by the bishop of Nuevo León.

The records found by Bolton in the parish house at Camargo included some for the mission at that place and some for the villa of Camargo.[34] A baptismal register, 1764–86, contains entries for both the mission of San Agustín of Laredo and for the villa, mostly after

[30] Lane, *Catholic Archives of Texas*, p. 83.

[31] Oberste, *Refugio Mission*, pp. 386–93.

[32] Lane, *Catholic Archives of Texas*, p. 91; letter from Sister M. Claude Lane, February 1, 1972. The first volume of the burial register is in the church of St. Augustine in Laredo, to which the records were returned after photostating.

[33] Bolton, *Guide to Arch. Mex.*, p. 447. Photocopies of the register of baptisms, April 21, 1807–February 21, 1828, and of the register of burials, May 16, 1807–November 18, 1825, are in the Bancroft Library of the University of California (Hammond, *Guide to Ms. Colls.*, p. 140).

[34] Bolton, *Guide to Arch. Mex.*, p. 450.

1770 for the latter. Another baptismal register is for the Mission of San José Camargo, 1770–1809. A marriage register of the Mission San Agustín of Laredo and the villa, 1764–96, contains entries only for the villa after 1770. Burial registers include one for the Mission of San Agustín of Laredo and the villa, 1764–97, and one for the Mission of San José of Camargo, 1772–1810. Separate records of the parish include baptismal registers from 1787, marriage registers from 1796, and burial registers from 1797; books of government from 1782; account books; and letters.

At the time of Bolton's survey, the parish church at Reynosa had a baptismal register of the Mission of Señor San Jochín del Monte de la Villa de Reynosa, 1790–1816 (containing also, in the latter part of the volume, marriages of persons of the villa), and a marriage register of the mission, 1790–1816. For the parish church of Reynosa, there were baptismal registers from 1800 (except for 1814–20); marriage registers from 1790; burial registers, 1830–45 and from 1850; and books of government, 1790–1827, containing communications from superiors for the government of the parish church.[35]

No records of the missions that were established at La Junta de los Ríos in 1683–84 have survived apparently, but the parish church of nearby Ojinaga, Chihuahua, where a presidio was established in 1760, has some records of interest for later years. A brief and incomplete examination of the church's records in 1949 revealed that they include records of marriages, 1798–1862, and petitions of soldiers stationed at the presidio for permission to marry women of the pueblo.[36] A few documents relating to the La Junta de los Ríos missions are in the archives of the Archdiocese of Santa Fe.[37]

In the cathedral at Saltillo, there are records of the parish church at Guerrero, Coahuila, where the Mission San Juan Bautista served as a base for missionary activities in Texas. These records include circulars of the bishop and ecclesiastical *cabildo* of Nuevo León, 1780–1804, 1831–50, which were circulated among the missions of Texas, and records of the chaplain of the Presidio del Río Grande.[38]

The parish church of Guadalupe in Ciudad Juárez holds records of the mission and parish of Nuestra Señora de Guadalupe as well as those of neighboring missions, including some in Texas.[39] The records

---

[35] Ibid., p. 449.

[36] Charles J. Kelley, "The La Junta Archives," *N. Mex. Hist. Rev.* 25 (Apr. 1950): 162–63.

[37] Angelico Chávez, O.F.M., *Archives of the Archdiocese of Santa Fe, 1678–1900* (Washington, 1957), pp. 27, 159, 160.

[38] Bolton, *Guide Arch. Mex.*, p. 443.

[39] Ibid., pp. 462–63.

of the church of Guadalupe include a register of baptisms from 1662, a register of burials from 1663, and a register of marriages from 1707. That church also has custody of records of the Mission San Antonio de Senecú, including a register of baptisms, 1719–22, 1772–1824, 1829–51; a register of marriages, 1706–23, 1772–1851; and a register of burials, 1772–1848. For San Antonio de Ysleta, the church of Guadalupe has a register of baptisms, 1792–98. Records of San Lorenzo mission include a register of baptisms, 1700–23, 1777–1847; register of marriages, 1777–1846; register of burials, 1778–1847; and a register of confirmations, 1833. Microfilm of the Guadalupe church records and the records of the missions, 1671–1899 (12 rolls), and Xerox copies of the Ysleta church baptismal records 1792–1803, with a translation, are in the collections of the University of Texas at El Paso. Records of the church of Guadalupe, 1730–1899 (approximately 5 feet), in the Catholic Archives of Texas in Austin, include baptismal, marriage, and burial records and are described as originals and copies.[40]

Since the El Paso region was part of New Mexico during the Spanish and Mexican regimes, the Archives of the Archdiocese of Santa Fe contain materials relating to the El Paso missions. A record of a visitation of the El Paso missions made by Juan Bautista Guevara, vicar of New Mexico, for the bishop of Durango, 1817 (book LXXXII), includes preliminary letters and instructions; inventories of the churches, sacristies, and fabrics; and materials relating to the churches of Guadalupe del Paso, San Lorenzo del Real, San Antonio de Senecú, San Antonio de Ysleta, and Purísima Concepción del Socorro.[41] Other materials concerning the missions mentioned above are in the general, loose, mission documents and the list of official communications (*patentes*) in the same repository.

Other Texas missions kept records like those described above. Information derived from the records is often embodied in the reports of friars sent to inspect the missions on behalf of the guardians of the missionary colleges in Mexico. The records of some missions were probably destroyed during Indian attacks and burnings of mission buildings. Other records were carried off to Mexico when the missions were closed, and others that were transferred to parish churches have since been lost.

In the years after 1821, when Mexico governed Texas, the Catholic church made little progress. The Franciscans departed but were not replaced by secular clergymen. Because the church favored the Spanish monarchy, the Mexican government did not support its activities and

[40] Lane, *Cath. Arch. Texas*, p. 91.

[41] Chávez, *Arch. Archdiocese of Santa Fe*, p. 193.

adopted regulatory legislation designed to control it.[42] The new colonies that were established by foreign empresarios experienced difficulty in obtaining appointments of clergymen and retaining the services of those who were designated. The administrator of the Diocese of Nuevo León designated Juan Nepomuceno de la Peña as vicar forane of Texas in 1824, but he seems to have been rather inactive in that position. On visits to San Felipe de Austin, the pastor of the Church of San Fernando in San Antonio, performed baptisms and marriages, but these visits were so infrequent that civil marriages had to be permitted.[43] In Nacogdoches, in the early 1820s, the chaplain served as pastor until the arrival, in 1828, of José Ignacio Galindo as parish priest.[44] He was succeeded, in 1830, by Fr. José Antonio Díaz de León, who had served as a Franciscan in the missions around San Antonio. After his death in 1834, he was not replaced because of the outbreak of the Texas Revolution. After the secularization of Refugio mission in 1830, Fr. Miguel Muro served as chaplain of the garrison and pastor of the townspeople at Goliad until his departure, in 1833, for the College of Zacatecas.[45] In 1829, the buildings at Refugio mission gave shelter to the Irish colonists brought in by McMullen and McGloin.[46] These colonists moved, in 1830, to the land on the Nueces River assigned to the empresarios, and founded the town of San Patricio. In 1830, Henry Doyle, the Irish priest who had come with the colonists, was authorized to build a chapel in the new settlement and repair the chapel at Refugio mission, in order to minister to persons who might settle there. In San Patricio, the Church of St. Patrick was erected on a site provided by the promoters.[47] St. Mary's Church was established at Victoria, at the time of its founding in 1824, by Martín de León. Fr. Michael Muldoon was pastor of San Felipe de Austin and vicar general of the foreign colonies in Texas during 1831–32, but after going to Mexico for a visit in 1832, he did not return to Texas.[48] The settlements in southwest Texas were burned by the Mexicans during their invasion of 1836. The revival of religious activities began with the arrival of John M. Odin in Texas, in 1840, as vicar prefect apostolic. His petition to the Congress of the Republic of Texas resulted in the

[42] Sister Mary A. Fitzmorris, *Four Decades of Catholicism in Texas, 1820–1860* (Washington, 1926), pp. 37–38.

[43] Barker, *Stephen F. Austin*, p. 261.

[44] Castañeda, *Our Catholic Heritage in Texas*, 6:332.

[45] Ibid., 330–31; Fitzmorris, *Catholicism in Texas*, p. 35.

[46] Oberste, *Refugio Mission*, p. 339.

[47] Fitzmorris, *Catholicism in Texas*, p. 22.

[48] Castañeda, *Our Catholic Heritage in Texas*, 6:341–42, 344–45.

act of January 13, 1841, declaring the churches of San Antonio, Goliad, and Victoria, the church lot at Nacogdoches, and the churches at the missions of La Purísima Concepción, San José, San Juan Capistrano, San Francisco de la Espada, and Refugio to be the property of the Catholic church.[49]

During 1930–31, Carlos E. Castañeda, with the support of the University of Texas and the Texas Knights of Columbus, examined the Fondo Franciscano (the records of the Holy Gospel Province in the Biblioteca Nacional) and selected documents on Texas for photostating.[50] The photostats from the Archivo de San Francisco el Grande, 1673–1800 (36 volumes), obtained by Castañeda are in the University of Texas Archives.[51] Though relating mostly to Texas, the collection also includes materials on New Mexico, California, and northern Mexico. Microfilm of selections of the archives of San Francisco el Grande (5 rolls), is in the Academy of American Franciscan History, Washington, D.C., and transcriptions and translations of the microfilm, prepared by Fr. Benedict Leutenegger, are in the Old Spanish Mission Historical Research Library at San José Mission, San Antonio, Texas. Photostats obtained by Castañeda and Fr. Paul Foik for the Texas Knights of Columbus from the Archivo de San Francisco el Grande are also in the Catholic Archives of Texas in Austin.[52]

The College of Santa Cruz of Querétaro, referred to above, was established in 1683 and was the first of several colleges whose purpose was to propagate the Catholic faith in Mexico.[53] The college trained missionaries, supplied them to the missions, and provided them with a place for recuperation after their labors. The guardian of the college had jurisdiction over the missionaries among the Indians. He was independent of the father provincial of the Franciscans at Mexico City, being subordinate to the Franciscan commissary general of the Indies at Madrid. In directing the operations of the college, the guardian was assisted by a council (discretory) of four members, selected from the older and more experienced members of the college. The guardian and the council directed the affairs of the college, passed on the fit-

---

[49] Gammel, *Laws of Texas*, 2:492.

[50] Knights of Columbus, Texas State Council, Historical Commission, *Minutes,* May 1931, p. 6; C. E. Castañeda, "Why I Chose History," *The Americas* 8 (Apr. 1952):479.

[51] Kielman, *Univ. of Texas Arch.*, p. 11; Castañeda and Dabbs, *Guide to Latin American Mss.*, p. 182.

[52] Lane, *Catholic Arch. Texas*, p. 87. Further information regarding the Holy Gospel Province and its records is in chapter nine, in the section on New Mexico.

[53] Michael B. McCloskey, O.F.M., *The Formative Years of the Missionary College of Santa Cruz of Querétaro, 1683–1733* (Washington, 1955), pp. 32–33.

ness of candidates for admission to the college, and adopted decrees for the governance of the college and the missionaries. The guardian was in regular communication with the missions, sent instructions to them, and received reports from them. He sent out visitors to the missions, to observe and report on their condition.

Soon after its founding, the College of Querétaro sent missionaries to Texas and maintained them there for nearly a hundred years. The operations of the Querétarans in Texas were supervised by a father president, who was selected by the college council.[54] In 1773, the Querétarans, having become responsible for the former Jesuit missions in Sonora, transferred the missions they had been conducting in Texas to the College of Guadalupe of Zacatecas.

The archives of the College of Santa Cruz of Querétaro were investigated by Herbert E. Bolton in 1908 and described in his guide, published a few years later. The archives contained important materials relating to the Franciscan missions in northern Mexico, Texas, and southern Arizona.[55] In 1908, the college was suppressed, and the convent that had housed it became a friary of the Franciscan Province of Michoacán. In 1917, one of the revolutionary armies seized the records, but when they were abandoned soon afterwards, individuals salvaged some of them.[56] Some of the records recovered by the Franciscans are now in Celaya, in the custody of the Michoacán Province. The records include reports, dating from 1692, on applicants wishing to join the order; necrology concerning missionaries of the college, 1703–1852; copybooks of circular letters and records of elections and canonical visitations, 1690–early nineteenth century; chapter book concerning elections, 1754–1876; book of decrees of the college, 1777–1853, containing minutes of the council of the college; book of investiture and professions, 1690–1855; documents relating to missions of the college — Río Grande, 1715–27, Sonora, 1766–1820, and Texas, 1718–72; and a book of deaths.[57]

---

[54] A tentative list of the presidents of the missions is in Habig, *Alamo Chain of Missions*, p. 272. The missions conducted by the Querétarans in Texas included: 1690, San Francisco de los Tejas; 1691, Santísimo Nombre de María; 1716, Nuestra Señora de la Purísima Concepción de los Hainai; 1716, San José de los Nazones; 1716, San Francisco Xavier de Horcasitas; 1718, San Antonio de Valero; 1720, San José de Aguayo; 1721, San Francisco de los Neches; 1722, San Francisco Xavier de Naxera; 1731, Nuestra Señora de la Purísima Concepción de Acuña; 1731, San Juan Capistrano; 1731, San Francisco Xavier de Horcasitas; 1749, Nuestra Señora de la Candelaria, 1749, San Ildefonso; 1757, Santa Cruz de San Sabá; 1761, Nuestra Señora de la Candelaria; 1762, San Lorenzo de Santa Cruz (Webb, *Handbook of Texas*, 2:568; O'Rourke, *Franciscan Missions in Texas*, pp. 64–76).

[55] Bolton, *Guide to Arch. Mex.*, pp. 387–92.

[56] McCloskey, *College of Santa Cruz of Querétaro*, p. 114.

[57] Canedo, "Some Franciscan Sources," p. 147.

The records had been used by official historians of the college. Isidro Félix de Espinosa, after serving as a missionary in Texas, became guardian of the college and, later, its historian. He wrote a *Crónica*[58] and a biography of Antonio Margil de Jesús and, for both works, drew upon his personal knowledge and the records of the college. A continuation of the history was prepared by Fr. Juan D. Arricivita, who was appointed historian of the college in 1787.[59]

Several repositories in the United States have reproductions of records of the College of Santa Cruz of Querétaro. Transcripts from those records relating to Texas missions are in the H. E. Bolton Collection in the Bancroft Library of the University of California. Other transcripts, obtained by William E. Dunn, are in the University of Texas Library and the Library of Congress. Photostats of letters, reports, and other documents from the college archives, 1706–67 (1,400 pages), are in the Catholic Archives of Texas in the chancery office of the Diocese of Austin.[60] In the winter of 1936–37, Fr. Marion A. Habig microfilmed selections from the college archives in Celaya for the Bancroft Library. A large part of the archives is available on microfilm (3 rolls, 6,000 pages), obtained in 1971 by Fr. Benedict Leutenegger, with the assistance of Pierson DeVries and Msgr. B. J. Janacek, for the Old Spanish Missions Historical Research Library at San José Mission, San Antonio, Texas.[61] That library plans to microfilm all the materials relating to Texas.

Early in the eighteenth century, the College of Our Lady of Guadalupe of Zacatecas began missionary work in Texas and other parts of northern Mexico. Authorized in 1703 under the auspices of the College of Santa Cruz of Querétaro, it opened near Zacatecas in 1707.[62] The new college sent five priests with the expedition of Capt. Domingo Ramón in 1716, to reoccupy Texas. Soon afterwards, Zacatecan missionaries participated with those from the College of Santa Cruz of Querétaro in the founding of missions in the San Antonio area. A succession of friars served as president of the Zacatecan missions in

---

[58] Originally published in Mexico in 1747, the work was republished by Lino Gómez Canedo, ed., *Crónica de los colegios de Propaganda Fide de la Nueva España* (Washington, 1964).

[59] *Crónica seráfica y apostólica del Colegio de Propaganda Fide de la Santa Cruz de Querétaro en la Nueva España* (Mexico, 1792). A microfilm negative of this publication is in Brown University Library.

[60] Lane, *Catholic Arch. Texas*, p. 87.

[61] Letter from Fr. Marion A. Habig, June 23, 1971. Father Habig was then attached to the Research Library, which is located at 6623 San José Drive, San Antonio, Tex., 78214.

[62] Alberto M. Carreno, "The Missionary Influence of the College of Zacatecas," *The Americas* 7 (Jan. 1951):304–07.

Texas from 1716 to 1830.[63] After the withdrawal of the Querétarans in 1773, the Zacatecan president supervised all of the missions in Texas. In accordance with a government decree, the college was abolished in 1908 and became a friary under the Franciscan Province of Jalisco (Guadalajara).

In 1908, H. E. Bolton found a depleted collection of records of the College of Guadalupe of Zacatecas in the old college building in the village of Guadalupe, outside Zacatecas, and described the materials relating to Texas and California in his guide.[64] The revolutionary forces of Francisco Villa destroyed some of the records in 1914 when they pillaged Zacatecas.[65] The community of friars took refuge in Texas in the 1920s, and, during that time, the Historical Commission of the Texas Knights of Columbus had photostats made of the old records they had brought with them.[66] The collection of correspondence, reports, diaries, personnel lists, and other documents, (1,200 pages) is in the Catholic Archives of Texas, in the chancery office of the Diocese of Austin.[67] Other records of the College of Guadalupe of Zacatecas, that were held for a time at Duns Scotus College at Hebbronville, Texas,[68] have been returned to Zacatecas. The greater part of the archives of the college has been lost, but some are still at Zacatecas.[69]

In the spring of 1971, Fr. Benedict Leutenegger, again with the assistance of Pierson DeVries and Msgr. B. J. Janacek, began a microfilming program in the archives of the College of Guadalupe of Zacatecas, in the friary near Zacatecas.[70] Eight rolls of microfilm (16,000 pages) and reproductions of five volumes were obtained at that time, and the plan is eventually to microfilm all remaining documents relating to Texas. The microfilm includes books of decrees, 1707–1859,

---

[63] A list of the names of the presidents is in Benedict Leutenegger and Marion A. Habig, *The Zacatecan Missionaries in Texas, 1716–1834, with a Biographical Dictionary* (Austin, 1973), p. 166. The Zacatecan missions in Texas included: 1716, Nuestra Señora de Guadalupe (Nacogdoches); 1716, Nuestra Señora de los Dolores de los Ais (San Augustine); 1716, San Miguel de Linares de los Adaes; 1720, San José y San Miguel de Aguayo (San Antonio); 1722, Nuestra Señora del Espíritu Santo; 1754, Nuestra Señora del Rosario de los Cujanes; 1756, Nuestra Señora de la Luz (El Atascosito); 1793, Nuestra Señora del Refugio (Webb, *Handbook of Texas*, 2:294; O'Rourke, *Franciscan Missions in Texas*, pp. 44–63; Hodge, *Handbook of American Indians*, passim.

[64] Bolton, *Guide to Arch. Mex.*, pp. 395–401.

[65] Carrera Stampa, *Archivalia mexicana*, p. 189.

[66] Knights of Columbus, Texas State Council, Historical Commission, *Minutes*, 1926, p. 21.

[67] Lane, *Catholic Arch. Texas.*, p. 88.

[68] Oberste, *Refugio Mission*, pp. 347, 355 n. 1, 365 n. 6, 371 n. 27, 31, 401.

[69] Habig, *Alamo Chain of Missions*, p. 274.

[70] Letter from Fr. Marion A. Habig, June 23, 1971.

containing minutes of the meetings of the father guardian and his council; books of visits of inspection, containing acts and elections of the triennial chapters held at the college; and books of deaths, containing notices of deaths of friars belonging to the college. Portions of the books of decrees which relate to friars who served in Texas have been published.[71] The Historical Research Library at San José Mission also has microfilm from the archives of the Franciscan Province of Jalisco (deposited in the Biblioteca Público in Guadalajara) containing materials relating to the American Southwest.

Along with other parts of north and northeastern New Spain, Texas was at first part of the Diocese of Guadalajara. In 1777, it became subject to the Diocese of Nuevo León, which included Nuevo Santander, Nuevo León, Coahuila and Texas, the district of Saltillo, and what had been part of the bishopric of Michoacán.[72] The seat of the Diocese of Nuevo León was at Linares until 1777, when it was moved to Monterrey. Texas continued under the Diocese of Nuevo León until 1836.

Bolton reported the archives of the Archbishopric of Guadalajara to be rich in material for the history of the Catholic church in northern Mexico, Texas, and Mexico.[73] Carlos E. Castañeda searched in these archives in 1930–31 and found documents relating to Fr. Antonio Margil de Jesús, Fr. Juan Agustín de Morfi's history of Texas, the original diary of the expedition of the Marqués de Aguayo into Texas in 1821, numerous documents on the San Sabá and San Xavier missions, a collection of De Mézière's letters, and copies of diaries of a number of expeditions made into Texas during the years 1673–1778.[74] About 3,000 pages of photostats were obtained and are now in the Catholic Archives of Texas in the chancery office of the Diocese of Austin.[75] In the archives of the archbishop of Linares, in Linares, are important documents for the history of the Catholic church in Coahuila and Texas.[76] Archives of the same archbishopric, in Monterrey, also contain material relating to the church in Texas.[77] In 1942, Castañeda and Fr. J. P. Gibson investigated the archives in the cathedral at Monterrey and obtained microfilm of letters of Joaquín de Arredondo, concerning the church in the movement for Mexican independence and

---

[71] Leutenegger and Habig, *Zacatecan Missionaries in Texas.*

[72] Bolton, *Guide to Arch. Mex.*, pp. 410, 415.

[73] Ibid., p. 382.

[74] Knights of Columbus, *Minutes*, May 1931, p. 33.

[75] Lane, *Catholic Arch. Texas*, p. 87.

[76] Carrera Stampa, *Archivalia mexicana*, pp. 151–52.

[77] Bolton, *Guide to Arch. Mex.*, p. 415.

the activities of the Gutiérrez-Magee expedition, Jean Lafitte, James Long, and others.[78] This microfilm is now in the Catholic Archives of Texas.[79]

Considerable material relating to the Franciscan missions in Texas is in the Archivo General de la Nación in Mexico City. Documents from the seventeenth to nineteenth centuries, in the section on Misiones, consist principally of correspondence of mission authorities with the viceroy.[80] In the Historia section, there is a collection of documents on the ecclesiastical and civil history of Texas, 1689–1779 (volumes 27–28), containing diaries of missionaries on expeditions into Texas; reports; representations; petitions by missionaries to the viceroy; and letters from missionaries and the commissary general of missions.[81] A copy of this compilation, made in 1792, was acquired by the Library of Congress in 1892.[82] Other volumes of the Historia section also contain materials on Texas missions, and additional materials are in other sections. The archives of the secretariat of the Hacienda contain accounts of the Texas missions.[83] The library of the Museo Nacional has a small quantity of miscellaneous documents relating to missions in Texas.[84] Documents collected in connection with the proposed canonization of Antonio Margil de Jesús are in the archives of the archbishop of Mexico, and reproductions from Mexican and Spanish archives, of which some information has already been presented in chapter four, in the section on New Mexico, include material on missions.[85]

In 1923, the Texas Knights of Columbus formed a historical commission, to collect materials relating to the history of the Catholic church in Texas, and thereafter gave financial support to the commission.[86] Paul J. Foik, the librarian of St. Edwards' University in Austin, became the chairman of the commission and directed its work, and the university became the headquarters and repository of its collections. After attempts to obtain reproductions from the Archivo General

[78] Knights of Columbus, *Minutes*, May 10, 1943, p. 15.

[79] Lane, *Catholic Arch. of Texas*, p. 91.

[80] Bolton, *Guide to Arch. Mex.*, pp. 67–75.

[81] Ibid., pp. 28–31. A copy made in 1852 of the documents in volumes 27 and 28 is in the Bancroft Library of the University of California.

[82] U.S. Library of Congress, *Handbook of Mss.*, p. 40.

[83] Bolton, *Guide*, p. 370.

[84] Ibid., pp. 197, 199, 200, 201.

[85] Lists of individual documents in the University of Texas Archives are in Castañeda, *Our Catholic Heritage in Texas*, 2:351–68; 3:414–39; 4:359–78.

[86] William H. Oberste, *Knights of Columbus in Texas, 1902–1952* (Austin, 1952), p. 171.

de Indias at Seville failed, the commission had copies made of reproductions that had previously been received by other American repositories.[87] Extensive photostat copies obtained from the Archivo General de la Nación in Mexico are from the Historia, Misiones, and Provincias Internas sections.[88] In 1948, the materials assembled under the auspices of the Knights of Columbus were given to the Texas Catholic Historical Society and moved to a building at Price Memorial College in Amarillo. In 1959, the society transferred the collection to Austin, a more central location in the state, where they were housed in the fireproof building of the chancery office of the Diocese of Austin.

Since the early 1950s, the Genealogical Society of the Church of Jesus Christ of Latter-Day Saints in Salt Lake City, in association with the Mexican Academy of Genealogy and Heraldry, has been microfilming vital statistics records in Mexican archives. By 1966, the society had microfilmed more than 50,000 rolls from 548 different Mexican archives. The microfilm includes records of baptisms, confirmations, births, marriages, and deaths, from parish archives dating from the sixteenth century.[89]

Other repositories have materials relating to the missions of Texas. The provincial records of Texas (Béxar Archives) in the University of Texas Archives, which are described in chapter eleven, in the section on Texas, contain considerable documentation relating to the establishment and relocation of missions, their administration, the construction and improvement of mission churches, and visitations of the bishop of Nuevo León. Xerox copies of 400 pages of these documents are in the Old Spanish Missions Historical Research Library at San José Mission, San Antonio. Letters of Fr. Francisco Hidalgo, 1705–16 (photocopies), relating to the Mission Nuestra Padre San Francisco de los Tejos are in the University of Texas Archives.[90] That repository also has another collection of documents concerning Nuestra Señora de los Dolores de la Punta, Nuestra Señora del Refugio, San Antonio de Valero, San Francisco Xavier, and San Juan Capistrano, 1691–1825 (5 inches, photocopies; source not given).[91] Documents accumulated during the inquiry into the proposed canonization of Fr. Antonio Margil de Jesús are in the San Jacinto Museum. The Bancroft Library of the University of California has some documents on Texas

[87] Lane, *Catholic Arch. of Texas*, p. 89.

[88] Ibid., p. 86.

[89] Nettie L. Benson, "Microfilming Projects in Mexico," *News from the Center* [for the Coordination of Foreign Manuscript Copying, Library of Congress], No. 7 (Spring 1970), p. 11.

[90] Kielman, *Univ. of Texas Arch.*, p. 173.

[91] Ibid., pp. 342–43.

missions, 1730–62 (58 pages), concerning the transfer of Nuestra Señora de la Purísima Concepción, San Francisco de los Neches, and San José de Los Nazonis to other sites; reports on the Amarillas presidio, and one on the Texas missions by Fr. Simón del Hierro, guardian of the College of Guadalupe of Zacatecas; and a collection of Franciscan papers on the administration of the order in the Indies, that includes documents on the beatification and canonization of Antonio Margil de Jesús.[92] Records of the Spanish Inquisition in Mexico, 1611–1796, are in the Library of Congress,[93] and other inquisition records, 1622–80, are in the New York Public Library. The latter repository has three letters of Antonio Margil de Jesús, 1716–18, and an extensive collection of his correspondence in the Archivo de la Recolección in Guatemala contains other letters regarding his service in east Texas.[94] A manuscript by Francisco Antonio Figueroa, entitled "Bezerro general, menlógico y cronológico de todos los religiosos . . .," in the Ayer Collection of the Newberry Library in Chicago, gives information regarding the members of the Holy Gospel Province up to 1700.[95]

Writings on Texas by Franciscans, many of which have been published, include diaries, reports, letters, memoirs, and histories.[96] Some of these documents were published in *Documentos para la historia de México* and have since been republished in both Spanish and English. Historians who have investigated archival sources for the history of the Southwest, and others using reproductions held by American repositories, have been publishing translations of this work for many years. Martín de Alarcón, the governor of Coahuila, led an expedition into Texas in 1718, establishing missions in the San Antonio area, and also journeyed into east Texas. Fr. Francisco Céliz, the chaplain of the expedition, prepared a diary that has been published from the manuscript in the Mexican Archivo General de la Nación.[97] A diary

---

92 Hammond, *Guide to Ms. Colls.*, pp. 141, 162.

93 U.S. Library of Congress, *Handbook*, pp. 386–87.

94 Lazaro Lamadrid, O.F.M., ed., "The Letters of Margil in the Archivo de la Recolección in Guatemala," *The Americas* 7 (Jan. 1951):324–25, 341–42.

95 Ruth L. Butler, *A Check List of Manuscripts in the Edward E. Ayer Collection* (Chicago, 1937):p. 129.

96 Lenhart, "Franciscan Historians of North America," pp. 16–21, describes some published and unpublished documents. See also Alexandre Masseron and Marion A. Habig, O.F.M., "Bibliography of English Franciscana," in Masseron and Habig, *The Franciscans: St. Francis of Assisi and His Three Orders* (Chicago, 1959), pp. 479–506.

97 Fritz L. Hoffman, trans. and ed., *Diary of the Alarcón Expedition into Texas, 1717–1719, by Fray Francisco Céliz* (Los Angeles, 1930). The manuscript of the journal was found by archivists in the Archivo General de la Nación, misplaced in a *Tierras* section volume, and information regarding it was communicated to Vito Alessio Robles who obtained transcripts. He supplied one to Hoffman and pub-

of a tour of the Texas missions by Fr. Gaspar José de Solís, made for the guardian of the College of Guadalupe of Zacatecas, is valuable for data on Indian tribes.[98] A report by Fr. José F. Lopez on an extended inspection of the Texas missions, made in 1785 for the bishop of Nuevo León, is one of the principal sources of information on the last years of the missions in Texas.[99]

Juan Agustín de Morfi, a Franciscan from Mexico City and author of a comprehensive diary on Texas and the northern provinces of Mexico, became the first historian of Texas. He accompanied Teodoro de Croix, the commandant general of the Interior Provinces, as chaplain and diarist on a tour of inspection of the northern provinces during 1777–78. In 1955, the University of Texas Archives bought volume three (August 26, 1779–June 1, 1781) of Morfi's diary from the Chicago Historical Society, which had acquired it with the Charles F. Gunther Collection, and later obtained volume two (November 12, 1777–August 25, 1779) from the same institution.[100] Volume one (August 4, 1777–November 11, 1777), in the Biblioteca Nacional, Mexico, and volume two, up to February 24, 1778, had been published earlier in Spanish.[101] All three volumes have recently been reedited and published, and Malcolm McLean has prepared an English translation for publication.[102] On his return to Mexico City from the tour of inspection, Father Morfi collected documents on the history of the missions in Texas. In 1931, C. E. Castañeda found an original draft of Morfi's manuscript in the Archivo de Convento Grande de San Francisco in the Biblioteca Nacional, obtained a copy for the Uni-

---

lished a Spanish version in *Universidad de México* 5 (1932–33), from which it was reprinted as *Unas paginas traspapeladas de la historia de Coahuila y Texas: El derrotero de la entrada a Texas del gobernador de Coahuila, sargento mayor Martín de Alarcón* (Mexico, 1933).

[98] Mattie A. Hatcher, ed. and Margaret K. Kress, trans., "Diary of a Visit of Inspection of the Texas Missions Made by Fray Gaspar José de Solís in the Year 1767–68," *Southw. Hist. Quar.* 35 (July 1931):28–76.

[99] J. Autry Dabbs, trans., "The Texas Missions in 1785," *Mid-America* 22 (January 1940):38–58.

[100] Malcolm D. McLean, "The Diary of Fray Juan Agustín de Morfi," *The Library Chronicle of the University of Texas* 5 (Spring 1956):38–39. Another copy of the diary is in the central archives of the Franciscans in Rome (Borges, "Documentación americana," p. 18).

[101] *Documentos para la historia de México*, 3d ser. 10:372–487; Vito Alessio Robles, ed., *Viaje de Indios y diario del Nuevo México, por el Rev. Fray Juan Agustín de Morfi* (Mexico, 1935). Another Spanish version edited by Mario Hernández y Sánchez-Barba was published in Madrid in 1958. The diary does not concern New Mexico, and in Texas, the party went only as far as San Antonio.

[102] Eugenio del Hoyo and Malcolm D. McLean, eds., *Diario y derrotero [Juan Agustín de Morfi]* 1777–1781 (Monterrey, 1967).

versity of Texas, and later published a translation.[103] Inasmuch as Morfi used archival sources that have since been depleted, his account is an important contribution to the history of Texas.

A collection of translated documents from the Galvin family papers relates to the San Sabá Mission, founded in 1757 and destroyed in 1758.[104] The compilation includes letters of missionaries, the presidio commander, Col. Diego Ortiz Parrilla, and other Texas officials; statements and depositions of Parilla, Miguel de Molina, the surviving missionary, and servants and soldiers; and minutes of Parrilla's interrogation of officers and soldiers.

In 1971, a new agency for collecting and publishing documents relating to the Spanish missions of Texas was founded. It developed from research that was done in the summer of 1969 for the interpretative program that is presented at San José Mission in San Antonio. The Old Spanish Missions Historical Research Library at San José Mission, established in the Franciscan friary just outside the grounds of the mission on March 19, 1971, has as its aims the collection and publication of documents on the missions, and the preparation of a documented history. Fr. Benedict Leutenegger, the resident archivist and curator, became the library's research-translator. The library has inaugurated a program for obtaining microfilm and Xerox copies of the archives of the Colleges of Santa Cruz of Querétaro and Guadalupe of Zacatecas, and other repositories in Mexico. Father Leutenegger and Fr. Marion A. Habig, a member of the board of trustees of the library and historian of the Franciscan St. Louis-Chicago Province, are preparing a volume of translations of decrees, relating to Texas, of the council of the College of Zacatecas, with biographical sketches of all Zacatecan missionaries who served in Texas. Compilations of translations of other documents that will be collected will also be published. Father Leutenegger has been appointed vice-postulator of the cause of the beatification and canonization of the Ven. Fr. Antonio Margil de Jesús, and is collecting his writings with a view to translating and publishing them.[105]

---

103 Carlos E. Castañeda, trans. and ed., *History of Texas, 1673–1779, by Fray Agustín Morfi*, 2 vols. (Albuquerque, 1935). A copy of the collection, made in 1792 by Manuel de Vega, that formed the basis of Morfi's history is in the Bancroft Library of the University of California.

104 Leslie B. Simpson, ed., and Paul D. Nathan, trans., *The San Sabá Papers: A Documentary Account of the Founding and Destruction of San Sabá Mission* (San Francisco, 1959).

105 Letters from Fr. Marion A. Habig, June 23, and July 9, 1971, the latter with a statement by Father Leutenegger regarding the Library of which Father Habig is a collaborator.

Part III
The
Records
of
California

19

History & Government

NOT LONG AFTER Hernando Cortés conquered Mexico in 1521, he sent out expeditions from its west coast to look for a passage through North America that would permit ships to travel west to the Orient. An expedition of 1533–34 discovered Lower California's Bay of La Paz, and, in 1535, Cortés himself went there to take possession in the name of the king of Spain. In 1539, Francisco de Ulloa sailed to the head of the Gulf of California and along the western coast of the peninsula, but did not find a western passage. Extending Ulloa's earlier voyage, Juan Rodríguez Cabrillo found San Diego Bay in 1542 and continued north to a cape near Fort Ross. Pedro de Unamuno, on a voyage from the Philippines, made a landing in 1587, probably at Morro Bay, and penetrated some distance inland before being attacked by Indians. In 1595, Sebastian Rodríguez Cermenho put in at San Francisco Bay and Monterey Bay and gathered much information on the California coast. In 1602, an expedition of three vessels, commanded by Sebastian Vizcaíno, explored the coast of California as far north as Cape Mendocino. Despite their interest in establishing a port in California for providing supplies and repairing galleons that sailed between the Philippine Islands and Mexico, after 1564 the Spanish did not occupy Upper California until long after they had made settlements in other sections of the Southwest, closer to New Spain.[1]

During the eighteenth century, land and sea expeditions were finally sent out by the Spanish to occupy Upper California, in order

---

[1] Andrew F. Rolle, *California: A History* (New York, 1969), pp. 36–55; John W. Caughey, *California: A Remarkable State's Life History* (Englewood Cliffs, N.J., 1970), pp. 24–30.

San Rafael Arcángel

Fort Ross

Sacramento River

Sierra

San Francisco Solano

Sonoma

Benicia

Sutter's Fort

San Francisco • ☩ San Francisco de Asís (Dolores)

☩ San José de Guadalupe

☩ Santa Clara de Asís

Branciforte
Santa Cruz
Monterey

San José

Nevada

☩ San Juan Bautista

San Carlos de Borromeo, Monterey

San Carlos de Borromeo del Carmel

Anza Trail

☩ Nuestra Señora de la Soledad

☩ San Antonio de Padua

☩ San Miguel Arcángel

☩ San Luís Obispo de Tolosa
San Luís Obispo

California

☩ La Purísima Concepción

☩ Santa Ynez

• ☩ Santa Barbara

Mojave
Desert

☩ San Buenaventura

☩ San Fernando Rey de España

• ☩ San Gabriel Arcángel
Los Angeles

☩ San Juan Capistrano

☩ San Luís Rey de Francia

Colorado River

San Pedro y ...

☩ San Diego de Alcalá

La Purísima
Concepción ☩☩

• San Diego

N

• Town or settlement

☩ Mission

Scale in Miles

0   40   80

to forestall Russian or English settlement. Early in 1769, the *San Carlos*, captained by Vicente Vilá, and later, the *San Antonio*, under Capt. Juan Pérez, left La Paz for San Diego, where they arrived in April. The members of the first land expedition, led by Capt. Fernando Rivera y Moncada, reached San Diego in May and erected a stockade. Late in June, the second land expedition, under Capt. Gaspar de Portolá, arrived from Loreto, Lower California. In 1769, Portolá led parties north from San Diego to San Francisco Bay and, in 1770, to Monterey Bay. A presidio that was built there was left in command of Lt. Pedro Fages, and missions were established at both San Diego and Monterey by the Franciscans.[2]

In succeeding years, the expansion of settlements was slow. Other missions were established (as related in chapter twenty-seven) until, by 1823, twenty-one missions had been founded by the Franciscans between San Diego and Sonoma. San José and Los Angeles began as civil settlements in 1777 and 1782 respectively, on sites favorable for agriculture and cattle raising. In the latter year, a presidio was located at Santa Barbara. Other towns developed about the missions and presidios. Despite the previous occupation of the country by the Spanish, the Russians constructed Fort Ross, north of Bodega Bay, in 1812. To check the Russian advance, a garrison was established on the northern frontier at Sonoma, in 1835, by Mariano Guadalupe Vallejo. The Russian venture proved unprofitable, and, in 1841, Fort Ross was sold to John A. Sutter.[3]

A land route from Sonora to California was opened in 1774, in order to supply the colonists and herds of livestock that were necessary for the development of California. The sea route was too long and hazardous and the trails from Lower California too unsuitable for passage of the large numbers of animals necessary to maintain the flow of supplies. To pioneer the route to California, Viceroy Bucareli chose Capt. Juan Bautista de Anza, commander of the frontier post of Tubac in Sonora, who early in 1774 had led a small party north along the valleys of the Magdalena and Santa Cruz rivers to the Gila River, down it to the Colorado River, and thence northwest across the San Jacinto Mountains to San Gabriel. In October, 1775, Anza conducted a colonizing party from Tubac to San Gabriel. From that mission he traveled with a smaller party, in June, 1776, to San Francisco, where he selected sites for a presidio and a mission which were founded later in the year.[4]

In the 1820s, an effort was made by several expeditions to find

---

[2] Rolle, *Calif.*, pp. 59–70; Caughey, *Calif.*, pp. 52–60.

[3] Ibid., pp. 106–07, 168.

[4] Ibid., pp. 79–80.

a route between California and Sonora, to replace the Anza trail which had been unsafe since 1781 when the Yumas destroyed the missions on the lower Colorado. During June and July, 1823, Capt. José Romero led an expedition from Tucson, via the lower Colorado River, to San Miguel, Lower California, and kept a diary that has been published.[5] Later in the same year, Captain Romero conducted a party eastward from San Gabriel, but had to return before reaching the Colorado.[6] Late in 1825, Romero set out on the return journey from San Gabriel to Tucson. In that year also, Col. José Figueroa, the military commander of Sonora, led an expedition from Tucson to the Colorado River. The reopened Sonora-California trail was used thereafter by Sonorans migrating to California.

The Spanish settlements were confined to the coastal areas of California. The great central valley, lying between the Coast Range and the Sierra Nevadas and inhabited by hostile Indians, was penetrated by military expeditions, but no settlements were made by either the Spanish or Mexicans. After 1806, Lt. Gabriel Moraga, and others, were particularly active in campaigns against these Indians,[7] knowledge of the southern part of the valley having been acquired earlier by the expeditions from Sonora led by Capt. Juan B. de Anza and Fr. Francisco Garcés.

In 1697, after earlier attempts by the Spanish government to occupy Lower California had failed, the Jesuits began the successful colonization of the peninsula with the establishment of a mission at Loreto. After the expulsion of the Jesuits from New Spain in 1767, the Spanish government took control of Lower California. When Upper California was established in 1769, it was made subordinate to the governor of Lower California at Loreto. In practice, however, the two colonies were governed separately. When the capital was shifted to Monterey in Upper California in 1777, a lieutenant governor was appointed at Loreto. In 1804, Upper California became an independent province under a governor at Monterey.[8]

The governor of California had charge of civil and military affairs. He supervised the pueblos, convoked the legislative assembly, and attended to the dispatch of a deputy to the Mexican congress, the repair of roads, and the support of schools. He was commander of the

---

[5] Lowell J. Bean and William M. Mason, trans. and eds., *Diaries and Accounts of the Romero Expeditions into Arizona and California, 1823–1826* (Los Angeles, 1962), pp. 14–24. Some of the other documents referred to in this book are not completely identified.

[6] Ibid., pp. 30–51, contains a diary, November 19, 1824–January 31, 1825, of this expedition by Lt. José María Estudillo.

[7] Rolle, *Calif.*, p. 109.

[8] Bancroft, *Hist. Calif.*, 1:306–07; 2:21; *New Catholic Encyclopedia*, 12:994–95.

troops and responsible for their support. He conducted relations with the Indians and sometimes sent military expeditions against them. The decisions of the governor in serious criminal cases were final.[9] He was responsible to the viceroy of New Spain or the commandant general in all except judicial matters, in which he was under the jurisdiction of the audiencia of Guadalajara,[10] but he actually ruled independently because of the remoteness of the province from Mexico City.

The founding of these northern frontier provinces led to the formation of a new territorial and administrative unit called the Interior Provinces, which was established by a royal decree of August 22, 1776.[11] Thereafter, the governor of Upper California was subordinate to the commandant general at Chihuahua, who was directly responsible to the crown. His primary duty was to protect the northern frontier from Indians and foreign encroachment. When the commandancy general was divided into three military districts in 1785, both Californias and neighboring Sinaloa and Sonora were placed in the third district. By a decree of December 3, 1787, the three military commands were consolidated into independent commandancies general called the Interior Provinces of the East and the Interior Provinces of the West, which included the Californias. When the two commandancies general were reunited in 1793, the Californias became directly subject to the viceroy.

Spanish rule in Upper California ended on April 11, 1822, when a junta, called by Gov. Pablo Vicente Sola, declared its adherence to the Mexican empire, which had been established in September, 1821, by Agustín Iturbide. Provincial electors, arranged for by the junta, chose Governor Sola as deputy to the Mexican Cortes, and elected Luís Arguello as his successor as governor. The official transfer of Upper California from Spanish to Mexican sovereignty took place on September 29, 1822, after the arrival of a representative of the Mexican government.[12]

Under the Mexican constitution of October, 1824, which established a republican form of government, Upper California became a territory and was placed, with Lower California, under one governor.[13] Early in 1825, José María de Echeandía was appointed governor of the

---

[9] Rolle, *Calif.*, pp. 82, 133, 152.

[10] Charles E. Chapman, *A History of California: The Spanish Period* (New York, 1930), p. 394; Theodore H. Hittell, *History of California*, 4 vols. (San Francisco, 1885–97), 1:509 ff.; Hubert H. Bancroft, *History of California*, 7 vols. (San Francisco, 1884–90), 1:637.

[11] Chapman, *Hist. Calif.*, pp. 310–20; Irving B. Richman, *California under Spain and Mexico, 1535–1847* (Boston, 1911), pp. 120–22.

[12] Hittell, *Hist. Calif.*, 2:44; Bancroft, *Hist. Calif.*, 2:451 ff.; Chapman, *Hist. Calif.*, p. 453; George Tays, "The Passing of Spanish California, September 29, 1822," *California Historical Society Quarterly* 15 (June 1936):141.

[13] Bancroft, *Hist. Calif.*, 3:2; Hittell, *Hist. Calif.*, 2:50.

Californias, with the title of commandant general. After attending to the affairs of Lower California, he arrived in San Diego to end Arguello's provisional governorship in November, 1825. Because this place was nearer Lower California and its climate suited his health better, Echeandía moved the capital and the government archives to San Diego, over the opposition of the people of Monterey.[14] Upon the appointment of Manuel Victoria as political chief, commandant general, and governor of Upper California, in 1830, the Californias were again separated, and the capital and archives were moved back to Monterey. The government house at that place was besieged during a revolt by the Californians in 1836, and its defenders used some of the records for cartridge wadding.

The post of military commandant of California was not always filled by the governor. Toward the end of 1836, Mariano Guadalupe Vallejo, who had been appointed military commandant of the northern district at Sonoma in 1835, became commandant general of the department, with the rank of colonel.[15] He surrendered the latter post in 1842 to Gov. Manuel Micheltorena, but was again placed in command of the northern frontier. In 1845, following the successful revolt against Micheltorena by insurgents led by José Castro and Juan B. Alvarado, Castro became the commandant general, and Pío Pico, the governor. When the latter moved to Los Angeles, Castro remained at Monterey, being represented in the south by a military commandant who occupied a post similar to that held by Vallejo in the north.

When the centralist system of government was established in Mexico in 1836, the two Californias were designated as one of the departments, which the country was divided into by a law of December 30, 1836. Pursuant to this law and the regulations of March 20, 1837, Gov. Juan B. Alvarado issued a decree on February 27, 1839, dividing the department into three districts.[16] Upper California was divided into two districts, the first of which extended from Sonoma to San Luís Obispo, with the head town at San Juan de Castro, and the second, from El Buchon to Santo Domingo on the peninsular frontier, with the head town at Los Angeles. District prefects were appointed by the governor, to exercise general authority over the town councils and local officials. Each of the districts was divided into two *partidos*, and subprefects, appointed by the prefects, were placed in charge of the second *partido* in each district — at Dolores (San Francisco mission)

---

[14] Hittell, *Hist. Calif.*, 2:80–81, 740–741.

[15] Bancroft, *Hist. Calif.*, 5:757.

[16] Ibid., 3:585, 639–40; Hittell, *Hist. Calif.*, 2:257–58; John W. Dwinelle, *The Colonial History of the City of San Francisco* (San Francisco, 1866), p. 38.

in the northern district, and Santa Barbara in the southern district. The seats of the *partidos* were known as *cabeceras*.

During the Spanish regime, provincial finances were handled by *habilitados*, who replaced the *guarda-almacenes*, or storekeepers, appointed under the regulations of 1781 issued by the commandant general.[17] These officials were selected at all presidios to manage finances (including the distribution of pay and rations), the procurement of supplies, the collection of taxes, and the keeping of accounts. The accounts had to be signed by the governor and the *alferez*, or royal treasury official, before being sent to Mexico. An *habilitado general* was appointed in 1791 to replace the factor, who had handled California business in Mexico since 1776.[18] His office was at Guadalajara, the seat of the *audiencia*. Prior to 1799, accounts of the *habilitados* relating to revenues were sent to the *habilitado* at Monterey for transmission to Mexico, but in that year, that official was appointed administrator general of royal exchequer revenues for California.[19]

The administration of revenues gave the Mexicans considerable trouble. In 1824, Mariano Estrada was appointed administrator general by the provincial deputation. He was relieved in 1825 by José María Herrera, who was appointed in Mexico to administer territorial finances. As *comisario subalterno de hacienda*, Herrera was largely independent of Governor Echeandía in financial matters, and was subordinate to the commissary general of the western states of Sonora and Sinaloa at Arizpe. The *habilitados* continued to serve under this official in collecting revenues at the presidios, but he took over much of their power. After the resignation of the *comisario* in September, 1827, there was no regular provincial official until the governor appointed Manuel Jimeno Casarin as acting commissary, or administrator of revenues, in November, 1828, and Juan Bandini as commissary at San Diego.[20]

Foreign trade was permitted by the Mexicans under a high tariff, which was the chief source of revenue during their rule. Ports of entry were designated at Monterey and San Diego, and at these places the customhouses were under the commissaries (mentioned above) that were appointed in 1828. A federal decree of September 30, 1829, established the customhouse at Monterey, with a staff consisting of an administrator, *contador*, commandant of the guard, and guard. Subordinate revenue officers were appointed at San Francisco, San Diego,

---

[17] Bancroft, *Hist. Calif.*, 1:335, 396–97, 629, 633–34.

[18] Ibid., 1:503 n. 6, 630–31; 2:421–22.

[19] Ibid., 1:634.

[20] Ibid., 2:513 n. 3; 3:13–14; 3:14, 59.

Santa Barbara, and Los Angeles.[21] In December, 1836, the departmental assembly replaced the old customs official at Monterey with a collector, who served about a year.[22] In 1838, the administrator was restored and continued in office,[23] functioning under the director general of revenues in Mexico.

Throughout the Spanish period, the commandants had judicial power over all criminal and civil cases except minor ones in the pueblos, which were heard by the alcaldes.[24] Appeals could be taken from the commandants to the governor, during these years, or to the Audiencia of Guadalajara. In 1826, Upper California was placed under the circuit court at Rosario, Sinaloa, although no cases appear to have been tried there. A federal law of May 23, 1837, provided for courts of first instance in each district, but appointments were not made, and alcaldes and, later, justices of the peace rendered decisions,[25] with the governor serving as the final appellate judge. Under the same law, appointments were made to a superior court in 1840, but some of the judges and the attorney general refused to serve, and the court did not begin operations until 1842.[26]

---

[21] Ibid., pp. 86 n. 51, 136, 240, 261, 377.

[22] Ibid., p. 474; 4:96; Hittell, *Hist. Calif.*, 2:233.

[23] Bancroft, *Hist. Calif.*, 4:96–98, 431–432.

[24] Ibid., 3:189–93.

[25] Michael Mathes, "Judicial Transformation in California, 1837–1851," *Los Angeles Bar Bulletin* 35 (September 1960):359–60.

[26] Bancroft, *Hist. Calif.*, 3:605; Hittell, *Hist. Calif.*, 2:309.

20

Provincial Records

AFTER ANNEXING TEXAS in December, 1845, the United States inherited a dispute over the area between the Nueces River and the Río Grande that was claimed by both Texas and Mexico. A clash that occurred in April, 1846, between Mexican forces, that had crossed over to the north of the Río Grande, and American troops, under General Zachary Taylor, marked the outbreak of the Mexican War. After the acquisition of Texas, American expansionist policy resulted in the dispatch of Commodore John D. Sloat to the Pacific Ocean, with orders to seize Monterey in the event of war with Mexico. After receiving word of the outbreak of war, Commodore Sloat sailed to the California coast and seized Monterey on July 7, 1846, and, within a few days, San Francisco, Sonoma, and Sutter's Fort also. Sloat was soon succeeded by Commodore Robert F. Stockton, who placed Capt. John C. Frémont, U.S. Army, who had brought an exploring party overland, and Lt. Archibald H. Gillespie, United States Marine Corps, a United States agent who had arrived on the scene, in command of a battalion of American volunteers. Stockton and Frémont then moved south to occupy southern California, and Los Angeles was captured on August 13. Lieutenant Gillespie was left in charge of Los Angeles, but incurred the hostility of the native Californians, and they drove him out. But in January, 1847, Stockton, Frémont, and Gen. Stephen W. Kearny, who had arrived overland from New Mexico, cooperated in recapturing Los Angeles.[1]

United States Army officers governed California for several years after its occupation. On March 1, 1847, General Kearny assumed control of the civil government and designated Monterey as capital. He

---

[1] Caughey, *Calif.*, pp. 166–70; Bancroft, *Hist. Calif.*, 5:234–37, 280, 284, 397.

was succeeded on May 31, 1847, by Col. Richard B. Mason, who was followed on February 26, 1849, by Gen. Persifor F. Smith. Under the terms of the treaty of Guadalupe Hidalgo of February 2, 1848, Mexico ceded California to the United States, but, because of the struggle in Congress over the extension of slavery in United States territory, California continued under military government. Responding to popular discontent, Gen. Bennett Riley, who had succeeded to the military governorship in April, 1849, authorized a convention to meet at Monterey to adopt a constitution for a state government. On December 20, 1849, Peter H. Burnett was inaugurated governor, and General Riley resigned the military governorship. Congress was less speedy in approving the action, and it was not until September 9, 1850, that California was admitted as a state.[2]

At the time of the American conquest of California in 1846, the provincial records were divided between Los Angeles and Monterey. Upon succeeding to the governorship in 1845, Pío Pico had moved the capital to Los Angeles, but José Castro, who was commandant, José Abrego, the provincial treasurer, and the customhouse officials had remained at Monterey.[3] The residents of the latter place showed a disposition to resist the removal of the archives but were overawed by threats of military force, and some of the archives were transferred to Los Angeles.[4]

Promptly, on the morning of July 7, 1846, American forces seized the records in the various public buildings at Monterey and carried them in blankets to the customhouse.[5] In January, 1847, the records in that building were in unlocked closets in a room, one end of which was used as a hospital.[6] The surgeon-in-charge and his hospital steward, believing the records to be of no value, used them as wastepaper. Lt. Henry W. Halleck, an aide to Gen. Stephen W. Kearny, observed them at that time but failed to examine them closely until several weeks later when he picked a paper up off the floor and found it to be part

---

[2] Bancroft, *Hist. Calif.*, 5:437; Caughey, *Calif.*, pp. 212–15.

[3] Chapman, *Hist. Calif.*, p. 483.

[4] Hittell, *Hist. Calif.*, 2:741; Bancroft, *Hist. Calif.*, 4:519–20.

[5] Deposition of José Abrego, Oct. 27, 1853, Records of the Bureau of Land Management, Board of Land Commissioners, California, Record of Evidence 3:309 (Record Group 49), National Archives (hereinafter cited as Bd. Land Commrs., Record of Evidence).

[6] Deposition of James L. Ord, Feb. 12, 1853, Bd. Land Commrs., Record of Evidence 2:572–73; also in United States vs. Neleigh, United States Supreme Court, Transcripts of Records, Dec. Term, 1861, No. 196, pp. 53–54 (hereinafter cited as U.S. Sup. Ct., Trans.). Ord was the surgeon-in-charge of the hospital.

of an *expediente*.[7] He reported the matter to Kearny, who ordered an examination of the records by William E. P. Hartnell, an Englishman long resident at Monterey who had occupied various positions under the Mexican government. The examination revealed that the papers were provincial and customhouse records. The collection was moved to a more secure place and locked up.

Other provincial records came into the hands of the Americans at Los Angeles. Before fleeing from that place in August, 1846, Gov. Pío Pico had a portion of the records of the departmental government boxed up and deposited in a large building owned by Luís Vignes, while other records were left in the government house.[8] When Commodore Stockton occupied Los Angeles the same month, he found that both furniture and public records had been removed from the government house.[9] On August 20, 1846, he issued a public order directing their return.[10] However, the records that were left behind by Pico in the government house were apparently destroyed by the Mexican forces under José María Flores, who occupied that building after the governor's departure.[11] Thomas O. Larkin, who had joined Stockton sometime before his entrance into Los Angeles, was told by Vignes of his possession of government records, and Larkin notified Stockton, who thereupon ordered Maj. John C. Frémont to seize them.[12] Frémont obtained the records, and after the outbreak of the revolt in southern California, conveyed them in bales on the backs of two mules to Sutter's Fort.[13] The records were evidently returned to Los Angeles after

[7] Deposition of Henry W. Halleck, Nov. 24, 1854, Bd. Land Commrs., Record of Evidence 5:706; United States vs. Bolton, U.S. Sup. Ct., Trans., Dec. Term, 1859, No. 164, p. 92. His opportunities for observation at Monterey were limited, for, during much of the first half of 1847, he was absent making surveys for fortifications at Los Angeles and San Francisco.

[8] Deposition of Pío Pico, Apr. 8, 1858, United States vs. Neleigh, U.S. Sup. Ct., Trans., Dec. Term, 1861, No. 196, p. 38.

[9] Stockton to Thomas Ewing, Nov. 19, 1849, enclosing Stockton to Frémont, Aug. 27, 1846, Records of the Office of the Secretary of the Interior, Division of Lands and Railroads, Letters Received (Record Group 48), National Archives (hereinafter cited as NA, SI, DLR, Lets. Recd.).

[10] Naval Records Collection of the Office of Naval Records and Library, Letters Sent Book of Commodore Robert F. Stockton (Record Group 45), National Archives, p. 206.

[11] Frederick A. Sawyer for the claimant, United States vs. Neleigh, U.S. Sup. Ct., Trans., Dec. Term, 1861, No. 196, p. 78.

[12] Deposition of Thomas O. Larkin, Mar. 7, 1854, Bd. Land Commrs., Calif., Record of Evidence 4:32–33; DeHaro vs. United States, U.S. Sup. Ct., Trans., Dec. Term, 1866, No. 420, pp. 32–33.

[13] Deposition of J. C. Frémont, May 7, 1858, United States vs. Neleigh, U.S. Sup. Ct., Trans., Dec. Term, 1861, No. 196, pp. 47–48; Bancroft, *Hist. Calif.*, 5:283 n. 36.

its recovery early in 1847. Papers of the departmental assembly, in two large boxes, were also deposited with Vignes and turned over to Stockton.[14] Some *expedientes* before the departmental assembly for action were also placed, by its secretary, in charge of Vignes at the time of Stockton's arrival, but the box containing them disappeared.[15]

Some of the records of the districts which had been set up under prefects in 1837 came into American hands. The prefect of the Monterey district went to Mexico about the time of the American occupation, leaving his records in his house, and, during his absence, some of them were removed by interested parties for their own use.[16] Upon his return to Monterey, he deposited some of the remaining papers in the archives office, under the charge of Halleck, and retained others, which he still had in his possession in 1853. Inasmuch as he had left certain records of the district in the hands of the alcalde at Monterey, the considerable collection of records still at Monterey may include records of the prefect of Monterey. An officer sent by Comdr. John B. Montgomery to the ranch of Francisco Guerrero, the late subprefect of the northern district of California, returned with him and the papers of his office to Yerba Buena.[17] Guerrero was freed, but his papers were retained. At Los Angeles, however, Frémont, if he found the records of the prefecture, evidently did not carry them away, or else they were returned at a later date. The archives of the prefecture of Los Angeles have been in the custody of the recorder of the county of Los Angeles for years, and consist of two large volumes for the years 1834–1850.[18]

Records carried off by the fleeing Mexican officials in 1846 were eventually recovered. Upon the approach of the Americans to Los Angeles in August, 1846, Pío Pico and the commandant, José Castro, fled, the former to Lower California and the latter to Sonora. The governor and his secretary, José Matías Moreno, according to tradition, carried off and buried government archives, but the latter retained

---

[14] J. D. Stevenson to Halleck, Sept. 7, 1847, *House Ex. Doc.* 17, 31 Cong., 1 sess., p. 180.

[15] Deposition of Agustín Olvera, June 29, 1854, Bd. Land Commrs., Calif., Record of Evidence 5:93.

[16] Deposition of Manuel Castro, Feb. 26, 1854, Bd. Land Commrs., Calif., Record of Evidence 2:611. Castro was the former prefect.

[17] John B. Montgomery to Francisco Guerrero, July 11, 1846, Naval Records Collection of the Office of Naval Records and Library, Letters Sent Book of Capt. John B. Montgomery, Commanding, U.S.S. *Portsmouth*, (Record Group 45) National Archives; Bancroft, *Hist. Calif.*, 5:240.

[18] Owen C. Coy, *Guide to the County Archives of California* (Sacramento, 1919), pp. 49, 241; Historical Records Survey, Southern California, *Inventory of the County Archives of California, No. 21, Los Angeles County (Los Angeles) County Clerk's Office*, (Los Angeles, 1943), p. 60.

some which were eventually transcribed for the library of Hubert Howe Bancroft.[19] From his refuge at Mulegé on the east coast of Lower California, Pío Pico reported on the end of the Mexican regime in Upper California.[20] Pío Pico, on his return to Upper California in 1848, was requested by Col. Richard B. Mason to surrender all official papers in his possession belonging to the archives of California, but whether he gave up any has not been ascertained.[21] From La Paz, Lower California, which was captured by Montgomery in April, 1847, a box of valuable records taken off by Castro, who used other papers for cannon wadding, was recovered.[22]

Instructions issued by the secretary of the navy to the commanders of naval forces operating in the Pacific Ocean contained no directions with regard to the archives of the province of Upper California.[23] But Commodore John D. Sloat, who was commanding at the time of the occupation, evidently gave oral instructions to his subordinates. Nor did the secretary of war give specific instructions on the subject of archives to General Kearny. Had the government at Washington issued some definite communication concerning them, more attention would have been given to their acquisition and greater care given to the records that were obtained. The Department of State, which had had long experience in the supervision of the territories, including some which had been taken over from Spain, should have advised the military departments of the importance of the Mexican records.

After General Kearny became military governor of California on March 1, 1847, he took steps to concentrate the provincial records at Monterey, which he had named capital. He ordered Frémont to bring all archives, public documents, and papers subject to his control pertaining to the government of California, to Monterey.[24] Soon after receiving this order, Frémont journeyed to Monterey, had an interview with Kearny, and promised to obey the order, but, following his return

---

[19] Bancroft, *Hist. Calif.*, 5:279 n. 27.

[20] George Tays, ed., "Pío Pico's Correspondence with the Mexican Government, 1846–1848." *Calif. Hist. Soc. Quar.* 13 (June 1934):99–149.

[21] Mason to Pío Pico, Feb. 21, 1849, *House Exec. Doc. 17*, 31 Cong., 1 sess., p. 694.

[22] Bayard Taylor, *Eldorado: or, Adventures in the Path of Empire*, 2 vols. (New York, 1850), 1:179.

[23] The instructions to both army and navy commanders are printed in "Mexican War Correspondence. Messages of the President of the United States and the Correspondence, Therewith Communicated, Between the Secretary of War and Other Officers of the Government, on the Subject of the Mexican War." Apr. 28, 1848, *House Exec. Doc. 60*, 30 Cong., 1 Sess., (Washington, 1848), pp. 153–65, 231–52.

[24] Kearny to Frémont, Mar. 1, 1847, *House Exec. Doc. 17*, 31 Cong., 1 Sess., pp. 289–90; Bancroft, *Hist. Calif.*, 5:440; Allan Nevins, *Frémont, the West's Greatest Adventurer*, 2 vols. (New York, 1928), 2:355.

to Los Angeles, he delayed. Not until after Kearny visited Los Angeles did Frémont obey his order and deliver the records to Monterey, in May, 1847, some in torn and mutilated condition after another journey on muleback.[25] These records included registers of land grants, which William Carey Jones later found in the custody of Halleck.[26] Informed by his aide, Halleck, of the records in the customhouse at Monterey, Kearny had William E. P. Hartnell, one of the customs officers there, remove them to the government house. Hartnell supervised the transfer of several cart-loads of records. He was appointed on March 10, 1847, to the position of translator and interpreter to the governor and served until the end of the military government.[27]

During the summer of 1847, Henry W. Halleck became the secretary of state of the military government of California and was made custodian of the Spanish records.[28] Halleck was a young lieutenant in the Corps of Engineers, skilled in Spanish, and a trained lawyer. Finding the records in great confusion and very mutilated, Halleck continued the work of arranging them and indexing the *expedientes*, which had been started by Hartnell, who became Halleck's assistant in this archival work. The records were kept, in 1847, in Gov. Richard B. Mason's office and were locked up except when Halleck and Hartnell were present; no other persons were allowed access to them. Deposits of records by individuals were always carefully endorsed as such upon their receipt. While Halleck was absent on military duty in Mexico from October, 1847, to June, 1848, Hartnell completed the index to the *expedientes* and a compilation of Mexican laws still in force in California.[29] Halleck remained in charge of the Spanish records until February, 1850, but as will be seen, the military government failed to bring together all the provincial records of California.

Some records of the regime of Capt. José María Flores, leader of the revolt in the Los Angeles area against the Americans in September,

---

25 John C. Frémont, *Memoirs of My Life. . . .* (Chicago, 1887), p. 553; John C. Frémont, "Conquest of California," *The Century Magazine*, n.s. 19 (April 1890): 928; James Wilson, *A Pamphlet Relating to the Claim of Señor Don José Y. Limantour, to Four Leagues of Land in the County Adjoining and Near the City of San Francisco* (San Francisco, 1853), p. 32.

26 Frémont, "Conquest of Calif.," p. 928; William C. Jones, "Report on the Subject of Land Titles in California," *Senate Exec. Doc.* 18, 31 Cong., 2 sess., Apr. 10, 1850, pp. 5–6.

27 *House Exec. Doc.* 17, 31 Cong., 1 sess., p. 290. He seems to have served as translator for the Americans from as early as October, 1846 (Walter Colton, *Three Years in California*, [New York, Cincinnati, 1850], p. 65).

28 Deposition of Henry W. Halleck, Nov. 25, 1854, Bd. Land Commrs., Calif., Record of Evidence 5:705.

29 Affidavit by Henry W. Halleck, Apr. 3, 1858, United States vs. Neleigh, U.S. Sup. Ct., Trans., Dec. Term, 1861, No. 196, p. 44.

1846, were captured by Frémont in December, 1846, at San Luís Obispo, when he was on his way to the recovery of Los Angeles.[30] Some of these records may have been deposited at Los Angeles, but others appear to have been carried to the east by Frémont. In July, 1848, his father-in-law, Sen. Thomas H. Benton, presented an original dispatch from Flores to José de Jesús Pico, the commandant at San Luís Obispo, to the United States Senate.[31] A letter from Flores to the minister of Hacienda, December 10, 1846, which turned up in the papers of Henry Dalton, a California merchant, has been printed.[32] Most of the records relating to Flores, who retreated to Sonora in January, 1847, have disappeared, although some, including letters and reports, found their way from private sources to the Bancroft collection.[33] Papers of Manuel Castro, a companion of Flores on his flight to Mexico who had also participated in the revolt, are in the Bancroft Library.[34] An original copy of the articles of capitulation, signed at Cahuenga by Frémont and Andrés Pico on January 13, 1847, is in the National Archives.[35] Letters from Flores to Andrés Pico are in the Coronel Collection in the Los Angeles County Museum.[36]

The customhouses were among the public buildings seized by the Americans when they occupied the ports of California, and with them, in most places, the customs records were obtained. The customs records at Monterey apparently remained there, under the charge of W. E. P. Hartnell, and became part of the provincial and departmental archives of California. Rafael Pinto, the collector at San Francisco, deposited the customs records with William A. Leidesdorff, the American vice-consul, and fled.[37] Commander Montgomery later attempted to gain pos-

---

[30] "Message of the President of the United States, Communicating the Proceedings of the Court Martial in the Trial of Lieutenant Colonel Frémont," Apr. 7, 1848, *Senate Exec. Doc. 33*, 30 Cong., 1 sess., pp. 378–79.

[31] *Congressional Globe*, 30 Cong., 1 sess., vol. 19, appendix, p. 984, contains the text of the letter dated Dec. 7, 1846.

[32] J. Gregg Layne, ed., "José María Flores," *Hist. Soc. South. Calif. Quar.* 17 (Mar. 1935):23–27.

[33] Bancroft, *Hist. Calif.*, 1:xlix; 5:320–21.

[34] Hubert H. Bancroft, *Literary Industries: A Memoir* (New York, 1891), pp. 415–26.

[35] This is an enclosure in a letter from Stockton to the secretary of the navy, Jan. 15, 1847, Naval Records Collection of the Office of Naval Records and Library, Letters Received from Officers Commanding Squadrons (Record Group 45), National Archives. In the same file with a letter from Stockton, Nov. 23, 1846, is a copy of Flores' proclamation of Sept. 24, 1846.

[36] Ruth Mahood, "The Coronel Collection," *Los Angeles County Museum Quarterly* 14, no. 4 (Autumn 1958):6.

[37] Bancroft, *Hist. Calif.*, 5:239; Hubert H. Bancroft, *California Pastoral, 1769–1848* (San Francisco, 1888), pp. 782–84.

session of the papers, but Leidesdorff refused to give them up. Pinto recovered them later, and, in 1878, presented them to Hubert Howe Bancroft.[38] Other customs records of the port of San Francisco are in the Vallejo Collection in the Bancroft Library, which also contains some letters from Pinto for the years 1839–42.[39] Papers of Juan Bautista Alvarado, Manuel Jimeno Casarin, Manuel Castanares, and Rafael González, customs officials at Monterey, and of Juan Bandini, customs collector at San Diego, are in the Bancroft Library.[40] That repository also has papers of William E. P. Hartnell, who is identified above. The Spanish archives of California in the Surveyor General's Office at San Francisco eventually comprised ten volumes of customhouse records, of which two were for the Monterey customhouse.[41]

The office of secretary of state of the military government of California was terminated upon the inauguration of the state government of California on December 20, 1849. In his capacity as an aide to Gen. Bennet Riley, commander of the Tenth Military Department, Halleck continued in charge of the California archives at Monterey until February, 1850, when, there being no other public official in the employ of the federal government to whom they could be entrusted, General Riley placed them in the care of Maj. Edward R. S. Canby, the assistant adjutant general of the department.[42] Inasmuch as this officer had charge of the military records of the department and those relating to civil affairs, it was logical to assign the care of the Spanish archives

---

38 Bancroft, *Hist. Calif.*, 1:lxx; 4:781; 5:239 n. 18; Bancroft, *California Pastoral*, pp. 783–84.

39 Doris M. Wright, comp., *A Guide to the Mariano Guadalupe Vallejo Documentos para la Historia de California, 1780–1875* (Berkeley, 1953), pp. 154–56.

40 Bancroft, *Hist. Calif.*, 1:xxxix, 748; 2:694, 710; 3:761; 4:692.

41 Rufus C. Hopkins, "The Spanish Archives of California," in Dwinelle, *Hist. San Fran.*, p. v.

42 Deposition of H. W. Halleck, Dec. 5, 1855, Bd. Land Commrs., Calif., Record of Evidence 20:350; *U.S. District Court, Northern District of California, No. 424, The United States vs. José Y. Limantour; Transcript of the Record from the Board of United States Land Commissioners, in Case No. 548* (San Francisco, 1857), p. 198; E. R. S. Canby to Alexander H. H. Stuart, secretary of the interior, Dec. 12, 1851, Records of the United States Senate, Senate Files, 51 Cong., 1 sess., Papers Accompanying S. file no. 1823 (Record Group 46), National Archives (hereinafter cited as NA, SF, 51 Cong., 1 sess., S. file no. 1823).

Canby had been at Monterey since early 1849, having relieved 1st Lt. William T. Sherman as assistant adjutant general of the Tenth Military Department on February 27, 1849. He continued to function in this position while in charge of the Spanish archives. Canby was absent from the departmental headquarters from March 9 to April 15, 1850, and was relieved during that period by 2nd Lt. John Hamilton: (Records of the Adjutant General's Office, Orders and Special Orders, Tenth Military Department, 1847–1850, Bk. 53, pp. 495, 503, (Record Group 94), National Archives; hereinafter cited as NA, AGO, Orders, 10th Mil. Dept.).

to him, also. Even had there been authority to do so, the employment of a competent civilian would have entailed the payment of compensation, whereas the importance of the records called for an officer-custodian responsible to the military authorities. Entering upon his duties as keeper of the archives on March 1, 1850, Major Canby was assisted for about two months by Hartnell, who resigned to accept a position with the county of Monterey.[43] The collection was moved to Sonoma in August, 1850,[44] along with the headquarters of the department, and, in October, another move was made to Benicia,[45] where the records were housed in a general depot constructed in 1849–50 by the quartermaster department of the United States Army.

Canby's work on the archives was largely connected with papers relating to land grants. He searched these papers in order to furnish copies or translations to individuals and United States officials, and he delved into the records of the departmental assembly for its action relative to land grants. He also made frequent examinations of the laws and decrees pertaining to land titles. So much of his time was thus spent that he had little left in which to arrange the records, but he did manage to prepare an index to the various registers of land titles.[46] He continued in charge of the California archives until his relief arrived on April 16, 1851.[47] Capt. Frederick Steele, acting assistant adjutant general, took charge of the Spanish archives on the departure of Canby.[48]

After the state government of California was organized on Decem-

---

[43] Certificate by Bennet Riley, July 9, 1851, Statement of Persifor F. Smith, July 9, 1851, NA, SF, 51 Cong., 1 sess., S. file no. 1823.

[44] Order No. 17, July 31, 1850, NA, AGO, Orders, 10th Mil. Dept., Bk. 53, p. 505.

[45] Ibid., Circular, Oct. 3, 1850, Bk. 53, p. 510.

[46] These indexes are in NA, SF, 51 Cong., 1 sess., S. file no. 1823, and, except the one for the first register (the first in Jones's list, referred to above), are arranged alphabetically by names of grantees, and give also the designation of the ranch, and the page number in the register. In the same file, with a letter from Canby to Sen. John R. J. Daniel, February 5, 1852, is a description of the principal series of records comprising the California archives.

[47] Following his return to the east, Canby presented, on July 16, 1851, a claim for compensation for his services as keeper of the archives to the secretary of the interior, who referred it to Senator Daniel on January 22, 1853. A bill passed the Senate in 1855, but after a new act created the Court of Private Claims, the claim was referred to that body, where it languished for over thirty years because of lack of prosecution by Canby. His widow withdrew the papers in December, 1887, for resubmission of the claim to the Senate, but without success. The papers relative to the claim are in NA, SF, 51 Cong., 1 sess., S. file no. 1823; see also *Senate Report* 472, 33 Cong., 2 sess.; Senate *Journal*, 50 Cong., 1 sess., p. 84.

[48] Orders Nos. 8 and 9, Apr. 15, 16, 1851, NA, AGO, Orders, 10th Mil. Dept., Bk. 255.

ber 20, 1849, it became interested in acquiring the provincial and land records of the Spanish and Mexican governments. The first act of the legislature, passed on January 5, 1850, instructed the new secretary of state to obtain all public records relating to the political, civil, and military history, and past administration of the state, from the former secretary of state of the territory of California.[49] An unsuccessful effort was made early in 1851 to obtain an order from the secretary of war for the transfer of the Spanish records, in the custody of Major Canby at Benicia, to the state.[50] However, some were transferred to the newly established Office of the United States Surveyor General of California. A California act of May 1, 1851, required the secretary of state to send an agent to Monterey to separate all records, not of a local character, from the Spanish archives then in the possession of the county recorder and county clerk, for deposit in the State Department.[51] This act resulted in the acquisition of a quantity of land papers, decrees, orders, proclamations, census returns, military papers, mission papers, custom-house records and communications from the Mexican government.[52] These presumably were the records recovered by Edwin M. Stanton in 1858. Another California enactment of March 20, 1866, made it the duty of the secretary of state to have the title papers of land claims derived from the Spanish and Mexican governments, in the United States Surveyor General's office, transcribed and translated into suitable books.[53] Under the supervision of Rufus C. Hopkins, eight volumes of transcripts were made during the years 1866–1871, together with eight volumes of translations and two volumes of maps. This collection is still available in the archives of the state at Sacramento. The state surveyor general subsequently published a "Report of Spanish or Mexican Grants in California, prepared by James S. Stratton."[54] This report contains a list of grants arranged alphabetically by the name of the grant, and a list of private grants classified by counties. A cor-

---

[49] Edwin L. Head, "Report on the Archives of the State of California," *Amer. Hist. Asso., Ann. Rep.*, 1915, p. 281; California, *Statutes*, 1850, p. 45.

[50] William M. Gwin to C. M. Conrad, Mar. 11, 1851, NA, WD, SW, Lets. Recd., file G 19 (72).

[51] California, *Statutes*, 1851, pp. 443–44.

[52] A list of these records is printed in *United States, Appellant, United States District Court, Northern District of California, No. 424; U.S. vs. José Y. Limantour; Trans. of the Record from the Bd. of U.S. Land Commrs., in Case No. 548*, pp. 267–72.

[53] California, *Statutes*, 1865–66, p. 312. An appropriation of $8,000 was made by the act of March 30, 1868, to continue the translation and transcription of the land records, and another of $1,000 was made for tracing the maps in a volume accompanying the *expedientes* (ibid., 1867–68, p. 672).

[54] California, Legislature, *Appendix to the Journals of the Senate and Assembly of the Twenty-Fourth Session* (Sacramento, 1881), 1:15–54.

rected version of the list appeared later.[55] In 1945, the state contracted with the Microstat Company of California for microfilming the Spanish maps and documents in its custody.

Among the claims confirmed by the Board of Land Commissioners (see below) were two belonging to José Y. Limantour, covering a considerable part of San Francisco and vicinity and worth millions of dollars. Jeremiah S. Black, who was appointed attorney general by President Buchanan on March 6, 1857, being informed of the fraudulent nature of some of Limantour's papers, decided, in consultation with the president and the heads of the other executive departments affected by the claims, to employ a special counsel to combat these and other claims. By this time, it was clear that fraud had been perpetrated in presenting claims to the board.[56]

The man selected for the mission to California was Edwin M. Stanton, a prominent Washington attorney, who had already been consulted by Black in regard to the California land cases. Stanton was instructed, on February 18, 1858, to proceed to San Francisco at his earliest convenience, to confer with the United States district attorney in regard to the cases pending before the district court, and, in particular, to investigate and defend the United States in the Limantour case.[57] He departed on February 21 by steamship from New York, accompanied by his son Eddie Stanton, Lt. Horace N. Harrison, United States Navy, and James Buchanan, a nephew of the president. The special attorney was provided with a letter of introduction from the commissioner of the General Land Office to James W. Mandeville, surveyor general at San Francisco, in which the latter was instructed to permit Stanton free access to the archives in his custody.[58] The party reached San Francisco on March 19, 1858.

---

[55] California, Surveyor General's Office, "Corrected Report of Spanish and Mexican Grants in California, Complete to February 25, 1886," in California, Legislature, *Appendix to the Journals of the Senate and Assembly of the Twenty-Seventh Session* . . . (Sacramento, 1887), 1:11–29.

[56] Jeremiah S. Black to President Buchanan, May 22, 1860, General Records of the Department of Justice, Attorney General's Letters Sent, Bk. A 3 (Record Group 60), National Archives, printed in "Expenditures on Account of Private Land Claims in California. . . . May 22, 1860," *House Exec. Doc.* 84, 36 Cong., 1 sess., pp. 30–31; Bancroft, *Hist. Calif.*, 6:541–43, 554; George C. Gorham, *Life and Public Services of Edwin M. Stanton*, 2 vols. (Boston and New York, 1899), 1:46–48; Homer S. Cummings and Carl McFarland, *Federal Justice, Chapters in the History of Justice and the Federal Executive* (New York, 1937), p. 134; Alston G. Field, "Attorney General Black and the California Land Claims," *Pacific Hist. Rev.* 4 (1935):239–40.

[57] J. S. Black to E. M. Stanton, NA, DJ, Atty. Gen. Lets. Sent, Bk. A 3, pp. 168–71.

[58] Thomas A. Hendricks to J. W. Mandeville, Feb. 18, 1858, Records of the Bureau of Land Management, General Correspondence, Bk. 2, p. 196 (Record Group 49), National Archives.

Stanton immediately set to work with great energy, and the lavish use of public funds, on the Spanish archives then in the custody of the surveyor general at San Francisco. A personal examination of these documents disclosed places where records had been abstracted and pages had been cut out.[59] By the middle of April, Stanton had in his employ, besides the persons brought with him, two clerks and six bookbinders. The office was refurbished and iron shelves and a safe were installed in the vault for safekeeping the records. Two acts of Congress, approved on May 18, 1858, facilitated Stanton's program. One of these empowered the secretary of the interior to collect and deposit in the Surveyor General's Office records that were in the unauthorized possession of individuals, allowed the use of search warrants by that official to recover concealed documents, and made tampering with records a misdemeanor;[60] the other prescribed a three-year term of imprisonment and a fine of $10,000 for fabricating or altering documents.[61] Aid was also afforded by the California legislature, which passed a resolution on April 16, 1858, authorizing the surveyor general to take over Spanish and Mexican records at Monterey and Sacramento that would be useful to the United States government.[62]

Thus fortified, Stanton undertook to accumulate the Spanish archives of California, at San Francisco, in order to have at his command the necessary documentary evidence to combat such claims as those of Limantour. Peter Della Torre, the United States attorney, following up a lead he had previously obtained, went with Stanton to the depot at Benicia in April, 1858, and returned with four large boxes of records which, upon further examination, were found to contain proof of the fraud attempted by Limantour.[63] James Buchanan made trips during the spring to Sacramento, Los Angeles, and San Diego to collect records.[64] The collection and transportation of records at Monterey was attended to by Edward L. Williams, an employee in the clerk's office there, and P. O. Minor, and the latter also brought

---

[59] Stanton to Black, April 16, 1858, Jeremiah S. Black Papers, Library of Congress.

[60] U.S., *Stats.*, 11:289–90.

[61] U.S., *Stats.*, 11:290–92.

[62] Calif., *Stats.*, 1858, pp. 357–58.

[63] Della Torre to Black, May 4, 1858, General Records of the Department of Justice, California Land Claim Transcripts (Record Group 60), National Archives (hereinafter cited as NA, DJ, Calif. Land Claim Trans.); *House Exec. Doc.* 84, 36 Cong., 1 sess., p. 13.

[64] Miscellaneous Treasury Account No. 135,241, vouchers 30–32, Records of the United States General Accounting Office (Record Group 217), National Archives (hereinafter cited as NA, GAO, Misc. Treas. Acct.); *House Exec. Doc.* 84, 36 Cong., 1 sess., p. 10; "Abstract of Disbursements by E. M. Stanton, Special Counsel of

records from San José.[65] A trip was also made to Los Angeles by James W. Mandeville, the surveyor general.[66]

Three months' work in the summer of 1858 on the part of Stanton and his staff, to which a copyist, four translators, a photographer, and a lithographer-artist had been added, was required to put the records in order.[67] Instead of arranging related records according to provenance, Stanton had them bound into large folio volumes in the segments in which they were received from Benicia, Sacramento, Monterey, etc. Historians who later searched the records, including Bancroft, Dwinelle, Eldredge, Engelhardt, and Hittell, found them difficult to use because of their lack of systematic arrangement. The reproduction of 287 sets of photographs of documents to be used as evidence in the Limantour case cost \$4,305.[68] A collection of documents to be introduced as archival exhibits in the same case was printed by O'Meara & Painter at a cost of \$1,871 for 150 copies. This volume also included a digest of laws and other documents from the archives, prepared by Rufus C. Hopkins who, along with John Clar, had been employed to translate the documents.[69]

The Spanish archives of California assembled in San Francisco formed an exceedingly valuable collection not only for land titles, but also for the history of California from its earliest settlement. The surveyor general reported the derivation of the collection as follows: Benicia 120 volumes, Sacramento 120 volumes, San José 6 volumes,

---

the United States in Relation to the Defence of Land Claims in California," in "Letter of the Secretary of the Treasury, . . . Relative to Amounts Paid on Account of Legal and Other Services in Investigating Land Titles in California in the Years 1857, 1858, 1859, 1860, and 1861." Dec. 8, 1862, *Senate Exec. Doc.* 2, 37 Cong., 3 sess., p. 11.

[65] NA, GAO, Misc. Treas. Acct. 135,241, vouchers 26 and 34; *House Exec. Doc.* 84, 36 Cong., 1 sess., p. 10; *Senate Exec. Doc.* 2, 37 Cong., 3 sess., p. 11.

[66] Mandeville to Thomas A. Hendricks, Oct. 12, 1858, U.S. Department of the Interior, Records of the Bureau of Land Management (Record Group 49), Letters Received from Surveyors General, California, National Archives (hereinafter cited as NA, DI, BLM, Lets. Recd., SG, Calif.).

[67] Vouchers signed by the members of Stanton's staff for the sums paid them by him are in NA, GAO, Misc. Treas. Acct. no 135,241; see also the statement in *House Exec. Doc.* 84, 36 Cong., 1 sess., p. 10, which contains the following misspellings: Brelawski for Bielawski, who made the photographic exhibits; Takrzewski for Zakrzewski, who was the lithographer-artist; Dunglada for Danglada, who copied a register from San Diego; and Lee & Care for Lee & Carl, who bound the archives volumes.

[68] "Letter of the Secretary of the Interior in Relation to the Amounts Paid to Different Persons on Account of Legal and Other Services for Investigating Land Titles in the State of California during the Years 1857, 1858, 1859, 1860 and 1861." Apr. 23, 1862, *Senate Exec. Doc.* 44, 37 Cong., 2 sess., p. 2.

[69] Rufus C. Hopkins, comp., *Digest of Mexican Laws, Circulars and Decrees, in the Archives of Upper California* (San Francisco, 1858).

Los Angeles 12 volumes, and Monterey 4 volumes — a total of 262 volumes.[70] Some of the records from Monterey proved to be purely local in character, and these were returned. The nearly 250,000 pages of records in the custody of the surveyor general covered the years from 1767 to 1848, and included provincial, departmental, military, mission, prefecture, customhouse, commissary, treasury, and local records. Besides official correspondence of the governors,[71] there were land records, laws, decrees, orders, proclamations, regulations, proceedings of the legislative assembly, military reports, journals, diaries, court proceedings, naturalization documents, election proceedings, and books of brands and marks. Lists of the series into which the records were bound, under the direction of Stanton, are available in print.[72]

Stanton remained in California until January, 1859, his departure being delayed by the illness of his son. For his legal services in California on behalf of the United States, he was paid $25,000;[73] his success played a part in his appointment as attorney general in 1860. Expenditures incurred in collecting, copying and translating Spanish and Mexican archives for use in the Limantour and other cases amounted to $5,186.50, while the cost of collecting, safekeeping, and binding the archives which were concentrated in the Surveyor General's Office in San Francisco was $4,416.98.[74] The traveling expenses of Stanton, Harrison, and Buchanan, and their room and board at the International Hotel during their stay in San Francisco, totalled $4,267.23.

---

[70] J. W. Mandeville to Thomas Hendricks, Oct. 19, 1858, NA, BLM, Misc. Lets. Recd.

[71] Part of the outgoing correspondence, 1834–38, of the governors was reported as missing from the collection (deposition of R. C. Hopkins, Aug. 27, 1862, *United States vs. the City of San Francisco*, U.S. Sup. Ct., Trans., Dec. Term, 1866, No. 287, p. 280).

[72] "Report of the Surveyor General of California," in U.S. Dept. of the Interior, *Annual Report*, 1880, p. 924, listing a total of 272 volumes; Bancroft, *Hist. Calif.*, 1:xxviii and *passim*, giving a total of 273 volumes; Zephyrin Engelhardt, *The Missions and Missionaries of California*, 4 vols. (San Francisco, 1908–15), 2:xxv–xxviii, presenting 28 series in 289 volumes. Other lists found by the author in the National Archives are also useful in showing the contents of the Spanish and Mexican archives of California. These lists are reproduced in Appendix B, the information for which was prepared in 1898 in the Surveyor General's Office when James M. Gleaves succeeded W. S. Green as the Surveyor General, and in Appendix C, the information for which was compiled by Worthington C. Ford of the Library of Congress.

[73] *Senate Exec. Doc.* 2, 37 Cong., 3 sess., p. 3; *Senate Exec. Doc.* 44, 37 Cong., 2 sess., p. 2; NA, GAO, Misc. Treas. Acct. No. 135,351.

[74] The United States in account with E. M. Stanton, NA, DJ, Calif. Land Claim Trans. The cost of the passage to California for Stanton and Harrison was $300 each. Passages for Stanton, Harrison, and Buchanan to New York cost $851.25. Buchanan was paid $300 a month for his services during the period of February 20, 1858, to February 1, 1859.

James F. Shunk, another special counsel, went to California in 1860, on orders of the attorney general, to examine the Spanish records and collect documents on a number of important California land cases then pending before the Supreme Court and the district courts of California.[75] This effort on the part of the government to prevent fraudulent land claims from being confirmed by the courts resulted in the accumulation of further documentation in Washington and in the court records. On his arrival in San Francisco early in October, 1860, Shunk conferred with the United States district attorney and agreed to furnish him with archival evidence connected with the land cases.[76] Shunk employed an attorney, John B. Williams, who had been a clerk in the District Attorney's Office, and a translator named Nye.[77] Together, they worked until near the end of February, 1861, searching for documents relating to the land cases, and preparing translations, tracings, and photographs. Shunk supplied the district attorney with material, sent memoranda on cases to the attorney general, and, on his return to Washington, took a box of photographs of documents, other papers, and books.[78]

Early in 1903, Herbert Putnam, the librarian of Congress, proposed the transfer of the Spanish archives of California from San Francisco to the Library of Congress. As part of a program for the acquisition of such records, his request was based on a report from Worthington C. Ford, chief of the Division of Manuscripts in the Library of Congress, following an inspection of the archives in the custody of the surveyor general.[79] In making the official request to the secretary of the interior for the transfer of the records, Putnam pointed out that the building in which they were housed was not fireproof, that the land office was not a natural permanent depository for such records, that only 20 or 25 volumes related to land titles, and that the rest, consisting of 302 volumes, had no bearing on the work of

---

[75] Jeremiah S. Black to J. F. Shunk, Sept. 5, 1860, Records of the Department of Justice, Attorney General's Letters Sent, Bk. B 2, National Archives.

[76] Shunk to Black, Oct. 12, 1860, Black Papers, Library of Congress.

[77] Ibid., Nov. 23, 1860; J. B. Williams to Black, Jan. 10, 1861, Black Papers, Library of Congress.

[78] Shunk's services and expenses cost the government $5,636 (NA, GAO, Misc. Treas. Acct. no. 140,778; *Senate Exec. Doc.* 44, 37 Cong., 2 sess.). In the Law Library of Congress is a small compilation by James F. Shunk, entitled "Photographic Exhibits in California Land Cases from the Mexican Archives," (San Francisco, 1861), containing samples of documents relating to land grants and signatures of California officials.

[79] Charles F. Gompertz to Herbert Putnam, Jan. 20, 1903, NA, DI, PM, Lets. Recd., p. 534; Notes of Mr. Samuel Gompertz on the attempt to remove the California Spanish archives to the Library of Congress, Records of the Bureau of Land Management, Surveyor General of California, National Archives; U.S. Library of Congress, *Report of the Librarian of Congress*, 1906, pp. 32–33.

the office.[80] Putnam's letter was accompanied by W. C. Ford's list of the 302 volumes of Spanish records, similar to the list published by Engelhardt in the work already cited.[81] On February 2, 1903, the secretary of the interior directed the commissioner of the General Land Office to instruct the United States surveyor general of California to have the 302 volumes of records designated in Ford's memorandum packed and shipped to the librarian of Congress.[82] This directive and its enclosures were transmitted to the surveyor general on February 4.[83] In his reply, that official pointed out that the act of May 18, 1858, required him to retain the records in his possession and asked how he could get around it.[84]

Agitation immediately developed in California against the removal of the Spanish records to Washington. Charles Gompertz, keeper of the archives, in a brief presented to George C. Perkins, United States senator from California, pointed out that papers pertaining to land were scattered throughout the collection of volumes, and that the records were necessary for the work of the Surveyor General's Office and were considerably used by California historians.[85] The aid of other politicians, as well as that of historians, was enlisted. A circular prepared by Prof. George Davidson and Zoeth S. Eldredge, historian, which was distributed to societies, libraries, clubs, and influential public men in the Pacific states, asserted that the records were as much a part of California as the Massachusetts archives were of Massachusetts and New England.[86] It further pointed out that if California had been one of the original states, it would have had title to the records. The removal of the records, it was averred, would be a great hardship on students of Pacific coast history. The circular elicited letters of protest addressed to the secretary of the interior. A letter

---

[80] Putnam to Hitchcock, Jan. 24, 1903, NA, DI, PM, Lets. Recd., p. 534.

[81] See Appendix C for a reproduction of Ford's list entitled "Spanish Archives in Land Office, San Francisco, California."

[82] Ethan Allen Hitchcock to W. A. Richards, Feb. 2, 1903, Records of the Bureau of Land Management, Division E, Special File, National Archives.

[83] W. A. Richards to W. S. Graham, Feb. 4, 1903, Records of the Bureau of Land Management, Division A, Letters Sent Press Copy Books, 13, National Archives.

[84] W. S. Graham to W. A. Richards, Feb. 13, 1903, NA, BLM, DI, Div. E, Spec. File.

[85] Gompertz to Perkins, Feb. 11, 1903, Records of the Bureau of Land Management, Surveyor General of California, Correspondence Relating to Attempt to Move Spanish Archives from San Francisco to Washington (Record Group 49), National Archives. Gompertz also wrote to Sen. Thomas R. Bard and to Benjamin I. Wheeler, president of the University of California at Berkeley.

[86] Notes of Gompertz, NA, BLM, GLO, SG Calif.; John Lombardi, "Lost Records of the Surveyor-General in California," *Pacific Hist. Rev.* 6 (December 1937): 364–66.

from Prof. Frederick J. Teggart, of the University of California, stressed the importance of the availability of the Spanish archives for the development of historical research on the Pacific coast.[87] Newspapers also became involved in the fight for the archives. On February 23, 1903, the state legislature adopted a resolution of protest against their removal.[88] As a result of a letter from Senator Perkins repeating the arguments of Gompertz and suggesting the procurement of more information,[89] as well as the general opposition,[90] the transfer order was suspended by the secretary of the interior on February 18, 1903.[91]

The Spanish archives remained in San Francisco, but nothing was done to improve their security. The commissioner of the General Land Office, on the direction of the secretary of the interior, sent a copy of Senator Perkins' letter to the surveyor general of California, and instructed him to report on certain queries to be found therein relative to the safety, accessibility, importance to the work of his office, and relevance to land claims of the Spanish archives.[92] In his report, the surveyor general enumerated 100 volumes containing documents relating to land matters and stated that, in many cases, the Spanish records were indispensable for the work of his office. He further stated that the records were housed on the third and fourth floors of a double brick structure, one of the most substantial in the city, which had been built originally for the United States Branch Mint.[93] The report was submitted to the secretary of the interior, who decided to allow the Spanish archives to remain in San Francisco. The opinion of the surveyor general as to the safety of the building was not shared by some users of the records, however, for Professor Davidson, in a letter which was forwarded by the president of the University of California to

---

[87] Teggart to Putnam, Feb. 16, 1903, Records of the Library of Congress, Librarian of Congress, Correspondence (Miscellaneous, Calif. Archives).

[88] Calif., *Stats.*, 1903, p. 680.

[89] Perkins to Hitchcock, Feb. 17, 1903, NA, SI, PM, Lets. Recd., p. 852.

[90] Letters were received in February, 1903, from Frank J. Brandon, secretary of the California Legislature; David Starr Jordan, president of Stanford University; Frank J. Symmes, president of the Merchants Association of San Francisco; Thomas J. Kirk, superintendent of public instruction at Sacramento; and, in March, 1903, from Josephine Tillman, corresponding secretary of the Daughters of California Pioneers Society, San Francisco (NA, SI, PM, Lets. Recd. and Lets. Sent).

[91] E. A. Hitchcock to W. A. Richards, Feb. 18, 1903, U.S. Department of the Interior, Bureau of Land Management (Record Group 49), Division E, Special File, Correspondence Relating to the Proposed Transfer of the Spanish Archives of California, 1903, File no. 32521, National Archives (hereinafter cited as NA, BLM, Div. E, Spec. File no.).

[92] W. A. Richards to W. S. Graham, Mar. 2, 1903, NA, BLM, Letters Sent Press Copy Book, p. 183.

[93] Graham to Richards, Mar. 23, 1903, NA, BLM, Div. E, Spec. File no. 55585.

Putnam, February 25, 1903, emphasized the extent to which the Spanish archives were used for research, urged their removal to a fireproof building, and recommended their duplication by photography and the deposit of copies in other places for security.[94] But neither annual reports nor correspondence of surveyors general of later years presents any evidence that further measures for the security of the records were taken.

In the San Francisco fire of April, 1906, started by the great California earthquake, nearly all the Spanish records were destroyed. Thus perished one of the largest collections of Spanish documents in the United States; only the land records escaped destruction. Previously there had been several disastrous fires in San Francisco, but unfortunately their lessons had not been taken to heart by federal officials.

Fortunately for those interested in researching the history of California, the Spanish records were considerably used and extensively copied during the last decades of the nineteenth century. California historians were responsible for the preservation of a wide range of material. Hubert Howe Bancroft, San Francisco publisher and bookseller, who was then gathering data for his *History of the Pacific States of North America*, employed fifteen "Spaniards" during 1876–77, under the direction of Thomas Savage, to copy, digest, and list the Spanish archives in the Surveyor General's Office.[95] A year's work, costing $18,000, produced enough material to fill sixty-three folio volumes, covering 1767–1846, which were used in the writing of Bancroft's *History of California*.[96] Bancroft's collection of transcripts, printed books, and manuscripts was housed, after 1881, in a brick building away from the business section of San Francisco, in the middle of a large lot at the corner of Valencia and Mission Streets, where it escaped the holocaust of 1906. The Bancroft Library, with its valuable transcripts and manuscripts, was purchased in 1905 by the University of

---

[94] Benjamin I. Wheeler to Herbert Putnam, Feb. 25, 1903, enclosing Davidson to Wheeler, Feb. 19, 1903, LC, Librarian of Congress, Corres.

[95] Hubert H. Bancroft, *Literary Industries* (San Francisco, 1890), pp. 471–72; John H. Caughey, *Hubert Howe Bancroft: Historian of the West* (Berkeley and Los Angeles, 1946), p. 108.

[96] This work contains a list of inhabitants for 1769–1800 in volume one, and a pioneer register containing biographical information, drawn from Spanish archives, mission records, and private manuscripts, in volumes two through five. The list and register have been reprinted: *California Pioneer Register and Index, 1542–1848, Including Inhabitants of California, 1769–1800 and List of Pioneers Extracted from The History of California by Hubert Howe Bancroft* (Baltimore, 1964), and *Register of Pioneer Inhabitants of California, 1542 to 1848 and Index to Information Concerning Them in Bancroft's History of California, Volumes I–V* (Los Angeles, 1964). Some of the entries in the register are meager and others are inaccurate. The 63-volume collection of copies, etc., has been microfilmed.

California, which has since maintained it as a separate (Bancroft) library. Beginning in the 1870s, Theodore Henry Hittell, a prominent San Francisco attorney, labored for many years in the Surveyor General's Office, copying and abstracting the California archives, and utilized the material in writing another general history of California. What became of the thousands of pages of copies he is said to have made has not been learned.[97] Father Zephyrin Engelhardt, historian of the Franciscan missions of California, procured copies in 1904 of many documents in the California archives, for publication in an extensive documentary compilation.[98] The value of this work is enhanced by the fact that the original records on which it was based are no longer extant.

Some of the documents of general interest, which formed part of the California archives, had been issued in either broadside or pamphlet form, and this fortunate multiplication of copies has resulted in the preservation, in libraries, of much of this kind of material. The types of documents included laws, decrees, proclamations, instructions, regulations, tables, orders, notices, manifestoes, reports, and expositions. Inasmuch as a survey of these materials in the California archives in the Surveyor General's Office had been made before their destruction, it is known that the collection of such materials in the Bancroft Library is largely complete.[99] A large collection of Mexican documents is also in the Sutro Library in the San Francisco Public Library.[100]

---

[97] G. W. Dickie, and others, "In Memoriam: Theodore Henry Hittell, Born April 5, 1830 — Died February 23, 1917." *Proceedings of the California Academy of Science*, 4th ser. 8 (June 17, 1918):15–16.

[98] Zephyrin Engelhardt, O.F.M., ed., *The Missions and Missionaries of California*, 4 vols. (San Francisco, 1908–15).

[99] Robert E. Cowan, *A Bibliography of the Spanish Press of California, 1833–1845* (San Francisco, 1919); George L. Harding, "A Check List and Census of California Spanish Imprints, 1833–1845," *Calif. Hist. Soc. Quar.* 12 (June 1933):130–36; Robert Greenwood, *California Imprints, 1833–1862: A Bibliography* (Los Gatos, Calif., 1961), imprints of 1833–45 on pp. 38–67. Some of these imprints are available on microfilm in the Library of Congress (William S. Jenkins, *Guide to the Microfilm Coll. of Early State Records, Supplement*, pp. 54–58, 128.

[100] Richard H. Dillon, "The Sutro Library," *News Notes of California Libraries* 51 (Apr. 1956):349–50.

21

Legislative Records

THE FIRST PROVINCIAL DEPUTATION, or legislature, of California met at Monterey on November 9, 1822. It consisted of the members of an electoral junta who had met earlier that year to select a deputy to the Mexican Cortes, and who were called together as a legislative body on the authority of a representative of the Mexican government, then in California, to oversee the transfer of that province from Spanish to Mexican jurisdiction.[1] The deputation was composed of six *locales*, or representatives, one from each presidio and pueblo district. It met thereafter from time to time at the will of the governors, being known after 1825 as the territorial deputation.[2] In 1828, the territory of California was divided into six districts for the purpose of choosing electors for the electoral college, which was to elect a deputy to the Mexican congress and four new members of the deputation.[3] After California became a department in 1837, in accordance with the new Mexican constitution, the territorial deputation became known as the departmental junta. A Mexican law of March 20, 1837, defined the powers of the junta regarding the enactment of measures on taxation, local government, education, industry, commerce, and the approval of land grants made by territorial officials.[4] After another constitutional

---

[1] Bancroft, *Hist. Calif.*, 2:462 ff.; Hittell, *Hist. Calif.*, 2:45.

[2] Bancroft, *Hist. Calif.*, 2:486, 614; Hittell, *Hist. Calif.*, 2:89, 96, 122, 179.

[3] Hittell, *Hist. Calif.*, 2:96. A document concerning the election of the elector at Santa Barbara is translated in Pablo Avila, trans. and ed., "Naming of the Elector-Designate, Santa Barbara, 1830," *Calif. Hist. Soc. Quar.* 27 (December 1948):333–38.

[4] Reynolds, *Spanish and Mex. Land Laws*, pp. 216–21.

change in Mexico, the legislature became known in 1843 as the departmental assembly. From the beginning, the legislature had a secretary who recorded its proceedings and kept its records.

The records of the legislative assembly seem to have been incomplete from the earliest days of American occupation. William C. Jones reported on the journals of the assembly in the custody of Henry W. Halleck as "very imperfect."[5] Ten years later, Rufus C. Hopkins, keeper of the California archives, in transmitting a transcript of the journal of 1845 to the attorney general, reported that there were no regular journals for the years 1841 and 1842, the only record for the latter year being for the session of May 31, and no journal for 1843.[6] The records for 1843 were said to have been destroyed in the San Francisco fire of 1849.[7] Copies of the journal of the assembly, February 1 to October 8, 1845, and January 3–23, 1846, are in the California land-grant transcripts in the records of the Department of Justice in the National Archives.[8] The journal for March 2 to July 24, 1846, has been printed in both Spanish and English.[9] The journal for October 23–30, 1834, is also in print.[10] The surveyor general of California had in his custody in 1852 one box of the proceedings of the legislative assembly of California. Inasmuch as those records were burned in 1906, the best collection of proceedings in existence is the transcripts and abstracts made for Hubert Howe Bancroft, now in the Bancroft Library of the University of California, comprising three volumes with a total of 996 pages.[11] A great many extracts from the assembly pro-

---

[5] W. C. Jones, *Land Titles in California: Report on the Subject of Land Titles in California*, Senate Exec. Doc. No. 18, 31 Cong., 2 Sess. (Washington, 1850), p. 4.

[6] Hopkins to Jeremiah Black, Nov. 4, 1859, General Records of the Department of Justice, Attorney General's Letters Received (Record Group 60), National Archives (hereinafter cited as NA, DJ, Atty. Gen. Lets. Recd.)

[7] U.S. District Court, Northern District of California, *The United States, Appellants vs. José Y. Limantour, Appellee*, Nos. 424 and 429; *Land Commission Exhibits* [San Francisco, 1858?], Exhibit D, pp. 7–8.

[8] NA, DJ, Calif. Land Claim Trans., No. 714, exhibit with deposition of José Castro, Mar. 12, 1855.

[9] United States vs. Bolton, U.S. Sup. Ct. Trans., Dec. Term 1859, No. 164, pp. 266–334.

[10] U.S. Supreme Court, *United States Appellant, Supreme Court of the United States*, No. 287, *The United States, Appellants vs. the City of San Francisco, and* No. 288, *the City of San Francisco, Appellant vs. the United States, Appeals from the Circuit Court of the United States for the Northern District of California* (Washington, 1866), pp. 109–28.

[11] Capt. Edward R. S. Canby examined the records of the legislative assembly and, in a letter to J. R. J. Daniel, February 5, 1852, stated that they consisted of 2,000 pages of either rough minutes of the proceedings or fair copies (NA, Senate Files, 51 Cong., 1 sess., papers accompanying S. file no. 1823).

ceedings are in the California land-grant transcripts in the records of the Department of Justice, and in the case records of the United States Supreme Court and United States District Courts at San Francisco and Los Angeles. Various decrees and resolutions of the assembly are printed in the compilations by Halleck, Jones, and Dwinelle, referred to in chapter twenty-four, in this section. Tables of approvals of land grants by the legislative assembly are in print.[12]

---

[12] Eugene B. Drake, *Jimeno's and Hartnell's Indexes of Land Concessions, from 1830 to 1846; also, Toma de Razón or Registry of Titles, for 1844–45; Approvals of Land Grants by the Territorial Deputation and Departmental Assembly of California, from 1835 to 1846, and a List of Unclaimed Grants* (San Francisco, 1861), pp. 51–59; "Alphabetical List of Approvals of Grants of Lands by the Departmental Assembly of California, Recorded in the Books of Sessions," in "Report of the Surveyor General of California," in U.S. Dept. of the Interior, *Annual Report,* 1880, pp. 912–16.

22

Archival Reproductions

A RECONSTRUCTION of the lost Spanish archives of California could be partially effected from the archives of Mexico and Spain.[1] In the Archivo General de la Nación in Mexico City there are original communications from the governors, other officials, and missionaries of Upper California to the viceroy, which often contain valuable enclosures, and copies or drafts of dispatches sent by the viceroy to California and Spain. Also, inasmuch as it was the practice among Spanish colonial officials to accumulate documents for transmission to Spain for action by the Spanish government, many documents of local origin are in the archives of Spain.

The Bancroft Library of the University of California at Berkeley has the principal collection of archival reproductions relating to California. The earliest acquisitions of transcripts from Mexican archives were obtained by H. H. Bancroft, probably in the 1870s. Amounting to thirty-two volumes, these transcripts include material on California and the Interior Provinces.[2] H. Morse Stephens, head of the university's history department from 1902 to 1919, initiated the search in European archives. On a sabbatical in 1909–10, Stephens investigated Spanish archives for materials on California and obtained some transcripts.[3] Herbert E. Bolton, as professor of American history at the university from 1911–40, built up a school for the study of Spanish

---

[1] For a description and bibliography regarding the Mexican and Spanish archives, see chapter four, in the section on New Mexico.

[2] Bancroft, *Literary Industries*, pp. 741–42; Bancroft, *North Mexican States*, 1:xx.

[3] Chapman, *Catalogue of Materials in the Archivo General de Indias*, pp. 11, 15, 56.

colonization in America.[4] He also served from 1916 to 1940 as director of the Bancroft Library, a position filled from 1940 to 1944 by Herbert I. Priestley, professor of Mexican history at the university, and from 1946 to 1965 by George P. Hammond, newly arrived from the University of New Mexico.

As related in the chapter on Texas, after 1913 the University of California participated in cooperative programs with other institutions for the procurement of transcripts from Mexican and Spanish archives. But the university also obtained reproductions from other sources. On the suggestion of H. M. Stephens, the Native Sons of the Golden West, a patriotic organization of Californians interested in promoting the history of California, undertook the sponsorship of traveling fellowships that enabled recipients to investigate the holdings of the archives of Spain, Mexico, and other places, relating to the history of California.[5] Beginning in 1930, Native Sons fellows obtained microreproductions from Mexican archives, many of which were deposited in the Bancroft Library.[6] Transcripts and photostats obtained by Bolton from Mexican, Spanish, and other archives, for his own publications, were also deposited in the library in 1955. In 1948–49, the Bancroft Library inaugurated a larger program, financed by the state legislature, for the procurement of microreproductions relating to early California and colonial Spanish America.[7] Under this program, microfilm totalling 865,000 frames was obtained from Mexican archives, by graduate students and faculty members, from the principal record groups in the Archivo General de la Nación, the Archivo Histórico de Hacienda, the Archivo de Defensa Nacional, the Archivo de Fomento, and the Biblioteca Nacional. Materials on Texas and New Mexico were also included.[8]

The Bancroft Library's acquisitions of reproductions from Spanish archives have been extensive. After 1911, numerous Native Sons of the Golden West fellowships were granted to graduate students of

---

[4] John F. Bannon, ed., *Bolton and the Spanish Borderlands* (Norman, Okla., 1964), pp. 8–10; Lawrence Kinnaird, "Bolton of California," *Calif. Hist. Soc. Quar.* 32 (June 1953) :98–100.

[5] Charles E. Chapman, "The Native Sons Fellowships," *Southw. Hist. Quar.* 21 (April 1918) :389–90.

[6] Tate, "Microphotography in Mexico," p. 358.

[7] Friends of the Bancroft Library, *Hammond*, p. 35; news note in *American Archivist* 11 (April 1948) :173–74.

[8] Descriptions of the materials copied are in Mary Ann Fisher, *Preliminary Guide to the Microfilm Collection in the Bancroft Library* (Berkeley, 1955), pp. 9–15; Richard W. Hale, Jr., *Guide to Photocopied Historical Materials in the United States and Canada* (Ithaca, N.Y., 1961), pp. 40–41, 210. The University of California has continued microfilming in Mexico.

the University of California, most of whom worked in Spanish archives on subjects being investigated for doctoral dissertations,[9] and quantities of these transcripts have been deposited in the Bancroft Library.[10] Charles E. Chapman, the Native Sons fellow who worked in Seville during 1912–14, gathered material that was embodied in his catalog, referred to above. The materials collected by the fellows and other scholars relate to exploration and settlement in the Interior Provinces, the Californias, New Mexico, and Texas, as well as to maritime explorations, and amount to thirty-five cartons.[11] The program to microfilm in foreign archives, inaugurated by the library in 1948, has resulted in the acquisition of 300,000 frames relating to the Pacific coast, many of which have been enlarged into photoprints for easier use. These reproductions from the Archivo General de Indias and the Archivo General de Simancas cover the years 1597–1821, but most are for the eighteenth century.[12]

Other repositories also have archival reproductions from Spanish and Mexican archives. Photostats from the Archivo General de Indias in Seville, 1596–1776 (300 items), that include accounts of Sebastián Vizcaíno's two voyages to the northwest coast, diaries of members of early expeditions to California, and documents relating to the early settlements and missions of California and the discovery of silver in Arizona in 1736, are in the Henry E. Huntington Library.[13] An extensive collection of photostats and transcripts on the Spanish exploration of the northwest coast of North America before 1800, assembled by Henry R. Wagner from the Archivo General de la Nación in Mexico, and the Archivo General de Indias and other Spanish archives, are in the Pomona College Library.[14] Copies of reproductions from the

---

[9] The names of the fellows, the subjects of their investigations, and the titles of their publications are in Hill, *American Missions in European Archives*, pp. 86–99.

[10] The transcripts, including many from the Archivo General de Indias, have been interfiled in alphabetical order with transcripts from other archives (Fisher, *Preliminary Guide*, p. 20).

[11] Hammond, *Guide to Ms. Colls.*, p. 149. Microfilm of documents in the British Museum in London relating to early Spanish activities in California, including an account of the port of Monterey, 1770, a description by Juan Bautista de Anza, 1773–74, and maps and plans of frontier presidios of New Spain are in the Bancroft Library (ibid., pp. 31, 72).

[12] Descriptions are in Fisher, *Preliminary Guide*, pp. 20–24.

[13] *Huntington Lib. Quar. Bul.* 8 (Feb. 1945):208.

[14] Wagner's activities in European archives are treated in his *Bullion to Books: Fifty Years of Business and Pleasure* (Los Angeles, 1942), p. 266 ff. He used the collection to prepare his *Spanish Voyages to the Northwest Coast of America in the Sixteenth Century* (San Francisco, 1929), and his *Spanish Explorations in the Strait of Juan de Fuca* (Santa Ana, Calif., 1933), both of which contain texts of documents.

Archivo General de la Nación in the Bancroft Library are also in the San Diego Historical Society Collections.[15] Reproductions in the Library of Congress, as already indicated in the section on Texas, include materials relating to California.[16] Adolph Sutro, book collector and public official of San Francisco, acquired copies of documents in the Spanish archives in Seville that have been published.[17] The San Francisco University Library has microreproductions from the Archivo General de Indias and the Vatican Archives. And photocopies of selections of California materials, 1532–1784 (3 volumes), from the Biblioteca Nacional, Mexico City, are in the University of the Pacific Library, Stockton, California.

Investigators in the Spanish archives also obtained reproductions of maps. The Lowery and Karpinski collections, mentioned in the section on Texas, chapter thirteen, contain photographs of maps that are in Spanish archives. In 1936, after completing his study of the cartography of the northwest coast, Henry R. Wagner presented his collection of 629 maps, consisting mostly of photostats of maps in European and American repositories, to the Pomona College Library.[18] Another Californian, Carl I. Wheat, collected photostats of maps, illustrating the development of the cartography of the Trans-Mississippi West, from European and American repositories and, in 1958, presented 1,200 maps to the Bancroft Library.[19] A chronological list of printed and manuscript maps relating to San Francisco Bay was published by Neal Harlow in 1950, and includes maps in Spanish and Mexican archives and Califor-

---

[15] Natl. Union Catalog of Ms. Colls., 1971, entry 1279.

[16] Hale, Guide to Photocopied Hist. Materials, p. 208.

[17] George B. Griffin, trans. and ed., Documents from the Sutro Collection (Los Angeles, 1891); reprinted by Donald C. Cutter, The California Coast (Norman, Okla., 1969). In 1906, the Sutro Library was partly destroyed by fire (Lota M. Spell, "The Sutro Library," Hisp. Am. Hist. Rev. 29 [August 1949]:452–54). Located at 2130 Fulton Street, San Francisco, the Sutro Library is now part of the California State Library. It has an extensive collection of Mexican pamphlets, including government and church publications, that were purchased by Adolph Sutro in Mexico during 1885–89. See California, State Library, Sutro Branch, Catalog of Mexican Pamphlets in the Sutro Collection (1623–1888), ed. by P. Radin (San Francisco, 1939–40).

[18] Henry R. Wagner, The Cartography of the Northwest Coast of America to the Year 1800 (Berkeley, 1937). A list of maps in volume 2, pp. 273–370, includes manuscript maps and gives their locations. See also Thomas W. Streeter, "Henry R. Wagner, Collector, Bibliographer, Cartographer, and Historian," Calif. Hist. Soc. Quar. 36 (June 1957):165–75.

[19] Carl I. Wheat, Mapping the Trans-Mississippi West, 1540–1861, Volume One, the Spanish Entrada to the Louisiana Purchase, 1540–1804 (San Francisco, 1957). Wheat illustrates his text with reproductions of maps and includes a chronological and descriptive list of maps ("bibliocartography") with their locations.

nia repositories.[20] And Spanish exploration and mapping of the head of the Gulf of California is illustrated in another published collection of over 100 printed maps.[21]

Maps of California in a variety of forms — manuscript, photostats, facsimiles, and printed — are in the Map Division of the Library of Congress,[22] the Henry E. Huntington Library, the Bancroft Library of the University of California, the University of California Library at Los Angeles, the Charles W. Bowers Memorial Museum at Santa Ana, California, the Sutro Collection in the San Francisco Public Library,[23] and the San Diego Historical Society.[24]

---

[20] Neal Harlow, *The Maps of San Francisco Bay from the Spanish Discovery in 1769 to the American Occupation* (San Francisco, 1950).

[21] Charles K. Fox, *The Colorado Delta: A Discussion of the Spanish Exploration & Maps* . . . (Los Angeles, 1936).

[22] Philip Lee Phillips, "Descriptive List of Maps of California and of San Francisco, to 1865, Inclusive, Found in the Library of Congress" [Washington, n.d.], Ms. A photostatic copy of this list is in the Henry E. Huntington Library. Early maps of California are listed in Justin Winsor, *The Kohl Collection of Maps (Now in the Library of Congress) Relating to America* (Washington, 1904).

[23] Charles B. Turrill, "Maps Showing the Californias in the Sutro Branch, California State Library; List of Maps and Authors and List of All Localities Indicated in Lower and Upper California" [San Francisco, 1917]. Photostat in the Map Division of the Library of Congress.

[24] For information regarding other collections of maps that include some relating to California, see chapters four and thirteen, in the sections on New Mexico and Texas.

23

Documentary Publications

ALTHOUGH NO COMPREHENSIVE, systematic documentary collection on Spanish and Mexican California has been published, there exists an extensive body of published materials derived from archival sources. The governments of Spain, Mexico, and California issued orders, decrees, and regulations in printed form, many of which have been reprinted in English translations; and other collections of documents, of limited scope, have also been published.[1] Soon after the acquisition of the Bancroft Collection by the University of California, professors of that institution organized the Academy of Pacific Coast History, to publish the original texts and English translations of documents in that collection. Under the general editorship of Frederick J. Teggart, diaries and logs of early sea voyages and land expeditions to California appeared in academy publications.[2] Late in 1911, H. E. Bolton proposed to the president of the University of California that a comprehensive body of documents on Spanish activities in the United States be published.[3] But no official sponsorship for such an undertaking was forthcoming.

Bolton himself prepared an extensive collection of documents on

---

[1] Titles of many documentary publications appear in the bibliographies by Cowan, Fahey, Greenwood, Harding, Mecham, Steck, Wagner, Winsor, and Wroth that are listed in the bibliography, where titles of other compilations that have been published recently also appear.

[2] Diaries of sea and overland journeys by captains, pilots, and missionaries are described in Charles J. G. M. Piette, O.F.M., "The Diarios of Early California, 1769–1784," *The Americas* 2 (Apr. 1946):409–22.

[3] Bannon, *Bolton*, p. 23.

Anza's exploratory and colonizing expeditions to California.[4] From Tubac on January 8, 1774, Lt. Col. Juan B. de Anza, along with Frs. Francisco T. H. Garcés, Juan Díaz, and Tomás Eixarch, and a party of soldiers, muleteers and servants, traveled north along the valleys of the Magdalena and Santa Cruz rivers to the Gila River, down it and the Colorado River, and thence northwest to San Gabriel where the party arrived on March 22. After visiting Monterey, Anza left San Gabriel on the return trip on May 5, taking a few men assigned by Pedro Fages, commandant at Monterey, as far as the Gila-Colorado junction, to learn the way across the desert. After parting with Father Garcés on the Gila on May 21, Anza was back at Tubac on May 27. Having pioneered a land route to California, Anza left Tubac in October, 1775, with a colonizing expedition that established San Francisco in 1776. He was accompanied by Fathers Garcés and Eixarch, who were going to the Yuma villages in Arizona, and by Fr. Pedro Font, who served as chaplain, diarist, and astronomer. Bolton's compilation on the Anza expedition consists chiefly of translations of documents obtained by him from repositories in Mexico, Spain, and the United States.[5] Anza's diaries of the first expedition, diaries by Fathers Díaz and Garcés, and Fr. Francisco Palóu's diary of an exploratory trip to the port of San Francisco in November, 1774, are in volume two of Bolton's work. Anza's diary of the second expedition, October 23, 1775–June 1, 1776; Father Font's short diary; Father Eixarch's diary of his winter on the Colorado River among the Yuma Indians, 1775–76; Father Palóu's account of the founding of San Francisco from his *Noticias de Nueva California;* and Lt. José J. Moraga's account of the same event are in volume three. A translation of Father Font's complete diary, September 29, 1775–June 1, 1776, (which is the best of the diaries), prepared from a copy of the original manuscript in the John Carter Brown Library, takes up volume four, which also contains Font's map of the expedition. A selection of correspondence, 1769–77, including communications between officials of Spain, Mexico, Sonora, and California and participants in the expeditions, especially Anza, Díaz, and Garcés, fills volume five. The correspondence is from the Archivo General de la Nación, Mexico City, the Archivo General de Indias, Seville, the Santa Barbara Mission Archives, and the Bancroft Library of the University of California. The correspondence concerns the origins, organization, equipment, and conduct of the expeditions. Bolton's own account of the expeditions, based on the foregoing materials, is

---

[4] Herbert E. Bolton, trans. and ed., *Anza's California Expeditions: An Outpost of Empire,* 5 vols. (Berkeley, 1930).

[5] Ibid., 2:vii–x; 3:vi–ix, contains lists of the diaries with their archival sources.

in volume one. The collection was his principal contribution to the history of California and the Southwest.

Other historians have prepared a number of important publications. Herbert I. Priestley edited an early description of California by Pedro Fages, a member of the first expedition to Monterey in 1769 and commandant at that place from 1770 to 1794.[6] Reprints of different editions of an account of August 16, 1770, of the Spanish occupation of California, originally published in Mexico in 1770 with a translation, have been published by George P. Hammond.[7] A facsimile of Miguel Costansó's narrative of the Portolá expedition to Monterey and a translation have been published.[8] Donald C. Cutter of the University of New Mexico has edited a diary of Gabriel Moraga,[9] and documents relating to a visit to Monterey, in 1791, by Capts. Alejandro Malaspina and José Bustamante y Guerra, two Spanish naval officers.[10] Ernest J. Burrus, the Jesuit historian, has published Capt. Fernando de Rivera y Moncada's diary, May 25, 1774–January 15, 1777, relating to his administration as governor of California, with related documents including correspondence with Fr. Junípero Serra, Juan Bautista de Anza, Pedro Fages, and the storekeepers at Monterey and San Diego; a report by Mariano Carillo on events at the San Diego mission up to 1772; and a eulogy on the Franciscan missionaries murdered by the Yuma Indians on the Colorado River in 1781.[11] A volume in the documentary series edited by José Porrúa Turanzas contains early reports, diaries, and journals relating to California.[12] Translations of documents relating to the exploration of the central valley of California, from the Bancroft Library and other repositories in California, have been published by S. F. Cook.[13] This collection includes formal reports to the

---

[6] Herbert I. Priestley, trans. and ed., *A Historical, Political, and Natural Description of California by Pedro Fages, Soldier of Spain* (Berkeley, 1937); reprinted from the *Catholic Hist. Review* 4 (January, April 1919):486–509, 71–90.

[7] George P. Hammond, trans. and ed., *Noticias de California: First Report of the Occupation by the Portolá Expedition, 1770* (San Francisco, 1958).

[8] Ray Brandes, trans. and ed., *The Costansó Narrative of the Portolá Expedition: Chronicle of the Spanish Conquest of Alta California* (Newhall, Calif., 1970).

[9] Donald C. Cutter, trans. and ed., *The Diary of Ensign Gabriel Moraga's Expedition of Discovery in the Sacramento Valley, 1808* (Los Angeles, 1957).

[10] Donald C. Cutter, trans. and ed., *Malaspina in California* (San Francisco, 1960).

[11] Ernest J. Burrus, ed., *Diario del Capitán Comandante Fernando de Rivera y Moncada, con un apéndice documental*, 2 vols. (Madrid, 1967).

[12] José Porrúa Turanzas, *Noticias y documentos acerca de los Californias, 1764–1795* (Madrid, 1959).

[13] Sherburne F. Cook, trans. and ed., "Colonial Expeditions to the Interior of California Central Valley, 1800–1820," University of California, *Publications, Anthropological Records* 16, no. 6 (Berkeley, 1960):239–92.

government and excerpts from letters and memoirs that supply the only available information regarding some explorations.

No microfilm publication of Spanish and Mexican records of California has been sponsored by the National Historical Publications Commission because of the unavailability of a central body of records, due to the destruction by fire of the provincial records in 1906. A microfilm publication of a different composition could be prepared from the reproductions of Mexican and Spanish archives and the archives and manuscripts in the Bancroft Library and other repositories in California. But the preparation of such a compilation would be a considerably more extensive project than was undertaken for the provincial records of Texas and New Mexico. Because such a project has not found a sponsor, individual editors, translators, and compilers will go on preparing separate publications, but their work would be facilitated if repositories would prepare more and better guides and inventories. Many finding aids fail to supply sufficient detail and are poorly indexed. An up-to-date, comprehensive bibliography of published documents relating to the whole Southwest would be a great aid to researchers.

24

Manuscript Collections

AT THE TIME THE UNITED STATES acquired California in 1846, not all of the Spanish and Mexican archives passed into the hands of its agents. Important masses of papers remained in the possession of officials at various places, but eventually most of these papers were acquired by repositories in California and elsewhere. The papers of other individuals also contain correspondence with California officials and other documents recording official transactions.

During the second half of the nineteenth century, Hubert Howe Bancroft, while engaged in historical investigations that resulted in his vast history of the Pacific slope, acquired by donation, purchase, or copying many collections of privately held papers relating to California. He assembled 50 collections of original papers in 110 volumes containing 40,000 documents.[1] Besides these collections of family papers, he also obtained scattered correspondence of 200 of the most prominent men in California, including Spanish and Mexican officials and Franciscan friars.[2] Governors represented in the Bancroft Collection by documents of various kinds include Felipe de Neve, Pedro Fages, José Joaquín Arrillaga, Pablo Vicente Sola, Luís Antonio Arguello, José María Echeandia, Manuel Victoria, José Figueroa, José Castro, Juan Bautista Alvarado, Pío Pico, and Manuel Micheltorena. Other

---

[1] Bancroft, *Hist. Calif.*, 1:48–49; Bancroft, *Calif. Pastoral*, p. 765; Bancroft, *Literary Industries*, pp. 383–439. The names of the persons whose papers were acquired are in these sources, and references to the acquisition of many of the collections are in the register of pioneers appended to the volumes of Bancroft's *Hist. Calif.*

[2] Bancroft, *Hist. Calif.*, 1:53–54. The titles of the various collections are listed in the bibliography in the front of volume one.

officials include Manuel Jimeno Casarin, secretary to Governor Alvarado, Juan Bandini, José María Covarrubias, and José Matias Moreno, secretaries to Governor Pico, and Carlos A. Carillo, deputy of Upper California in the Mexican Congress, 1831–32. Army officers' papers include those of Fernando de Rivera y Moncada, commandant of Upper California, 1774–77; José Francisco Ortega, commandant at San Diego, 1773–81, Santa Barbara, 1781–84, and Monterey, 1787–91; and José de la Guerra y Noriega, commandant at Santa Barbara, 1815–42. Members of the legislative assembly whose papers are in the Bancroft Library include Juan Bautista Alvarado, Juan Bandini, José Joaquín Estudillo, Rafael Gómez, Rafael González, Manuel Jimeno Casarin, Agustín Olvera, and Manuel Requena. Other army officers and soldiers represented in the Bancroft Collection include Antonio María Pico, Ygnacio del Valle, Antonio del Valle, José Joaquín Estudillo, Domingo Carilla, José Carillo, Juan María Osuna, Valentín Cota, Antonio Francisco Coronel, and Miguel Avila. Manuel Castro, an official at Monterey, presented some papers in 1875, and more at a later date. Numerous diaries, journals, and ship logbooks relate to the early expeditions from Mexico to California and, later, to Upper California.[3] Other items include a commentary by Pedro Fages on the report of Capt. Nicolás Soler, November 8, 1787, on the Santa Barbara presidio; the report of Miguel Costansó, December 17, 1794, on the project for fortifying the presidios of Upper California; and a report by Costansó and others, July 13, 1795, on aid for Upper California. Manuscripts collected by Bancroft, relating to Mexico, include viceroy decrees and instructions,[4] recollections, historical narratives, chronicles, and historical notes of a number of prominent figures.[5]

Other materials in the Bancroft Library include Fr. Pedro Font's short journal of the second Anza expedition from Sonora to San Francisco, 1775–76 (79 pages); documents relating to the exploration of the northern California coast, 1773–91 (70 pages); logbooks considered to be those of the frigate *Princesa* on round-trip voyages from San Blas to San Francisco, February 11–November 21, 1779, under Ignacio Arteaga, and of another voyage from San Blas to Santa Barbara and

---

[3] Entries relating to these documents are in the bibliography of Bancroft's *Hist. Calif.*, 1, and in Herbert I. Priestley, *Franciscan Explorations in California* (Glendale, Calif., 1946).

[4] H. H. Bancroft, *History of Mexico*, 6 vols. (San Francisco, 1883–88), contains the titles in vol. 1, and other information passim. A selection of the instructions has been published; Mexico, Viceroyalty, *Instrucciones que los virreyes de Nueva España dejaron a sus sucessores* (Mexico, 1867).

[5] Bancroft, *Calif. Pastoral*, pp. 769–92. In print is: Pío Pico, *Don Pío Pico's Historical Narrative*, ed. by Martine Cole and Henry Welcome, trans. by Arthur P. Botelle (Glendale, Calif., 1973).

other California ports, in 1782, under Esteban José Martínez; and a diary by Martínez of another voyage of that ship, February 17–December 5, 1789.[6] Various collections of Mexican records include some from the viceroyalty; manuscript and printed copies of Spanish royal decrees; Mexican viceregal orders, and other documents, 1675–1819 (3 volumes); and account books of the royal treasurer at Guadalajara, 1622–1738 (3 volumes).[7] Documents relating to the second Conde de Revilla Gigedo include instructions issued during his term as viceroy, 1789–94 (2 volumes), and documents constituting his residencia, or the defense of his administration, 1795–1802 (266 pages).[8] There are also extensive Spanish and Mexican decrees from the sixteenth through the nineteenth centuries (9 volumes, and 788 and 724 pages) relating to civil and ecclesiastical administration.[9]

The principal collection of papers acquired by Bancroft were those of Mariano Guadalupe Vallejo, who was commander and director of colonization on the northern frontier, 1835–36; commandant general of California, 1836–42; and again commander of the northern frontier after 1842. Obtained in 1875, largely through the efforts of Enrique Cerruti, Bancroft's agent, the collection contains fifty volumes of documents (1780–1875) consisting so preponderantly of archival material that they can be regarded as the official archives of the Mexican government in northern California.[10] Composed of correspondence and other documents, including land papers, the collection is important for military and political affairs, relations with the missions and the Indians, economic matters, and the colonization of the north. The collection contains letters of numerous governors and other officials, including José Abrego, a local official at Monterey and member of the territorial deputation; Ignacio Martínez, an official at San Francisco; and Juan del Prado Mesa, military commander at Santa Clara, San Francisco, and San José. Part of the Vallejo manuscripts consists of papers of relatives and friends, including J. B. R. Cooper and Thomas O. Larkin. Military records of San Francisco, 1813–33, include rosters and accounts.

Papers of Americans and other foreigners who settled in California during the Mexican period were also obtained by Bancroft. The most important of these collections are the papers of Thomas O. Larkin,

[6] Hammond, *Guide to Ms. Colls.*, pp. 72, 75, 113, 122.

[7] Ibid., pp. 36, 90, 134–36.

[8] Ibid., pp. 193–94.

[9] Ibid., pp. 230–31.

[10] Doris M. Wright, *A Guide to the Mariano Guadalupe Vallejo Documentos para la Historia de California, 1780–1875* (Berkeley, 1953).

who was a merchant at Monterey and United States consul there from 1843 to 1846. Larkin's papers, 1822–56 (36 volumes and 181 folders), contain letters received, letters sent when he was United States consul, and other business papers.[11] Other Monterey merchants whose papers are in the Bancroft Library include John B. R. Cooper and William E. P. Hartnell. Hartnell's papers, 1820–47, include business records of Mc-Culloch, Hartnell & Co., and correspondence, land grants, and his diary when he was *visitador general* of California missions, 1839–40.[12] The papers of Henry D. Fitch, 1827–58, a ship captain, merchant, and minor official at San Diego, were presented to Bancroft by his widow, Josefa C. Fitch, who also dictated a narration.

The Bancroft Collection of manuscripts, other historical materials, and books, was purchased by the University of California, through the efforts of Prof. H. M. Stephens, in November, 1905.[13] The collection was moved in 1906 from the Valencia Street building in San Francisco where it had been housed for twenty-five years, surviving the famous fire of 1906, to a building at the university in Berkeley. The Bancroft Library, as it became known, was the nucleus of a larger collection of manuscripts and other materials on the history of California and the west. Beginning in the 1930s, the Bancroft Library utilized the Works Progress Administration to prepare photographic reproductions of the Vallejo and other manuscript collections for the use of researchers, in order to preserve the originals from further wear and tear.[14]

Additions have been made to the manuscript holdings of the Bancroft Library since its acquisition by the University of California. These accessions were obtained largely through the fund-raising efforts of the Friends of the Bancroft Library, an organization that was founded by G. P. Hammond when he became director of the Bancroft Library

---

[11] Documents by Mexican officials and reports by Larkin to the U.S. secretary of state on conditions in California are printed in G. P. Hammond, ed., *The Larkin Papers: Personal, Business, and Official Correspondence of Thomas Oliver Larkin, Merchant and United States Consul in California*, 10 vols. (Berkeley and Los Angeles, 1951–64). Letters from Larkin to Abel Stearns and William A. Leidesdorff, 1831–56, partly concerned with political and military matters are in John A. Hawgood, ed., *First and Last Consul Thomas Oliver Larkin and the Americanization of California: A Selection of Letters* (San Marino, 1962). Other Larkin letters, written to Faxon D. Atherton, 1842–53, concerning the activities of Mexican officials and the American occupation, are in Doyce B. Nunis, Jr., ed., "Notes and Documents: Six New Larkin Letters," *South. Calif. Quar.* 49 (Mar. 1967):65–103.

[12] Susanna B. Dakin, *The Lives of William Hartnell* (Stanford, 1949), pp. 298–99.

[13] John W. Caughey, in *Hubert Howe Bancroft: Historian of the West* (Berkeley and Los Angeles, 1946), pp. 350–63, relates the long story of the acquisition.

[14] About 1950, the Bancroft Library began the preparation of a general guide to its manuscript collections. Volumes 1 and 2 are cited in this book. Volume 3, concerning California manuscripts, was still in preparation in 1976.

in 1946. The Thomas W. Norris collection of California manuscripts, 1770s–1900s (3,000 items), includes letters of M. G. Vallejo, John A. Sutter, and others. Originals or copies of documents by or about Gov. Gaspár de Portolá, 1703–85 (20 folders), relate to his career as a soldier, explorer, and administrator in Upper and Lower California.[15] An extensive collection of papers of Count Revilla Gigedo, viceroy of New Spain, 1789–94, were obtained as a gift from Irving Robbins of Palo Alto.[16] A 1960 purchase in Mexico included fragments of the journal of Gov. Fernando Rivera y Moncada.[17]

The Henry E. Huntington Library at San Marino has acquired, by purchase or gift, important manuscripts of Mexican officials and others, relating to California. The papers of José de Gálvez, 1763–94 (734 items), contain correspondence, orders, proclamations, reports, and other documents concerning the years he served as *visitador general* of New Spain, when the early expeditions to Upper California were being conducted.[18] The Gálvez collection consists mainly of original letters received by viceroys of New Spain from Gálvez, and copies of letters to him, indicating that they had come from the records of the viceroyalty. A diary of Capt. Juan Bautista de Anza, January–May 1777, relating to his overland expedition from Sonora to Monterey, is a contemporary copy.[19] The journal of José Longinos Martínez, a surgeon and naturalist who made the first scientific expedition to Lower and Upper California in 1791–92, was obtained through Henry R. Wagner, who found it in Mexico.[20] The instructions of Count Revilla Gigedo to his successor in office, June 1794 (1 volume), is one of a series of such documents emanating from the viceroys of New Spain. Papers of another viceroy, the Marqués de Branciforte, 1795–1800, concern the administration of the Pious Fund, the fortifications and defense of the Californias, and foreign ships and seamen. Four letter books of Viceroy Juan Ruiz de Apodaca, 1816–21, contain contemporary copies of official correspondence with the Spanish minister of war, giving details on occurrences in Mexico. The papers of Mariano Guadalupe Vallejo,

---

[15] *Bancroftiana* 17 (November 1957); Hammond, *Guide to Ms. Colls.*, p. 184.

[16] News note in *Pacific Hist. Rev.* 26 (May 1957):209.

[17] Other fragments of Rivera's journal are in the Franciscan Academy, Washington, D.C., and the California Historical Society Collection.

[18] John C. Parish, "California Books and Manuscripts in the Huntington Library," *Huntington Library Bulletin*, No. 7 (Apr. 1935):26–30. Descriptions of most of the Huntington Library collections are also in the *Natl. Union Catalog of Ms. Colls.*

[19] Parish, "Calif. Books and Mss.," p. 31.

[20] Published by Lesley B. Simpson, trans. and ed., *Journal of José Longinos Martínez: Notes and Observations of the Naturalist of the Botanical Expedition in Old and New California and the South Coast, 1791–1792* (San Francisco, 1961). In 1939–40, Simpson, a professor of Spanish at the University of California, found materials relating to Longinos in the Archivo General de la Nación, Mexico.

1833–88 (257 items), contain correspondence and other documents relating to the defense of the northern frontier and relations with missions and the Indians.[21] The Huntington Library has many other manuscripts for the years 1769–1845, including missionaries' letters, logbooks, diaries, orders, instructions, and royal orders, relating to the occupation of California, exploration, the administration of missions, and commerce with Mexico.[22] William A. Leidesdorff was a ship captain and merchant at San Francisco, where he served after October, 1845, as the United States vice-consul. The Leidesdorff papers, 1840-67 (502 items), contain personal, official, and business manuscripts, including letters from Thomas O. Larkin and John A. Sutter.[23] The Abel Stearns papers, 1806–1935 (12,500 items), include correspondence and personal, business, and legal manuscripts. Stearns arrived in California from Massachusetts in 1829 and became a merchant and rancher at Los Angeles.

Repositories in other places in California have collections containing materials relating to Spanish and Mexican activities. The Antonio Francisco Coronel Collection, 1770–1912 (10 feet), in the Los Angeles County Museum Library, contains manuscripts and publications relating to southern California.[24] That repository has the Del Valle family papers, 1818–1920 (approximately 1,000 items), including papers of Antonio Seferino del Valle, an army officer at San Francisco and Monterey, and his son Ygnacio, a soldier, rancher, and wine merchant.[25] The same repository also has manuscript collections that were assembled by the Historical Society of Southern California, relating to families in southern California and the history of California and the Southwest (2 volumes and 10 bundles). The Library of the University of California at Los Angeles has papers of Juan Bandini, 1837–89 (1 box and 2 volumes); Manuel Castro and family, 1837–70 (approximately 50 items); Archibald H. Gillespie (a Marine Corps officer who served as an emissary from Washington to John C. Frémont), 1845–60 (900 items); Abel Stearns papers, 1837–68 (143 items); William H. Davis letters, 1842–82; and the large Robert E. Cowan Collection containing materials relating to California and the American west.[26] Some

---

[21] Parish, "Calif. Books and Mss.," p. 34.

[22] Reproductions of 34 mission documents, 1806–51 (290 pp.), from the collections of the Huntington Library have been presented to the Archives of the Archdiocese of Los Angeles by Doyce B. Nunis, Jr.

[23] Parish, "Calif. Books and Mss.," pp. 35, 38–41.

[24] Mahood, "Coronel Collection," pp. 4–7; *Natl. Union Catalog of Ms. Colls.*, 1961, entry 1145.

[25] *Natl. Union Catalog of Ms. Colls.*, 1961, entry 1625.

[26] University of California at Los Angeles, Library, *Guide to Special Colls.*, p. 5 ff.

materials concerning the legal history of the Palos Verdes ranch, 1840–84 (226 items), are in the Palos Verdes Public Library.[27] Records of California businessmen, dating from 1826, are in the California State Library at Sacramento, and include the business papers of William H. Davis, a merchant at San Francisco after 1838. Papers of Henry D. Fitch, a storekeeper at San Diego and surveyor of public lands, are in the San Diego Historical Society Collection. That society also has papers from the Pío Pico family, some from the family of José Antonio Yorba, a soldier and landowner of San Diego, and a miscellaneous collection, dating from 1769, that contains papers of other early Californians. Papers of Pedro Fages, 1775, William A. Leidesdorff, 1845–74, and ship logbooks, dating from 1821, are in the California Historical Society collections at San Francisco.[28]

Second only to the Vallejo collection, for the pre-1846 history of California, are the De la Guerra family papers in the Santa Barbara Mission Archives. Joseph Antonio de la Guerra y Noriega was commandant at Santa Barbara from 1815 to 1842, treasurer and financial adviser for the Franciscans, and deputy to the Mexican Congress in 1827. In 1924, Fr. Joseph Thompson, O.F.M., a great grandson of De la Guerra, found the papers in the hands of a cousin in the old family home in Santa Barbara, and in the home of a family connection there.[29] He obtained permission to deposit them in the safe at the Santa Barbara Mission, and later, while he was working on a biography of De la Guerra, the papers were deposited in the safe at St. Joseph's Friary in Los Angeles. He later placed the papers in the Huntington Library, where they were arranged in folders in alphabetical order by names of authors, by Miss Haydée Noya, a Spanish linguist and librarian, and microfilmed. Following the final deposit of the original papers and a microfilm in the new archive-library of the Santa Barbara Mission, Fr. Maynard J. Geiger, its archivist, made a calendar of 817 pages, to facilitate the work of researchers. Xerox copies of the papers were also prepared. Microfilm and Xerox copies of the papers, and a copy of Geiger's calendar, are in the Huntington Library, and a microfilm is also in the American Academy of Franciscan History, near Potomac, Maryland. Seven volumes of transcripts made in 1877 are in the Bancroft Library of the University of California. The De la Guerra papers, 1798–1885 (12,000 pages), half of which antedate 1846, consist of official and

---

[27] Historical Records Survey, Southern California, *Inventory of the Bixby Collection in the Palos Verdes Library and Art Gallery* (Los Angeles, 1940).

[28] James De T. Abajian, "Preliminary Listing of Manuscript Collections in Library of California Historical Society," *Calif. Hist. Soc. Quar.* 33 (Dec. 1954):373, 374.

[29] Maynard J. Geiger, O.F.M., "History of the Santa Barbara De la Guerra Family Documents," *South. Calif. Quar.* 54 (Fall 1972):278.

personal papers, including many letters written to De la Guerra and his son Pablo by military and civil officers of Mexico and California, missionaries of Upper and Lower California, and merchants, lawyers, ranchers, businessmen, relatives and friends; decrees of the Mexican government; and a variety of business papers, ship logbooks, censuses, and presidio reports.

Other miscellaneous collections of Spanish documents on California are in the Pacific School of Religion Library, Berkeley; the Southwest Museum Library, Los Angeles; the Pasadena Public Library; the Junípero Serra Museum of the San Diego Historical Society; the Charles W. Bowers Memorial Museum, Santa Ana; the Sutro Library in the San Francisco Public Library; and the Stanford University Library.

Repositories in other places in the United States have manuscripts relating to California. Reports by Gov. Pedro Fages on the presidios at San Diego, 1788, and San Francisco, 1791; Capt. Nicolás Soler's report on the Santa Barbara presidio, 1788; and a statistical report on the Monterey presidio, 1791; are in the Beinecke Collection of Western Americana in the Yale University Library.[30] In the same collection, there is a volume of the proceedings of the trial of Francisco Berdusco, February–December 1835, for complicity in a plot to overthrow Gov. José Figueroa; Gov. Luís Arguello's oath of allegiance to Emperor Iturbide, April 2, 1823; and several documents of 1824–26 relating to the Junta de Fomento de California, which is referred to in chapter twenty-five, footnote eight.[31] A report by Lt. José Cortes, Royal Corps of Engineers, on the defenses of the northern provinces of New Spain, 1799 (1 volume), is in the Manuscript Division of the Library of Congress. That repository also has six communications of 1819 from the viceroy, Juan Ruiz de Apodaca (Count of Venadito), to the Spanish government, relating to the defense of the northern frontier. Dispatches from Thomas O. Larkin, United States consul at Monterey, 1834–48, are in the National Archives (General Records of the Department of State, Record Group 59). These dispatches are available on microfilm publication M–138, and are printed in volumes 2–5 of *The Larkin Papers*, cited above. A diary of Miguel de Campa, O.F.M., chaplain on a voyage of the *Santiago* to California in 1775, and a report by Visitador General José de Gálvez on conditions in Mexico, California, Sonora, and the northern provinces of New Spain, 1768–78, are in the Ayer Collection in the Newberry Library, Chicago, Illinois.[32] A collection of royal decrees, let-

---

[30] Goddard, Kritzler, and Hanna, *Catalogue of the Beinecke Collection of Western Americana*, pp. 10–11.

[31] Ibid., pp. 6, 11, 49–50.

[32] Ruth L. Butler, *A Check List of Manuscripts in the Edward E. Ayer Collection* (Chicago, 1937), pp. 123, 129.

ters and instructions of the viceroy of New Spain, seventeenth and eighteenth centuries (3 feet), in the William L. Clements Library of the University of Michigan, Ann Arbor, Michigan, includes material relating to California.[33] Another collection of Mexican records in that repository includes a defense by Count Juan Vicente Revilla Gigedo of his administration as viceroy and his instruction of 1794 to his successor,[34] and, in a volume of miscellaneous Mexican manuscripts, there is a report by the Marqués de Sonora on the condition of the Californias in 1772.[35] A volume of Mexican military records, 1793–1803, in the New York Historical Society Collection includes muster rolls and other records of soldiers stationed at San Fernando and Santa Rosa, California.[36] José de Gálvez's instruction to his successor, December 31, 1771, is in the New York Public Library.[37] Letters of Manuel Micheltorena to Manuel Castañares and others, 1842–44 (8 items), are in the Latin American Collection in the University of Texas Library.[38]

---

[33] William S. Ewing, *Guide to the Manuscript Collections in the William L. Clements Library* (Ann Arbor, 1953), p. 198.

[34] Ibid., p. 233.

[35] Howard H. Peckham, *Guide to the Manuscript Collections in the William L. Clements Library* (Ann Arbor, 1942), pp. 184–85.

[36] New York Historical Society, *Survey of the Manuscript Collections in the New-York Historical Society* (New York, 1941), p. 44; *Natl. Union Catalog Ms. Colls.*, 1965, entry 1527.

[37] New York Public Library, *The Dictionary Catalog of the Manuscript Division*, 2 vols. (New York, 1967), 1:28.

[38] Castañeda and Dabbs, *Guide*, pp. 5–6.

25

Land Records

UNDER SPANISH RULE in Upper California, free grants of land were made to encourage settlement and to develop agriculture and grazing. The laws of the Indies allowed each pueblo four square leagues of land, and it was intended that the presidios and missions be converted into pueblos and given the same allowances.[1] The commandants of the new settlements at San Diego and Monterey were authorized, by instructions of the viceroy of 1773, to make grants within the limits of the town or mission.[2] A regulation of 1781, designed to stimulate emigration from old Mexico, authorized the pueblos to grant house lots and agricultural tracts to new settlers, who were also to be supplied with livestock, agricultural implements, and government pastureland, and were to be paid for several years.[3] Under this regulation, the distribution of land within the four square leagues was handled by the alcaldes and *ayuntamientos*. The captains of presidios were directed, in 1791, to grant house lots and fields to soldiers and settlers within four square leagues. Government land was used as pasture, and settlers were obligated to do militia duty and sell surplus produce to the presidios. Settlements recognized by the United States as entitled to the four square leagues allotted to pueblos included San Francisco, Sonoma, Monterey, Santa Barbara, San Diego, San José, and Los Angeles.[4]

---

[1] Bancroft, *Hist. Calif.*, 1:607–08; William W. Robinson, *Land in California* (Berkeley and Los Angeles, 1948), pp. 34, 40. A square league contained about 4,438 acres.

[2] Bancroft, *Hist. Calif.*, 1:608; Hittell, *Hist. Calif.*, 1:516–17.

[3] Bancroft, *Hist. Calif.*, 1:336, 346; Hittell, *Hist. Calif.*, 1:522.

[4] Hittell, *Hist. Calif.*, 2:751; Robinson, *Land in Calif.*, p. 60.

Under both Spanish and Mexican governments, Franciscan missions were allowed to occupy land, which was worked by the Indians, but ownership of the land continued to be held by the government.[5] An instruction of 1786 authorized the governor to make concessions for ranching and farming outside the limits of pueblos.

The Mexican government adopted a more liberal land-grant system and, consequently, made over 600 of the 800 land grants which were presented to United States officials for confirmation.[6] A national colonization law of August 18, 1824, and regulations of November 21, 1828, authorized the governor to make grants of eleven square leagues to heads of families, private persons, and empresarios who were to contract for the introduction of colonists.[7] A Mexican commission was created in 1824 to promote the settlement and development of Upper and Lower California.[8] The empresario contracts were to be approved by the supreme government in Mexico, and the other grants, by the territorial deputation. The secularization of mission lands, during 1834–36, which had comprised a sixth of the area of Upper California, was followed by a great increase in grants for ranches, and most of the 500 ranches that existed in Upper California by 1846 were carved out of mission lands.[9] The governors made numerous grants, in payment for civil or military services rendered to the government of California, that did not have to be approved by the departmental assembly. After 1837, the prefects, with the consent of the governor, could grant small

---

[5] Hittell, Hist. Calif., 2:749; Robinson, Land in Calif., p. 25.

[6] Robinson, Land in Calif., p. 67.

[7] Ibid., pp. 65–66; Hittell, Hist. Calif., 2:750.

[8] The proceedings of this commission were printed in Mexico City in 1827 and are reprinted in Keld J. Reynolds, trans. and ed., "Principal Actions of the California Junta de Fomento, 1825–1827," Calif. Hist. Soc. Quar. 24 (December 1945):289–320; 25 (March–December 1946):57–78, 149–68, 267–78, 347–67. The colonization project of José María Híjar and José María Padrés, initiated in 1834 with official approval, failed the next year after difficulties arose between Híjar and the governor of California. The regulations of the company have been reprinted in Keld J. Reynolds, ed., "The Reglamento for the Híjar and Padrés Colony of 1834," Hist. Soc. South. Calif. Quar. 28 (Dec. 1946):142–75. A list of the names of 239 persons is in C. Alan Hutchinson, "An Official List of Members of the Híjar-Padrés Colony for Mexican California, 1834," Pacific Hist. Rev. 11 (Aug. 1973):407–18.

[9] Robinson, Land in Calif., p. 61. Lists of ranch grants are given in the following publications: "Report of the Surveyor General of California," in U.S. Department of the Interior, Annual Report, 1880 (Washington, 1880), pp. 899–912; Bancroft, Hist. Calif., 1:661–63, 683 n. 14; 2:711–13 n. 5; 3:655 n. 5; 5:619 n. 1; Robinson, Land in Calif., pp. 56–57; William W. Robinson, Ranchos Become Cities (Pasadena, 1938), pp. 219–34; William E. Smythe, The History of San Diego, 2 vols. (San Diego, 1908), 1:112–13; Robert G. Cowan, Ranchos of California: A List of Spanish Concessions, 1775–1822, and Mexican Grants, 1822–1846 (Fresno, Calif., 1956), pp. 12–113.

tracts within the common lands of the towns, and house lots in the towns. In 1839, John A. Sutter, a Swiss immigrant, founded a settlement that became known as Sutter's Fort, on the American River near its junction with the Sacramento River. The governor of California made a grant of eleven square leagues to Sutter, who renamed the settlement New Helvetia. Americans arriving overland settled around the fort, and in 1848 the town of Sacramento was laid out there.[10] Surveys of the land grants were not made regularly by either the Spanish or Mexican governments; descriptions based on landmarks were usually indefinite and caused much trouble for United States land commissioners who later became engaged in investigating and confirming titles. Late in 1844, however, Jasper O'Farrell, an emigrant from Ireland with a background in engineering and the Spanish language, was appointed government land surveyor of Upper California. By 1846, he had surveyed at least twenty-one land grants, and accurate maps by him are in the land records of California.[11]

Early laws and regulations concerning land grants in California required the keeping of pertinent records. The book of grants (*toma de razón*), required by the regulation of 1781, was kept by the secretary of the provincial government and was found among the records at Monterey by American officials.[12] Alcaldes were obliged, under a law of 1789, to keep a record of all pueblo grants. The procedure resulted in the accumulation of a number of documents for each grant; these were filed together in separate *expedientes*, bearing numbers and names, and were kept in the custody of the secretary. A complete *expediente* included the following papers: the original petition of the applicant to the governor, the sketch (*diseño*) of the land solicited, the report (*informe*) of the local official, the decree of concession, the approval of the departmental assembly, the governor's certificate, and a copy (*borrador*) of the title.[13] This documentation was incomplete more often than not, for the procedures and conditions of occupation

---

[10] The text of the grant of June 18, 1841, and of a later one of February 5, 1845, for 22 square leagues, which was disallowed by the United States government, are printed in "Petition of John A. Sutter, Praying Compensation for Land Owned by Him in California, and Held under Mexican Grants, ..." Jan. 15, 1866, *Senate Misc. Doc.* 38, 39 Cong., 1 sess., pp. 8–9. The 1841 grant is also in William Hartnell, trans., and Neal Harlow, ed., *A Faithful Translation of the Papers Respecting the Grant Made by Governor Alvarado to J. A. Sutter* (Sacramento, 1942), pp. 5–7.

[11] Geoffrey Mawn, "Agrimensor y Arquitecto: Jasper O'Farrell's Surveying in Mexican California." *South. Calif. Quar.* 56 (Spring 1974):1–12.

[12] See the description of these records by W. C. Jones below.

[13] Other samples of the documents in the *expedientes* are in: Joseph J. Hill, *The History of Warner's Ranch and Its Environs* (Los Angeles, 1927), pp. 194–221; Donaldson, *Public Domain*, pp. 382–94.

were seldom entirely complied with. The approval of the departmental
assembly, the certificate for which was frequently missing from the
expediente, was recorded in its minutes.[14]

Land records became an early concern of the government at
Washington, for, under the treaty of Guadalupe Hidalgo (1848) when
California was acquired from Mexico, legitimate titles had to be
respected. To ascertain what titles were valid, it was necessary to
investigate Mexican laws and regulations relating to land grants and
the records pertaining to them. Henry W. Halleck presented a report
on this subject, on March 1, 1849, to Colonel Mason, who forwarded it
to Washington. From his examination of the archives which he had collected, Halleck prepared a treatise on Spanish and Mexican laws and
regulations governing grants or sales of public lands in California, to
which he appended translations of laws by William E. P. Hartnell.[15]
He found that there were imperfections in most of the titles and
expressed the opinion that some were fraudulent.

The Departments of the Interior and State sent out an agent, in
1849, with instructions to locate and report on the archives relating
to land grants.[16] The attorney selected for this mission was William
Carey Jones, a son-in-law of Senator Thomas H. Benton, who was
familiar with both the Spanish language and Spanish colonial titles.
Jones reached Monterey in September, having come by steamship
from Panama, and later visited San José, San Francisco, San Diego,
and Los Angeles to examine records. Among the old archives at Monterey, which he reported as imperfect and disordered,[17] he found the

---

14 An "Alphabetical list of approvals of grants of land, by the departmental
assembly of California, recorded in the books of sessions," is printed in the "Report
of the Surveyor General of California," in U.S. Dept. of the Interior, *Annual Report*,
1880, pp. 912–16.

15 Henry W. Halleck, "Report on the Laws and Regulations Relative to Grants
or Sales of Public Lands in California, March 1, 1849," in *House Exec. Doc.* 17, 31
Cong., 1 sess., Jan. 24, 1850, pp. 118–82, printed also in John A. Rockwell, ed., *A
Compilation of Spanish and Mexican Law, in Relation to Mines, and Titles to Real
Estate, in Force in California, Texas and New Mexico. . . .* (New York, 1851), pp.
431–88. Halleck's original report has not been found. It may have been transmitted
with a letter from the secretary of war to the secretary of the interior, January 14,
1850, but it is not with the letter in the letters received file of the latter official,
nor has it been found elsewhere.

16 Justin Butterfield to W. C. Jones, July 5, 1849, NA, DI, BLM, Lets. Sent, PLC,
vol. 16, pp. 76–82, printed in *House Exec. Doc.* 17, 31 Cong., 1 sess., pp. 113–15,
and Rockwell, ed., *Spanish and Mexican Law*, pp. 425–29; John M. Clayton to
W. C. Jones, July 12, 1849, General Records of the Department of State, Instructions to Special Agents, vol. 1 (Record Group 59), National Archives, pp. 278–79.
Printed in *House Exec. Doc.* 17, 31 Cong., 1 sess., pp. 116–17, and Rockwell, *Spanish
and Mex. Law*, pp. 429–30.

17 W. C. Jones to Thomas Ewing, Sept. 30, 1849, Records of the Office of the
Secretary of the Interior, Division of Lands and Railroads, Letters Received (Record

principal records relating to land grants. These records consisted of a register of farms and cattle brands and marks, containing information on the boundaries of several of the missions, the pueblos of San José and Branciforte, and a record of twenty grants made between 1784 and 1825 and two made in 1829; registers of land grants, May 22, 1833–May 9, 1836, January 18, 1839–December 8, 1843, and January 8, 1844–December 23, 1845; and a file of land-grant records (*expedientes*) containing file numbers 1 to 579.

Besides information relative to land records, Jones's report contains data regarding land-grant procedure, and documentary appendixes with texts in English of various laws, regulations, instructions, etc. relative to land grants and missions, which were copied for him by Bayard Taylor.[18] Jones also compiled a list of land grants that is included in his report. In Mexico City, on his return from California, he obtained admission to the archives in order to make further investigations, particularly in those relative to missions, on which he presented considerable historical data. Jones gave a more favorable view of the land-title situation in California than Halleck had; he believed that most of the titles were valid and that the few fraudulent ones could easily be detected.

Robert Greenhow, another American traveler to Mexico and California who, for many years, had been translator and librarian of the Department of State, was also interested in land records. He was sent to Mexico City in 1850 by that department to obtain information relative to claims of American citizens against Mexico,[19] and to search the archives for material relating to land claims in California.[20] During his sojourn of six months or so in Mexico City, he gathered a large collection of transcripts relating to California, especially to the public

---

Group 49), National Archives; printed in *House Exec. Doc.* 17, 31 Cong., 1 sess., pp. 117–18.

[18] The original report by Jones entitled "Report on the Subject of Land Titles in California made in pursuance of instructions from the Secretary of State and the Secretary of the Interior by William Carey Jones, April 10, 1850," is in the Records of the Bureau of Land Management, Private Land Claims Division, series K, vol. 192 (Record Group 49), National Archives. It was printed in Washington in 1850 in pamphlet form and also as *Senate Exec. Doc.* 18, 31 Cong., 2 sess. The copy from which the latter printing was made is in the Records of the United States Senate (Record Group 46), National Archives. All the appendixes are with the original report except no. 2, and they are in Spanish with English headings. Two of the appendixes — no. 15: Figueroa's regulation of Aug. 9, 1824, and no. 17: Alvarado's regulation of Jan. 17, 1839 — are broadsides, which were probably extra copies found by Jones in the records at Monterey.

[19] Daniel Webster to Greenhow, Apr. 22, 1850, NA, DS, Instructions to Special Agents, Bk. 1, p. 306.

[20] Ishbel Ross, *Rebel Rose: Life of Rose O'Neal Greenhow, Confederate Spy* (New York, 1955), p. 32.

lands, from the archives of Mexico.[21] Late in 1850, he and his wife moved to San Francisco, and subsequently, while employed as an assistant law agent of the United States in San Francisco, he translated documents in his own collection and others in printed compilations, with the intention of publishing a work of his own — but it never appeared. He died early in 1854 from an injury sustained in a fall. His wife, who had gone east for a visit, returned to California that year, recovered her husband's papers, and waged a successful suit against the city of San Francisco for damages because of her spouse's death. The fate of the collection of transcripts has not been ascertained.

Frémont did not deliver all the records which had come into his possession at Los Angeles to Monterey in 1847. He retained a small quantity, relating evidently to land grants, to present at Washington for examination by the government. Some of these, including documents relating to the grant to General Castro, were lost in the mountains on Frémont's overland journey.[22] Papers concerning the grant to Fr. Eugenio MacNamara in 1846 for the colonization of Irish families, which Frémont reported to be part of a scheme to place California under British protection, were delivered to Washington.[23] These papers were evidently also held back by Frémont for use in his defense in a court martial, that resulted in his resignation from the army. The concession to MacNamara and related correspondence have been published.[24]

The passage by Congress of legislation for the settlement of

---

[21] In a letter to the secretary of state, June (no day) 1850, Greenhow stated that he had been investigating laws and records about California lands and expressed the opinion that Jones' report was designed to protect the claim of Frémont to Mariposa and Jones' own claim to the mission lands of San Luís Rey, which he had purchased for $20,000: General Records of the Department of State, Dispatches from Special Agents, Bk. 18 (Record Group 59), National Archives; Greenhow to Samuel D. King, Jan. 28, 1853, enclosure King to John S. Wilson, Mar. 5, 1853, NA, BLM, Misc. Lets. Recd. Greenhow's communication is a seven-page bibliographical essay concerning printed documentary works embodying Spanish and Mexican land laws and regulations. Transcripts by the Greenhows, that do not appear to relate particularly to California lands, are in the Bancroft Library of the University of California (Hammond, Guide to Ms. Colls., p. 125).

[22] Deposition of J. C. Frémont, May 7, 1858, United States vs. Neleigh, U.S. Sup. Ct., Trans., Dec. Term, 1861, No. 196, p. 48.

[23] Deposition of J. C. Frémont, Feb. 28, 1848, "California Claims in Senate of the United States," Feb. 23, 1848, Senate Report 75, 30 Cong., 1 sess., p. 14; Frémont, Memoirs, p. 553.

[24] Senate Report 75, 30 Cong., 1 sess., pp. 22–25 (English), 77–83 (Spanish). The file in the records of the United States Senate in the National Archives, from which this report was prepared, contains the English translations, and copies of the Spanish versions. The original Spanish documents are with a letter from Frémont to the secretary of state, Mar. 1, 1848, in General Records of the Department of State, Miscellaneous Letters Received (Record Group 59), National Archives.

private land claims in California resulted in the transfer of the Spanish records to the permanent custody of the United States Surveyor General for California. An act of Congress, approved March 3, 1851, provided for the appointment of a board of land commissioners to examine evidence and decide upon the validity of private land claims, for a surveyor general to attend to the surveying of confirmed claims, and for a law agent to look after the public interests.[25] Samuel D. King, a former clerk in the General Land Office, was appointed surveyor general. Presenting an instruction from the secretary of war,[26] he took over two boxes of Spanish records, consisting of bundles of disordered papers of various kinds and dates, from the commanding officer at Benicia in July, 1851.[27] After consulting with the collector of customs and Sen. William M. Gwin, who had brought the letter from the secretary of war, King employed Ramón De Zaldo, a native of Spain, to arrange and index the land records. In subsequent correspondence, this employee was referred to as the keeper of the archives and translator. The surveyor general used a passageway in the basement of the customhouse for an office, pending the completion of a new "fireproof" building next door in which he agreed to rent two rooms. Iron safes were sent to him from New York for safekeeping the records, and he had some tin boxes made with locks.

Other precautions were also taken in connection with the Spanish records transferred to the surveyor general. Upon approving the measures taken by that official, the commissioner of the General Land Office directed the preparation of an abstract of the land papers or, when necessary, facsimile copies, for the use of that office.[28] The surveyor general was also instructed to allow only persons in public service to use the records, and to make them available to the Board of Land Commissioners. An assistant to the keeper of the archives was employed in March, 1852, to complete the indexing of the miscellaneous papers and, at the same time, to supply the Board of Land Commissioners with documents. The preparation of facsimile copies of the land papers was not insisted upon, after King pointed out the labor and expense it would involve, but an alphabetical abstract of land titles was furnished to the General Land Office with a covering letter of

---

[25] U.S., *Stats.*, 9:631–34.

[26] Charles M. Conrad to Persifor F. Smith, Major General commanding the Pacific Division, Mar. 14, 1851, Records of the Office of the Secretary of War, Military Book, Letters Sent, vol. 31 (Record Group 107), National Archives.

[27] Samuel D. King to Justin Butterfield, July 14, 1851, NA, BLM, Lets. Recd. SG; "Report of the Surveyor General of California," in U.S. Department of the Interior, *Annual Report*, 1851, p. 49.

[28] Butterfield to King, Sept. 11, 1851, NA, BLM, Lets. Sent, PLC, Bk. 17; printed in *Senate Exec. Doc. 26*, 32 Cong., 1 sess., pp. 7–8.

July 28, 1852,[29] and an additional list of 311 land documents was transmitted on August 12.[30] An index of the Spanish archives was furnished the same month by the surveyor general to the Board of Land Commissioners, together with copies of the other lists.[31] In 1853, the commissioner of the General Land Office approved a suggestion of the surveyor general that certified copies of documents be furnished to the courts and the Board of Land Commissioners, and that the originals not be allowed to leave the office.[32] De Zaldo was succeeded as keeper of the archives by John Clar, a native of the Mediterranean region, on July 16, 1853, and the latter, in 1855, by Rufus C. Hopkins, a Virginian, who remained in the position until 1878.

For many years after the Surveyor General's Office was opened in San Francisco, it continued to receive records pertaining to grants from grantees of lands in California, pursuant to the act of Congress of March 4, 1851.[33] These records were eventually arranged and bound as follows:

> Book No. 1 — Register of Brands and Marks.
> Book No. 2 — Record of Grants from 1833 to 1836.
> Book No. 3 — Registry of Titles, 1841, 1842, and 1843.
> Book No. 4 — Registry of Titles, 1844 and 1845.
> Book No. 5 — Record of Possessions, 1835 to 1842.
> Book No. 6 — Record of Possessions, 1835 to 1840.
> Book No. 7 — Registry of Possessions from 1841 to 1842.[34]

---

[29] This abstract entitled: "Index to Land Titles in Upper California Derived from the Spanish and Mexican Governments Rec'd with S. Genl's. letter of 28 July 1852," is in the Records of the Bureau of Land Management (Record Group 49), Private Land Claims Records No. 183, National Archives. It gives the following information: names of grantees, nature of the action by the California government, date, by whom granted, situation, name of locality, the *expediente* number, and remarks.

[30] King to Butterfield, Aug. 12, 1852, NA, BLM, Lets. Recd., SG, Calif., transmitting the list, which is not present with the letter. A copy is bound with the index of records referred to in the next footnote.

[31] Receipt of the index and the two lists, which were transmitted in a letter of the surveyor general of August 20, 1852 (not found), was acknowledged by a letter from Hiland Hall and Harry Thornton to S. D. King, September 7, 1852 (NA, BLM, Board of Land Commissioners California, Letter Book 17). The index is also among the records of the board, printed in an appendix. A copy of the index, bearing the title "Schedule of Documents on File in the Spanish and Mexican Archives of the Office of the U.S. Surveyor General for California" (being part of a Schedule of Articles Belonging to the U.S. Surveyor General's Office), is filed with the letter from John C. Hays to Thomas A. Hendricks, Sept. 9, 1857 (NA, BLM, Lets. Recd., SG, Calif., E–6547).

[32] John S. Wilson to John C. Hays, Sept. 13, 1853, NA, BLM, Lets. Sent, PLC, Bk. 19.

[33] U.S., *Stats.*, Vol. 9, Sect. 8, p. 632.

[34] "Report of the Surveyor General of California," in U.S. Dept. of the Interior, *Annual Report*, 1888, p. 402.

In the adjudication of Spanish and Mexican land claims, the records in the custody of the surveyor general became very important. The Board of Land Commissioners relied chiefly on the *expedientes* in the possession of that officer, but it also accepted documents from claimants, and proofs that they had occupied the land. During its deliberations from 1851 to 1856, the board adjudicated 813 claims covering over 12,000,000 acres of land. Transcripts of its proceedings and decisions were sent, pursuant to an act of Congress approved August 31, 1852, to the attorney general, and by the terms of the same act, appeals were automatically taken to the United States District Court at San Francisco.[35] In handling these cases, the attorney general was assisted by the district attorneys at San Francisco and Los Angeles, both of whom were appointed in 1850, and the law agent at San Francisco, a position first filled in 1853. Yet this array of officials failed to bring together and utilize, during the period the board was operating, all available records in California relating to land claims.

Although not all archives of the Mexican government had been collected in San Francisco, and insufficient use had been made of those in the custody of the surveyor general, Peter Della Torre, who had only taken the oath of office as district attorney for the Northern District of California on July 13, 1857, was already on the track of evidence against the Limantour claim before the appointment of Stanton in February, 1858. On behalf of the government, E. L. Williams examined the archives at Sacramento in the office of the secretary of state, in January, 1858, and found archives of the Mexican government.[36] In these records and others, which Williams, who was deputy recorder of Monterey County, was persuaded to bring to San Francisco from Monterey, enough evidence was discovered to refute the Limantour claim.[37] Della Torre proposed to have Williams, to whom he gave credit for demonstrating the spuriousness of the seals used by Limantour, search the archives at Santa Barbara and Los Angeles for further material. Soon afterwards, Stanton arrived and took over the direction of the investigation; he later also employed Williams in the Limantour case.

During the intensive searching in the archives in the Surveyor General's Office occasioned by Stanton's activities, the keeper of the

---

[35] U.S., *Stats.*, 10:99.

[36] Affidavit of E. L. Williams, Oct. 18, 1858, Records of the Department of Justice, Letters Received by the Attorney General, National Archives (hereinafter cited as NA, DJ, Lets. Recd. AG).

[37] Della Torre to Jeremiah S. Black, NA, DJ, Lets. Recd. AG. Correspondence of Della Torre with Stanton and Black, 1857–62, relative to his claim for compensation for services connected with California land claims, is in Records of the United States Senate, Senate File 58A–E1. Some of the correspondence between Della Torre and the Dept. of Justice is printed in *Senate Rep.* 311, 48 Cong., 1 sess.

archives, Rufus C. Hopkins, found a valuable index to the land concessions made by the Mexicans. The first part, for the years 1830 to 1844, had been prepared by Manuel Jimeno Casarin, who, as secretary, had charge of the records from 1843 to 1845, while the continuation for 1844 to 1846 had been compiled by W. E. P. Hartnell in 1847–48. Stanton had twenty-five copies of the Jimeno index printed in 1858, in order to preserve the worn original and make copies available for use.[38] Both indexes and a registry of titles were prepared for publication by Eugene B. Drake, who was an archives clerk in the Surveyor General's Office in 1859.[39]

After years of hard usage, the land papers were in such bad condition that measures for their preservation became necessary. Beginning in 1879, annual appropriations were made for copying the original title papers and documents, filed in the 813 land claims presented to the Board of Land Commissioners, with translations, into record books, and also all the *expedientes* and Spanish records, books, etc. relating to Mexican land grants in California. The translating seems to have been largely the work of John Clar, previously a clerk in the Surveyor General's Office and serving as translator in the early 1880s, and James Alexander Forbes, translator and head of the "Spanish Archives Department" from about 1883 to 1891. When completed in 1888, the transcripts and translations comprised twenty-eight large volumes, with indexes numbering 18,200 pages.[40] The contents of the volumes are shown in two compilations which were prepared and published at the beginning of the work. The most complete lists of their kind available in print, these compilations are titled as follows: "Catalogue of the Original Expedientes or Records in Relation to Land Claims in Upper California under the Spanish and Mexican Governments, with References to Registries of the Same, Arranged in Alphabetical Order, now on File in the Spanish Archives of the Office of the United States Surveyor-General for California,"[41] and a "List of Original Documents in Cases presented to the United States Land Commission, now on File in the Office of the United States Surveyor General for Califor-

---

[38] Manuel Jimeno Casarin, *Jimeno's Index of Land Concessions, from 1830 to 1845, and the "Toma de Razón," or Registry of Titles for 1844–45, in the Archives of the Office of the Surveyor General of the United States for California* (San Francisco, [1858]).

[39] Eugene B. Drake, comp., *Jimeno's and Hartnell's Indexes of Land Concessions, from 1830 to 1846, Also, Toma de Razón or Registry of Titles, for 1844–45: Approvals of Land Grants by the Territorial Deputation and Departmental Assembly of California, from 1835 to 1846, and a List of Unclaimed Grants* (San Francisco, 1861).

[40] "Report of the Surveyor General of California," in U.S. Dept. of the Interior, *Annual Report*, 1888, pp. 402–03.

[41] Ibid., 1880, pp. 173–238.

nia."[42] The alphabetical arrangement of the catalog makes it possible to use it as an index, for it contains the names of the claimants, the localities of the grants, and the *expediente* numbers. The catalog covers the registers of land grants (*tomas de razón*), previously described, as well as the file of *expedientes*. It also contains an alphabetical list of the names of ranches, lists of *expedientes* in numerical order, and a list of approvals of grants of land by the departmental assembly.

In the 1880s, the Surveyor General's Office also undertook the preparation of an abstract, in English, of the general, civil, political, and military archives of the country, preliminary to their indexing. This abstract was completed in 1890, after a careful investigation of the 280,639 pages of Spanish manuscripts.[43] To facilitate reference to the volumes of Spanish records, they were arranged differently and numbered from 1 to 302. The indexing became a regular part of the work of the keeper of the archives, and by 1904, volume 138 had been reached. Beginning in 1900, summaries in English of the contents of each volume were placed on their back covers. The position of keeper of the archives was filled towards the end of the 1890s by Charles F. Gompertz, a native of England appointed from Alameda County, who served until about 1909. An inventory of the records, prepared in 1898, is printed in an appendix.

Further acquisitions of records were made by the Surveyor General. After diligent efforts, some records which properly belonged to the archives of San Francisco were obtained from Los Angeles in 1888.[44] Officials of Los Angeles refused to give up other records in their possession, but an accession from San Diego was collated and classified by the Surveyor General's Office.[45]

The private land-grant records, as arranged by the Surveyor General's Office, consisted of several series. The private land-grant files, 1784–1846 (7½ feet), contained petitions for land, the governors' references to local authorities for reports, the reports, the governors' concessions, the reports of actions of the legislative assembly, the title or patent, the reports of measurement, depositions by witnesses, judicial proceedings, *diseños*, notices of sales, boundary disputes, land suits, wills, and correspondence.[46] The 579 files (*expedientes*) covered

---

[42] Ibid., pp. 799–858.

[43] Ibid., 1890, p. 359.

[44] Ibid., 1888, p. 403; 1892, p. 418.

[45] Ibid., 1892, p. 418.

[46] The California land-grant records are described in Jacob N. Bowman, Index of the Spanish-Mexican Private Land Grant Records and Cases of California ([Berkeley], 1958), p. g–k; and in U.S. Survey of Federal Archives, *Inventory of Federal Archives in the States, Series VIII, The Department of the Interior, No. 5, California* pt. 1, (San Francisco, 1941), pp. 6–9.

grants in Upper California and 30 grants, petitioned for or granted by Upper California governors, in Lower California. The unclassified *expedientes* were miscellaneous *expedientes*, including petitions and rejected petitions, 14 petitions and grants of land in Lower California, and 13 grants made but not claimed in the United States tribunals. Almost 100 of the 315 *expedientes* in the series were related to papers in the private land-claim files described above. A series of deposited *expedientes* consisted of papers deposited in the Surveyor General's Office by claimants or others. Almost half of the 21 files in that series related to claims in the tribunals, and the remainder were ungranted petitions or unclaimed grants. Only parts of the private land-claim *expedientes* and unclassified *expedientes*, and one of the deposited *expedientes*, survived the fire of 1906 that destroyed the Surveyor General's Office. The surviving parts of the files described above are in the Bureau of Land Management Records (Record Group 49) in the National Archives. The California State Archives has transcripts of the private land-grant records that were made before the fire.

The register of land grants issued (*toma de razón*) was kept in the governor's office in the custody of his secretary. It has been ascertained from the testimony of persons who were familiar with the land records that there were eight registers for 1784–1846,[47] but only the register for 1839–43 has survived. This register was loaned to Capt. Joseph L. Folsom in May, 1851, for use in a lawsuit, and he reported to the surveyor general that the book burned up in a fire which occurred that month. For years this register was believed to be lost, but in 1914, the California State Library bought a book which was identified in 1942 by Jacob N. Bowman, an authority on California land titles, as the lost *toma de razón*.[48] Photostats of this register are in the California State Archives and the Bancroft Library of the University of California at Berkeley. No information has been uncovered on the third register, 1836–38, or the fifth register, 1841–43. The first register, 1784–1832, the second register, 1833–36, and the sixth register, 1844–45, were burned in 1906. The seventh register, which was used at Los Angeles until April, 1846, and the eighth register, which was used from May 1, 1846, until the end of the Mexican regime later that year, were

---

[47] Jacob N. Bowman, "The Lost Toma de Razón, a Register of Land Claims Comes to Light," *Calif. Hist. Soc. Quar.* 21 (Dec. 1942):311–12. Juan B. Alvarado, who was in command during the civil commotions of 1837–38, deposed that no record or register of land titles was kept during that time (deposition of Juan B. Alvarado, Mar. 7, 1853, Records of the Bureau of Land Management, Board of Land Commissioners, California, Record of Evidence, vol. 2 [Record Group 49], National Archives, p. 637). W. C. Jones examined some of the land registers; his description is cited above.

[48] Bowman, "Lost Toma de Razón," p. 311.

in a box with other records that were placed in the home of Luís Vignes for safekeeping, in August, 1846, and were probably destroyed soon afterwards, as no information of a later date, regarding the seventh and eighth registers, has come to light. Several of the registers are available in transcript. The entries for 1784–1831 were in the register of the general division of the Spanish archives, of which a transcript is in the Bancroft Library. Transcripts of the titles that comprised the second, fourth, and sixth registers are in the California State Library. The sixth register has been published, together with indexes by Jimeno and Hartnell.[49] Abstracts of the entries in various registers are also in print.[50] Other indexes, prepared by Major Canby while he was in charge of the land records, are mentioned above in chapter twenty.

The private land-grant *expedientes* included rough sketches (*diseños*) showing the location, area, boundaries, and geographical features of the grant requested, that were prepared to accompany the petition to the governor.[51] Usually free-hand ink drawings, although sometimes in color, the *diseños* also showed ranch and farm structures, cultivated lands, vineyards, roads, mills, and bridges. Some original *diseños* are in the land-grant *expedientes* in the National Archives, and certified copies of many others are in the United States District Court records and the California State Archives. Original copies and transcripts of some *diseños* are in the Bancroft Library; others are in the records of the Bureau of Land Management in Washington. Still other *diseños* are in published documents of the United States Congress. An index to the *diseños* and other maps is in the Bancroft Library and clerk's office of the United States District Court in San Francisco.

An index to the private land-grant case records, that was begun by Jacob N. Bowman, historian of the California State Archives, as a revision of the index in Hoffman's *Reports of Land Cases*,[52] was expanded to include the transcripts of land records in the California State Library, and other materials in the Bancroft Library, the National Archives, and published congressional documents. This index enables the searcher to find all pertinent records relating to individual land grants, and it also contains an index of petitioners, grantees, claimants, and patentees. Copies of the index are in the Bancroft Library, the

---

[49] E. B. Drake's compilation previously cited in footnote thirty-nine.

[50] "Report of the Surveyor General of California," in U.S. Dept. of the Interior, *Annual Report*, 1880, pp. 860–99.

[51] R. A. Donkin, "The Diseño: A Source for the Geography of California, 1830–46," *Mid-America* 40 (Apr. 1958), p. 98.

[52] Ogden Hoffman, *Reports of Land Cases Determined in the United States District Court for the Northern District of California June Term, 1853 to June Term, 1858, Inclusive* (San Francisco, 1862).

clerk's office of the United States District Court in San Francisco, and the National Archives. A card index of witnesses' names in the private land-grant records, and an index of maps (*diseños*, sketches, surveys), are in the Bancroft Library and the clerk's office of the United States District Court.

The Spanish and Mexican land-grant records that survived the San Francisco fire of 1906 remained in the custody of the Surveyor General's Office in that city. When that office was discontinued in 1925, the district cadastral engineer, in charge of the Public Survey Office, became the custodian of the records. That office and the records were moved in 1932 to Glendale, where the land records were examined in 1936 by the Survey of Federal Archives. After an inspection of the land records by Philip M. Hamer, the national director of the Survey of Federal Archives, in 1937, they were sent to the National Archives. In 1939, these records were accessioned for permanent preservation in that institution.

The records of the Surveyor General's Office transferred to the National Archives in 1937 also included records relating to private land claims in California. These records comprise an index to complete *expedientes;* an index to incomplete *expedientes;* an alphabetical list of 580 complete *expedientes;* an alphabetical list of 315 incomplete *expedientes;* a list of documents relative to land claims deposited in the Spanish archives since the annexation of California to the United States, 1849–87; correspondence, lists, affidavits, and petitions concerning certified copies of land documents furnished by the surveyor general to the Board of Land Commissioners, 1852–53; a docket of district court land cases (1 volume); receipts for patents, 1857–98 (2 volumes); and transcripts by C. F. Gompertz of incomplete *expedientes,* numbers 75–315.

Other records of the surveyor general of California that had been in the custody of the Public Survey Office in Glendale in 1936 remained in California.[53] An appropriation that was made by Congress on June 22, 1906,[54] enabled the surveyor general to replace some of the records, such as survey plats and tract books, from transcripts in the General Land Office in Washington. The Bureau of Land Management Land Office in Sacramento, in which the operation of that bureau in California has been consolidated, has files of field notes of surveys, survey plats, and tract books. In the records of the surveyor general in the Federal Records Center in San Francisco, there is a file of American

[53] U.S. Survey of Federal Archives, California, *Inventory of Federal Archives in the States, Dept. of the Interior, Calif.,* pp. 8–14.

[54] U.S., *Stats.*, 34:429.

documents relating to Spanish and Mexican land grants, 1856–90 (1 foot), containing survey notes, court orders, surveyors' depositions, and other records.[55]

The validity of private land claims in California was decided by a Board of Land Commissioners, authorized by an act of March 3, 1851.[56] That act required land claimants to present titles obtained from the Spanish or Mexican governments, documentary evidence, and the testimony of witnesses, to the board. The corporate authorities of towns (pueblos) in existence on July 7, 1846, were to present claims to land within the town, rather than the individual holders of the lots. The board was to report to the secretary of the interior on all mission lands, lands held by civilized Indians, and lands occupied and cultivated by pueblo or ranchero Indians. Besides the commissioners appointed by the president, the board was to have a law agent, to protect the interests of the United States, and a secretary, to serve as interpreter and records keeper.

The board held hearings from 1851 to 1856, mostly in San Francisco although some hearings were held in Los Angeles in 1852, to consider claims presented in the Southern Judicial District. The surveyor general of California was instructed, on July 3, 1852, to furnish the board with facsimile copies of records relating to claims presented to the board.[57] Although the board relied chiefly on private land-claim records in the custody of the surveyor general, it also accepted documents from claimants, such as proofs of occupation. The board adjudicated 809 claims, covering over 12 million acres of land, and approved the majority of the claims.[58] Some claims were withdrawn; others were rejected because of fraud or serious defects.

Upon the board's dissolution in 1856, its records were divided between the Surveyor General's Office in San Francisco and the General Land Office in Washington, in accordance with instructions from the latter office.[59] The Surveyor General's Office received the case files accumulated by the board, a bar docket, a register of witnesses, an index to decisions, an index to journals, an index to records, blotter

---

[55] U.S. Federal Records Center, San Francisco, *Preliminary Inventory of the Records of the Bureau of Land Management (Record Group 49)*, comp. by John P. Heard (San Francisco, 1969), p. 7.

[56] U.S., *Stats.*, 9:631; Robinson, *Land in Calif.*, p. 100.

[57] John Wilson to S. D. King, July 3, 1852, Records of the Bureau of Land Management, Letters Sent Relating to Private Land Claims, vol. 18 (Record Group 49), National Archives (hereinafter cited as NA: BLM, Lets. Sent PLC).

[58] Robinson, *Land in Calif.*, pp. 105–06.

[59] Thomas A. Hendricks to the Board of Commissioners, Nov. 10, 1855, NA, BLM, Lets. Sent PLC, vol. 21.

journals with rough minutes of the proceedings of the board, an index to original minutes, an index to localities, an index to Spanish and Mexican archives in the Surveyor General's Office, an index to land titles, a key to the catalog of the contents of box number thirty in the Surveyor General's Office, an index to registered papers, a subpoena docket, a register of papers filed with petitions, a trial docket, and miscellaneous papers comprised of letters and receipts.[60]

Part of the board's case files, and other records that had been deposited in the Surveyor General's Office in 1856, were burned when that office was destroyed by fire in 1906. In 1937, the remainder of the board's records were transferred from the Public Survey Office in Glendale to the National Archives in Washington for repair, and were accessioned by the National Archives in 1939 and assigned to Record Group 49, Records of the Bureau of Land Management. The original private land-claim cases numbered 813 files, but less than 600 are now extant, and those that have survived are incomplete.[61] These files contain title papers; copies of *expedientes* from Spanish and Mexican archives; originals or transcripts of deeds, wills, assignments, and other instruments showing transfers of title; decrees; orders of the Spanish government; certificates of legislative approval; and *diseños*. An index to these case files has been prepared by the National Archives.[62] Other records include a general index of Spanish and Mexican archives in the Surveyor General's Office, an index to land titles received from the surveyor general, a key to the catalog of the contents of box number thirty in the Surveyor General's Office, an index to lands granted and persons to whom they were conceded (copy of Jimeno-Hartnell index), an index to land holdings, an index to land titles granted between 1833 and 1836, and an index to land cases with docket numbers assigned by the board.

More extensive are the records of the Board of Land Commissioners that were sent to the General Land Office in 1856 and are now part of the records of the Bureau of Land Management in the National Archives. The record of evidence (21 volumes) contains copies of documents relating to claims considered by the board. The record of petitions (2 volumes) contains copies of petitions of claimants or others

[60] List of the Papers, Documents and Books Turned over to, and Deposited with the U.S. Surveyor General of California, by the Late Board of Commissioners, Mar. 19, 1856, Records of the Board of Land Commissioners, No. 188, Records of the Bureau of Land Management (Record Group 49), National Archives.

[61] John Lombardi, "Lost Records of the Surveyor-General in California," *Pacific Historical Review* 6 (December 1937):368.

[62] U.S. National Archives, Alphabetical Index to the California Board of Land Commissioners Expedientes for Private Land Claims in California, Record Group 49, Records of the General Land Office ([Washington], 1969).

requesting confirmation of claims. The record of decisions (3 volumes) contains copies of opinions of the board, transmitted to the commissioner of the General Land Office, and copies of decrees of confirmation or denial. A docket (1 volume) serves as a finding aid to land claims and the action of the board thereon. The journal of the proceedings of the board (4 volumes) contains minutes of its sessions and copies of documents relating to the formation and personnel of the board. A letters-sent book, February 14, 1852–February 18, 1856 (1 volume), contains copies of letters sent by the board's members and its secretary. An index to private land claims (1 volume) is an alphabetical index to localities, names of original grantees, and names of present claimants, with names of counties and docket numbers. An index to the records of the United States Land Commission serves as an index to the records described above. Maps bound in three volumes are tracings of sketches (*diseños*) submitted in support of land claims. Microreproductions of the foregoing records are in the Bancroft Library of the University of California at Berkeley.

The records of the Bureau of Land Management contain other records that are important for the history of land claims in California. The private land-claim papers in the Washington National Records Center contain titles, survey plats, field notes of surveys, abstracts of title, evidence and testimony regarding claims, court decisions, appeals, correspondence, and other documents relating to the settlement of the claims (93 boxes; microfilm in the Bancroft Library).[63] Survey plats of private land grants (24 volumes) in the Cartographic Records Branch of the National Archives present graphically not only the boundaries of the claims, but other features of the land they covered (see additional description in chapter seven, in the section on New Mexico). In the same repository are plats of rejected surveys (3 volumes); an index of California private land claims (photostat of the original in the Bureau of Land Management); and a small file of oversize maps and plats of California private land grants that were removed from the private land-claim papers described above, with a list of the same. A file of field notes of surveys, ca. 1883–1918, in the National Archives includes a section on California, and another file of rejected field notes also includes some California material.

When land claims were finally approved, patents (deeds) signed by the president were issued to claimants. Record copies of the patents are in books in the Bureau of Land Management in Washington.

---

[63] U.S. National Archives, *Preliminary Inventory of the Land-Entry Papers*, p. 12. See also U.S. National Archives, Alphabetical Index to the California Private Land Claims Dockets, Record Group 49, Records of the General Land Office ([Washington], 1969).

Microfilm of the land records of the Bureau of Land Management in Washington relative to public lands in California was received by the United States Land Office in Sacramento in April, 1957. This microfilm had been prepared as part of a records improvement program for land records of the western states, which has been described in chapter seven, in the section on New Mexico. The microfilm for California was later sent to Portland, Oregon, where preparation of new records for California was under way, their installation in Sacramento being planned for the fall of 1970.

Other records relating to California private land claims are also in the National Archives. Certified copies of the proceedings of the Board of Land Commissioners were furnished to the United States District Courts and the United States attorney general, in accordance with an act of Congress of August 31, 1852.[64] The California land-claim transcripts, 1851–56 (25 feet), in the records of the Department of Justice (Record Group 60) accessioned by the National Archives in October, 1937, relate to most of the cases adjudicated by the board, and contain, besides the board's proceedings, copies of documentary evidence from the Spanish and Mexican archives including land-grant *expedientes*, petitions to the board, extracts of proceedings of the legislative assembly of Upper California, maps, testimony of witnesses, depositions presenting evidence as to grants, and the board's decisions. The transcripts relate to grants to pueblos and missions as well as to individuals. A docket book of California land cases, ca. 1858 (Record Group 60), serves as a finding aid to the transcripts described above. Microfilm of the transcripts was obtained by the Bancroft Library in 1965. The attorney general's correspondence file contains material relating to the role of the Department of Justice in appeals from decisions of the board to United States District Courts and the Supreme Court. This file contains not only correspondence, but also case memoranda prepared from the land-claims transcripts by law assistants. The transcripts are valuable not only for land claims, but also for biographical information and for data on local history contained in the great many depositions. Photographic exhibits relating to the cases of Luco vs. the United States and the United States vs. Limantour are in the Records of the United States Senate (Record Group 46).

The records of United States courts are also important sources of documents for the history of California private land grants. Appeals in cases which were not confirmed by the Board of Land Commissioners were taken first to United States District Courts at San Francisco and Los Angeles. When the latter court was closed in 1866, its

---

[64] U.S., *Stats.*, 10:99.

records were transferred to the court at San Francisco, where they were interfiled with its case records. In 1961, the District Court at San Francisco deposited its records of private land-grant cases in the Bancroft Library. The district courts' private land-grant case files, 1852–1942 (100,000 pages) contain testimonies, transcripts of the Board of Land Commissioners' copies of land-grant *expedientes* with translations, *diseños*, wills, briefs, opinions, decrees, mandates, papers on court actions, and photographic exhibits.[65] Included are 458 cases for the Northern District (San Francisco) and 398 for the Southern District (Los Angeles). All but 109 of the 2,031 *diseños*, sketches, surveys, and maps are filed separately in the case files.[66] During 1939–42, a Works Progress Administration project flattened the rolls in which the records had been kept and placed them in canvas-covered folders, suitably labeled. The *diseños*, which had previously been removed from the rolls, were mounted on heavier paper, covered with silk gauze, and refiled in separate steel drawers. Indexes to the *diseños* and other maps are in the Bancroft Library and the clerk's office of the United States District Court in San Francisco. Numerous briefs of cases tried before the courts of California are in print.[67] Decisions of the courts, relative to California land cases, are in *Federal Cases*.[68] The earlier opinions of Judge Ogden Hoffman had already been published, but that compilation is useful primarily for the appended index to private land-grant cases.[69] More complete is Bowman's "Index to the Spanish-Mexican Private Land Grant Records and Cases," which has been cited in footnote forty-six. A few land cases that appeared before the United States Circuit Court for California are also interfiled among the land-grant case files of the District Court for the Northern District of California, to which the Circuit Court records were transferred in 1912. Certified transcripts of records of 114 cases appealed to the Supreme Court, and other documents in its appellate case files, are in the National Archives

---

[65] U.S. Survey of Federal Archives, California, *Inventory of Federal Archives in the States, Series II, Federal Courts, No. 5, California* (San Francisco, 1939), p. 37; Bowman, Index to Spanish-Mexican Private Land Grant Records and Cases, page m.

[66] Described and some reproduced in Robert H. Becker, *Diseños of California Ranchos: Maps of Thirty-Seven Land Grants, 1822–1846, from the Records of the United States District Court, San Francisco* (San Francisco, 1964).

[67] Robert E. Cowan and Robert G. Cowan, *A Bibliography of the History of California, 1510–1930*, 4 vols. (San Francisco, 1933–64), 2:341–75.

[68] *The Federal Cases: Comprising Cases Argued and Determined in the Circuit and District Courts of the United States from the Earliest Times to the Beginning of the Federal Register*, 30 vols. (St. Paul, 1894–97).

[69] Hoffman, *Reports of Land Cases*, appendix 1, pp. 1–109; reprinted in *Federal Cases*, 30:1217–57.

(Record Group 267).[70] Reports on Supreme Court cases have been published in the *United States Supreme Court Reports*.[71]

Other records held by the District Court in San Francisco include a land-case register, 1853–1903; an index to land-case opinions, 1854–71; a docket of land cases, 1853–58; and minutes and decree books from 1851. The National Archives has, for the Northern District, microfilm of the judgment and decree book, 1851–1950 (41 volumes); and minutes, 1851–1949 (106 volumes); and, for the Southern District, a judgment and decree book in land cases, September 1, 1855–December 9, 1865 (1 volume); minutes, January 2, 1851–April 11, 1866 (5 volumes); and minutes of the Circuit Court, July 2, 1855–December 31, 1911 (39 volumes).

Collections of documents relating to California land grants that were made by claimants, law firms, land surveyors, and others are now in manuscript repositories in the state. Records of Halleck, Peachy and Billings, a law firm that handled many important cases, are in the University of California at Los Angeles Library, the Bancroft Library of the University of California at Berkeley, and the Henry E. Huntington Library. Papers relating to the José Y. Limantour land-grant case, 1842–88 (2 boxes, 1 portfolio), are in the Bancroft Library. Materials in the Huntington Library include a collection of documents in pamphlet form on California land titles (19 volumes), made by Henry E. Wills; manuscripts relating to the Limantour, Mariposa, and Peralta cases; the Chipman–Dwinelle papers relating to the Encinal San Antonio, a ranch that was part of the Peralta grant and the present site of Alameda; and other land-claim papers in the Henry R. Wagner collection. Survey notes, field books, maps, and other papers, 1849–1900 (approximately 1,400 items), of Alfred Solano, George Hansen, and Sidney B. Reeve, surveyors of Los Angeles County, also in the Huntington Library document the transition from ranches to cities. Other collections in the same repository are the Jasper O'Farrell papers, ca. 1845–50, containing rough surveys and sketches of California ranches and towns, and the Henry H. Haight papers, 1846–85, containing material relating to land titles in San Francisco. Field notes of Hansen and Solano on Los Angeles surveys, 1855–90 (7 volumes), are in the Library of the University of California at Los Angeles. Records of the

---

[70] U.S. National Archives, *Preliminary Inventory [No. 139] of the Records of the Supreme Court of the United States, (Record Group 267)*, comp. by Marion M. Johnson (Washington, 1962), pp. 6–7.

[71] *United States Supreme Court Reports: Cases Argued and Decided in the Supreme Court of the United States* (Newark and Rochester, N. Y., 1882–). The reports are published in chronological order, but digests that serve as indexes are available.

Quicksilver Mining Co., 1851–1920 (1 foot), in the Stanford University Library relate to its operations in New Almaden and its land claims and legal disputes with the New Almaden Co.[72] California title and abstract companies have also compiled records relating to private land grants.

After the state government of California was organized on December 20, 1849, it became interested in acquiring the provincial and land records of the Spanish and Mexican governments. The first act of the legislature, passed on January 5, 1850, instructed the secretary of state to receive, from the late secretary of state of the territory of California, all public records relating to the political, civil, and military history of the state, and its past administration.[73] An unsuccessful effort was made early in 1851 to obtain an order from the secretary of war for the transfer of the Spanish records in the custody of General Smith at Benicia to the state.[74] Instead, part of the records were transferred to the newly established Office of the United States Surveyor General of California. Another California act, of May 1, 1851, directed the secretary of state to send an agent to Monterey to separate all records not of a local character from the Spanish archives then in the possession of the county recorder and county clerk, for deposit in the State Department.[75] As a result of these two acts, some of the Spanish records of California were placed in the custody of that department at Sacramento, and presumably were the records recovered by Stanton in 1858. Another California enactment, of March 20, 1866, made it the duty of the secretary of state to have the title papers of land claims derived from the Spanish and Mexican governments, in the United States Surveyor General's Office, transcribed and translated into suitable books.[76] From 1866–71, Rufus C. Hopkins supervised the transcribing of eight volumes of transcripts, eight volumes of translations, and two volumes of maps. This collection is still available in the California State Archives at Sacramento (microfilm in the Bancroft Library). The state archives also has an index volume to the records, and copies of surveys and plats relating to land claims (5 volumes).[77]

---

[72] Information regarding some of the manuscripts described is from the *Natl. Union Catalog of Ms. Colls.*, and from finding aids cited in chapter twenty-four in this section, entitled "Manuscript Collections."

[73] Calif., *Stats.*, 1850, p. 45; Edwin L. Head, "Report on the Archives of the State of California," American Historical Association, *Annual Report*, 1915, p. 281.

[74] William W. Gwin to C. M. Conrad, Mar. 11, 1851, NA, WD, SW, Lets. Recd., file G 19 (72).

[75] Calif., *Stats.*, 1851, p. 443.

[76] Ibid., 1865–66, p. 312.

[77] Bowman, Index of the Spanish-Mexican Private Land Grant Records, pp. n–o.

The California surveyor general subsequently published a "Report of Spanish or Mexican Grants in California, prepared by James S. Stratton."[78] This report contains a list of grants, arranged alphabetically by the name of the grant, and a list of private grants, classified by counties. A corrected version of the former list appeared later.[79] In 1945, the state made a contract with the Microstat Company of California to microfilm the Spanish documents in its custody.

An act of the California legislature of April 4, 1850, provided for county recorders, who were to keep records of deeds, mortgages, and other documents relating to real estate, including those received from Mexican authorities at the time of the change of government.[80] The recorders of forty California counties have recorded private land-grant patents. J. N. Bowman's researches revealed that thirteen patents had been issued which were not recorded in these offices, and that there were a number of confirmations of claims for which no patents were issued. Several of the recorders' offices, including those in Santa Cruz and Santa Rosa, have some loose records concerning grants, and those and other offices have records of alcalde and pueblo grants, correspondence, and other papers. Real estate transactions that occurred after 1850 are more easily ascertained from the records developed by title insurance companies.[81] Maps of ranch grants under the Mexican regime, in some California counties, are in the custody of the counties.[82]

---

[78] California, Surveyor General, "Report of the Surveyor-General of the State of California, from August 1st, 1879, to August 1st, 1880," *Appendix to the Journals of the Senate and Assembly of the Twenty-Fourth Session* (Sacramento, 1881), 1:15–54.

[79] California, Surveyor General, "Corrected Report of Spanish and Mexican Grants in California, Complete to February 25, 1886," in "Report of the Surveyor-General of the State of California, from August 1, 1884, to August 1, 1886," *Appendix to the Journals of the Senate and Assembly of the Twenty-Seventh Session* (Sacramento, 1887), 1:11–29.

[80] Calif., *Stats.*, 1849–50, pp. 151–2.

[81] Robinson, *Land in Calif.*, p. 227.

[82] Edward L. Chapin, Jr., *A Selected Bibliography of Southern California Maps* (Berkeley, 1953), pp. 89, 114, 120.

26

Records of Local Jurisdictions

LOCAL GOVERNMENT IN CALIFORNIA was similar to that of other Spanish colonies in the New World. Three forms of settlement were utilized in California, following the usual scheme of Spanish colonization — the mission, the presidio, and the pueblo.

The mission establishments were conducted by members of the Franciscan order who, at first, had extensive civil authority, exercising it with the aid of Indian alcaldes.[1]

The presidios were garrisoned by soldiers, under commandants who had civil and judicial authority within their respective districts, and were located at San Diego, Monterey, Santa Barbara, and San Francisco. Throughout the Spanish period, the presidios were ruled, in most respects, according to the regulations of 1772 and 1781,[2] with the governor exercising military, civil, and judicial authority throughout the province.

The only pueblos, or civil settlements, in California during the Spanish regime were those established at San José (1777), Los Angeles (1781), and Branciforte (1797; soon defunct), near the present city of Santa Cruz.[3] The regulation issued by Gov. Felipe de Neve in Octo-

---

[1] Chapman, *Hist. Calif.*, p. 395.

[2] Bancroft, *Hist. Calif.*, 1:206–07, 333–34. An English translation of the rules and regulations for presidios on the frontier, September 10, 1772, is in John Galvin, ed., and Adelaide Smithers, trans., *The Coming of Justice to California: Three Documents* (San Francisco, 1963), pp. 3–45. The regulation of October 24, 1781, is in John E. Johnson, trans., *Regulation for Governing the Province of the Californias* (San Francisco, 1929).

[3] Dwinelle, *Colonial Hist. San Francisco*, pp. 14–15; Florian Guest, O.F.M., "The Establishment of the Villa de Branciforte," *Calif. Hist. Soc. Quar.* 41 (Mar. 1962):29.

ber, 1781, called for the appointment of ordinary alcaldes and other municipal officers for the first two years after a pueblo was organized, and their election thereafter by the citizens of the pueblo.[4] However, the most important official at a pueblo during the Spanish period was the *comisionado* (commissioner), the representative of the central government, who was usually a corporal or sergeant. He enforced the governor's decrees, collected taxes, regulated the conduct of the people and kept the peace, made grants of land, and supervised farming and public works. The alcaldes and *ayuntamientos* (town councils) were subordinate to the commissioners.

The commissioners heard civil and criminal cases and presented testimony regarding them to the presidio commander. They had full responsibility in minor criminal cases and probably in some civil cases. The commissioner was subordinate to the presidio commander, who also took an active part in the government of the town. The commander imposed judicial sentences for the punishment of crimes and rendered decisions in civil cases. And he confirmed the election of alcaldes and *regidores*, subject to the approval of the governor.

Under the Mexican regime, alcaldes displaced commissioners as the chief local officials, and more pueblos were organized. Town councils were established at Santa Barbara in 1826 and Monterey about 1827; and others came into existence during the 1830s at San Diego, Santa Cruz, San Luís Rey, San Rafael, San Antonio, and San Francisco.[5] Yerba Buena, which eventually became part of the city of San Francisco, was laid out by direction of Gov. José Figueroa in 1835.[6] Some of the new pueblos were former missions, which were secularized under the Mexican law of August 17, 1833, and enactments of the territorial deputation. These mission pueblos included Sonoma, San Juan Bautista, San Juan Capistrano, and San Luís Obispo. The town councils were composed of the alcalde (mayor), *regidores* (councilmen), and a *sindico procurador* (attorney) who acted as a prosecutor.

The alcalde exercised legislative, executive, and judicial authority.[7] He presided over the town council, appointed its committees, voted on

---

[4] Theodore Grivas, "Alcalde Rule," in *Military Governments in California, 1846–1850* (Glendale, Calif., 1963), p. 152. The provisions of this and other regulations relating to the government of towns are given in Francis F. Guest, O.F.M., "Municipal Government in Spanish California," *Calif. Hist. Soc. Quar* 46 (Dec. 1967):309–12.

[5] Bancroft, *Hist. Calif.*, 3:703; Hittell, *Hist. Calif.*, 2:203–06; Benjamin F. Gilbert, "Mexican Alcaldes of San Francisco, 1835–1846," *Journal of the West* 2 (July 1963):245–56.

[6] Bancroft, *Hist. Calif.*, 3:708–709; Hittell, *Hist. Calif.*, 2:201–203.

[7] Grivas, "Alcalde Rule," pp. 158–65.

its legislation, and supervised pueblo finances. He enforced the acts of the town council and ordinances and decrees of the governor and provincial deputation, proclaiming these, as well as acts of the Mexican Congress, to the townspeople. After the town council had approved a petition for a grant of pueblo land, the alcalde made the grant. In his judicial capacity, the alcalde settled disputes by arbitration or by trying minor civil and criminal cases and rendering decisions, over which no appeal could be made. Disputes involving military personnel and clergymen were settled by their superiors in California or Mexico. The jurisdiction of the alcalde and *ayuntamiento* extended over much of the territory contiguous to the pueblo.

The *ayuntamientos* were dissolved at the end of 1839, pursuant to the Mexican law of March 20, 1837, establishing a centralized departmental system of government and replacing the *ayuntamientos* by justices of the peace appointed by the governor.[8] The records of the *ayuntamientos* were transferred at this time to the justices of the peace, and the functions of the commandants and alcaldes were largely taken over by departmental prefects and subprefects, who were charged with the supervision of local affairs. The new system of justices of the peace lasted only until 1843 when the alcaldes were formally restored, the term having been applied, popularly, to the justices. The *ayuntamientos* were reestablished at the beginning of 1844, pursuant to the governor's proclamation of November 14, 1843.[9] Suppressed at this time, the prefectures were restored in 1845 by act of the departmental assembly.[10] Two districts were established: Los Angeles district with the three *partidos* of Los Angeles, Santa Barbara, and San Diego; and the Monterey district with the two *partidos* of Monterey and Yerba Buena. *Ayuntamientos* were to continue at Los Angeles and Monterey, and in the other *partidos* there were to be municipal juntas composed of the justices of the peace and two citizens, presided over by the subprefect.

Once under United States rule, the local archives of California were transferred to American alcaldes, who were appointed by the military governor or elected, pursuant to the proclamation issued by Commodore Stockton. Testimony subsequently taken in land cases shows that the records were not properly safeguarded during these years, that unauthorized access to them was allowed, and that some papers

---

[8] Bancroft, *Hist. Calif.*, 3:586, 616–17, 654–55, 675–76, 696–97, 705–06, 729–30; Gilbert, "Mexican Alcaldes," pp. 246, 248.

[9] Bancroft, *Hist. Calif.*, 4:358.

[10] Ibid., pp. 533, 685–86.

were taken from the records and others were mutilated. An act of the California legislature of February 18, 1850, created twenty-seven counties[11] (a number of which embraced the former Mexican pueblos) as follows:

County	County Seat
San Diego	San Diego
Los Angeles	Los Angeles
Santa Barbara	Santa Barbara
San Luís Obispo	San Luís Obispo
Monterey	Monterey
Branciforte	Santa Cruz
San Francisco	San Francisco
Santa Clara	San José
Sonoma	Sonoma

The records of the alcaldes and *ayuntamientos* were transferred, in accordance with an act of the California legislature of February 28, 1850, to the county clerks and recorders of deeds of the newly created counties.[12] In 1858, Stanton's agents took the records of some localities to San Francisco and deposited them in the Surveyor General's Office. The records of several towns were still in the custody of that office in 1866,[13] but some were returned before the fire of 1906.

An extensive collection of records of Monterey is in the custody of Monterey County at Salinas. The documents include criminal proceedings of the Monterey court, March 10, 1807–November 12, 1843 (volumes 1–5). Other materials (volumes 6–16) include papers on military affairs, March 1, 1781–January 3, 1843; papers from the prefect's office, July 17, 1837–November 7, 1849; papers regarding tithes, missions, religious affairs, and the conversion of the Indians, July 23, 1782–February 12, 1844; cases and papers connected with Indians, January 11, 1833–June 5, 1848; land grants, sales, transfers, suits, and location claims, 1803–49; powers of attorney, 1834–49; register of cattle brands, 1835–49; papers on the probate of estates and wills, 1830–48; papers relating to claims against the Mexican government for payment for military services, 1841–42, 1846–47; naturalization papers, 1829–42; papers on political affairs, schools, censuses, and elections, August 25, 1828–March 10, 1849; alcalde and *ayuntamiento* records, August 28, 1828–February 1, 1850; official acts of the judges of first instance and *jueces del campo*, October 25, 1842–January 31, 1846;

---

[11] Calif., *Stats.*, 1849–50, pp. 58–63.

[12] Ibid., p. 81.

[13] Rufus C. Hopkins, "The Spanish Archives of California," in Dwinelle, *Colonial Hist. San Francisco*, p. v.

and papers regarding ships at sea, 1833–49. An English translation of the Spanish records in volumes 6–16 and the deeds of grants (volumes A and C) fills two volumes, and an alphabetical name index is in another volume. A 500-page index to volumes 6–16 of the Spanish archives, prepared by Alexander S. Taylor and John Ruurd in 1858–59, shows the document number, names of parties, volume and page numbers of the archives, date of the document, and kind of document.[14]

Other records held by Monterey County include deeds of grants, 1822–50 (volume A), containing a record of grants of lots in Monterey, showing the name of the grantee, date, description of the property granted, and date recorded. Grants to land outside the municipality of Monterey, many in the vicinity of San Juan Bautista, are in volume C. Deeds, 1828–49 (volumes A–D), contain a record of deeds, grants, and other instruments affecting title to real property, showing the names of grantors and grantees and descriptions of the property. Certificates of sheriff sales, 1825–49, is a chronological record of sales to satisfy debts, showing the names of debtors and creditors, descriptions of property, date of judgment, date of sale, amount of judgment, and signature of the sheriff.

Transcripts and abstracts of the Monterey records, prepared by Thomas Savage in 1877 for H. H. Bancroft, are in the Bancroft Library of the University of California. A microfilm of this one-volume compilation is in the Library of Congress.[15]

Another collection of Monterey municipal records, purchased by the Henry E. Huntington Library in February, 1959, consists of correspondence and documents, 1828–54 (1,337 items), including the *ayuntamiento* minutes for 1833, 1834, and 1836.[16] About 1962, the Huntington Library obtained microfilm of all sixteen of the volumes of Monterey records held by the county recorder at Salinas.

Only some of the Los Angeles records survived the hostilities of the period of the American conquest. After José M. Flores was defeated by the Americans, the records disappeared, but in 1849, the local Catholic priest delivered them to the alcalde.[17] When the records were

---

[14] The description of the Monterey records is from the Historical Records Survey, Northern California, Report on California Pre-Statehood Records [No. 1], Feb. 6, 1939 (Ms. in possession of the author; copy supplied by the Historical Records Survey).

[15] Jenkins, "Miscellaneous," in *Guide to Microfilm Collection of Early State Records*, p. 58.

[16] Henry E. Huntington Library, *Annual Report*, 1958–59, p. 7. These records were obtained from Mr. and Mrs. Wilford R. Holmans of Pacific Grove, Calif., collectors of Californiana.

[17] William W. Robinson, ed., "Abel Stearns on the California Los Angeles Archives," *Hist. Soc. South. Calif. Quar.* 19 (Sept.–Dec. 1937):141–42; Stephen C. Foster, "I Was Los Angeles' First American Alcalde," *Hist. Soc. South. Calif. Quar.* 31 (Dec. 1949):318–21.

arranged and indexed by order of the town council in 1850, many documents, such as concessions of town lands and certain record books, were found to be missing. But the Los Angeles records, 1823–52 (some continued into the American period), did include alcalde correspondence and other records from 1823, *ayuntamiento* minutes from 1832,[18] judicial records of civil and criminal cases, records of the Los Angeles prefecture from 1834, a register of cattle brands and marks, 1833–52,[19] and notarial records. Besides correspondence and other documents concerning the relations of the pueblo and prefecture with the Mexican and provincial governments, the collection includes petitions for land, claims for mines, deeds, mortgages, contracts, bankruptcy papers, wills,[20] inventories of personal and household goods, orders regarding horse races, court-martial papers, papers on ecclesiastical matters, censuses, decrees and proclamations, and other documents emanating from the Mexican government.[21]

The Los Angeles records had become so worn and fragile by the 1930s that the Historical Society of Southern California initiated measures for their preservation. Through an agreement made by the society, the County Recorder's Office (custodian of the records), and the Henry E. Huntington Library, a program for photostating, transcribing, and translating the documents began in 1934–35.[22] The Huntington Library made photostats of the documents for the County Recorder's Office, which, in 1938, allowed the original records to be deposited in the library. Photostats were also supplied to the Historical Society of Southern California. Typists and translators of the State Emergency

---

[18] A collection of documents derived from the minutes is published in Marco R. Newmark, "Ordinances and Regulations of Los Angeles, 1832–1888," *Hist. Soc. South. Calif. Quar.* 30 (Mar. 1948):26–41; extracts pertaining to Indians are in William W. Robinson, ed., "The Indians of Los Angeles As Revealed by the Los Angeles City Archives," *Hist. Soc. South. Calif. Quar.* 20 (Dec. 1938):156–72; and other extracts are in H. J. Lelande, ed., "Extracts from the Los Angeles Archives," *Hist. Soc. South. Calif., Annual Publication* 6, pt. 3 (1905):242–52.

[19] Reproductions of the cattle brands and information regarding the persons who registered them are in Ana B. Packman, "California Cattle Brands and Earmarks," *Hist. Soc. South. Calif. Quar.* 27 (Dec. 1945):127–49.

[20] M. R. Harrington, trans., "Will of Don Tomás Antonio Yorba, Year of 1845," *Hist. Soc. South. Calif. Quar.* 33 (Mar. 1951):67–73.

[21] Owen C. Coy, *Guide to the County Archives of California* (Sacramento, 1919), pp. 49, 241–42; Historical Records Survey, Southern California, *Inventory of the County Archives of California, No. 20, Los Angeles County (Los Angeles) County Clerk's Office* (Los Angeles, 1943), pp. 59–60.

[22] Marion Parks, "Translating and the Spanish Records of Los Angeles County," *Hist. Soc. South. Calif. Quar.* 17 (Mar. 1935):28–29; W. N. Charles, "Transcription and Translation of the Old Mexican Documents of the Los Angeles County Archives," *Hist. Soc. South. Calif. Quar.* 20 (June 1938):84–88; Henry E. Huntington Library, *Tenth Annual Report*, 1936–37, p. 16.

Relief Administration and the Works Progress Administration prepared transcriptions and translations, copies of which were eventually furnished to the County Recorder's Office. Indexes were also prepared.

In 1959, the Los Angeles County clerk transferred court records of 1839–82, including criminal cases, 1839–50, civil cases, 1839–44, and other records in Spanish, 1840–50, to the Los Angeles County Law Library.[23] The Los Angeles Archives has translations of Los Angeles archives, 1826–45 (3 volumes, 1,500 pages), including citizen petitions, *ayuntamiento* proceedings, a register of voters of 1830, and censuses of 1836 and 1844.[24] Transcripts and extracts from the Los Angeles Archives, 1821–50 (5 volumes), that were made in 1876 by Benjamin Hayes and two assistants, for H. H. Bancroft, are in the Bancroft Library.[25]

A number of censuses of Los Angeles that are in various repositories have been published. Some of these resulted from the religious law that required missionaries to verify, on lists of inhabitants furnished by military and civilian officials, the names of those who had or had not complied with the obligation of receiving penance and the Eucharist during the Easter season. A 1781 census gives data about the first twelve settlers of Los Angeles and their families.[26] A 1790 padrón, giving the names, ages, occupations, and birthplaces in Mexico and Spain of the men, and the names and ages of wives and children, has been published from a translation in the Eldredge papers in the Bancroft Library.[27] Three censuses of Los Angeles, that have been published from original documents in the De La Guerra papers in the Santa Barbara Mission Archives include a list of February 4, 1816, prepared by Sgt. Guillermo Cota, containing information on the ownership or nonownership of land, the use of land, other occupations, and the date of arrival in the pueblo of seventy married men, twelve single men, and four widowers; an unsigned list of January 20, 1823, giving the names of men capable of bearing arms and the kinds of weapons they possessed; and a list of February 15, 1823, prepared by Sergeant Cota, showing the names of retired soldiers and artillerymen, their wives,

---

[23] *Natl. Union Catalog of Ms. Colls.*, 1961, entry 1312.

[24] Letter from Stanley B. Gordon, City Archivist, Office of the City Clerk, Los Angeles, Nov. 13, 1975.

[25] A collection of documents derived from transcripts in the Bancroft Library and other sources in Thomas W. Temple II and Marion Parks, trans., "Documents Pertaining to. the Founding of Los Angeles," *Hist. Soc. South. Calif. Quar.* 15 (1931):117–263.

[26] Thomas W. Temple II, trans., "First Census of the Los Angeles District," *Hist. Soc. South. Calif., Ann. Pub.* 15 (1931):148–49.

[27] Mrs. Joseph M. Northrop, ed. "Padrón (Census) of Los Angeles, 1790," *South. Calif. Quar.* 41 (June 1959):181–82.

and children over nine years of age, who were obliged to fulfill the sacraments.[28] Lists of Los Angeles inhabitants prepared by Fr. José de Miguel of Mission San Gabriel, April 15, 1804, and June 1, 1812, and an unsigned one of June, 1823, all supplying data similar to the list of February 15, 1823, have also been published from copies of the originals in the Alexander S. Taylor Collection in the Chancery Archives of the Archdiocese of San Francisco.[29] The 1836 census has been published in facsimile,[30] and the 1844 census has been published in typescript.[31] These censuses show the names of men, women, and children in Los Angeles and its surrounding jurisdictions, their ages, places of residence, occupations, and marital status. The 1844 census is followed by a surname index. Both censuses include foreigners, and separate lists of foreigners on the censuses have been published.[32]

Two early maps of the Los Angeles area are also available. A map of Los Angeles, prepared in 1849 for the Los Angeles Council by Lt. Edward O. C. Ord, United States Army, and William R. Hutton, is in the Henry E. Huntington Library.[33] Ord's map covers only the heart of the grant of four square leagues made to the pueblo of Los Angeles. A revised, enlarged map, prepared by Lothar Seebold in 1872, is in a vault in the City Clerk's Office.[34]

Municipal records of San Francisco were seized at the time of the American occupation, but some were lost later. Comdr. John B. Montgomery, with men from the U.S.S. *Portsmouth*, took formal possession of Yerba Buena and the nearby presidio on July 9, 1846. Lt. J. S. Missroon proceeded on July 11 to the mission Dolores, which was then the headquarters of the alcalde, and seized a collection of public documents.[35] These were carried back to Yerba Buena and, after being

---

28 Maynard J. Geiger, O.F.M., trans. and ed., "Six Census Records of Los Angeles and Its Immediate Area between 1804 and 1823," *South. Calif. Quar.* 54 (Winter 1972):322–34.

29 Ibid., pp. 316–22, 334–41.

30 J. Gregg Layne, ed., "The First Census of the Los Angeles District [1836]," *Hist. Soc. South. Calif. Quar.* 18 (Sept.–Dec. 1936):81–99, plus 54 pages of the census.

31 Marie E. Northrop, ed., "The Los Angeles Padrón of 1844 as Copied from the Los Angeles City Archives," *Hist. Soc. South. Calif. Quar.* 42 (Dec. 1960):360–417.

32 Layne, "First Census," p. 87; Thomas W. Temple II, "Some Notes on the 1844 Padrón de Los Angeles," *Hist. Soc. South. Calif. Quar.* 17 (Dec. 1960):422.

33 "Acquisitions," *Huntington Lib. Quar.* 25 (May 1962):259.

34 William W. Robinson, *Maps of Los Angeles from Ord's Survey of 1849 to the End of the Boom of the Eighties* (Los Angeles, 1966), pp. 9, 14. Seebold's map is also published in J. Gregg Layne, "Edward Otho Cresap Ord," *Hist. Soc. South. Calif. Quar.* 17 (Dec. 1935):139.

35 Missroon to Montgomery, July 11, 1846, "Report of the Secretary of the Navy, Dec. 5, 1846," *House Doc.* 4, 29 Cong., 2 sess. (Washington, 1846), p. 656; Bancroft, *Hist. Calif.*, 5:240.

packed, sealed, and labeled, were placed in the customhouse, then serving as a military barracks. An inventory of these records, prepared in January, 1846, when an exchange of officials occurred, shows they dated from the founding of the *ayuntamiento*.[36] On examining the records in the office of the first alcalde of San Francisco, early in 1850, Henry W. Halleck found them to contain a large mass of records of the alcalde's office under the Mexican government, and military documents and correspondence dating back to the establishment of the presidio by the Spanish.[37] Subsequently, he was unable to locate these early records, and it was presumed that they were destroyed in the burning of public offices during disastrous fires that swept the city in 1850 and 1851. Nor were Mayor Teschemacker and John W. Dwinelle, the city's counsel in its case before the United States district and circuit courts involving the title to the pueblo grant, subsequently able to locate the records.[38]

The extant records of the alcalde of San Francisco during the Mexican period are in the custody of that city. A record book of Alcalde Francisco Guerrero, 1839–43 (1 volume, 64 pages), contains chronological notes regarding appointments, petitions, reports, and other official actions, with information as to the nature of the actions and the names of the persons involved. Land records date from 1824 and are accompanied by English translations and indexes.[39]

The long legal battle over the pueblo grant to San Francisco, and litigation in other cases involving large tracts of land and extensive investigations of the California archives in the Surveyor General's Office and local archives, resulted in the publication of much documentary material. On behalf of the city, a commission transcribed the records in the recorder's and mayor's offices and prepared a schedule

---

[36] José de la Cruz Sánchez, "The Inventory of all the Archives [of Yerba Buena] from the Foundation of the *Ayuntamiento* in 1835, to the End of the Present Year. [1845]," *The Pioneer: or, California Monthly Magazine* 1 (March 1854):142–44. This inventory is also printed in the transcripts of the cases of the United States vs. Limantour, exhibit O, pp. 33–34, cited in chapter twenty, and the United States vs. the City of San Francisco, pp. 99–100, cited in chapter twenty-one.

[37] Deposition of Henry W. Halleck, Mar. 14, 1854, Bd. Ld. Commrs., Record of Evidence 4:72–73; the United States vs. the City of San Francisco, U.S. Sup. Ct., Trans., Dec. Term, 1866, No. 287, pp. 38–40. In the case of Hart vs. Burnett (California, Supreme Court, *Reports of Cases*, 5:551), it is stated that nearly all the old pueblo archives were lost in 1851.

[38] Deposition of H. F. Teschemacker, Aug. 29, 1862, U.S. Sup. Ct., Trans., Dec. Term, 1866, No. 287, p. 382; Deposition of John W. Dwinelle, Sept. 2, 1862, ibid., p. 381. See also Bancroft, *Hist. Calif.*, 2:703. Accounts of the San Francisco fires of 1849–51 are in ibid., 6:202–6.

[39] Historical Records Survey, Northern California, *Inventory of the County Archives of California, No. 39, the City and County of San Francisco (San Francisco)*, Volume II (San Francisco, 1940), pp. 83–85; Coy, *Guide to the County Archives*, pp. 410–11.

of miscellaneous original grants of lots and privileges on the water-front, made by alcaldes, *ayuntamientos,* and others,[40] and a synopsis of all beach and waterfront lots on the east side of the city.[41] Alfred Wheeler, a member of the commission, published a report containing the titles to all lots within the corporate limits of San Francisco.[42] John W. Dwinelle published several editions of his brief in the 1860s, which contain numerous documents, a schedule of grants made by municipal authorities of San Francisco, 1835–46,[43] and a copy of the record of land grants kept by Alcalde Francisco Guerrero during 1839–43.[44] The transcript of the record of the Supreme Court of this case also contains documents.[45] The Limantour case, involving a fraudulent claim to a large part of San Francisco, necessitated extensive investigations that resulted in the printing of several volumes, including one of archival exhibits containing much material of a general nature derived from the California archives, and another of exhibits obtained from the records of the United States Board of Land Commissioners.[46]

The Bancroft Library of the University of California has official documents of early San Francisco that were assembled from the Cowan, Honeyman, and T. W. Norris collections in that repository. The collection includes official correspondence of various alcaldes and justices of the peace, proclamations, documents relating to criminal and other court proceedings, land-grant papers, and other papers, 1835–57 (2 boxes).[47]

Records of San Diego are among the Spanish records formerly in the custody of the United States Surveyor General of California and

---

[40] San Francisco, Commission to Enquire into City Property, *Report on the Condition of the Real Estate within the Limits of the City of San Francisco, and the Property Beyond, within the Bounds of the Old Mission Dolores* (San Francisco, 1851).

[41] San Francisco, Commission to Enquire into City Property, *Report on the Condition of the Beach and Water Lots in the City of San Francisco, Made in Pursuance of an Ordinance of the City Council of Said City* (San Francisco, 1850).

[42] Alfred Wheeler, *Land Titles in San Francisco, and the Laws Affecting the Same, with a Synopsis of All Grants and Sales of Land within the Limits Claimed by the City* (San Francisco, 1852).

[43] Dwinelle, *Colonial Hist. of San Francisco,* pp. 113–4, addendum 78.

[44] Ibid., pp. 162–67, addendum 86.

[45] United States, Appellant, *Supreme Court of the United States, No. 287, The United States, Appellants, vs. the City of San Francisco, and No. 288, the City of San Francisco, Appellant, vs. the United States* (Washington, 1966).

[46] United States District Court, Northern District of California, *The United States, Appellants, vs. José Y. Limantour, Appellee, Nos. 424 and 429, Archive Exhibits* (San Francisco? 1858?); United States District Court, Northern District of California, *The United States vs. José Y. Limantour, Appellee, Nos. 424 and 429, Land Commission Exhibits* (San Francisco, 1858).

[47] *Natl. Union Catalog Ms. Colls.,* 1971, entry 772.

now in the Records of the Bureau of Land Management (Record Group 49) in the National Archives. Letters sent by the alcalde and *ayuntamiento*, June 1835–September 1839 (1 volume), are copies of letters to local and provincial officials on a variety of subjects.[48] A record of letters sent by the alcalde of San Diego, 1834–35, contains synopses of outgoing letters. Microfilm and xerox copies of these San Diego records are in the Junípero Serra Museum in San Diego, the museum of the San Diego *Union* (newspaper), and the Bancroft Library. Other original records of San Diego, 1830–50, concerning political, judicial, ecclesiastical, and commercial matters; and Indians, titles to public lands, and the title of the pueblo of San Diego; are in the San Diego Historical Society Archives.[49] That repository also has a copy of the San Diego court records, 1835–39.

Transcripts of San Diego records, 1826–50, in the Bancroft Library concern the activities of the commandant, alcalde, *ayuntamiento*, prefect, and justices of the peace. H. H. Bancroft bought these transcripts in 1874 from Benjamin Hayes, who also prepared an index that accompanies the transcripts.

Records of San José are in the custody of the county recorder of Santa Clara County. A deed book, 1836–46 (1 volume), contains copies of deeds showing the names of grantors and grantees and the description and location of the property. Papers (*expedientes*) of ranches, 1840–50 (1 box), consist of certified copies of papers and grants relating to ranches. A record of cattle marks and brands, 1834–52 (65 pages, the reverse pages of the deed book described above), includes drawings of brands. A list of individuals holding property in the jurisdiction of San José, 1806 (2 pages), is pasted onto the back cover of the deed book.[50] An unofficial record book is the log book of the ship *Sterling*, 1844 (150 pages), recording events connected with its voyage

---

[48] Lombardi, "Lost Records of the Surveyor-General," p. 369.

[49] San Diego Historical Society, *A Guide to the Research Collections of the San Diego Historical Society* (San Diego, 1964), pp. 10–11.

[50] Historical Records Survey, Northern California, *Inventory of the County Archives of California, No. 44, Santa Clara County (San José)* (San Francisco, 1939), pp. 171–72; Coy, *Guide to County Arch.*, p. 473. An examination of the Spanish and Mexican records at San José early in the American period revealed that they consisted of criminal trial proceedings, election returns, estate papers, prefecture papers, censuses, alcalde's correspondence, petty cases before the alcalde's court, correspondence of the priests of the Santa Clara mission, papers of the court of justice, correspondence from the governors, petitions for land, papers of the court of first instance, and military correspondence. These records spanned the years 1777 to 1846, but there were few records for 1844–46 (U.S. District Court, California [Northern District], *United States Appellant, In the United States District Court, Northern District of California, The United States vs. Andrés Castillero, No. 420, "New Almaden," Transcript of the Record*, [San Francisco, 1859–61], pp. 813–14). An inventory of the records of San José, dated November 10, 1846, is in ibid., pp. 810–12.

around Cape Horn and calls at California ports. Transcripts of the San José records (6 volumes), made by Thomas Savage in 1877, are in the Bancroft Library. Correspondence in Spanish, dating from 1792, is in the city's Historical Museum. A digest has been prepared in English, and microfilm copies of the correspondence is in the City Clerk's Office and the Bancroft Library.[51]

The Spanish and Mexican records at Santa Cruz, 1787–1845 (more than 500 items), include materials on the founding of Branciforte, which was absorbed by Santa Cruz.[52] Documents of 1796–1803 (250 pages), relating to Branciforte, and a census of November, 1801, are in the Latin American Collection of the University of Texas Library (William B. Stephens Collection).[53]

Some records of other pueblos have survived. San Luís Obispo was founded in 1844 on lands of the mission of the same name, and was ruled during 1844–46 by justices of the peace. Among the county records at San Luís Obispo are alcalde prestatehood records, 1840–50, which only include, however, eleven documents for 1840–46, and a register of cattle brands and ranch seals, 1840–50, on one sheet.[54] Deeds begin in 1842 and contain a record of conveyances of title to real estate showing the date, names of grantor and grantee, and a description of the property. Other material relating to San Luís Obispo is in the Bancroft Library. In 1846, the Mexican alcalde at Sonoma retired to his ranch, taking his records with him, but was pursued by Americans who seized the records.[55] Some Sonoma records were destroyed during the Bear Flag Revolt,[56] but the Sonoma County records at Santa Rosa include land records, 1836–54 (1 volume), containing grants made by Mariano Guadalupe Vallejo, director of colonization on the northern frontier; lists of grants; and a register of cattle brands, 1843–56.[57] H. H. Bancroft, after conducting searches for the records of Santa Barbara, concluded that, except for a few land titles, they had been lost.[58]

Manuscripts concerning New Helvetia, the trading and agricul-

---

[51] Letter to Henry P. Beers from Francis L. Greiner, city clerk of San Jose, Aug. 16, 1977.

[52] Coy, *Guide to County Arch.*, p. 484.

[53] Spell, *Research Materials for the Study of Latin America*, p. 14.

[54] Historical Records Survey, Northern California, *Inventory of the County Archives of California*, No. 41, San Luís Obispo (San Francisco, 1939), p. 207.

[55] Deposition of José S. Berreyesa, July 21, 1853, NA, BLM, Bd. Ld. Commrs., Calif., Record of Evidence 3:21.

[56] Hoffman, *Reports of Cases*, p. 93.

[57] Coy, *Guide County Arch.*, pp. 522–24.

[58] Bancroft, *Calif. Pastoral*, p. 268; Bancroft, *Hist. Calif.*, 3:653; 5:630.

tural settlement made by John A. Sutter in 1839, on the American River near its junction with the Sacramento River, are in several repositories. Transcripts of Sutter's correspondence, 1839–48, and a copy of a diary, 1845–48, are in the Bancroft Library.[59] The New Helvetia diary has been published from the original manuscript in the Society of California Pioneers.[60] Other Sutter papers, 1840–79 (235 items), consisting in part of copies from originals in the records of the United States House of Representatives and the Bancroft Library, are in the California State Library.[61] Sutter letters that were privately owned have also been published.[62] Papers relating to the Sutter land grant near Sacramento, 1851–65 (1 box), are in the Wakeman Bryerly papers in the Maryland Historical Society Collection.[63] Papers of Lt. Edward M. Kern, 1845–62, in the Henry E. Huntington Library cover the period when he was in command of Sutter's Fort, during the Bear Flag Revolt and the American conquest of California.[64]

The local records described above should be used for microfilm publications. Such publications would make these records more accessible to historians, thus promoting the writing and recording of the history of California and the Southwest, and would provide security copies of these valuable records.

---

[59] Bancroft, *Hist. Calif.*, 1:lxxxii; 2:685; 4:134 n. 23; Richard H. Dillon, *Fool's Gold: The Decline and Fall of Captain John Sutter of California* (New York, 1967), p. 360. Another copy of the diary is in the T. H. Hittell papers in the Sutro Library in San Francisco. Sutter's reminiscences, also in the Bancroft Library, have been published: Erwin G. Gudde, ed., *Sutter's Own Story: The Life of General John Augustus Sutter and the History of New Helvetia in the Sacramento Valley* (New York, 1936).

[60] John A. Sutter, *New Helvetia Diary: A Record of Events Kept by John A. Sutter and His Clerks at New Helvetia, California from September 9, 1845 to May 25, 1848* (San Francisco, 1939). Douglas S. Watson, ed., *The Diary of Johann August Sutter* (San Francisco, 1932), contains the text of a diary for 1838–50. In it, there is a reference, in September 1845 (p. 27), to the burning of some of Sutter's papers, while they were in the custody of John S. Fowler, his agent.

[61] *Natl. Union Catalog Ms. Colls.*, 1962, entry 4747.

[62] John A. Sutter, *Six French Letters: Captain John Augustus Sutter to Jean Jacques Vioget, 1842–1843* (Sacramento, 1942). The survey of Sutter's grant, which was done by Vioget, is reproduced in this publication. It was the first modern land survey in California.

[63] *Natl. Union Catalog Ms. Colls.* 1967, entry 1349.

[64] Ibid., 1961, entry 1848; Robert V. Hine, *Edward Kern and American Expansion* (New Haven, 1962), p. 163.

27

Ecclesiastical Records

CALIFORNIA WAS A FIELD of Franciscan missionary activity from the time of the founding of its earliest settlements throughout the Spanish and Mexican periods. Fr. Junípero Serra accompanied the expedition of Gov. Gaspár de Portolá to Monterey in 1769, and, on July 16, he established the Mission San Diego de Alcalá there. During Serra's presidency of the California missions, he founded eight other missions: San Carlos de Borromeo at Monterey (1770), which was moved to Carmel in 1771; San Antonio de Padua (1771), near Jolon, Monterey County; San Gabriel Arcángel (1771), San Luís Obispo (1772), and San Francisco de Asís (1776), usually referred to as Dolores, located in San Francisco; and San Juan Capistrano (1775), Santa Clara de Asís (1777), and San Buenaventura (1782), at Ventura. The missions were carefully sited among populous Indian tribes, where there was land for agriculture and grazing, and plentiful water.[1] Under Serra's direction, the missions were conducted according to the system that had been tried in Texas and the Sierra Gorda in Mexico. Livestock was introduced, agriculture was started, vineyards and orchards were planted, and trades were taught. The missionaries had charge of both the spiritual and temporal activities of mission residents, and they made prosperous communities out of the missions. They also ministered to the spiritual needs of the Spaniards and Mexicans at nearby presidios, pueblos, and ranches.

In later years, particularly during the presidency of Fr. Fermín Francisco de Lasuén, the chain of Franciscan missions was completed

---

[1] R. Louis Gentileore, "Missions and Mission Lands of Alta California," *Association of American Geographers, Annals* 51 (Mar. 1961):49. This article includes maps.

by filling in the gaps between the older missions. The new missions included Santa Barbara (1786); La Purísima Concepción (1787), near the present town of Lompoc in Santa Barbara County; Santa Cruz (1791), on the San Lorenzo River; Nuestra Señora de la Soledad (1791), in the Salinas Valley; San Juan Bautista (1797), near Irvington in Alameda County; San Miguel Arcángel (1797), in the upper Salinas Valley in San Luís Obispo County; San Fernando Rey (1797), on the road to Los Angeles; and San Luís Rey de Francia (1798), in San Diego County. Santa Ynez Mission was established in 1804, at what became Solvang, to minister to the Indians east of the Coast Range. First opened in 1817 as an *asistencia* to San Francisco de Asís, San Rafael Arcángel became an independent mission in 1822. The last and northernmost mission, San Francisco Solano, was established at Sonoma in 1823.[2] The missions were located on or near the coast. Explorations were made into the interior to select other mission sites, but none was ever established.

In 1780, Francisco Garcés and other missionaries from the Franciscan College of Santa Cruz of Querétaro did attempt to establish two missions in southeastern California, to convert the Yuma Indians and serve as a way station on the overland trail from Mexico to the California missions. La Purísima Concepción was located on the western bank of the lower Colorado River, where Fort Defiance was later built.[3] Mission San Pedro y San Pablo de Bicuñer was located nearby. But missionaries and other inhabitants of both missions were massacred by the Yuma Indians in July 1781, and no further missionary activities took place in the area.

After the Mexican Revolution, the missions of California were neglected, and, during the 1830s and 1840s, they were gradually secularized. Under a plan of secularization adopted by the territorial deputation in pursuance of decrees of 1833–34 of the Mexican Congress, the missionaries were to be relieved of their temporal responsibilities, and the mission properties were to be placed in charge of administrators appointed by the governor.[4] The temporalities were to be distributed among the neophytes at the missions, and the land was to be turned

---

[2] The earliest and still the most comprehensive treatment of mission history is Fr. Zephyrin Engelhardt's *Missions and Missionaries of California*, 4 vols. (San Francisco, 1908–15). See also Ralph B. Wright, John B. Anderson, and Benjamin M. Watson, eds., *California's Missions* (Los Angeles, 1950), and California Division of Beaches and Parks, *California Historical Landmarks* (Los Angeles, 1965). The names of Indian tribes associated with the various missions are given in the mission sketches in Hodge, *Handbook of American Indians*, passim, and in Swanton, *Indian Tribes of North America*, pp. 478–529.

[3] California Division of Beaches and Parks, *California Historical Landmarks*, p. 58.

[4] Hittell, *Hist. Calif.*, 2:181–88.

over to pueblos that were to be organized at them, according to existing law. But lack of financial support forced the missionaries to sell their cattle for the value of the hides, and other unsaleable property was neglected. Agricultural and other activities declined, the neophytes drifted away, and most of the missionaries departed for other fields or returned to Franciscan monasteries in Mexico or Europe. A few of the missionaries, whose superiors opposed secularization, lingered on at the missions to care for the few Indians who remained.

The transition of the mission buildings to parish churches or other church establishments was gradual. In 1842, the recently appointed Roman Catholic bishop of the Californias obtained the transfer of San Luís Obispo and San Miguel from Fr. Narciso Durán of the Franciscans, and placed priests in charge of these missions, which became the first regular Roman Catholic parishes in California.[5] In 1843, the bishop designated a parish priest for San Buenaventura. The bishop had established himself at Santa Barbara Mission, and a decree of the California assembly of May 28, 1845, reserved that mission for his residence. He assigned priests to San Gabriel in 1851 and San José in 1855, and turned Santa Clara over to the Society of Jesus, which inaugurated Santa Clara University in 1851 in the old mission buildings.

During 1845–46, the Mexican government sold some of the other missions. Then, on March 22, 1847, Col. S. W. Kearny, commander of United States military forces in California, ordered that, until adjudication occurred, the missions of San José, Santa Clara, Santa Cruz and San Juan Capistrano were to be under the charge of Catholic priests, as they were when the United States flag was raised. A claim for the mission properties, presented by Archbishop Joseph S. Alemany to the United States Land Commission, was decided favorably on December 18, 1855,[6] but the confirmation covered only land occupied by church buildings, cemeteries, and gardens. After surveys were made, patents for the land were issued to the archbishop by the United States government. The mission churches have since been restored or reconstructed.[7]

Missions in California established by the Franciscan College of San Fernando were headed by a president who was selected by the college. The president corresponded with missionaries, officials of California and Mexico, and the guardian of the college; received reports from the missionaries; and transmitted reports on the status of the missions to the guardian. The terms of the presidents were as follows: 1769–84, Junípero Serra; 1773–74 (acting), 1784–85 (acting), Fran-

---

[5] Francis J. Weber, *A Biographical Sketch of Right Reverend Francisco García Diego y Moreno, First Bishop of California 1785–1846* (Los Angeles, 1961), p. 28.

[6] Hoffman, *Reports of Land Cases,* appendix, pp. 83–84; Robinson, *Land in California,* pp. 31–32.

[7] The addresses of the missions are in the *Official Catholic Directory,* 1976.

cisco Palóu; 1785–1803, Fermín F. de Lasuén; 1804–12, Estevan Tapis; 1812–15, José F. Señán; 1815–20, Mariano Payeras; 1820–23, José F. Señán; 1823–24 (ad interim), Vicente Francisco de Sarría; 1824–27, Narciso Durán; 1827–31, José Bernardo Sánchez; 1831–38, Narciso Durán; and 1838–46, José Joaquín Jimeno.[8]

A commissary prefect, who served in California after 1812, relieved the president of some of his duties. He issued instructions to the missionaries, attended to business affairs, conducted investigations, and made canonical visitations throughout the territory. The commissary prefects were Vicente Francisco de Sarría (1812–18, 1824–32?), Mariano Payeras (1820–23), Ildefonso Arreguía (1832–36?), Narciso Durán (1838–46), and José Joaquín Jimeno (1846–53).

While Serra was president of the California missions, he maintained his headquarters at San Carlos de Borromeo (Carmel), as did his successors until 1812. José Señán was at San Buenaventura when appointed president in 1815 and made that mission his headquarters during his two terms as president. While Mariano Payeras was president (1820–23), he continued to reside at La Purísima Concepción, where he had been stationed since 1804. Narciso Durán resided at San Carlos during his first term (1827–31), and at Santa Barbara during his second term (1831–38). And José Bernardo Sánchez dwelt at San Gabriel during his term (1831–38).

In January, 1833, a group of Franciscans from the College of Guadalupe of Zacatecas, of which Francisco García Diego y Moreno was the commissary prefect and Rafael Moreno the president and vice-commissary prefect, arrived in California to take over the missions north of San Miguel from the College of San Fernando.[9] Narciso Durán, the president of the Fernandino missions, transferred the missions of Soledad, San Carlos, San Juan Bautista, Santa Cruz, San José, Santa Clara, San Rafael, and San Francisco Solano to the Zacatecans. García Diego and Moreno installed themselves at Santa Clara Mission, but García Diego left for Mexico in 1836 to promote the establishment of a bishopric in California, and Moreno was succeeded in 1838 by José González Rubio, followed in 1843 by José Antonio Anzar. The latter had his headquarters at San Juan Bautista.

The records of the father presidents of the California missions are at Santa Barbara Mission. This mission is the only one that has remained under the control of the Franciscans since its founding. It became the logical repository of the records of the California Franciscan missions. The original records in the Santa Barbara Mission

---

[8] Data for this list was found in the brief biographical sketches in Maynard J. Geiger, O.F.M., *Franciscan Missionaries in Hispanic California, 1769–1848* (San Marino, 1969).

[9] Ibid., p. 159; Weber, *García Diego y Moreno*, p. 6; Bancroft, *Hist. Calif.*, 3:318.

Archives have been augmented by the acquisition of transcripts from various sources. Fr. Zephyrin Engelhardt, historian of the California missions and a resident at Santa Barbara Mission from 1900 to 1934, obtained transcripts of materials in the Bancroft Library of the University of California and the Taylor Collection in the chancery office of the Archdiocese of San Francisco. Other acquisitions of transcripts were made by Fr. Theodore Arentz, an archivist at Santa Barbara. On becoming archivist of the Santa Barbara Mission Archives in 1937, Fr. Maynard J. Geiger examined the manuscripts and transcripts, arranged them in several series, numbered the documents, placed them in folders, and prepared a calendar. The calendar presents descriptive information regarding the documents, indicates their origins, and gives data on those that have been published.[10]

The 3,000 documents in the Santa Barbara Mission Archives constitute the principal collection of materials for the history of the California Franciscan missions. The series designated California missions documents, 1640–1853, includes correspondence of the presidents and commissaries prefect with missionaries and Spanish and Mexican officials; missionaries' correspondence; reports to the viceroy on the condition of the missions; decrees and orders of the viceroy and the governor of California; correspondence with the guardian of the College of San Fernando and the bishops of Durango, Sonora, and the Californias; circulars from the commissary general of the Indies; papal documents; correspondence with the commandant general of the Interior Provinces; special reports by the presidents; lists of missionaries; and account books.[11] Lists of Franciscan missionaries serving in California, 1796–1821, prepared by the president for submission to the governor of California, contain biographical information on the missionaries.[12] Statistical tables on California missions, 1784–1831 (1798, 1805, 1824, 1825, 1830 missing), supply data on the spiritual and material growth of the missions. General biennial reports, 1793/94–1827/28 (1819/20, 1821/22, 1823/24, missing), contain a page of statistics, followed by brief narratives on the condition of the missions, the Indians, mission life, industry, and other matters. Annual and biennial reports of individual missions, 1776–1832, prepared by the missionaries, give statistics regarding baptisms, marriages, deaths, and the number of Indians living at the missions, and describe livestock, and agricultural and building operations.[13] The collection includes reports of December 31,

---

[10] Maynard J. Geiger, O.F.M., *Calendar of Documents in the Santa Barbara Mission Archives* (Washington, 1947).

[11] Geiger, *Calendar of Documents*, pp. 47–180.

[12] Ibid., pp. 242–43.

[13] Ibid., pp. 244–47, gives information on the reports for each mission.

1840, and January 7, 1841, from missions under the jurisdiction of the College of Guadalupe of Zacatecas. Statistical tables on the spiritual condition of the missions, 1811–21 (20 items), give data on baptisms, marriages, deaths, and the number of Indians living at each mission. General spiritual reports, 1808–31 (22 items; 1824 missing), contain statistics on the number of Easter communions, confessions, and viatica for each year in all the missions. Spiritual reports for individual missions, 1808–32, give statistics for communions, confessions, and viatica.[14] Inventories of missions and church property, 1834–58, are available for a number of places.[15] Diaries of exploration by friars for mission sites and new routes of communication, 1777–1822 (16 items), include journeys into the San Joaquín Valley, the Sacramento Valley, and the Mojave Desert.[16]

Reproductions of some of the holdings of the Santa Barbara Mission Archives are in other repositories. Edward F. Murray copied twelve volumes of transcripts for H. H. Bancroft, that are now in the Bancroft Library of the University of California at Berkeley. Some of the entries in these transcripts consist only of the titles of documents. The Henry E. Huntington Library has microfilmed other manuscripts in the Santa Barbara Mission Archives and supplied it with photoprint enlargements so that the original documents could be retired from use.[17]

The Serra manuscripts in the Santa Barbara Mission Archives have been supplemented by an extensive collection of photoreproductions from other repositories. Even before his appointment as archivist at Santa Barbara, Father Geiger was assigned the task of searching for Serra's writings and other materials relating to him, and obtaining copies.[18] His searches continued for years and resulted in the procurement of photoreproductions from more than 100 repositories in the United States, Spain, and Mexico that total more than 8,000 documents.[19] The climax of Geiger's work was a lengthy, documented biography of Serra.[20]

---

14 Ibid., pp. 248–50.

15 Ibid., pp. 253–54, gives a list of the inventories.

16 Ibid., pp. 254–56, gives a list of the diaries.

17 Henry E. Huntington Library, *18th Annual Report* (1944–45), (San Marino, Calif., 1946), p. 11.

18 Maynard J. Geiger, O.F.M., "In Quest of Serrana," *The Americas* 1 (July 1944):97–103.

19 A calendar of part of the Serra collection is in Geiger, *Calendar of Documents,* pp. 1–46.

20 Geiger, *The Life and Times of Fray Junípero Serra,* O.F.M., 2 vols. (Washington, 1959). A list of documents with archival sources is in ibid., 2:406–67.

The California missions kept a variety of records, in books supplied by the College of San Fernando. The register of baptisms (*libro de los bautismos*) contains the entry number of the individual baptized, his Christian name, status (adult or child), date, place of residence, age, Indian name, notation of previous instruction (in the case of adults), admonition given to sponsors, physical condition or social relationship of the baptized, and the signature of the priest with his rubric.[21] Much less information was given in the register of marriages because of the availability of information in the baptismal registers. The register of deaths (*libro de muertos*) contains the Christian and Indian names of the deceased, names of his parents, husband or wife, his marital status, and whether he was an adult or child. The Indian's occupation is sometimes noted. The entries further show the place of death, the place and date of burial, and the place of the individual's origin. Note is made of the sacrament received before death and the circumstances of death, if unusual, followed by the priest's signature.[22] Most of the entries in the registers relate to Indian neophytes, but several thousand are for Spaniards or Mexicans living in the vicinity of the missions. The registers contain entries for 89,124 baptisms, 25,348 marriages, and 65,848 deaths, up to 1834.[23] The registers supply much personal information on the missionaries, including their daily activities and the dates of their arrival and departure. Confirmation registers contain further information on individuals who were given that religious rite.

Other records were usually kept by the missions. Census rolls (*padrones*) contain the names of all Indians, entered in alphabetical order by their Christian name, with birthplace, date of baptism, age at baptism, and the individual's entry number in the baptismal register. The books of official letters (*libros de patentes*) contain transcriptions of circulars of Franciscan superiors, the king, the viceroy, and the bishop, as well as the annual reports of the missions. The annual reports supply statistics on baptisms, marriages, and deaths, Indians living at the missions, livestock and agricultural production, the names of missionaries in charge, and information on building operations. Biennial reports give summary information on mission population, baptisms and marriages, deaths of Indians and whites, and the number of male and female Indians, adults and children. The annual reports were sent to the father president of the California missions, who prepared sum-

---

[21] Maynard J. Geiger, O.F.M., *Mission Santa Barbara, 1782–1965* (Santa Barbara, 1965), p. 28.

[22] Ibid., pp. 32–34.

[23] Jacob N. Bowman, "The Parochial Books of the California Missions," *Hist. Soc. South. Calif. Quar.* 43 (Sept. 1961):310.

mary reports from them, copies of which were sent to the governor of California, for the viceroy, and to the College of San Fernando. Inventories list church and mission furniture, stores, and livestock. Books of invoices contain invoices of furnishings and supplies sent by ship from Mexico, with the prices paid for the materials.

In 1847–48, several officers of the United States Military Government of California, under instructions from Lt. Henry W. Halleck, collected mission records.[24] By the end of May, 1848, a large pile of mission records had been assembled at Monterey.[25] These records passed, along with other Spanish and Mexican records of California, into the custody of the United States Surveyor General for California, who had in his custody, in 1852, two boxes of papers relating to missions. The description of records in the Surveyor General's Office, prepared by Worthington C. Ford for the Library of Congress in 1903 (referred to in chapter twenty), lists mission records, 1785–1846 (11 volumes), that perished in the fire of 1906.

Mission records that have survived and are now in the custody of the chancery office of the Archdiocese of San Francisco (445 Church Street, San Francisco 94114) include the following:[26]

San Francisco de Asís (Dolores): Register of baptisms, Aug. 10, 1776–1870 (2 vols.). Register of marriages, Jan. 7, 1777–1859 (1 vol.). Register of deaths, Dec. 21, 1776–1856 (2 vols.). Account book, 1805–28 (1 vol.).

San José: Register of baptisms, Sept. 2, 1797–May 8, 1859 (2 vols.). Register of marriages, Sept. 24, 1797–May 17, 1859 (1 vol.). Register of deaths, Sept. 18, 1797–1837 (1 vol.).

San Rafael: Register of baptisms, Dec. 14, 1817–1839; register of marriages, Feb. 22, 1818–39; register of deaths, Jan. 13, 1818–39 (all in one volume).

Mission records in the custody of the chancery office of the Archdiocese of Los Angeles (1531 West Ninth Street, Los Angeles 90015) include:[27]

---

[24] See the letters from Halleck to Col. J. D. Stevenson, Sept. 7, 1847; to Capt. J. E. Brackett, Sept. 18, 1847; and to Capt. J. L. Folsom, Sept. 18, 1847, *in House Ex. Doc.* 17, 31 Cong., 1 sess., pp. 393–94, 396, 397.

[25] Richard B. Mason to Stephen C. Foster, May 31, 1848, ibid., p. 558.

[26] Francis J. Weber, "The San Francisco Chancery Archives," *The Americas* 20 (January 1964):316; Bowman, "Parochial Books," pp. 311–13. The records have been microfilmed as a security measure. The latest closing dates for the mission (and parish) records in the sources cited throughout this list are used rather than breaking the dates off at the end of the mission period in 1834 or the end of the Mexican regime in 1846, in order to make the list as useful as possible to researchers.

[27] Francis J. Weber, "The Los Angeles Chancery Archives," *The Americas* 21 (Apr. 1965):411; Bowman, "Parochial Books," pp. 311–13.

San Buenaventura: Book of official letters, 1806–42 (1 vol.).

San Diego de Alcalá: Book of official letters, 1806–42 (1 vol.).

San Fernando Rey: Register of baptisms, Sept. 18, 1797–1855. Register of marriages, Feb. 6, 1798–1854 (1 vol.). Register of deaths, Apr. 7, 1798–1852 (1 vol.). Book of letters and inventories, 1806–47 (1 vol.).

Mission records in the custody of the chancery office of the Diocese of Monterey (580 Fremont Boulevard, Monterey 93940) include:[28]

San Antonio de Padua: Register of baptisms, Aug. 14, 1771–1882 (3 vols.). Register of marriages, May 1, 1773–1872 (1 vol.). Register of deaths, May 10, 1819–1872 (1 vol.). Register of confirmations, 1778–1872 (1 vol.).

San Carlos de Borromeo (Carmel): Register of baptisms, Dec. 26, 1770–1896 (6 vols.). Register of marriages, Nov. 10, 1772–1908 (2 vols.). Register of deaths, June 3, 1770–1915 (3 vols.). Register of confirmations, 1778–1896 (1 vol.).

San Juan Bautista: Register of baptisms, 1797–1843 (2 vols.).

San Luís Obispo: Register of baptisms, Oct. 1, 1772–Feb. 21, 1821 (1 vol.). Register of marriages, 1772–1824 (1 vol.). Register of deaths, Oct. 4, 1772–1838 (1 vol.). Register of confirmations, 1778–1906 (1 vol.). Book of official letters and inventories, 1806–16. Census rolls, 1775–1836.

San Miguel: Register of deaths, 1798–1858 (1 vol.).

Santa Cruz: Register of baptisms, 1791–1857 (2 vols.). Register of marriages, Nov. 6, 1791–1902 (1 vol.). Register of deaths, 1791–1894 (2 vols.). Register of confirmations, 1793–1902 (1 vol.).

Nuestra Señora de la Soledad: Register of baptisms, Nov. 1791–1854 (1 vol.). Register of marriages, 1791–1854 (1 vol.).

Mission records in the Santa Barbara Mission Archives (Franciscan Fathers, Old Mission, Santa Barbara 93105) include:[29]

San José: Register of deaths, Feb. 16, 1837–April 25, 1859 (1 vol.). Register of confirmations, Mar. 19, 1835–Sept. 8, 1855 (1 vol.).

San Luís Obispo: Book of official letters and inventories, 1806–09 (transcripts, 15 pp.).

San Luís Rey: Register of baptisms, July–Aug. 1827; Mar. 1-13, 1828 (4 pp.). Book of official letters and inventories, 1806–33 (1 vol.). Census rolls, 1798–1834; 1811–20 (2 vols.). Registers of baptisms, marriages, and deaths had disappeared by 1847.

---

[28] The data are from a list of records supplied by the Very Rev. Philip Maxwell, Chancery Office, Monterey [Apr. 1971]. These records were transferred from Fresno to Monterey when the Diocese of Monterey was established in 1967, because the new diocese embraced the territory where the missions were located.

[29] Geiger, *Calendar of Documents*, pp. 250–52; Geiger, *Mission Santa Barbara*, pp. 28–32, 255–56.

Santa Barbara: Register of baptisms, Dec. 31, 1786–Sept. 14, 1858 (1 vol.). Register of marriages, Feb. 3, 1787–July 5, 1857 (1 vol.). Register of burials, Aug. 8, 1787–Dec. 30, 1841 (1 vol.). Books of official letters, Nov. 28, 1791–Jan. 20, 1843 (1 vol.). Annual reports, 1787–1836 (in book of official letters). Book of orders, Nov. 13, 1798–July 27, 1848 (1 vol.). Account books, 1805–18; 1813–15; 1816–22 (3 vols.). Account book of seeds and harvests, and record of masses, 1787–1807 (1 vol.). Account book of merchandise, Jan. 1, 1842 (1 vol.). Book of accounts with the presidio, 1794–ca. 1805 (1 vol.). Census rolls, 1815; Dec. 5, 1840. Invoices of goods delivered to the mission, 1787–1811 (1 vol.). Microfilm of the Santa Barbara mission records is in the Bancroft Library.

Santa Ynez: Account book, 1830–38 (1 vol.).

Nuestra Señora de Soledad: Register of confirmations, May 7, 1792–Apr. 29, 1795 (1 vol.).

Mission records in the custody of parishes include the following:[30]

La Purísima Concepción (Rectory, Santa Ynez Mission, 1760 Mission Drive, Solvang 93463): Register of baptisms, Apr. 9, 1788–1850 (1 vol.). Register of marriages, May 10, 1788–1850 (1 vol.). Register of deaths, Feb. 14, 1789–1850 (2 vols.). Account book, 1806–34 (1 vol.). The mission has a set of reproductions of the registers. An English translation of the account book, made by the Works Projects Administration, is in the Santa Barbara Mission Archives and the Bancroft Library of the University of California.

San Antonio de Padua (Rectory, San Antonio Mission, Jolon 93928): Register of burials, Aug. 27, 1771–May 10, 1819.

San Buenaventura (Rectory, San Buenaventura Mission, 211 East Main Street, Ventura 93001): Register of baptisms, Apr. 27, 1782–1873 (2 vols.). Register of marriages, Aug. 30, 1782–1893 (1 vol.). Register of deaths, Apr. 15, 1782–1912 (2 vols.). A book of inventories, 1790–1809, is in the San Buenaventura Mission Museum, 225 East Main Street.

San Diego de Alcalá (San Diego Mission, 10818 San Diego Mission Road, San Diego 92120): Register of baptisms, Oct. 1, 1775–1846 (2 vols.). Register of marriages, Nov. 10, 1775–1938 (2 vols.). Register of deaths, Nov. 6, 1775–1880 (2 vols.). Register of confirmations, 1789–1904 (2 vols.). The register of deaths for 1831–49 is missing. All the registers of this mission were burned in an Indian uprising of 1775; the entries in the books before that date were entered in the new books without dates. A few original pages of the marriage register for 1813 are in the San Diego Historical Society Collection (Junípero Serra

---

[30] The data in this section are from Bowman, "Parochial Books of the Calif. Missions," *passim.*

Museum, 2727 Presidio Drive). That repository also has English translations of the baptismal, marriage, and death registers, and microfilm of the registers.[31] The society's holdings include a register of burials in Campo Santo cemetery, 1769–1804 (typescript), and a register of burials at Presidio Hill, San Diego, 1780 (typescript). Copies of the baptismal and burial records are in the San Diego Public Library.

San Francisco de Asís (Rectory, Dolores Mission, 3321 Sixteenth Street, San Francisco 94114): Register of baptisms, Aug. 10, 1776–1856 (2 vols.). Register of marriages, Jan. 7, 1777–1860. Register of deaths, Dec. 21, 1776–1856 (2 vols.). A book of confirmations, 1838–40, is in the Orradre Library, University of Santa Clara.

San Francisco Solano (Rectory, St. Francisco Church, 469 Third Street, Sonoma 95476): Register of baptisms, 1840–68. Register of marriages, 1840–1908. Register of deaths, 1840–78.

San Gabriel (Rectory, Mission San Gabriel, 537 West Mission Drive, San Gabriel 91776): Register of baptisms, Nov. 27, 1771–1855 (3 vols.). Register of marriages, Dec. 15, 1774–1855 (1 vol.). Register of deaths, Aug. 6, 1774–1855 (2 vols.).

San Juan Bautista (Rectory, San Juan Bautista Mission, San Juan Bautista 95045): Register of baptisms, July 11, 1797–1931 (2 vols.). Register of marriages, Oct. 5, 1797–1934 (1 vol.). Register of deaths, Sept. 23, 1797–1934 (1 vol.).

San Juan Capistrano (Rectory, San Juan Capistrano Mission, San Juan Capistrano 92675): Register of baptisms, Dec. 19, 1776–1853 (2 vols.). Register of marriages, Jan. 23, 1777–1915. Register of deaths, July 13, 1777–1850.

San Luís Obispo (Rectory, San Luís Obispo, 941 Chorro, San Luís Obispo 93402): Register of baptisms, Dec. 14, 1821–1869 (vol. II).

San Miguel (Rectory, San Miguel Mission, San Miguel 93451): Register of baptisms, July 25, 1797–1861 (1 vol.). Register of marriages, Jan. 24, 1797–1860 (1 vol.).

Santa Ynez (Rectory, Santa Ynez Mission, 1750 Mission Drive, Solvang 93463): Register of baptisms, Sept. 17, 1804–50 (1 vol.). Register of marriages, Dec. 16, 1804–50 (1 vol.). Register of deaths, Jan. 23, 1805–60 (1 vol.).

Mission records in the Bancroft Library (University of California, Berkeley 94720) include the following:[32]

San Antonio de Padua: Census rolls, 1803–34. Inventories, 1836; 1845 (in A. Pico, Papeles varios). Loose documents, 1774–1837, con-

---

[31] San Diego Historical Society, *Guide to Research Collections*, pp. 8, 34.

[32] Letters from William M. Roberts, Reference Librarian, Bancroft Library, University of California, Mar. 19, Apr. 27, 1971, with lists of records and copies of catalog cards.

sisting mostly of matrimonial investigations, marriage dispensations, reports on the activities of the mission, and a few letters. Records of sacraments administered to neophytes, 1828; 1833 (in Sarría's sermons).

San Diego de Alcalá: Inventory book, 1777–84, containing lists of church and mission property, stores, and livestock.

San Fernando Rey: Alphabetical list of neophytes.

San Francisco Solano (acquired with the Guadalupe Vallejo papers): Register of baptisms, Apr. 4, 1824–1839 (1 vol.). Register of marriages, May 2, 1824–1839 (1 vol.). Register of deaths, Dec. 26, 1823–1839 (1 vol.).

San José: Book of official letters and inventories, June 6, 1807–July, 1844.

Santa Ynez: Inventory, 1845 (in A. Pico, Papeles varios).

Soledad: Census rolls, 1818–34.

Records of the Santa Clara Mission in the Orradre Library (University of Santa Clara, Santa Clara 95053) include the following: Register of baptisms, June 6, 1777–June 8, 1862 (3 vols.). Register of marriages, Jan. 12, 1778–Aug. 15, 1863 (1 vol.). Register of burials, June 22, 1777–Dec. 22, 1866 (2 vols.). Register of confirmations, Nov. 11, 1779–Nov. 29, 1896 (1 vol.). Book of official letters and inventories, 1806–46 (1 vol.).[33]

The missionaries attended to the spiritual needs of the military and civilian population of California, so there were few secular churches during the mission era. A presidial church was active at Santa Barbara from 1782 and was succeeded eventually by a parochial church. An adobe church that was started at Los Angeles in 1784 was replaced in 1822 by a new structure, which was dedicated to Nuestra Señora la Reina de los Angeles.[34] But, as in the past, the missionary at San Gabriel continued to minister to the church until the arrival of a resident priest in 1832. The missionaries at San Diego, San Francisco, and Santa Cruz served the presidios at those places during the mission period. A chapel constructed at the presidio of Monterey, in the last decade of the eighteenth century, is still the parish church of Monterey.[35] In 1803, a chapel was constructed at San José where mass was said, when necessary, to provide viaticum for the dying.[36]

---

[33] Letters from Arthur M. Spearman, S.J., Archivist, Orradre Library, University of Santa Clara, Mar. 16, Apr. 7, 1971, with lists of records.

[34] J. Thomas Owen, "The Church by the Plaza: A History of the Pueblo Church of Los Angeles," *Hist. Soc. South. Calif. Quar.* 42 (Mar. 1960):5–28.

[35] Maynard J. Geiger, O.F.M., "The Royal Presidio Chapel of San Carlos, Monterey, Capital of Colonial California," *The Americas* 9 (Oct. 1952):207.

[36] Guest, "Municipal Govt. in Spanish Calif.," p. 325.

Records of the presidio chapel of Monterey and the successor Church of Our Lady of Sorrows in the rectory of the church (21 Sola Street, Santa Barbara 93105) include the register of baptisms, 1782–1846; register of marriages, 1782–1885; and the register of confirmations, 1783; 1790–94; 1831–46.[37] The register of deaths, 1782–1873, of that church is in the Santa Barbara Mission Archives.[38]

The records of the Church of Our Lady Queen of the Angels are in the rectory of the church, 100 Sunset Boulevard, Los Angeles 90012. Baptisms and deaths are recorded in separate registers, that date from 1826. Other registers of marriages and confirmations begin in 1827.[39] Microfilm of these records is in the Henry E. Huntington Library in San Marino.

In 1795, Father Lasuén was appointed commissioner of the Holy Office of the Inquisition, and in 1796, the bishop of Sonora extended his faculties to Lasuén, with the authority to delegate them to the missionaries, and designated Lasuén as his vicar forane and ecclesiastical judge for California.[40] In May, 1779, Pope Pius VI established the Diocese of Sonora, embracing the states of Sinaloa and Sonora and Upper and Lower California.[41] The bishop never visited Upper California, but he corresponded with the president of the Franciscan missions there and considered the missionaries' activities sufficient for the spiritual welfare of both the Indians and the white colonists. The archives of the bishop of Sonora in Hermosillo contain correspondence and other documents, from 1795, relating to Upper California.[42] Correspondence of the bishops is also in the Archivo General de la Nación.

In April, 1840, Pope Gregory XVI separated Upper and Lower California from the Diocese of Sonora and organized them into the Diocese of the Californias, designating San Diego as the see. But, on arriving at San Diego in December, 1841, Bishop Francisco García Diego y Moreno decided that it was unsatisfactory and established himself at Santa Barbara Mission, where he remained until his death in 1846.[43] The parishes of California, which were being augmented by the transfer of mission churches from the Franciscans, came under

---

37 Bowman, "Parochial Books," pp. 313, 315 n. 25; Geiger, *Mission Santa Barbara*, pp. 34, 254.

38 Geiger, *Calendar of Santa Barbara Mission Archives*, p. 251.

39 Historical Records Survey, Southern California, *Guide Ms. Colls. Calif.*, p. 14.

40 Geiger, *Franciscan Missionaries in Hispanic California*, 1769–1848, p. 140.

41 Francis J. Weber, "The Development of Ecclesiastical Jurisdiction in the Californias," American Catholic Historical Society, *Records* 75 (June 1964):98.

42 Bolton, *Guide Arch. Mex.*, p. 467; Carrera Stampa, *Archivalia mexicana*, p. 181.

43 Weber, *García Diego y Moreno*, pp. 26–28; Geiger, *Mission Santa Barbara*, pp. 120–21.

the charge of the new bishop. He trained priests for the churches, appointed them to curacies, made pastoral visits, and, in 1844, established a seminary at Santa Ynez Mission. In 1842, he summoned José María González Rubio from San José to serve as his secretary.

Records of the bishop of the Californias are in several repositories. The book of administration (*libro de gobierno*), 1840–1929 (1 volume), in the chancery office of the Archdiocese of Los Angeles, contains the administrative acts of the first bishop and his successors at the see of Monterey.[44] The book of matrimonial dispensations and declarations of nullity (*libro primero de decretos y dispensias*), 1840–99 (1 volume); roman documents, decrees, and faculties, 1840–96 (1 volume); and a historical documents collection dating from 1840 are in the same repository. A copybook of letters sent (*libro borrador*), 1840–82 (1 volume), is in the chancery office of the Archdiocese of San Francisco (Xerox copy in the chancery office of the Archdiocese of Los Angeles),[45] where Bishop García Diego's diary is also located. An account book, 1842–54 (1 volume), and translations of a few outgoing letters of Bishop García Diego, 1844–46, are in the Santa Barbara Mission Archives.[46]

A new Franciscan missionary college, the College of San Fernando, was opened in Mexico City in 1731 by the College of Santa Cruz of Querétaro. After the crown approved its establishment in 1733, the new college elected its own guardian and became independent of Querétaro.[47] Its purpose was to supply missionaries for work among the Indians on the frontier, and it became active in Mexico and in Lower and Upper California. Its organization and operations were similar to those of the College of Santa Cruz of Querétaro.

After the suppression of the Jesuits in 1767, the viceroy entrusted their missions in Lower California to the Franciscan College of San Fernando, and, soon afterwards, the establishment of missions in Upper California began under Junípero Serra. In 1833, the northern missions in California were transferred to the Franciscan College of Guadalupe of Zacatecas. (Concerning this college and its records, see chapter eighteen, in the section on Texas.) Following the secularization of the missions, Santa Barbara, the last mission remaining under the jurisdiction of the Franciscans, separated from the College of San Fernando in 1853 and became the College of Our Lady of Sorrows. The College of San Fernando in Mexico was abolished in 1908, becoming a religious

---

[44] Weber, "Los Angeles Chancery Archives," p. 417.

[45] Weber, "San Francisco Chancery Archives," p. 317.

[46] Geiger, *Calendar of Documents*, pp. 163, 166, 168–70.

[47] Maynard J. Geiger, O.F.M., "The Internal Organization and Activities of the San Fernando College, Mexico (1734–1858)," *The Americas* 6 (July 1949):4; McCloskey, *Missionary College of Santa Cruz of Querétaro*, pp. 111, 289.

house of the Province of the Holy Gospel. But the records of the college had already been dispersed, for, in that same year, H. E. Bolton was unable to find any there.

Archives of the College of San Fernando are in several repositories in Mexico. Some of the archives are in a collection that was acquired by the Biblioteca del Museo Nacional about 1905 from Alfonso Lancaster-Jones, a former representative of Mexico in England, in a series of documents relating to missions of California, 1767–1802 (6 volumes).[48] These volumes contain correspondence of missionaries and officials of the college, and correspondence and regulations of the viceroy of New Spain. Typescripts and photocopies from these records, 1768–1802 (123 folders), and from the papers of Fr. Agustín Fischer, 1770–73 (5 folders), and a collection on the missions of the Californias and northern Mexico compiled by Fr. Francisco Xavier Castro on the instruction of Fr. Rafael Verger, guardian of the college, are in the Bancroft Library.[49] Other archives of the college, formerly held by the secretaría de Hacienda, are now in the Archivo General de la Nación. The ten volumes in this collection include the book of decrees, 1734–1858, of which there is a typewritten copy in the Santa Barbara Mission Archives. Microreproductions from this collection are in the Bancroft Library.[50] Other letters of the college in the Biblioteca Nacional include a volume of letters of Junípero Serra.

Other materials relating to Franciscan missions in California are in repositories in Mexico. The archival sections mentioned in chapter thirteen, in the section on Texas, as well as those on the Interior Provinces and the Californias, in the Archivo General de la Nación in Mexico contain correspondence, reports, representations, and other documents relating to the California missions.[51] Documents in the archives of the College of Guadalupe of Zacatecas, including a book of miscellaneous correspondence, 1833–52, relate to the Zacatecan missions in California.[52] Accounts relating to the Fernandino missions, and other materials relating to synods, the Pious Fund, freights, and bequests to missions are in the archives of the secretariat de Hacienda.[53] In the Temporalidades section of the Archivo Histórico de Hacienda

---

[48] Bolton, *Guide Arch. Mex.*, p. 194; Geiger, "San Fernando College," p. 31. Chronological lists of the contents of each volume are in Bolton, pp. 194–201.

[49] Fisher, *Preliminary Guide*, p. 14; Hammond, *Guide to Ms. Colls.*, p. 141.

[50] Fisher, *Preliminary Guide*, p. 10.

[51] Bolton, *Guide Arch. Mex.*, passim.

[52] Ibid., pp. 399–400.

[53] Ibid., p. 372. Some documents from those archives, including one addressed by the College of San Fernando to the king, February 26, 1825, have been published: Mexico, Ministerio de Hacienda y Crédito Público, *Las Misiones de la Alta California* (Mexico, 1914), pp. 29–88.

are memoranda of goods required by the missions, 1805–08, and documents relating to the secularization of the missions and their division between the colleges of San Fernando and Zacatecas.[54] Other documents relating to the Pious Fund are in the archives of the Mexican House of Deputies.[55] Reproductions from Mexican archives in the Bancroft Library, the Library of Congress, and the University of Texas Archives contain materials relating to California (see chapter thirteen, in the section on Texas). An account book of San Carlos Mission, 1770–1828, is in the Archivo General de la Nación. A collection of reproductions (20 volumes, Xerox) from the Misiones section of the Archivo General de la Nación is in the Academy of American Franciscan History, Potomac, Maryland.

The Bancroft Library of the University of California at Berkeley has many original manuscripts and transcripts relating to California's Franciscan missions, acquired mostly by Hubert H. Bancroft. A collection titled Archivo de las misiones, 1796–1856 (4 boxes, 1 portfolio), consisting partly of transcripts, includes correspondence, circular letters, reports, accounts, censuses, and other papers.[56] Transcripts of mission registers are available for La Purísima Concepción, San Antonio de Padua, San Buenaventura, San Diego de Alcalá, San Francisco Solano, San Gabriel Archángel, San José, San Juan Bautista, San Juan Capistrano, San Luís Obispo, San Miguel, San Rafael, Santa Barbara, Santa Clara, Santa Cruz, and Santa Ynez, and for the parish churches of Monterey and Santa Barbara. Statistical reports on the missions date from 1769. Papers of individual friars, including correspondence, reports, memorials, and representations, include some each for Junípero Serra, Francisco Palóu, Fermín Francisco Lasuén, Vicente Francisco Sarría, and Luís Antonio Martínez (missionary at San Luís Obispo for thirty-two years), and Mariano Payeras' notes on the missions, 1815, 1816, and other years.[57] There are also copies and extracts of the Alexander S. Taylor Collection in the archives of the Archdiocese of San Francisco, and of mission materials in the Archives of Santa Barbara Mission. A copy of a census of Santa Barbara Mission, June 1, 1834, is in the Eldredge papers in the Bancroft Library, as are documents on the Pious Fund of the Californias (5 items, 936 pages; originals and copies), relating to bequests, financial management, and litigation.[58]

---

[54] Mexico, Ministerio de Hacienda y Crédito Público, *Guía del Archivo Histórico de Hacienda*, leaves 53, 63–65.

[55] Carrera Stampa, *Archivalia mexicana*, p. 96.

[56] *Natl. Union Catalog of Ms. Colls.*, 1971, entry 694.

[57] Bancroft, *Hist. Calif.*, 1:52 n. 58.

[58] Hammond, *Guide to Ms. Colls. of the Bancroft Lib.*, 2:182.

Other materials on missions, in the Bancroft Library, are in the papers of officials who were concerned with the administration of the missions during the period of secularization. Mission documents, 1828–46, are in the papers of Andrés Pico, who had charge of San Luís Rey from 1834–42 and was commissioner in charge of preparing inventories of mission property in 1846.[59] The Juan Bandini papers contain documents on San Gabriel Mission for the years 1838–40, when Bandini was its administrator.[60] As inspector of missions during 1839–40, William E. P. Hartnell kept a diary, that is among his papers in the Bancroft Library.[61]

Other repositories in California have materials on the Franciscan missions. Letters of Fr. José Francisco de Paula Señán, 1806–23 (42 items), in the library of St. John's Seminary at Camarillo are mainly addressed to the president of the College of San Fernando, concerning conditions at San Buenaventura where Señán served from 1798 to 1825.[62] Other manuscripts on missions, in the same repository, include replies of seventeen missions, in 1731, to a questionnaire of the College of San Fernando on agricultural and industrial activities of the missions,[63] and an inventory of the temporalities of San Fernando Mission, April 29, 1843, when it was transferred to the parish priest. The library of the University of California at Los Angeles has letters of Juan Crespi, November 24, 1769, and June 11, 1770, and other documents on the California missions. The San Diego Public Library has a long letter of Fr. Luís Jayme, describing conditions at the mission in San Diego.[64] Letters of Catholic missionaries in California, 1772–1849 (8 volumes), a collection assembled by Alexander S. Taylor, that is now in the chancery office of the Archdiocese of San Francisco, consists chiefly of correspondence between civil officials and missionaries of both Upper and Lower California.[65] A chronological index to the Taylor Collection was prepared in English by John Ruurd of Monterey. The Bancroft Library of the University of California has five volumes of copies and extracts from the Taylor Collection and a copy of the index. Photoreproductions of the Taylor Collection are in the Santa Barbara Mission Archives, the Academy of American Franciscan History in

[59] Bancroft, *Hist. Calif.*, 1:lxx, 47 n. 46; 4:776–77.

[60] Ibid., 1:xxx, 49 n. 49; 2:709.

[61] Ibid., 1:liii; 3:778.

[62] *Natl. Union Catalog of Ms. Colls.*, 1961, entry 2737.

[63] St. John's Seminary Library, *One Hundred Manuscripts and Books from the Estelle Doheny Collection* (Los Angeles, 1950), p. 15.

[64] Addressed to Rafael Verger, the father guardian of San Fernando College, the letter is published in facsimile and translation in Maynard J. Geiger, O.F.M., *Letter of Luís Jayme, O.F.M., San Diego, October 17, 1772* (Los Angeles, 1970).

[65] Weber, "San Francisco Chancery Archives," pp. 315–16.

Potomac, Maryland, the Henry E. Huntington Library in San Marino, California, and the chancery office of the Archdiocese of Los Angeles. Documents on the Pious Fund, 1839–1902 (3 volumes), in the chancery office of the Archdiocese of San Francisco were presented by the heirs of John T. Doyle, who was the legal adviser to the Catholic church in the suit involving the fund.[66] Other manuscripts relating to Santa Cruz Mission and other Franciscan missions in California are in the Henry E. Huntington Library, and still other mission manuscripts are in the Charles W. Bowers Memorial Museum at Santa Ana. The Santa Barbara College Library in Goleta has a history of Carmel Mission, 1784 (microfilm), by Fr. Junípero Serra.

Manuscripts relating to the Franciscan missions in California that are in other repositories include both originals and reproductions. Four letters from Viceroy Bucareli to the guardian of the College of San Fernando, 1772–76, relating to the California missions, and a letter from Fr. Fermín F. de Lasuén to Father Palóu, December 13, 1787, are in the Beinecke Collection of Western Americana in the Yale University Library.[67] A contemporary copy of Pedro Font's diary of 1775–76 is in the Manuscript Division of the Library of Congress.[68] Juan Crespi's diary, 1769–70, Junípero Serra's diaries of 1769 and 1770, and letters of Francisco Palóu, 1772, 1773, are in the Edward E. Ayer Collection in the Newberry Library in Chicago.[69] Letters of Rafael Verger, guardian of the College of San Fernando and later bishop of Monterey, are in the Boston Public Library. A contemporary copy of Juan Crespi's diary of his trip from San Diego to Monterey, March 24–April 17, 1770, is in the New York Public Library.[70] Fr. Pedro Font's original diary of the second Anza expedition from Tubac to San Gabriel, September 29, 1775–June 1, 1776, is in the John Carter Brown Library, Providence, R.I. Serra's diary of his overland trip to San Diego in 1769, other Serra papers, 1766–75, and other diaries and documents relating to California missions, are in the Thomas Gilcrease Institute of American History and Art in Tulsa, Oklahoma.[71] Franciscan materials on California in the W. B. Stephens Collection

---

[66] Ibid., p. 316.

[67] Goddard, Kritzler, and Hanna, *Catalogue of the Beinecke Collection of Western Americana,* pp. 38, 47.

[68] Vicente Cortés Alonso and Mathias C. Kieman, "Manuscripts Concerning Mexico and Central America in the Library of Congress, Washington, D.C.," *Americas* 18 (Jan. 1962):273.

[69] Butler, *Check List of Mss,* pp. 126, 145, 149, 150.

[70] Published in Charles J. G. M. Piette, O.F.M., ed., "An Unpublished Diary of Fray Juan Crespi, O.F.M.," *The Americas* 3 (July, Oct. 1946, Jan. 1947):102–14, 234–43, 368–81.

[71] Clevy L. Strout, *A Catalog of Hispanic Documents in the Thomas Gilcrease Institute* (Tulsa, 1962), pp. 28–31, 117.

in the University of Texas Library, Latin America Collection, include copies of correspondence of Junípero Serra, January 27, 1774–June 4, 1777 (38 items), relating to the condition and progress of the missions; letters of Rafael Verger to various Franciscan missionaries, 1770–74; a few letters of Vicente de Mora, 1774–76; a diary of Esteban José Martínez, July 19–21, 1774; letters of Francisco Palóu to Serra and Verger, 1774; a list of the presidents of the California missions, 1774–76; and documents of 1788 and 1790 relating to the Pious Fund.[72] Fr. Juan Buenaventura Bestart's historical memoirs of the College of San Fernando are in the Genaro García Collection in the same repository.

Letters and reports of early California missionaries, including Frs. Juan Crespi, Junípero Serra, and Francisco Palóu, and Fr. Rafael José Verger, guardian of the College of San Fernando, are in the British Museum, London. Typescripts of these records (216 pages), made in 1910, are in the Bancroft Library of the University of California.[73]

In Europe, materials relating to Franciscan missions in California are in various Spanish and Franciscan archives. Documents of the eighteenth century in the Archivo General de Indias in Seville include letters of viceroys of Mexico to the king and the Council of the Indies, letters of Fr. Junípero Serra and others to the viceroy, and other documents.[74] Other documents are in the Real Academia de la Historia in Madrid and the Museo Naval.[75] Materials in the General Archives of the Franciscan Order in Rome are largely documents that have been published, although usually from other copies. These include Fr. Juan Crespi's diary of the expedition to California, 1775, and diaries by Frs. Juan Díaz, Francisco Garcés, and Pedro Font, relating to the Anza expeditions to California.[76] An account by Fr. Gerónimo Boscana of the Indians of San Juan Capistrano, 1812–22, is in the Bibliothèque Nationale, Paris.

Many documents from the archival and manuscript collections described above have been published. Franciscans who served as chaplains on the early expeditions to California were the best diarists of the trips, and they also accompanied and chronicled explorations into the interior of California.[77] Historians have translated, edited, and pub-

---

[72] Castañeda and Dabbs, *Guide to Latin American Mss.*, pp. 3, 8–12, 13–14.

[73] Hammond, *Guide to Ms. Colls.*, p. 46.

[74] Chapman, *Catalogue of Materials in the Archivo General de Indias*, passim.

[75] Lejarza, "Los Archivos Españoles y la Misionología," pp. 556, 566.

[76] Borges, "Documentación americana," pp. 26, 35, 36, 103–04, 112.

[77] Piette, "Diarios of Early Calif.," pp. 409–22; Herbert I. Priestley, *Franciscan Explorations in California*, ed. by Lillian E. Fisher (Glendale, Calif., 1946), pp. 151–57.

lished Franciscan diaries for more than a hundred years.[78] The Academy of Pacific Coast History *Publications,* published in Berkeley in 1909–19, included accounts of the early expeditions to California, and Fr. Narciso Durán's diary of the expedition on the Sacramento and San Joaquín rivers in 1817. In 1927, Herbert E. Bolton republished Fr. Juan Crespi's diaries of his journeys to Mexico and Lower and Upper California.[79] Bolton's five-volume compilation on Anza's California expeditions (described in chapter twenty-three) includes diaries on the first expedition of 1774 by Frs. Juan Díaz and Francisco T. H. Garcés; Fr. Francisco Paloú's journal of the expedition to San Francisco Bay; Fr. Pedro Font's diary of the expedition of 1775–76; and correspondence of Garcés, Díaz, Junípero Serra, Fermín Francisco de Lasuén, and others. Translations of letters of several Franciscans who participated in the occupation of California, and of José de Gálvez, visitor general of New Spain, prepared from copies made from a vellum bound volume of manuscripts offered for sale in San Francisco about 1931, have been published.[80] A diary by Fr. Juan Vizcaíno of the voyage of the *San Antonio* from Lower California to San Diego, February–April 1769, has been published.[81] John Galvin, the California collector, has issued a journal by Fr. Miguel de la Campa of a coasting voyage from Monterey in 1775,[82] and a hitherto unpublished narrative of the same year by Fr. Vicente Santa María, relating to the first sea expedition into San Francisco Bay.[83] Letters and reports written from the San Francisco mission by Fr. Martin de Landaeta to his superiors, 1800–07, have been published from the originals in the Archivo General de la Nación, Mexico City.[84] A small collection of correspondence of early

[78] The titles of many publications are in Francis J. Weber, *A Select Guide to California Catholic History* (Los Angeles, 1966), and John T. Ellis, *A Guide to American Catholic History* (Milwaukee, 1959). See also the titles of other bibliographies in the bibliography of this book.

[79] H. E. Bolton, trans. and ed., *Fray Juan Crespi, Missionary-Explorer on the Pacific Coast, 1769–1774* (Berkeley, 1927).

[80] Douglas S. Watson and Thomas W. Temple II, trans. and ed., *The Expedition into California of the Venerable Padre Fray Junípero Serra and His Companions in the Year 1769, as Told by Fray Francisco Paloú, and Hitherto Unpublished Letters of Serra, Paloú, and Gálvez* (San Francisco, 1934).

[81] Arthur Woodward, trans. and ed., *The Sea Diary of Fr. Juan Vizcaíno to Alta California, 1769* (Los Angeles, 1959).

[82] John Galvin, trans. and ed., *A Journal of Explorations Northward along the Coast from Monterey in the Year 1775 [by] Fr. Miguel de la Campa* (San Francisco, 1964).

[83] John Galvin, trans. and ed., *The First Spanish Entry into San Francisco Bay, 1775: The Original Narrative, Hitherto Unpublished, by Fr. Vicente Santa María, and Further Details by Participants* (San Francisco, 1971).

[84] José C. Valades, ed., *Noticias acerca del Puerto de San Francisco (Alta California)* (México, D.F., 1949).

California missionaries, 1769–92, derived from Mexican and Spanish archives and from the British Museum, has been published by Lino Gómez Canedo, the Franciscan scholar.[85]

Franciscans are not only the narrators of missionary activities in California, but have long been among the principal historians of those activities. Francisco Palóu, a longtime missionary in California, wrote, from documents and personal observations, a life of Junípero Serra, that was published in Mexico in 1787 and is regarded as the most important history of early California.[86] On the basis of a long study of the documentation on Serra, Maynard J. Geiger published an English translation of Palóu's life of Serra with extensive critical notes, in 1955.[87] Palóu himself prepared, for the College of San Fernando, a compilation of letters and diaries, with his own comment, of which a transcript by Francisco García Figueroa was found in the Mexican archives and published in Mexico in 1857[88] and San Francisco in 1874.[89] A corrected version of the compilation was later prepared by H. E. Bolton, directly from Figueroa's transcript, and published in English.[90] Palóu's letters of 1767–87, in volume four of Bolton's publication, are valuable for Franciscan activities in California.

Other Franciscans have prepared documentary compilations on the work of members of their order in California. After a preliminary investigation into the history of the Franciscans in California, Fr. Zephyrin Engelhardt concluded that a documentary history was necessary to present their true history. Using the records at Santa Barbara Mission, where he became a resident in 1900, and other materials in repositories in California, he prepared his *Missions and Missionaries of California*, published in four volumes in 1908–15. This extensive source work contains translations of many documents, and extracts from other documents. Engelhardt later wrote histories of a number of the California missions.

---

[85] Lino Gómez Canedo, O.F.M., ed., *De México a la Alta California, una gran epopeya misional* (México, D.F., 1969).

[86] Francisco Palóu, O.F.M., *Relación histórica de la vida y apostolicas tareas del venerable Padre Fray Junípero Serra y de las misiones que fondo en la California septentrional* (Mexico, 1787). Evaluations of this and the works of other Franciscan historians have been brought together in Francis J. Weber, "California's Serrana Literature," *South. Calif. Quar.* 51 (Dec. 1969):325–46. Palóu's life of Serra was published under the title *Viajes misionales por la Alta California* in Mario Hernández y Sánchez-Barba, *Viajes por Norteamérica (Biblioteca Indiana): Libros y fuentes sobre América y Filipinas,* (Madrid, 1958), 2:629–782.

[87] Maynard J. Geiger, O.F.M., trans. and ed., *Palóu's Life of Fray Junípero Serra* (Washington, 1955).

[88] *Documentos para la Historia de México,* 4th ser., vols. 5–7.

[89] Francisco Palóu, O.F.M., *Noticias de la Nueva California* (San Francisco, 1874).

[90] H. E. Bolton, ed. and trans., *Historical Memoirs of New California, by Fray Francisco Palóu, O.F.M.,* 4 vols. (Berkeley, 1926).

While Geiger was collecting manuscripts of Junípero Serra, Charles J. G. M. Piette, a Belgian Franciscan, was also assembling Serra's writings to publish them. Piette was furnished with copies of the materials found by Geiger, and he also made investigations of his own in repositories and libraries in the United States and Mexico. He became a resident member of the Academy of American Franciscan History, which published his biography of Serra, in which there are excerpts of Serra's writings in French.[91] After Piette's death in 1948, the Academy undertook the job of completing the compilation of Serra's writings. The transcripts obtained by Piette were checked by Fr. Benjamin G. Sanz in repositories in California and Mexico, and other photoreproductions were obtained from Spain. The published work includes the Spanish texts and English translations of Serra's outgoing letters to the College of San Fernando, to missionaries in California, governors and military officers of California, viceroys of Mexico, and to Teodoro de Croix, the commandant general of the Interior Provinces.[92] In this compilation, the derivations of the documents are indicated.

The Academy of American Franciscan History (located near Potomac, Maryland) was founded in 1944, to locate and collect materials on Franciscan history and to publish documents and other historical works. The principal undertaking of the academy has been the collection and publication of the correspondence of the presidents of the California missions. Reproductions of documents have been obtained from repositories in Mexico, the United States, and Europe. After the initial collecting by Frs. Benjamin Gento and Lazaro Lamadrid, Fr. Finbar Kenneally edited the writings of Fermín Francisco de Lasuén.[93] This compilation includes Lasuén's outgoing letters to Franciscan missionaries, the College of San Fernando, and civilian officials; reports on the San Diego and San Carlos missions; and biennial and statistical reports on the California missions. Only English translations of the outgoing letters are included; the incoming letters were collected but not published.

Correspondence of other presidents has been collected and in 1978 is in various stages of preparation for publication. Photoprints of the original writings of the other presidents, and rough translations prepared by the academy staff, have been supplied to specialists in the

---

[91] Charles J. G. M. Piette, O.F.M., *Le Secret de Junípero Serra, fondateur de la California-Nouvelle, 1769–1784*, 4 vols. (Washington, 1949–57).

[92] Antonine Tibesar, O.F.M., ed., *Writings of Junípero Serra*, 4 vols. (Washington, 1955–57). Another Serra letter since discovered has also been published in Francis J. Weber, trans. and ed., *A Letter of Junípero Serra: A Bicentennial Discovery* (Boston, 1970).

[93] Finbar Kenneally, O.F.M., ed., *Writings of Fermín Francisco de Lasuén*, 3 vols. (Washington, 1965–1971).

history of the Southwest who are doing the editing. Fr. Antonine Tibe-sar, director of the academy, is editing the writings of Narciso Durán.[94] The academy itself, with the assistance of the Franciscan provinces in the United States, is financing the publication of the writings. When completed, the multivolumed series will provide a valuable source for the history of Spanish and Mexican California.

The academy has contributed materials for the compilation of the writings of José Francisco Señán, who served at San Buenaventura from 1798 to 1823, and as president of the California missions from 1812–15 and 1820–23.[95] This compilation also includes other Señán letters from collections in St. John's Seminary, the Bancroft Library, the Archivo Histórico de Hacienda (Mexico), and the Taylor Collection in the chancery office of the Archdiocese of San Francisco. A fuller collection of Señán's writings will be published by the academy.

The adjudication that occurred after the United States acquired Upper California, regarding the Mexican government's nonpayment of income from the Pious Fund of the Californias to the Catholic church in California, produced further documentation. That fund originated in 1697 when the Jesuits were authorized to establish missions in Lower California, with the understanding that the Spanish crown would not provide financial support. The Jesuits succeeded in raising funds from individuals not only for the current operation of the missions, but also for a permanent endowment.[96] When the Jesuits were expelled from the Spanish possessions in 1767, the crown took over the management of the fund for the Dominican missions in Lower California and the Franciscan missions in Upper California. The Mexican government later assumed control of the fund and, in 1842, placed the capital in the national treasury and acknowledged an annual indebtedness of six percent for religious support of the California missions. This payment was not made after the transfer of California to the United States. Later, the California prelates presented a claim to the Mexican and American Mixed Claims Commission, that was established under a convention of 1868 to determine the validity of claims

---

[94] Interview with Fr. Antonine Tibesar, Sept. 30, 1971. Letters of Durán to the College of San Fernando, 1806–27, written mostly while he was a missionary at San José, and some for 1825–27, when he was president, have been published: Francis Price, ed. and trans., "Letters of Narciso Durán," *Calif. Hist. Soc. Quar.* 37 (June, September 1958):97–128, 241–65. To facilitate its researches, the academy has sponsored the preparation of a catalog of Franciscan documents in the National Library of Mexico for publication.

[95] Lesley B. Simpson, ed. and Paul D. Nathan, trans., *The Letters of José Señán, O.F.M., Mission San Buenaventura, 1796–1823* (San Francisco, 1962).

[96] *New Catholic Encyclopedia*, 9:379.

of the citizens of each country against the government of the other. A decision favorable to the California prelates was rendered, and some payments were made by the Mexican government; but it later defaulted and never resumed payments. Pursuant to an award made in 1902 by the Permanent Court of Arbitration at The Hague, Mexico again made payments until 1914. A settlement finally reached by the United States and Mexico in 1967 provided for the payment of a lump sum.[97]

---

[97] The various efforts to settle this dispute resulted in several publications containing Spanish and Mexican documents; the titles are in Kenneth M. Johnson, *The Pious Fund* (Los Angeles, 1963), and Francis J. Weber, *The United States versus Mexico, the Final Settlement of the Pious Fund* (Los Angeles, 1969).

Part IV
The
Records
of
Arizona

28

History &
Government

ABOUT 1561, FRANCISCO DE IBARRA was appointed governor and captain general, for the purpose of conquering and ruling the northern regions of New Spain.[1] The kingdom of Nueva Vizcaya, as Ibarra named the territory, embraced what became the modern states of Durango, Chihuahua, Sinaloa, and Sonora, and the southern parts of Coahuila. The town of Durango was founded in 1563 and became the capital of the kingdom, but much of the time the captain general had his headquarters in Parral, in what is now southern Chihuahua, because of its better location for the superintendence of military and Indian affairs, and its greater economic importance. The captain general moved back to Durango in the middle of the eighteenth century, but the accumulated archives remained at Parral.[2] The captain general exercised both political and military authority, and appointed *alcaldes mayores* and other officials in the towns.

During the Spanish period, the area that became southern Arizona and northern Sonora was known as Pimería Alta. It was the northwestern frontier of New Spain and was inhabited by Pima, Papago, and other Indians. It was subordinate to Sonora, an area that extended from the Yaqui River on the south to the Gila River on the north, and included southern Arizona throughout the Spanish and Mexican periods. The administrator was both the principal civil official (*alcalde mayor*) and the military commander. He was located at San Juan

---

[1] Bancroft, *Hist. North Mex. States,* 1:102.

[2] Robert C. West, "The Municipal Archives of Parral, Chihuahua, Mexico," in *Handbook of Latin American Studies, 1940, No. 6, Selective Guide* (Cambridge, 1941), p. 523.

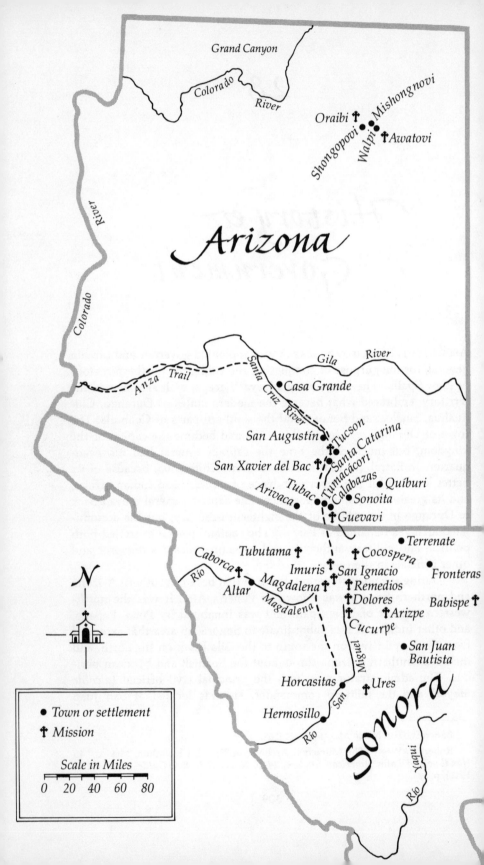

Grand Canyon

Colorado River

Oraibi ✝ Mishongnovi
Shongopovi Walpi ✝ Awatovi

Arizona

Colorado River

Santa Cruz River

Gila River

Anza Trail

● Casa Grande

San Augustín ✝ Tucson
Santa Catarina
San Xavier del Bac ✝ ✝ Tumacácori
Tubac Calabazas ● Quíburi
Arivaca ● ● ✝ Sonoita
✝ Guevavi

Tubutama ✝ ✝ Cocospera ● Terrenate
Caborca
Río ✝ Imuris ✝ San Ignacio ● Fronteras
Altar Magdalena ✝ ✝ Remedios
Magdalena ✝ Dolores ✝ Babispe
✝ Arizpe
Cucurpe
● San Juan
Bautista

Horcasitas ●

Hermosillo ● ✝ Ures

Río San Miguel

Sonora

Río Yaqui

N

● *Town or settlement*
✝ *Mission*

Scale in Miles
0 20 40 60 80

Bautista, where a garrison was usually maintained for the protection of Sonora. In 1693, Sonora was separated from Sinaloa, its neighbor on the south, and given its own governor, whose headquarters were at San Juan Bautista. During the seventeenth and early eighteenth centuries, the governors of both provinces were responsible to the captain general of Nueva Vizcaya. Then in 1734, Sinaloa and Sonora were joined with the other coastal provinces of Rosario, Culiacán, and Ostimuri into a single jurisdiction called Sinaloa and Sonora, that was independent of the captain general of Nueva Vizcaya. The capital of newly formed Sinaloa and Sonora was supposed to be at San Felipe de Sinaloa, but for all practical purposes it was at San Juan Bautista, Pitic (Hermosillo), or Horcasitas, where the management of affairs required the governor to spend most of his time.[3]

To protect the settlements of Sonora from the Apaches, whose raiding parties came down continually from the region they occupied between the Gila River valley and the upper Río Grande in New Mexico, the Spanish established presidios at Fronteras and Janos, late in the seventeenth century.[4] Mounted troops from Fronteras patrolled in Pimería Alta, but it was not until 1742 that the presidio of Terrenate was established, nineteen miles southeast of Guevavi, just south of the present international boundary, for the protection of missions in Pimería Alta.[5] Troopers from Terrenate patrolled the Guevavi area and escorted the missionaries on their rounds. After the Pima revolt of 1751, a garrison was established in 1752 at Santa Ana, a settlement south of San Ignacio, and in 1753, Gov. Diego Ortiz Parilla, of Sonora, located a presidio at Tubac, on the west bank of the Santa Cruz River north of Tumacácori.[6] The line of presidios was soon strengthened by the addition of others at Altar, Horcasitas, and Buenavista, in Sonora. In the 1750s and 1760s, expeditions made up of contingents from Fronteras, Terrenate, Tubac, and Janos marched north as far as the Gila River, to punish the Apaches, but neither the marches nor the presidios had much impact on those elusive Indians.

Pursuant to a royal regulation of 1772, a realignment and strengthening of the cordon of presidios was undertaken. Terrenate was moved north into Arizona in 1775 to Quiburi, near present Fairbank, and became the presidio of Santa Cruz.[7] But severe attacks by the Apaches

---

[3] Bancroft, *Hist. North Mex. States*, 1:232–33, 255, 272, 520. The *alcalde mayor*, although possessing nominal jurisdiction over Pimería Alta, seldom interfered with the Jesuits.

[4] Ibid., p. 272.

[5] John L. Kessell, "The Puzzling Presidio: San Phelipe de Guevavi, Alias Terrenate," *N. Mex. Hist. Rev.* 41 (Jan. 1966):33.

[6] Ibid., p. 34.

[7] Ibid., p. 38.

forced its abandonment, and in 1780, it was moved south to Las Nutrias, and again in 1787, to the abandoned mission at Suamca. In 1775, the presidio of Fronteras was moved north into the San Bernardino Valley, in the vicinity of the present international boundary, but Indian attacks forced its withdrawal in 1780. In late 1776, the presidio of Tubac was moved fifty miles along the Santa Cruz River to the Pima and Sobaipuri village near Tucson, a location selected for the protection of the over-land route to California and the mission at San Xavier del Bac.[8] The commander at Tucson was Capt. Pedro Allande y Saabedra, who, in the 1780s, led several campaigns to the Gila River. Capt. José Zúñiga, the commandant from 1794 to 1810, explored a route from that post toward Santa Fe, getting as far as Zuñi from whence he sent runners to the capital of New Mexico.[9] During this period, a provincial militia corps was created to strengthen the presidios.[10]

For many years, the viceroy of New Spain exercised authority over officials in Sinaloa and Sonora, as in other parts of Mexico. In 1776, in an effort to improve administration, the northern provinces were set up as the Interior Provinces, with authority in both military and civil matters given to a commandant general whose headquarters were, initially, at Arizpe, Sonora. In 1787, Sonora, Nueva Vizcaya, New Mexico, and the Californias became the Western Interior Prov-inces, under a commandant general at Chihuahua. The Western Interior Provinces were reunited with the Eastern Interior Provinces in 1792, and, in 1813, the Western Interior Provinces, consisting of Sonora, Sinaloa, Nueva Vizcaya, and New Mexico, were placed under a com-mandant at Durango.

The governors of the Mexican provinces were replaced, in 1786, by governor intendants, who were under the civil, military, judicial, and financial authority of the viceroy, the commandant general, or the audiencia. The intendancy of Arizpe included Sonora and Sinaloa. The intendancy of Durango, corresponding to Nueva Vizcaya, included modern Durango and Chihuahua and had its seat at Durango. Locally, subdelegates appointed by the intendants replaced the *alcaldes mayores* and *corregidores*. In judicial matters, Sonora, like other parts of north-ern Mexico, came under the Audiencia of Guadalajara.[11]

---

[8] Sidney B. Brinckerhoff, "The Last Years of Spanish Arizona, 1786–1821," *Ariz. and the West* 2 (Spring 1967):7.

[9] Jack Holterman, "José Zúñiga, Commandant of Tucson," *The Kiva* 22 (Nov. 1956):1–4.

[10] William A. DePalo, Jr., "The Establishment of the Nueva Vizcaya Militia dur-ing the Administration of Teodoro de Croix, 1776–1783," *N. Mex. Hist. Rev.* 48 (July 1973):223.

[11] Bancroft, *Hist. North Mex. States*, 1:670–72, 674–75, 676–79.

The liberal Spanish constitution of 1820 introduced changes in the governmental system of Sinaloa and Sonora, as in other provinces on the northern frontier. Deputies were sent to the Cortes in Madrid, and a provincial deputation was inaugurated at Arizpe to legislate matters pertaining to the province. Local self-government was handled through *ayuntamientos* that were organized in the towns.[12]

During the years following 1821, when Mexico was becoming independent of Spain, other changes in the government of Sonora were made. But the failure of the new central government to grant a greater measure of self-government caused disturbances in Sonora, and resulted in extensive destruction of the archives that had been accumulated at Arizpe. A decree adopted in February, 1824, in response to agitation in Sonora, provided for the union of the two provinces of Sinaloa and Sonora as the Internal State of the West, and was approved by representatives of the two provinces in October, 1825. This state was divided into the five departments of Arizpe, Horcasitas, Fuerte, Culiacán and San Sebastián. The state functioned under a governor, a vice-governor, a legislature, and a supreme court at Fuerte. Local administration was handled by alcaldes and missionaries. The two departments of Arizpe and Horcasitas became the state of Sonora in 1831, with the capital at Hermosillo. On the south, the boundary of Sonora was eighteen miles south of Alamos, and on the north, the state extended to the Colorado and Gila rivers, thus embracing southern Arizona. The other areas of Sonora became a department in 1837, but after a period of civil war between the federalists and centralists, the federal system provided for in the constitution of 1831 was again adopted, and, in 1847, Sonora once more became a state, with a governor and legislature at Ures. The capital was returned to Hermosillo in 1878.[13]

The presidial system established by the Spanish on the northern frontier was continued by the Mexican government, but with inadequate financial support. The military establishment in Sinaloa and Sonora continued under the commandant general at Chihuahua until 1826, when the Internal State of the West was provided with its own commandant general at Arizpe.[14] Nearly 800 officers and soldiers garrisoned the presidios at Tucson, Tubac, Fronteras, Santa Cruz, Altar, Buenavista, Horcasitas or Pitic, Bacoachi, and Babispe. Two active state companies of militia were available for service, but locally such companies were not usually organized. Without the support of federal or

---

[12] Ibid., 2:635.

[13] Ibid., p. 637 n. 36, 646, 664.

[14] Ibid., p. 638. Sinaloa was given its own commander in 1835.

state forces, the presidial companies were unable to do much more than protect their immediate areas. Tucson and Tubac were attacked in the 1830s and 1840s by Apaches, whose raids also extended to settlements farther south. So harassed was the frontier that many settlers, ranchers, and miners were forced to withdraw.[15] Then in the fall of 1848, many Mexicans joined the California gold rush, and those who remained were forced to take refuge at Tucson. Before 1852, however, a small group of Mexican soldiers reoccupied the presidio of Tubac.

In 1846, after the outbreak of the Mexican War, forces under Gen. Stephen W. Kearny marched across the territory south of the Gila River, but the territory was not occupied, and the treaty of 1848, concluding the war, established the international boundary at the Gila.[16] The United States then became interested in the strip south of the Gila, for a route for a southern railroad to California, and it was purchased from Mexico for $10,000,000 under the Gadsden treaty of December 30, 1853. Finally, on March 10, 1856, possession of the region was effected when United States dragoons replaced the Mexican troops at Tucson. In 1851, that part of Arizona north of the Gila had been placed, for administrative purposes, under the territory of New Mexico, and, after the United States acquired the strip south of that river, it was made part of Doña Ana County, in the territory of New Mexico.[17] An act of Congress of February 24, 1863, created the Arizona territory, and included in its boundaries the western portion of the Gadsden purchase.[18]

---

[15] Ibid., p. 653; Robert C. Stevens, "The Apache Menace in Sonora, 1831–1849," *Ariz. and the West* 6 (Autumn 1964):219–21.

[16] Bancroft, *Ariz. and N. Mex.*, p. 479.

[17] Ibid., pp. 503–04.

[18] Ibid., p. 509.

29

Spanish & Mexican Records

THE ONLY RECORDS from Spanish settlements in the Gadsden purchase area that have survived are those of the missions, which are described in chapter thirty-four. With the approach of Lt. Col. Phillip St. George Cooke, United States Army, to Tucson in December, 1846, the Mexicans evacuated the town, carrying off all public property. For documentary sources on the activities of the Spanish and Mexicans in Arizona, recourse must be had to the archives of Mexico, Spain, Sonora, Nueva Vizcaya, and Chihuahua, where the superior authorities accumulated and preserved records. Inasmuch as military personnel and missionaries who served in Arizona came from Mexico and returned there after performing their service, information regarding them can be found in the records of Spanish towns and churches south of the border, especially in Sonora.

Several archives in Mexico City have materials relating to Sonora and Arizona. Correspondence, reports, diaries, and other documents are in the Archivo General de la Nación, especially in the Historia and Provincias Internas sections. These concern political and financial administration, military affairs, ecclesiastical affairs, relations with the Indians, explorations and expeditions, and mining.[1] Similar documentation is also available for Sinaloa and Nueva Vizcaya, with which Sonora was associated during the seventeenth and eighteenth centuries. In the Archivo Histórico de Hacienda, Sección de Temporalidades, there are documents concerning the exploration of the Colorado River, 1729 and 1763, another by Capt. Juan Mateo Manje on the condition

---

[1] Bolton, *Guide to Arch. Mex.*, passim.

of Sonora, 1722, and papers of 1755–60 regarding hostilities of the Apaches, Seris, and Pimas.[2]

Since Arizona was subordinate to Spanish and, later, Mexican officials in Sonora, the Archivo Histórico del Estado Sonora in Hermosillo contains much pertinent material. These archives have over 800,000 pages of official correspondence, reports, memoranda, executive decrees, minutes, and debates of the state legislature; judicial records; and other materials dating from the early years of the eighteenth century. These documents concern general administration, appointments and elections of officials, presidios, relations with the Indians, taxes and monopolies, and the establishment of missions and administration of their community property.[3] Included are documents on the establishment of the colony at the junction of the Gila and Colorado rivers, the expeditions to California, 1772–83, and American fur traders on the Gila and Colorado rivers in the 1820s. The documents are arranged chronologically, and the archivo has manuscript inventories.

The documents in the Archivo General de Notarias begin in the eighteenth century and contain materials relating to business and legal transactions (see the description of notarial archives in chapter seventeen, in the section on Texas).

Archives at Durango date from the early years of the colonial period, covering Nueva Vizcaya as well as the state of Durango.[4] In the Archivo del Estado, Professor Bolton found a large, unclassified collection that included correspondence of governors, intendants, and military commandants; reports of inspections of presidios; decrees; royal cédulas; proclamations; proceedings of criminal and civil trials; probate records, residencias of various officials; files of the royal accountant and royal treasury; and accounts extending from the sixteenth to the eighteenth centuries. A portion of the political and military records of the province and state were deposited in the Federal Jefatura de Hacienda. The records of the intendancy of Durango, in several hundred poorly arranged bundles, were in the same place. The records of the ayuntamiento, dating from 1583, were in the best condition and included royal cédulas, correspondence, proceedings of the sessions, reports of elections, ordinances, proclamations, and autos on various

---

[2] Mexico, Ministerio de Hacienda y Crédito Público, Guía del Archivo Histórico de Hacienda, siglos XVI a XIX (Mexico, 1940–45), leaves 55, 56, 57, 73, 84–85.

[3] Bolton, Guide to Arch. Mex., pp. 465–67; Carrera Stampa, Archivalia mexicana, pp. 180–81. Two volumes of a new catalog of the state archives of Sonora have been published: Cynthia Radding de Murrieta and Maria Lourdes Torres Chávez, Catálogo del Archivo Histórico del Estado Sonora (Hermosillo, 1974–75).

[4] Bolton, Guide to Arch. Mex., pp. 407–08; Carrera Stampa, Archivalia mexicana, pp. 132–33.

subjects. These municipal records are of more than local interest. The separate file of notarial archives, consisting of documents relating to legal and business transactions, date from the beginning of the seventeenth century.

The Parral (Chihuahua) archives, 1631–1821, are important for the history of that part of northern Mexico known in the seventeenth and eighteenth centuries as Nueva Vizcaya, and they include much material on trade and commerce, Indian affairs, military history, slavery, social history, civil and criminal lawsuits, mining, and government. These archives are especially important because of the destruction of the archives at Chihuahua and Santa Fe. As part of a microfilm project in the Parral archives, a finding aid regarding these records was produced. After a preliminary investigation of the Parral archives by a group of Arizonans, including George W. Chambers, of the publishing firm of Arizona Silhouettes, Renato Rosaldo and Robert R. Anderson, of the Department of Romance Languages of the University of Arizona, and Charles C. DiPeso, director of the Amerind Foundation of Dragoon, Arizona, it was decided that the archives needed arranging and indexing.[5] These tasks were accomplished in 1959–60 during five trips to Parral, where continuous work was carried on by a small staff. The documents were arranged chronologically within each calendar year, according to the following classification:[6]

> 1. Administrative Business and War Measures *(Causas administrativos y guerras)*, consisting of military reports concerning native activity and official visits, reports pertaining to such administrative activities as the location of royal stores for tax purposes, reports of governors and other officials, and other matters pertaining to administration on the federal level.
> 2. Land and Mining Claims *(Minas, Solares y Terrenos)*, consisting of records of land cases and mining property, including sales of ranches and other properties.
> 3. Protocols *(Protocolos)*, consisting of formal protocols written during the course of a year by various city officials concerned with city and provincial business, public records, wills, etc.
> 4. Civil Actions *(Causas civiles)*, consisting of records

---

[5] Holmes, "Southwestern Archival Legacy," p. 538; Samuel B. Freedman, "Microfilming in Mexico," *Library Journal* 85 (Nov. 1, 1960):3926–31. Freedman had charge of the microfilming.

[6] Parral (Mexico), Archivo, *English Translation of the Index to El Archivo de Hidalgo del Parral, 1631–1821*, trans. by Consuelo P. Boyd (Tucson, 1971). Available in Spanish in 1961. See also Robert R. Anderson, "A Note on the Archivo de Hidalgo del Parral," *Ariz. and the West* 4 (Winter 1962):381–85.

of court cases concerned with money and materials, and culture transactions at the civil court level, including cases concerning enforced slavery.

5. Criminal Actions *(Causas criminales)*, consisting of records of federal cases, including murders, theft, rape, etc.

6. Unclassified Material *(Papeles varios)*, consisting of unidentified documents or parts of documents that could not be otherwise classified or properly indexed.

The index to the Parral archives is actually a brief calendar giving the frame number of the microfilm, the classification number, and an English summary of the documents with the names of persons involved. Entries for individual documents have no dates nor place names except where land is involved, and the calendar is not indexed.

In Spain, where matters were submitted for information, decision, and instruction, extensive documentation also accumulated in government archives. The most important repository of materials relating to New Spain is the Archivo General de Indias in Seville. Its holdings concern administration and affairs in Sonora, Arizona, Sinaloa, and Nueva Vizcaya.[7] Included are documents on the presidios of Tubac, Tucson, Fronteras, Terrenate, Janos, and Horcasitas, and on the Pima, Apache, and Yuma Indians. Included also is material on various individuals such as Capt. Juan Bautista de Anza, commander at Tubac and explorer of the route to California, and Govs. Agustín de Vildosola and Diego Ortiz Parrilla. Diaries of Capt. Juan M. Manje, 1699 and 1701, concerning his travels with Fr. Eusebio F. Kino are in the Biblioteca Nacional in Madrid.[8] That repository also has other documents on Sonora, including a report by Capt. Gabriel A. Vildosola of August 14, 1766.

---

[7] Chapman, *Catalogue of Materials in the Archivo General de Indias*, passim.

[8] Ernest J. Burrus, S.J., *Kino and Manje: Explorers of Sonora and Arizona* (Rome, Italy, and St. Louis, Mo., 1971), p. 283.

30

Archival Reproductions

In 1966, the Arizona Historical Society collaborated with the Mexican National Institute of Anthropology and History on a microfilm project in the Archivo Histórico del Estado de Sonora, which was then housed in the University of Sonora Library at Hermosillo. Documents selected for microfilming by Dr. Wisberto Jiménez Moreno and Fr. Kieran McCarty, O.F.M., filled forty-one rolls. The filmed materials relate to military and Indian affairs (especially to campaigns against the Apaches), public lands, and the administration of the province during the Spanish and Mexican periods. A duplicate of the microfilm was purchased by the Arizona Historical Foundation and placed in the Hayden Memorial Library of Arizona State University, Tempe, Arizona, for the use of persons investigating the history of the Southwest and Mexico. A calendar of the documents is being prepared in English by Consuelo P. Boyd at the Hayden Memorial Library, and documents of special interest and others concerning Arizona are being translated. Father McCarty has been editing the microfilm at the Arizona Historical Society and translating important documents relating to southern Arizona.[1]

The Bancroft Library of the University of California has supplied the Arizona Historical Society with microfilm and Xerox copies of materials relating to Spanish and Mexican Arizona that are described in Bolton's guide. These include documents on political, military, and religious affairs; correspondence on land and sea expeditions; campaigns against the Apaches, Comanches, and Seris; military records

---

[1] Letter from Donald L. DeWitt, Archivist, Arizona Historical Society, Dec. 6, 1972, with a list of microfilm rolls; *Jour. Ariz. Hist.* 7 (Winter 1966):207.

concerning presidios and soldiers; records relating to lawsuits and investigations; and diaries and journals of missionaries and soldiers. This collection amounts to 152 rolls, and a typewritten guide is available.

The University of Arizona has also done microfilming in Sonora. In 1964 and 1966, the university microfilmed materials in the executive section of the state archives at Hermosillo that included mining records, selected military reports, and some concerning Yaqui Indian relations (17 rolls). A continuation of the project on a cooperative basis with the University of Sonora is planned.[2]

In the summer of 1960, the Micro Photo Division of the Bell & Howell Company microfilmed the Parral archives, after the archives had been arranged by the group of Arizonans referred to above.[3] The Parral archives, 1631–1821, consist of more than 260,000 pages on 324 rolls of film. The microfilm negative is held by the Micro Photo Division (Wooster, Ohio 44691), from which copies can be purchased for $5,000. A set of the microreproductions was given to the public library at Parral, and there is another set in Mexico at the Instituto Tecnológico y de Estudios Superiores de Monterrey. In the United States, sets were available in 1972 at the University of Alabama, the University of Arizona, the University of California at Berkeley, Fort Lewis College at Durango, Colorado, Northern Illinois University at DeKalb, the University of Minnesota, the State University of New York at Stony Brook, the State University of New York at Buffalo, Temple University at Philadelphia, the University of Texas at Austin, the University of Texas at El Paso, Texas Agricultural and Mechanical College, Texas Christian University at Fort Worth, Tulane University at New Orleans, the University of Utah, and the Library of Congress.

The Library of the University of Texas at El Paso has photo-reproductions from several places in Mexico. In 1969, it microfilmed the presidial archives of Janos, Chihuahua, which were then in the church at that place. The Janos archives, 1721–ca. 1900 (36 rolls), contain correspondence, payrolls, receipts, and other documents relating primarily to military affairs.[4] The Janos archives are also available on microfilm at the El Paso Centennial Museum and the University of Arizona Library. Microfilm from the Durango archives is also in the Library of the University of Texas at El Paso. Under the Texas Consortium for Microfilming Mexican Archival Resources, initiated in

---

[2] Letter from Joseph F. Park, Curator, Western Collection, University of Arizona Library, Sept. 22, 1970.

[3] Freedman, "Microfilming in Mexico," pp. 3926–31.

[4] Letter from Leon C. Metz, Archivist, University of Texas at El Paso, Feb. 12, 1970.

1969, the University of Texas at El Paso has been microfilming documents on civil, military, and judicial affairs, dating from 1584, in the Durango archives.[5] The microfilming of documents (1710–1940) in the Chihuahua *ayuntamiento* archives was completed in 1973.[6] Microfilm of the archives of Durango is in the Academia Mexicana de la Historia, Biblioteca, Mexico City, and in the Museo Nacional de Antropologia, as well as in the Library of the University of Texas at El Paso.

Reproductions from Mexican repositories are also in the Bancroft Library of the University of California, Berkeley. Official correspondence of Sonora, 1766–70 (7 volumes, photocopies), were collected by Sherburne F. Cook from the Biblioteca Nacional in 1940.[7] Included in this correspondence are letters of Govs. Juan de Pineda and Enrique de Grimarest of Sonora, Capt. Juan Bautista de Anza, Visitor Gen. José de Gálvez, and Col. Domingo Elizondo, the leader of an expedition against the Seri Indians, for which preparations were made by Capt. Lorenzo Cancio Bonadares, commander of the presidio at Buenavista. Other items are photocopies of Juan Mateo Manje's "Luz de Tierra Incógnita" and his diaries (which are mentioned in chapter thirty-one), and a privately held manuscript narrative by Captain Manje of the journey he made with Father Kino, November 2–December 2, 1697, down the San Pedro and Gila rivers.[8] Selected typescripts from the Archivo del Estado at Hermosillo, Sonora, 1777–1848 (5 folders), include documents concerning Philip Nolan in Texas, 1797–1800, and American trappers on the Gila River in 1826 and the Colorado River in 1828.[9]

---

[5] Torok, *Guide to Colls. Univ. of Texas at El Paso Archives*, p. A 3.

[6] Ibid., p. A 2; *American Archivist* 37 (Jan. 1974):146. Greenleaf and Meyer, *Research in Mexican History*, pp. 110, 150.

[7] Hammond, *Guide to Ms. Colls.*, p. 83.

[8] Ibid., p. 120; Herbert E. Bolton, *Rim of Christendom: A Biography of Eusebio Francisco Kino, Pacific Coast Pioneer* (N.Y., 1936), p. 610. The narrative is printed in Burrus, *Kino and Manje*, pp. 353–56.

[9] Hammond, *Guide to Ms. Colls.*, p. 96.

31

Documentary Publications

THE MOST EXTENSIVE COLLECTION of published documents on Sonora and Pimería Alta is still that assembled in 1790–92 by Fr. Francisco García Figueroa, and partly published in Mexico City in 1853–57 in the *Documentos para la historia de México*. In that publication, volumes one and two of the fourth series contain materials for the ecclesiastical and civil history of Sonora, and volumes three and four contain materials for Nueva Vizcaya.[1] The compilation includes letters, reports, memorials, relations, notices, geographical descriptions, and diaries, by Jesuits, Franciscans, army officers, and others. These volumes have been one of the chief sources for English translations prepared by American historians. The Spanish texts are not without errors, however, so translators will be well advised to obtain photocopies of the original documents from the repositories in Mexico.

An important contributor to the early documentation on Pimería Alta was Juan Mateo Manje, who became an officer in the Flying Company of Sonora in 1693, served as *alcalde mayor* at times, and for many years was a prominent citizen of the province. He accompanied Father Kino on nine of his exploring expeditions between 1694 and 1701, keeping journals that supplement those of Kino. In 1720–21, he prepared a book entitled "Luz de Tierra Incógnita," of which the original manuscript has been lost.[2] In the first part of the book (copy in

---

[1] García Figueroa's Colección de memorias de Nueva España became part of the Historia section in the Archivo General de la Nación, Mexico. The volumes of that section from which the materials were selected for publication are described in Bolton, *Guide to Arch. of Mex.*, pp. 21–26.

[2] Burrus points out in his *Kino and Manje* (p. 282) that the editorial policy applied to Manje's "Luz de Tierra Incógnita" resulted in a completely altered text, not free from errors.

the Biblioteca Nacional, Mexico), he presents a historical account of the Spanish conquest of the New World, especially northwestern New Spain, and describes the Indian tribes, mineral resources, adaptability of the country for agriculture and livestock raising, and activities of the religious orders. The second part, containing seven diaries of his travels with Kino, was first published in the *Documentos para la historia de México* (fourth series, volume 1, pages 226–343, Mexico, 1856). Both parts were published in a modernized and more exact text in 1926.[3] Harry J. Karns retraced the Kino and Manje trails, in an effort to locate the historic sites mentioned in Manje's diaries, and published an English translation of the 1926 Spanish text in 1954.[4]

A critical edition of Manje's journals concerning his expeditions with Kino, and other documents relating to the history of the borderlands, have been published in E. J. Burrus's *Kino and Manje: Explorers of Sonora and Arizona.* The documents are based on the autograph manuscripts of Manje in the Biblioteca Nacional in Madrid, the Archivo General de la Nación in Mexico, and the most reliable, available texts. After a long discussion in English of the explorers' expeditions and plans, embodying critical comment on the documents, Burrus presents thirty documents in Spanish, half of which are published for the first time.[5] Two versions of some diaries are included, because of differences in contents and chronology. Manje's journals of two short trips with Kino in 1698 have been lost, and his account of the expedition of February—April, 1702, was prepared from Kino's diary, to which he added his own reflections and interpretations. Other documents by Manje include his plan of 1706 for the development of Pimería Alta, and his plea of 1735, along with other citizens, to Gov. Manuel de Huidobro for defensive measures against raids by hostile Indians. Manje's journals are valuable not only for his and Kino's exploring activities, but also for information regarding the Indians, the desert landscape including its products and resources, the missions and missionaries, and Spanish settlement. (A compilation of Manje's letters would be an important contribution to the history of the borderlands.) Another diary, by Capt. Diego Carrasco, an officer who accompanied Kino on the expedition of 1698 to the Gila and Colorado rivers, also appears from internal evidence to have been prepared from Kino's

---

[3] Francisco Fernández del Castillo, ed., *Luz de tierra incógnita en la América septentrional y diario de las exploraciones en Sonora (Publicaciones* del Archivo General de la Nación 10, México, D.F., 1926).

[4] Harry J. Karns, trans. and ed., *Unknown Arizona and Sonora, 1693–1721* (Tucson, 1954). Manje prepared some maps but none of them has been found.

[5] The introduction is on pp. 5–278, the documents on pp. 279–584. A chronological list of Manje's journals, with information on places previously published and the archival sources, is on p. 283. Other documents in this compilation are mentioned below, in chapter 34 ("Ecclesiastical Records").

own diary. Burrus's exceptional background for his task has resulted in an outstanding book.

Early in 1975, the Arizona State Museum, with the financial support of grants from the National Historical Publications and Records Commission and the National Endowment for the Humanities, began work on an extensive documentary publication on the Southwest. The project was under the direction of Charles W. Polzer, whose earlier archival work (noted in chapter thirty-four) was to be utilized. Documents were collected from archive sources in the United States, Mexico, Spain, and other places in Europe (see "List of Repositories"). Documents were selected for publication in both Spanish and English on civil-military relations and the Franciscans and Jesuits.

A small number of publications have been prepared by individuals interested in southwestern history. A short diary of Kino's expedition of 1697, by Lt. Cristóbal Martín Bernal, is available in translation.[6] John L. Kessell has translated an account of the expedition led by Capts. Bernardo Bustamante and Gabriel A. de Vildosola against the Apaches on the upper Gila River, prepared by Fr. Bartholomé Saenz who served as chaplain;[7] and Capt. Juan B. de Anza's report to the governor of Sonora on a 1766 expedition against the Apaches.[8] A diary of three expeditions by Lt. Col. Pedro Fages against the Yuma Indians, after their massacre of missionaries and settlers at the Colorado River settlements, has been published.[9] In the spring of 1795, Capt. José Zúñiga, commander of the presidio of Tucson, led a party of soldiers and Apache scouts from Sonora to the Zuni village in western New Mexico, from whence an Indian courier was sent with a message to the governor of New Mexico. A translation of the diary of the expedition, prepared by George P. Hammond, then of the University of Southern California, from the manuscript in the Archivo General de Indias has been published.[10] Compilations of published documents relating to the presidios at Tubac and Tucson would be worthwhile undertakings.

---

[6] Fay J. Smith, trans. and ed., "Diary of Lieutenant Cristóbal Martín Bernal," in Fay J. Smith, John L. Kessell, and Francis J. Fox, S.J., *Father Kino in Arizona* (Phoenix, 1966), pp. 35–47.

[7] John L. Kessell, trans. and ed., *Spaniard and Apache on the Upper Gila, 1756: An Account of the Bustamante-Vildosola Expedition by Father Bartholomé Saenz, S.J.* (Santa Fe).

[8] John L. Kessell, trans. and ed., "Anza, Indian Fighter: The Spring Campaign of 1766," *Jour. Ariz. Hist.* 9 (Fall 1968):158–63. A compilation of Anza's letters and other documents relating to Arizona would be a valuable publication.

[9] Herbert I. Priestley, trans. and ed., *The Colorado River Campaign, 1781–82: Diary of Pedro Fages* (Berkeley, 1913).

[10] G. P. Hammond, trans. and ed., "The Zúñiga Journal, Tucson to Santa Fe: The Opening of a Spanish Trade Route, 1788–1795," *N. Mex. Hist. Rev.* 6 (Jan. 1931): 40–65.

32

Manuscript Collections

In Arizona, where statehood was not attained until 1912 and governmental and educational institutions developed slowly because of the meager population, only a few repositories have developed collections of historical materials. The Department of Library and Archives in Phoenix, which grew out of the territorial library, has been mainly concerned with the care of records of the territorial and statehood periods, but its holdings do include some documents of Junípero Serra and Francisco T. H. Garcés.[1] It also has a collection of maps of the Southwest and Mexico. The state historian, a position created in 1909, collected data for historical works such as Farish's *History of Arizona*. The Arizona Pioneers' Historical Society, organized at Tucson in 1884, has had a succession of historical secretaries who collected manuscript materials on the history of the territory, the state and, more recently, on the colonial period.[2] After being housed for years in quarters provided by the University of Arizona, the society acquired its own fireproof building in 1955, at 949 East Second Street, near the university campus.

Because of inactivity as a collecting agency for many years after its organization, the Arizona Historical Society has not acquired much original material on the Spanish and Mexican periods. The principal collection is that named for Jesús José Aguiar, a treasury official of Cosalá, Sinaloa, who assembled it, and which was preserved in later years by Eustaquio and Alezandro Buelna, also of Sinaloa. The Aguiar Collection was one of many presented to the society by William J.

---

[1] Hilton, *Handbook of Hispanic Source Materials*, p. 2.

[2] Eleanor B. Sloan, "Seventy-Five Years of the Arizona Pioneers' Historical Society, 1884–1959," *Ariz. and the West* 1 (Spring 1959):66–67.

Holliday, an Indianapolis steel manufacturer and collector of western Americana who maintained a winter home in the foothills of the Catalina Mountains in Tucson. The Aguiar Collection (over 500 items) consists of governmental decrees of the Internal State of the West (*Occidente*) and its successors, Sinaloa and Sonora, May 14, 1825– October 26, 1835, arranged chronologically in binders; miscellaneous volumes relating to the same provinces and Mexico, containing holograph copies of regulations and instructions for the operation of municipal government, and the conduct of mayors and parties in litigation; and official publications of the government of Sinaloa, concerning fiscal matters, laws, and regulations, 1783–1944. A published calendar describes the individual documents in English, by province.[3]

Other manuscripts in the Arizona Historical Society Collection are much less extensive. A few reports by Gov. Manuel de Huidobro, June 12, 1843 (31 pages), concern an uprising by Yaqui, Pima, Mayo and·other Indians. Other holdings include the appointment of Josef de Castro as the *alférez* (ensign) of the presidio of Tucson, 1782; a census of Tubac, ca. 1830, giving a list of the *vecinos* (citizens) and the members of their families; papers relating to Tucson collected by Capt. Donald W. Page; Mexican land records, 1824–65 (1 inch, typescripts and English translations); and a collection of maps dating from 1580. Letters of Teodoro de Croix, commandant general of the Interior Provinces, to José de Gálvez, 1774–80 (45 pages, typescript), concern the inspection and functioning of the presidio of Tucson.[4]

The Bancroft Library of the University of California also has materials, acquired in part by H. H. Bancroft from Alphonse L. Pinart. These include documents for the history of Sonora, 1784–1877 (7 volumes, extracts from manuscript and printed matter);[5] and documents for the history of the north Mexican states, 1816–46 (2 volumes, manuscript and printed), including material on the history of Chihuahua.[6] In the same repository, there are documents relating to the Indians of Sonora, 1825–27; a collection of Sonora materials that includes correspondence of officials; and letters and diaries of Capt. Juan B. de Anza, 1766–80, concerning his expedition to California, 1774–76, and his expeditions against the Comanches, 1779, and the Moquis,

---

[3] Paul H. Ezell and Greta Ezell, *The Aguiar Collection in the Arizona Pioneers' Historical Society* (San Diego, 1964).

[4] Charles C. Colley, *Documents of Southwestern History: A Guide to the Manuscript Collections of the Arizona Historical Society* (Tucson, 1972), pp. 5, 38, 104, 108, 130, 151.

[5] Hammond, *Guide to Ms. Colls.*, pp. 173–74.

[6] Ibid., p. 43; Bancroft, *Hist. North Mex. States*, 1:xxxix.

1780.[7] In another Pinart collection consisting of manuscripts relative to northern Mexico, ca. 1768–1833? (106 items, originals and copies), there is correspondence of Lt. Ignacio Pérez with the missionaries at Tumacácori and other missions, 1821–23, concerning his failure to pay for cattle purchased from them and his relations with local officials. Two other small collections on northern Mexico, 1824–41 (68 items) and 1842–61 (312 items), containing originals and copies of letters and other documents, relate to political, military, and ecclesiastical matters. Materials concerning the Tubac presidio include a report of Roque Ibarra, the acting commandant, on a campaign against the Apaches, 1842–43; statistics on the infantry at Tubac; and data regarding occurrences at that presidio. Reports from Andrés B. Centeno, another commander at Tubac, furnish information relating to its population, needs, and relations with the Apaches and the officials at Tucson. Reports and letters of the commandant at Tucson, 1842–46, 1855, concern Indian relations, presidio supplies, and occurrences.[8]

A journal of the captain of cavalry of the presidio of Tubac, September 17, 1773, is in the Thomas Gilcrease Institute of American History and Art, Tulsa, Oklahoma.

---

[7] Bancroft, *Ariz. and N. Mex.*, p. xxv.

[8] Hammond, *Guide to Ms. Colls.*, pp. 174–76.

33

Land Records

FEW LAND GRANTS WERE MADE in southern Arizona. Grants of four
square leagues were made to the presidios of Tucson and Tubac, where
the commandants were authorized to make grants to individuals.
Ranches that developed around the missions and *visitas* (Indian settlements) established by Fr. Eusebio Kino in the Spanish period had
to be abandoned because of Indian hostility. Following Mexican Independence, a law of the State of the West, adopted May 20, 1825,
limited grants to ranchers to four square leagues. Land grants were
made in the Santa Cruz and San Pedro valleys, and extensive ranching
operations developed along the present international boundary.[1]

Before the establishment of the intendant system, land grants in
Sonora and Sinaloa, which included Arizona, came under the jurisdiction of the Real Audiencia of Guadalajara. District officials handled
the preliminary proceedings, including surveying, evaluating, and sell-
ing the land at public auction, and compiled *expedientes*.[2] A file of
papers was transmitted to Guadalajara, and, after examination and
approval, a title was registered and delivered to the grantee.[3] Under
the intendant system, local proceedings were taken care of by the sub-
delegate and forwarded to the intendant at Arizpe for approval and
issuance of the title. The *expediente* was transmitted by the intendant

---

[1] Ray H. Mattison, "Early Spanish and Mexican Settlements in Arizona," *N. Mex.
Hist. Rev.* 21 (Oct. 1946):282, 286, 288–89. This article contains brief histories of
the individual land grants in Arizona.

[2] R. C. Hopkins to J. A. Williamson, July 6, 1879, Records of the Bureau of Land
Management, Miscellaneous Letters Received, file O–33312 (Record Group 49),
National Archives (hereinafter cited as NA, BLM, Misc. Lets. Recd.).

[3] Hopkins to Williamson, May 15, May 31, 1879, NA, BLM, Misc. Lets. Recd., files
O–22636, O–26676.

through the commandant general to the viceroy, by whom it was referred to the attorney general for further approval. In Mexico City, the grant was registered by the attorney general and the Real Tribunal y Audiencia de la Contaduria, and then the *expediente* was returned to Arizpe for deposit in the archives. The foregoing system was followed until the establishment of Mexican Independence in 1821. From 1821–1825, a provisional commissary general of the treasury exercised supervision over the granting of lands.[4] A law of the Mexican Congress of August 4, 1824, gave the revenue derived from the sale of public lands to the states, thus permitting them to assume the management of public lands. In Sonora, the treasury department performed this function, and *expedientes* and other records relating to land grants passed into its hands.

The Gadsden treaty of 1853, which effected the purchase of the region south of the Gila River, contained a provision that recognized the validity of land titles in the ceded territory,[5] but it was many years before United States officials undertook the settlement of private land claims in earnest. Although the treaty contained a provision to the effect that land grants would be considered valid only when they were found duly recorded in the archives of Mexico, it did not stipulate an arrangement whereby copies of the land records could be obtained by the United States. Even after the establishment of the Territory of Arizona as a separate surveying district, by an act of Congress of July 11, 1870,[6] and the appointment of John Wasson as surveyor general of Arizona, in February, 1871,[7] there was more delay. The appropriation act approved July 15, 1870, made it the duty of the surveyor general, under instructions issued by the secretary of the interior, "to ascertain and report upon the origin, nature, character and extent of the claims to land in said Territory under the laws, usages and customs of Spain and Mexico,"[8] and to accomplish this, he was given the same powers and duties bestowed upon the surveyor general of New Mexico by the eighth section of the act approved July 22, 1854.[9] But instructions were not forthcoming from the Department of the Interior for a number of years, and funds were not provided by Congress for an even longer period.

Consideration of the matter in the department finally resulted in

---

[4] Bolton, *Guide Arch. Mex.*, pp. 379–80.

[5] U.S., *Stats.*, Vol. 10, Art. 6, p. 1035.

[6] U.S., *Stats.*, 16:230.

[7] W. W. Custis to John Wasson, Feb. 7, 1871, Records of the Bureau of Land Management, Letters Sent to the Surveyor General, Arizona, Bk. 1 (Record Group 49), National Archives (hereinafter cited as NA, BLM, Lets. Sent to SG., Ariz.).

[8] U.S., *Stats.*, 16:304.

[9] U.S., *Stats.*, 10:308.

the dispatch of an agent to investigate land records in Mexico. In October, 1872, the acting secretary of the interior appointed Rufus C. Hopkins, keeper of the Spanish archives in the Office of the Surveyor General of California, to visit such states of Mexico as might be necessary to examine official records of land grants made in United States territory.[10] In the execution of this task, he was to make such transcripts and indexes as were required to supply needed information relative to the grants. Hopkins found at Ures, the capital of Sonora, a collection of land records containing *expedientes* extending back to 1661, from which he made extracts of documents relating to grants in Arizona proper and those near the border between that territory and Sonora.[11] He also made copies of pertinent entries from a register of land grants (*toma de razón*) for 1831 to 1849, and from a list of *expedientes* originally made in 1808 but kept up-to-date since that time. Information he obtained relative to land-grant procedure necessitated his extending his trip, and he traveled overland to Guaymas, armed with a Henry rifle and six-shooter for protection against the Indians, where he sailed for Acapulco. He reached Mexico City in March, 1873, and, with the help of the American minister, gained admission to the Archivo General de la Nación.

What ultimately became of the extracts and notes that Hopkins obtained at Ures, Sonora, has not been ascertained. In February, 1873, he sent them from Guaymas to his son Henry, who was employed in the United States Surveyor General's Office in San Francisco. Hopkins probably took them to Tucson later, when he became employed in the Surveyor General's Office there (where his son also became attached).

Shortly before the arrival of Hopkins in Mexico City in 1873, Thomas H. Nelson, the American minister at that place, had addressed an inquiry to the Mexican minister of foreign affairs.[12] He did this after the receipt of an instruction from the secretary of state, which had been dispatched pursuant to a Senate resolution calling for the procurement of information on the condition of records in Mexico relating to grants of land in the territories of Arizona and New Mexico.

---

[10] B. R. Cowen to Hopkins, Oct. 18, 1872, Records of the Office of the Secretary of the Interior, Letter Book, Land, Vol. 14 (Record Group 48), National Archives.

[11] R. C. Hopkins, Guaymas, Mexico, to B. H. Bristow, Feb. 7, 1873, NA, BLM, Misc. Lets. Recd., K-38219. Hopkins seems to have utilized this visit to Sonora to make a report to the Texas Pacific Railroad Company regarding Spanish and Mexican land grants in Arizona (Hopkins to John Wasson, Feb. 9, 1880, Records of the Bureau of Land Management, Private Land Claim Dockets, No. 6, El Paso de los Algodones [Record Group 49], National Archives, hereinafter cited as NA, BLM, PLC Dockets).

[12] Nelson to Hamilton Fish, Mar. 15, 1873, General Records of the Department of State, Diplomatic Despatches from Mexico, Vol. 47, No. 791 (Record Group 59), National Archives. Enclosed is a copy of a letter from Nelson to Juan M. Lafragua, Mar. 3, 1873, making the inquiry referred to.

Neither the Mexican minister of foreign affairs nor the American minister followed up on the matter, assuming that Hopkins had furnished whatever information had been desired, but the receipt of further instructions from Washington in 1874 reopened the correspondence.[13] According to a report from the director of the Archivo General de la Nación, there were no pertinent land records in that institution, but since the area in question was subordinate to the Audiencia of Guadalajara, he suggested that there might be records in Guadalajara, if they had escaped the conflagration of 1859.[14] The notary public in the mortgage office of the secretary of the government of the state of Jalisco at Guadalajara, in charge of the archives of the suppressed special land tribunal, reported that there were no title deeds in the records naming locations in Arizona and New Mexico, but that since Arizona had been part of Sonora, some of the records might relate to grants in Arizona.[15] A search was also made of the records of the Supreme Tribunal of Justice of the State of Jalisco at Guadalajara, but with no results.

In 1879, Hopkins went on another mission to Sonora. J. A. Williamson, commissioner of the General Land Office, had pointed out that there were no archives or copies of archives relating to land grants in the region obtained by the Gadsden treaty, where the construction of railroads and development of resources increased incentive to fabricate land titles, and had urged the dispatch of Hopkins to obtain copies of Mexican land records as a precautionary measure.[16] Secretary of the Interior Schurz responded by appointing Hopkins to undertake the investigation.[17] Instructions were soon sent to Hopkins by Williamson to proceed to Ures, Sonora, and procure transcripts and abstracts of land records.[18] Hopkins left San Francisco for Tucson in April, 1879, and, after a trip by stage of over twenty days, reached

---

[13] Hamilton Fish to John W. Foster (successor to Nelson), Apr. 14, 1874, General Records of the Department of State, Diplomatic Instructions to Mexico, Vol. 19 (Record Group 59), National Archives.

[14] Foster to Fish, May 7, 1874, NA, DS, Despatches from Mexico, Vol. 51, No. 142, enclosing a letter to Juan M. Lafragua, Apr. 29, 1874, and a reply from that official, Apr. 29, enclosing a communication from F. P. de Urquidi, Mar. 22, 1873, all printed in *Senate Exec. Doc.* 3, 43 Cong., 2 sess., pp. 2–4.

[15] Foster to Fish, July 16, 1874, NA, DS, Despatches from Mexico, Vol. 51, No. 165, enclosing a letter from J. M. Lafragua, June 3, 1874, with subenclosures, all printed in *Senate Exec. Doc.* 3, 43 Cong., 2 sess., pp. 4–6.

[16] Williamson to Carl Schurz, Feb. 24, 1879, Records of the Office of the Secretary of the Interior, Appointments Division, Letters Received, file 160A. 1879 (Record Group 48), National Archives.

[17] Schurz to Williamson, Feb. 26, 1879, NA, BLM, Misc. Lets. Recd., file N–98980.

[18] Williamson to Hopkins, Mar. 4, 1879, Records of the Bureau of Land Management, Letters Sent, Miscellaneous Private Claims, Bk. 36 (Record Group 49), National Archives (hereinafter cited as NA, BLM, Lets. Sent, Misc. Priv. Claims).

Ures on April 30.[19] Hopkins was courteously received by Governor
Serna, who directed subordinate officials to afford him every facility
and assistance required for the pursuit of his work. His examination
revealed that the land records of Sonora dated from 1661 and comprised about 1500 *expedientes*, totalling some 110,000 pages.[20] From
this mass, he selected some 1200 to 1500 pages relative to grants in
Arizona, but, on learning that for every sheet of certified copy he
would have to pay a stamp tax of fifty cents, he decided to abstract
the information required for determining the titles of grants and their
locations instead of obtaining complete transcripts. He also made a
list of all grants in the archives, down to the year 1854. During the
latter part of May, while the records were being moved to the new
capital at Hermosillo, he prepared a lengthy historical account of the
land-grant procedure followed in northern Mexico during the Spanish
and Mexican regimes.[21] He again found the register of land grants for
1831 to 1849, which he had examined in 1873, and communicated his
intention to copy it. His inspection of the records confirmed tradition-
ary reports of the destruction of records during the many revolutions
which had devastated the country. Incomplete grants in the archives
were likely, he feared, to be discovered by manipulators and utilized
for fraudulent ends. From Hermosillo, where he had followed the
archives sometime after the middle of May, Hopkins returned late in
June to Tucson. With the expectation of finding additional records at
Arizpe, Sonora, left behind when the capital was moved to Ures in
1839, he traveled to that place in July, but found nothing.[22]

From Tucson, where he had obtained employment in the office
of the United States Surveyor General as a clerk and translator in
August, 1879, Hopkins transmitted a report on his mission to the
General Land Office in Washington in March, 1880.[23] Besides a copy
of his appointment and instructions, this report contains an account
of his mission, based on his letters of the preceding year. The abstracts
of land grants prepared by Hopkins from the original *expedientes*
appear on pages 17–131 of the report. Concerning the land grants,

---

[19] Hopkins to Williamson, May 1, 1879, NA, BLM, Misc. Lets. Recd., file O–19137.

[20] Hopkins to Williamson, May 15, June 15, 1879, NA, BLM, Misc. Lets. Recd.,
files O–22636, O–28885.

[21] Hopkins began this historical account in his letter of May 15, 1879, cited in
footnote 20, and concluded it in another of May 31, 1879, NA, BLM, Misc. Lets.
Recd., file O–26676.

[22] Hopkins to Williamson, Aug. 1, 1879, NA, BLM, Misc. Lets. Recd., file O–37536.

[23] Report of R. C. Hopkins, Special Agent, in Relation to Mexican Land Grants
in the Territory of Arizona, Mar. 6, 1880, Records of the Bureau of Land Management, Private Land Claims, No. 184.

he stated that some were partly or entirely within the limits of the state of Sonora, and only a survey would reveal the exact locality. He considered the *expedientes* to be manifestly genuine, without simulation of signatures, interpolations, changes of dates, or other indications of bad faith. The record of abstracts is followed, on pages 136–169, by a list of *expedientes* of grants.

According to instructions issued to the surveyor general of Arizona, John Wasson, on January 9, 1877, it was his duty to report on all land titles in Arizona that had originated before the United States acquired sovereignty over the area.[24] The reports were to be so prepared as to enable Congress to discriminate between bona fide and fraudulent claims. Since he was to ascertain the origin, nature, and extent of claims under the laws, usages, and customs of Spain and Mexico, the surveyor general was instructed to acquaint himself with the land system that Spain had utilized in her colonies. He was to apply to the surveyor general of New Mexico for archives relating to grants of land in Arizona. Such records as were assembled were to be arranged chronologically, bound, listed, and abstracted. To guard the public against fraudulent or antedated claims, he was to test the title papers against genuine signatures and official registers or abstracts. Original title papers were to be required of claimants, and, if they could not be produced, their loss had to be accounted for, and only authenticated copies were to be accepted in their place.

During 1879, the surveyor general completed preparations for the reception and consideration of private land claims. In addition to the examination of land records in Mexico, printed materials concerning Spanish and Mexican land procedures were collected. An iron safe was obtained for the protection of original title papers to be submitted by claimants, and other records. Among the claims filed, after the opening of the office on September 1, were several for large and valuable tracts of land. The claim known as El Paso de los Algodones embraced five square leagues at the junction of the Colorado and Gila rivers, including part of the town of Yuma, property of the Southern Pacific Railroad, and the El Sopori claim of over thirty square leagues near Tucson. Suspicions were aroused regarding the validity of these grants, and, in January, 1880, Hopkins was sent to Hermosillo, Sonora, by the surveyor general, with instructions to make a careful examination of the records pertaining to these grants and the one for La Punta del Sargento, which had been made on the same date in 1838 to the

---

[24] J. A. Williamson to John Wasson, Jan. 9, 1877, NA, BLM, Letter Book, Misc. Private Claims, Bk. 33.

grantee of the El Paso de los Algodones grant.[25] Pursuant to Wasson's directions, Hopkins compared the paper, penmanship, color of ink, and signatures with rubrics in the records of these grants with the same elements in records of other grants of the same year, and reported that the claims were fraudulent, the title papers antedated, and the signatures forged.[26] Subsequently, Hopkins returned to Hermosillo with a photographer and procured photographic copies of the records pertaining to the three grants.[27] In August, 1880, the surveyor general sent transcripts and photographic exhibits to the commissioner of the General Land Office, with a recommendation that the claim be rejected.[28] Congress failed to act upon the claim, and it was presented, in 1892, to the Court of Private Land Claims; the order of that court for the confirmation of 21,700 acres was appealed by the government to the Supreme Court, which reversed the decision.[29] The experience gained from these cases pointed out the necessity of comparing title papers filed by claimants with original land records in Mexico.

A more general investigation of Mexican archives relative to land grants was contemplated in 1881. Hopkins was instructed to examine and report on any records of Spanish and Mexican land grants in Arizona, that were still extant in Chihuahua, Alamos, Fuerte, Culiacán, Ymurio, and any other places which might have records.[30] The places named were political capitals or towns in which records had been kept. Knowledge of the records in these places was required to support claims for which no records could be found in Arizpe, Ures, or Hermosillo. Hopkins did visit Chihuahua, but seems to have withdrawn from the quest at that point, in order to return to Hermosillo for further photographic evidence against the El Sopori claim.[31] As a result of archival searches and exhibits in this case also, the surveyor general submitted a report, to the General Land Office in December, 1881,

25 Wasson to Hopkins, Jan. 14, 1880, Records of the Bureau of Land Management, Surveyor General of Arizona, Letters Sent Relating to Private Land Claims (Record Group 49), National Archives (hereinafter cited as NA, BLM, SG Ariz., Lets. Sent PLC).

26 Hopkins to Wasson, Feb. 9, 1880, NA, BLM, PLC Dockets No. 6, El Paso de los Algodones; Wasson to J. A. Williamson, Feb. 14, 1880, NA, BLM, SG Ariz., Lets. Sent PLC; House Report 1585, 51 Cong., 1 sess.

27 Wasson to Hopkins, June 24, 1880, NA, BLM, SG Ariz., Lets. Sent PLC; Wasson to Henry Buchanan, Aug. 20, 1880, NA, BLM, SG Ariz., Lets. Sent, PLC. Wasson expressed satisfaction with the clear photographs received from Buchanan, a Tucson photographer with whom Wasson had contracted out the work in Hermosillo.

28 Wasson to Williamson, Aug. 12, 1880, NA, BLM, SG Ariz., Lets. Sent PLC; the undated report by Wasson on the claim is in ibid., p. 317.

29 Mattison, "Early Ariz. Settlements," pp. 324–25.

30 Wasson to Hopkins, May 16, 1881, NA, BLM, SG Ariz., Lets. Sent PLC.

31 Wasson to Hopkins, June 25, 1881, acknowledging a letter from Chihuahua,

in which he recommended the rejection of the claim on grounds that the title papers were forged, antedated, and invalid under article six of the Gadsden treaty.[32] In the following year, continued investigation of the records of the northern states of Mexico was recommended,[33] and searches seem to have been made in subsequent years.[34]

A reinvestigation of the Tres Alamos grant of ten square leagues on the San Pedro River led, in 1886, to still further searches in the land records at Hermosillo. Professor J. George Hilzinger, a reputable Spanish scholar of the Pacific coast, was employed by the surveyor general of Arizona, to examine such documents as might be found in the archives at Hermosillo and make copies or photographs of them.[35] Hilzinger arrived in Hermosillo in May, 1886, shortly after the archives had been moved to the new capitol.[36] He searched the records in both the treasurer's and secretary of state's offices, finding numerous differences between original petitions of claimants in the records of the latter office and certified copies filed by claimants in Tucson.[37] He recommended a more extended search in the records of the secretary of state's office for documents relating to land claims, and also a more thorough examination of the land records of Sonora. G. C. Wharton, an inspector attached to the General Land Office who had spent some time in 1886 attempting to ascertain the location of the Tres Alamos grant, was again sent to the aid of the surveyor general of Arizona. Early in 1887, the surveyor general sent him to Guaymas, to examine court records related to the claim and look again into land records at Hermosillo.[38] As a result of these investigations the surveyor general recommended against the confirmation of this grant, also.[39]

NA, BLM, SG Ariz., Lets. Sent PLC; Wasson to N. C. McFarland, Aug. 13, 1881, NA, BLM, Lets. Recd., file N–55751; Wasson to Hopkins, Aug. 27, 1881, NA, BLM, SG Ariz., Lets. Sent PLC.

[32] Wasson to McFarland, Dec. 9, 1881, NA, BLM, SG Ariz., Lets. Sent PLC; Mattison "Early Ariz. Settlements," pp. 303–04.

[33] "Report of the Surveyor General of Arizona," July 31, 1882, in U.S. Dept. of the Interior, *Annual Report*, 1882, pp. 254–55.

[34] "Report of the Surveyor General of Arizona," July 7, 1885, ibid., 1885, p. 478.

[35] William A. J. Sparks to John Hise, Apr. 21, 1886, NA, BLM, Lets. Sent to SG Ariz., Bk. 2; Hise to Hilzinger, May 19, 1886, NA, BLM, SG Ariz., Lets. Sent PLC.

[36] Hilzinger to Hise, June 10, 1886, *Senate Exec. Doc.* 29, 50 Cong., 1 sess., pp. 25–26.

[37] The petition and a translation thereof by Hilzinger, and an earlier translation by R. C. Hopkins, who had left the employ of the Surveyor General of Arizona in 1886, are printed in ibid., pp. 19–21, with other documents.

[38] G. C. Wharton weekly report, Feb. 12, 1887, NA, BLM, Misc. Lets. Recd., file A–18990; Hise to Wharton, Feb. 14, 1887, NA, BLM, Phoenix, PLC Lets.; Wharton to William Walker, Mar. 22, 1887, NA, BLM, Misc. Lets. Recd., file A–37516.

[39] *Senate Exec. Doc.* 29, 50 Cong., 1 sess., pp. 5–18; Mattison, "Early Ariz. Settlements," p. 317.

The efforts of the federal government to combat the Peralta-Reavis claim for 12,740,000 acres of land in Arizona and New Mexico, which was presented to the surveyor general of Arizona in 1883 by James Addison Reavis, led to further archival investigations.[40] Later the same year, the surveyor general sent Rufus C. Hopkins to Guadalajara and Mexico City in a fruitless effort to find additional documentary evidence in the archives, relating to the grants.[41] Study of available documents later enabled the surveyor general to discredit the claim in his report of 1889 to the General Land Office. In February, 1893, Reavis filed a petition in the Court of Private Land Claims at Santa Fe, New Mexico. Will M. Tipton, an investigator for the court, examined archives at Hermosillo, Guadalajara, and in the Bravis district of Chihuahua.[42] Severo-Mallet-Prevost, a New York law firm employed as a special counsel in the case, investigated the archives at Guadalajara, Mexico City, and Madrid, and Reavis's activities at those places prior to the claim.[43] As a result of these investigations, the government was able to prove, during the trial in 1895, that Reavis had inserted fabricated documents regarding the grant into the archives of Mexico and Spain, and thus to demonstrate that his claim was fraudulent.

The activities of the surveyor general of Arizona, connected with the confirmation of private land claims, resulted in an accumulation of files of Spanish land-grant records. In the late 1930s, when the Survey of Federal Archives examined the land records in the Office of the Cadastral Engineer of the General Land Office at Phoenix, there were two files. The private land-grant records, 1767–1908 (6½ feet),

---

[40] Mattison, "Early Ariz. Settlements," pp. 325–327. A full account with bibliographical data appears in Donald M. Powell, *The Peralta Grant: James Addison Reavis and the Barony of Arizona* (Norman, Okla., 1960).

[41] J. W. Robbins to N. C. McFarland, Nov. 7, 1883, *Senate Exec. Doc.* 177, 48 Cong., 1 sess., pp. 2–3; Powell, *Peralta Grant,* pp. 50–51; United States Defendant, *In the United States Court of Private Land Claims Santa Fe District, James Addison Peralta-Reavis and Doña Sofia Loreto Micaela de Peralta de la Córdoba (Husband and Wife,) Plaintiffs, vs. The United States of America, Peralta Grant No. 110* (Santa Fe, 1895), pp. 177, 471–473, 809–811, 859, 874. After leaving the employ of the Surveyor General of Arizona, Rufus C. Hopkins did some translations, among them a collection entitled *Muniments of Title of the Barony of Arizona, and Translation into English* (San Francisco, 1893).

[42] *Peralta-Reavis vs. The United States,* pp. 388, 399; Will M. Tipton, "The Prince of Imposters," *Land of Sunshine* 8 (March 1899):164. Reavis, who had sold quit claims while the Surveyor General was investigating his claim, was sentenced to the penitentiary.

[43] *Peralta-Reavis vs. The United States,* pp. 407, 877–880; Powell, *Peralta Grant,* pp. 117–123. The evidence in the Peralta-Reavis case became a classic example of spurious documentation and was exhibited by the Department of Justice at the Chicago World's Fair and other expositions.

included grants, title papers, original Spanish documents, translations of the documents, and laws; affidavits, depositions, reports, petitions, notices, decrees, testimony, contracts, conveyances, powers of attorney, quit claim deeds, declarations, maps, sketches, field notes, opinions, reports of the surveyor general, applications for survey, correspondence, briefs, leases, defendant exhibits, plats, and decisions of the secretary of the interior; and opinions, orders, and decrees of the Court of Private Land Claims.[44] The second file of Spanish land-grant records, 1866–1908 (6 feet), contained the same kinds of documents.[45]

In 1955, the State Office of the Bureau of Land Management at Phoenix, then the custodian of the records of the former surveyor general of Arizona, proposed the transfer of the Spanish land-grant records to the National Archives, since they were no longer needed by that office. Later in the year, however, the state supervisor of the bureau was authorized to allow the Arizona State Department of Library and Archives to microfilm the records, and, accordingly, under an agreement made early in 1956, the records were microfilmed during that year on 26 rolls of microfilm.[46] Then, the original Spanish land-grant records were accessioned by the National Archives in October, 1958.

Other records of the surveyor general of Arizona relating to private land claims were received by the National Archives from the Land Office at Phoenix, in June, 1960, and placed in Record Group 49.[47] A journal of private land claims, 1879–95 (4 volumes), contains copies of Spanish documents, translations, and other documents relating to the claims. A docket of private grants (1 volume) is a record of the documents recorded in the journal described above and the actions of the Court of Private Land Claims on the claims. Another volume contains a duplicate copy of Rufus C. Hopkins' report on his mission to Sonora in 1879, which is referred to above. Private land-grant papers (5 boxes), contain a variety of documents similar to those in the pri-

---

[44] U.S. Survey of Federal Archives, *Inventory of Federal Archives in the States, Series VIII, The Department of the Interior, No. 3, Arizona* (Tucson, 1939), pp. 10–11. The reports on serials (nos. 469–495) on which the inventory was based contain lists of documents for each land grant. These reports are in the records of the U.S. Work Projects Administration, Survey of Federal Archives (Record Group 69), National Archives.

[45] U.S. Survey of Federal Archives, *Inventory of Federal Archives, Dept. of the Interior, Ariz.* pp. 11–12. The report on serials (no. 466) in the W.P.A. records referred to above contains lists of records of each grant.

[46] Letter from E. I. Rowland, State Supervisor, Bureau of Land Management, Phoenix, Ariz., Jan. 16, 1958.

[47] The description of records that follows is based upon a personal examination of the records.

vate land-grant records described above. Other items include surveyor general letters sent relating to private land claims, September 1, 1879–May 13, 1895 (3 volumes), and letters received relating to private land claims from the commissioner of the General Land Office, April 9, 1879–December 12, 1881 (1 volume). Other records in the National Archives containing material relating to land grants in Arizona are described in chapter seven, in the section on New Mexico.

Other records of the surveyor general of Arizona are now in the Federal Records Center for Region Nine at Bell, California. A file of letters received from the commissioner of the General Land Office, January, 1870–June, 1925 (67 volumes), includes decisions and instructions relative to Spanish and Mexican land grants, and surveys of the grants. A letters-sent book of the surveyor general, September, 1879–June, 1882 (1 volume), contains copies of letters sent regarding the examination of titles to private land claims. Other records include the proceedings of the Court of Private Land Claims, July, 1891–April, 1904 (1 volume), containing minutes and copies of legal documents relating to Arizona claims, and a register of documents filed with the court, February, 1892–June, 1899 (1 volume).[48] The court's case files relating to land grants in Arizona and related records, are described above in chapter seven, in the section on New Mexico, where there is also a description of a file relating to the Peralta-Reavis claim.[49]

A small collection of Arizona land-grant documents, 1825–1930 (200 items), is in the Arizona Historical Society Collection at Tucson.

In the same year in which the four original counties of Arizona were established, another act of the Arizona legislature, approved November 7, 1864, provided for the recording of grants of land received from the Mexican or United States governments in each county.[50] Inasmuch as most of the Gadsden Purchase, including Tucson and Tubac, was embraced by Pima County, it was the one primarily affected by the act. Under the provisions of the act, the county acquired copies of land grants made by Mexico in what became Arizona from collections of records in Mexico. Bound into one volume, this collection is in the Recorder's Office at Tucson.[51] In the same custody, there is an

---

48 U.S. Federal Records Center, Bell, Calif., *Preliminary Inventory of the Records of the Bureau of Land Management* (Record Group 49), comp. by Gilbert Dorame (Los Angeles, 1966), pp. 15–18.

49 Records of the Bureau of Land Management's central office in Washington, D.C., also contain materials relating to land grants in Arizona; see the description of these records in the section on New Mexico, chapter seven.

50 Arizona (Terr.), *Acts*, 1864, pp. 39–40.

51 Historical Records Survey, Arizona, *Inventory of the County Archives of Arizona, No. 10, Pima County (Tucson)* (Phoenix, 1938), pp. 41–42.

old book of records containing material relating to a number of Spanish and Mexican land grants, and two registers prepared in 1862, one of claims to lots in Tucson and the other of claims to the mission of Tucson, both containing entries for claims antedating the transfer of the territory to the United States. Records of claims to lots in presidios and pueblos had to be recreated during the American period, for the archives in which the grants made by the commandants had been recorded had perished.[52]

---

[52] "Report of the Surveyor General of Arizona," July 23, 1883, in U.S. Dept. of the Interior, *Annual Report*, 1883, p. 214; Wasson to Williamson, Dec. 25, 1879, BLM, SG Ariz., Lets. Sent PLC.

34

Ecclesiastical Records

SPANISH OCCUPATION OF PIMERÍA ALTA, on the northwestern frontier of New Spain, was furthered by the establishment of missions. The Society of Jesus, which was founded in 1534 and had become active in missionary work in foreign lands, was the order that introduced Christianity into the area. Fr. Eusebio Francisco Kino pioneered the missionary work of the Jesuits in Pimería Alta, after several years of labor in Lower California. In 1687, he established a mission at Dolores, on the San Miguel River in Sonora, and made that place his headquarters for the next twenty-four years while he founded other missions in Pimería Alta, visited Indian villages, and explored the region as far north as the Gila and Colorado rivers.[1] During the 1690s, he visited the Indians in the Santa Cruz River valley of southern Arizona, and in 1701, he established missions at Guevavi, near the later settlement of Nogales, and at San Xavier del Bac, south of present Tucson.[2] (These missions languished after the death of Kino in 1711, but were later revived.) The other missions established by Kino, on the upper waters of the rivers in northern Sonora, were Remedios, near the head of the San Miguel River, Magdalena, San Ignacio, Imuris, and Cocospera, farther west on the Magdalena River, and Santa María Suamca, near the head of the Santa Cruz River and not far from the present inter-

---

[1] Earl Jackson, *Tumacácori's Yesterdays* (Santa Fe, 1951), p. 18; Bancroft, *Ariz. and N. Mex.*, p. 352.

[2] John L. Kessell, *Mission of Sorrows: Jesuit Guevavi and the Pimas, 1691–1767* (Tucson, 1970), pp. 28–32. Maps showing the locations of the missions are in Bancroft, *Ariz. and N. Mex.*, p. 353; Kessel, *Guevavi*, p. 2; John A. Donohue, S.J., *After Kino: Jesuit Missions in Northwest-New Spain, 1711–1767* (Rome, St. Louis, 1969); and in Burrus, *Kino and Manje*.

national boundary. Farther west, on the Altar River, were Caborca, Tubutama, Sáric, and other missions. The missionaries taught the Indians agricultural and construction methods, introduced domestic animals, and made the missions the source of supplies for the presidios.

After the unsuccessful initial advance of the Jesuits into northern Pimería Alta at the beginning of the eighteenth century, contact was maintained with the Indians in that area by Fr. Luis Velarde, Kino's successor at Dolores, and by Fr. Agustín de Campos, at San Ignacio. Indians from the north visited the two missions, and recordings were made of their baptisms and marriages.[3] Campos also made tours to the north where he ministered to the Indians, but, unlike Kino, he kept no record of his travels. In these years, as in later times, the failure of the Spanish crown to give support and the hostility of the Apaches hindered the expansion and growth of the mission frontier. Eventually, in 1732, Juan Bautista de Anza, captain of Fronteras Presidio, escorted three new missionaries to the north. Fr. Ignacio X. Keller was taken to Suamca, on the headwaters of the Santa Cruz River. Farther down the river, Fr. Juan B. Grazhoffer was stationed at Guevavi, and Fr. Phelipe Segesser was stationed at San Xavier del Bac.[4] Indian settlements (*visitas*) that were served by the missionary at Guevavi included Sonoita, Arivaca, Tumacácori, and Tubac; and those served by the missionary of San Xavier del Bac were San Agustín, Santa Catarina, and Casa Grande. The missionaries rode circuit, performing baptisms and marriages and recording deaths. For nearly twenty years after the transfer of Fr. Gaspar Stiger from Guevavi and San Xavier to San Ignacio in 1736, except for a short residence by Fr. Francisco Pauer in 1751, San Xavier del Bac was also a *visita* of Guevavi.

The remaining years of Jesuit tenure in northern Pimería Alta were no more successful than the earlier ones. During the revolt of the Pima Indians in November, 1751, the missionaries at Guevavi and San Xavier del Bac were forced to flee south for their lives.[5] The buildings at the former place were ransacked, and those at the latter were destroyed. The missionaries and settlers at Tubutama garrisoned themselves in the church at first, but later fled to San Ignacio. The missionaries at Caborca and Sonoita, in Sonora, were killed by the Indians, and the mission property was destroyed. After Fr. Francisco Xavier Pauer became the missionary at Guevavi in 1753, he made visits to Tumacácori, Tubac, Tucson, and San Xavier del Bac. In 1758, Calabazas, a new settlement of Indians just below the junction of the Santa

---

[3] Kessell, *Guevavi*, pp. 32–39; Donohue, *After Kino*, pp. 10–12.

[4] Kessell, *Guevavi*, pp. 43, 54; Donohue, *After Kino*, pp. 68–69.

[5] Kessell, *Guevavi*, pp. 106–07, 137.

Cruz River and Sonoita Creek, also became a *visita* of Guevavi. After his brief sojourn at San Xavier del Bac, in 1756, was terminated by Indian hostility, Fr. Alonso Espinosa returned there in 1757 to reestablish the mission on a permanent basis.[6] Attempts by Fr. Bernardo Middendorf to establish missions at Santa Catarina in 1756 and Tucson in 1757 were thwarted by Indian attacks which forced him to flee. Thereafter, Tucson continued as a *visita* of San Xavier del Bac. The Pima and Papago Indians tolerated the missions in Pimería Alta, because they provided refuges for their families and places of recuperation when they returned from warring expeditions,[7] but the Apaches continually harassed both the red and white settlers in the Santa Cruz Valley and made it necessary for the missionaries to have escorts on their travels.

By becoming too powerful in political affairs and too contentious in religious and educational spheres, the Jesuits incurred the enmity of European heads of state. In 1767, after the French and Portuguese governments had already expelled the Jesuits, Charles III of Spain ordered their expulsion from New Spain. In 1777, the Society of Jesus was suppressed by the Pope and was not restored until 1814. Upon receipt of the king's order of expulsion in Sonora in 1767, the missionaries of Pimería Alta were conducted by military escort to Mátape, where fifty-one of them were assembled from the missions of Sinaloa and Sonora.[8] From that point, they were conducted on the long journey to Spain, some dying on the way from hardship and deprivation. The survivors were imprisoned at Cádiz from whence, in 1775, most of the Sinaloa and Sonora missionaries were taken to various religious houses in Spain. The former Jesuit missions in Pimería Alta were placed in charge of royal commissioners, who wasted their property.[9]

Since the Franciscans were already active in missions in New Mexico and Texas, they were the logical choice to take over the Jesuit missions in Sonora. The Jesuit missions of Pimería Alta and Baja were soon occupied by Franciscan missionaries of the College of Santa Cruz

[6] Ibid., p. 139; Donohue, "Unlucky Jesuit Mission of Bac," pp. 133–34.

[7] Bancroft, *Hist. North Mex. States*, 1:564–66.

[8] Peter M. Dunne, S.J., "The Expulsion of the Jesuits from New Spain, 1767," *Mid-America* 19 (Jan. 1937):21; Kessell, *Guevavi*, pp. 179–86. Donohue, *After Kino*, pp. 150–2.

[9] Bancroft, *Hist. North. Mex. States*, 1:576. See ibid., p. 563 n. 23, for the names of missionaries who served in the Pimería Alta missions, pp. 578–80 for a list of Jesuits who served in Sonora and Sinaloa and their dates of service, and p. 543 for a list of missionaries in Pimería Alta in 1750. Another list of Sonoran missionaries is in Rafael de Zelis, S.J., *Catálogo de los sugetos de la Compañía de Jesús que formaban la Provincia de México el día del arresto, 25 junio de 1767* (Mexico, 1871), pp. 134–35.

of Querétaro, which sent fourteen of its members to Sonora.[10] Fr. Juan C. Gil de Bernabé arrived at Guevavi in the summer of 1768, but was carried away sick in 1771.[11] The Indians soon deserted the mission, and it was never reoccupied. Fr. Francisco T. H. Garcés reached San Xavier del Bac in June, 1768, and from that base, carried on missionary work and explorations among the Papagos, Pimas, Yumas, and Apaches.[12] A large adobe brick church that was constructed at Bac by the Franciscans is still standing. Early in the Franciscan era, Tumacácori was raised to mission status by the assignment of a resident missionary. Franciscans served as chaplains at Tubac and, later, at Tucson.[13]

Franciscans continued to serve as missionaries at San Xavier del Bac and Tumacácori until measures adopted by the Mexican government for the expulsion of Spaniards and the secularization of missions forced their withdrawal.[14] Both missions were abandoned by the late 1820s. Restoration of the church at San Xavier del Bac was begun in 1906 by the bishop of Tucson, with the Franciscans returning permanently in 1912. It has served as the mission church of the Papago Indians for many years.[15] Tumacácori was made a national monument in 1908 to protect the ruins of the mission, and the church has been reroofed. Entries in the parish registers regarding inhabitants of the villages of Arizona were made by the parish priest at San Ignacio, Sonora, into the 1840s.[16]

Late in 1775, Frs. Francisco T. H. Garcés and Tomas Eixarch, Franciscan friars, selected sites for missions among the Yuma Indians at the junction of the Gila and Colorado rivers. Garcés went on to Cali-

---

[10] Marion A. Habig, O.F.M., "The Builders of San Xavier del Bac," *Southw. Hist. Quar.* 41 (Oct. 1937):156–57.

[11] Kessell, *Guevavi*, p. 190.

[12] *New Catholic Encyclopedia*, 6:283.

[13] Bancroft, *Hist. North. Mex. States*, 1:563 n. 23; Victor R. Stoner, "Fray Pedro Antonio de Arriquibar, Chaplain of the Royal Fort at Tucson," ed. by Henry F. Dobyns, *Ariz. and the West* 1 (Spring 1959):74. Lists of the names of Franciscans who served in Pimería Alta and Sonora are in Bancroft, *Hist. North. Mex. States*, 1:689 n. 56; and in Zephyrin Engelhardt, O.F.M., *The Franciscans in Arizona* (Harbor Springs, Mich., 1899), pp. 222–23. A list prepared January 3, 1791 by Henrique de Grimarest, an official at Arizpe, contains the names of twenty-six Franciscans who served in Sonora in 1790, fifteen of whom are not in Bancroft's lists cited above (Henry F. Dobyns and Paul H. Ezell, eds., "Sonoran Missionaries in 1790," *N. Mex. Hist. Rev.* 34 (Jan. 1959):52–54. This list is from the Archivo General de la Nación, Misiones, vol. 13.

[14] Bancroft, *Ariz. and N. Mex.*, p. 406.

[15] Nancy W. Newhall, *Mission San Xavier del Bac* (San Francisco, 1954), pp. 31–32.

[16] Jackson, *Tumacácori's Yesterdays*, pp. 55–56.

fornia with Juan Bautista de Anza, while Eixarch wintered among the Indians to prepare them for mission life.[17] Garcés returned in 1780 with three more missionaries and some soldiers and settlers, and established the missions of Purísima Concepción and San Pedro y San Pablo de Bicuñer on the western side of the Colorado, that eventually became southeastern California. These missions served as way stations on the road to the coast settlements in California. In July, 1781, the Yumas massacred Garcés and his companion, Fr. Juan A. Barreneche, at Concepción, Frs. Juan Díaz and Matías Moreno at Bicuñer, and all of the other persons at the two missions. The missions were not reestablished, and the Anza trail to California was not used for many years.

During most of the period from 1768 until the end of the mission era, the missions in southern Arizona were subordinate to the Franciscan College of Santa Cruz of Querétaro. In 1783, however, the missions of Pimería Baja and Alta formed into the Custody of San Carlos of Sonora, of which Fr. Sebastián Flores became the superior.[18] The arrangement was not successful, and, in 1791, the missions were again placed under the college, to which they remained subordinate until the suppression of the missions.

Only fragments of the records of the missions of Arizona have survived. Historians have found none for San Xavier del Bac.[19] Fragmentary baptismal, marriage, and burial records of Guevavi, 1739–67, are in a book entitled "Tubaca y Otros" in the archives of the Diocese of Tucson.[20] Fragments of Tubac mission books in the Bancroft Library of the University of California, Berkeley, California, include a register of marriages and burials, 1814–24, and an entry for a burial on January 12, 1848.[21] A book entitled "De Calabasas Bautismos," in the archives

---

[17] Bancroft, *Ariz. and N. Mex.*, p. 717. Eixarch kept a diary of his winter on the Colorado, which is mentioned below.

[18] Engelhardt, *Franciscans in Ariz.*, pp. 171–73: Habig, "Builders of San Xavier del Bac," pp. 157–162. Information regarding the College of Santa Cruz of Querétaro and its records is in chapter 18, in the section on Texas.

[19] Bishop John B. Salpointe took the records of San Xavier del Bac to Tucson, to keep them from being lost. He later sent three books containing records of baptisms and burials to Washington, for exhibit at Philadelphia (testimony of John B. Salpointe, June 17, 1895, in *United States Defendant in the United States Court of Private Land Claims, Santa Fe District, James Addison Peraltareavis and Doña Sofia Loreto Micaela de Peraltareavis ... Plaintiffs vs. the United States of America, Defendant, No. 110, Peralta Grant*, (Santa Fe, 1895), pp. 950–52. It is possible that the writer who furnished the list of missionaries at San Xavier del Bac, 1768–1828, published in the Tucson *Dos Republicas*, Sept. 16, 1877, used the records of that mission. The list is reproduced in Bancroft, *Ariz. and N. Mex.*, p. 379 n. 12.

[20] Kessell, *Guevavi*, pp. 68 n. 51, 208.

[21] Bancroft, *Ariz. and N. Mex.*, pp. xxxvii, 383 n. 22; Hammond, *Guide to Ms. Colls.*, p. 181.

of the Diocese of Tucson, contains fragmentary baptismal, marriage, and burial records of Tumacácori, 1768–1825.[22] Microfilms of these records are in the Arizona Historical Society Collection, the University of Arizona Library, and the St. Louis University Library.

Censuses of mission settlements listing the names of residents were sometimes made by missionaries. A 1796 census of Tumacácori, made by Fr. Mariano Bordoy, gives the names and ethnic groups of 103 people, including married couples, widowers, single men, widows, girls, and boys, and contains a report on the condition of the mission. Except for three Spaniards, the listees were Papago, Yaqui, Opata, and Pima Indians. This census was found by Antonio Nakayama, a Mexican historian, in the archives of the bishop of Sinaloa (Culiacán), and was copied in 1949 by Alfred P. Whiting, who later published it.[23] A census of Tucson was found by the same historian in the same repository and was sent by the bishop of Sinaloa to the bishop of Los Angeles, who sent it, in 1942, to the bishop of Tucson for the archives of the diocese.[24] This census was first published by Bernice Cosulich in the *Arizona Daily Star*, October 18, 1942, and has been republished from a manuscript of the census given to the Arizona Historical Society by George Chambers in 1969. The date of 1820 has been ascribed to both published versions, but Henry F. Dobyns presents evidence, based on a study of the careers of soldiers listed in the census and other material, that indicates the Tucson census was prepared in January, 1797, at the time of a visit by the vicar general of the Diocese of Sonora for presentation to him.[25] Compiled by Fr. Pedro de Arriquibar, chaplain of the presidio, the census contains the names of heads of households and their wives; the number of children and servants; the names of 27 men who were unmarried or did not have their families with them; and the names of 102 soldiers and 79 Spanish settlers — a total of 395 persons, some of whose descendants are now living in southern Arizona.[26]

The fragments that remain of the mission books supply information on the history of the missions, the missionaries who served at them, the Pimas and Papagos attached to them, and the white settlers in

---

[22] Stoner, "Fray Pedro Antonio de Arriquibar," p. 74 n. 15; Kessell, *Guevavi*, pp. 68 n. 51, 208.

[23] Alfred F. Whiting, ed., "The Tumacácori Census of 1796," *The Kiva* 19 (Fall 1953):1–12.

[24] Stoner, "Fray Pedro Antonio de Arriquibar," p. 75 n. 23.

[25] Henry F. Dobyns, "The 1797 Population of the Presidio of Tucson," *Jour. Ariz. Hist.* 13 (Autumn 1972):205.

[26] Karen S. Collins, ed., "Fray Pedro de Arriquibar's Census of Tucson, 1820," *Jour. Ariz. Hist.* 11 (Spring 1970):18–22. An inventory of the chapel is with the census but is not published.

the surrounding country. The records of the head missions contain entries concerning the *visitas* that were visited by the missionaries. The missionaries ministered to the military personnel at the presidios of Tubac and Tucson, baptizing their children, performing marriages, and administering the last rites — all duly recorded in the registers. The same services were performed for whites in the neighborhoods of the missions. The Guevavi record book has been described as the most important single source for the history of that mission.

The records of the missions in northern Sonora are useful for information regarding the Indians, missionaries, and Spaniards who lived in southern Arizona. Indians from Arizona frequently visited the missions in Sonora, which were more regularly supplied with missionaries, taking along their children for baptism, and women whom they wished to marry. Padres attached to the missions made tours of the Indian towns in Arizona, baptizing children, performing marriages, and administering the last rites. Missionaries and chaplains moved around; those who served in Arizona served at other times at different places in Sonora. Spanish military personnel served in the presidios of Sonora on both sides of what became the Arizona-Sonora boundary. Wherever service was rendered, whether north or south of the border, the Jesuits and Franciscans made regular recordings in their mission books.

Alphonse Louis Pinart, a French linguist and collector who traveled in Sonora, collected the records of a number of missions. These were later acquired by Hubert H. Bancroft, whose collection was purchased in 1905 by the University of California at Berkeley.[27] These Sonora mission records are as follows:[28]

San Francisco del Atí: Register of baptisms, 1757–1827 (1 vol., 85 pp.), including some entries from San Antonio de Oquitoa and Tubutama.

La Purísima Concepción de Caborca: Register of baptisms, 1764–69; 1820–22 (2 folders, 10, 6 pp.). Register of burials and marriages, 1790–1803 (1 folder, 14 pp.).

Santiago de Cocóspera: Register of baptisms, 1822–36 (1 folder). Register of burials, 1822–36 (1 folder).

Nuestra Señora del Pópulo del Bisanig (visita): Register of baptisms, 1780–1803 (1 folder, 65 pp.). Register of marriages, 1762–78 (1 folder, 20 pp.).

---

[27] Pinart is reported to have stolen the records of Magdalena mission (Lange and Riley, *Journals of Adolph F. Bandelier*, 2:250), and apparently acquired others in the same fashion (Kessell, *Guevavi*, p. 32 n. 29).

[28] Hammond, *Guide to Ms. Colls.*, pp. 177, 180–82. All of these mission records in the Pinart Collection in the Bancroft Library are on microfilm which can be borrowed on interlibrary loan.

San Antonio de Oquitoa: Register of baptisms, Jan. 27, 1757–Jan. 26, 1845 (1 folder); also includes records of episcopal visitations in 1821 and 1845, and of a visitation by a commissary prefect in 1822.

San Diego de Pitiqui (visita): Register of baptisms, 1772–1801; 1826 (2 folders, 64 pp.). Register of marriages, 1772–78 (1 folder, 8 pp.). Register of burials, 1768–97 (1 folder, 10 pp.).

San Ignacio de Cabórica: Register of baptisms, 1720–1812 (2 folders), with record of episcopal visitations in 1825 and 1837. Register of marriages, 1713–37 (2 folders), and fragments of a census report, 1768. Register of burials, 1697–1788 (1 vol.).

San Pedro y San Pablo de Tubutama: Register of baptisms *(bautismos)*, 1768–1806 (1 folder, 49 pages), includes its *visita*, Santa Teresa.

Santa María Magdalena: Register of baptisms *(bautismos)*, 1698–1824 (4 folders). Register of marriages and burials *(casamientos y entierros)*, 1702–1825 (3 folders).

Santa María Suamca: Register of baptisms *(bautismos)*, 1732–68 (1 folder), with a record of an episcopal visitation in 1737. Register of baptisms and marriages *(bautismos y casamientos)*, 1743–55 (1 folder). Register of marriages and burials *(casamientos y entierros)*, 1736–68 (1 folder).

Jesuit missions established on the northern frontier of Mexico from the early 1600s on were under the jurisdiction of the father provincial of that order, in Mexico City. He selected missionaries for service on the frontier, appointed visitors to inspect the missions, sent out instructions, and received reports, on the basis of which he reported to the father general in Rome. Another official in Mexico was the father procurator, who purchased supplies for the missions. Father visitors made periodic visits to the missions to ascertain their condition and supervise their activities and, using information gathered on the tours, prepared reports for transmittal to the father provincial. After 1725, the father visitors were under a visitor general, or vice provincial, who was designated for northern New Spain. The vice provincial inspected missions, examined their records and financial conditions, and, after consulting the local visitor, transferred missionaries.[29] The missionary in charge of a group of missions was known as the father rector. In Pimería, he was located at Dolores and, later, at San Ignacio.

The records of the Jesuit father provincial and of colleges, houses, and missions throughout Mexico, that were seized at the time of the expulsion in 1767, have been preserved in public archives. The principal repository of the Jesuit central archives is the Archivo General de la Nación in Mexico City (primarily the Historia and Misiones sec-

---

[29] Donohue, *After Kino*, pp. 20, 22, 30, 31–34, 43, 44, 61, 84.

tions). Correspondence of Sonoran missionaries, relations, declarations, reports, diaries, and catalogs of personnel are in the Historia section.[30] Kino's important historical memoir of Pimería Alta, prepared from manuscripts in his possession at Dolores that have since disappeared, makes up most of volume twenty-seven of the Misiones section.[31] Missionaries wrote annual letters to their superiors, who prepared reports from them on the condition of the missions, that were sometimes sent with copies of letters from the missionaries to the father provincial in Mexico City. The missionaries also wrote directly to the father provincial at times. These letters, running from 1573 to 1763, are also in the Misiones section.[32] Reproductions of the annual letters, obtained by H. E. Bolton in 1937, are in the Bancroft Library of the University of California,[33] which also has microfilm of twenty-seven volumes of material relating to the Jesuits from the Archivo General de la Nación.[34] Other documents on the Sonora missions are in the Archivo Histórico del Instituto Nacional de Antropología e Historia, México, D.F.[35]

Documents on the Jesuits are in other repositories in Mexico City also. The Archivo Histórico de Hacienda contains Jesuit materials that were in the Colegio Maximo de San Pedro y San Pablo, the major Jesuit seminary in Mexico City, and the business office of the Mexican Province, which was also located in Mexico City. The Ramo de Temporalidades in this repository contains 121 bundles, mostly from the Jesuit procurator's files, that include papers relating to Jesuit properties, lists of supplies to be furnished to the missions by the procurator, letters and memorials of missionaries, and letters and reports of the father visitor to the father provincial.[36] In the same repository, there are censuses of San Xavier del Bac and Tucson, 1766, giving the names of individuals in family groups.[37] These archives have been largely unexploited until recently and will probably be shown to contain other materials on Pimería Alta. Reproductions from the Archivo Histórico de Hacienda are in the Pius XII Memorial Library at St. Louis University

[30] Bolton, *Guide to Arch. Mex.*, pp. 23–24, 52–55; see especially vols. 16–17:308, 333, 391–93 of the Historia section.

[31] Ibid., p. 74.

[32] Ibid., pp. 74–75; Peter J. Dunne, S.J., "Jesuit Annual Letters in the Bancroft Library," *Mid-America* 20 (Oct. 1938):264.

[33] Dunne, "Jesuit Annual Letters," p. 265.

[34] Fisher, *Preliminary Guide*, p. 12.

[35] Carrera Stampa, *Archivalia mexicana*, p. 48.

[36] Donohue, *After Kino*, p. 10 n. 9, and passim; Mexico, Ministerio de Hacienda y Crédito Público, *Guía del Archivo Histórico de Hacienda*, leaves 73, 74, 76; Greenleaf and Meyer, *Research in Mexican History*, p. 78.

[37] Mexico, *Guía del Archivo Histórico de Hacienda*, leaves 73, 84–85.

and in the University of San Francisco Library, San Francisco, California. A collection of royal orders and decrees on the expulsion of the Jesuits, 1767–70, and later ones of 1774–94, are in the Biblioteca Nacional, where there is also a record of the proceedings of a conference of ecclesiastical and military officers at San Ignacio, May 15–17, 1754, on Indian unrest in Pimería Alta.[38] An undated diary by Father Kino is in the records of the Secretaria de Relaciones Exteriores.[39]

Letters of Father Kino that were discovered in Guanajuato, Mexico, in the possession of a Jesuit of the Province of Mexico, have been reported as being in preparation for publication by Fr. Perez Alonso, S.J.[40]

Sonora was part of the Diocese of Durango at first, but, pursuant to a royal order of February 4, 1781, it was placed, along with Sinaloa and the Californias, in the new Diocese of Sonora.[41] The see was at Arizpe, where the new bishop arrived in 1783. Bishops visited Pimería in 1725 and 1737,[42] and in 1821, the bishop of Sonora visited Arizona.[43] An apparently incomplete collection of records of the Archdiocese of Durango includes material on the administration of church revenues.[44] A record of proceedings of the cathedral cabildo of Durango is in the Museo Nacional in Mexico City. The archives in the episcopal residence of the bishop of Sonora in Hermosillo, dating from 1795, include correspondence and other documents, some of which relate to Arizona.[45] Selections from these documents are on microfilm in the University of Arizona Library.

Materials concerning the Franciscan missions of Pimería Alta are also in Mexican archives. Missionary letters, reports, memorials, diaries, and reports of visitations, and communications of officials of the College of Santa Cruz of Querétaro and the bishop of Sonora, dating from 1768, are in various sections of the Archivo General de la Nación.[46] The writers of these documents include Antonio de los Reyes,[47] Francisco T. H. Garcés, Francisco A. Barbastro, and Juan Díaz, visitor

---

[38] Bolton, *Guide to Arch. Mex.*, pp. 19, 210; Kessell, *Guevavi*, p. 134 n. 35.

[39] Bolton, *Guide*, p. 235.

[40] Southwestern Mission Research Center, Inc., Tucson, Ariz., *SMRC Newsletter*:1 (February 1967).

[41] Bancroft, *Hist. North. Mex. States.*, 1:678.

[42] Donohue, *After Kino*, pp. 17, 83.

[43] Bancroft, *Ariz. and N. Mex.*, p. 406.

[44] Bolton, *Guide to Arch. Mex.*, p. 408.

[45] Ibid., p. 467.

[46] Ibid., pp. 23, 25, 26, 28, 32, 37, 38, 71, 72, 92, 151, 153, 179, 199, 452.

[47] Documents by Father Reyes that have been published include a report on the missions of Sonora: Antonio de los Reyes, O.F.M., *Copia del manifiesto estado de la provincias de Sonora, en 20 de avril de 1772* (México, D.F., 1945), and a memorial

of the missions of Sonora. The documents supply information on the condition and administration of the missions, financial support of the missionaries, the custody of San Carlos of Sonora, and the relations with the college. Other records for Sonora of the same nature, 1766–1820, are in the records of the College of Santa Cruz of Querétaro, along with decrees and reports of the council of the college.[48] The Fondo Franciscano in the Biblioteca Nacional includes documents on Sonora and Sinaloa for 1529–1847.[49] A representation of Francisco Barbastro, ca. 1782, protesting the establishment of the Custody of San Carlos of Sonora is in the public library at Guadalajara.[50]

The activities of the Jesuits in Mexico and other parts of North and South America were carried on under the general direction of the headquarters of the Society of Jesus in Rome. The Generalate, as the headquarters was known, became the custodian of the central archives of the society (Archivum General). Considerable destruction of the society's records occurred at the time of its suppression in 1777, but extensive and valuable series of the records have been preserved.[51] The Archivum Romanum Societatis Iesu (ARSI) includes outgoing and incoming letters, catalogs of institutions and personnel of the Jesuit provinces, acts of the general and provincial congregations, general and particular histories of the society, documents on controversial matters, manuscripts of Jesuits, death notices, and two original maps, 1695, 1696–97, by Fr. Eusebio F. Kino. Included in the holdings of the Generalate are the annual letters received from the father provincial of the Mexican Province. Some of the series relating to Mexico are incomplete, but the extant materials supplement those in the Archivo General de la Nación in Mexico, and other collections of Jesuit documents.[52] Another branch of the Jesuit central archives is the Fondo Gesuitico in Rome,

---

on the condition of the missions that includes a census of the missions: "Memorial sobre las misiones de Sonora, 1772," *Boletín del Archivo General de México* 9 (1938):276–320.

[48] Bolton, *Guide to Arch. Mex.*, pp. 388–91.

[49] Carrera Stampa, *Archivalia mexicana*, p. 111.

[50] Bolton, *Guide to Arch. Mex.*, p. 382. A published report by Father Barbastro and some related documents concerning the missions of Sonora and Sinaloa have been published: Lino Gomez Canedo, ed., *Sonora hacia fines del siglo XVIII; un informe del misionero franciscano Fray Francisco Antonio Barbastro, con otros documentos complementarios* (Guadalajara, 1971).

[51] A history of the general archives of the Society of Jesus is in Thomas Hughes, S.J., *A History of the Society of Jesus in North America, Colonial and Federal*, 3 vols. in 4 (New York, 1907–19), 1:46–79.

[52] Additional description of the records is in Ernest J. Burrus, S.J., "Mexican Historical Documents in the Central Jesuit Archives," *Manuscripta* 12 (Nov. 1968):133–61; and Josephus Teschitel, S.J., "Archivum Romanum Societatis Iesu, (ARSI)," *Archivum* 4 (1954):145–52.

consisting of the records of the Procurator General of the society. He was the treasurer of the society and the chief liaison officer with the various papal congregations.

Until recent years, the archives of the Society of Jesus in Rome were closed to historical investigators, except those who were members of the society. However, Herbert E. Bolton gained access and searched in those archives for documents on Eusebio F. Kino, obtaining photoreproductions on materials that he found. More recently, Ernest J. Burrus, a member of the Jesuit Historial Institute, supervised the microfilming of Jesuit documents for the Knights of Columbus Vatican Film Library in the Pius XII Memorial Library at St. Louis University (3655 West Pine Boulevard, St. Louis, Missouri 63108).[53] The 185 rolls of microfilm in that repository contain documents on Jesuit activities in North and South America during the years 1570–1850.[54]

Measures taken by the Jesuits to record and publish their own history include the establishment of a Jesuit Historical Institute in Rome. It publishes a historical journal *(Archivum Historicum Societatis Iesu)*, a collection of monographs *(Biblioteca Instituti Historici Societatis Iesu)*, and a documentary publication series *(Monumenta Historica Societatis Iesu)* which was taken over in 1929 from Spanish Jesuits who had founded it in Madrid in 1894.

Copies of the microfilm collected by Burrus on the Jesuits in northern Mexico and Arizona, during his many years of investigations in Mexican, European, and United States repositories, are in the Knights of Columbus microfilm collection in St. Louis. For use in his publication projects, he also has microfilm of most of the materials in Rome. In 1970, Fr. Charles W. Polzer, a Jesuit of the Province of California and a historian, did research in Mexico City on the Jesuits, in the Archivo General de la Nación and the Archivo Histórico de Hacienda, Ramo de Temporalidades.[55] Microfilm that he obtained from that section relating to missions and *visitas* in Arizona, and to correspondence of missionaries of Sonora, Sinaloa, Chihuahua, and Lower California, is also in the Knights of Columbus microfilm collection, and a copy is in the Kino House in Tucson. This house was established in May, 1969, as the residence and field office of the American section of the Jesuit Historical Institute, with Father Polzer in charge. Kino House also has copies of some of the Jesuitica in the Pius XII Memorial Library at St. Louis

---

[53] Burrus, "Research Opportunities in Italian Archives," pp. 440–41, 451.

[54] John F. Bannon, S.J., "The Saint Louis University Collection of Jesuitica Americana," *Hisp. Amer. Hist. Rev.* 37 (Feb. 1957):82–88, describes the microfilmed series.

[55] Letter from Charles W. Polzer, S.J., Nov. 20, 1972; *SMRC Newsletter* 4 (Nov. 1970).

University and several rolls of microfilm of privately owned mission records, that are made available to scholars. Investigations into materials in Mexican archives relating to the Jesuits were still being pursued and in 1973 were under the charge of Félix Zubillaga, S.J., of the Jesuit Historical Institute in Rome.

Other sources relating to missions and missionaries are in the Arizona Historical Society. The papers of Fr. Victor R. Stoner, an early investigator of Arizona mission history, include typed and photographic extracts from Arizona and Sonora mission records, and other material on Fr. Eusebio F. Kino, the Hopi Indians, Fr. Marcos de Niza, and Coronado.[56] Other items include letters of Jesuit missions of Lower California and northern Mexico, 1697–1745 (165 pages, typed), and burial records of Father Kino, 1711 (photocopies). Original manuscripts concerning the travels of Fr. Jacobo Sedelmayr, that were presented to the society by W. J. Holliday, include his 1746 relation, his 1748 diary, an anonymous diary of 1750, and a letter to the viceroy regarding the pacification of the Indians of Pimería Alta.[57] Materials concerning the Franciscans include Fr. Antonio de los Reyes' report on the administration of the missions of Sonora, 1772 (40 pages, photostat); a file of documents by Fathers Reyes and Barbastro, 1781–92, on the dispute over the Custody of San Carlos (in the Byron Ivancovich Collection);[58] and a 1797 inventory of the furnishings of the chapel of the presidio of Tucson.[59] Microfilm of miscellaneous documents on eighteenth-century church activities, from the cathedral archives at Hermosillo and Culiacán, and the Jesuit papers in St. Louis University Library are also in the society's holdings.

The Bancroft Library of the University of California has some small collections of Jesuit and Franciscan materials. Included are letters on the banishment of the Jesuits from Mexico.[60] A collection of materials for the history of Sonora, 1658–1778 (964 pages), consisting of transcripts from the Archivo General de la Nación, Mexico, contains letters and reports by missionaries, among them several by Jacobo Sedelmayr, 1746–49.[61] Documents for the ecclesiastical and civil history of Nueva Vizcaya, ca. 1596–1750 (766 pages), consist of reports, correspondence, and other documents relating to the activities of Jesuit and

---

[56] Colley, *Guide to Ms. Colls. Ariz. Hist. Soc.*, p. 178.

[57] Ibid., p. 168.

[58] Ibid., p. 120.

[59] Ibid., pp. 28, 166.

[60] Bancroft, *Hist. North Mex. States*, 1 :xxxii, xxxviii.

[61] Bancroft, *Literary Industries*, p. 630; Hammond, *Guide to Ms. Colls. of the Bancroft Lib.*, p. 227. Most of these materials were printed in the *Documentos para la historia de México*, 3rd and 4th series.

Franciscan missionaries and governmental and military matters.[62] Selected documents from the archives of the College of Santa Cruz of Querétaro on the missions of Sonora, 1729–1842 (5 folders; typescripts and photocopies), are in the Bancroft Library.[63] Original Kino items include a report of May 3–November 4, 1698, concerning Apache hostilities and aid in resisting them given by the Pimas and Sobaipuris; a report of February 5, 1703, to the viceroy on the history of existing missions and plans for additional ones in Pimería Alta and Upper California; and a report of May 10, 1704, to the king, describing his mission work.[64] Papers of Phelipe Segesser de Brunegg, 1689–1761 (377 pages, photocopies), include correspondence with his family in Switzerland, with fellow Jesuits, and others, and lists of supplies for the missions.[65] A long letter written by Fr. Bernardo Middendorff, March 3, 1757, describing his journey, with the expedition of Gov. Juan Antonio de Mendoza of Sonora, from his mission at Tucson to the Gila River, has been published.[66] Papers of Fr. Diego Bringas de Manzaneda, 1773–95 (18 pages, photocopies and typescripts), include a large scale map of a journey he made in 1795 from Sonora to the Gila River, on an expedition for which no diary has been discovered; a smaller map by Bringas; a geographical description of Sonora, without date or signature (probably prepared between 1772 and 1775); a sketch map of the province; and an unsigned census of the missions of Sonora.[67] Other items are inventories of property at Tumacácori and San Xavier del Bac. Materials relating to the Jesuits and Franciscans in Pimería Alta are also in other repositories. A lengthy account of the Pima uprising of 1751 and its aftermath by Fr. Salvador Ignacio de la Peña,

---

[62] Hammond, *Guide to Ms. Colls.*, p. 60.

[63] Ibid., p. 93.

[64] Ibid., pp. 107, 219.

[65] Ibid., p. 213.

[66] Morgan and Hammond, *Guide to Ms. Colls., Bancroft Lib.*, p. 78. A facsimile and an English translation of this letter are in Arthur D. Gardiner, trans. and ed., "Letter of Father Middendorff, S.J., Dated from Tucson 3 March 1757," *The Kiva* 22 (June 1957):1–10.

[67] Hammond, *Guide to Ms. Colls.*, p. 24. These documents and a translation of the geographical description are printed in Paul H. Ezell, "Fray Diego Bringas: A Forgotten Cartographer of Sonora," *Imago Mundi* 13 (October 1956):151–58. A report by Bringas reviewing the history of the region during the eighteenth century until early 1796, summarizing the findings of his 1795 trip to the Gila River and urging the king to reestablish missions and presidios on the northern Pima frontier, is on the University of Arizona's microfilm copy of the Civezza Collection, and is also available on another microfilm copy from the cathedral archives in Hermosillo. A translation of this report has been prepared by Bernard L. Fontana, ethnologist at the Arizona State Museum, and Daniel Matson, lecturer in anthropology at the University of Arizona, for publication (letter from Bernard L. Fontana, February 28, 1973).

missionary at Cucurpe and secretary on Fr. Joseph de Utrera's visitation to Pimería in 1754, is in the Library of the University of California at Los Angeles (microfilm in the University of Arizona Library).[68] Letters written by Father Kino to the Duchess of Aveiro of Madrid, a benefactress of foreign missions, and to several fathers, 1680–87 (33 items), relating to Lower California and Sonora, were purchased in 1922, for $18,750, from Maggs Brothers of London by the Henry E. Huntington Library, San Marino, California.[69] Copies of an inventory and census of San Xavier del Bac, June 29, 1768, are in the Santa Barbara Mission Archives.[70] An original letter from Father Kino to Fr. Juan de Estrada, November 2, 1698, and another to Fr. Antonio Leal, April 8, 1702, are in the Beinecke Collection of Western Americana at Yale University, New Haven, Connecticut.[71] In the same collection, there is an account by Fr. Juan Ortiz Zapata of a visitation to the missions of Nueva Vizcaya in 1693, with a general description and history of that province written by an unknown Jesuit late in the seventeenth century; a letter from Fr. José Ximenez, guardian of the College of Santa Cruz of Querétaro to the viceroy, December 24, 1808, urging the establishment of missions on the Gila River, and the viceroy's reply of January 6, 1809; a report by Fr. Juan A. Balthasar on the missionaries of Sonora, 1744; and a communication from Viceroy Revilla Gigedo to Balthasar, February 22, 1753, with an opinion of February 15, 1753.[72] Diaries by Fr. Francisco T. H. Garcés of his expeditions of 1774–75 and 1775–76 (mentioned later) are in the Manuscript Division of the Library of Congress.[73] Garcés' diary of 1775–76, and one by Fr. Pedro Font, who accompanied Anza on his 1775–76 expedition to California, were bought by the Library of Congress in 1901 from Dr. Nicolas León of Guadalupe Hidalgo, Mexico. Another copy of the Garcés diary of 1775–76 was purchased from Dr. León in 1897 by the Bureau of American Ethnology of the Smithsonian Institution. Copies of letters of Father Garcés, including one to Fr. Diego Jiménez, 1762; one to Captain Anza, July 29, 1768; and three to Gov. Juan de

[68] Kessell, *Guevavi*, p. 108 n. 47.

[69] Herbert E. Bolton, "Archives and Trails," *Calif. Monthly* 37 (October 1936):40.

[70] Geiger, *Calendar of Santa Barbara Mission Archives*, p. 253.

[71] Published in Yale University Library, Beinecke Rare Book and Manuscript Library, *Stevenson and Kino: Manuscripts from the Edwin J. Beinecke Collection of Robert Louis Stevenson and the Frederick W. and Carrie S. Beinecke Collection of Western Americana* (New Haven, 1963), and in Ernest J. Burrus, S.J.., *La Obra cartográfica de la provincia mexicana de la Compañia de Jesús (1567–1967)*, 2 vols. (Madrid, 1967), 1:149–65, 171–74.

[72] Goddard, Kritzler, and Hanna, *Catalogue of the Beinecke Collection*, pp. 5, 46, 57, 85.

[73] U.S. Library of Congress, *Handbook of Mss.*, p. 22.

Pineda of Sonora, 1768–69; are in the Newberry Library, Chicago, Illinois.[74] Kino's diary of his expedition with Capt. Diego Carrasco, from Dolores to the Gila River and the Gulf of California, September 22–October 18, 1698, is in the Thomas Gilcrease Institute of American History and Art in Tulsa, Oklahoma.[75] The diary that Fr. Tomás Eixarch kept of his winter on the Colorado River among the Yuma Indians, December 4, 1775–May 11, 1776, was copied by Fr. Pedro Font, a member of Anza's second expedition, and is part of Font's complete diary in the John Carter Brown Library, Providence, Rhode Island.[76]

Extensive materials relating to the Jesuits in Sonora, Lower California, and Sinaloa in the seventeenth and eighteenth centuries, and some relating to the Franciscans, are in the Latin American manuscript section in the University of Texas Library. The W. B. Stephens Collection (microreproductions in the University of San Francisco Library) includes missionary letters, reports and diaries; inventories of missions;[77] reports on visitations; general reports on the missions; and catalogs of missionaries. The writers include Eusebio F. Kino, Jacobo Sedelmayr, Bernardo Middendorff, Agustín de Campos, José Garrucho, and Visitors General José de Utrera, Ignacio Lizasoaín, and Manuel Aguirre.[78] In the same collection, there is another version of Francisco T. H. Garcés's diary of 1775–76,[79] which one specialist considers to be the original manuscript.[80] Another Franciscan item is a long account by Fr. Francisco Antonio Barbastro, July 9, 1788, of the missionary affairs of the Custody of San Carlos of Sonora.[81]

Fr. Kieran McCarty, superior and historian at San Xavier del Bac, has been collecting materials on the history of the Franciscan missions in northern Sonora and southern Arizona for a number of years. He has microfilmed the records of many of the missions in Sonora, sometimes flying to inaccessible places in crop-dusting airplanes. The materials that he has assembled have been placed in the Oblasser Library at San Xavier del Bac, which was named for Fr. Bonaventure Oblasser, a predecessor at the mission for many years who had been a collector of

---

[74] Butler, *Check List of Mss.*, p. 129.

[75] Strout, *Catalog of Hispanic Documents*, p. 24.

[76] Piette, "Diarios of Early Calif.," p. 419 n. 18. It was published in Bolton, trans. and ed., *Anza's Calif. Expeditions*, 3:311–81.

[77] Translation of inventories of Guevavi, 1737, 1761, and of San Xavier del Bac, 1737, 1765, are in Kessell, *Guevavi*, pp. 195–205.

[78] Castañeda and Dabbs, *Guide to the Latin American Mss.*, pp. 4, 5, 6, 148, 149; Donohue, *After Kino*, passim.

[79] Castañeda and Dabbs, *Guide*, pp. 163–64.

[80] Piette, "Diaries of Early Calif.," p. 419 n. 18.

[81] Castañeda and Dabbs, *Guide*, p. 36.

a variety of things. In 1972, Father McCarty was working on a history of the Franciscan missions, 1768–1848, which will be published by the Academy of American Franciscan History. Father McCarty and Daniel S. Matson are preparing a translation of the correspondence of Fr. Francisco T. H. Garcés for publication by the Arizona Historical Foundation.[82]

Materials relating to the activities of the Jesuits and Franciscans in Pimería Alta are in various European repositories. Documents concerning both orders are in the Archivo General de Indias in Seville,[83] and the Archivo Histórico Nacional,[84] the Real Academia de la Historia,[85] and the Biblioteca de Archivo General del Ministerio de Hacienda in Madrid.[86]

The records of the procurator of the Society of Jesus in Seville, who represented the overseas provinces from 1574, are reported to have been lost.[87] H. E. Bolton obtained transcripts and other reproductions from Spanish, French, German, and Italian repositories, for his works on Father Kino; these are now in the Bolton Collection of the Bancroft Library of the University of California at Berkeley. Documents by Jesuits, relating to Pimería Alta, are in the Fr. Marcellino de Civezza Collection in the Pontificio Ateneo Antoniano in Rome, and microfilm of selections of these, 1767–1800, is in the University of Arizona Library.[88] In the same repository, there is microfilm of "Cartas de las misiones de la Compañía de Jesús en la Baja California y Norte de México," found by Father Burrus in Barcelona, Spain.[89] From the time of his departure from Spain for Mexico until his death, Fr. Phelipe Segesser wrote letters to his family in Switzerland. Segesser's letters, 1730–62, in the Segesser von Brunegg family archives in Lucerne, Switzerland (microfilm in the Bancroft Library of the University of California, Berkeley, and the University of Arizona Library; 369 exposures), include several written from Guevavi, San Xavier del Bac, and San Ignacio during 1731–34.[90] Gottfried Bernard Middendorff, one of the German Jesuits who arrived in Pimería Alta in 1756, kept a diary

---

[82] *SMRC Newsletter* 1 (Nov. 1967); 2 (Mar. 1968); 3 (Feb. 1969); 4 (July 1970).

[83] Chapman, *Catalogue of Materials in the Archivo General de Indias*, passim.

[84] Shepherd, *Guide to Spanish Arch.*, p. 28.

[85] José Tudela, *Los manuscritos de América en las Bibliotecas de España* (Madrid, 1954), pp. 287–96.

[86] Spain, Dirección General de Archivos y Bibliotecas, *Guía de las bibliotecas de Madrid* (Madrid, 1953), p. 54.

[87] E. J. Burrus, trans. and ed., "Kino's First Report on His First Permanent Mission," *Manuscripta* 5 (Oct. 1961):165 n. 4.

[88] Borges, "Documentacíon americana," passim.

[89] Kessell, *Guevavi*, p. 161 n. 19.

[90] Ibid., p. 59 n. 35.

(Aus dem Tagebuch des Mexicanischen Missionarius, Gottf. Bernh. Middendorff, 1754–1776), which is in the Library of the Ignatiushaus, Bonn, West Germany.[91] Selected documents relating to the Jesuits in America and the Philippines, 1653–1752 (28 folders, typescript), from Haupstaatarchiv, Munich, in the Bancroft Library include communications by Phelipe Segesser and Jacobo Sedelmayr.[92] Documents on the Franciscans in Arizona, including some by Francisco Garcés, Francisco A. Barbastro, Antonio de los Reyes, and others, some of which are also in the Archivo General de la Nación, Mexico, or have been published, are in the General Archives of the Franciscans in Rome.[93]

On instruction of the father general of the Society of Jesus, Fr. Eusebio F. Kino wrote at Dolores, over a long period, his "Favores Celestiales," a historical account of missionary activities, explorations, Indian troubles, and other matters of Pimería Alta and, to a lesser extent, Lower California, from 1687 to 1707.[94] Completed in 1710 from Kino's papers which have since disappeared, the original manuscript of the "Favores Celestiales" was found by H. E. Bolton in 1907 in the Archivo General de la Nación, Mexico. While that repository published the Spanish version in installments,[95] Bolton reworked and edited for publication an English translation, prepared for him by Elizabeth H. West.[96] Kino's historical memoir is the principal source on the period

---

[91] Ibid., p. 53 n. 16. A relation by Segesser, written at Tecoripa in 1737, describing the daily life of a missionary has been published in English from a photocopy of a German version published in 1886 in the *Katholische Schweitzerbläte*, (Luzerne, Switzerland). Theodore E. Treutlein, trans. and ed., "Document: The Relation of Philipp Segesser," *Mid-America* 27 (July 1945), pp. 139–87. Bernard L. Fontana and Daniel S. Matson are preparing translations of Segesser's letters, 1730–34, for publication in book form.

[92] Theodore E. Treutlein, "Jesuit Travel to New Spain (1678–1756)," *Mid-America* 19 (Apr. 1937) :111 n. 23.

[93] Hammond, *Guide to Ms. Colls. of the Bancroft Lib.*, p. 224.

[94] H. E. Bolton, "Father Kino's Lost History: Its Discovery and Its Value," Bibliog. Soc. Amer., *Papers* 6 (1911) :21–23.

[95] Mexico, Archivo General de la Nación, *Las Misiones de Sonora y Arizona; comprendiendo: la crónica titulada: "Favores Celestiales y la relación diaria de la entrada al norueste" por el Padre Eusebio Francisco Kino (Kühn), (Publicaciones* del Archivo General de la Nación 8 [Mexico, 1913–22]). This publication and the modernized Spanish version of the "Favores Celestiales," published in Madrid (Mario Hernandez y Sanchez-Barba, ed., *Viajes misionales por la Pimería Alta*, Madrid, 1958), contain so many errors that they are unreliable. The only diary by Kino covering his trip to find the mouth of the Gila River, September 21–October 18, 1698, that has been found is also in the *Publicaciones* del Archivo General de la Nación 8:395–409; and in English in Smith, Kessell, and Fox, *Father Kino in Arizona*, pp. 8–29. The latter publication also contains a bibliography of Kino's writings, pp. 106–22.

[96] H. E. Bolton, ed., *Historical Memoir of Pimería Alta: A Contemporary Account of the Beginnings of California, Sonora, and Arizona, by Father Eusebio Francisco Kino, S.J., Pioneer Missionary, Explorer, Cartographer, and Ranchman, 1683–1711*, 2 vols. (Cleveland, 1919).

and contains many quotations from correspondence with his superior and other missionaries, from seven diaries he kept of exploring expeditions made primarily in what became United States territory, and from documents by or information from the journals of army officers and others who accompanied him.

Bolton had planned to publish Kino's other writings from reproductions obtained from Mexico and a number of European archives which he visited in the summer of 1933. After using these materials for a biography of Kino, however, he turned to other aspects of southwestern history.[97]

In 1957, the superior general of the Society of Jesus established the Jesuit Historical Institute at St. Louis University, St. Louis, Missouri, as the American division of the Institutum Historicum Societatis Iesu in Rome.[98] It was to be responsible for compiling and editing documentary collections on the history of the Jesuits in North America. Ernest J. Burrus, an American Jesuit who had been attached to the Institutum since 1950, became the director of the institute, which was provided with a board of advisers composed of Jesuits attached to several Jesuit universities in the United States. Father Burrus had been working for more than a decade on the history of the Jesuits in Mexico and has continued to specialize in the history of the Jesuits in the borderlands.

Burrus has energetically searched in repositories in Mexico, the United States, and Europe, and has found manuscripts on the Jesuits that eluded H. E. Bolton. He has authored numerous publications, some of them documentary in content, with the assistance of members of the Institutum. His compilation of Kino's correspondence obtained from the Archivum Romanum Societatis Iesu is composed of communications to and from Kino's superiors in Mexico City and Rome, concerning the missions of Lower California and Sonora during 1689–1704.[99] His compilation of Kino's correspondence with the generals of the Society of Jesus concerns the same areas.[100] More extensive is his compilation of Kino's letters to the Duchess of Aveiro, published from

---

[97] Bolton's *Rim of Christendom* contains a list of Kino's published and manuscript writings, with places of publication and names of repositories, on pp. 598–605.

[98] "Announcement," *Manuscripta* 1 (July 1957) 102–103.

[99] E. J. Burrus, trans. and ed., *Kino Reports to Headquarters: Correspondence from New Spain with Rome*, (Rome, 1954).

[100] E. J. Burrus, trans. and ed., *Correspondencia del P. Kino con los generales de la Compañía de Jesús, 1682–1707* (Mexico City, 1961). Other publications on Kino include his report to the viceroy in 1703, embodying a plan for the development of Pimería Alta, and a letter to the procurator in Seville, of Jesuit missions, which are listed in the bibliography.

the originals in the Henry E. Huntington Library.[101] Since these letters were written during the years 1680–87, they are of primary interest for the history of Lower California where Kino had served before going to Pimería, but the collection does contain three letters of 1687 written at Dolores. An English translation of the foregoing compilation was published by the Jesuit Historical Institute in 1965 as the first volume of a projected series on "Sources for the History of the Americas," which is to cover South as well as North America, the Philippine Islands and the Mariana Islands.

The publications by Burrus, mentioned above, laid the groundwork for more extensive compilations on the Jesuits. His *Kino and Manje*, also mentioned above, does not include Kino's diaries, because a separate Spanish-English edition of them, with critical commentary, is being prepared with Fr. Charles W. Polzer. Several documents by Jesuits were included, however, in *Kino and Manje*. Among them is a journal by Fr. Juan María de Salvatierra of his 1701 expedition with Kino and Manje to the head of the Gulf of California, which convinced them all that Lower California was a peninsula.[102] Because earlier Spanish and English versions[103] of Fr. Luis J. Velarde's description of Pimería Alta in 1716 are unreliable, that document[104] is published, along with his 1717 plan for the development of Pimería Alta.[105] The remaining documents are a letter of May 15, 1752 from Fr. Juan A. Balthasar, provincial of the Mexican Jesuits, to the Spanish provincials, emphasizing the dependence of the Mexican Province on Spain for manpower, and his eulogy of Kino, published originally in his *Apostólicos Afanes*.[106] Burrus has also undertaken, with Fr. Félix Zubillaga, a volume to be entitled "The Borderlands of the Eighteenth Century: Documents on Sonora, Sinaloa, Lower California, and Arizona."

Burrus's carefully edited compilations provide extensive documentation on the Kino period, and plans in course for volumes on later years will result in one of the best series available on an area of missionary expansion in United States territory. But, unlike Reuben G.

[101] Burrus, ed., *Kino escribe a la Duquesa: Correspondencia del P. Eusebio Francisco Kino con la Duquesa de Aveiro y otros documentos* (Madrid, 1964).

[102] Burrus, *Kino and Manje*, pp. 587–618.

[103] Rufus K. Wyllys, trans. and ed., "Padre Luís Velarde's Relación of Pimería Alta, 1716," *N. Mex. Hist. Rev.* 6 (Apr. 1931):111–57. This translation was prepared from the Spanish version in *Documentos para la historia de México*, 4th ser. 1:226–402. Another English translation is in Karns, trans., *Unknown Arizona and Sonora*, pp. 221–67.

[104] Burrus, *Kino and Manje*, pp. 619–75.

[105] Ibid., pp. 680–708.

[106] Ibid., pp. 712–26.

Thwaites' *Jesuit Relations*, it is not a systematic, chronological series presented in a uniform format.[107]

Translations of other documents relating to the missions of Pimería Alta have been published by American scholars. A descriptive report, of July 31, 1732, to the bishop of Durango from the missionaries newly established at the missions of San Xavier del Bac, Guevavi, and Santa María Suamca; royal cédulas of 1728 and 1733 regarding the missions of Pimería Alta; and a report of Capt. Juan Bautista de Anza, January 7, 1737, on the discovery of silver at Arizonac, near Guevavi; have been published from a longhand pamphlet then owned by Henry R. Wagner of San Marino, California.[108] Fr. Juan A. Balthasar made an official visitation to the Sonora missions in 1744, and prepared a report for submission to the father provincial in Mexico, that was critical of the government's nonsupport of Sinaloa.[109] A report of the bishop of Durango to the king, June 19, 1745, supported Fr. Jacobo Sedelmayr's recommendation to establish new missions in the north on the Gila, Colorado, and Azul rivers, and urged the construction of a presidio for their defense.[110]

The interest of the Spanish government in expanding the mission system northward to the Gila and Colorado rivers, in order to provide way stations on the road to Lower California, resulted in further explorations by the Jesuits. After an earlier trip to Casa Grande in Arizona in 1736, Fr. Ignacio Keller, the missionary at Suamca, reached the Salt River in 1737, but, when traveling north of the Gila River in 1743 to visit the Hopis, his party was attacked by Apaches.[111] He was succeeded as an explorer by Jacobo Sedelmayr, who had made several journeys north between 1737 and 1743 from his base at Tubutama.[112] Accounts of his later expeditions of 1746, 1748, and 1750 have been published from manuscripts in the Arizona Historical Society.[113] His 1746 relation

---

[107] R. G. Thwaites, ed., *The Jesuit Relations and Allied Documents: Travels and Exploration of the Jesuit Missionaries in New France, 1610–1791; the Original French, Latin, and Italian Texts, with English Translations and Notes; Illustrated by Portraits, Maps, and Facsimiles*, 73 vols. (Cleveland, 1796–1901).

[108] George P. Hammond, trans. and ed., "Pimería Alta after Kino's Time," *N. Mex. Hist. Rev.* 4 (July 1929):225–38.

[109] Peter M. Dunne, S.J., trans. and ed., *Juan Antonio Balthasar, Padre Visitador to the Sonora Frontier, 1744–45: Two Original Reports* (Tucson, 1957).

[110] Ronald L. Ives, trans. and ed., "The Report of the Bishop of Durango on Conditions in Northwestern Mexico in 1745," *Hisp. Am. Hist. Rev.* 19 (Aug. 1939): 314–17.

[111] Donohue, *After Kino*, p. 80; Kessell, *Guevavi*, p. 98.

[112] Donohue, *After Kino*, pp. 79, 112–15.

[113] Peter M. Dunne, trans. and ed., *Jacobo Sedelmayr, Missionary Frontiersman, Explorer in Arizona and Sonora: Four Original Manuscript Narratives* (Tucson, 1955).

gives a review of exploration in Pimería from the time of Kino, with historical, geographical and ethnological information and accounts of his own journeys, in which he touched the Gila, Salt, and Colorado rivers and the Bill Williams Fork.[114] His diary concerning his trip of 1748, when he reached the Yumas on the Gila River but failed to reach the mouth of the Colorado River, is available.[115] His second effort, in November–December, 1750, to reach the mouth of the Colorado by traveling down the Gila River also failed when members of his military escort became ill, but an unnamed ensign in the party authored a narrative of this expedition.[116]

A new group of German Jesuits arrived in Pimería Alta in 1756. Ignaz Pfefferkorn was assigned to Atí at first and later to Guevavi (1761–63) and Cucurpe. Joseph Och became assistant to Fr. Gaspar Stiger at San Ignacio (1756–58). Bernardo Middendorff opened a mission at Tucson in January, 1757, but, due to Indian hostility, was forced to flee with the military detachment in May. In the same year, Miguel Gerstner was assigned to Guevavi. While serving in Pimería Alta, Pfefferkorn kept voluminous notes, some of which he managed to save at the time of the Jesuit expulsion from Pimería Alta in 1767. During his eight years of captivity in Spain and, later, Germany, he wrote a lengthy work, augmenting his own material with that of other Jesuits, including Jacobo Sedelmayr, that he published in 1794–95 in Cologne, Germany.[117] Theodore E. Treutlein of San Francisco State College, who has made a specialty of the writings of German Jesuits, has published a translation.[118] This work is important for the geographical, historical and ethnographical information it contains concerning Sonora, some of which must have been obtained at Guevavi.

Joseph Och kept notes and prepared reports on his travels and

---

[114] Published in Spanish in *Documentos para la historia de México,* 3d ser. 1:pt. 2, this relation was used to prepare an earlier English translation: Ronald L. Ives, trans. and ed., "Sedelmayr's relación of 1746," U.S. Bureau of American Ethnology, *Bulletin* 123 (Washington, 1939):97–117.

[115] This document was dated 1749 by Dunne, but the correct date is 1748; see Donohue, *After Kino,* p. 120 n. 20.

[116] The last document in Dunne's compilation is a letter from Sedelmayr to the Count of Revilla Gigedo, the viceroy of New Spain, June 25, 1751, urging the northern expansion of the missionary frontier (pp. 77–80).

[117] Ignaz Pfefferkorn, S.J., *Beschreibung der Landschaft Sonora samt andern Merwürdigen Nachrichten von den Innern Theilen New-Spaniens und Reise aus Amerika bis in Deutschland,* 2 vols., (Köln am Rheine, 1794–95). A projected third volume never appeared.

[118] Treutlein, trans. and ed., *Sonora, a Description of the Province* (Albuquerque, 1949). Treutlein also authored an unpublished University of California doctoral dissertation on "Jesuit Travel in America, 1678–1756, as Recorded in the Travel Diaries of German Jesuits, 1934."

observations during the eight years (1756–64) that he served at the missions of San Ignacio, Cumuripa, Baseraca, and Guásavas, until illness forced him to retire to Mexico City. He burned or lost most of his papers but apparently kept some notes, and, from these and his memory of the impressions he had recorded, he prepared reports concerning his travels, the Indians of Sonora, and its government and economy, that were published in Germany.[119] A translation of these reports has been prepared by Theodore E. Treutlein.[120] Och's reports are valuable for conditions in Sonora at the time he served there, and contain information regarding fellow missionaries, including Middendorff and Gerstner, who served in Arizona. The German Jesuits were better prepared scholastically and scientifically than most of their Spanish colleagues, and their more voluminous writings are important contributions.[121] They wrote letters from Sonora and Arizona in the seventeenth and eighteenth centuries to colleges, religious houses, and relatives and friends in Germany. Some of these communications were published in *Der Neue Welt-Bott*,[122] a compilation edited by Joseph Stöcklein that also contains translations from the *Lettres Edifiantes*.[123] *Der Neue Welt-Bott* is one of the great sources of information on travel and missionary activity, but the material on northern Mexico appears to be limited.[124]

In 1863, Buckingham Smith, American antiquarian, collector of Hispanic Americana, and secretary of the American legations in Mexico, 1850–52, and Spain, 1852–58, issued a printing of the "Rudo Ensayo," a historical and descriptive account of northern Mexico west of the Sierra Madre, and southern Arizona, prepared about 1761–62 by

---

[119] Joseph Och, S.J., "Nachrichten von Seinen Reisen nach dem Spanischen Amerika; seinem dortigen Aufenthalte vom Jahr 1754 bis 1767, und Rückkehr nach Europa 1768," in Christoph G. von Murr, ed., *Nachrichten von Verschiedenen Laendern des Spanishchen Amerika*, 2 vols. (Halle, 1809–11), 1:1–292.

[120] Theodore E. Treutlein, trans. and ed., *Missionary in Sonora: The Travel Reports of Joseph Och, S.J., 1755–1767* (San Francisco, 1965).

[121] T. E. Treutlein, "Non-Spanish Jesuits in Spain's American Colonies," in Adele Ogden, ed., *Greater America: Essays in Honor of Herbert E. Bolton* (Berkeley, 1945), pp. 230–31.

[122] Joseph Stöcklein and others, eds., *Der Neüe Welt-Bott: Allerhand so lehrals Geist-Reiche Brief Scrifften un Reis-Beschreibungen welche von denen Missionariis der Gesellschafft Jesu aus beyden Indien und andern über Meer Gelegnen Ländern seit An. 1642 biss auf des Jahr [1750]*, 5 vols. (Augsburg, 1726–58).

[123] *Lettres édifiantes et curieuses, écrites des missions étrangeres par quelques missionaires de la Compagnie de Jésus*, 34 vols. (Paris, 1703–76). Most of the North American letters in this compilation relate to Canada and the United States.

[124] See the list of letters to Auguste Carayon in the appendix, *Bibliographie historique de la Compagnie de Jésus ou catalogue des ouvrages relatifs a l'histoire des Jésuites depuis leur origine jusqu'a nos jours* (Paris, London, Leipzig, 1864), pp. 546–70.

an unknown Jesuit.[125] A Cuban author and historian living in Philadelphia prepared an English translation of the Spanish version that appeared in 1894,[126] and a reprint of the translation came out in 1951.[127] Soon afterwards, it was demonstrated, through evidence in the work itself and in letters of Juan Nentuig to the father provincial in the Archivo Histórico de Hacienda, that Nentuig, a missionary on the Sonora frontier after 1749, wrote the work in 1762.[128] Nentuig's work is valuable for its information on the geography, ethnology, and natural history of the area; the condition of Jesuit missions and churches; mining camps; and settlements and events for the years after 1750. A new annotated translation, prepared from Nentuig's original manuscript embodying the proofs of his authorship, would be a worthwhile undertaking.[129]

The Jesuits made important contributions to the cartography of Pimería Alta. Fr. Eusebio F. Kino traveled northward many times on foot and horseback, traversing the region between the Magdalena River, the Gila and San Pedro rivers, and the Colorado. He sought not only converts to Christianity, but geographical information, and recorded his findings in letters, reports, diaries, and maps that delineated, for the first time, the geography of Pimería Alta. His principal geographical quest was to try and discover whether Lower California was an island or a peninsula, but, although he reached the mouth of the Colorado River and learned enough to believe that Lower California was a peninsula, he did not obtain complete proof.[130] Bolton gave considerable attention to Kino's geographical discoveries,[131] but E. J. Burrus

---

[125] *Rudo ensayo, tentativa de una prevencional descripción geographica de la Provincia de Sonora, sus terminos y confines: o major collecion de materiales para hacerla quien lo supiere major* (Albany, N.Y., 1863).

[126] Eusebio Guiteras, trans., "Rudo Ensayo," Amer. Cath. Hist. Soc., *Records* 5 (1894):99–264.

[127] *Rudo Ensayo, by an Unknown Jesuit Padre, 1763* (Tucson, 1951).

[128] Alberto F. Pradeau, "Nentuig's 'Description of Sonora,'" *Mid-America* 35 (April 1953):81–83. Nentuig was a native of Silesia. Microreproductions of Nentuig's letters, 1764–67, are in the Bancroft Library of the University of California.

[129] The original manuscript of Nentuig's work is in the Archivo General de la Nación (Historia, vol. 393), which published another Spanish version entitled *Descripción geográfica natural y curiosa de la Provincia de Sonora*, redactado por German Viveros (Mexico, 1971).

[130] Burrus, *Kino and Manje*, pp. 107, 120–21, 126, 134–35. The peninsularity of California was demonstrated in 1746 when Fr. Ferdinand Consag traveled east along the coast of the Gulf of California as far as the mouth of the Colorado River, and Fr. Jacobo Sedelmayr reached that point after traveling northwest from Caborca.

[131] Bolton, *Rim of Christendom*, p. vii; pp. 606–10 contains a list of Kino's maps, with descriptive data.

has recently made a more systematic investigation of Kino's map-making activities. The results of Burrus' searches for Kino's maps in repositories in Europe, the United States, and Mexico, and his study of their use by European cartographers, led him to conclude that Kino's maps were the most extensive and significant cartographical series in the history of New Spain.[132] In his published study, Burrus includes reproductions of Kino's principal maps, with extensive description.[133] Other Jesuits who made cartographical contributions included Luís Velarde, Juan A. Balthasar, Ignaz Keller, Jacobo Sedelmayr, Gaspar Stiger, Bernardo Middendorff, Juan Nentuig, and Ignacio Pfefferkorn.[134]

Histories of Jesuit activities in the Province of Mexico incorporating archival materials were prepared in the eighteenth century. The *Apostólicos Afanes de la Compañía de Jesús*, published anonymously in Barcelona in an effort to promote missions in Sonora, has been credited to Fr. Juan A. Balthasar, vice provincial in that province in 1744, and to Fr. José Ortega.[135] The first part of the book, by Ortega, concerns the Nayarit missions, and the remainder, prepared by Balthasar from Kino's "Favores Celestiales" and Sedelmayr's and Keller's reports, concerns the explorations of Fathers Kino, Keller, Sedelmayr, and Consag. More comprehensive is Alegre's *Historia*, which he undertook on the instruction of the father provincial, after being summoned from Yucatan to Mexico City in 1764. In preparing the history, he used the archives of the province, as well as obtained information from other Jesuits, and he sometimes quoted whole letters or parts of letters in the text.[136] The manuscript of Alegre's history remained in Mexico when the Jesuits were expelled in 1767. It was published in Mexico

---

[132] Ernest J. Burrus, S.J., *Kino and the Cartography of Northwestern New Spain* (Tucson, 1965), p. 13.

[133] Ibid., pp. 13–20, contains "A Chronological List of Kino's Cartographical Productions."

[134] A description of their maps in chronological order is in E. J. Burrus, *La Obra cartográfica de la provincia mexicana de la Compañía de Jesús (1567–1967)*, 1:15–116, and pp. 126–33 contain a list of maps prepared by historians between 1900 and 1967. Volume one also contains a few cartographical reports by Kino, Manje, and Velarde, and volume two contains reproductions of Jesuit maps, including some by Kino and Nentuig.

[135] *Apostólicos afanes de la Compañía de Jesús escritos por un padre de la misma sagrada religion de su Provincia de México* (Barcelona, 1954). Juan B. Iguiniz deals with the authorship in the introduction to the edition that appeared under the same title in Mexico City in 1944. See also Burrus, *Kino and Manje*, pp. 6, 713 n. 3–5, 737. Another edition was entitled *De los principios, progress y decaimiento de la espiritual conquesta de la Pimería Alta por la muerte del Padre Eusebio Francisco Kino de los nuevos progresos, varios descubrimientos y estado presente de la Pimería Alta* (Mexico, 1887).

[136] Ernest J. Burrus, S.J., "Francisco Javier Alegre: Historian of the Jesuits in New Spain," *Archivum Historicum Societatis Iesu* 20 (Ian–Iun, 1953):448–54.

City in 1841–42 by Carlos M. Bustamante, the Mexican writer who was promoting the effort to obtain the reestablishment of the Jesuits in Mexico.[137] The original two-volume manuscript, covering the years 1577–1763, is in the Joaquín García Icazbalceta Collection in the University of Texas Library.[138] A new edition of Alegre's history, by Fathers Burrus and Zubillaga, contains a revised text based on various manuscript copies, a bibliography, an introduction concerning the author, and comprehensive notes.[139] Alegre's work is especially important because some of the manuscripts on which it was based are no longer extant. Volume four on the years 1676–1766 contains chapters relating to Pimería Alta and Arizona.

Part of volume three of Arricivita's history of the College of Santa Cruz of Querétaro is concerned with Franciscan activities in Sonora.[140]

The most extensive traveler among the Franciscans in Arizona was Francisco T. H. Garcés, who served as the missionary at San Xavier del Bac after 1768. In that year and in 1770, he made trips to the Pima and Papago villages on the Gila River, to bring the Indians under the influence of the church, and, in 1771, he went again to the Gila and Colorado rivers, to select sites for missions. In 1774, he accompanied the Anza exploring expedition to San Gabriel in California and, on returning, went on his own to visit one of the Yuma tribes on the Colorado River. He set off with Anza's colonizing party in October, 1775, but, after leaving it at the junction of the Gila and the Colorado, he went up the latter river to the Mohave Desert and traversed California to San Gabriel. From that place, he traveled, by way of the Tulare valley, back to the Mohave, on to the Moqui country, and back to the Mohave, thence down the Colorado to Yuma, and back to San Xavier del Bac. His detailed account of his expedition is a major contribution to the history, geography, and ethnology of a large area of the Southwest. The first English translation of Garcés' narrative was published by Elliott Coues,[141] a naturalist and editor of journals on

---

[137] Bancroft, *Hist. of Mex.*, 3:449.

[138] Burrus, "Francisco Javier Alegre," p. 455; Castañeda and Dabbs, *Guide to Latin American Mss.*, p. 29.

[139] F. J. Alegre, S.J., *Historia de la Provincia de la Compañía de Jesús de Nueva España*, 4 vols., ed. by Ernest J. Burrus, S.J. and Félix Zubillaga, S.J. (Rome, 1956– 60). The four volumes make up volumes nine, thirteen, sixteen, and seventeen, of the *Biblioteca Instituti Historici, S.J.* Kino's "Favores Celestiales" was the principal source used by both Ortega and Alegre.

[140] Juan D. Arricivita, O.F.M., *Crónica seráfica y apostólica del Colegio de Propaganda Fide de la Santa Cruz de Querétaro en la Nueva España* (Mexico, 1792). Arricivita was appointed historian of the college in 1787.

[141] Elliott Coues, trans. and ed., *On the Trail of a Spanish Pioneer: The Diary and Itinerary of Francisco Garcés (Missionary Priest) in His Travels through Sonora, Arizona, and California, 1775–1776*, 2 vols. (New York, 1900).

travel and exploration in the American West, where he had served as an Army surgeon and naturalist with government surveys. Coues used the copy of the Garcés diary in the Bureau of American Ethnology (which was the most detailed one available to him), another copy then on loan to that bureau, and the Spanish version which had been published in Mexico in 1854.[142] The published diary is devoted mainly to the expedition of 1775–76, but it contains a brief treatment of the *entradas* of 1768–74.[143] A new translation of Garcés diary, prepared by John Galvin from a contemporary copy in his own collection and a Spanish version that he edited, has appeared recently.[144]

In 1964, the Southwestern Missions Research Center was organized in Tucson by Fr. Charles W. Polzer, Bernard L. Fontana, James Murphy, Walter Fathauer, Mrs. Byron Ivancovich, and William W. Wasley. The center became affiliated with the Arizona Historical Society and, by late 1972, had 275 members, mostly in the Southwest. The center serves as a coordinating agency for persons engaged in historical and anthropological studies relating to the Southwest, and helps to prevent further duplication of field research and the reproduction of research materials already copied. Information regarding projects under way is disseminated in a *Newsletter*, issued irregularly since February, 1967.

---

[142] *Documentos para la historia de México*, 2nd ser. 1:225–374. Other copies of the Garcés diary are in the Archivo General de la Nación, Mexico City, the Archivo General de Indias, Seville, and the Franciscan archives in Rome.

[143] Garcés's diary of the Anza expedition to California, 1773–74, is in the compilation by Bolton on *Anza's California Expeditions*, described in chapter 23, in the section on California. The diaries of his earlier expeditions of 1770 and 1771 seem not to have been published, although they are available in the Archivo General de la Nación, México, Historia section, vol. 396.

[144] John Galvin, trans. and ed., *A Record of Travel in Arizona and California, 1775–1776: A New Translation* (San Francisco, 1965); J. Galvin, *Diario de exploraciones en Arizona y California en los años de 1775 y 1776 [por] Fray Francisco Garcés* (Mexico, 1968). Galvin's translation differs little from that of Coues, and lacks the copious notes supplied by the latter.

Part V

Reference Material

Appendix A

Repositories

Arizona

Phoenix   Arizona Department of Library and Archives
U.S. Bureau of Land Management, Arizona State Office

Tucson   Arizona Historical Society
Roman Catholic Diocese of Tucson, Chancery Archives
San Xavier del Bac Mission, Oblasser Library
University of Arizona Library

California

Berkeley   Pacific School of Religion Library
University of California, Bancroft Library

Camarillo   St. John's Seminary Library

Claremont   Pomona College Library

Fresno   Roman Catholic Diocese of Monterey-Fresno, Chancery Archives

Jolon   San Antonio Mission

Laguna Niguel   Federal Archives and Records Center (formerly at Bell, California)

Los Angeles   Los Angeles County Law Library
Los Angeles County Museum Library
Office of the City Clerk
Office of the County Recorder
Roman Catholic Archdiocese of Los Angeles, Chancery Archives
Roman Catholic Church, Our Lady Queen of the Angels Church

[369]

California (cont.)	Southwest Museum
	University of California at Los Angeles Library
Palos Verdes	Palos Verdes Public Library
Pasadena	Pasadena Public Library
Sacramento	California State Archives
	California State Library
	U.S. Bureau of Land Management, California Land Office
San Bruno	Federal Archives and Records Center (formerly at San Francisco)
San Diego	San Diego Historical Society
	San Diego de Alcalá Mission
	San Diego Public Library
San Francisco	California Historical Society
	California State Library, Sutro Library
	City Archives
	Dolores Mission
	Roman Catholic Archdiocese of San Francisco, Chancery Archives
	Society of California Pioneers
	U.S. District Court, Northern District of California
San Gabriel	San Gabriel Archangel Mission
San José	San José Historical Museum
San Juan Bautista	San Juan Bautista Mission
San Juan Capistrano	San Juan Capistrano Mission
San Luís Obispo	San Luís Obispo Mission
San Marino	Henry E. Huntington Library and Art Gallery
San Miguel	San Miguel Mission
Santa Ana	Charles W. Bowers Memorial Museum
Santa Barbara	Our Lady of Sorrows Church
	Santa Barbara Mission Archives
Santa Clara	University of Santa Clara, Orradre Library
Solvang	Santa Ynez Mission
Sonoma	San Francisco Church
Stanford	Stanford University Library
Ventura	San Buenaventura Mission
Canada	
Montreal	McGill University Library

Colorado
Denver

Colorado State Archives
Federal Archives and Records Center
State Historical Society of Colorado
U.S. Bureau of Land Management, Colorado
Land Office

Connecticut
New Haven

Yale University Library

District of Columbia

Library of Congress, Law Library
Library of Congress, Manuscript Division
National Archives
Supreme Court Library
U.S. Bureau of Land Management,
Department of the Interior
Washington National Records Center

England
London

British Museum

France
Paris

Bibliothèque Nationale

Illinois
Chicago

Newberry Library, Edward E. Ayer Collection

Italy
Rome

Order of Friars Minor (Franciscans), Central
Archives
Pontificio Ateneo Antoniano, Marcellino de
Civezza Collection
Roman Catholic Curia, Sacred Congregation
for the Propagation of the Faith
(Propaganda Fide) Archives
Vatican Library
Society of Jesus (Jesuits), Archivum
Romanum Societatis Iesu

Maryland
Baltimore
Potomac

Maryland Historical Society
Academy of American Franciscan History

Massachusetts
Boston

Boston Public Library

Massachusetts (cont.)
Cambridge   Harvard University, Gray Herbarium
Harvard University, Peabody Museum

Mexico
Camargo
  (Tamaulipas)   Archivo de la Iglesia Parroquial

Celaya
  (Guanajuato)   Franciscan Province of Michoacán

Chihuahua
  (Chihuahua)   Archivo del Ayuntamiento
Archivo General del Estado

Ciudad Juárez
  (Chihuahua)   Archivo de la Iglesia Parroquial
Archivo Municipal

Culiacán (Sinaloa)   Archivo del Obispado de Sinaloa

Durango
  (Durango)   Archivo del Arzobispado de Durango
Archivo del Estado de Durango
Archivo Municipal

Guadalajara
  (Jalisco)   Archivo del Arzobispado de Guadalajara
Biblioteca Público

Hermosillo (Sonora)   Archivo del Obispado de Sonora
Archivo General del Gobierno del Estado

Linares
  (Nuevo León)   Archivo del Obispado de Linares

Matamoros
  (Tamaulipas)   Archivo de la Iglesia Parroquial
Archivo Municipal

México
  (Distrito Federal)   Academia Mexicana de la Historia, Biblioteca
Archivo del Arzobispado de México
Archivo de Relaciones Exteriores (Ministerio
  de Relaciones Exteriores)
Archivo General de la Nación
Archivo Histórico de Hacienda (Ministerio de
  Hacienda y Crédito Público)
Archivo Histórico Militar Mexicano
  (Secretaria de Defensa Nacional)
Biblioteca del Museo Nacional
Biblioteca Nacional
Cámaro de Diputados, Archivo
Instituto Histórico del Antropológia e
  Historia, Biblioteca

Monterrey
  (Nuevo León)
	Archivo del Arzobispado de Monterrey
	Archivo del Estado de Nuevo León
	Instituto Tecnológico y de Estudios Superiores
	  de Monterrey

Parral (Chihuahua)	Archivo de Hidalgo del Parral Biblioteca Público
Ojinaga (Chihuahua)	Archivo de la Iglesia Parroquial
Reynoso (Tamaulipas)	Archivo de la Iglesia Parroquial
Saltillo (Coahuila)	Archivo del Obispado de Coahuila Archivo del Estado de Coahuila
Zacatecas (Zacatecas)	Archivo del Estado de Zacatecas Colegio de Guadalupe de Zacatecas, Biblioteca

Michigan

Ann Arbor	University of Michigan, William L. Clements Library
Detroit	Detroit Public Library

Missouri

St. Louis	St. Louis University Library
	St. Louis University, Pius XII Memorial
	  Library, Knights of Columbus Vatican
	  Film Library

New Mexico

Albuquerque	University of New Mexico Library
Las Vegas	New Mexico Highlands University Library

Santa Fe	Historical Society of New Mexico
	New Mexico State Records Center and
	  Archives
	Roman Catholic Archdiocese of Santa Fe,
	  Chancery Archives
	U.S. Bureau of Land Management, New
	  Mexico State Office

New York

New York	New-York Historical Society New York Public Library

Oklahoma

Tulsa	Thomas Gilcrease Institute of American History and Art

Rhode Island
Providence   Brown University, John Carter Brown Library

Spain
Cadiz   Escuela Real de Navegación
Madrid   Academia de la Historia
                              Archivos Militares
                              Archivo General de Ministerio de Hacienda
                              Archivo Histórico Nacional
                              Biblioteca Central Militar
                              Biblioteca del Palacio Real
                              Biblioteca Nacional
                              Ministerio de Asuntos Exteriores
                              Museo de Ciencias Naturales
                              Museo Naval
                              Real Academie de la Historia
Sevilla   Archivo General de Indias
                              Biblioteca Colombina
Simancas   Archivo General
Toledo   Biblioteca Pública

Switzerland
Lucerne   Segesser von Brunegg Family Archives

Texas
Angleton   Brazoria County, County Clerk's Office
Austin   Austin Public Library
                              Catholic Archives of Texas (Texas Catholic
                                  Historical Society)
                              Roman Catholic Diocese of Austin, Chancery
                                  Archives
                              Texas General Land Office
                              Texas State Library, Archives Division
                              University of Texas, Eugene C. Barker Texas
                                  History Center, Texas Archives
                              University of Texas Library, Latin American
                                  Collection
Bay City   Matagorda County, County Clerk's Office
Belleville   Austin County, County Clerk's Office
Dallas   Dallas Historical Society
                              Southern Methodist University, De Golyer
                                  Foundation Library
                              Southern Methodist University, Hendren
                                  Library
Denton   North Texas State College Library

Texas (cont.)

El Paso	University of Texas at El Paso Library
Galveston	Rosenberg Library
Gonzales	Gonzales Memorial Museum
Houston	Houston Public Library
Laredo	Laredo Junior College
	St. Augustin Church
	Webb County, County Clerk's Office
Lubbock	Texas Technological University Library
Nacogdoches	Nacogdoches County, County Clerk's Office
Refugio	Our Lady of Refuge Church
	Dawgood Library
	District Court, Clerk's Office
San Antonio	Alamo Museum
	Bexar County, County Clerk's Office
	Lady of the Lake College, Archives
	Old Spanish Mission Historical Research Library, San José Mission
	Roman Catholic Archdiocese of San Antonio, San Fernando Cathedral Archives
	St. Mary's University Library
	Trinity University Library
San Augustine	San Augustine County Clerk's Office
San Jacinto	San Jacinto Museum
Waco	Baylor University, Texas History Collection

Utah

Salt Lake City	Genealogical Society of the Church of Jesus Christ of Latter Day Saints

West Germany

Bonn	Ignatiushaus Bibliothek
Munich	Haupstaatarchis

Wisconsin

Madison	State Historical Society of Wisconsin

Appendix B

Documentary List of California Archives

No 1. General Index of the Spanish & Mexican Archives in the Office of the U.S. Surv^r General, for California[1]

Index of Documents in the Archives of California—

Period of the Spanish domination, 1767 to 1821 & 22

Box n⁰. 1	Official Correspondence 1767 to 1786 inclusive
Box n⁰. 2	Official Correspondence 1787 to 1790 inclusive
Box n⁰. 3	Official Correspondence 1791 to 1796 inclusive
Box n⁰. 4	Official Correspondence 1797 to 1800 inclusive
Box n⁰. 5	Official Correspondence 1801 to 1821 & 22 inclusive
Box n⁰. 6	Copy-books of the correspondence of Governor Neve from 1775 to 1782–.
	Copy-books of the correspondence of Governor Fages from 1782 to 1791.
	Copy-books of the correspondence of Governor Arrillaga from 1792 to 1794.
Box n⁰. 7	Copy-books of the correspondence of Governor Borica from 1794 to 1800.
Box n⁰. 8	Copy-books of the correspondence of Governor Arrillaga from 1800 to 1814.
	Copy-books of the correspondence of Governor Sola from 1814 to 1821 & 22.

---

[1] Records of the Bureau of Land Management (Record Group 49), California Board of Land Commissioners No. 1, National Archives. This index was transmitted by a letter from Samuel D. King, Surveyor General of California, to the Board, Aug. 20, 1852. The circumstances under which the "General Index to the Spanish and Mexican Archives" was prepared can be ascertained in Chapter 25.

Box no. 9   Papers relating to the Presidios of Monterey, San Diego, San Francisco, Santa Barbara & Loreto—
Box no. 10   Ditto, do. do.
Box no. 11   Papers relating to the Missions—
Box no. 12   Papers relating to the Missions—
Box no. 13   Several unclassed papers of the Spanish epoch, mostly of little importance and without date or incomplete—

Mexican Epoch 1821 & 22 to 1846 & 48

Box no. 14   Copy-books of Official Correspondence, 1822 to 1828 inclusive—
Box no. 15   Copy-books of Official Correspondence, 1829 to 1831 inclusive—
Box no. 16   Copy-books of Official Correspondence 1838 to 1844
Box no. 17   Mexican Decrees & Correspondence, 1821 to 1830.
Box no. 18   Mexican Decrees & Correspondence, 1830 to 1833—
Box no. 19   Mexican Decrees & Correspondence, 1834 to 1837.
Box no. 20   Mexican Decrees & Correspondence, 1838 to 1843—
Box no. 21   Mexican Decrees & Correspondence, 1843 to 1846.
Box no. 22   Mexican Laws.
Box no. 23   Official communications to the Governors from the Subordinate Authorities of California, and also petitions and letters from other parties. 1820 to 1839. 1840 to 1846.
Box no. 24   Communications from the different Alcaldes to the Governors—
Box no. 25   Official Communications from the Governments of the different States of Mexico to the Government of the State of California 1821 to 1846.
             Official Communications from the Revenue Department "Dirrecion General de Rentas" to the Chief Official of the Custom house at Monterey—
Box no. 26   Documents relating to the Secularization of the Missions—
Box no. 27   Naturalization Documents.
Box no. 28   Sundry documents—
Box no. 29   Sundry books of miscellaneous character, and destitute of importance—
Box no. 30   Records of Proceedings relating to Mexican Land Claims which are either void from a denial of the Authorities to grant the lands petitioned for, or incomplete from the proceedings being unfinished, or from the want of part of the papers constituting evidence—
Box no. 31   Proceedings of the Legislative Assemblies of California during the Mexican epoch—
Box no. 32   Papers relating to Lower California 1846, 47 & 48.

Box n⁰. 33 Several unclassified papers of the Mexican epoch,
mostly of little importance, and without date or
incomplete—

C Six boxes containing 579 Records of Proceedings
concerning Mexican Claims, of which there is a
classified Index—

There is also a book entitled Registro de Sitios, frenos
y Señales, containing some Spanish grants, and a
few Mexican grants made in the first years of the
Mexican epoch—

There are besides Some old Spanish Indexes of the
Presidial Archives, which do not reach the year
1800, and which rather Serve to Show what there
was, than what there is in the Archives, Since many
of the documents therein Specified are missing—

Appendix C

Office of U. S. Surveyor General.

Contents of Large Case, Marked No. 1—but designated as No. 4 in the Inventory of property transferred by W. S. Green to J. M. Gleaves, March 31st 1898.[1]

Vols.
1– 52	Provincial State Papers. Benicia. Military—Years, 1767–1821
53– 87	Department State Papers. Benicia. Military.
88–109	Provincial State Papers.
110–120	Provincial Records.
121–122	Provincial State Papers. Presidios.
123–124	Provincial State Papers. Benicia—Miscellaneous.
125	Provincial State Papers. Indices—1773–1819.
126–136	State Papers—Military and Political Sacramento Series.

Contents of Large Case, Marked No. 2, but designated as No. 3 in the Inventory of property transferred by W. S. Green to J. M. Gleaves, March 31st 1898.

Vols.
137–139	State Papers, Sacramento Series. Military and Political
140–141	State Papers, Superior Decrees & Dispatches Sacramento Series

---

[1] Enclosure with a letter from James M. Gleaves, Surveyor General for California, to the Commissioner of the General Land Office, March 31, 1898, Letters Received from Surveyors General, file no. 35104, Records of the Bureau of Land Management (Record Group 49), National Archives. The list of records was prepared when J. M. Gleaves succeeded W. S. Green as Surveyor General for California. For references to other lists in print see Chapter 20.

Vols.

142   State Papers—Provincial Records—Sacramento Series
143   State Papers—Presidios & Missions miscellaneous—
        Sacramento Series
144   State Papers Miscellaneous—Sacramento Series
145–146   State Papers—Missions & Colonizations
147–148   State Papers—Missions & Colonizations
149–157   State Papers—Missions & Colonizations
158–162   Departmental State Papers Monterey.
163–169   Departmental State Papers San José.
170–184   Departmental State Papers Los Angeles.
185–191   Los Angeles Archives.
192–193   Departmental State Papers—Naturalization.
194–197   Legislative Papers.
198   State Papers—Miscellaneous—Benicia.
199–200   Departmental State Papers—Benicia.
201   Departmental State—Memorials & Reports.
202   Departmental State Papers—Miscellaneous. Benicia.
203   Departmental State Papers—Dispatches from other
        Departments.
204   Departmental State Papers—Official Correspondence
        and Reports.
205–208   Departmental State Papers
209   Departmental State—Books.
210–211   Departmental State Papers
212–213   Departmental State Papers—Miscellaneous.
214–215   Departmental State Papers—Presidios
216–229   Departmental State Papers—Records—Books.
230–231   Departmental State Papers—Departmental Payments
232–237   Departmental State Papers—Prefectures & Juzgados.
        (Benicia)
238–239   Departmental State Papers—Juzgados
240–260   Superior Government State Papers
261   Departmental State Papers—Superior Government
        Decrees & Dispatches—Benicia.
262–263   Departmental State Papers—Customhouse—(Monterey).
264–271   Departmental State Papers—Customhouse—(Benicia).
272–276   Departmental State Papers—Commissary & Treasury—
        (Benicia).
278–279   Mexican Archives—Lower California. Years—1847–1848.

Appendix D

Spanish Archives in Land Office
San Francisco, California[1]

302 volumes, as follows:–	No. of Volumes[2]
Provincial, Military 1767–1820	51
Departmental Military 1821–1845.	37
Provincial State Papers, 1767–1822.	21
Provincial Records, 1775–1822.	12
Provincial State Papers Presidio (military posts) 1780–1821.	2
Provincial State Papers Presidio Benicia Misc. 1770–1821. (Diary, etc.)	2
Provincial State Papers Presidio Indexes 1773–1819.	
State Papers Sacramento Series Missions & Presidios, 1780–1845.	14
State Papers Sacramento Series Despatches, 1770–1845.	2
State Papers Provincial Records, 1770–1821.	1
State Papers Misc. 1821–1845.	2
State Papers—Mission & Colonization (no date)	2

---

[1] Enclosure with a letter from Herbert Putnam, Librarian of Congress, to Ethan A. Hitchcock, Secretary of the Interior, Jan. 24, 1903, Records of the Bureau of Land Management (Record Group 49), Division E, Special File "E" Box 8, Package 1, National Archives. As explained in Chapter 20, this list was prepared by Worthington C. Ford, head of the Division of Manuscripts in the Library of Congress.

[2] The figures under the heading "Volumes" are the total number of volumes in each series of records, as given on the opposite side of the page.

	No. of Volumes
State Papers—Missions 1785–1846.	11
Departmental State Papers—Monterey. (No dates).	I–VI (But we find 5 missing)
Departmental State Papers—San Jose. (No dates)	7
Departmental State Papers—Los Angeles (No dates). (Prefectures & Courts)	8
Departmental State Papers	
Decrees & Dispatches–	1
Proclamations–	2
Miscellaneous	1
City Los Angeles	1
of corres. [pondence]	2
Los Angeles—archives—civil (No dates).	7
Dept. State Papers—Naturalization (1819–1846).	2
Legislative Records, 1822–1846.	4
State Papers—Benicia—Misc. 1773–1829.	1
Dept. State Papers—Benicia—Misc. 1821–1846.	2
Dept. State Papers—Benicia—Memorials & Reports 1826–1844.	1
Dept. State Papers—Misc. 1830–1846.	1
Dept. State Papers—Despatches from other Departments. 1823–1845.	1
Dept. State Papers—Benicia—Official correspondence and reports.	1
Departmental State Papers—1821–1846.	11
Departmental Record Books—1822–1845, Kept by Secretary of Assembly.	14
Departmental Payments–	2
Departmental State Papers—Benicia, Prefect & Courts.	6
Departmental State Papers, Benicia Courts.	2
Supr. Gov't State Papers (Mexico) (Decrees & Despatches)	21
Dept. State Papers—Supr. Gov. Decree & Despatches.	1
Dept. State Papers—Custom House, Monterey–	2
Dept. State Papers—Custom House, Benicia.	8
Dept. State Papers, Commissary & Treasury.	6
Mexican Archives—Lower California.	23

Bibliography

CONTENTS

Bibliography

BIBLIOGRAPHIES

Cadden, John P. *The Historiography of the American Catholic Church, 1785–1943*. Washington, The Catholic University of America Press, 1944. (The Catholic University of America, *Studies in Sacred Theology*, No. 82).

California Library Association, Committee on Local History. *California Local History: A Centennial Bibliography*. Ed. by Ethel Blumann and Mable W. Thomas. Stanford, Stanford University Press, 1950.

California, State Library, Sacramento; Sutro Branch, San Francisco. *Catalogue of Mexican Pamphlets in the Sutro Collection (1623–1888)*. Prepared by the personnel of the Works Progress Administration. Ed. by P. Radin. San Francisco, California State Library, 1939–40.

California, University, Bancroft Library. *Index to Printed Maps*. Boston, G. K. Hall, 1964.

Carayon, Auguste. *Bibliographie historique de la Compagnie de Jésus ou catalogue des ouvrages relatifs a l'histoire des Jésuites depuis leur origine jusqu'à nos jours*. Paris, Auguste Durand; London, Barthes and Lowell; Leipzig, A. Franck, 1864.

Chapin, Edward L., Jr. *A Selected Bibliography of Southern California Maps*. With a foreword by Clifford H. MacFadden. Berkeley, University of California Press, 1953.

Cowan, Robert E. *A Bibliography of the Spanish Press of California, 1833–1845*. San Francisco, n. p., 1919.

——. *A Bibliography of the History of California, 1510–1930*. 4 vols. San Francisco, John Henry Nash, 1933–64. Volume four by Robert G. Cowan published in Los Angeles.

Ellis, John T. *A Guide to American Catholic History.* Milwaukee, Bruce Publishing Co., 1959.

Fahey, Herbert. *Early Printing in California, from its Beginning in the Mexican Territory to Statehood, September 9, 1850.* San Francisco, Book Club of California, 1956. Appended: "Bibliography of Imprints," 1833–50, pp. 95–132.

Greenwood, Robert, Seiko J. Suzuki, and Marjorie Pulliam, eds. *California Imprints, 1833–1862: A Bibliography.* Los Gatos, The Talisman Press, 1961.

Handbook of Latin American Studies, 1935–. Prepared by a number of scholars for the Hispanic Foundation in the Library of Congress. Cambridge, Harvard University Press, 1936–51; Gainesville, University of Florida Press, 1951–.

Harding, George L. "A Census of California Spanish Imprints, 1833–1845." *California Historical Society Quarterly* 12 (June 1933): 125–36.

Haynes, Henry W. and Justin Winsor. "Critical Essay on the Sources of Information — Editorial Note — Early Explorations of New Mexico." In Justin Winsor, ed., *Narrative and Critical History of America,* 2:473–504. Boston, New York, Houghton, Mifflin, 1884.

Historical Records Survey, Illinois. *Check List of New Mexico Imprints and Publications, 1784–1876; Imprints, 1834–1876; Publications, 1784–1876.* [Lansing?]* Michigan, Historical Records Survey, 1942.

————. Texas. *Texas Newspapers, 1813–1939: A Union List of Newspaper Files Available in Offices of Publishers, Libraries, and a Number of Private Collections.* Houston, San Jacinto Museum of History Association, 1941. (San Jacinto Museum of History Association, *Publications,* Vol. 1.)

Hodge, Frederick W. "Bibliography of Fray Alonso de Benavides." Museum of the American Indian, Heye Foundation, *Indian Notes and Monographs* 3 (1919):1–39.

Jenkins, John H. *Cracker Barrel Chronicles: A Bibliography of Texas Town and County Histories.* Austin, The Pemberton Press, 1965.

Ker, Annita M. *Mexican Government Publications: A Guide to the More Important Publications of the National Government of Mexico, 1821–1936.* Washington, Government Printing Office, 1940.

López, E. Y. *Bibliografía de Sonora.* Hermosillo, Ediciones Fátima, 1960.

Mecham, J. Lloyd. "The Northern Expansion of New Spain, 1522–1822: A Selected Descriptive Bibliographical List." *Hispanic American Historical Review* 7 (May 1927):233–76.

Millares Carlo, Agustín. *Repertorio bibliográfico de los archivos mexi-*

---

*Information within brackets is assumed to be correct but is not verifiable by the author.

canos y de los europeos y norteamericanos de interés para la historia de México. Mexico, Instituto Bibliográfico Mexicano, 1959. (Universidad Nacional Autonoma, Biblioteca Nacional de Mexico, Instituto Bibliográfico Mexicano, [Publicación] Núm. 1.)

Phillips, Philip Lee. "Descriptive List of Maps of California and of San Francisco, to 1865, inclusive, Found in the Library of Congress." [Washington, D.C.] Typescript. Photostatic copy in the Henry E. Huntington Library, San Marino, Calif.

Powell, Donald M. *Arizona Gathering II, 1950–1969: An Annotated Bibliography.* Tucson, University of Arizona Press, 1973.

Rader, Jesse L. *South of Forty from the Mississippi to the Rio Grande: A Bibliography.* Norman, University of Oklahoma Press, 1947.

Raines, Cadwell W. *A Bibliography of Texas: Being a Descriptive List of Books, Pamphlets, and Documents Relating to Texas in Print and Manuscript since 1536.* Austin, Gammel, 1896.

San Diego 200th Anniversary, Inc. Historical Research, Archival Material, Libraries Committee. *San Diego, California: A Bicentennial Bibliography, 1769–1969.* Ed. by Ronald Louis and Silveira de Braganza. San Diego, San Diego 200th Anniversary, Inc. 1969.

Shelton, Wilma L. *Checklist of New Mexico Publications, 1850–1953.* Albuquerque, University of New Mexico Press, 1954.

Steck, Francis B. *A Tentative Guide to Historical Materials on the Spanish Borderlands.* Philadelphia, The Catholic Historical Society of Philadelphia, 1943.

Streeter, Thomas W. *Bibliography of Texas, 1795–1845.* 5 vols. Cambridge, Harvard University Press, 1955–60.

Streit, Robert. *Americanische Missionliteratur (Bibliotheca Missionum: Veroffentlichungen des Internationalen Instituts für Missionswissenschaftliche Forschung,* Vols. 2–3). Aachen, Xaverius Verlagsbuchhandlung A.–G., 1924, 1929.

Swadesh, Frances L. *20,000 Years of History: A New Mexico Bibliography with an Ethnohistorical Introduction.* Santa Fe, Sunstone Press, 1973.

Turrill, Charles B. "Maps Showing the Californias in the Sutro Branch, California State Library: List of Maps and Authors and List of All Localities Indicated in Lower and Upper California. [San Francisco] 1917. Photostat in the Map Division, Library of Congress.

Vance, John T. *The Background of Hispanic American Law: Legal Sources and Juridical Literature of Spain.* Washington, Catholic University of America Press, 1937.

Vollmar, Edward R., S. J. *The Catholic Church in America: An Historical Bibliography.* New Brunswick, N.J., The Scarecrow Press, 1956.

Wagner, Henry R. *The Spanish Southwest, 1542–1794: An Annotated*

Bibliography. Albuquerque, The Quivira Society, 1937. (Quivira Society *Publications,* Vol. 7.)

Wagner, Henry R. and Charles L. Camp, *Henry R. Wagner's The Plains and the Rockies: A Bibliography of Original Narratives of Travel and Adventure, 1800–1865.* Columbus, Ohio, Long's College Book Co., 1953.

Wallace, Andrew, ed. *Sources & Readings in Arizona History: A Checklist of Literature Concerning Arizona's Past.* Tucson, Arizona Historical Society, 1965.

Weber, Francis J. *A Select Guide to California Catholic History.* Los Angeles, Westernlore Press, 1966.

Winsor, Justin. "Spanish North America: Critical Essay on the Sources of Information." In his *Narrative and Critical History of America,* 8:246–70. Boston, New York, Houghton, Mifflin, 1889.

Winther, Oscar O. *A Classified Bibliography of the Periodical Literature of the Trans-Mississippi West (1811–1957).* Bloomington, Indiana University Press, 1961.

MANUSCRIPTS AND ARCHIVES

Manuscripts

Beers, Henry P. Correspondence Files. Numerous letters to and from archival institutions, historical societies, libraries, historians, and others, some of which are cited in the footnotes of this work. These files consist of several hundred communications, amounting to three linear inches.

Black, Jeremiah S. Papers. Manuscript Division, Library of Congress.

Staunton, Edwin M. Papers. Manuscript Division, Library of Congress.

U.S. Library of Congress, Manuscript Division. Correspondence Files; Letters Sent Books.

United States National Archives

U.S. Congress, House of Representatives. House Files. Records of the U.S. House of Representatives (Record Group 233).

U.S. Congress, Senate. Senate Files. Records of the United States Senate (Record Group 46).

U.S. Department of the Interior, Records of the Bureau of Land Management (Record Group 49).

California Board of Land Commissioners
> Letters Sent Book, 1852–54.
>> List of Papers, Documents and Books Turned over to and Deposited with the U.S. Surveyor General of California by the Late Board of Commissioners to Ascertain & Settle the Private Land Claims in Said State, March 19, 1856. No. 188.
> Record of Evidence.

Division E, Special File, Correspondence Relating to the Proposed Transfer of the Spanish Archives of California, 1903.

General Correspondence, Including Surveyors General of Oregon, Washington, and California—Letters Sent, 1855–59.

Letters Received from Surveyors General.

Letters Received from the Surveyor General of California: Schedule of Documents on File in the Spanish and Mexican Archives of the Office of the U.S. Surveyor General for California. Enclosure John C. Hays to Thomas A. Hendricks, September 9, 1857, being part of a Schedule of Articles Belonging to the U.S. Surveyor General's Office, File E6547.

Letters Sent Relating to Miscellaneous Private Claims.

Letters Sent Relating to Private Land Claims, 1850–60, vols. 17–23.

Letters Sent to Surveyors General.

Letters Sent to Surveyors General of Arizona, 1863–84.

Letters Sent to Surveyors General of California, 1851–59.

Letters Sent to Surveyors General of Colorado, 1861–77.

Miscellaneous Letters Received.

Private Land Claims Division.

Index to Land Titles in Upper California Derived from the Spanish and Mexican Governments Rec'd with Surveyor General's Letter of July 28, 1852 (file B 28835–1852).

Private Land Claim Papers.

Report of Rufus C. Hopkins, Special Agent, in Relation to Mexican Land Grants in the Territory of Arizona, March 6, 1880, Private Land Claims, No. 184.

Report on the Subject of Land Titles in California made in Pursuance of Instructions from the Secretary of State and the Secretary of the Interior by William Carey Jones, April 10, 1850, Series K, vol. 192.

Surveyor General of Arizona, Letters Sent Relating to Private Land Claims, 1879–95 (3 vols.).

Surveyor General of California, Letters Sent by Samuel Gompertz, July, 1905–August, 1907 (1 vol.). Notes of Samuel Gompertz on the Attempt to Remove the California Spanish Archives to the Library of Congress, 1903.

U.S. Department of the Interior, Records of the Office of the Secretary of the Interior (Record Group 48).

Appointments Division, Letters Received.

Division of Lands and Railroads.

Letters Received.

Letters Sent Books, 1849–57 (3 vols.).

Miscellaneous Letters Received.

Register of Letters Received.

Division of Territories and Island Possessions, Letters to the Secretary of the Interior from the State Museum of New Mexico, 1923.

Letters Sent Book, Land.

Miscellaneous Letters Sent.

Patents and Miscellaneous Division.

    Letters Received.

    Letters Received Relating to the Territory of Arizona, 1868–1907.

    Letters Received Relating to the Territory of Colorado, 1868–85.

    Letters Received Relating to the Territory of New Mexico, 1854–1907.

    Letters Sent Book, 1849–53 (1 vol.).

U.S. Department of Justice, General Records of the Department of Justice (Record Group 60).

Attorney General's Letters Received.

Attorney General's Letters Sent, 1857–63 (5 vols.).

California Land Claims Transcripts, 1852–56.

Cuaderno o libro de actas de sesiones públicas correspondiente al presente año 1845 (Journal of the Department Assembly of California, 1845 [binding title]).

U.S. Department of the Navy, Naval Records and Library Collection (Record Group 45).

Letters Received by the Secretary of the Navy from Commanding Officers of Squadrons.

Letters Sent Book of Capt. John B. Montgomery, Commanding U.S.S. *Portsmouth*, 1844–47 (3 vols.).

Letters Sent Book of Robert F. Stockton, 1843–47 (Photostat).

U.S. Department of State, General Records of the Department of State (Record Group 59).

Despatches from Special Agents. In volume 15, there is a report to the Secretary of State by Thomas Butler King on his mission to California during 1849, dated March 22, 1850.

Diplomatic Despatches.

Diplomatic Instructions.

Domestic (Outgoing) Letters.

Instructions to Special Agents.

Miscellaneous (Incoming) Letters.

Territorial Papers of New Mexico Territory, 1851–72 (4 vols.).

U.S. General Accounting Office, Records of the United States General Accounting Office (Record Group 217).

Miscellaneous Treasury Accounts.

U.S. Land Office, Phoenix, Arizona, Private Land Claims

Letters, 1879–92 (2 vols.).

U.S. National Archives and Records Service, Records of the National Archives and Records Service (Record Group 64).

Civil Archives Division, National Resources Branch, Correspondence Files.

U.S. War Department, Records of the Adjutant General's Office (Record Group 94).

Letters Received from Stephen W. Kearny.

Letters Sent by the Military Governors and the Secretary of State of California, March 1, 1847–September 23, 1848 (3 vols.).

Military Book, Letters Sent.

Orders and Special Orders, 10th Military Department, 1847–51. Books 53, 255.

Records of U.S. Army Commands (Record Group 98).

Benecia Barracks, Letters Sent, 1852–59. Book 109.

Tenth Military Department, Letters Received, May 1846–March 1849; Letters Sent Book, 1847–50 (vols. 1–2).

U.S. Work Projects Administration (Records of the Work Projects Administration) (Record Group 69).

Survey of Federal Archives, Reports on Serials (Nos. 469–95) Public Survey Office, Office of the Cadastral Engineer, Phoenix, Arizona. Reports on Serials (No. 535) Supervisor of Surveys, Denver, Colorado.

United States Supreme Court

U.S. Supreme Court. Transcripts of Records and Briefs in United States Cases Decided by the Supreme Court of the United States. In the library of the Supreme Court.

PRINTED MANUSCRIPTS AND ARCHIVES

Mexico

Documentos para la historia de México. 20 vols. Mexico, Imprint varies, 1853–57.

García Icazbalceta, Joaquín, ed. *Colección de documentos para la historia de México.* 2 vols. Libreria de J. M. Andrade, Mexico, 1858, 1866.

Hernández y Dávalos, Juan E., ed *Colección de documentos para la guerra de independencia de México de 1808 a 1821.* 6 vols. Mexico, J. M. Sandoval, 1877–82.

Mexico (Viceroyalty). *Instructions for Governing the Interior Provinces of New Spain, 1786.* Trans. and ed. by Donald E. Worcester. Berkeley, The Quivira Society, 1951. (Quivira Society, *Publications*, Vol. 12.)

Mexico (Viceroyalty). *Instrucciones que los virreyes de Nueva España dejaron a sus sucesores.* Mexico, Imprenta Imperial, 1867.

_____. *Reglamento para todos los presidios de las Provincias Internas de esta governación, hecho. por el· Exc^mo Señor Marqués de Casa-Fuerte. . . .* [Mexico, 1729]. Printed in Rivera y Villalón, *Diario y derrotero* (pp. 198–234), listed under Journals.

_____. *Rules and Regulations for the Presidios to be Established on the Frontier Line of New Spain. Ordered by Our Lord the King in a Decree of September 10, 1772, By Order of His Lordship the Most Excellent Viceroy of this Kingdom. Reprinted in Mexico in the Printing Office of Don Joseph Antonio Hogal, Calle de Tiburcio, in the Year 1773.* In John Galvin, ed. and Adelaide Smithers, trans. *The Coming of Justice to California: Three Documents,* pp. 3–45. San Francisco, John Howell Books, 1963.

Mexico, Laws, Statutes, etc. "Provisional Regulation for the Interior Government of the Departments [March 20, 1837]." In San Francisco (District) Legislative Assembly, *Minutes of the Proceedings of the Legislative Assembly of the District of San Francisco, From March 12th, 1849 to June 4th, 1849, and A Record of the Proceedings of the Ayuntamiento or Town Council of San Francisco, from August 6th, 1849, until May 3d, 1850, with an Appendix,* pp. 249–77. San Francisco, Towne & Bacon, 1860.

Pacheco, Joaquín F., Francisco de Cárdenas, and Luis Torres de Mendoza. *Colección de documentos inéditos relativos al descubrimiento, conquista y colonización de la posessiones españolas de América y Oceania. . . .* 42 vols. Madrid, n. p., 1864–84.

Reynolds, Matthew G. *Spanish and Mexican Land Laws, New Spain and Mexico.* St. Louis, Buxton & Skinner, Stationery Co., 1895.

Rockwell, John A. *A Compilation of Spanish and Mexican Law, in Relation to Mines, and Titles to Real Estate, in Force in California, Texas, and New Mexico. . . .* New York, J. S. Voorhies, 1851.

Schäfer, Ernst. *Indice de la colección de documentos inéditos de Indias editada por Pacheco, Cárdenas, Torres de Mendoza, y otros (1 serie, tomos 1–42) y la Real Academia de la Historia (2 serie, tomos 1–25).* 2 vols. (Consejo Superior de Investigaciones Científicas, Instituto "Gonzalo Fernández de Oviedo"). Madrid, Gráficas Ultra, S.A., 1946–47.

Thomas, Alfred B., trans. and ed. *Teodoro de Croix and the Northern Frontier of New Spain, 1776–1783, from the Original Documents in the Archives of the Indies, Seville.* Norman, University of Oklahoma Press, 1941.

White, Joseph M., ed. *A New Collection of Laws, Charters, and Local Ordinances of the Governments of Great Britain, France and Spain, Relating to Concessions of Land in Their Respective Colonies,*

Together with the Laws of Mexico and Texas on the Same Subject. 2 vols. Philadelphia, T. & J. W. Johnson, 1839.

Arizona

Baldonado, Luis, O.F.M., trans. and ed. "Missions San José de Tumacácori and San Xavier del Bac in 1774." *The Kiva* 24 (April 1959): 21-24.

Bolton, Herbert E., ed. *Kino's Historical Memoir of Pimería Alta; A Contemporary Account of the Beginnings of California, Sonora, and Arizona by Father Eusebio Francisco Kino, S.J., Pioneer Missionary Explorer, Cartographer, and Ranchman, 1683–1711.* 2 vols. Cleveland, Arthur H. Clark, 1919.

Burrus, Ernest J., S.J., ed. *Correspondencia del P. Kino con los generales de la Compañía de Jesús, 1682–1707.* Mexico, Editorial Jus, 1961.

——————. *Kino escribe a la Duquesa: Correspondencia del P. Eusebio Francisco Kino con la Duquesa de Aveiro y otros documentos.* Madrid, Ediciones José Porrúa Turanzas, 1964. *(Colección Chimalistac de libros y documentos acerca de la Nueva España, 18.)*

——————, trans. and ed. *Kino Reports to Headquarters: Correspondence from New Spain with Rome; Original Spanish Text of Fourteen Unpublished Letters and Reports with English Translation and Notes.* Rome, Institutum Historicum Societatis Iesu, 1954. *Supplement, Facsimiles of Documents and Kino's 1683 Map of Lower California.* Rome, 1954.

——————. *Kino Writes to the Duchess: Letters of Eusebio Francisco Kino, S.J., to the Duchess of Aveiro.* Rome, St. Louis, Jesuit Historical Institute, 1965. *(Sources and Studies for the History of the Americas, vol. 1.)*

——————. "Kino's First Report on His First Permanent Mission." *Manuscripta* 5 (October 1961):164–69.

——————. *Kino's Plan for the Development of Pimería Alta, Arizona & Upper California: A Report to the Mexican Viceroy.* Tucson, Arizona Historical Society, 1961.

Collins, Karen, S., ed. "Fray Pedro de Arriquibar's Census of Tucson 1820." *Journal of Arizona History* 11 (Spring 1970):14–22.

Cosulich, Bernice. *Tucson Census, 1820.* Tucson, Arizona Silhouettes, 1953.

Dobyns, Henry F. and Paul H. Ezell. "Sonoran Missionaries in 1790." *New Mexico Historical Review* 34 (January 1959):52–54.

Ezell, Paul H., trans. and ed. "Fray Diego Bringas, a Forgotten Cartographer of Sonora." *Imago Mundi* 13 (October 1956):151–58.

Gardiner, Arthur D., trans. and ed. "Letter of Father Middendorff, S.J., Dated from Tucson 3 March 1757." *The Kiva* 22 (June 1957): 1–10.

Gómez Canedo, Lino, ed. *Sonora hacia fines del siglo XVIII: Un informe del misionero franciscano Fray Francisco Antonio Barbastro, con otros documentos complementarios.* Guadalajara, Librería Font, 1971. (*Documentación Historia Mexicana*, No. 4).

Hammond, George P., trans. and ed. "Pimería Alta after Kino's Time." *New Mexico Historical Review* 4 (July 1929):220–38.

Hernández y Sánchez-Barba, Mario. *Viajes misionales por la Pimería Alta: Estudio preliminar y notas aclaratorias.* Madrid, Aguilar, 1958. (*Bibliotecá Indiana: Libros y fuentes sobre América y Filipinas*, 2:87–255.)

Hopkins, Rufus C. *Muniments of Title of the Barony of Arizona and Translation into English.* San Francisco, The Bancroft Co., 1893.

Ives, Ronald L., trans. and ed. "The Report of the Bishop of Durango on Conditions in Northwestern Mexico in 1745." *Hispanic American Historical Review* 19 (August 1939):314–17.

Kessell, John L., trans. and ed. "Documents of Arizona History: A Personal Note from Tumacácori, 1825." *Journal of Arizona History* 6 (Autumn 1965):145–51.

————. "Father Eixarch and the Visitation at Tumacácori." *The Kiva* 30 (February 1965):77–81.

Lettres édifiantes et curieuses, écrites des missions étrangères par quelques missionaires de la Compagnie de Jésus. 34 vols. Paris, 1702–76.

Mexico, Archivo General de la Nación. *Las misiones de Sonora y Arizona: Comprendiendo: La Crónica titulada; "Favores Celestiales" y la "Relación diaria de la entrada al Noroeste" por el padre Eusebio Francisco Kino (Kühn)."* Versión paleográfica e indice por Francisco Fernández del Castillo, con noticias biobibliográficas del padre Kino y sus exploraciones y fundaciones por el dr. Emilio Böse. Mexico, Editorial "Cultura," 1913–22. (*Publicaciones del Archivo General de la Nación, 8.*)

Murr, Christoph G. von, ed. *Nachrichten von Verschiedenen Laendern des Spanischen America: Aus eigenhandigen Aufsaetzen eigniger Missionare der Gesellschaft Jesu.* 2 vols. Halle, J.C. Hendel, 1809–11.

Reyes, Antonio de los, O.F.M., *Copia del manifiesto Estado de las provincias de Sonora, en 20 de abril de 1772.* Mexico, Ed. Vargas Rea, 1945.

————. "Memorial sobre las misiones de Sonora [julio 6, 1772]." *Boletín del Archivo General de Mexico* 9 (enero-febrero-marzo 1938):276–320.

Stöcklein, Joseph et al, eds. *Das Neue Welt-Bott: Allerhand so lehr-als Geist-Reiche Brief Scrifften und Reis-Beschreibungen Welche von denen Missionariis der Gesellschafft Jesu aus beyden Indien und andern über Meer Gelegnen Ländern seit An. 1642 biss auf das Jahr [1750]. 5 vols. Augsburg, 1726–58.*

Treutlein, Theodore E., trans. and ed. "The Relation of Philipp Segesser." *Mid-America* 27 (July 1945):139–87.

Venturi, Pietro Tacchi, "Nuove Lettere Inedite del P. Eusebio Francesco Chino d. C. d. G.," *Archivum Historicum Societatis Iesu,* 3 (1934):248–64.

Whiting, Alfred T., ed. "The Tumacácori Census of 1796." *The Kiva* 19 (Fall 1953):1–12.

Yale University Library, Beinecke Rare Book and Manuscript Library. *Manuscripts from the Edwin J. Beinecke Collection of Robert Louis Stevenson and the Frederick W. and Carrie S. Beinecke Collection of Western Americana.* [New Haven, 1963].

California

Academy of Pacific Coast History, Berkeley, Calif. *Publications.* Volumes 1–4, 1909–1919. Berkeley, University of California Press, 1910–19.

Avila, Pablo, trans. and ed. "Naming of the Elector-Designate, Santa Barbara, 1830." *California Historical Society Quarterly* 27 (December 1948):333–38.

Bean, Lowell J. and William M. Mason, trans. and ed. *Diaries and Accounts of the Romero Expeditions into Arizona and California, 1823–1826.* Los Angeles, Ward Ritchie Press, 1962.

Becker, Robert H. *Diseños of California Ranchos: Maps of Thirty-Seven Land Grants, 1822–1846, from the Records of the United States District Court, San Francisco.* San Francisco, Book Club of California, 1964.

Bolton, Herbert E., trans. and ed. *Historical Memoirs of New California by Fray Francisco Palóu, O.F.M.* 4 vols. Berkeley, University of California Press, 1926.

Brooks, B. S. "Alcalde Grants in the City of San Francisco." *The Pioneer: or, California Monthly Magazine* 1 (March, April, May, June 1854):129–44, 193–200, 258–64, 321–29; 2 (July 1854):1–15.

Charles, W. N., trans. and ed. "Transcription and Translation of the Old Mexican Documents of the Los Angeles County Archives." *Historical Society of Southern California Quarterly* 20 (June 1938): 84–88.

Cook, Sherburne F., trans. and ed. "Colonial Expeditions to the Interior of California Central Valley, 1800–1820." *University of California Publications, Anthropological Records* 16, no. 6 (1960):239–92.

Cutter, Donald C., trans. and ed. *The California Coast.* Norman, University of Oklahoma Press, 1969.

Cutter, Donald C. *Malaspina in California*. San Francisco, John Howell Books, 1960.

Drake, Eugene B., comp. *Jimeno's and Hartnell's Indexes of Land Concessions, from 1830 to 1846: Also, Toma de Razón or Registry of Titles, for 1844–'45; Approvals of Land Grants by the Territorial Deputation and Departmental Assembly of California, from 1835 to 1846; and a List of Unclaimed Grants.* Compiled from the Spanish Archives in the U.S. Surveyor General's Office. San Francisco, Kenny & Alexander, Booksellers, 1861.

Engelhardt, Zephyrin, O.F.M. *The Missions and Missionaries of California.* 4 vols. San Francisco, The James H. Barry Company, 1908–15.

Figueroa, José. *The Manifesto which the General of Brigade, Don José Figueroa, Commandant-General and Political Chief of U. California, Makes to the Mexican Republic.* Monterey, 1835. Also San Francisco, San Francisco Herald Office, 1855, and Oakland, Biobooks, 1952.

Flores, José Manuel. [Letter to José de Jesús Pico, Dec. 7, 1846] *Congressional Globe for the First Session, Thirtieth Congress, Appendix*, 25:984. Washington, Blair & Rives, 1848.

Font, Pedro, O.F.M. *San Francisco Bay and California in 1776: Three Maps, with Outline Sketches Reproduced in Facsimile from the Original Manuscript Drawn by Pedro Font, Chaplain and Cartographer to the Expedition Led by Juan Bautista de Ansa. . . .* With an explanation by Irving B. Richman. Providence, R. I., Merrymount Press, 1911.

Geiger, Maynard J., O.F.M., trans. and ed. *Letter of Luís Jayme, O.F.M., San Diego, October 17, 1772.* Los Angeles, Dawson's Book Shop, 1970.

———, trans. and ed. "Six Census Records of Los Angeles and Its Immediate Area between 1804 and 1823." *Southern California Quarterly* 54 (Winter 1972):313–52.

Gómez Canedo, Lino, O.F.M., ed. *De México a la Alta California, una gran epopeya misional.* Mexico, Editorial Jus, 1969, (Colección México Heroico, Num. 103.)

Griffin, George B., trans. and ed. *Documents from the Sutro Collection.* Los Angeles, Franklin Printing Co., 1891. (Historical Society of Southern California, *Publications* 2, pt. 1.)

Hammond, George P., ed. *The Larkin Papers: Personal, Business and Official Correspondence of Thomas Oliver Larkin, Merchant and United States Consul in California.* 10 vols. Berkeley, University of California Press, 1951–64.

———, trans. and ed. *Noticias de California, First Report of the Occu-*

pation by the Portolá Expedition, 1770. San Francisco, The Book Club of California, 1958.

Harrington, M. R., trans. "Will of Don Tomás Antonio Yorba, Year of 1845." Historical Society of Southern California Quarterly 33 (March 1951):67–73.

Hartnell, William, trans., and Neal Harlow, ed. A Faithful Translation of the Papers Respecting the Grant Made by Governor Alvarado to J. A. Sutter. Sacramento, Sacramento Book Collectors Club, 1942. Reprinted from the original pamphlet published in 1850 by John Plumbe.

Hawgood, John A., ed. First and Last Consul: Thomas Oliver Larkin and the Americanization of California, a Selection of Letters. San Marino, The Huntington Library, 1962.

Hopkins, Rufus C., comp. Digest of Mexican Laws, Circulars and Decrees, in the Archives of Upper California. San Francisco, O'Meara & Painter, 1858.

Hutchinson, A. Alan, ed. "An Official List of Members of the Híjar-Padrés Colony for Mexican California, 1834." Pacific Historical Review 40 (August 1973):407–18.

Jimeno Casarin, Manuel. Jimeno's Index to Land Concessions, from 1830 to 1845, and the "Toma de Razón," or Registry of Titles for 1844–45, in the Archives of the Office of the Surveyor General of the United States for California. San Francisco, Lee & Carl, [1858].

Johnson, John E., trans. Regulations for Governing the Province of the Californias, Approved by His Majesty by Royal Order, dated October 24, 1781. San Francisco, The Grabhorn Press, 1929.

Kenneally, Finbar, O.F.M., ed. Writings of Fermín Francisco de Lasuén. 2 vols. Washington, Academy of American Franciscan History, 1965.

Layne, J. Gregg, "The First Census of the Los Angeles District [1836]." Historical Society of Southern California Quarterly 18 (September–December 1936):81–99. With facsimile, pp. 1–54.

————. "José María Flores." Historical Society of Southern California Quarterly 17 (March 1935):23–27.

Lelande, H. J., trans. "Extracts from the Los Angeles Archives." Historical Society of Southern California, Annual Publications 6, pt. 3 (1905):242–52.

Mexico. Archivo General de la Nación. Photographic Exhibits in California Land Cases from the Mexican Archives. [Collected by] James F. Shunk. San Francisco, 1861. Photographic reproductions.

Mexico. Ministerio de Hacienda y Crédito Público. Las misiones de la Alta California. Mexico, Tipografía de la Oficina Impresora de Estampillas, 1914. (Colección de documentos históricos, vol. 2.)

Newmark, Marco R., trans. and ed. "Ordinances and Regulations of Los Angeles, 1832–1888." *Historical Society of Southern California Quarterly* 30 (March 1948):26–41.

Northrop, Mrs. Joseph M., ed. "Padrón (Census) of Los Angeles, 1790." *Southern California Quarterly* 41 (June 1959):181–82.

Northrop, Marie E., ed. "The Los Angeles Padrón of 1844 as Copied from the Los Angeles City Archives." *Historical Society of Southern California Quarterly* 42 (December 1960):360–417.

Nunis, Doyce B., Jr., ed. "Notes and Documents: Six New Larkin Letters." *Southern California Quarterly* 49 (March 1967):65–103.

Palóu, Francisco, O.F.M. *Noticias de la Nueva California, escritos por el Rev. Padre Francisco Palóu.* 4 vols. San Francisco, Imprenta de Edouardo Bosqui y Cia, 1874. (California Historical Society, *Publications,* ed. by John T. Doyle).

————. "Viajes misionales por la Alta California." In Mario Hernández y Sánchez-Barba, ed. *Viajes por Norteamérica,* pp. 629–782. Madrid, Aguilar, 1958. *(Biblioteca Indiana: Libros y Fuentes sobre América y Filipinas, 2.)*

Pico, Pio. *Don Pio Pico's Historical Narrative.* Ed. and introduction by Martin Cole and Henry Welcome: trans. by Arthur P. Botello. Glendale, Calif., Arthur H. Clark Co., 1973.

Porrúa Turanzas, José. *Noticias y documentos acerca de las Californias, 1764–1795.* Madrid, José Porrúa Turanzas, 1959. *(Colección Chimalistac de libros y documentos acerca de la Nueva España, 5).*

Price, Francis, trans. "Letters of Narciso Durán." *California Historical Society Quarterly* 37 (June, September 1958):97–128, 241–65.

Priestley, Herbert I., trans. and ed. *A Historical, Political and Natural Description of California by Pedro Fages, Soldier of Spain.* Berkeley, University of California Press, 1937.

Reynolds, Keld J., trans. and ed. "Principal Actions of the California Junta de Fomento, 1825–1827." *California Historical Society Quarterly* 24–25 (December 1945–December 1946):57–58, 149–68, 267–78, 347–67.

————. "The Reglamento for the Híjar and Padrés Colony of 1834." *Historical Society of Southern California Quarterly,* 28 (December 1946):142–75.

Robinson, William W., trans. and ed. "The Indians of Los Angeles As Revealed by the Los Angeles City Archives." *Historical Society of Southern California Quarterly* 20 (December 1938):156–72.

San Francisco, Alcalde. "Copy of Original Spanish Records of Land Grants Contained in a Book Entitled 'Blotter of Francisco Guerrero while Alcalde at Various Times, 1839–1843'; of Record in the Recorders Office of the County of San Francisco.'" In John W.

Dwinelle, *The Colonial History of the City of San Francisco*, pp. 162–71. San Francisco, 1866.

Simpson, Lesley B., ed., and Paul D. Nathan, trans. *The Letters of José Señán, O.F.M., Mission San Buenaventura, 1796–1823.* San Francisco, John Howell for the Ventura County Historical Society, 1962.

Sutter, John A. *Six French Letters: Captain John Augustus Sutter to Jean Jacques Vioget, 1842–1843.* Sacramento, The Nugget Press, 1942.

Tays, George, ed., "Pio Pico's Correspondence with the Mexican Government, 1846–1848." *California Historical Society Quarterly* 13 (June 1934):99–149.

Temple, Thomas W. II, trans. "First Census of Los Angeles." Historical Society of Southern California, *Annual Publications* 15 (1931): 148–49.

———— and Marion Parks, trans. "Documents Pertaining to the Founding of Los Angeles." Historical Society of Southern California, *Annual Publications* 15 (1931):117–263.

Tibesar, Antonine, O.F.M., ed. *Writings of Junípero Serra.* 4 vols. Washington, Academy of American Franciscan History, 1955–56. (*Publications* of the Academy of American Franciscan History, *Documentary Series, Vols.* 4–7.)

Valades, José C., ed. *Noticias acerca del Puerto de San Francisco (Alta California).* Por Martín Landaeta. Mexico, Antigua Librería Robredo de José Porrúa e Hijos, Sucs., 1949. (*Biblioteca histórica mexicana de obras inéditos,* 22.)

Watson, Douglas S. and Thomas W. Temple II, trans. and eds. *The Expedition into California of the Venerable Padre Fray Junípero Serra and His Companions in the Year 1769, as Told by Fray Francisco Palóu, and Hitherto Unpublished Letters of Serra, Palóu, and Gálvez: the Whole Newly Translated and Arranged.* San Francisco, Nueva California Press, 1934.

————. "La carta de Flores." *California Historical Society Quarterly* 12 (June 1933):147–54.

Weber, Francis J., trans. and ed. *A Letter of Junípero Serra to the Reverend Father Preacher Fray Fermín Francisco de Lasuén: A Bicentennial Discovery.* Boston, David R. Godine, 1970.

New Mexico

Adams, Eleanor B. and Angelico Chavez, trans. and eds. *The Missions of New Mexico, 1776: A Description by Fray Francisco Atanasio Domínguez.* Albuquerque, University of New Mexico Press, 1956.

Bandelier, Adolph F. "An Outline of the Documentary History of the

Zuñi Tribe." *Journal of American Ethnology and Archaeology* 3 (1892):1–115.

Bloom, Lansing B., ed. *Antonio Barreiro's Ojeada sobre Nuevo México.* Santa Fe, El Palacio Press, 1928. (Historical Society of New Mexico, *Publications in History*, Vol. 5.)

Carroll, H. Bailey and J. Villasana Haggard, trans. and eds. *Three New Mexico Chronicles: The Exposición of Don Pedro Bautista Pino 1812; the Ojeada of Lic. Antonio Barreiro 1832; and the Additions by Don José Agustín de Escudero, 1849.* Albuquerque, The Quivira Society, 1942. (Quivira Society, *Publications*, Vol. 11.)

Dunham, Harold H., ed. "Sidelights on Santa Fe Traders, 1839–1846." *Westerners Brand Book, Denver Annual* 6 (1950):263–82. Contains despatches of Manuel Alvarez.

Hackett, Charles W., ed. *Historical Documents Relating to New Mexico, Nueva Vizcaya and Approaches Thereto, to 1773.* 3 vols. Washington, Carnegie Institution of Washington, 1923, 1926, 1937. (Carnegie Institution of Washington, *Publication*, No. 330.)

————, ed., and Charmion C. Shelby, trans. *Revolt of the Pueblo Indians of New Mexico and Otermín's Attempted Reconquest, 1680–1682.* 2 vols. Albuquerque, University of New Mexico Press, 1942. (*Coronado Cuarto Centennial Publications, 1540–1940*, ed. by George P. Hammond, Vols. 8–9.)

Hammond, George P., ed. and Agapito Rey, trans. *Narratives of the Coronado Expedition, 1540–1542.* Albuquerque, University of New Mexico Press, 1940. (*Coronado Cuarto Centennial Publications, 1540–1940*, ed. by G. P. Hammond, Vol. 2.)

———— and ————. *Obregon's History of 16th Century Explorations in Western America, Entitled Chronicle, Commentary, or Relation of the Ancient and Modern Discoveries in New Spain and New Mexico, Mexico, 1584.* Los Angeles, Wetzel Publishing Co., 1928.

———— and ————. *Oñate, Colonizer of New Mexico, 1595–1628.* Albuquerque, University of New Mexico Press, 1953. (*Coronado Cuarto Centennial Publications, 1540–1940*, ed. by G. P. Hammond, Vols. 5–6.)

———— and ————. *The Rediscovery of New Mexico, 1580–1594: The Explorations of Chamuscado, Espejo, Castaño de Sosa, Morlete and Leyva de Bonilla and Humaña.* Albuquerque, University of New Mexico Press, 1966. (*Coronado Cuarto Centennial Publications, 1540–1940*, ed. by G. P. Hammond Vol. 3.)

Hodge, Frederick W., ed., and Gilberto Espinosa, trans. *History of New Mexico, by Gaspar Pérez de Villagrá, Alcalá, 1610.* Los Angeles, The Quivira Society, 1933. (Quivira Society, *Publications*, ed. by G. P. Hammond, Vol. 4.)

———— and Charles F. Lummis, eds., and Mrs. Edward E. Ayer, trans.

The Memorial of Fray Alonso de Benavides. Chicago, Privately Printed, 1916.

———— and George P. Hammond, eds., and Agapito Rey, trans. *Fray Alonso de Benavides' Revised Memorial of 1634, with Numerous Supplementary Documents Elaborately Annotated.* Albuquerque, University of New Mexico Press, 1945. (*Coronado Cuarto Centennial Publications, 1540–1940, Coronado Historical Series,* ed. by G. P. Hammond, Vol. 4.)

Loomis, Noel M., ed., and Abraham P. Nasatir, trans. *Pedro Vial and the Roads to Santa Fe.* Norman, University of Oklahoma Press, 1967.

Lummis, Charles F., trans. and ed. "Letter of the Father Fray Silvestre Vélez de Escalante, written on the 2d of April, in the Year 1778." *Land of Sunshine* 12 (March–April 1900):247–50, 309–14. Printed also in R. E. Twitchell, ed., *Spanish Archives of New Mexico,* 2:268–80.

Lynch, Cyprian J., ed., and Peter P. Forrestal, trans. *Benavides Memorial of 1630.* Washington, Academy of American Franciscan History, 1954. (*Publications* of the Academy of American Franciscan History, *Documentary Series,* Vol. 2.)

Maas, Otto, ed. *Misiones de Nuevo Mejico: Documentos del Archivo General de Indias* (Sevilla). Madrid, Imprenta Hijos de T. Minuesa de los Ríos, 1929.

————. *Viajes de misioneros franciscanos á la conquista del Nuevo México: Documentos del Archivo General de Indias* (Sevilla). Sevilla, Imprenta de San Antonio C. de San Buenaventura, 1915.

Moorhead, Max L. "Notes and Documents [Mexican Report on American Invasion of New Mexico]." *New Mexico Historical Review* 26 (January 1951):68–82.

Morfi, Juan Agustín. *Descripción geográfica del Nuevo México.* México, Vargas Rea, 1947. (*Biblioteca Aportación Histórica.*)

Olmstead, Virginia L., trans. and ed. *New Mexico Spanish & Mexican Colonial Censuses 1790, 1823, 1845.* Albuquerque, New Mexico Genealogical Society Inc., 1975.

Padilla, José León, defendant. *History of the Las Vegas Grant: Containing a Correct Literal Translation of the Original Spanish Papers* . . . . East Las Vegas, J. A. Caruth, Printer, 1890.

Perrigo, Lynn I., trans. "New Mexico in the Mexican Period as Revealed in the Torres Documents." *New Mexico Historical* Review 29 (January 1954):28–40.

————. "The Personal Interests of Juan Gerónimo Torres." *New Mexico Historical Review* 26 (April 1951):159–64.

————. "Provincial Statutes of 1824 to 1826." *New Mexico Historical Review* 27 (January 1952):66–76.

Perrigo, Lynn I. "Some Laws and Legal Proceedings of the Mexican Period." *New Mexico Historical Review* 26 (July, October 1951): 244-47, 335–41.

Porrúa Turanzas, José. *Documentos para servir a la historia del Nuevo Mexico, 1538–1778.* Madrid, José Porrúa Turanzas, 1962. *(Colección Chimalistac de libros y documentos acerca de la Nueva España, 13).*

Reeve, Frank D., ed. "The Charles Bent Papers." *New Mexico Historical Review* 29–31 (July 1954–July 1956).

————. "Documents Concerning Bishop Crespo's Visitation, 1730." *New Mexico Historical Review* 28 (July 1953):222–33.

Thomas, Alfred B., trans. and ed. *After Coronado: Spanish Exploration Northeast of New Mexico, 1696–1727; Documents from the Archives of Spain, Mexico, and New Mexico.* Norman, University of Oklahoma Press, 1936.

————. *Forgotten Frontiers: A Study of the Spanish Indian Policy of Don Juan Bautista de Anza, Governor of New Mexico, 1777–1787, from the Original Documents in the Archives of Spain, Mexico and New Mexico.* Norman, University of Oklahoma Press, 1932.

————. *The Plains Indians and New Mexico, 1751–1777: A Collection of Documents Illustrative of the History of the Eastern Frontier of New Mexico.* Albuquerque, University of New Mexico Press, 1940.

Tyler, S. Lyman, ed., and H. Darrel Taylor, trans. "The Report of Fray Alonso de Posada in Relation to Quivira and Teguayo." *New Mexico Historical Review* 33 (October 1958):285–314.

Weber, David J., trans. and ed. *The Extranjeros: Selected Documents from the Mexican Side of the Santa Fe Trail, 1825–1828.* Santa Fe, Stagecoach Press, 1967.

Texas

Abstract of the Constitution, Laws, and other Documents Having Reference to, and Including the Impresario Grants and Contracts Made by the State of Coahuila and Texas to and with John Charles Beales: Also, Deeds of the Same from Him to John Woodward; To Which Is Appended an Argument Sustaining the Rights and Titles of John Woodward. New York, Narine Co's Print, 1842.

Alessio Robles, Vito, ed. *Memoria [de Miguel Ramos Arizpe] sobre el Estado de las Provincias Internas de Oriente presentada a las Cortes de Cádiz.* Mexico, Bibliófilos mexicanos, 1932.

Amsler, Robert, ed. "A Prospectus for the Wavell Colony in Texas." *Southwestern Historical Quarterly* 56 (April 1953):543–51.

Barker, Eugene C., ed. *The Austin Papers.* 3 vols. Washington, Government Printing Office, 1924, 1928. (American Historical Association, *Annual Report* [1919]:2, pts. 1 and 2, [1928]2.)

————. *The Austin Papers, October, 1834–January, 1837, Volume III.* Austin, University of Texas Press, 1926.

————. "Descriptions of Texas by Stephen F. Austin." *Southwestern Historical Quarterly* 28 (October 1924):98-121.

————. "General Austin's Order Book for the Campaign of 1835." *Texas State Historical Association Quarterly* 11 (July 1907):1–55.

————. "Journal of the Permanent Council (October 11–27, 1835." *Texas State Historical Association Quarterly* 7 (April 1904):249–78.

————. "Journal of Stephen F. Austin on His First Trip to Texas, 1821" *Texas State Historical Association Quarterly* 7 (April 1904): 286–307.

————. "Minutes of the Ayuntamiento of San Felipe de Austin, 1828–1832." *Southwestern Historical Quarterly* 21–24 (January 1918–October 1920).

Beers, Henry P., ed. "Stephen F. Austin and Anthony Butler: Documents." *Southwestern Historical Quarterly* 62 (October 1958): 233–40.

Benson, Nettie L., trans. and ed. "A Governor's [Manuel María de Salcedo] Report on Texas in 1809." *Southwestern Historical Quarterly* 71 (April 1968):603–15.

————. *Report That Dr. Miguel Ramos de Arizpe, Priest of Bourbon and Deputy in the Present General and Special Cortes of Spain for the Province of Coahuila, One of the Four Eastern Interior Provinces of the Kingdom of Mexico, Presents to the August Congress on the Natural, Political and Civil Condition of the Provinces of Coahuila, Nuevo León, Nuevo Santander, and Texas of the Four Eastern Provinces of the Kingdom of Mexico.* Austin, University of Texas Press, 1950.

Bolton, Herbert E., trans. and ed. *Athanase de Mézières and the Louisiana-Texas Frontier, 1768–1780; Documents Published for the First Time, from the Original Spanish and French Manuscripts, Chiefly in the Archives of Mexico and Spain.* 2 vols. Cleveland, Arthur H. Clark, 1914.

Campbell, Elsie, trans. "Spanish Records of the Civil Government of Ysleta, 1835." Master's thesis, Texas Western College, 1950.

Castañeda, Carlos E., trans. "Statistical Report on Texas by Juan N. Almonte." *Southwestern Historical Quarterly* 28 (January 1925): 177–222.

Chabot, Frederick C., ed. *Texas in 1811: The Las Casas and Sambrano Revolutions.* San Antonio, Yanaguana Society, 1941. (Yanaguana Society, *Publications* 6.)

————. *Texas Letters.* San Antonio, Yanaguana Society, 1940. (Yanaguana Society, *Publications* 5.)

Dabbs, J. Autrey, trans. "The Texas Missions in 1785 [Report by Fray José F. López]." *Mid-America* 22 (January 1940):38–58.

Davis, Robert E., ed., and Thomas W. Walker, trans. *The Diary of William Barret Travis, August 30, 1833–June 26, 1834.* Waco, Texas, Texian Press, 1966.

Documents Relating to a Grant of Land Made to John Charles Beales and José Manuel Royuela in Texas. New York, 1833.

Documents Relating to Grants of Lands Made to Don Estevan Willson [sic] and Dr. Richard Exeter, in Texas. New York, 1831.

Edman, Grace A., trans. "A Compilation of Royal Decrees in the Archivo General de la Nación Relating to Texas and Other Northern Provinces of New Spain, 1719–1799." Master's thesis, University of Texas, 1930.

Espinosa, José Manuel, trans. "Population of the El Paso District in 1792." *Mid-America, n.s. 12 (January 1941):61–84.*

Freeman, John D. *Memorial of Doctor John Charles Beales, et als., vs. The United States, Narrating the Establishment of a Mexican Colony on the Río Grande, under Grants from the Mexican State of Coahuila and Texas, Its Destruction by the Results of the Rebellion in Texas in 1835, the Forcible Expulsion of Colonists from Their Lands and the Subsequent Denial Alike of All Legislative and Judicial Remedies, and Praying of Congress the Ordinary Relief in the Premises.* [Washington? 1870?]

Galveston Bay and Texas Land Company. *Address to the Reader of the Documents Relating to the Galveston Bay & Texas Land Company, Which Are Contained in the Appendix.* New York, G. F. Hopkins & Son, 1831.

Garrett, Kathryn, ed. "The First Constitution of Texas, April 17, 1813." *Southwestern Historical Quarterly* 40 (April 1937):290–308.

Garrison, George P., ed. "The Prison Journal of Stephen F. Austin." *Texas State Historical Association Quarterly* 2 (January 1899): 183–210.

Gómez Canedo, Lino., O.F.M. *Primeras exploraciones y poblamiento de Texas, 1686–1694.* Monterrey, Instituto Tecnológico y de Estudios Superiores de Monterrey, 1968.

Gulich, Charles A., Jr., Katherine Elliott, Winnie Allen, and Harriet Smither, eds. *The Papers of Mirabeau Bonaparte Lamar.* 6 vols. Austin, A. C. Baldwin and Sons, Printers, 1921–28.

Hackett, Charles W., ed., and Charmion C. Shelby and Mary R. Splawn, trans. *Pichardo's Treatise on the Limits of Louisiana and Texas: An Argumentative Historical Treatise with Reference to the Verification of the True Limits of the Provinces of Louisiana and Texas; Written by Father José Antonio Pichardo* .... 4 vols. Austin, University of Texas Press, 1931–46.

Hafen, LeRoy R., ed. "[Antonio] Armijo's Journal of 1829–30: The Beginning of Trade between New Mexico and California." *Colorado Magazine* 27 (April 1950):120–31.

Hatcher, Mattie A., trans. "Descriptions of the Tejas or Asinai Indians, 1691–1722." *Southwestern Historical Quarterly* 30 (January, April 1927):206–18, 283–304; 31 (July, October 1927):50–62, 150–80.

_____. "Texas in 1820: Report on the Barbarous Indians of the Province of Texas, by Juan Antonio Padilla." *Southwestern Historical Quarterly* 23 (July 1919):47–60.

_____ and Margaret K. Kress, trans. "Diary of a Visit of Inspection of the Texas Missions Made by Fray Gaspar José de Solís in the Year 1767–68." *Southwestern Historical Quarterly* 35 (July 1931): 28–76.

Hunnicutt, Helen M., trans. and ed. "Election of Alcaldes in San Fernando, 1750." *Southwestern Historical Quarterly* 54 (January 1951):333–36.

McLean, Malcolm D., ed. *Papers Concerning Robertson's Colony in Texas.* 2 vols. Fort Worth, Texas Christian University Press, 1974–75. In progress.

Morfi, Juan Agustín, O.F.M. *History of Texas, 1673–1779, by Fray Juan Agustín Morfi.* 2 vols. Trans. and ed. by Carlos E. Castañeda. Albuquerque, The Quivira Society, 1935. (Quivira Society, *Publications,* ed. by G. P. Hammond, Vol. 6.)

Mullins, Marion D., ed. *The First Census of Texas, 1829–1836, to Which are Added Texas Citizenship Lists, 1821–1845, and Other Early Records of the Republic of Texas.* Washington, National Genealogical Society, 1959. (National Genealogical Society, *Special Publications,* No. 22.)

Osborn, Mary M., ed. "The Atascosita Census of 1826." *Texana* 1 (Fall 1963):299–321.

Perry, Carmen, trans. and ed. *The Impossible Dream by the Rio Grande: A Documented Chronicle of the Establishment and Annihilation of San José de Palafox.* San Antonio, St. Mary's University Press, 1971.

Petition to Congress Made by the Heirs of Dr. John Charles Beales and the Howard University of Washington for the Confirmation of the Title to a Certain Grant of Land in New Mexico Known as the Arkansas Grant. New York, S. C. Law, 1880.

Porrúa Turanzas, José, ed. *Documentos para la historia eclesiástica y civil de la Provincia de Texas, o Nuevas Philipinas, 1720–1779.* Madrid, Ediciones José Porrúa Turanzas, 1961. (*Colección Chimalistac de libros y documentos de la Nueva España,* 12.)

Simpson, Lesley B., ed., and Paul D. Nathan, trans. *The San Sabá Papers: A Documentary Account of the Founding and Destruction of San Sabá Mission.* San Francisco, John Howell Books, 1959.

Taylor, Virginia H. and Juanita Hammons, trans. and eds. *The Letters of Antonio Martínez, Last Spanish Governor of Texas, 1817–1822.* Austin, Texas State Library, 1957.

Texas, General Land Office. *Abstract of All Original Texas Land Titles Comprising Grants and Locations to August 31, 1941.* 8 vols. Austin, 1941–42. Other compilations of abstracts were published in 1841, 1852, and 1859.

————, ————. *An Abstract of the Original Titles of Records in the General Land Office.* Houston, National Banner Office–Niles & Co., Printers, 1838. Reprinted, Austin, Pemberton Press, 1964.

————. Laws, Statutes, etc. *Translation of the Laws, Orders and Contracts, on Colonization, from January 1821, up to 1829, in Virtue of Which Col. Stephen F. Austin Introduced and Settled Foreign Emigrants in Texas.* Columbia, Texas. Reprinted by Borden & Moore, 1837.

Wallace, Ernest and David M. Vigness, eds. *Documents of Texas History, Volume I (1528–1846).* Lubbock, Texas Technological College Library, 1960.

Wavell, Arthur. "Account of the Province of Texas." In Henry G. Ward. *Mexico in 1827*, 1:547–59. 2 vols. London, Henry Colburn, 1828.

West, Elizabeth H., trans. and ed. "Bonilla's Brief Compendium of the History of Texas, 1772." *Texas State Historical Association Quarterly* 8 (July 1904):3–78.

————. "Diary of José Bernardo Gutiérrez de Lara, 1811–1812." *American Historical Review* 34 (October 1928, January 1929): 55–77, 281–94.

Williams, Amelia W. and Eugene C. Barker, eds. *The Writings of Sam Houston, 1813–1863.* 8 vols. Austin, The University of Texas Press, 1938–43.

Winfrey, Dorman H., James M. Day, George R. Nielsen, and Albert D. Pattillo, eds. *Texas Indian Papers, 1825–1843.* Austin, Texas State Library, 1959.

Winkler, Ernest W., ed. "Documents Relating to the Organization of the Municipality of Washington, Texas." *Texas State Historical Association Quarterly* 10 (July 1906):96–100.

————. *Manuscript Letters and Documents of Early Texians*, Austin, The Steck Company, 1937.

Journals and Diaries

Anza, Juan Bautista de. "Anza, Indian Fighter: The Spring Campaign of 1766." Trans. and ed. by John L. Kessell. *Journal of Arizona History* 9 (Fall 1968):155–63.

————. "Anza's Complete Diary, 1774," "Anza's Diary from Tubac to San Gabriel, 1774," "Anza's Return Diary, 1774," and "Anza's Diary of the Second Anza Expedition, 1775–1776." In Herbert E.

Bolton, trans. and ed., *Anza's California Expeditions*, 2:1–130, 131–211, 213–43; 3:1–200. 5 vols. Berkeley, University of California Press, 1930.

Armijo, Antonio. "Armijo's Journal of 1829–30: The Beginning of Trade Between New Mexico and California." Ed. by LeRoy R. Hafen. *Colorado Magazine* 27 (April 1950):120–31.

Balthasar, Juan Antonio, S.J. *Juan Antonio Balthasar, Padre Visitador to the Sonora Frontier, 1744–45: Two Original Reports*. Trans. and ed. by Peter M. Dunne, S.J. Tucson, Arizona Historical Society, 1957.

Berlandier, Jean L. *The Indians of Texas in 1830 by Jean Louis Berlandier*. Ed. by John C. Ewers and trans. by Patricia R. Leclercq. Washington, Smithsonian Institution Press, 1969.

Campa, Miguel de la, O.F.M. *A Journal of Explorations Northward along the Coast from Monterey in the Year 1775 [by] Fr. Mig¹ de la Campa*. Trans. and ed. by John Galvin. San Francisco, John Howell Books, 1964.

————. *Unas páginas traspapeladas de la historia de Coahuila y Texas: El derrotero de la entrada a Texas del gobernador de Coahuila, sargento mayor Martín de Alarcón*. Redactó por Vito Alessio Robles. Mexico, Sección Editorial, 1933.

Carrasco, Diego. "Diego Carrasco's Diary [September 22–October 18, 1698]." In Ernest J. Burrus, S.J., ed. and trans., *Kino and Manje: Explorers of Sonora and Arizona*, pp. 554–77. Rome and St. Louis, Jesuit Historical Institute, 1971.

Castaño de Sosa, Gaspar. *A Colony on the Move: Gaspar Castaño de Sosa's Journal, 1590–1591*. Ed. by Albert H. Schroeder and trans. by Dan S. Matson. Santa Fe, School of American Research, 1965.

Céliz, Francisco, O.F.M. *Diary of the Alarcón Expedition into Texas, 1718–1719*. Trans. and ed. by Fritz L. Hoffman. Los Angeles, The Quivira Society, 1935. (The Quivira Society, *Publications*, Vol. 5.)

Chovel, Rafael and Jean L. Berlandier. *Diario de viaje de la Comisión de Límites que puso el gobierno de la Republica, bajo la dirección del Exmo. Sr. General de Division D. Manuel de Mier y Teran*. Mexico, Tipografía de Juan R. Navarro, 1850.

Costansó, Miguel. *The Costansó Narrative of the Portolá Expedition; First Chronicle of the Spanish Conquest of Alta California*. Trans. and ed. by Ray Brandes. Newhall, Calif., Hogarth Press, 1970.

Crespi, Juan, O.F.M. "An Unpublished Diary of Fray Juan Crespi, O.F.M., (San Diego to Monterey, April 17 to November 11, 1770)." Ed. by Charles J. G. Piette. *The Americas* 3 (July–October 1946, January 1947):102–13, 234–42, 368–81.

————. *Fray Juan Crespi, Missionary-Explorer on the Pacific Coast,*

1769–1774. Trans. and ed. by Herbert E. Bolton. Berkeley, University of California Press, 1927.

Díaz, Juan, O.F.M. "Díaz's Diary from Tubac to San Gabriel, 1774" and "Return Journey, 1774." In H. E. Bolton, trans. and ed., *Anza's California Expeditions,* 2:247–90, 293–306.

Domínguez, Francisco A., O.F.M. and Silvestre Vélez de Escalante, O.F.M. *The Domínguez-Escalante Journal: Their Expedition through Colorado, Utah, Arizona and New Mexico in 1776.* Trans. by Fray Angelico Chávez and ed. by Ted J. Warner. Provo, Utah, Brigham Young University Press, 1976.

Eixarch, Tomás, O.F.M. "Eixarch's Diary of His Winter on the Colorado, 1775–1776." In H. E. Bolton, trans. and ed., *Anza's California Expeditions,* 3:311–81.

Escobar, Francisco de, O.F.M. "Father Escobar's Relation of the Oñate Expedition to California, 1605." Trans. and ed. by H. E. Bolton. *Catholic Historical Review* 5 (April 1919):19–41.

Fages, Pedro. *The Colorado River Campaign, 1781–1782: Diary of Pedro Fages.* Trans. and ed. by Herbert I. Priestley. Berkeley, University of California Press, 1913. (Academy of Pacific Coast History, *Publications,* Vol. 3.)

Font, Pedro, O.F.M. *Font's Complete Diary: A Chronicle of the Founding of San Francisco* [1775–76]. Translated from the Original Spanish Manuscript. Berkeley, University of California Press, 1930. (H. E. Bolton, trans. and ed., *Anza's California Expeditions,* Vol. 4.)

————. "Font's Short Diary of the Second Anza Expedition, 1775–1776." In H. E. Bolton, trans. and ed., *Anza's California Expeditions* 3:201–307.

Garcés, Francisco T. H., O.F.M. *Diario de exploraciones en Arizona y California en los años de 1775 y 1776 [por] Fray Francisco Garcés.* Ed. by John Galvin. Mexico, Universidad Nacional Autonoma de Mexico, 1968. (Instituto de Investigaciones Históricas Cuadernos: Serie documental, no. 6.)

————. "Garcés Diary from Tubac to San Gabriel, 1774"; "Garcés Brief Account, 1774"; and "Garcés Diary of His Detour to the Jalchedunes, 1774." In H. E. Bolton, trans. and ed., *Anza's California Expeditions,* 2:309–60, 363–72, 375–92.

————. *On the Trail of a Spanish Pioneer: The Diary and Itinerary of Francisco Garcés (Missionary Priest) in His Travels Through Sonora, Arizona, and California, 1775–1776.* 2 vols. Trans. and ed. by Elliott Coues. New York, Francis P. Harper, 1900.

————. *A Record of Travel in Arizona and California, 1775–1776: A New Translation.* Trans. and ed. by John Galvin. San Francisco, John Howell, 1965.

Lafora, Nicolás de. *The Frontiers of New Spain: Nicolás de Lafora's Description, 1766–1768.* Trans. and ed. by Lawrence Kinnaird.

Berkeley, Calif., The Quivira Society, 1958. (Quivira Society, *Publications*, Vol. 13.)

————. *Nicolás de Lafora: Relación del viaje que hizo a los presidios internos en la frontera de la América septentrional, perteneciente al rey de España.* Liminar bibliográfico y anotaciones por Vito Alessio Robles. Mexico, Editorial Pedro Robredo, 1939.

————. "Viaje a los presidios internos de la América septentrional." Estudio preliminar y notas aclaratoricas por Mario Hernández y Sánchez-Barba. In *Viajes por Norteamérica*, pp. 252–327. Madrid, Aguilar, 1958. (*Biblioteca Indiana: libros y fuentes sobre América y Filipinas*, 2.)

Manje, Juan Mateo. *Luz de tierra incógnita en la América septentrional y diario de las exploraciones en Sonora.* Versión, notas y índice por Francisco Fernández del Castillo. Mexico, Talleres Gráficos de la Nación, 1926. (*Publicaciones* del Archivo General de la Nación, vol. 10.)

————. "Manje's Records of His Expeditions with Kino [1694–1701]." In Ernest J. Burrus, S. J., *Kino and Manje: Explorers of Sonora and Arizona*, pp. 282–519. St. Louis, Rome, Jesuit Historical Institute, 1971.

————. *Unknown Arizona and Sonora, 1693–1721: From the Fernández del Castillo version of Luz de tierra incógnita.* This is an English translation by Harry J. Karns and associates of pt. 2 of *Luz de Tierra* . . . . Tucson, Arizona Silhouettes, 1954.

Martín Bernal, Cristóbal. "Diary of Lieutenant Cristóbal Martín Bernal." Trans. and ed. by Fay J. Smith. In Fay J. Smith, John L. Kessell, and Francis J. Fox., S.J., *Father Kino in Arizona*, pp. 35–47. Phoenix, Arizona Historical Foundation, 1966.

Martínez, José Longinos. *Journal of José Longinos Martínez: Notes and Observations of the Naturalist of the Botanical Expedition in Old and New California and the South Coast, 1791–1792.* San Francisco, John Howell Books, 1961.

Montoya, Juan de. *New Mexico in 1602: Juan de Montoya's Relation of the Discovery of New Mexico.* Ed. by George P. Hammond and trans. by Agapito Rey. Albuquerque, The Quivira Society, 1938. (Quivira Society, *Publications*, vol. 8.)

Moraga, Gabriel. *The Diary of Ensign Gabriel Moraga's Expedition of Discovery in the Sacramento Valley, 1808.* Trans. and ed. by Donald C. Cutter. Los Angeles, Glen Dawson, 1957.

Morfi, Juan Agustín, O.F.M. *Diario y derrotero, 1777–1781.* Ed. by Eugenio del Hoyo and Malcolm McLean. Monterrey, Instituto Tecnológico y de Estudios Superiores de Monterrey, 1967. (*Noticias geográficas e históricas del noreste de México 2*, Instituto Tecnológico y de Estudios Superiores de Monterrey. Series: *Historia*, 5.)

————. *Viaje de Indios y diario del Nuevo México, por el Fray Juan*

Agustín de Morfi. Con una introducción bibliográfica y anotaciones por Vito Alessio Robles. Mexico, Antigua Librería Robredo de José Porrúa e Hijos, 1935.

Morfi, J. A. "Viaje de Indios y diario del Nuevo Mexico." Estudio preliminar y notas aclaratorias por Mario Hernández y Sánchez-Barba. In *Viajes por Norteamérica.* Madrid, Aguilar, 1958. pp. 329–431. (Biblioteca Indiana: libros y fuentes sobre America y Filipinas, 2.)

Nentuig, Juan. *Descripción geográfica natural y curiosa de la Provincia de Sonora.* Edición preparada, con una introducción histórica, notas, apéndice e índice analitico, por German Viveros. Mexico, Archivo General de la Nación, 1971.

————. "Rudo Ensayo." Trans. by Eusebio Guiteras. *American Catholic Historical Society Records* 5 (1894):99–264.

[————]. *Rudo Ensayo, by an Unknown Jesuit Padre, 1673.* First published in an edition of 150 copies by Buckingham Smith, 1863. Translated by Eusebio Guiteras and published in vol. 5, no. 2, of the Records of the American Catholic Historical Society of Philadelphia, June 1894. Tucson, Arizona Silhouettes, 1951.

————. *Rudo ensayo, tentativa de una prevencional descripción geographica de la provincia de Sonora, sus terminos y confines: O mejor colección de materiales para hacerla quien lo supiere mejor.* Ed. by Buckingham Smith. [Albany, N.Y., Munsell, Printer] 1863.

Och, Joseph. *Missionary in Sonora: The Travel Reports of Joseph Och, S.J., 1755–1767.* Trans. and ed. by Theodore E. Treutlein. San Francisco, California Historical Society, 1965.

————. *Nachrichten von Seinen Reisen nach dem Spanischen Amerika, seinem dortigen Aufenthalte vom Jahr 1754 bis 1767, und Rückkehr nach Europa 1768.* In Christoph G. von Murr, ed. *Nachrichten von Verschiedenen Laendern des Spanischen Amerika.* 2 vols. Halle, J. C. Hendel, 1809–11.

O'Conor, Hugo de. *Informe de Hugo de O'Conor sobre el estado de las Provincias Internas del Norte, 1771–76.* Texto original con prólogo del Lic. Enrique González Flores; anotaciones por Francisco R. Almada. Mexico, Editorial Cultura, 1952.

Palóu, Francisco, O.F.M. "Palóu's Diary of the Expedition to San Francisco, 1774." In H. E. Bolton, trans. and ed., *Anza's California Expeditions,* 2:395–456.

Perea, Estevan de, O.F.M. "Estevan de Perea's Relacion." Trans. and ed. by Lansing B. Bloom. *New Mexico Historical Review* 8 (July 1933): 211–35.

Perez de Luxán, Diego. *Expedition into New Mexico Made by Antonio de Espejo, 1582–1583, as Revealed in the Journal of Diego Perez de Luxán, a Member of the Party.* Ed. by George P. Hammond and trans. by Agapito Rey. Los Angeles, The Quivira Society, 1929. (Quivira Society, *Publications,* Vol. 1.)

Pfefferkorn, Ignaz, S.J. *Beschreibung der Landschaft Sonora samt andern merkwürdigen Nachrichten von den inneren Theilen Neu-Spaniens und Reise aus Amerika bis in Deutschland, nebst einen landcharte von Sonora.* 2 vols. Köln am Rheine, Auf Kosten des Verfassers gedrukt in der Langenschen buchhandlung, 1794–95.

—————. *Sonora, a Description of the Province.* Trans. and ed. by Theodore E. Treutlein. Albuquerque, University of New Mexico Press, 1949. *(Coronado Cuarto Centennial Publications, 1540–1940,* ed. by George P. Hammond, Vol. 12.)

Rivera y Moncada, Fernando de. *Diario del Capitán Comandante Fernando de Rivera y Moncada, con un apéndice documental.* Madrid, Ediciones José Porrúa Turanzas, 1967. *(Colección Chimalistac,* vols. 24–25.)

Rivera y Villalón, Pedro de. *Diario y derrotero de la caminado, visto y observado en la visita que hizo a los presidios de la Nueva España septentrional el Brigadier Pedro de Rivera.* Con una introducción y notas por Vito Alessio Robles. Mexico, Taller Autográfico, 1946. (Archivo Histórico Militar Mexicano, Num. 2.)

Saenz, Barthólome, S.J. *Spaniard and Apache on the Upper Gila 1756: An Account of the Bustamante-Vildósola Expedition by Father Barthólome Saenz, S.J.* Santa Fe, Stagecoach Press, 197-.

Salvatierra, Juan María de, S.J. "Complete Text of Salvatierra's Journal [January–May 21, 1701]." In Ernest J. Burrus, S.J., *Kino and Manje: Explorers of Sonora and Arizona,* pp. 587–618. Rome and St. Louis, Jesuit Historical Institute, 1970.

Sánchez, José María. "A Trip to Texas in 1828." Trans. by Carlos E. Castañeda. *Southwestern Historical Quarterly* 29 (April 1926): 249–88.

Santa María, Vicente. *The First Spanish Entry into San Francisco Bay, 1775: The Original Narrative, Hitherto Unpublished, by Fray Vicente Santa María, and Further Details by Participants.* Trans. and ed. by John Galvin. San Francisco, John Howell Books, 1971.

Sedelmayr, Jacobo. *Jacobo Sedelmayr, Missionary, Frontiersman, Explorer in Arizona and Sonora: Four Original Manuscript Narratives.* Trans. and ed. by Peter M. Dunne, S.J. Tucson, Arizona Pioneers' Historical Society, 1955.

—————. "Sedelmayr's Relación of 1746." Trans. and ed. by Ronald L. Ives. U.S. Bureau of American Ethnology, *Bulletin* 123, pp. 97–117. Washington, Government Printing Office, 1939.

Solís, José Gaspar de, O.F.M. *The Solís Diary of 1767.* Trans. by Peter P. Forrestal. [Austin, Texas]. *(Preliminary Studies of the Texas Catholic Historical Society,* ed. by Paul J. Foik, Vol. 1, No. 6 [March 1931].)

Sutter, Johann A. *The Diary of Johann August Sutter.* Ed. by Douglas S. Watson. San Francisco, The Grabhorn Press, 1932.

Sutter, Johann A. *New Helvetia Diary: A Record of Events Kept by John A. Sutter and His Clerks at New Helvetia, California from September 9, 1845, to May 25, 1848.* San Francisco, The Grabhorn Press, 1939.

Tamarón y Romeral, Pedro. *Bishop Tamarón's Visitation of New Mexico, 1760.* Trans. and ed. by Eleanor B. Adams. Albuquerque, Historical Society of New Mexico, 1954. (Historical Society of New Mexico, *Publications in History,* vol. 15.)

————. *Demostración del vastísimo obispado de la Nueva Vizcaya– 1765: Durango, Sinaloa, Sonora, Arizona, Nuevo México, Chihuahua y porciones de Texas, Coahuila y Zacatecas.* Con una introducción bibliográfica y anotaciones por Vito Alessio Robles. México, Antigua Librería Robredo de J. Porrúa e Hijos, 1937.

————. "Viajes pastorales y descripción de la diócesis de Nueva Vizcaya." Estudio preliminar y notas aclaratorias por Mario Hernández y Sánchez-Barba. In *Viajes por Norteamérica,* pp. 945–1062. Madrid, Aguilar, 1958. (*Biblioteca Indiana: libros y fuentes sobre América y Filipinas* 2.)

Vargas, Diego de. [Journal of an Expedition to Taos, 1696. Journal of a Reconnaissance from El Paso to Santa Fe, 1692.] In Ralph E. Twitchell, *The Leading Facts of New Mexican History,* 4:340–54, 403–29. Cedar Rapids, Iowa, Torch Press, 1917.

Velarde, Luís, S.J. "Padre Luís Velarde's Relación of Pimería Alta, 1716." Trans. by Rufus K. Wyllys. *New Mexico Historical Review* 6 (April 1931):111–57.

————. "Velarde's Description of Pimería Alta." In Ernest J. Burrus, *Kino and Manje, Explorers of Sonora and Arizona,* pp. 622–75. Rome and St. Louis, Jesuit Historical Institute, 1971.

Vélez de Escalante, Silvestre, O.F.M. "Father Escalante's Journal with Related Documents and Maps." Trans. and ed. by Herbert S. Auerbach. *Utah Historical Quarterly* 11 (January–October 1943):1–142.

————. "Fray Silvestre Vélez de Escalante to Provincial Fray Isidro Murillo, Zuñi, April 30, 1776, with a Literal Copy of the Diary He Kept during His Journey to the Hopi Pueblos in 1775." *New Mexico Historical Review* 38 (April 1963):118–38.

————. *Pageant in the Wilderness: The Story of the Escalante Expedition to the Interior Basin, 1776, Including the Diary and Itinerary of Father Escalante.* Trans. and ed. by Herbert E. Bolton. Salt Lake City, Utah Historical Society, 1950.

Vizcaino, Juan, O.F.M. *The Sea Diary of Fr. Juan Vizcaino to Alta California, 1769.* Trans. and ed. by Arthur Woodward. Los Angeles, Glen Dawson, 1959. (*Early California Travel Series,* Vol. 49.)

Zárate Salmerón, Gerónimo de. *Relaciones: An Account of Things Seen and Learned by Father Gerónimo de Zárate Salmerón from the*

Year 1538 to the Year 1626. Trans. by Alicia R. Milich, foreword by Donald C. Cutter. Albuquerque, Horn and Wallace, 1966.

――――. "Relating all the Things That Have Been Seen and Known in New Mexico as well by Sea as by Land from the Year 1538 till That of 1626." Ed. and trans. by Charles F. Lummis. *Land of Sunshine* 11 (November 1899):337–46; 12 (December 1899, January, February 1900):39–48, 104–13, 180–87.

Zúñiga, José. "The Zúñiga Journal, Tucson to Santa Fe: The Opening of a Spanish Trade Route, 1788–1795." Ed. and trans. by George P. Hammond. *New Mexico Historical Review* 6 (January 1931):40–65.

PRINTED SOURCES

Arizona (Territory), Laws, Statutes, etc. *Acts, Resolutions, and Memorials.* Prescott, Office of the Arizona Mines, 1865.

Binkley, William C., ed. *Official Correspondence of the Texas Revolution, 1835–1836.* 2 vols. New York, D. Appleton-Century, 1936.

Bloom, Lansing B., ed. "Bourke on the Southwest, VII." *New Mexico Historical Review* 10 (October 1935):271–322.

――――. "Historical Society Minutes, 1859–1863." *New Mexico Historical Review* 18 (July, October 1943):247–311, 394–428.

――――. [Letters of Lansing B. Bloom, November 26, 1938, April 1939.] *New Mexico Historical Review* 13 (July 1938): 334–36; 14 (January, April 1939):115–20, 200–03.

――――. "A Student's Day in Seville." *El Palacio* 24 (June 9, 1928): 446–49.

California, Laws, Statutes, etc. *The Statutes of California.* San José, San Francisco, Sacramento, 1850–1903.

Carnegie Institution of Washington, Department of Historical Research. *Report of the Department of Historical Research*, 1905–[1928]. [Washington, Carnegie Institution, 1905–29.] Extracted from the *Year Book* of the Carnegie Institution of Washington.

Colton, Walter. *Three Years in California.* New York, A. S. Barnes & Co.; Cincinnati, H. W. Derby & Co., 1850.

Connor, Seymour D., Howard Lackman, and Margaret K. Howard, eds. *Texas Treasury Papers: Letters Received in the Treasury Department of the Republic of Texas, 1836–1846.* 4 vols. Austin, Texas State Library, 1955–56. Vol. 4 ed. by Virginia H. Taylor and Mrs. B. Brandt.

Espinosa, José Manuel, ed. "Memoir of a Kentuckian [Samuel Ellison] in New Mexico, 1848–1884." *New Mexico Historical Review* 13 (January 1937):1–13.

Federal Cases: Comprising Cases Argued and Determined in the Cir-

cuit and District Courts of the United States from the Earliest Times to the Beginning of the Federal Reporter. . . . 30 vols. St. Paul, West Publishing Co., 1894–97.

Frémont, John C. *Memoirs of My Life by John Charles Frémont.* Chicago and New York, Belford, Clarke & Company, 1887.

Gammel, Hans P. N. *The Laws of Texas, 1822–1897.* 10 vols. Austin, The Gammel Book Company, 1898.

Gray, William F. *From Virginia to Texas, 1835: Diary of Col. Wm. F. Gray Giving Details of His Journey to Texas and Return in 1835–1836 and Second Journey to Texas in 1837.* Houston, Gray, Dillaye & Co., 1909.

Haggard, Juan V. and Malcolm D. McLean. *Handbook for Translators of Spanish Historical Documents.* [Austin] University of Texas, 1941.

Halleck, Henry W. "Report on the Laws and Regulations Relative to Grants or Sales of Public Lands in California, March 1, 1849." *House Executive Document* No. 17, 31 Congress, 1 Session, January 24, 1850, Serial 573. [Washington, 1850.] pp. 118–82. Also in J. A. Rockwell, ed., *Compilation of Spanish and Mexican Laws,* pp. 431–98.

Henry E. Huntington Library and Art Gallery. *Annual Report, 1927/28–1969/70.* San Marino, Calif., 1929–70.

Hoffman, Ogden. *Reports of Land Cases Determined in the United States District Court for the Northern District of California, June Term, 1853 to June Term, 1858, Inclusive.* San Francisco, Numa Hubert, 1862.

Jones, William C. *Land Titles in California: Report on the Subject of Land Titles in California, Made in Pursuance of Instructions from the Secretary of State and the Secretary of the Interior . . . together with a Translation of the Principal Laws on the Subject and Some Other Papers Relating Thereto.* Washington, Gideon & Co., Printers, 1850. Also published in *Senate Executive Document* No. 18, 31 Congress, 2 Session, Serial 589. Both include a "List of Private Grants in California, As Recorded in the Archives at Monterey."

Knights of Columbus, Texas State Council, Historical Commission. *Minutes of the Regular Meetings.* Austin, 1926–48.

Lange, Charles H. and Carroll L. Riley, eds. *The Southwestern Journals of Adolph F. Bandelier, 1880–1882, 1883–1884.* 2 vols. Albuquerque, University of New Mexico Press, 1966, 1970.

New Mexico, Commission of Public Records. *First Annual Report, 1960–61.* Santa Fe, 1961.

New Mexico (Territory), Governor. *Messages of the Governor to the Territorial Legislature, 1847–1909.* Printed as pamphlets and usually in the House of Representatives Journal or in the Legislative Council Journal. See the list in Shelton, *Checklist of New Mexico Publications*, pp. 143–47.

————, ————. *Report of the Governor of New Mexico to the Secretary of the Interior, 1879–1911*. Washington, Government Printing Office, 1879–1911.

————, Laws, Statutes, etc. *Laws [or Acts] of the Territory of New Mexico*. Santa Fe, 1852–1909. See the list in Shelton, *Checklist of New Mexico Publications*, pp. 187–97.

————, Librarian. "Report of Samuel Ellison, Librarian of the Territory of New Mexico for the Years 1882 and 1883." In *Official Reports of the Territory of New Mexico, for the Years 1882 and 1883*. Santa Fe, 1884. pp. 31–57.

————, Secretary. *Report, 1897–1911*. Published with the governor's message, in the Council and House Journals or the Legislative Manual. See the list in Shelton, *Checklist of New Mexico Publications*, pp. 102–03.

New Mexico Historical Society. *Report, 1903/04–*. Santa Fe, 1905–. Issued in various forms: with the Governor's Message; as publications of the society; and in the *New Mexico Historical Review*.

Newberry Library. *Report of the Trustees, 1940, 1941*. Chicago, Newberry Library, 1941–42.

Official Catholic Directory, 1970. New York, P. J. Kenedy Sons, 1970.

San Francisco, Commission to Enquire into City Property. *Report on the Condition of the Beach and Water Lots in the City of San Francisco, Made in Pursuance of an Ordinance of the City Council of Said City, Creating a Commission to Enquire into City Property*. San Francisco, Evening Picayune, 1850.

————, ————. *Report on the Condition of the Real Estate within the Limits of the City of San Francisco, and the Property Beyond, within the Bounds of the Old Mission Dolores, Made in Pursuance of an Ordinance of the Common Council of Said City, Creating a Commission to Enquire into City Property*. San Francisco, Evening Picayune, 1851.

Sayles, John and Henry. *Early Laws of Texas: General Laws from 1836 to 1879, . . . also Laws of 1731 to 1835, as Found in the Laws and Decrees of Spain Relating to Land in Mexico, and of Mexico Relating to Colonization; Laws of Coahuila and Texas; Laws of Tamaulipas; Colonial Contracts; Spanish Civil Law; Orders and Decrees of the Provisional Government of Texas*. 3 vols. St. Louis, The Gilbert Book Co., 1888.

Smyth, George W. "The Autobiography of George W. Smyth." *Southwestern Historical Quarterly* 36 (January 1933):200–14.

Texas (Republic), Congress, House of Representatives. *Journals of the House of Representatives of the Republic of Texas*, 1st Congress,

1st Session through 9th Congress, extra Session, 1836–45. Austin, Columbia, Houston, Washington, Texas, 1836–45. For publication details see Streeter, *Bibliography of Texas,* vol. 2.

Texas (Republic), Congress, Joint Committee on Public Lands. *Evidence in Relation to Land Titles Taken Before Joint Committee on Public Lands.* Austin, Whiting's Press, 1840.

————, Department of Agriculture, Insurance, Statistics, and History. "Report of the Classifier and Translator of Manuscripts in the Texas State Library." In *Twenty-Ninth Annual Report of the Commissioner of Agriculture, Statistics and History for the Year 1903,* pp. xiii–xxvi. Austin, Von Boeckmann-Jones Co., 1904.

————, General Land Office. *Report of the Commissioner of the General Land Office,* 1954/56–1967/68. [Austin, 1956–69.]

————, Legislature, State Historical Survey Committee. *Report to the Governor and the Fifty-Fourth Legislature.* Austin, n. p., [1955].

————, Library and Historical Commission. *Biennial Report,* 1909/10–1944/46. Austin, San Antonio, 1911–46.

U.S. Congress (Congressional Series arranged by serial numbers). "Land Claims—Between the Rio Hondo and the Sabine; Report of the Register and Receiver of the Land District South of Red River, in Louisiana, upon Land Claims Situated between the Rio Hondo and the Sabine, November 1, 1824." *House Executive Document* No. 49, 24 Congress, 1 Session. Serial 287.

————. "Occupation of Mexican Territory, December 22, 1846." *House Executive Document* No. 19, 29 Congress, 2 Session. Serial 499.

———— "Message of the President of the United States Communicating the Proceedings of the Court Martial in the Trial of Lieutenant Colonel Frémont, April 7, 1848." *Senate Executive Document* No. 33, 30 Congress, 1 Session. Serial 507.

———— "California Claims . . . Report of the Committee on Military Affairs, to Which Was Referred the Memorial of John Charles Frémont. . . , February 23, 1848." *Senate Report* No. 75, 30 Congress, 1 Session. Serial 512.

———— "Report of Lieut. J. W. Abert, of His Examination of New Mexico, in the Years 1846–47, February 10, 1848." *House Executive Document* No. 41, 30 Congress, 1 Session. Serial 517.

———— "Mexican War Correspondence. Messages of the President of the United States, and the Correspondence, Therewith Communicated, Between the Secretary of War and Other Officers of the Government upon the Subject of the Mexican War, April 28, 1848." *House Executive Document* No. 60, 30 Congress, 1 Session. Serial 520.

———— "California and New Mexico. Message from the President of the United States, Transmitting Information in Answer to a

Resolution of the House of the 31st of December, 1849, on the Subject of California and New Mexico, January 24, 1850." *House Executive Document* No. 17, 31 Congress, 1 Session. Serial 573.

———— "Report of the Secretary of the Interior, Communicating a Copy of the Instructions Given to the Commissioners Appointed under the Act to Ascertain and Settle the Private Land Claims in California, February 3, 1852. *Senate Executive Document* No. 26, 32 Congress, 1 Session. Serial 614.

———— "Archives—New Mexico; Memorial of the Legislative Council of New Mexico in Regard to the Archives of the Territory, February 4, 1854." *House Miscellaneous Document* No. 50, 33 Congress, 1 Session. Serial 741.

———— "Report [of the] Committee of Claims . . . for the Relief of Lieutenant Colonel E. R. S. Canby, February 1, 1855." *Senate Report* No. 472, 33 Congress, 2 Session. Serial 775.

———— "Land Claims—New Mexico, February 12, 1857." *House Executive Document* No. 73, 34 Congress, 3 Session. Serial 906.

———— "New Mexico—Private Land Claims. . . , Documents. . . , February 10, 1860." *House Executive Document* No. 14, 36 Congress, 1 Session. Serial 1047.

———— "Expenditures on Account of Private Land Claims in California, May 22, 1860." *House Executive Document* No. 84, 36 Congress, 1 Session. Serial 1056.

———— "To Confirm Certain Land Claims in the Territory of New Mexico, April 2, 1860." *House Report* No. 321, 36 Congress, 1 Session. Serial 1068.

———— "Letter of the Secretary of the Interior, . . . in Relation to the Amounts Paid to Different Persons on Account of Legal and Other Services for Investigating Land Titles in the State of California during the Years 1857, 1858, 1859, 1860, April 23, 1862." *Senate Executive Document* No. 44, 37 Congress, 2 Session. Serial 1122.

———— "Private Land Claims in New Mexico. . . . The Reports of the Surveyor General and Papers in Four Private Land Claims in New Mexico, May 16, 1862." *House Executive Document* No. 112, 37 Congress, 2 Session. Serial 1137.

———— "Letter of the Secretary of the Treasury, . . . Relative to Amounts Paid on Account of Legal and Other Services in Investigating Land Titles in California in the Years 1857, 1858, 1859, 1860, and 1861, December 8, 1862." *Senate Executive Document* No. 2, 37 Congress, 3 Session. Serial 1149.

———— "Petition of John A. Sutter, Praying Compensation for Land Owned by Him in California, and Held under Mexican Grants, . . . , January 15, 1866." *Senate Miscellaneous Document* No. 38, 39 Congress, 1 Session. Serial 1239.

———— "Public Buildings in New Mexico, Letter from the Secretary of the Interior, Transmitting Report of the Condition of the Public Buildings in Mexico, December 12, 1867." *House Executive Document* No. 33, 40 Congress, 2 Session. Serial 1330.

U.S. Congress. "Condition of the Records and Documents of Mexico Relating to the Land Now Embraced within the Territories of Arizona and New Mexico, also to Their Place of Custody and Deposit and to the Method of Procuring Authentic Transcripts of Such Records and Documents, December 10, 1874." *Senate Executive Document* No. 3, 43 Congress, 2 Session. Serial 1629.

———— "Report of the Commissioner of the General Land Office Concerning a Tract of Land in Colorado Patented to Charles Beaubien, March 29, 1882." *Senate Executive Document* No. 142, 47 Congress, 1 Session. Serial 1990.

———— "Letter from the Secretary of the Interior, Transmitting Correspondence Relative to Surveys in Arizona and California and Recommending Increase of Clerical Hire in the Office of the Surveyor General, May 29, 1884." *Senate Executive Document* No. 177, 48 Congress, 1 Session. Serial 2167.

———— "Report: The Committee on Claims . . . for the Relief of . . . Heirs of the Northern District of California, Peter Della Torre, Deceased . . . , March 12, 1884." *Senate Report* No. 311, 48 Congress, 1 Session. Serial 2174.

———— "Letter from the Acting Secretary of the Interior, Transmitting Report from the Surveyor General of Arizona on the Tres Alamos Tract, No. 17, December 19, 1887." *Senate Executive Document* No. 29, 50 Congress, 1 Session. Serial 2504.

———— "Forfeiture of the El Paso de los Algodones Grant, in Arizona, April 19, 1880." *House Report* No. 1585, 51 Congress, 1 Session. Serial 2811.

———— "Reproducing Plats of Survey Destroyed at San Francisco, May 4, 1906." *House Document* No. 771, 59 Congress, 1 Session. Serial 4990.

U.S. Court of Private Land Claims, Santa Fe. "Final Report of the United States Attorney for the Court of Private Land Claims of the Business Transacted from July 1, 1891, to June 30, 1904, and Résumé of Results Thereof." In U.S. Department of Justice, *Annual Report of the Attorney General of the United States for the Year 1904*, pp. 95–109. Washington, Government Printing Office, 1904.

————. *United States, Defendant. In the United States Court of Private Land Claims, Santa Fe District, James Addison Peralta Reavis and Doña Sofía Loreto Micaela de Peralta de la Córdoba (Husband and Wife) Plaintiffs, vs. The United States of America, Defendant, No. 110, Peralta Grant.* Santa Fe, New Mexican Printing Company, 1895.

U.S. Department of the Interior. *Annual Report of the Secretary of the Interior*, 1849–1963. Washington, 1849–1963. Printed in the Congressional serial set and in a Department of the Interior set.

U.S. Department of Justice. *Annual Report of the Attorney General of the United States* . . . 1870–1905. Washington, Government Printing Office, 1871–1905.

U.S. Department of the Navy. *Report of the Secretary of the Navy*, December 5, 1846 *(House Document* No. 4, 29 Congress, 2 Session. Serial 497). Washington, Ritchie & Heiss, 1846.

U.S. District Court, California (Northern District). *United States, Appellant. The United States vs. Andrés Castillero, No. 420, "New Almaden." Transcript of the Record* . . . . 4 vols. San Francisco, 1859–61.

————. *In the District Court of the United States for the Northern District of California. No. 429. The United States vs. José Y. Limantour, Appellee. Transcript of the Record, Printed by Order of P. Della Torre, Esq. U.S. Attorney.* San Francisco, Whitton, Towne & Co., Printers and Publishers, 1858.

————. *The United States, Appellants, vs. José Y. Limantour, Appellee. Nos. 424 and 429. Archive Exhibits, A, B, C, D, E, F, G, H, I, J, K, M, N, O, P, Q, R, S, T, U, V, W, X, Y, YY, Z, ZZ. Filed on the Part of the United States, P. Della Torre, U.S. Attorney.* [San Francisco? 1858?]

————. *The United States, Appellants, vs. José Y. Limantour, Appellee. Nos. 424 and 429. Land Commission Exhibits, A, B, C, D, E, F, G, H, I, J, K, L, M, N, O, P, Filed on the Part of the United States. P. Della Torre, U.S. Attorney* [San Francisco? 1858?]

————. *The United States Appellants vs. José Y. Limantour, Appellee, Nos. 424 and 429, Spanish Exhibits, A, B, C, D, E, Filed on the Part of the United States, P. Della Torre, U.S. Attorney* [San Francisco? 1858?]

U.S. General Land Office (and Bureau of Land Management, from 1946) 1817–1963. The reports for 1817–48 are in the U.S. Treasury Department, *Annual Report of the Secretary of the Treasury on the State of the Finances* in the Congressional Series; and the reports for 1849–1963 are in the U.S. Department of the Interior, *Annual Report of the Secretary of the Interior.*

U.S. Laws, Statutes, etc. *The Statutes at Large of the United States of America,* 1789–. Boston, C. C. Little and J. Brown, 1845–51; Boston, Little, Brown and Company, 1855–73; Washington, Government Printing Office, 1875–.

U.S. Library of Congress. *Annual Report of the Librarian of Congress,* 1866–1968. Washington, Government Printing Office, 1866–1969.

U.S. Supreme Court. *United States, Appellant. Supreme Court of the United States, No. 287. The United States, Appellants, vs. the City of San Francisco, and No. 288, the City of San Francisco, Appellant, vs. the United States. Appeals from the Circuit Court of the United States for the Northern District of California, December Term 1866. Filed October 4, 1866.* Washington, Government Printing Office, 1866.

U.S. Supreme Court. *United States Supreme Court Reports: Cases Argued and Decided in the Supreme Court of the United States.* Newark and Rochester, Lawyers' Cooperative Publishing Co., 1882–.

U.S. Surveyor General of New Mexico. "Reports." In the *Reports of the Secretary of the Interior,* listed above under the Department of the Interior.

Wilcox, Sebron S. [Letter of Seb. S. Wilcox to Walter P. Webb, Jan. 25, 1941.] *Southwestern Historical Quarterly* 44 (April 1941):499.

GUIDES, INVENTORIES, CATALOGS, ETC.

Abajian, James DeT. "Preliminary Listing of Manuscript Collections in Library of California Historical Society." *California Historical Society Quarterly* 33 (December 1954):372–76.

"Bandelier Collection of Copies of Documents Relative to the History of New Mexico and Arizona." In *Report of the United States Commission to the Columbian Historical Commission at Madrid, 1892–93, with Special Papers,* pp. 305–26. House Executive Document No. 100, 53 Congress, 3 Session, Serial 3322. Washington, Government Printing Office, 1895.

Barker, Eugene C. "Report on the Public Archives of Texas." American Historical Association, *Annual Report* 2 (1901):353–58.

Bolton, Herbert E. *Guide to Materials for the History of the United States in the Principal Archives of Mexico.* Washington, Carnegie Institution, 1913. (Carnegie Institution of Washington, *Publication* No. 163.)

————. "Spanish Mission Records at San Antonio." *Texas State Historical Association Quarterly* 10 (April 1907):297–307.

Borges, Pedro, O.F.M. "Documentación americana en el Archivo General O.F.M. de Roma." *Archivo iber-americano* 19 (enero-junio 1959):5–119.

Bowman, Jacob N. "California Private Land Grant Records in the National Archives." January 24, 1956. Photostat in National Archives Library.

————. "Index of Private Land Grants and Land Grant Papers." Manuscript in the Bancroft Library, University of California. Berkeley, 1942.

————. "Index of the Spanish-Mexican Private Land Grant Records and Cases of California." Berkeley, 1958. Xerox copy in the

National Archives from original in the Bancroft Library, University of California.

————. "The Parochial Books of the California Missions." *Historical Society of Southern California Quarterly* 43 (September 1961): 303–15.

Burrus, Ernest J., S.J. *A History of the Southwest: A Study of the Civilization and Conversion of the Indians in Southwestern United States and Northwestern Mexico from the Earliest Times, Volume I, Catalogue of the Bandelier Collection in the Vatican Library*. Rome, Jesuit Historical Institute, 1969.

Butler, Ruth L. *A Check List of Manuscripts in the Edward E. Ayer Collection*. Chicago, The Newberry Library, 1937.

California, State Library. "Index to Spanish Archives on File in the State Library, XIV—Spanish Archives Collected in Monterey in 1851, by Order of the Legislature." In United States, Appellant. *U. S. District Court, Northern District of California, No. 424: The United States vs. José Y. Limantour; Transcript of the Record from the Board of United States Land Commissioners, in Case No. 548, Filed February 29, 1856*, pp. 267–72. San Francisco, Whitton, Towne & Co's Excelsior Steam Presses, 1857.

————, Surveyor General. "Corrected Report of Spanish and Mexican Grants in California, Complete to February 25, 1886." In *Report of the Surveyor-General of the State of California from August 1, 1884, to August 1, 1886, Appendix to the Journals of the Senate and Assembly of the Twenty-Seventh Session . . .* , 1:11–29. Sacramento, 1887. Also published separately in Sacramento, 1886.

————, ————. "Report of Spanish or Mexican Grants in California, prepared by James S. Stratton." In *Report of the Surveyor-General of the State of California, from August 1st, 1879, to August 1st, 1880*. California, Legislature, *Appendix to the Journals of the Senate and Assembly of the Twenty-Fourth Session*, 1:15–54. Sacramento, 1881.

————, University, Los Angeles, Library. *Guide to Special Collections in the Library of the University of California at Los Angeles*. Los Angeles, 1958. (UCLA Library, *Occasional Papers* No. 7.)

Carrera Stampa, Manuel. *Archivalia mexicana*. Mexico, Editorial Jus, S.A., 1952. (Universidad Nacional Autonoma de México, *Publicaciones del Instituto de Historia*, 1st ser., Num 27.)

Castañeda, Carlos E. *A Report on the Spanish Archives in San Antonio, Texas*. San Antonio, Yanaguana Society, 1937.

———— and Jack A. Dabbs. *Guide to the Latin American Manuscripts in the University of Texas Library*. Cambridge, Harvard University Press, 1939. (Committee on Latin American Studies, American Council of Learned Societies, *Miscellaneous Publication*, No. 1.)

———— and ————. *Independent Mexico in Documents: Indepen-*

dence, Empire and Republic; A Calendar of the Juan B. Hernández y Dávalos Manuscript Collection. Mexico, Editorial Jus, 1954.

Cavazos Garza, Israel. *Catálogo y síntesis de los protocolos del Archivo Municipal de Monterrey, 1599–1700, 1700–1725.* Monterrey, Instituto Tecnológico y de Estudias Superiores de Monterrey, 1966, 1973. (Indices de los archivos del noreste de Mexico, 2; Instituto Tecnológico y de Estudias Superiores de Monterrey, *Publicaciones, Series: Historia* 4.)

Chapman, Charles E. *Catalogue of Materials in the Archivo General de Indias for the History of the Pacific Coast and the American Southwest.* Glendale, Arthur H. Clark Co., 1919. (University of California, *Publications in History,* Vol. 8.)

Chávez, Angelico, O.F.M. *Archives of the Archdiocese of Santa Fe, 1678–1900.* Washington, Academy of American Franciscan History, 1957. *(Publications* of the Academy of American Franciscan History, *Bibliographical Series,* Vol. 3.)

————. "Some Original New Mexico Documents in California Libraries." *New Mexico Historical Review* 25 (July 1950):244–53.

Colley, Charles C. *Documents of Southwestern History: A Guide to the Manuscript Collections of the Arizona Historical Society,* Tucson, Arizona Historical Society, 1972.

Connor, Seymour V. *A Preliminary Guide to the Archives of Texas.* [Austin], Texas State Library, 1956.

Cowan, Robert G. *Ranchos of California: A List of Spanish Concessions, 1775–1822, and Mexican Grants, 1822–1846.* Fresno, Academy Library Guild, 1956.

Coy, Owen C. *Guide to the County Archives of California.* Sacramento, California State Printing Office, 1919. (California Historical Survey Commission, *Publication.)*

Daly, Lowrie J. "Microfilmed Materials from the Archives of the Sacred Congregation 'De Propaganda Fide.'" *Manuscripta* (November 1966):139–44.

Day, James M.; Ann B. Dunlap; Mike Smyers; and Kenneth Parker. *Maps of Texas, 1527–1900: The Map Collection of the Texas State Archives.* Austin, The Pemberton Press, 1964.

Day, James M. and Donna Yarbrough. *Handbook of Texas Archival and Manuscript Depositories.* Austin, Texas Library and Historical Commission, 1966. (Texas State Library, *Monograph Series,* No. 5.)

Díaz, Albert J. *A Guide to the Microfilm of Papers Relating to New Mexico Land Grants.* Albuquerque, University of New Mexico Press, 1960. (University of New Mexico *Publications, Library Series,* No. 1.)

————. *Manuscripts and Records in the University of New Mexico Library.* Albuquerque, University of New Mexico Library, 1957.

————. "University of New Mexico Special Collections." *New Mexico Historical Review* 33 (July, October 1958):235–51, 316–21.

Dixon, Ford. "Texas History in Maps: An Archival and Historical Examination of the James Perry Bryan Map Collection." *Texana* 5 (Summer, Fall, 1967):99–116, 238–67.

Edwards, Mrs. Ben C. *Chronological List of Framed Documents from Dr. Wm. E. Howard Collection* [in the Daughters of the Republic of Texas Library]. San Antonio, 1950.

Evans, G. Edward. "A Guide to Pre-1750 Manuscripts in the United States Relating to Mexico and the Southwestern United States, with Emphasis on Their Value to Anthropologists." *Ethnohistory* 17 (Winter-Spring 1970):63–90.

Ewing, William S. *Guide to the Manuscript Collections in the William L. Clements Library.* Ann Arbor, Clements Library, 1953.

Ezell, Paul and Greta. *The Aguiar Collection in the Arizona Pioneers' Historical Society.* San Diego, San Diego State College Press, 1964.

Fish, Carl R. *Guide to the Materials for American History in Roman and Other Italian Archives.* Washington, Carnegie Institution, 1911. (Carnegie Institution of Washington, *Publication*, No. 128.)

Fisher, Mary Ann. *Preliminary Guide to the Microfilm Collection in the Bancroft Library.* Berkeley, University of California, 1955.

Geiger, Maynard J., O.F.M. *Calendar of Documents in the Santa Barbara Mission Archives.* Washington, Academy of American Franciscan History, 1947. (*Publications* of the Academy of American Franciscan History, *Bibliographical Series*, Vol. 1.)

Genealogical Society of the Church of Jesus Christ of Latter-Day Saints. *Major Genealogical Record Sources in Mexico.* (Genealogical Society, *Research Paper*, Series H, No. 2.) [Salt Lake City], 1970.

Goddard, Jeanne; Charles A. Kritzler; and Archibald Hanna. *A Catalogue of the Frederick W. & Carrie S. Beinecke Collection of Western Americana, Volume I, Manuscripts* [in the Yale University Library]. New Haven and London, Yale University Press, 1965.

Gómez Canedo, Lino, O.F.M. *Los archivos de la historia de America, período colonial española.* 2 vols. México, D.F. Comisión de Historia. 1961. (Instituto Panamericano de Geografía e Historia, Comisión de Historia. *Publicación* Num. 225.)

Greenleaf, Richard E. and Michael C. Meyer. *Research in Mexican History: Topics, Methodology, Sources, and a Practical Guide to Field Research.* Lincoln, University of Nebraska Press, 1973.

Hale, Richard W., Jr. *Guide to Photocopied Historical Materials in the United States and Canada.* Ithaca, N. Y., Cornell University Press, 1961.

Hamer, Philip M. *A Guide to Archives and Manuscripts in the United States.* New Haven, Yale University Press, 1961.

Hammond, George P. *A Guide to the Manuscript Collections of the Bancroft Library, Volume II.* Berkeley and Los Angeles, University of California Press, 1972. (Bancroft Library, *Bibliographical Series, Volume 2: Manuscripts Relating Chiefly to Mexico and Central America.*)

Hilton, Ronald. *Handbook of Hispanic Source Materials and Research Organizations in the United States.* Stanford, Stanford University Press, 1956.

Historical Records Survey, Arizona. *Inventory of the County Archives of Arizona, No. 10, Pima County (Tucson).* Phoenix, The Historical Survey, 1938.

————, Colorado. *Inventory of the County Archives of Colorado, No. 2, Alamosa County (Alamosa).* Denver, The Historical Records, Survey, 1942.

————, ————. *Inventory of the County Archives of Colorado, No. 12, Costilla County (San Luis).* Denver, The Historical Records Survey, 1938.

————, ————. *Inventory of the County Archives of Colorado, No. 11, Conejos County (Conejos).* Denver, The Historical Records Survey, 1938.

————, New Mexico. *Inventory of the County Archives of New Mexico, No. 1, Bernalillo County (Albuquerque).* Albuquerque, The Historical Records Survey, 1938.

————, ————. *Inventory of the County Archives of New Mexico, No. 4, Colfax County (Ratón).* Albuquerque, The Historical Records Survey, 1937.

————, ————. *Inventory of the County Archives of New Mexico, No. 7, Doña Ana County (Las Cruces).* Albuquerque, The Historical Records Survey, 1940.

————, ————. *Inventory of the County Archives of New Mexico, No. 17, Mora County (Mora).* Albuquerque, The Historical Records Survey, 1941.

————, ————. *Inventory of the County Archives of New Mexico, No. 23, Sandoval County (Bernalillo).* Albuquerque, The Historical Records Survey, 1939.

————, ————. *Inventory of the County Archives of New Mexico, No. 31, Valencia County (Los Lunas).* Albuquerque, The Historical Records Survey, 1940.

————, Northern California. *Inventory of the County Archives of California, No. 20, Napa County (Napa).* San Francisco, The Northern California Historical Records Survey Project, 1941.

————, ————. *Inventory of the County Archives of California, No. 36, San Benito County (Hollister).* San Francisco, The Northern California Historical Records Survey Project, 1940.

————, ————. *Inventory of the County Archives of California, No. 39. The City and County of San Francisco (San Francisco), Volume II.* San Francisco, The Northern California Historical Records Survey Project. 1940.

————, ————. *Inventory of the County Archives of California, No. 41, San Luis Obispo (San Luis Obispo).* San Francisco, The Northern California Historical Records Survey Project, 1939.

————, ————. *Inventory of the County Archives of California, No. 44, Santa Clara County (San Jose).* San Francisco, The Northern California Historical Records Survey Project, 1939.

————, Southern California. *Guide to Depositories of Manuscripts in the United States: California.* Los Angeles, The Southern California Historical Records Survey Project, 1941.

————, ————. *Inventory of the Bixby Records Collection in the Palos Verdes Library and Art Gallery.* Los Angeles, The Southern California Historical Records Survey Project, 1940.

————, ————. *Inventory of the County Archives of California, No. 20, Los Angeles County (Los Angeles) County Clerk's Office.* Los Angeles, The Southern California Historical Records Survey Project, 1943.

————, Texas. *Inventory of the Colonial Archives of Texas, No. 3, Municipality of Brazoria, 1832–1837 (Brazoria County Courthouse, Angleton, Texas).* San Antonio, The Texas Historical Records Survey, 1937.

————, ————. *Inventory of the Colonial Archives of Texas, 1821–1837, Municipality of San Felipe de Austin (Austin County Courthouse, Belleville, Texas).* San Antonio, 1938. Xerox copy of manuscript in the University of Texas Library.

————, ————. *Inventory of the County Archives of Texas, No. 28, Caldwell County (Lockhart).* San Antonio, The Texas Historical Records Survey, 1941.

————, ————. *Inventory of the County Archives of Texas, No. 75, Fayette County (Lagrange).* San Antonio, The Texas Historical Records Survey, 1940.

Hoffman, Ogden. "Table of Land Claims, Presented to the Commission Pursuant to the Provisions of the Act of Congress of March 3d, 1851, Entitled 'An Act to Ascertain and Settle the Private Land Claims in the State of California.' " In Hoffman, *Reports of Land Cases Determined in the United States District Court for the Northern District of California,* appendix 1. San Francisco, 1862. Also in *The Federal Cases,* 30:1217–57, listed under "Printed Sources."

Howard, William E. *Calendar of the Howard Collection of Texana: A Collector's Item.* [Dallas, 1944]

Hoyo, Eugenio del. *Indice del Ramo de Causas Criminales del Archivo Municipal de Monterrey.* Monterrey, Instituto Tecnológico y de Estudios de Monterrey, 1963. (Instituto Tecnológico y de Estudios Superiores de Monterrey, *Serie de Historia* 2.)

Jenkins, Myra E. *Calendar of the Mexican Archives of New Mexico, 1821–1846.* Santa Fe, State of New Mexico Records Center, 1970.

————. *Guide to the Microfilm of the Spanish Archives of New Mexico, 1621–1821, in the Archives Division of the State of New Mexico Records Center.* Santa Fe, State of New Mexico Records Center, 1967.

————. *Guide to the Microfilm Edition of the Mexican Archives of New Mexico, 1821–1846, in the Archives Division of the State of New Mexico Records Center.* Santa Fe, State of New Mexico Records Center, 1969.

Jenkins, William S., comp., and Lillian A. Hamrick, ed. *A Guide to the Microfilm Collection of Early State Records.* Prepared by the Library of Congress in association with the University of North Carolina. Washington, Photoduplication Service, Library of Congress, 1950. *Supplement.* Comp. and ed. by W. S. Jenkins. Washington, 1951.

Kenneally, Finbar, O.F.M., ed. *United States Documents in the Propaganda Archives: A Calendar.* 5 vols. Washington, Academy of American Franciscan History, 1966–74. (Publications of the Academy of American Franciscan History.)

Kielman, Chester V. *Guide to the Microfilm Edition of the Béxar Archives, 1717–1803.* Austin, University of Texas Archives, 1967.

————. *Guide to the Microfilm Edition of the Béxar Archives, 1804–1821.* Austin, University of Texas Archives, 1969.

————. *Guide to the Microfilm Edition of the Béxar Archives, 1822–1836.* Austin, University of Texas Archives, 1971.

————. *The University of Texas Archives: A Guide to the Historical Manuscripts in the University of Texas Library.* Austin, University of Texas Press, 1967.

Lane, (Sister) M. Claude. *Catholic Archives of Texas: History and Preliminary Inventory.* Houston, Sacred Heart Dominican College, 1961.

Mexico, Dirección de Archivo Histórico Militar. *Guía del Archivo Histórico Militar de México, formado de orden de la Dirección del Archivo Militar.* Prólogo de Vito Alessio Robles. México, D.F., Taller Autográfico, 1948.

————, Ministerio de Hacienda y Crédito Público. Archivo. *Guía del Archivo Histórico de Hacienda, Siglos XVI a XIX.* Mexico, Los talleres de impresiones de estampillas y valores de la Sría. de hda., 1940–45.

Miller, David J. "Private Land Claims [Adjudicated]; Private Land Claims Not Yet Adjudicated." In New Mexico (Territory), Secretary's Office, *The Legislative Blue-Book of the Territory of New Mexico*, pp. 129–34. Santa Fe, Charles W. Greene, Public Printer, 1882.

Morgan, Dale L. and George P. Hammond, eds. *A Guide to the Manuscript Collections of the Bancroft Library.* Berkeley and Los Angeles, University of California Press, 1963. (Bancroft Library *Publications, Bibliographical Series*, Volume 1: *Pacific and Western Manuscripts, except California.*)

Murrieta, Cynthia R. de and María L. Torres Chávez. *Catálogo del Archivo Histórico del Estado Sonora.* 2 vols. Hermosillo, Centro Regional del Noreste, Instituto Nacional de Antropología e Historia, Secretaría de Educación Pública, 1974–75.

New Mexico, State Records Center and Archives. *Calendar of the Mexican Archives of New Mexico, 1821–1846.* Prep. by Myra Ellen Jenkins. Santa Fe, State of New Mexico Records Center and Archives, 1970.

————. *Calendar of the Spanish Archives of New Mexico, 1621–1821.* Santa Fe, State of New Mexico Records Center and Archives, 1968.

New-York Historical Society. *Survey of the Manuscript Collections in the New-York Historical Society.* New York, The New-York Historical Society, 1941.

Parish, John C. "California Books and Manuscripts in the Huntington Library." *Huntington Library Bulletin*, No. 7 (April 1935), pp. 1–58.

Parral, Mexico, Archivo. *English Translation of the Index to El Archivo de Hidalgo del Parral, 1631–1821.* Trans. by Consuelo P. Boyd. Tucson, Arizona Silhouettes, 1971.

————. "Index to El Archivo de Hidalgo del Parral, 1631–1821. Tucson, Arizona Silhouettes, 1961. Photocopy in the Library of Congress.

Peckham, Howard H. *Guide to the Manuscript Collections in the William L. Clements Library.* Ann Arbor, University of Michigan Press; London, H. Milford, Oxford University Press, 1942.

Read, Benjamin M. *Chronological Digest of the "Documentos Inéditos del Archivo de las Indias."* Albuquerque, Albright & Anderson, 1914.

Río, Ignacio del. *Guía del archivo franciscano de la Biblioteca Nacional de México. Vol. 1. Guías, no. 3.* Mexico, Instituto de Investigaciones Bibliográficas, Universidad Nacional Autonoma de México, 1975.

Rubio Mañé, Jorge Ignacio. *El Archivo General de la Nación, México, D.F.*, pp. 63–169. México, D.F., Editorial Cultura, 1940. Also published in *Revista de la historia de América* 9 (1940):63–169.

Saint John's Seminary, Camarillo, California, Library, Estelle Doheny

Collection. *One Hundred Manuscripts and Books from the Estelle Doheny Collection in the Edward L. Doheny Memorial Library, St. John's Seminary, Camarillo, California.* Los Angeles, Anderson & Ritchie, 1950.

Sánchez, José de la Cruz. "The Inventory of All the Archives [of Yerba Buena] from the Foundation of the Ayuntamiento in 1835, to the End of the Present Year [1845]." *The Pioneer: or, California Monthly Magazine* 1 (March 1854):142–44.

San Diego Historical Society. *A Guide to the Research Collections of the San Diego Historical Society Located in the Serra Museum, Presidio Hill, Birthplace of California.* San Diego, The Society, 1964.

San Jacinto Museum of History, San Jacinto Monument, Texas. *A Check List of Manuscripts Including a Transcript of a Letter from the Battleground, an Eyewitness Account of the Battle of San Jacinto.* San Jacinto, San Jacinto Museum of History Association, 1949.

Santos, Richard G. "An Annotated Survey of the Spanish Archives of Laredo at Saint Mary's University of Texas." *Texana* 4 (Spring 1966):41–46.

————. "Documentos para la historia de México en los archivos de San Antonio, Texas." *Revista de Historia de América* 63–64 (enero–diciembre, 1967):343–49.

Scholes, France V. "Manuscripts for the History of New Mexico in the National Library in Mexico City." *New Mexico Historical Review* 3 (July 1928):301–23.

Shepherd, William R. *Guide to the Materials for the History of the United States in Spanish Archives.* Washington, Carnegie Institution, 1907. (Carnegie Institution of Washington, *Publication*, No. 91.)

Sherburne, George et al. "*Huntington Library Collections.*" *Huntington Library Bulletin*, No. 1 (May 1931), pp. 33–106.

Smithsonian Institution. *Catalogue of the Berlandier Manuscripts Deposited in the Smithsonian Institution, Washington, D.C.* New York, Folger & Turner, Printer, 1853.

Spain. Archivo General de Simancas. *Guía del Archivo General de Simancas.* [Madrid], Dirección General de Archivos y Bibliotecas; [Valencia, Tipografía Moderna], 1958.

————. Archivo Histórico Nacional. *Guía del Archivo Histórico.* Por Luis Sánchez Belda. [Madrid], 1958.

————. Dirección General de Archivos y Bibliotecas. *Guía de los archivos de Madrid.* Madrid, Nuevas Gráficas, 1952.

————. ————. *Guía de las bibliotecas de Madrid.* Madrid, Talleres Gráficos Escelices, 1953.

Spell, Lota M. *Research Materials for the Study of Latin America at the University of Texas.* Austin, University of Texas Press, 1954.

Strout, Clevy L. *A Catalog of Hispanic Documents in the Thomas Gilcrease Institute.* Tulsa, The Thomas Gilcrease Institute of American History and Art, 1962.

Taylor, Virginia H., trans. and ed. "Calendar of the Letters of Antonio Martínez, Last Spanish Governor of Texas, 1817–1822." *Southwestern Historical Quarterly* 59 (January–April, 1956):372-81, 473–86; 60 (July 1956–April 1957):80–99, 292–305, 387–400, 533–47; 61 (July–October 1957):125–46, 288–304.

———. *The Spanish Archives of the General Land Office of Texas.* Austin, Lone Star Press, 1955.

Texas, General Land Office. "Key to the Spanish Archives of the General Land Office of Texas." Photostat in possession of the author, supplied by the Texas General Land Office.

Torok, Mildred. *Guide to Collections: The University of Texas at El Paso Archives.* [El Paso], 1972.

Tudela, José. *Los manuscritos de América en las bibliotecas de España.* Madrid, Ediciones Cultura Hispánica, 1954.

Twitchell, Ralph E. *The Spanish Archives of New Mexico.* 2 vols. Glendale, Calif., The Arthur H. Clark Co., 1914.

U.S. Federal Records Center, Bell, California. *Preliminary Inventory of the Records of the Bureau of Land Management (Record Group 49).* Comp. by Gilbert Dorane. Los Angeles, 1966.

———, San Francisco, California. *Preliminary Inventory of the Records of the Bureau of Land Management (Record Group 49).* Comp. by John P. Heard. San Francisco, 1969.

U.S. Library of Congress. *Archives of Government Offices Outside of Washington (House Document* No. 1443, 62 Congress, 3 Session. Serial 6501.) Washington, Government Printing Office, 1913.

———, Division of Maps. *The Lowery Collection: A Descriptive List of Maps of the Spanish Possessions within the Present Limits of the United States, 1502–1820.* Prep. by Woodbury Lowery; ed. by Philip Lee Phillips. Washington, Government Printing Office, 1912.

———, Manuscript Division. *Handbook of Manuscripts in the Library of Congress.* Washington, Government Printing Office, 1918.

———, ———. *Manuscripts on Microfilm: A Checklist of the Holdings in the Manuscript Division.* Comp. by Richard B. Bickel. Washington, Government Printing Office, 1975.

———, ———. *The National Union Catalog of Manuscript Collections, 1959/61–1974.* 12 vols. 1959–61, Ann Arbor, Mich., J. W. Edwards, Inc., 1962; 1962, Hamden, Conn., The Shoe String Press, Inc., 1964; 1963/64–74, Washington, Library of Congress, 1965–1975.

U.S. National Archives. "Alphabetical Index to the California Board of Land Commissioners Expedientes for Private Land Claims in California," Records of the General Land Office (Record Group 49). [Washington], 1969. Typed manuscript.

————. "Alphabetical Index to the California Private Land Claims Dockets," Records of the General Land Office (Record Group 49). [Washington, 1969]. Typed manuscript.

————. *Guide to the National Archives of the United States.* Washington, Government Printing Office, 1974.

————. "Land Grant Records That Survived a Great Fire." *Historical Society of Southern California Quarterly* 26 (March 1944):38–44.

————. *List of Cartographic Records of the General Land Office (Record Group 49).* Comp. by Laura E. Kelsay. Washington, The National Archives, 1964. (*Special Lists* No. 19.)

————. "Preliminary Inventory of the Cartographic Records of the Bureau of Land Management (Record Group 49)." Comp. by Laura E. Kelsay. [Washington], 1965. Typed manuscript.

————. *Preliminary Inventory of the Land-Entry Papers of the General Land Office.* Comp. by Harry P. Yoshpe and Philip B. Brower. Washington, The National Archives, 1949. (*Preliminary Inventories* No. 22.)

————. *Preliminary Inventory of the Records of the Supreme Court of the United States (Record Group 267).* Comp. by Marion M. Johnson. Washington, The National Archives, 1962. (*Preliminary Inventories* No. 139.)

————. "Records of Mexican Land Claims in California." Prep. by Ralph G. Lounsbury. [Washington, n.d.] Typed manuscript.

U.S. Survey of Federal Archives, Arizona. *Inventory of Federal Archives in the States, Series VIII, The Department of the Interior, No. 3, Arizona.* Tucson, The Survey of Federal Archives, 1939.

————, California. *Inventory of Federal Archives in the States, Series II, Federal Courts, No. 5, California.* San Francisco, The Survey of Federal Archives, 1939.

————, ————. *Inventory of Federal Archives in the States, Series V, Department of Justice, No. 5, California.* San Francisco, The Survey of Federal Archives, 1939.

————, ————. *Inventory of Federal Archives in the States, Series VIII, The Department of the Interior, No. 8, California.* San Francisco, The Survey of Federal Archives, 1941.

————. ————. "Lists of Maps in the Spanish and Mexican Land Claims Cases in the United States District Court for the Northern District of California." San Francisco, 1940. Typescript in the National Archives.

U.S. Surveyor General of California. "Alphabetical List of Approvals of Grants of Land, by the Departmental Assembly of California, Recorded in the Book of Sessions." In U.S. Department of the Interior, *Annual Report,* 1880 pp. 912-16. Washington, Government Printing Office, 1880.

————. "Alphabetical List of Names of Ranchos, the Claims of Which Have Been Acted upon by the Former Governments." In U.S. Department of the Interior, *Annual Report,* 1880, pp. 899–912. Washington, Government Printing Office, 1880.

————. "Catalogue of the Original Expedientes or Records in Relation to Land Claims in Upper California under the Spanish and Mexican Governments, with References to Registries of the Same, Arranged in Alphabetical Order, Now on File in the Spanish Archives of the Office of the United States Surveyor-General for California." In U.S. Department of the Interior, *Annual Report,* 1880, pp. 859–99. Washington, Government Printing Office, 1880.

————. "List of Original Documents in Cases Presented to the United States Land Commission, Now on File in the Office of the United States Surveyor General for California." In United States Department of the Interior, *Annual Report,* 1880, pp. 799–858. Washington, Government Printing Office, 1880.

————. "List of Original Land Grants on File in the Land Commission Papers of the United States Surveyor General's Office for California." In U.S. District Court, California (Northern District), *The United States, Appellants vs. José Y. Limantour, Appellee, Nos. 424 and 428, Land Commission Exhibits* . . . . [San Francisco, 1958]. Exhibit K.

U.S. Surveyor General of New Mexico. "List of Documents Relating to Grants of Land by the Spanish and Mexican Governments in the Archives of the Office of the Surveyor-General of New Mexico, June 30, 1885." In U.S. Department of the Interior, *Annual Report,* 1885, 1:535–52. Washington, Government Printing Office, 1885. Also in *House Executive Document* No. 1, 49 Congress, 1 Session. Serial 2378.

————. "Private Land Claims Against the Public Domain in New Mexico on File in the Office [of the] United States Surveyor-General for New Mexico, June 30, 1885." In U.S. Department of the Interior, *Annual Report,* 1885, 1:554–61. Washington, Government Printing Office, 1885. Also in *House Executive Document* No. 1, pt. 5, 49 Congress, 1 Session. Serial 2378.

————. "Schedule of Documents Relating to Grants of Land by the Spanish and Mexican Governments, Forming the Archives of the Surveyor General of New Mexico—Abstract of the Grants of Lands Selected from the Public Records of the Territory, Found in the Archives of Santa Fe, New Mexico." In U.S. Department of the

Interior, *Annual Report*, 1856, pp. 413–32, 433–39. *(Senate Executive Document* No. 5, 34 Congress, 3 Session. Serial 875.) Washington, A.O.P. Nicholson, Printer, 1856. Also in *House Executive Document* No. 1, 34 Congress, 3 Session. Serial 893.

Van den Eynde, Damian, O.F.M. "Calendar of Spanish Manuscripts in John Carter Brown Library." *Hispanic American Historical Review* 16 (November 1936):564–607.

Vaughan, John H. "A Preliminary Report on the Archives of New Mexico." *American Historical Association, Annual Report*, 1909, pp. 465–90.

Weber, Francis J. "The Los Angeles Chancery Archives." *The Americas* 21 (April 1965):410–20.

————. "The San Francisco Chancery Archives." *The Americas* 20 (January 1964):313–21.

Withington, Mary C. *A Catalogue of Manuscripts in the Collection of Western Americana Founded by William Robertson Coe, Yale University Library*. New Haven, Yale University Press, 1952.

Wright, Doris M. *A Guide to the Mariano Guadalupe Vallejo Documentos para la Historia de California, 1780–1875*. Berkeley, University of California Press, 1953.

SECONDARY PUBLICATIONS

Books

Aberle, Sophie de B. *The Pueblo Indians of New Mexico: Their Land, Economy and Civil Organization*. [Menasha, Wis., 1948]. (Memoirs Series of the American Anthropological Association, No. 70.)

Alegre, Francisco J., S.J. *Historia de la Provincia de la Compañía de Jesús de Nueva España*. 4 vols. Ed. by Ernest J. Burrus, S.J. and Félix Zubillaga. Rome, Institutum Historicum, S.J., 1956–60. *(Biblioteca Instituti Historici S.J.*, Vols. 9, 13, 16, 17.)

Almada, Francisco R. *Diccionario de historia, geografía y biografía sonorenses*. Chihuahua, Propiedad Asegurada, 1952.

Anderson, George B. *History of New Mexico, Its Resources and People*. 2 vols. Los Angeles, Chicago, New York, Pacific States Publishing Co., 1907.

Arricivita, Juan D., O.F.M. *Crónica seráfica y apostólica del Colegio de Propaganda Fide de la Santa Cruz de Querétaro en la Nueva España*. Mexico, F. de Zúniga y Ontiveros, 1792.

Balthasar, Juan A., S.J., and José de Ortega, S.J. *Apostólicos afanes de la Compañía de Jesús, escritos por un padre de la misma sagrada religion de su provincia de México*. Barcelona, Por Pablo Nadal, 1754. Reimpreso en México por L. Alvarez de la Cadena, 1944.

————. *De los principios, progreso y decaimiento de la espiritual con-*

quista de la Pimería Alta por la muerte del Padre Eusebio Francisco Kino: De los Nuevos progresos, varios descubrimientos y estado presente de la Pimería Alta. Mexico, Tipografía de E. Abadiano, 1887.

Bancroft, Hubert Howe. *California Pastoral, 1769–1848.* San Francisco, The History Company, Publishers, 1888.

————. *California Pioneer Register and Index, 1542–1848: Including Inhabitants of California, 1769–1800, and List of Pioneers Extracted from the History of California by Hubert Howe Bancroft.* Baltimore, Regional Publishing Co., 1964.

————. *History of Arizona and New Mexico, 1530–1888.* San Francisco, The History Co., 1889.

————. *History of California.* 7 vols. San Francisco, The History Company, 1884–90.

————. *History of Mexico.* 6 vols. San Francisco, The History Company, 1883–88.

————. *History of the North Mexican States and Texas.* 2 vols. San Francisco, A. L. Bancroft, 1884, 1889.

————. *Literary Industries.* San Francisco, The History Company, 1890.

————. *Register of Pioneer Inhabitants of California, 1542 to 1848, and Index to Information Concerning Them in Bancroft's History of California, Volumes 1–8.* Los Angeles, Dawson's Book Shop, 1964.

Bandelier, Adolph F. A. *Final Report of Investigations among the Indians of the Southwestern United States Carried on Mainly in the Years from 1880 to 1885.* Cambridge, Mass., J. Wilson and Son, 1890, 1892. (Archaeological Institute of America, *Papers, American Series,* No. 3, pt. 1, and No. 4, pt. 2.)

Bannon, John F., ed. *Bolton and the Spanish Borderlands.* Norman, University of Oklahoma Press, 1964.

Barker, Eugene C. *The Life of Stephen F. Austin, Founder of Texas, 1793–1836: A Chapter in the Westward Movement of the Anglo-American People.* Nashville, Dallas, Cokesbury Press, 1925.

Barnes, Will C. *Arizona Place Names.* Revised and enlarged by Byrd H. Granger. Tucson, University of Arizona Press, 1960.

Beck, Warren A. *New Mexico: A History of Four Centuries.* Norman, University of Oklahoma Press, 1962.

Beck, Warren A. and Ynez D. Haase. *Historical Atlas of California.* Norman, Okla., University of Oklahoma Press, 1974.

———— and ————. *Historical Atlas of New Mexico.* Norman, Okla., University of Oklahoma Press, 1969.

Bishop, Curtis K. and Bascom Giles. *Lots of Land.* Austin, The Steck Company, 1949.

Blair, Eric L. *Early History of Grimes County.* [Austin], 1930.

Bolton, Herbert E. *Rim of Christendom: A Biography of Eusebio Francisco Kino, Pacific Coast Pioneer.* New York, The Macmillan Company, 1936.

————. *Texas in the Middle Eighteenth Century: Studies in Spanish Colonial History and Administration.* Berkeley, University of California Press, 1915.

Bowden, J. J. "Private Land Claims in the Southwest." 6 vols. Houston, 1969. Typewritten copy in the Library of Congress, Law Library.

————. *Spanish and Mexican Land Grants in the Chihuahua Acquisition.* El Paso, Texas Western Press, 1971.

Bradfute, Richard W. *The Court of Private Land Claims. The Adjudication of Spanish and Mexican Land Grant Titles, 1891–1904.* Albuquerque, University of New Mexico Press, 1975.

Branda, Eldon S., ed. *The Handbook of Texas: A supplement. Volume III.* Austin, The Texas State Historical Association, 1976.

Brayer, Herbert O. *Pueblo Indian Land Grants of the "Río-Abajo," New Mexico.* [Albuquerque], University of New Mexico Press, 1939.

————. *William Blackmore: The Spanish-Mexican Land Grants of New Mexico and Colorado, 1863–1878.* Denver, Bradford-Robinson, 1949.

Brinckerhoff, Sidney B. and Odie B. Faulk. *Lancers of the King: A Study of the Frontier Military System of New Spain, with a Translation of the Royal Regulations of 1772.* Phoenix, Arizona Historical Foundation, 1965.

Brown, John H. *Life and Times of Henry Smith, the First American Governor of Texas.* Dallas, A. D. Aldridge & Co., 1887.

Burrus, Ernest J., S.J. *Kino and Manje, Explorers of Sonora and Arizona, Their Vision of the Future: A Study of Their Expeditions and Plans with an Appendix of Thirty Documents.* Rome, Italy and St. Louis, Mo., Jesuit Historical Institute, 1971. (*Sources and Studies for the History of the Americas,* Vol. 10.)

————. *Kino and the Cartography of Northwestern New Spain.* Tucson, Arizona Historical Society, 1965.

————. *La Obra cartográfica de la Provincia Mexicana de la Compañía de Jesús (1567–1967).* 2 vols. Madrid, Ediciones José Porrúa Turanzas, 1967. (*Colección Chimalistac de libros y documentos acerca de la Nueva España,* 1.)

California, Division of Beaches and Parks. *California Historical Landmarks.* [Sacramento], California State Printing Office, [1965].

Castañeda, Carlos E. *Our Catholic Heritage in Texas, 1519–1936.* 6 vols. Austin, Von Boeckmann-Jones Co., 1936–50.

———— and Early Martin, Jr. *Three Manuscript Maps of Texas by*

Stephen Austin: With Biographical and Bibliographical Notes. Austin, Privately Printed, 1930.

Caughey, John W. *California: A Remarkable State's Life History.* Englewood Cliffs, N.J., Prentice-Hall, Inc., 1970.

————. *Hubert Howe Bancroft, Historian of the West.* Berkeley and Los Angeles, University of California Press, 1946.

Chabot, Frederick C. *Misión La Purísima Concepción: Being an Account of Its Founding in East Texas.* . . . San Antonio, The Naylor Co., 1935.

————. *With the Makers of San Antonio: Genealogies of the Early Latin, Anglo-American, and German Families with Occasional Biographies.* . . . San Antonio, Artes Graficas, 1937.

Chapman, Charles E. *A History of California: The Spanish Period.* New York, The Macmillan Company, 1930.

Chávez, Angelico, O.F.M. *The Cathedral of the Royal City of the Holy Faith of Saint Francis.* Santa Fe, 1947.

————. *Origins of New Mexico Families in the Spanish Colonial Period.* Santa Fe, The Historical Society of New Mexico, 1954.

Cleland, Robert G. *This Reckless Breed of Men: The Trappers and Fur Traders of the Southwest.* New York, Alfred A. Knopf, 1950.

Coan, Charles F. *A History of New Mexico.* 3 vols. Chicago, The American Historical Society, 1925.

Crocket, George L. *Two Centuries in East Texas: A History of San Augustine County and Surrounding Territory from 1685 to the Present Time.* Dallas, Southwest Press, 1932.

Cummings, Homer S. and Carl McFarland. *Federal Justice: Chapters in the History of Justice and the Federal Executive.* New York, The Macmillan Company, 1937.

Dakin, Susanna B. *The Lives of William Hartnell.* Stanford, Stanford University Press, 1949.

Davis, William W. H. *El Gringo: or, New Mexico and Her People.* New York, Harper Brothers, 1857.

Dillon, Richard H. *Fool's Gold: The Decline and Fall of Captain John Sutter of California.* New York, Coward-McCann, Inc., 1967.

Donaldson, Thomas. *The Public Domain: Its History with Statistics (House Miscellaneous Document No. 45, pt. 4, 47 Congress, 2 Session. Serial 2158.)* Washington, Government Printing Office, 1884.

Donohue, John A., S.J. *After Kino: Jesuit Missions in Northwestern New Spain, 1711–1767.* Rome and St. Louis, Jesuit Historical Institute, 1969. (*Sources and Studies for the History of the Americas,* Vol. 6.)

Dwinelle, John W. *The Colonial History of the City of San Francisco: Being a Narrative Argument in the Circuit Court of the United States for the State of California for Four Square Leagues of Land*

Claimed by that City and Confirmed to It by that Court. San Francisco, Towne & Bacon, 1866.

Engelhardt, Zephyrin, O.F.M. *The Franciscans in Arizona.* Harbor Springs, Mich., Holy Childhood Indian School, 1899.

Espinosa, Isidro Félix de, O.F.M. *Crónica de los Colegios de Propaganda Fide de la Nueva España.* Ed. by Lino G. Canedo, O.F.M. Washington, Academy of American Franciscan History, 1964. (Academy of American Franciscan History, *Franciscan Historical Classics,* Vol. 2.)

Espinosa, José M. *Crusaders of the Rio Grande: The Story of Don Diego de Vargas and the Reconquest and Founding of New Mexico.* Chicago, Institute of Jesuit History, 1942.

Federal Writers' Project. *California: A Guide to the Golden State.* New York, Hastings House, 1939.

Fitzmorris, (Sister) Mary A. *Four Decades of Catholicism in Texas, 1820–1860.* Washington, Catholic University of America, 1926.

Fox, Charles K. *The Colorado Delta: A Discussion of the Spanish Exploration & Maps.* . . . Los Angeles, 1936.

Friends of the Bancroft Library. *GPH: An Informal Record of George P. Hammond and His Era in the Bancroft Library.* [Berkeley] University of California, 1965.

Garrison, George P. *Texas: A Contest of Civilizations.* Boston, New York, Houghton, Mifflin, 1903.

Geiger, Maynard J., O.F.M. *Franciscan Missionaries in Hispanic California, 1769–1848.* San Marino, The Huntington Library, 1969.

————. *The Life and Times of Fray Junípero Serra, O.F.M.; or, the Man who Never Turned Back (1713–1784): A Biography.* 2 vols. Washington, Academy of American Franciscan History, 1959. (*Publications* of the Academy of American Franciscan History, *Monograph* Series, Vols. 5–6.)

————. *Palóu's Life of Fray Junípero Serra.* Washington, Academy of American Franciscan History, 1955. (*Publications* of the Academy of American Franciscan History, *Documentary Series,* Vol. 3.)

————. *Mission Santa Barbara, 1782–1965.* Santa Barbara, Calif., Franciscan Fathers of California, 1965.

Gorham, George C. *Life and Public Services of Edwin M. Stanton.* 2 vols. Boston, New York, Houghton, Mifflin, 1899.

Grivas, Theodore. *Military Governments in California, 1846–1850.* Glendale, Calif., Arthur H. Clark, Co., 1963.

Gudde, Erwin G. *California Place Names. The Origin and Etymology of Current Geographical Names.* Berkeley and Los Angeles, University of California Press, 1969.

Habig, Marion A., O.F.M. *The Alamo Chain of Missions: A History of San Antonio's Five Old Missions.* Chicago, Franciscan Herald Press, 1968.

Hafen, LeRoy R. and Ann W. *The Old Spanish Trail, with Extracts from Contemporary Records and Including Diaries of Antonio Armijo and Orville Pratt.* Glendale, Calif., Arthur H. Clark, Co., 1954.

Hall, Frederic. *The History of San José and Surroundings.* San Francisco, A. L. Bancroft and Company, 1871.

Hallenbeck, Cleve. *Land of the Conquistadores.* Caldwell, Idaho, The Caxton Printers, Ltd., 1950.

――――. *Spanish Missions of the Old Southwest.* Garden City, N. Y., Doubleday, Page and Company, 1926.

Hamrick, Alma W. *The Call of the San Sabá: A History of San Sabá County.* San Antonio, The Naylor Co., 1941.

Hansen-Taylor, Marie and Horace E. Scudder, eds. *Life and Letters of Bayard Taylor.* 2 vols. Boston, Houghton, Mifflin, 1885.

Harlow, Neal. *The Maps of San Francisco Bay from the Spanish Discovery in 1769 to the American Occupation.* San Francisco, Grabhorn Press, 1950.

Hatcher, Mattie A. *The Opening of Texas to Foreign Settlement, 1801–1821.* Austin, Texas, The University, 1927. (University of Texas *Bulletin*, No. 2714, April 8, 1927.)

Heusinger, Edward W. *Early Exploration and Mission Establishments in Texas.* San Antonio, The Naylor Co., 1936.

Hewett, Edgar L. and Wayne L. Mauzy. *Landmarks of New Mexico.* Albuquerque, University of New Mexico Press, 1953.

Hill, Joseph J. *The History of Warner's Ranch and Its Environs.* Los Angeles, Privately Printed, 1927.

Hill, Roscoe R. *American Missions in European Archives.* Mexico, Instituto Panamericano de Geografía e Historia, 1951. (Instituto Panamericano de Geografía e Historia, Misiones Americanos en los Archivos Europeos 2, *Publicación*, Num. 108.)

Hine, Robert V. *Edward Kern and American Expansion.* New Haven, Yale University Press, 1962.

Hittell, Theodore H. *History of California.* 4 vols. San Francisco, vols. 1–2, Pacific Press Publishing House and Occidental Publishing Co., 1885; vols. 3–4, N. J. Stone & Company, 1897.

Hodge, Frederick W., ed. *Handbook of American Indians North of Mexico.* 2 vols. New York, Pageant Books, Inc., 1959. (Smithsonian Institution, Bureau of American Ethnology, *Bulletin* No. 30.)

Hogan, William R. *The Texas Republic: A Social and Economic History.* Norman, University of Oklahoma Press, 1946.

Horgan, Paul. *The Centuries of Santa Fe.* New York, E. P. Dutton, 1956.

Hughes, Anne E. *The Beginnings of Spanish Settlement in the El Paso District.* Berkeley, University of California Press, 1914. (University of California, *Publications in History*, Vol. I, No. 3.)

Hughes, Thomas, S.J. *A History of the Society of Jesus in North America, Colonial and Federal, Text Vol. I.* 3 vols. in 4. London, New York, Longmans, Green and Co., 1907–17.

Huson, Robert. *Refugio County Basic Titles: Refugio County General, Colonial Grants, Four League Grant to Town of Refugio.* Refugio, Texas, Refugio Mission Title Co., 1951.

Jackson, Earl. *Tumacácori's Yesterdays.* Santa Fe, Southwestern Monuments Association, 1951. (Southwestern Monuments Association, Popular Series No. 6.)

Johnson, Kenneth M. *The Pious Fund.* Los Angeles, Dawson's Book Shop, 1963.

Keleher, William A. *Maxwell Land Grant: A New Mexico Item.* Santa Fe, The Rydal Press, 1942.

————. *Violence in Lincoln County, 1869–1881.* Albuquerque, University of New Mexico Press, 1957.

Kelly, Henry W. *Franciscan Missions of New Mexico, 1740–1760.* Albuquerque, University of New Mexico Press, 1941. (Historical Society of New Mexico, *Publications in History*, Vol. 10, April 1941.)

Kemp, Louis W. *The Signers of the Texas Declaration of Independence.* Houston, The Anson Jones Press, 1944.

Kennedy, William. *Texas: the Rise, Progress, and Prospects of the Republic of Texas.* 2 vols. London, R. Hastings, 1841.

Kessell, John L. *Mission of Sorrows: Jesuit Guevavi and the Pimas, 1691–1767.* Tucson, University of Arizona Press, 1970.

Kubler, George. *The Rebuilding of San Miguel at Santa Fe in 1710.* Colorado Springs, Taylor Museum, 1939.

Lockwood, Francis C. *Pioneer Days in Arizona from the Spanish Occupation to Statehood.* New York, The Macmillan Company, 1932.

Masseron, Alexandre and Marion A. Habig, O.F.M. *The Franciscans: St. Francis of Assisi and His Three Orders.* Chicago, Franciscan Herald Press, 1959.

McCloskey, Michael B., O.F.M. *The Formative Years of the Missionary College of Santa Cruz of Querétaro, 1683–1733.* Washington, Academy of American Franciscan History, 1955. (*Publications* of the Academy of American Franciscan History, *Monograph Series*, Vol. 2.)

McConnell, Joseph C. *The West Texas Frontier: or, A Descriptive History of Early Times in Western Texas. . . .* 2 vols. Jacksboro, Tex., Gazette Print, 1933; Palo Pinto, Tex., Texas Legal Bank and Book Co., 1939.

Merriman, Roger B. *The Rise of the Spanish Empire in the Old World and in the New.* 4 vols. New York, The Macmillan Company, 1918–34.

Nevins, Allan. *Frémont, The West's Greatest Adventurer: Being a Biography.* . . . 2 vols. New York, London, Harper & Brothers, 1928.

New Catholic Encyclopedia. 15 vols. Prepared by the editorial staff of the Catholic University of America. New York, McGraw-Hill, 1967.

Newhall, Nancy W. *Mission San Xavier del Bac.* San Francisco, Five Associates, 1954.

Nichols, Ruth G. and S. W. Lifflander. *Samuel May Williams, 1795–1858: Biography by Ruth G. Nichols. Calendar to Samuel May Williams Papers Compiled by Ruth G. Nichols and S. W. Lifflander.* Galveston, Rosenberg Library Press, 1956.

Oberste, William H. *History of Refugio Mission.* Refugio, Texas, Refugio Timely Remarks, Publisher, 1942.

————. *Knights of Columbus in Texas, 1902–1952.* Austin, Von Boeckmann-Jones Company, 1952.

————. *Texas Irish Empresarios and Their Colonies: Power & Hewetson, McMullen & McGloin; Refugio-San Patricio.* Austin, Von Boeckmann-Jones Co., 1953.

O'Rourke, Thomas P. *The Franciscan Missions in Texas (1690–1793).* Washington, Catholic University of America, 1927. (Catholic University of America, *Studies in American Church History,* Vol. 5.)

Palóu, Francisco, O.F.M. *Life of Fray Junípero Serra.* Trans. and ed. by Maynard J. Geiger, O.F.M. Washington, Academy of American Franciscan History, 1955. (Academy of American Franciscan History, *Publications, Documentary Series,* Vol. 3.)

————. *Relación histórica de la vida y apostólicas tareas del Venerable Padre Fray Junípero Serra y de las misiones que fondó en la California Septentrional.* Mexico, Imprenta de Don Felipe de Zúñiga y Ontiveros, 1787.

Parmenter, Mary F., Walter R. Fisher, and Lawrence E. Mallette. *The Life of George Fisher (1795–1873) and the History of the Fisher Family in Mississippi.* Jacksonville, Fla., H. & W. B. Drew Company, 1959.

Pearce, Thomas M. *New Mexico Place Names. A Geographical Dictionary.* Albuquerque, University of New Mexico Press, 1965.

Piette, Maximin Charles J. G. *Evocation de Junípero Serra, Fondateur de la Californie.* Washington, Academy of American Franciscan History, 1946.

————. *Le Secret de Junípero Serra, Fondateur de la Californie-Nouvelle, 1769–1784.* Washington, Academy of American Franciscan History, 1949.

Polzer, Charles W., Thomas C. Barnes, and Thomas H. Naylor, comps. *Documentary Relations of the Southwest. Project Manual.* Tucson, Arizona State Museum, 1977.

Pool, William C. *A Historical Atlas of Texas*. Maps by Edward Triggs and Lance Wren. Austin, Encino Press, 1975.

Powell, Donald M. *The Peralta Grant: James Addison Reavis and the Barony of Arizona*. Norman, University of Oklahoma Press, 1960.

Priestley, Herbert I. *Franciscan Explorations in California*. Ed. by Lillian E. Fisher. Glendale, Calif., Arthur H. Clark, Co., 1946.

――――. *The Mexican Nation: A History*. New York, The Macmillan Company, 1925.

Read, Benjamin M. *Illustrated History of New Mexico*. Santa Fe, New Mexican Printing Co., 1912.

Richardson, Rupert N., Ernest Wallace, and Adrian N. Anderson. *Texas, the Lone Star State*. Englewood Cliffs, N. J., Prentice-Hall, Inc., 1970.

――――, and Carl C. Rister. *The Greater Southwest: The Economic, Social and Cultural Development of Kansas, Oklahoma, Texas, Utah, Colorado, Nevada, New Mexico, Arizona, and California from the Spanish Conquest to the Twentieth Century*. Glendale, Calif., Arthur H. Clark, Co., 1934.

Richman, Irving B. *California under Spain and Mexico, 1535–1847*. Boston, Houghton, Mifflin, 1911.

Rister, Carl C. *Comanche Bondage: Dr. John Charles Beales's Settlement of La Villa de Dolores on Las Moras Creek in Southern Texas of the 1830's.* . . . Glendale, Calif., Arthur H. Clark, Co., 1955.

Robinson, William W. *Land in California: The Story of Mission Lands, Ranchos, Squatters, Mining Claims, Railroad Grants, Land Scrip Homesteads*. Berkeley, University of California Press, 1948.

――――. *Maps of Los Angeles from Ord's Survey of 1849 to the End of the Boom of the Eighties*. Los Angeles, Dawson's Book Shop, 1966.

――――. *Ranchos Become Cities*. Pasadena, San Pasqual Press, 1939.

Rolle, Andrew F. *California: A History*. New York, Thomas Y. Crowell Company, 1969.

Ross, Ishbel, *Rebel Rose: Life of Rose O'Neal Greenhow, Confederate Spy*. New York, Harper & Brothers, 1954.

Rowland, Leon. *Los Fundadores*. Fresno, Academy of California Church History, 1951. (Academy of California Church History, *Publication* No. 3.)

Royce, Josiah. *California from the Conquest in 1846 to the Second Vigilance Committee in San Francisco.* . . . Boston, New York, Houghton, Mifflin, 1887.

Santos, Richard G. *A Preliminary Report on the Archival Project in the Office of the County Clerk in Bexar County*. San Antonio, [1966].

Schmidt, Charles F. *History of Washington County, [Texas]*. San Antonio, The Naylor Co., 1949.

Scholes, France V. *Church and State in New Mexico, 1610–1650.* Albuquerque, University of New Mexico Press, 1937. (Historical Society of New Mexico, *Publications in History,* Vol. 7.)

————. *Troublous Times in New Mexico, 1659–1670.* Albuquerque, University of New Mexico Press, 1942. (Historical Society of New Mexico, *Publications in History,* Vol. 11.)

Scott, Florence J. *Historical Heritage of the Lower Río Grande.* San Antonio, The Naylor Co., 1937.

Sibley, Marilyn M. *Travelers in Texas, 1761–1860.* Austin, University of Texas Press, 1967.

Simmons, Marc. *Spanish Government of New Mexico.* Albuquerque, University of New Mexico Press, 1968.

Smith, Fay J., John L. Kessell, and Francis J. Fox, S.J. *Father Kino in Arizona.* Phoenix, Arizona Historical Foundation, 1966.

Smythe, William E. *The History of San Diego.* 2 vols. San Diego, The History Company, 1907.

Sonnichsen, Charles L. *Pass of the North: Four Centuries on the Río Grande.* El Paso, Texas Western Press, 1968.

Southwestern Mission Research Center. *SMRC Newsletter* 1–9. Tucson, 1967–77.

Sutter, John A., ed. *Sutter's Own Story: The Life of General John Augustus Sutter and the History of New Helvetia in the Sacramento Valley.* Edited by Erwin G. Gudde. New York, G. P. Putnam's Sons, 1936.

Swanton, John R. *The Indian Tribes of North America.* Washington, Government Printing Office, 1952. (Smithsonian Institution, Bureau of American Ethnology, *Bulletin* No. 145.)

Taylor, Bayard, *Eldorado: or, Adventures in the Path of Empire, Comprising a Voyage to California, via Panamá: Life in San Francisco and Monterey. . . .* 2 vols. New York, George P. Putnam, 1850.

Taylor, Paul S. *An American-Mexican Frontier: Nueces County, Texas.* Chapel Hill, University of North Carolina Press, 1934.

Texas, Legislature, House of Representatives. *Biographical Directory of the Texas Conventions and Congresses, 1832–1845.* Austin, n.p., 1941.

Twitchell, Ralph E. *The Leading Facts of New Mexican History.* 5 vols. Cedar Rapids, Ia., The Torch Press, 1911–17.

Wagner, Henry R. *Bullion to Books: Fifty Years of Business and Pleasure.* Los Angeles, The Zamorano Club, 1942.

————. *The Cartography of the Northwest Coast of America to the Year 1800.* 2 vols. Berkeley, University of California Press, 1937.

————. *Sixty Years of Book Collecting.* Los Angeles, The Zamorano Club, 1952.

————. *Spanish Explorations in the Strait of Juan de Fuca.* Santa Ana, Calif., Fine Arts Press, 1933.

Wagner, Henry R. *Spanish Voyages to the Northwest Coast of America in the Sixteenth Century*. San Francisco, California Historical Society, 1929. (California Historical Society, *Special Publication No. 4*.)

Webb, Walter P., H. Bailey Carroll, Llerena B. Friend, May Joe Carroll, and Louise Nolen, eds. *The Handbook of Texas*. 2 vols. Austin, The Texas State Historical Association, 1952.

Weber, Francis J. *A Biographical Sketch of Right Reverend Francisco García Diego y Moreno, First Bishop of the Californias, 1785–1846*. Los Angeles, The Borromeo Guild, 1961.

————. *The United States versus Mexico: The Final Settlement of the Pious Fund*. Los Angeles, Historical Society of Southern California, 1969.

Westphall, Victor. *The Public Domain in New Mexico, 1854–1891*. Albuquerque, University of New Mexico Press, 1965.

Wheat, Carl I. *Mapping the Trans-Mississippi West, 1540–1861, Volume One. The Spanish Entrada to the Louisiana Purchase, 1540–1804*. San Francisco, Institute of Historical Cartography, 1957.

Wheeler, Alfred. *Land Titles in San Francisco, and the Laws Affecting the Same, with a Synopsis of All Grants and Sales of Land within the Limits Claimed by the City*. San Francisco, Alta California Steam Printing Establishment, 1852.

Wilson, James. *A Pamphlet Relating to the Claims of Señor Don José Y. Limantour, to Four Leagues of Land in the County Adjoining and Near the City of San Francisco, California*. San Francisco, Whitton, Towne & Co., 1853.

Wooten, Dudley G., ed. *A Comprehensive History of Texas, 1685 to 1897*. 2 vols. Dallas, William G. Scarff, 1898.

Wortham, Louis J. *A History of Texas, from Wilderness to Commonwealth*. 5 vols. Fort Worth, Wortham-Molyneaux Company, 1924.

Wright, Ralph B., John B. Anderson, and Benjamin M. Watson. *California's Missions*. Los Angeles, The Sterling Press, 1950.

Writers Program, Arizona, *The Grand Canyon State: A State Guide*. Ed. by Henry G. Alsberg and Harry Hansen. Completely revised by Joseph Miller. New York, Hastings House, 1966.

Writers Program, California. *California. A Guide to the Golden State*. New revised edition, ed. by Harry Hansen. New York, Hastings House, 1967.

Writers' Program, New Mexico. *New Mexico: A Guide to the Colorful State*. New York, Hastings House, 1940.

Writers Program, New Mexico. *New Mexico. A Guide to the Colorful State*. Ed. by Henry G. Alsberg. New and completely revised edition by Joseph Miller. New York, Hastings House, 1962.

Writers Program, Texas. *Texas. A Guide to the Lone Star State.* New Revised edition, ed. by Harry Hansen. New York, Hastings House, 1969.

Yoakum, Henderson. *History of Texas from Its First Settlement in 1685 to Its Annexation to the United States in 1846.* 2 vols. New York, Redfield, 1855.

Zelis, Rafael de, S.J. *Catálogo de los sugetos de la Compañía de Jesús que formaban la Provincia de México el día del arresto, 25 de junio de 1767.* Mexico, Impr. de I. Escalante y Ca., 1871.

Articles

Adams, Eleanor B. "The Chapel and Cofradia of Our Lady of Light in Santa Fe." *New Mexico Historical Review* 22 (October 1947): 327–41.

―――. "Fray Francisco Atanasio Domínguez and Fray Silvestre Vélez de Escalante. *Utah Historical Quarterly* 44 (Winter 1976):40–58.

Almada, Francisco R. "El Archivo de la Comandancia General de las Provincias Internas." *Boletín de la Sociedad Chihuahuense de estudios históricos* 1, num. 3 (julio 1938): 71–73.

Alter, J. Cecil. "Father Escalante's Map." *Utah Historical Quarterly* 9 (January, April 1941):64–72.

Anderson, Clinton P. "The Adobe Palace." *New Mexico Historical Review* 19 (April 1944):97–122.

Anderson, Robert R. "A Note on the Archivo de Hidalgo del Parral." *Arizona and the West* 4 (Winter 1962):381–85.

Avila, Pablo, trans. and ed. "Naming of the Elector-Designate, Santa Barbara, 1830." *California Historical Society Quarterly* 27 (December 1948):333–38.

Bacarisse, Charles A. "The Union of Coahuila and Texas." *Southwestern Historical Quarterly* 61 (January 1958):341–49.

Baker, Charles C. "Mexican Land Grants in California." *Southern California Historical Society, Annual Publication* 9, pt. 3 (1914): 236–42.

Bannon, John F., S.J. "Herbert Eugene Bolton: His Guide in the Making." *Southwestern Historical Quarterly* 73 (July 1969):35–55.

―――. "The Saint Louis University Collection of Jesuitica Americana." *Hispanic American Historical Review* 37 (February 1957): 82–88.

Barker, Eugene C. "General Arthur Goodall Wavell and Wavell's Colony in Texas, a Note." *Southwestern Historical Quarterly* 47 (January 1944):253–55.

―――. "The Government of Austin's Colony, 1821–1831." *Texas State Historical Association Quarterly* 21 (January 1918): 223–52.

Barker, Eugene C. "Lester Gladstone Bugbee, Teacher and Historian." *Southwestern Historical Quarterly* 49 (July 1945):1–32.

————. "Professor George Pierce Garrison: An Appreciation." *University of Texas Record* 10 (January 8, 1911):190–94.

————. "Private Papers of Anthony Butler." *The Nation* 92 (June 15, 1911):600–01.

————. "To Whom Credit Is Due." *Southwestern Historical Quarterly* 54 (July 1950):6–12.

Barton, Henry W. "The Anglo-American Colonists under Mexican Militia Laws." *Southwestern Historical Quarterly* 65 (July 1961): 61–71.

Benson, Nettie L. "Microfilming Projects in Mexico." *News from the Center* [for the Coordination of Foreign Manuscript Copying, Library of Congress], No. 7 (Spring 1970), pp. 11–16.

————. "Texas Failure to Send a Deputy to the Spanish Cortes, 1810–1812." *Southwestern Historical Quarterly* 64 (July 1960):14–35.

Blake, Robert B. "Locations of the Early Spanish Missions and Presidios in Nacogdoches County." *Southwestern Historical Quarterly* 41 (January 1938):212–24.

Bloom, Lansing B. "Beginnings of Representative Government in New Mexico." *New Mexico Historical Review* 21 (April 1946):127–34.

————. "Ledgers of a Santa Fe Trader." *New Mexico Historical Review* 21 (April 1946):135–39.

————. "New Mexico under Mexican Administration." *Old Santa Fe* 1 (July 1913–April 1914):3–49, 131–75, 235–87, 347–68; 2 (July 1914–April 1915):3–56, 119–69, 223–77, 351–80.

Bolton, Herbert E. "Archives and Trails." *California Monthly* 37 (October 1936):19, 40–42.

————. "Father Kino's Lost History: Its Discovery, and Its Value." Bibliographical Society of America, *Papers* 6 (1911):9–34.

————. "The Founding of Missions on the San Gabriel River, 1745–1749." *Southwestern Historical Quarterly* 17 (April 1914):323–78.

————. "The Mission as a Frontier Institution in the Spanish-American Colonies." *American Historical Review* 23 (October 1917):42–61.

————. "Records of the Mission of Nuestra Señora del Refugio." *Southwestern Historical Quarterly* 14 (October 1910):164–66.

Borges, Pedro, O.F.M. "Notas sobre el disaparecido archivo matritense de la Comisario General de Indias." *Archivo Ibero-Americano* 26 (avril–septiembre 1966):113–64.

Bowman, Jacob N. "The Lost Toma de Razón: A Register of Land Claims Comes to Light." *California Historical Society Quarterly* 21 (December 1942):311–20.

Brinckerhoff, Sidney B. "The Last Years of Spanish Arizona, 1786–1821." *Arizona and the West* 9 (Spring 1967):5–20.

Brown, Madie D. "Gen. M. G. Vallejo and H. H. Bancroft." *California Historical Society Quarterly* 29 (June 1950):149–59.

Bugbee, Lester G. "The Old Three Hundred: A List of Settlers in Austin's Colony." *Southwestern Historical Quarterly* 1 (October 1897):108–117.

————— and Eugene C. Barker. "Report on the Béxar Archives." American Historical Association, *Annual Report* 1 (1902):357–63.

Burrus, Ernest J., S.J. "The Bandelier Collection in the Vatican Library." *Manuscripta* 10 (July 1966):67–84.

—————. "Bandelier's Manuscript Sources for the Study of the American Southwest." In *Homenaje a Don José María de la Peña y Cámara*, pp. 29–48. Madrid, Ediciones José Porrúa Turanzas, 1969.

—————. "Francisco Javier Alegre, Historian of the Jesuits in New Spain (1729–1788)." *Archivum Historicum Societatis Iesu* 22 (Ian–Iun 1953):439–509.

—————. "An Introduction to Bibliographical Tools in Spanish Archives and Manuscript Collections Relating to Hispanic America." *Hispanic American Historical Review* 35 (November 1955):443–83.

—————. "Mexican Historical Documents in the Central Jesuit Archives." *Manuscripta* 12 (November 1968):133–61.

—————. "Research Opportunities in Italian Archives and Manuscript Collections for Students of Hispanic American History." *Hispanic American Historical Review* 39 (August 1959):428–63.

Cadenhead, Evie E., Jr. "The G. R. G. Conway Collection in the Gilcrease Institute: A Checklist." *Hispanic American Historical Review* 38 (August 1958):373–82.

Carr, Ralph. "Private Land Claims in Colorado." *The Colorado Magazine* 25 (January 1948):10–30.

Carreño, Alberto M. "The Missionary Influence of the College of Zacatecas." *The Americas* 7 (January 1951):297–320.

Castañeda, Carlos E. "A Great Literary Collection." *Mexican Life* 16 (September 1940):30–31, 51–54.

—————. "Why I Chose History." *The Americas* 8 (April 1952):475–83.

Chapman, Charles E. "The Archivo General de Indias." *Southwestern Historical Quarterly* 21 (October 1917):145–55.

—————. "The Native Sons' Fellowships." *Southwestern Historical Quarterly* 21 (April 1918):389–94.

Chávez, Angelico, O.F.M. "Addenda to New Mexico Families." *El Palacio* 62 (November–December 1955):324–39; 63 (May–December 1956):166–74, 236–48, 317–19, 367–76; 64 (March–August 1957):123–6, 178–91, 246–8.

—————. "El Vicario Don Santiago Roybal." *El Palacio* 55 (August 1948):231–52.

—————. "New Names in New Mexico, 1820–1850." *El Palacio* 64 (September–December 1957):291–318, 367–80.

Chávez, Angelico, O.F.M. "Santa Fe Church and Convent Sites in the Seventeenth and Eighteenth Centuries." *New Mexico Historical Review* 24 (April 1949):85–93.

Connor, Seymour V. "The Evolution of County Government in the Republic of Texas." *Southwestern Historical Quarterly* 55 (October 1951):163–200.

Cortés Alonso, Vicenta and Mathias C. Kieman, O.F.M. "Manuscripts Concerning Mexico and Central America in the Library of Congress, Washington, D.C." *The Americas* 18 (January 1962):255–96.

Dabney, Lancaster E. "Louis Aury: the First Governor of Texas under the Mexican Republic." *Southwestern Historical Quarterly* 42 (October 1938):108–16.

DePalo, William A., Jr. "The Establishment of the Vizcaya Militia during the Administration of Teodoro de Croix, 1776–1783." *New Mexico Historical Review* 48 (July 1973):223–49.

"Destruction of Spanish and Mexican Archives in New Mexico by United States Officials." Reprint from *Santa Fe Weekly Post*, April 30, 1870, and the *Albuquerque Republican* [n.d.]. Photostat in the National Archives Library.

Dickie, G. W., Leverett M. Loomis, and Ransom Pratt. "In Memoriam: Theodore Henry Hittell, Born April 5, 1830–Died February 23, 1917." California Academy of Science, *Proceedings*, 4th ser. 8 (June 17, 1917):1–25.

Dillon, Richard H. "The Sutro Library." *News Notes of California Libraries* 51 (April 1956):338–52.

Dobyns, Henry F. "The 1797 Population of the Presidio of Tucson." *Journal of Arizona History* 13 (Autumn 1972):205–09.

Donkin, R. A. "The Diseño: A Source for the Geography of California, 1830–46." *Mid-America* 40 (April 1958):92–105.

Donohue, John A., S.J. "The Unlucky Jesuit Mission of Bac." *Arizona and the West* 2 (Summer 1960):127–39.

Dunham, Harold H. "New Mexican Land Grants with Special Reference to the Title Papers of the Maxwell Grant." *New Mexico Historical Review* 30 (January 1955):1–22.

Dunne, Peter M., S.J. "Jesuit Annual Letters in the Bancroft Library." *Mid-America* 20 (October 1938):263–72.

————. "The Expulsion of the Jesuits from New Spain, 1767." *Mid-America* 19 (January 1937):3–30.

Dutton, Bertha P. "The Museum of New Mexico." *El Palacio* 56 (January 1949):3–20.

Eckhart, George B. "Missions in Texas Along the Río Grande and in Adjacent Areas." *Southwestern Historical Quarterly* 63 (January 1960):606–07.

————. "Spanish Missions of Texas, 1680–1800: An Outline of Spanish Mission History in Texas from 1680 to 1800." *The Kiva* 32 (February 1967):73–95.

Ellis, Florence H. "Tomé and Father J. B. R. [John Baptist Ralliere]." *New Mexico Historical Review* 30 (April, July 1955):89–114, 195–220.

Espinosa, José Manuel. "Vélez de Escalante's 'Authorship' of the So-Called 'Anonymous' Manuscript in A.G.N., Historia, Tomo 2." *Hispanic American Historical Review* 22 (May 1942):422–25.

Estep, Raymond. "The First Panhandle Land Grant." *Chronicles of Oklahoma* 36 (Winter 1958):358–70.

————. "The Le Grand Survey of the High Plains—Fact or Fancy." *New Mexico Historical Review* 29 (April 1954):81–96, 141–53.

Faye, Stanley. "Commodore Aury." *Louisiana Historical Quarterly* 24 (July 1941):611–97.

Field, Alston G. "Attorney-General Black and the California Land Claims." *Pacific Historical Review* 4 (September 1935):235–45.

Fields, Dorothy L. "David Gouverneur Burnet." *Southwestern Historical Quarterly* 49 (October 1945):215–32.

Foscue, Edwin J. "Agricultural History of the Lower Rio Grande Valley Region." *Agricultural History* 8 (July 1934):124–37.

Foster, Stephen C. "I Was Los Angeles' First American Alcalde." *Historical Society of Southern California Quarterly* 31 (December 1949):318–21.

Freedman, Samuel B. "Microfilming in Mexico." *Library Journal* 85 (November 1, 1960):3926–31.

Frémont, John C. "Conquest of California." *The Century Magazine,* n.s. 41 (April 1890):917–28.

Friend, Llerena. "E. W. Winkler and the Texas State Library." *Texas Libraries* 24 (May–June 1962):89–114.

Garver, Lois. "Benjamin Rush Milam." *Southwestern Historical Quarterly* 38 (October 1934, January 1935):79–121, 177–202.

Geiger, Maynard J., O.F.M. "History of the Santa Bárbara De la Guerra Family Documents." *Southern California Quarterly* 54 (Fall 1972):277–84.

————. "In Quest of Serrana." *The Americas* 1 (July 1944):97–103.

————. "The Internal Organization and Activities of San Fernando College, Mexico (1734–1858)." *The Americas* 6 (July 1949):3–31.

————. "The Royal Presidio Chapel of San Carlos, Monterey, Capital of Colonial California." *The Americas* 9 (October 1952):207–11.

Gentilcore, R. Louis. "Missions and Mission Lands of Alta California." Association of American Geographers, *Annals* 51 (March 1961):46–72.

Gilbert, Benjamin F. "Mexican Alcaldes of San Francisco, 1835–1846." *Journal of the West* 2 (July 1963):245–56.

Gómez Canedo, Lino G., O.F.M. "Some Franciscan Sources in the Archives and Libraries of America." *Americas* 13 (October 1956): 141–74.

Graf, Leroy P. "Colonizing Projects in Texas South of the Nueces, 1820–1845." *Southwestern Historical Quarterly* 50 (April 1947): 431–48.

Griffin, Grace G. "Foreign American History Manuscript. Copies in the Library of Congress." *Journal of Documentary Reproduction* 3 (March 1940):3–9.

Guest, Florian, O.F.M. "The Establishment of the Villa de Branciforte." *California Historical Society Quarterly* 41 (March 1962):29–50.

Guest, Francis F., O.F.M. "Municipal Government in Spanish California." *California Historical Society Quarterly* 46 (December 1967):307–36.

Gumm, Clark L. "The Foundation of Land Records." *Our Public Lands* 7 (October 1957):4–5, 12–14.

Habig, Marion A., O.F.M. "The Builders of San Xavier del Bac." *Southwestern Historical Quarterly* 41 (October 1937):154–65.

————. "The Franciscan Provinces of Spanish North America." *The Americas* 1 (July, October 1944–January 1945):88–96, 215–30, 330–44.

————. "Mission San José y San Miguel de Aguayo, 1720–1824." *Southwestern Historical Quarterly* 71 (April 1968):496–516.

Hafen, Le Roy R. "Mexican Land Grants in Colorado." *Colorado Magazine* 4 (May 1927):81–93.

Haggard, J. Villasana. "The House of Barr and Davenport." *Southwestern Historical Quarterly* 49 (July 1945):66–88.

Hammond, George P. "Manuscript Collections in the Spanish Archives in New Mexico." In *Archives and Libraries: Papers Presented at the 1939 Conference of the American Library Association*, pp. 80–87. Chicago, American Library Association, 1939.

————. "The Use of Microphotography in Manuscript Work in New Mexico." In *Archives and Libraries: Papers Presented at the 1939 Conference of the American Library Association*, pp. 98–102. Chicago, American Library Association, 1939.

Hanke, Lewis. "Materials for Research on Texas History in European Archives and Libraries." *Southwestern Historical Quarterly* 59 (January 1956):335–43.

————. "Mexican Microfilm Developments." *Library of Congress Quarterly Journal* 6 (August 1949):9–13; 8 (February 1951):12–14.

Harllee, William C. "Sterling Clack Robertson." In *Kinfolks: A Genealogical and Biographical Record . . .* , 3:2813–65. New Orleans, Searcy & Pfaff, Ltd., 1937.

Harrison, Robert W. "Public Land Records of the Federal Government." *Mississippi Valley Historical Review* 41 (September 1954): 277–88.

Hatcher, Mattie. "The Municipal Government of San Fernando de Béxar, 1730–1800." *Texas State Historical Association Quarterly* 8 (April 1905):277–352.

Head, Edwin L. "Report on the Archives of the State of California." American Historical Association, *Annual Report*, 1915, pp. 277–309.

Henderson, Mary V. "Minor Empresario Contracts for the Colonization of Texas, 1825–1834." *Southwestern Historical Quarterly* 31 (April 1928):295–324; 32 (July 1928):1–28.

Hodge, Frederick W. "Biographical Sketch and Bibliography of Adolphe Francis Alphonse Bandelier." *New Mexico Historical Review* 7 (October 1932):353–70.

Holmes, Oliver W. "Managing Our Spanish and Mexican Southwestern Archival Legacy." *Southwestern Historical Quarterly* 71 (April 1968):527–41.

Holterman, Jack. "José Zúñiga, Commandant of Tucson." *The Kiva* 22 (November 1956):1–4.

Hopkins, Rufus C. "The Spanish Archives of California." In John W. Dwinelle. *The Colonial History of the City of San Francisco . . . ,* pp. v–ix. San Francisco, Townes & Bacon, 1866.

Houston, Virginia Taylor. "Surveying in Texas." *Southwestern Historical Quarterly* 65 (October 1961):204–33.

Houze, Robert A. "The Texas Consortium for Microfilming the Mexican Archives." *Texas Library Journal* 45 (Fall 1969):120–22, 185–86.

Jenkins, Myra Ellen. "The Juan de Villagutierre y Sotomayor Manuscript." *El Palacio* 67 (June 1960):108.

Jones, O. Garfield. "Local Government in the Spanish Colonies as Provided by the Recopilación de Leyes de los Reynos." *Texas State Historical Association Quarterly* 19 (July 1915):65–90.

Jones, Oakah L., Jr., "Pueblo Indian Auxiliaries in New Mexico, 1763–1821." *New Mexico Historical Review* 38 (April 1962):81–109.

Karpinski, Louis C. "Manuscript Maps Relating to American History in French, Spanish and Portuguese Archives." *Mississippi Valley Historical Review* 14 (December 1927):437–39.

Keleher, William A. "Law of the New Mexico Land Grant." *New Mexico Historical Review* 4 (October 1929):350–71.

Kelley, Charles J. "The La Junta Archives." *New Mexico Historical Review* 25 (April 1950):162–63.

Kelley, J. Charles. "The Historic Indian Pueblos of La Junta de los Ríos." *New Mexico Historical Review* 27 (October 1952):257–95; 28 (January 1953):21–51.

Kessell, John L. "The Puzzling Presidio: San Phelipe de Guevavi, alias Terrenate." *New Mexico Historical Review* 41 (January 1966): 21–46.

Kielman, Chester V. "The Béxar Archives Microfilm Project in the University of Texas Archives." *Texas Library Journal* 44 (Spring 1968):17–18.

Kinnaird, Lawrence. "Bolton of California." *California Historical Society Quarterly* 32 (June 1953):97–103.

Kinney, John M. "The Texas Consortium to Microfilm Mexican Archival Resources." *College and Research Libraries* 32 (September 1971):386–80.

Lamadrid, Lazaro, O.F.M. "The Letters of Margil in the Archivo de la Recolección in Guatemala." *The Americas* 7 (January 1951): 323–55.

Laumbach, Verna. "Las Vegas before 1850." *New Mexico Historical Review* 8 (October 1933):241–64.

Layne, J. Gregg. "Edward Otho Cresap Ord." *Historical Society of Southern California Quarterly* 17 (December 1935):139–42.

Lejarza, Fidel de. "Los Archivos españoles y la misionología." *Misionalia hispanica* año 4, num. 12 (1947):525–85.

Lenhart, John M. "Franciscan Historians of North America." In *Franciscan History of North America*, pp. 21–29. (The Franciscan Educational Conference, *Report of the Eighteenth Annual Meeting, Santa Barbara, California*, August 2–4, 1936.) Washington, The Franciscan Educational Conference, 1937.

Lombardi, John. "Lost Records of the Surveyor-General in California." *Pacific Historical Review* 6 (December 1937):361–71.

Lutz, Paul V. "Government Loses Suit for Documents." *Manuscripta* 19 (Fall 1967):9–11.

Mahood, Ruth. "The Coronel Collection." *Los Angeles County Museum Quarterly* 14 (Autumn 1958):4–7.

Manrique, Jorge A. "Una colección importante para la historigrafia del noroeste." *Historia mexicana* 16 (avril–junio 1967):636–43.

Mathes, Michael. "Judicial Transformation in California, 1837–1851." *Los Angeles Bar Bulletin* 35 (September 1960):359–64.

Mattison, Ray H. "Early Spanish and Mexican Settlements in Arizona." *New Mexico Historical Review* 21 (October 1946):273–327.

Mawn, Geoffrey. "'Agrimensor y Arquitecto': Jasper O'Farrell's Surveying in Mexican California." *Southern California Quarterly* 56 (Spring 1974):1–12.

McLean, Malcolm D. "The Béxar Archives." *Southwestern Historical Quarterly* 50 (April 1947):493–96.

————. "The Diary of Fray Juan Agustín de Morfi." *The Library Chronicle of the University of Texas* 5 (Spring 1956):38–39.

————. "Report on the Compilation of the Sterling C. Robertson Papers." *Southwestern Historical Quarterly* 47 (April 1944):411–12; 48 (April 1945):556–58.

Muir, Andrew F. "Humphrey Jackson, Alcalde of San Jacinto." *Southwestern Historical Quarterly* 88 (January 1965):361–65.

————. "The Municipality of Harrisburg, 1835–1836." *Southwestern Historical Quarterly* 56 (July 1952):36–50.

O'Hara, John F., C.S.C. "The Benavides Memorials." *Catholic Historical Review* 3 (April 1917):76–78.

Owen, J. Thomas. "The Church by the Plaza: A History of the Pueblo Church of Los Angeles." *Historical Society of Southern California Quarterly* 42 (March 1960):5–28.

Packman, Ana B. "California Cattle Brands and Earmarks." *Historical Society of Southern California Quarterly* 27 (December 1945): 127–49.

Pañdzić, Basile. "Les Archives Générales de l'Ordre des Frères Mineurs." *Archivum* 4 (1954):153–64.

Parks, Marion. "Translating the Spanish Records of Los Angeles County." *Historical Society of Southern California Quarterly* 17 (March 1935):28–29.

Patterson, Jerry E. "Spanish and Spanish American Manuscripts in the Yale University Library." *Yale University Library Gazette* 31 (January 1957):110–33.

Pattison, William D. "Use of the U. S. Public Land Survey Plats and Notes as Descriptive Sources." *Professional Geographer*, n.s. 8 (January 1956):10–14.

Piette, Charles J. G. M., O.F.M. "The Diarios of Early California, 1769–1784." *The Americas* 2 (April 1946):409–22.

Platón, Jaime S. "The Spanish Archives of Laredo." *Texas Libraries* 22 (January–February 1960):12–13.

Poldervaart, Arie. "The New Mexico Law Library—A History." *New Mexico Historical Review* 21 (January 1946):47–68.

Potts, Charles S. "Early Criminal Law in Texas: From Civil Law to Common Law, to Code." *Texas Law Review* 21 (April 1936):394–406.

Pradeau, Alberto F. "Nentuig's 'Description of Sonora.'" *Mid-America* 35 (April 1953):81–90.

"Ralph Emerson Twitchell." *New Mexico Historical Review* 1 (January 1926):78–85.

Rather, Ethel Z. "DeWitt's Colony." *Texas State Historical Association Quarterly* 8 (October 1904):95–192.

————. "Texas History Materials in Saltillo." *Southwestern Historical Quarterly* 7 (January 1904):244–45.

Robinson, William W., ed. "Abel Stearns on the California and Los

Angeles Archives." *Historical Society of Southern California Quarterly* 19 (September–December 1937):141–43.

Rowland, Kate M. "General John Thomas Mason." *Texas State Historical Association Quarterly* 11 (January 1908):163–98.

Santos, Richard G. "A Preliminary Survey of the San Fernando Archives." *Texas Libraries* 28 (Winter 1966–67):152–72.

Scholes, France V. "Civil Government and Society in New Mexico in the Seventeenth Century." *New Mexico Historical Review* 10 (April 1935):71–111.

————. "Problems in the Early Ecclesiastical History of New Mexico." *New Mexico Historical Review* 7 (January 1932):32–74.

————. "Research Activities of Lansing B. Bloom in Foreign Archives." *New Mexico Historical Review* 21 (April 1946):100–09.

————. "Royal Treasury Records Relating to the Province of New Mexico, 1596–1683." *New Mexico Historical Review* 50 (January 1975):5–23.

———— and Lansing B. Bloom. "Friar Personnel and Mission Chronology, 1598–1629." *New Mexico Historical Review* 19 (October 1944):319–36; 20 (January 1945):58–82.

Sena, José D. "Archives in the Office of the Cadastral Engineer at Santa Fe." *El Palacio* 36 (April 11–18, 1934):113–21.

Sharp, Jay W. "The Maps of the Stephen F. Austin Collection in the Eugene C. Barker Texas History Center." *Southwesetern Historical Quarterly* 64 (January 1961):388–97.

Sloan, Eleanor B. "Seventy-Five Years of the Arizona Pioneers' Historical Society, 1884–1959." *Arizona and the West* 1 (Spring 1959):66–70.

Spell, Lota M. "The Grant and First Survey of the City of San Antonio." *Southwestern Historical Quarterly* 66 (July 1962):73–89.

————. "The Sutro Library." *Hispanic American Historical Review* 29 (August 1949):452–54.

Stevens, Robert C. "The Apache Menace in Sonora, 1831–1849." *Arizona and the West* 6 (Autumn 1964):211–22.

Stoner, Victor R. "Fray Pedro Antonio de Arriquibar, Chaplain of the Royal Fort at Tucson." Ed. by Henry F. Dobyns. *Arizona and the West* 1 (Spring 1959):71–79.

Streeter, Thomas W. "Henry R. Wagner, Collector, Bibliographer, Cartographer, and Historian." *California Historical Society Quarterly* 36 (June 1957):165–72.

Tanodi, Aurelio Z. "Institución notarial hispanoamericana." *Archivum* 12 (1962):31–53.

Tate, Vernon D. "Microphotography in Mexico." *Inter-American Bibliographical and Library Association, Proceedings,* 1940, pp. 352–60.

Tays, George. "The Passing of Spanish California, September 29, 1822." *California Historical Society Quarterly* 15 (June 1936): 139–42.

Temple, Thomas W. II. "Some Notes on the 1944 Padrón de Los Angeles." *Historical Society of Southern California Quarterly* 42 (December 1960):418–22.

Teschitel, P. Josephus. "Archivum Romanum Societatis Iesu (ARSI)." *Archivum* 4 (1954):145–52.

Tipton, Will M. "The Prince of Impostors." *The Land of Sunshine* 8 (February, March 1899):107–18, 161–70.

Townes, John C. "Sketch of the Development of the Judicial System of Texas." *Texas State Historical Association Quarterly* 2 (July 1898):29–53.

Treutlein, Theodore E. "Jesuit Travel to New Spain (1678–1756)." *Mid-America* 19 (April 1937):104–23.

————. "Non-Spanish Jesuits in Spain's American Colonies." In Adele Ogden, ed., *Greater America: Essays in Honor of Herbert E. Bolton*, pp. 219–42. Berkeley, University of California Press, 1945.

True, C. Allen. "John A. Williams, Champion of Mexico in the Early Days of the Texas Revolution." *Southwestern Historical Quarterly* 47 (October 1943):107–19.

Van den Eynde, Damián, O.F.M. "The Franciscan Manuscripts in the John Carter Brown Library, Providence, R. I., U.S.A." *Archivum Franciscanum Historicum* annus 31 (January–April 1938):219–22.

Van Hook, Joseph O. "Mexican Land Grants in the Arkansas Valley." *Southwestern Historical Quarterly* 40 (July 1936):58–75.

Vigness, David M. "Don Hugo O'Conor and New Spain's Northeastern Frontier." *Journal of the West* 6 (January 1967):27–40.

Walters, Paul H. "Secularization of the La Bahía Missions." *Southwestern Historical Quarterly* 54 (January 1951):287–300.

Warner, Ted J. "Frontier Defense." *New Mexico Historical Review* 41 (January 1966):5–19.

Weber, Francis J. "California Serrana Literature." *Southern California Quarterly* 61 (December 1969):325–46.

————. "The Development of Ecclesiastical Jurisdiction in the Californias." *American Catholic Historical Society of Philadelphia, Records* 75 (June 1964):93–102.

————. "Roman Archives of Propaganda Fide." *American Catholic Historical Society, Records* 76 (December 1965):245–48.

Well, George H. "Saving the Archives: The Dash to Fort Union." *Our Public Lands* 3 (April 1953):4, 14.

West, Robert C. "The Municipal Archive of Parral, Chihuahua, Mexico." In *Handbook of Latin American Studies*, No. 6, 1940, pp. 523–29. Cambridge, Harvard University Press, 1941.

West, Robert G. "Validity of Certain Spanish Land Grants in Texas." *Texas Law Review* 2 (June 1924):435–44.

Wilcox, Sebron S. "Laredo during the Texas Republic." *Southwestern Historical Quarterly* 42 (October 1938):83–107.

————. "The Spanish Archives of Laredo." *Southwestern Historical Quarterly* 49 (January 1946):341–60.

Winkler, Ernest W. "Some Historical Activities of the Texas Library and Historical Commission." *Southwestern Historical Quarterly* 14 (April 1911):294–304.

Wroth, Lawrence C. "The Frontier Presidios of New Spain: Books, Maps, and a Selection of Manuscripts Relating to the Rivera Expedition, 1724–1728." Bibliographical Society of America, *Papers* 45 (Third Quarter 1951):191–218.

Wuthenau, A. von. "The Spanish Military Chapels in Santa Fe and the Reredos of Our Lady of Light." *New Mexico Historical Review* 10 (July 1935):175–94.

Zimmerman, James F. "The Coronado Cuarto Centennial." *Hispanic American Historical Review* 20 (February 1940):158–62.

TITLES FOUND TOO LATE TO BE EXAMINED

Almaráz, Felix D., Jr. "The Making of a Boltonian: Carlos E. Castañeda of Texas — the Early Years." *Red River Valley Historical Review* 1 (Winter 1974):329–50.

Dobyns, Henry F. *Spanish Colonial Tucson: A Demographic History.* Tucson, University of Arizona Press, 1976.

Ericson, Carolyn R. *Nacogdoches — Gateway to Texas: A Biographical Directory, 1773–1849.* Fort Worth, Tex., Arrow-Curtis Printing Co., 1974.

Lickteig, Franz-Bernard. "The Propaganda Fide Archives and Carmel in the United States." *Carmel Sword* 26 (October 1976):18–43.

McCarty, Kieran R., trans. and ed. *Desert Documentary: The Spanish Years, 1767–1821.* Tucson, Arizona Historical Society, 1976. (Arizona Historical Monograph no. 4.)

Mexico. Archivo General de La Nación. *Indice del ramo de Californias.* By Roberto Villasenor and Beatriz Arteaga. Mexico, Archivo General de la Nación, 1977. (Guías y catalogos.)

————. *Inventario de ramos, guías e indices, actualizado al mes de marzo de 1977.* By Cristina Urrutia de Stebelski and others. Mexico, Archivo General de la Nación, 1977.

Minge, Ward A. *Acoma: Pueblo in the Sky.* Albuquerque, University of New Mexico Press, 1976.

Rodriguez de Librija, Esperanza. *Indice analytico de la guía del Archivo Histórico de Hacienda.* Mexico, Archivo General de la Nación, 1975. (Colección documental no. 2.) An index to the *Guía del Archivo Histórico de Hacienda* published in 1940–45.

Index

472 INDEX

becomes national monument, 343;
census of, 345; corresp. of, 327;
given resident missionary, 343;
inventory of, 353; report on, 345
Twitchell, Ralph E.: calendars by, 17, 22;
catalog by, 19; criticism of, 20 n. 56;
coll. of, 40, 41; saves Spanish
archives, 16; work of, on N. Mex.
land records, 52

Ugalde, Juan de, 138
Ulloa, Francisco de, 199
Unamuno, Pedro de, 199
Union catalog, archival reproductions of, 121
United States Army: governs Calif., 207–8;
occupies Ariz., 315; occupies N.
Mex., 9; occupies Sonora, 314;
occupies Texas, 167
U.S. Attorney, N. Mex., 10 n. 9
U.S. Attorney, San Francisco, 218
U.S. Attorney General: corresp. file of, re
Calif. land claims, 264; sends Shunk
to Calif., 221; supplied with
transcripts of Calif. Board of Land
Commrs. proceedings, 255
U.S. Bureau of Land Management: archives of,
re land in Southwest, 54–57; diseños
in records of, 259; established, 49 n.
28; and land patents of Calif., 263;
land surveys of, in Southwest, 54;
and private land claim papers,
53–54; records Ariz. land grants,
337, 338 n. 49; records Calif. land
claims, 263
U.S. Bureau of Land Management, State
Office, Denver, Colo., private land
claim records in, 53–54, 60
U.S. Bureau of Land Management, State
Office, Phoenix, Ariz.: repository of
Ariz. land records, 337; survey
records of, 54
U.S. Bureau of Land Management, State Office,
Sacramento, Calif.: survey records
held by, 260; records improvement
program of, 264
U.S. Bureau of Land Management, State
Office, Santa Fe., N. Mex.: 49 n. 28;
legislative records held by, 29; and
microfilm of land grant records, 50;
records of, transferred to State
Records Center, 51
U.S. Circuit Court for California, Calif. land
cases of, 265, 266
U.S. Commissioner of the General Land Office,
instructions re: abstract of Calif.
land papers, 253; Spanish archives of
Calif., 223
U.S. Congress: act of, re Calif. land claims,
218, 252–53; act of, re territorial
archives, 18; appropriation of, for
microfilming, 22 n. 68; authorizes
annexation of Texas, 102; authorizes
Court of Private Land Claims, 57;
land grant documents published by,
47 n. 12, 259; report of, on Colo.
land claims, 59
U.S. Department of Justice: Calif. land claim
transcripts of, 227, 264; exhibits
Peralta-Reavis documents, 336 n. 43;
prepares case re Santa Cruz records,
66
U.S. Department of State: Alvarez dispatches
held by, 42; negligence of, re Calif.

records, 211; sends Greenhow to
Mexico and Calif., 251; sends Jones
to Calif., 250; Texas constitution
held by, 136
U.S. District Attorney, San Francisco, 221
U.S. District Cadastral Engineer: of Glendale,
Calif., 260; of Phoenix, Ariz., 336;
of Santa Fe, N. Mex., 49
U.S. District Court, Los Angeles: case records
of, 228; records of, re Calif. land
cases, 264–65, 266
U.S. District Court, San Francisco: appeals to,
re Calif. land claims, 255; case
records of, 228; index of, to Calif.
diseños, 265; records of, re Calif.
land cases, 221, 264–65, 266; and
reproductions of diseños, 259
U.S. District Court, Santa Fe: custodian of
territorial court records, 58 n. 55;
land cases of, 221
U.S. District Land Office, Santa Fe, 49 n. 28
U.S. General Land Office: Calif. Board of Land
Commrs. records sent to, 261; and
letters from Surv. Gen. of N. Mex.,
53; map files of, 56; merged into
Bureau of Land Management, 49 n.
28; supplied with abstract of Calif.
land titles, 253
U.S. House of Representatives, Sutter papers
in records of, 281
U.S. Library of Congress
Archives obtained by: of N. Mex., 18; of
Spanish Inquisition in Mexico, 194;
of Zuñi mission, 82
Ford's mission to Calif. for, 289
Mss. obtained by: Berlandier, 139; Cortes
report, 245; Font's diary, 299;
Garcés diaries, 354; García Figueroa
coll., 140; Mason letters, 132 n. 22;
Talamantes Pichard coll., 140
Microfilm obtained by, of: Archivo
General de Indias, 120; calendar of
Matamoros archives, 115; Coahuila
Congress proceedings, 116; Dept. of
Nacogdoches, 112; Mexican state
archives, 120; Monterey records,
273; Nacogdoches ayuntamiento
proceedings, 170 n. 61; Parral
archives, 320; San Felipe (Texas)
ayuntamiento proceedings, 172;
Spanish archives, 35; Texas censuses,
108 n. 18; Texas land records, 151
Reproductions obtained by, of: Calif.
mission records, 297; Escalante
letter, 25; Franciscan materials on
Texas, 192; Holy Gospel Province,
80; Mexican archives, 82, 232–33;
Miera y Pacheco's map, 88; N. Mex.
archives, 24; N. Mex. land records,
46; N. Mex. legislative records, 29;
Propaganda Fide archives, 83;
Spanish archives, 33, 119
Transcripts obtained by, of: Mexican
archives, 35, 113, 114; San Antonio
ayuntamiento minutes, 165; Spanish
archives, 119 and n. 34
U.S. Library of Congress, Geography and Map
Division, reproductions of maps
obtained by, 121–22, 233 and n. 22
U.S. National Archives
Archives accessioned by: Ariz. land grant
archives, 337; Bureau of Land
Management records, 54; of Calif.